THE COMPLETE
Venison
COOKBOOK

THE COMPLETE
Venison
COOKBOOK

by

Harold W. Webster, Jr.

QUAIL RIDGE PRESS

Preserving America's Food Heritage

Printed in Canada

QUAIL RIDGE PRESS
P. O. Box 123 • Brandon, MS 39043
1-800-343-1583
info@quailridge.com • www.quailridge.com

Illustrations by M. Kathryn Thompson

ISBN-13: 978-0-937552-70-4 • ISBN-10: 0-937552-70-4

*First printing, September 1996 • Second, December 1996
Third, July 1997 • Fourth, December 1998 • Fifth, January 2001
Sixth, July 2003 • Seventh, October 2005 • Eighth, May 2007
Ninth, January 2009 • Tenth, January 2010 • Eleventh, January 2011*

Library of Congress Cataloging-in Publication Data
Webster, Jr., Harold W,
     The Complete Venison Cookbook; over 900 recipes
inspired by American cooks, early settlers & Native Americans /
by Harold W. Webster, Jr.
        p. cm.
     Includes bibliographical references and index.
     ISBN-13: 978-0-937552-70-4
     ISBN-10: 0-937552-70-4 (pbk.)
     1. Cookery (Venison) I. Title.
TX751.W43 1996
641,6'91--dc20
                             96-2875
                             CIP

Dedication

Winston Churchill once said, "Writing a book was a great adventure." I agree with Sir Winston,

This book is dedicated to all my friends and family in Mississippi, Maine, Nevada, Arkansas and in other locales, who have contributed their venison, recipes, opinions, patience, support, and appetites to make my great adventure come true.

To Anne, who tried her very best not to interrupt me while I was writing, and who discovered along the way that venison does not have to taste bad.

My sincere thanks to the Breland and Rounsaville families of Leakesville, Mississippi, and to my relatives at Dubard Plantation, who so generously allowed me to hunt on their land.

And to my parents, who always encouraged me to develop my own ideas, pursue my goals, march as my conscience may dictate, and to explore and travel the world without the limitations of self-imposed restrictions.

Hunters for the Hungry

Established as a cooperative effort by members of the hunting community, the "Hunters for the Hungry" movement brings together hunters, sportsmen's associations, meat processors, state meat inspectors and hunger relief organizations to help feed America's hungry. Sportsmen nationwide have donated hundreds of thousands of pounds of venison to homeless shelters, soup kitchens and food banks.

You can show that hunters care about their community by donating your extra game meat to feed deserving families.

Each year donations of game have multiplied. These relief organizations now find themselves turning away thousands of pounds of game meat because they cannot offset the processing and packaging costs. In addition to donating your extra game, your financial contributions can help offset the costs of large scale processing, packaging, storage and distribution.

The National Rifle Association Is supporting "Hunters for the Hungry" programs through its Hunters for the Hungry Information Clearinghouse. As part of the NRA Association's Hunter Services Division, the clearinghouse puts interested individuals in touch with programs in their area and fosters public awareness through education, fund-raising and publicity.

For information about "Hunters for the Hungry" activities in your local area, contact the Hunters for the Hungry Information Clearinghouse at:

1-800-492-HUNT • e-mail: contact@nra.org
web site: www.nrahq.org/hunting/hunterhungry.asp

Contents

About the Author

Harold Webster was raised in Nelliesburg, Mississippi, and comes from a family of early settlers who have been hunting, cooking and eating venison in Mississippi since before 1795. A graduate of the University of Arkansas, and a veteran of the Marine Corps, he now resides in Leakesville and Jackson, Mississippi.

Harold has hunted and cooked venison across the United States from Maine to Nevada. He has traveled and explored the world, and along the way, has sampled and enjoyed some of the world's greatest local cuisines. He has feasted on wild boar with high chiefs in the mountain forests of Pago Pago, dined on local venison with Lacadone Indians in the steamy jungles of Quintana Roo, savored Riso Nero on Napoleon's island of Elba, enjoyed Smoked Prosciutto in the beautiful city of Florence, was taught how to roll sushi in Tokyo, and learned the fine art of making Venison and Crab Boudin in Dominic You's Barataria. He is frequently asked to be a guest chef.

The author is also an accomplished restorer of antique wooden sailing vessels, a builder of fine Appalachian dulcimers, a sky diver, potter, white-water kayak racer, amateur historian, pilot, wood and metal worker, back-packer, builder of stain glass windows, competitive marksman, blue-water sailor, weaver, scuba diver, builder of experimental aircraft, amateur marine archaeologist, lithographer, country-philosopher, and a life-long professional educator.

Introduction

Venison does not have to taste bad!

This is the reason that I chose to develop and compile a history of recipes that would make cooking and eating venison a pleasure rather than an ordeal. There is absolutely no reason why venison should not taste as good as the finest grain-fed beef.

The Complete Venison Cookbook contains over 900 recipes, 700 or so of which feature venison; the remainder either complement venison or are used in the preparation of venison recipes.

Please note that some recipes call for Homemade Butter, Tomato Catsup, Mayonnaise, etc., all of which recipes appear in the book if they are capitalized. But do not hesitate to use bought butter, catsup, mayonnaise, etc.

In Colonial America, venison was the primary source of large game meat for the family table. The Colonial cook knew hundreds of ways to prepare and preserve game. The most prized delicacy of all was venison. Early Americans had few domesticated animals. These animals were far too precious to be killed for the table.

Today many cooks are afraid to prepare venison because they have heard about its alleged dryness, toughness, and unpleasant flavor. Outstanding venison dishes are very easy to prepare, once a few basic harvesting and cooking procedures have been learned.

If you do not hunt, or do not have ready access to domestic venison, you will find listed in the Appendix several firms that raise and ship farm-raised venison. Since it is illegal to buy, sell or trade in indigenous deer species, some of these suppliers have imported European, Australian, or Oriental deer, and breed them specifically for this market. These suppliers will be able to provide you with the exact cuts of venison that you require. Some of these firms also market prepared venison products. Other firms have fresh venison air shipped from Europe and New Zealand daily.

Venison is a fine, delicately textured, and virtually fat-free meat. Many cuts are very similar to veal. Other cuts, such as chops, look like pork. Round steaks, although smaller, have the appearance of beef. Stew meat and ground venison also resemble beef. Even though many cuts of venison look like other meats, venison has one overall characteristic that distinguishes it from other meats: venison is a low- or no-fat meat and needs additional moisture in cooking.

Venison responds best to slow and very moist cooking. Fast frying can turn a thinly cut chop or steak into something closely resembling harness leather. Dry roasting will give you a piece of very dry meat. Frying venison should be done very quickly: brown the outside, but leave the inside less than medium. Many outstanding recipes call for quickly browning, then slowly cooking in a gravy over very low heat.

For dry roasting, larding (inserting thin strips of moist meat such as bacon, salt pork or beef or pork fat into the venison) and/or wrapping the roast with moist meats such as bacon or salt pork is recommended. These moisturizing techniques are almost a must. Ground venison for burgers, sausages, and other ground venison recipes need to have a small amount of beef suet or pork fat, bacon, or mushrooms ground in with the venison.

If you have a meat smoker, an interesting variation is to smoke bacon, beef, or pork fat. The smoked meat additive is especially good when making recipes which call for ground venison such as for burgers, meat loaves, meatballs and sausages. Smoked bacon sides are available, but they are expensive. By smoking your own meat additive, you not only save money, but you can control the amount of smoked flavor in the meat.

When in doubt about cooking venison: (1) cook to less than medium done, (2) cook very slowly, (3) cook in moist recipes, and (4) when dry roasting large cuts, either lard and/or wrap the roast in moist meats.

As with other types of meat, the tenderest cuts come from the muscle groups that are used the least. The neck is one of the toughest cuts because it is in almost constant motion from either grazing or looking around. The tenderest muscle group is the little tenderloin, closely followed by the long backstrap. Venison chops cut from the part of the backbone which contains the tenderloin and/or the backstrap are among the finest cuts of meat you can find. Fore and hindquarters are used to make roasts, large steaks, stew, and ground meat. Although somewhat less tender than the backstrap, fine steaks can be cut from the top half of the quarters. These quarter muscle groups need care to prevent toughening while cooking. When they are used as large roasts, slow cooking to less than medium, and larding with moist

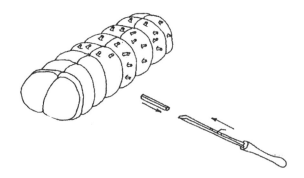

Larding a Roast with a Larding Needle

meats will prevent their drying out during the dry-roasting process. Chops should be cut thicker than one would cut from pork. Round steaks can be cut the same thickness as one would cut from beef. Quick browning and very slow cooking for chops and steaks make for outstanding meals.

Native Americans and early settlers harvested deer in a way that we did not rediscover until the early 1980s. They quietly stalked or waited for their game. With one well-placed arrow or musket ball, the deer was harvested quickly and cleanly. This method of deer hunting produced venison that was mild flavored and sweet smelling.

When I first began trying to cook venison, I could not stand the wild taste. I wondered: "If venison tastes this bad, how could my early Mississippi ancestors stand to eat it?" I knew that when Jacob Curry settled in the Spanish Territory of what is now Mississippi in the late 1790s, venison was a mainstay in his family's diet. It was not until the mid 1980s, in Leakesville, Mississippi, that I found out why many of the old families preferred venison to beef: they harvested their deer by still-hunting, and cooked their venison in moist recipes. My attitude towards venison was changed forever.

While visiting with old family friends in Leakesville, I have had occasion to be invited over to the Rounsavilles' and Brelands' for venison Sunday dinner or barbecues. The venison that I was served was glorious. Mary Sue Rounsaville makes venison stew and chops that will melt in your mouth. Curtis Breland's smoked venison roasts have no equal. Mary Sims makes a stew that is as good as, and possibly better, than any type of stew that you have ever eaten. When Anne and I were first dating, Mary Sim's Stew was the first meal that I cooked for her. I don't know if it helped her to make up her mind, but we did marry and Anne still likes the stew.

What I didn't know about the venison I was served, was that a few of these old Greene County Scots and Frenchmen would occasionally ease out to the woods and harvest a deer in the quiet of the early evening. This was the hunting that they really enjoyed. At first, they didn't talk much about this to me. This was the venison they served to their families and to special invited guests.

I don't remember anyone telling me how the venison used in those particular recipes was harvested. When I would ask what made the venison taste so good, I would be blessed with sympathetic smiles and mumbled replies. It wasn't time for me to know the secret. For the time being, I would have to be satisfied with little real information. Hunting magazines, large generic cookbooks, and general game cookbooks did provide a few basic recipes. These recipes featured descriptions of complicated marinades which were promoted as a means of masking the "wild taste" of venison. I was not a very successful venison chef. In time the secrets would be shared with me and my adventure would begin.

Low-Fat and Low-Sodium Venison Recipes: Since venison is virtually fat free, you can convert many of these recipes to Low, or Fat Free and Low, or No Sodium. You can substitute fresh mushrooms in ground venison recipes instead of pork or beef fat; use safflower oil instead of olive oil; use margarine instead of butter; use salt substitutes instead of salt; use other low/no fat and low/no sodium prepared products; and use skimmed milk instead of whole milk (substitutions should not be made in baked goods or sauces).

I recommend that you experiment with substituting the fat with ground fresh mushrooms because mushrooms can provide water and prevent the ground venison from tasting dry. This substitution procedure has not been tested on all of these recipes. You will need to experiment. Make your ground venison or sausage by beginning with 25% (by weight) of mushrooms to 75% (by weight) of venison. Break off a small piece and fry it. If the ground venison is dry, add more mushrooms to the mixture and test it again.

Nutritional Analysis: The most misunderstood fact about game is the idea that because game is full flavored, it is heavy (i.e., caloric, fatty, etc.). Nothing could be farther from the truth. Game is low in fat and cholesterol, high in protein. The chart below shows this clearly.

100 gr. (3.6 oz.)	Calories	Fat gr.	Cholesterol mg.	Protein gr.
Chicken w/skin	239	17.90	83	18.2
Beef (bottom Round)	214	9.76	92	31.0
Beef (ground)	265	18.40	85	24.0
Pork (shoulder)	219	10.64	101	19.0
Venison	159	3.30	66	25.0

Source of Nutritional Analysis: D'Artagnan, Inc.

In addition to venison cooking and preserving recipes, I have included chapters with a wide variety of recipes for Venison Sauces, Marinades and Gravies. These recipes provide the creative cook with the resources needed to modify existing recipes, and to experiment with new ones.

Also included are recipes for Side Dishes, Salads, Breads, Desserts, Drinks & Punch. Some of these recipes are over 250 years old. All of them will provide tasty accompaniments to your venison. Many of these recipes have come from Colonial dinner, luncheon or feast menus on which venison was the main course. If you like to experiment, I have included in Lagniappe (a little something extra), recipes for making some of the required cooking ingredients from scratch, like Homemade Butter. When called for in a recipe, these can be found by locating their page number in the index. Feel free to substitute similar ingredients, recipes or packaged products.

1

Processing Your Venison

How you kill, clean, age, and package your venison will determine how your venison will taste when you cook it. If you treat your venison like the fine piece of meat that it is, you will be rewarded with some of the finest meat that you have ever put in your mouth.

If prime beef were killed, cleaned, aged, and packaged the way I have seen some venison processed, it would not be fit to eat. If you were to take fine grain-fed livestock and run it at full speed for several hours, shoot it badly, let it run wounded before dying, let the beef lie in the woods several hours before finding it, wait several hours before field dressing, and then immediately butcher and freeze the meat in plain paper, how do you think that fine piece of beef would taste? I suspect that you would return it immediately to the meat market for a refund.

When beef is slaughtered, the animals are well rested and are dispatched quickly. Still-hunting deer accomplishes the same thing. The deer are calm and rested. They are usually grazing. There is no adrenaline or lactic acid built up in the muscles to spoil the taste. With still-hunting, the hunter has most of the control. The hunter can decide if the deer meets the harvesting criteria. The hunter can wait until the deer is in position for a well-placed shot, and the hunter has the time to take accurate aim. This is how our ancestors did it.

Venison, as with beef, should be cooled as quickly as possible. The cooling process begins when you quickly eviscerate the carcass and begin allowing cool air to circulate inside the body cavity. If it will be several hours before you get back to camp, the venison should be field dressed, with the hide left on, and the body cavity propped open. At camp, since the hide is a good insulator, the hide should be removed as soon as possible so that the carcass can begin cooling on all sides. After skinning and dressing, the carcass can be cut down the backbone to make two halves to further facilitate the cooling process.

If you hunt and eat venison because you have a fat-restrictive diet, identify the recipes that meet the constraints of your diet before you go hunting. Make note of the cuts of meat that you will need to prepare these recipes. This is the time to begin making your butchering decisions. Included in this book are many recipes that are diet restrictive in and of themselves. Other recipes can be modified to meet specific dietary restrictions. Have a butchering plan. There is nothing worse than having a fine cut of venison and not having the proper recipe to prepare it properly. Plan ahead. But if you have been given venison, you will find a recipe that will work with the cut of meat that you have been given.

Many camps now have walk-in coolers. The cooler should be pre-cooled to 34 to 36 degrees. This cooling process is the same method used to age fine beef. The carcass can be hung in the cooler to age from three to five days. This cooling process allows the meat to tenderize itself, and the cold temperature prevents the growth of unwanted bacteria. If a cooler is not available to you, butcher and wrap the meat in serving sizes and freeze immediately. When you place the meat in the freezer, spread it out. If you stack the meat in one area, it may take several days for the center of the pile to freeze.

Some Mississippi venison processors do not recommend the aging of venison. Venison does not have the protective fat layer that beef has. Without the fat layer, the outer layer of skin tends to dry out and become hardened, there is measurable weight loss by evaporation, and the hardened skin makes the venison difficult to cut. The author has recorded an average 11.25% weight loss when hanging venison in a commercial/temperature-controlled cooler for 4 days.

If you have a walk-in cooler that will constantly maintain 34 to 36 degrees, the tenderizing effect of aging 3 to 4 days is worth the effort and loss of carcass weight. Some venison processors recommend that you consider leaving the skin on if you are going to age your venison in a cooler. They say that this helps prevent dehydration. I prefer to skin my deer and wrap the outer side of the carcass in a layer of plastic wrap. Skinning a deer after several days in a cooler can be difficult. The hide may contain dirt and insects that you don't want to be in your cooler. The plastic wrap will minimize the weight loss and will allow the meat to cool on all sides.

If you do not have a commercial quality meat cooler, do not attempt to age your venison by hanging it in the open air or in any area that is cooled by natural air.

The temperatures between night and day will vary considerably. At night the temperature may drop below 32 degrees and the meat will freeze and then thaw as the day warms. As the day warms, bacteria may begin to grow. This cooling, freezing, warming, cooling cycle will ruin the best venison and may be very hazardous to your health.

It has been recommended by one venison processor that if you do not have a commercial quality cooler, then you might wish to divide the venison into the quarter and the back sections and totally immerse all the parts in an ice chest full of ice water for 2 to 3 days. Replace the ice as it melts. Do not allow the venison just to sit in cool water. Keep the ice chest full of ice. The ice/water soaking may help in removing blood, keep the outer skin moist, prevent weight loss, and may somewhat age the venison without the inconveniences of dehydration and outer skin hardening that will occur in a cooler. This is also a good way to transport your venison home.

In medieval times and in early America, a rule of thumb was to let the game hang until the skin could be slipped off the carcass. This was especially true in Europe, where ducks were hung by the neck and were not considered ready to eat until the neck separated from the body and the duck fell to the ground. In some areas of the world this method of tenderizing is still practiced. Most of us would rather not have our game aged quite that much.

The Old World's demand for exotic spices was not to improve the flavor, but to mask the over-ripe condition of the game. Many of our best wild game marinades and spice mixtures were developed during this time and have been handed down to us. Today we use spices and marinades primarily to flavor, and to some degree to tenderize game. Old World cooks used marinades to make game more acceptable to the nose rather than to satisfy the palate.

It wasn't until the 1920s that home refrigerators were available to the average American consumer. Prior to that time home processors were limited to the use of cold weather, the spring house, the ice box (which required the delivery of block ice from the community ice house) to keep food cool, or preservation methods such as dehydration, canning, curing or pickling. As far back as Roman times and until the early 1900s, ice was sawn from lakes during the winter and stored or shipped to other parts of the world for summer cooling.

In the area around Phippsburg, Maine, you can still see the dams that were built on the river to make lakes so that ice could be commercially sawn during the winter. In many parts of the world, the cutting and shipping of natural ice was a major industry. Early Roman Emperors and the Moguls of India would have their ice brought down from the Italian Alps and the mountains of India in the summer to cool their food and to make their iced drinks.

Native Americans and early American settlers would clean and begin cooling their game as soon as it was killed. They knew that this would not only lighten the return load but they also knew that the sooner they began the cooling process, the better the meat would be. Without the means to store raw meat, these early residents and settlers quickly cooked what they needed, and preserved the remainder by either using salt or by dehydration. In Northern areas, where the temperature may not rise above freezing for months, venison could be left to naturally freeze and used throughout the winter as needed.

When your cooling and aging process is complete, you will have to make some decisions as to how you will butcher your venison. These decisions are not always easy. The butchering decisions you make now will determine what recipes you will be able to use.

You cannot have chops, tenderloins, back steaks, hindquarter roasts, eye of round and round steaks from the same side of the deer. When making these decisions, I view the carcass as three separate pieces: the neck section and two body halves.

As a general rule, I take my large cuts of meat such as tenderloin, backstrap, fore and hindquarters, and whole rib sections from one side. From the other side I take round steaks, chops, spare ribs and small roasts. From the remaining pieces and scraps, I save the larger pieces for stew meat, and the smaller chunks—neck, brisket and flank—I grind for hamburger or sausage.

By saving the larger chunks as roasts, you will have the option later on to convert it to stew meat, ground meat, sausage, jerky, steaks, hamburgers, meatballs, meat loaves, or to use in pâtés. Fore and hindquarters, whole rib sections, and whole back sections with tenderloin and backstrap can be frozen whole. At a later date they can be thawed and butchered for recipes requiring quantities of meat for making large batches of jerky, sausage, or hamburger.

Without a plan, most of us have the tendency to freeze pieces of venison in too large a portion. I package and freeze some large cuts of meat such as deboned fore and hindquarters. I usually do this because I am planning on using that particular cut for a recipe that calls for a large roast, or I may be planning on using it for a large sausage or jerky-making project. As a rule, I try to package my meat in one-serving sizes. Steaks and chops are wrapped individually and stored singularly or in twos or threes in ziplock bags. Stew meat and meat destined for sausage or hamburger is usually packaged in 1-lb. and 2 lb. packages. When I select meat for one particular recipe, I had much rather thaw 2 packages than have unneeded venison left over. Once venison is thawed, do not refreeze the raw meat. After cooking, many recipes can be frozen.

Many camps divide the venison between all those who have hunted during the season. At the camp where I hunt in Leakesville, we cut most of our venison into round steaks, chops, backstraps, small roasts and stew meat. By doing this, we are able to make a simple and equitable distribution to all hunters. From a practical point of view, we cannot cut the meat to individual specifications. Some years, Bill Rounsaville will send several of the deer and wild hog carcasses to be professionally made into bulk sausage links. This is some of the best-tasting sausage that I have ever put in my mouth.

When possible, I enjoy hunting alone, or with my good friends Don Blake or Jake Von Toble of Las Vegas, and with Curtis Breland or Bill Rounsaville of Leakesville. With these friends, we have the time to pass over those deer that do not meet our exact harvesting needs. We can also take the time to butcher our venison according to the recipes and the special cuts of meat that we may require.

Mike McAlpine, another hunting friend and co-worker of mine, believes in freezing his venison in larger pieces. While developing recipes for this book, Mike brought me at least 1½ deer, in large pieces, to keep in the office freezer. The plan was for me to have a ready source of large cuts of meat so that I could work out some of my more challenging recipes, In return, I would bring Mike samplings of the dishes. One Friday, when I went to the freezer to select a cut of meat for my weekend cooking, I found that somebody had left the freezer door partially open. All the meat had thawed and it was a stinking mess. We are both still fussin'. This was in March and deer season didn't open again until the next Fall.

The Rival® Electric Food Slicer (see Appendix) is worth the cost if you want to accurately cut large amounts of deboned venison steaks or backstraps. For cutting chops or steaks which still have the bone inside, you will need either a hand meat saw or a commercial meat band saw. If you only butcher an occasional deer, the hand saw will serve you well. Hand saws cost about $30.00 and mine has served me well for many seasons. Some camps have purchased commercial electric meat saws and they are outstanding pieces of equipment. One camp at which I hunt has an electric saw. The saw is nice when we are butchering 5 or 6 deer on a Sunday afternoon. Considering the cost and the time it takes to clean the saw with hot soapy water, you can butcher one deer in about the same amount of time with a hand saw. The benefit of the electric saw is the ability to butcher large amounts of meat in a short period of time and to be able to accurately cut venison in consistently sized pieces. For roasts made from quarters you can

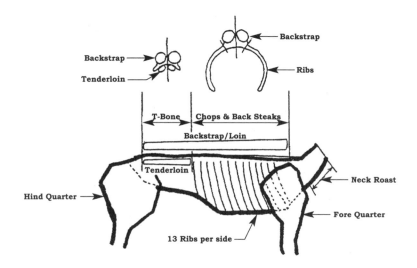

Basic Butchering Chart

obtain the same degree of accuracy by slicing the meat down to the bone with a sharp knife and then using your hand saw to saw through the leg bone.

If you do not have the butchering skills, and/or a meat cooler, you can still process your venison in a very respectable manner, When I was living in Las Vegas, Nevada, Don Blake, Jake Von Tobel and I would hunt on the edge of the picturesque Jarbridge Wilderness Area of Idaho. We hunted with a pioneer farm family in Deeth, Nevada. Deeth is located at the end of a sixty-five mile long dirt road that decreases in quality the farther you drive. Deeth is a twelve hour drive, due north from Las Vegas.

We hunted mule deer on horseback. Our friends acted as our guides. We would field-dress our deer in the mountains, leaving the hide on, and transport the carcass back to their ranch house on horseback. In the barn, we would finish dressing the deer by removing the skin and head, and prop open the carcass and let it hang in the cold barn. The carcass would be covered with cheesecloth netting to protect the meat. The high altitude and cold mountain air acted like a cooler.

We would only hunt for two or three days. When we were ready to leave, the carcasses would be wrapped in fresh cheesecloth and a water-proof blanket, and quickly driven back to Las Vegas. That evening the venison would be delivered to a firm that specialized in cold storage, aging, and the butchering of large game.

In many respects, the use of a commercial meat processing firm may be superior to doing the work yourself. For a small fee, these firms will age, cut to your specifications, and professionally wrap and fast-freeze your venison. Many firms will also make your venison into sausage.

Professional processors utilize freezer paper to package meat. If you will be keeping your venison frozen for more than six months, I recommend that you completely seal each of the packages in two layers of heavy-duty plastic kitchen wrap. This plastic wrap will prevent evaporation and assist in preventing freezer burn. Although somewhat expensive, home vacuum sealing machines will virtually eliminate freezer burn. Before investing in one of these sealing machines, check with your venison processor to see if they have this service. For an additional charge, some firms will exhaust all air, heat-seal, and fast-freeze your venison in heavy plastic. If you do decide to purchase you own vacuum sealer, I recommend the Professional Foodsaver® Vacuum Sealer (see Appendix).

Most modern hunting rifles are capable of consistently shooting 1-inch groups at 80 yards with most brands of ammunition. With a scoped rifle, if you take your time and slowly squeeze off your shot, there is no reason why you cannot consistently shoot 1¼-inch groups at 80 yards. With a 1¼-inch shot group, you can easily hit the head of a grazing deer.

Rifles with sequential serial numbers will have different shooting characteristics. These minor differences are primarily the results of different rifling buttons being used to make the lands and grooves on different rifle barrels.

When I first purchased my old Winchester Model 70, .30-06-caliber hunting rifle, I spent many hours at the range testing every type of ammunition that I could find. Of all the ammunition I tested, including some rather sophisticated match hand loads, I found that, out to 100 yards, my rifle liked one of the least expensive ammunitions best. There is much to be said for the more expensive ammunitions that have special expansion characteristics. But nothing will beat a well-placed shot. From a bench rest, my old rifle with its favorite ammunition will consistently shoot 1-inch or less groups at 100 yards.

I have found that my shooting accuracy is in direct proportion to my confidence in the accuracy of my rifle.

To maintain my confidence, I retest the zero of my rifle 3 or 4 times during the hunting season. Normally my rifle is still zeroed. But on occasions I have found that minor sight adjustments were in order. These rifle accuracy confirmation tests allow me to focus on controlling me, concentrate on the game, and not worry about whether or not my rifle will shoot to the point of aim. The time spent on the target paper will confirm that if you do your part, the rifle will do its part.

With my Thompson Center Renegade, .54 caliber, open sight, black powder rifle, I can constantly shoot 1+-inch groups at 40 yards, 2½-inch groups at 60 yards and 8-inch groups at 80 yards. My friends at Dubard Plantation use modern in-line black powder rifles. These fine rifles are capable of unbelievable accuracy. Take your muzzle loader to the range and experiment with powder loads and different types of bullets. Black powder rifles can provide a surprising degree of accuracy.

Because of the arched trajectory of the large slow moving black powder bullet, I have to apply a little "Kentucky" elevation for shots between 40 yards and 80 yards. Since I have zeroed my rifle at known range and fired it at different ranges, I know where the impact point of my bullet will be at these ranges. I am not a good judge of distances. I arrive at my hunting site early enough in the afternoon to pace off 40, 60 and 80 yards in several directions and place a limb or a stick at each distance.

At my age, my eyes are not as good as they used to be. Primitive weapon hunting regulations require the use of open sights. Since my old eyes do not focus well with open sights, I no longer attempt shots at over 60 yards with my black powder rifle, I have never attempted a head shot with my muzzle loader. If my eyes were younger, I too would own one of those new super accurate in-line black powder rifles, and head shots would be in order.

During the primitive weapons hunting season, I zero my old black powder rifle each day that I hunt by shooting one 3-shot group and making sight adjustments if needed. The fourth, or game shot, will be right on. If I have not fired the rifle at game during the day, I either pull or fire the lead out before leaving the field. When I get home, I completely disassemble my rifle and clean it thoroughly with hot soapy water and black powder solvent. The next day that I hunt, I follow the same routine.

If you can hit an area the size of a pack of cigarettes at 100 yards with your sporting rifle, or 40 yards with your black powder rifle, you can make a head shot. With a head shot, the deer just lays down. The hunter is able to quickly recover the game, carry it back to camp, and begin the cooling and butchering process. With head shots, deer are not wounded. There is no wasted meat. The hunter will usually either make a quick and clean shot, or he will probably miss completely. You are in control. If you take your time, and if you have a well-zeroed rifle, the chances of missing a head shot are very small.

When I have had the opportunity to hunt mule deer in the mountains of the Western states, the shooting ranges were usually 150+ yards. At these ranges, head shots are not practical. This is where your confidence in the zero of your rifle can mean the difference between a well placed shot, a miss, or worse: a wounded deer that cannot be found. If you are confident that your rifle will hit where you aim, then all you have to do is squeeze the trigger when your sight is aligned.

When I was a young boy, my father once told me that he knew the trick to hitting the target every single time. I asked him, "How?" And he said, "If it ain't lined up, don't pull the trigger." Dad learned his shooting "trick" because his Uncle Jake could only afford to buy him one shell at a time from the county store in Oak Ridge, Mississippi. What he shot with that one shell was what the family ate. His "trick" has served me well.

Very few people can hold the sight exactly on target all the time; I cannot. High power rifle competition marksmen use the technique of squeezing the trigger only when the sights are perfectly aligned with the target. When the sights drift off the target, they stop squeezing. When the sights drift back on target, they begin to squeeze again. After several cycles of squeezing and stopping, the rifle goes off on target without any conscious effort on the shooters part.

For more information on home packaging, storing and preserving your venison, see the chapters on Freezing, Canning, Smoking & Curing; Sausage; Corned Venison; and Jerky.

2

Elegant Venison

Elegant Venison is dedicated to providing you with venison recipes that will define and enhance the most elegant of your dining occasions. Each and every recipe will provide you with a culinary centerpiece.

Many of these recipes are quite simple to prepare. Other recipes will challenge all of your culinary skills.

The elegant Crown Roast of Venison, Classic French Venison Pâté, and Elegant Venison Wellington will challenge you and will draw praise from your guests.

No less elegant, but as simple to prepare, are Minted Venison Chops in Puff Pastry, Roast Venison Tenderloin with Blackberry Sauce, and Spinach-Stuffed Smoked Venison Backstrap.

With any of these recipes, you and your guests will experience a truly unique and memorable dining experience

Apple-Currant Stuffed Venison Chops

6 venison chops, cut 1¼" to 1½ " thick
1½ cups garlic croutons
½ cup apple, chopped
½ cup Cheddar cheese, shredded
2 Tbsp. dried currants
2 Tbsp. butter, melted

2 Tbsp. orange juice
¼ tsp. salt
⅛ tsp. cinnamon
Apple-Orange Cranberry Liqueur
   Sauce

Preheat oven to 350 degrees. Cut a small pocket in the side of each venison chop. Mix together the croutons, apple, cheese and currants. In another bowl, combine melted butter, orange juice, salt and cinnamon. Pour butter mixture over the crouton mixture and mix gently. Stuff the venison chops with the butter-crouton mixture. Place the stuffed chops in a shallow baking dish and bake uncovered for 1 hour. Cover the dish with aluminum foil and bake for another 15 minutes. Serve with Apple-Orange Cranberry Liqueur Sauce. Serves 6.

Apple-Stuffed Venison Sausage Roll

2 lbs. Country Venison Sausage
2 cups apples, chopped fine
⅓ cup onions, chopped fine
1 cup soft bread crumbs

1 cup wheat germ
2 Tbsp. dark brown sugar
Hot Cumberland Sauce

Preheat oven to 350 degrees. Dry Country Venison Sausage; lay on a dish towel; press into a rectangle about ½" thick. Make stuffing by mixing apples, onions, bread crumbs, wheat germ and brown sugar. Spread the apple mixture on sausage. Leave a ½" clean border around the edges of the sausage. Lift the long side of dish towel and roll stuffed sausage, jelly-roll style, away from you. Roll the sausage roll back and forth between dish towel. Press the edges and ends to seal the sausage. Bake in a shallow pan for about 1 hour. Serve sliced on a winter evening. Recipe can be doubled. Serve with Hot Cumberland Sauce. Serves 4 to 6.

Bird Breasts of Venison

4 venison top of round steaks, cut ¼" thin
4 slices salt pork, cut ¼" thin, finely chopped
2 cups cracker crumbs
salt
pepper
¼ tsp. poultry seasoning
¼ tsp. lime juice
⅛ tsp. onion juice
3 eggs, beaten

4 smoked bacon slices
cotton string
salt
pepper
2 cups White Cream Gravy
4 pieces toasted bread
parsley sprigs
4 broccoli heads, steamed
4 cherry tomatoes, halved

Pound venison until it is thin. Cut the venison into 4 pieces 4" x 2". Each piece will make one bird's breast. Mix together salt pork, cracker crumbs, salt, pepper, poultry seasoning, lime juice, and onion juice. Moisten the pork mixture with the beaten egg. Divide the pork mixture into 4 equal parts. Spread the pork mixture thinly on each piece of venison. Roll and wrap each breast with a piece of bacon; tie with cotton string or secure with a toothpick. Season with salt and pepper and cover with White Cream Gravy. Cover and cook in a heavy skillet very slowly and over low heat for 20 to 35 minutes. Serve on toast and garnish with parsley, broccoli heads and cherry tomatoes. Serves 4.

Boudin Blanc Chevreuil

A fine and very perishable French delicacy. Either eat or freeze immediately.

½ lb. venison backstrap or front quarter
½ lb. deboned chicken or rabbit
¼ lb. lard or shortening
2 tsp. salt
1 tsp. white pepper
⅛ tsp. cloves
⅛ tsp. nutmeg
⅛ tsp. ginger

¼ tsp. cinnamon
2 cups onions, chopped
½ cup bread crumbs
¼ cup warm cream
3 eggs, beaten
32mm sausage casings (required)
butter, melted
Brown Rice Pilau

Combine venison, chicken or rabbit and grind through a fine disc. Mix the meat mixture with the lard and add salt, pepper, cloves, nutmeg, ginger, cinnamon. Add the onions to the meat mixture and regrind. Soak the bread crumbs in cream. Add crumbs to beaten eggs. Mix all ingredients together. Fill casings, twisting and tying with string at 6" intervals. Heat a large pot of water to the boiling point. Place sausages into a wire basket, do not crowd. Lower wire basket in the boiling water; reduce heat to 190 degrees and cook for about 20 minutes. If sausages rise to the top of the water, prick them to release air. Remove from water; brush with melted butter and grill until browned. Serve with Brown Rice Pilau. Serves 4 to 6.

Cacciastecca à la Haroldo é Anna

A variation of Bistecca Florentine with touches of Anna and Haroldo.

1 large top of round steak, cut 2"thick
4 Tbsp. extra virgin olive oil
2 Tbsp. parsley, minced
2 garlic cloves, minced
½ tsp. salt

½ tsp. pepper
2 tsp, lemon juice
1 Tbsp. butter
1 lemon, cut into wedges
1 tomato, cut into wedges

Prepare a mixture of olive oil, parsley, garlic, salt and pepper, and 1 teaspoon lemon juice. Place mixture and steaks in a heavy 1-gallon ziplock plastic bag. Exhaust as much air as possible. Place in a refrigerator for 2 to 4 hours. Remove the steaks from the zip-lock bag. Drain off surplus marinade and broil steak under a very hot broiler for 3 to 8 minutes on each side. *Do not overcook.* Serve the steak on a hot platter, with a large lump of butter on top. Garnish around platter with parsley sprigs, lemon and tomato wedges. Serves 2 to 4.

Deer can live as long as 10 to 12 years in the wild.

Chevreuil à la Mode

2 Tbsp. butter
4 lbs. deboned venison hindquarter roast,
   rolled and tied (from a young and
   tender deer)
¼ cup white onion, chopped
2 cups dry white wine
½ cup hot water
1½ tsp. salt
½ tsp. thyme

¼ tsp. black pepper
3 whole cloves
½ bay leaf
1 sprig parsley
12 small white onions, peeled
6 med. carrots, pared and quartered
   lengthwise
2 Tbsp. flour

Melt butter over medium-high heat in a large Dutch oven. Add tied venison and brown well on all sides. During the last few minutes of browning, add chopped onions. Add wine, water, salt, thyme, pepper, cloves, bay leaf and parsley. Bring to a boil. Reduce heat and simmer, covered, for 3 hours. Add whole onions and carrots. Cover and simmer 1 hour or until the venison is fork tender. Remove the venison to a heated serving platter. Lift out vegetables with a slotted spoon and place around the venison. Keep warm. Skim off the excess fat from the top of the cooking liquid. Combine ¼ cup cold water with the flour. Gradually stir flour mixture into the liquid in the Dutch oven. Bring to a boil and cook, stirring constantly, until the mixture is smooth and thickened. Strain gravy and serve with meat and vegetables. Serves 8 to 10.

Chevreuil Bourguignonne

5 lbs. venison, cut in 1½" square pieces
1 tsp. Accent or MSG
1 Tbsp. salt
¼ tsp. pepper
½ lb. salt pork
1 med. white onion, chopped
1 clove garlic, minced
3 cups dry red wine

1 bay leaf
¼ cup parsley chopped, divided
1 tsp. thyme
12 pearl onions, peeled
additional dry red wine, if needed
1 lb. mushrooms, sliced
3 Tbsp. flour

Combine Accent, salt and pepper and sprinkle over venison. Cut salt pork into small cubes. Heat a Dutch oven over medium-high heat. Add salt pork and cook until golden brown. Remove salt pork pieces and reserve; add venison to hot fat, a few pieces at a time; brown well on all sides and remove. Add chopped onion and cook until the onion is just tender. Return salt pork and venison to the Dutch oven. Add garlic, wine, bay leaf, parsley (reserve ½ Tbsp.), thyme and pearl onions. Cover and simmer for about 3 hours or until the venison is tender. Add additional wine if necessary. Add mushrooms during the last 15 minutes of the cooking time. Combine the flour with a little cold water to make a fluid paste. Gently stir flour into the venison mixture, stirring constantly and gently, until the mixture is thickened. Serves 12.

Classic French Venison Pâté

½ lb. venison loin cut into ¼" strips
1 (⅞-oz.) can diced truffles and juice
4 Tbsp, Cognac
pinch of salt
pinch of black pepper
pinch of thyme
pinch of allspice
1½ Tbsp. green onions, minced
½ cup onion, finely minced
2 Tbsp. butter
½ cup Madeira
¾ lb. (1½ cups) lean pork, finely ground smoked bacon strips
¾ lb, (1½ cups) venison, finely ground

½ lb. pork fat, finely ground
2 eggs
1½ tsp. salt
⅛ tsp. pepper
pinch allspice
½ tsp. thyme
2 med. garlic cloves, chopped fine
fresh pork fat or fat salt pork cut into very thin strips, or salt pork
½ lb. lean boiled ham cut into ¼" strips
1 bay leaf

Mix the venison strips, truffles and juice, cognac, salt, pepper, thyme and allspice and green onions and set aside. Cook onions in butter until they are just tender. When onions are tender, place them in a large bowl. Add Madeira to the onion skillet; boil and reduce by ½ the volume. Mix onions and reduce Madeira. To the onions and Madeira mixture, add ground venison, pork, pork fat, eggs, salt, pepper, allspice, thyme and garlic. With a spoon, beat vigorously until the mixture is thoroughly blended. Fry a small piece of the mixture and taste. Adjust the seasonings to taste. Place pork fat strips or salt pork between pieces of waxed paper and pound until it is ⅛-inch thick. Place the pounded slices of pork into a saucepan; cover with cold water; bring to a boil and simmer for 10 minutes. Remove pork from the pan; rinse in cold water and dry with paper towels.

Line the bottom and sides of an 8-cup terrine, baking dish, casserole or loaf pan with the pork fat. Heat oven to 350 degrees. Drain the venison strips and reserve the marinade. Beat marinade into ground meat mixture. Spoon ⅓ of the ground meat mixture into the bottom of mold. Cover ground meat mixture with ½ of the marinated venison strips and ½ of the ham strips. Arrange the diced truffles down the center of strips. Cover with second ⅓ of the ground meat mixture and the remaining ½ marinated venison and ham strips. Top with remaining ⅓ of the ground meat mixture. Place bay leaf on top of this mixture. Cover top of meat with a layer of smoked bacon strips. Cover top of mold tightly with aluminum foil. Set the mold in pan of hot water. The water should come no more than ½ way up the side of the mold. Bake for 1½ to 2 hours. The pâté is done when it slightly shrinks away from the sides of the mold or when the smoked bacon runs clear when it is pierced.

Remove pâté pan from water pan. Place a piece of aluminum foil or a smaller loaf pan on top of the Pâté and weigh it down with 2 bricks or canned goods. Cool thoroughly and then place in the refrigerator for 3 hours before serving. Turn pâté out onto a platter. Cut into slices. Makes about 18 slices.

Cornbread Fried Venison Chops
with Pumpkin Seed Sauce

½ cup hulled pumpkin seeds
2 Tbsp. extra-virgin olive oil
3 cloves garlic, minced
1 large onion, diced
2 to 4 tomatilloes, husked and diced
1 cup chicken stock
8 Tbsp. (1 stick) butter, cut in small chunks
3 Tbsp. plus 1 tsp. chopped fresh cilantro
    for garnish
salt and pepper to taste
3 large red bell peppers
½ cup extra-virgin olive oil
8 thick-cut venison chops
3 large eggs, beaten
3 cups Skillet Buttermilk
    Cornbread, finely crumbled
salt and pepper to taste
safflower or canola oil for frying

In a small dry skillet, toast pumpkin seeds over medium heat; remove and allow to cool. Heat olive oil in a saucepan over medium heat and sauté garlic and onion until they are just tender. Add tomatilloes and ½ cup chicken stock and simmer uncovered for 10 minutes. Add toasted pumpkin seeds and remaining chicken stock; cook over very low heat for 5 minutes. Remove from heat and purée in a food processor. Return to the pan and whisk in butter and chopped cilantro. Season with salt and pepper to taste. Set aside in a warm place.

Purée bell peppers with olive oil, season with salt and pepper, and transfer to a small squeeze bottle. Place venison chops in a bowl and pour eggs over to coat. Spread Skillet Buttermilk Cornbread crumbs out on a large cookie sheet. Dredge the egg-coated venison in the crumbs. Pour oil to a depth of about ½" into a large heavy skillet and heat over medium-high heat. Add breaded venison to the pan and fry for about 2 minutes on each side, or until golden brown. *Do not overcook*; venison should be slightly pink in the center. Drain on paper towels. To serve, coat plates with pumpkin-seed sauce. Arrange venison chops in the center of the plate. Squeeze the red pepper purée in a decorative pattern over the chops. Garnish with cilantro sprigs. Serves 4,

Mock Venison Goose Breasts

12 thin slices (¼") venison top round steak
salt
pepper
12 apple sections, cored and peeled
6 prunes, cut in half
1 med. onion, grated
1 egg
1 Tbsp. water
fine dry bread crumbs
butter
Venison Soup Stock or beef
    broth

Pound and rub the venison slices with salt and pepper. Lay a section of apple and half a prune on each slice; top with a little grated onion then roll and tie with string. Beat egg well and add water. Divide the crumbs in two separate dishes. Dip venison rolls in the crumbs, then in the egg, then again in the crumbs. Brown in butter; add a little Venison Soup Stock or beef broth; cover and gently simmer for about 2 hours or until the meat is tender. Baste a few times while cooking and add more liquid if necessary. Carefully remove the strings and place breasts on a platter. Pour a little of the gravy from pan around the breasts. Gravy may be reduced to a thicker consistency if desired. Serves 6.

Elegant Venison Wellington

1 (4 lb. to 4½ lb.) boneless venison
   hindquarter
salt and pepper to taste
Butter Pastry
Duxelles

1 egg, beaten with 1 Tbsp. water
sesame seeds
Tomatoes Stuffed with Horseradish
   Cream
fresh basil sprigs

Tie hindquarter with butchers' twine and place venison on a rack in a shallow baking pan. Sprinkle with salt and pepper. Roast at 360 degrees for 20 minutes. Remove roast from the oven and let stand until cool. Roll Butter Pastry on a floured surface into a rectangle which is about 3" longer than roast and 12" to 13" wide. Press Duxelles into the rolled pastry; leave an inch uncovered around all the edges. Place the venison on the pastry. Moisten pastry edges with water and fold over the venison; press the edges firmly together. Trim off excess pastry from ends so that only a single layer of pastry covers ends of the roast. Place venison roast, seam-side-down, in a shallow baking pan. Cut small seasonal decorations from pastry trimmings and place the decoration on the top. Brush the pastry with beaten egg and sprinkle with the sesame seeds. Bake at 400 degrees for 30 to 35 minutes or until browned. Remove from the oven and let stand for 15 to 20 minutes before slicing. Serve with Tomatoes with Horseradish Cream. Place fresh basil sprigs on platter around roast. Serves 3 to 4.

Crown Roast of Venison

1 or 2 whole venison rib sections with
   loins attached
½ tsp. garlic salt
⅛ tsp. black pepper
1 lb. to 3 lb. Venison and Bacon Burger
1 (20-oz.) can apple slices with juice,
   chopped
⅓ cup apple cider

10 slices dried bread; cut into ½-inch
   cubes
2 Tbsp. raisins
¾ tsp. salt
1 tsp. cinnamon
½ tsp. cardamom
¼ tsp. allspice
Apple-Orange Cranberry Liqueur Sauce

Note: The assembly of the crown is difficult. It is recommended that you take two whole rib sections, with loins still attached, to a butcher and have them assemble the crown roast. If you would like to try to assemble your own: cut off rib tips even and about 6" above the backbone. Place the two rib roasts end to end on meat board. Cut two small slits behind the adjoining ribs and tie together with cotton twine. Cut two small slits on the end ribs; pull together, meat side toward center, and tie, forming a crown roast. Or, pull both ends of 12-rib roast into a circle and tie, forming a crown.

   Mix garlic salt and pepper together; rub mixture into all sides of roast. Place seasoned roast, bone ends up, in a shallow roasting pan. Cook Garlic Venison Sausage in a skillet until brown, drain excess grease. Combine next 8 ingredients with sausage; stir enough to moisten dried bread. Fill center of crown roast with sausage mixture; cover with aluminum foil. Insert meat thermometer into center of roast. Bake at 325 degrees for 2 or 3 hours or until meat thermometer reads 135 to 140 degrees. (Time varies according to size and age of animal.) Add decorative frills for the top of each crown point, (available at local butcher shop.) Serve with Apple-Orange Cranberry Liqueur Sauce. Serves 10 to 14.

Filet De Chevreuil, Due De Roquefort
Mlle. Dabney

½ cup celery, chopped coarsely
1 small onion, sliced
1 bay leaf, crumbled
¼ tsp. dried rosemary
3½ to 4 lb. top round from doe or young deer
butter
salt
black pepper
2 Tbsp. cognac

3 cups sifted flour
½ cup shortening
ice water
½ lb. Roquefort cheese
1 egg yolk
1 Tbsp. whole milk
1 cup chicken broth
1 truffle, minced (optional)

Heat oven to 350 degrees. Place celery, onion, bay leaf and rosemary in the bottom of a roasting pan. Cover venison filet with a generous coating of butter. Sprinkle with salt and pepper. Place on top of celery mixture in baking pan. Bake 30 minutes. Remove venison from the oven. Warm cognac and pour over venison. Ignite with a match and allow flames to burn out. Let meat stand in pan and cool completely while preparing pastry covering. Sift together flour and 1 tsp. salt into a mixing bowl. Cut in shortening with a pastry blender until the consistency of cornmeal. Add about 4 Tbsp. ice water, or enough to make the dough stick together. Shape into a ball, wrap in waxed paper and chill. On a lightly floured board, roll dough into a rectangle about ⅛" thick. Remove venison from the pan, leaving vegetables in the pan. Force the Roquefort cheese through a sieve and mix it into a paste. Spread cheese over the top and sides of the filet. Place the filet on the center of the pastry. Wrap the pastry around the filet, trimming the edges as needed. Secure the ends with a small amount of cold water. Place the venison on a baking sheet.

Beat together the egg yolk and the milk. Brush the top of the pastry with egg yolk mixture. Bake at 450 degrees for 15 minutes or until the pastry is browned. While the venison is baking, remove the fat from the top of the liquid in the vegetable roasting pan. Add chicken broth and place over medium heat. Simmer, stirring constantly to scrape the bits from the bottom of the pan. Remove from heat and strain. Chop truffle and add to sauce. Let simmer about 15 minutes to blend flavors. Stir in 1 Tbsp. softened butter just before serving. Remove venison to a heated serving platter. Cut venison in generous slices and serve with truffle sauce. Serves 6 to 8.

French Choucroute

1 med. onion, sliced
1 Tbsp. vegetable oil
2 lbs. venison spare ribs
1½ lbs, venison loin chops
2 med. apples, cored and cut into wedges
48 oz. canned sauerkraut
2 Tbsp. light brown sugar
1 tsp. cloves, ground
2 med. garlic cloves, minced
1 bay leaf

⅛ tsp. black pepper
1 cup dry white wine
4 oz. bratwurst
4 oz. knockwurst
4 oz. weiners
4 oz. kielbasa sausage
12 med. potatoes peeled and steamed
12 new onions, peeled and steamed
12 baby carrots, peeled and steamed

Cook the sliced onion in vegetable oil in a Dutch oven for about 5 minutes or until just tender; remove from heat. Cut venison spareribs into 3 rib portions and add to the onions. Trim venison chops and add to Dutch oven. Add apples. Mix Sauerkraut, brown sugar, cloves, garlic, bay leaf, black pepper, and wine; and pour over meat. Cover and bake in a 375-degree oven for about 1½ hours or until all meat is tender. Place Venison Bratwurst in an unheated skillet with 2 to 3 Tbsp. water and cook over low heat 5 to 8 minutes. Uncover and cook 5 to 8 minutes more or until the water has evaporated and the bratwurst is cooked through.

Place knockwurst, Venison Frankfurters and kielbasa in a large pot; cover sausages with water; cover pot and simmer 5 to 10 minutes or until heated through. Mound sauerkraut onto a deep/wide serving platter. Arrange meats and sausages around and on top of the sauerkraut. Arrange potatoes, onions, and carrots around the side of the platter. Serves 12.

Minted Venison Chops in Puff Pastry

12 venison chops, cut 1" thick with 6" rib
salt & pepper
2(17 ¼-oz.) pkgs. frozen puff pastry sheets
  (4 sheets total)

3 Tbsp. fresh mint, chopped
1 egg yolk
3 Tbsp. water
Cranberry and Almond Conserve

Cut chops and leave 6" to 8" of rib attached. Scrape meat off rib making a 'handle' on the chop. Trim off all fat from edge of venison chops. Preheat electric broiler. It is not necessary to preheat a gas broiler. Arrange chops on rack in broiler pan. Season with salt and pepper. Broil 3 to 4 inches from the heat for 2 minutes. Turn chops over and broil for 2 minutes. Remove chops to baking sheet; cover with plastic wrap. Freeze chops for 1 hour.

While chops are in freezer, thaw puff pastry according to package directions. On floured surface, gently unfold 1 sheet of pastry. Press pastry together at the 2 fold seams to seal. Roll out to a 12-inch square. Cut in 4 (6" by 6") squares, trimming edges evenly, Repeat with 2 more sheets of pastry, making 12 squares in all. Roll out last sheet of pastry and cut out 12 (½" by 1") decorative shapes with small cutters. Wrap and refrigerate pastry. To assemble: Work with 2 squares of puff pastry at a time, keeping remaining squares refrigerated. After chops have been in freezer 1 hour, remove from freezer. Position 1 chop in center of each pastry square. Top each chop with ¾ teaspoon mint. Starting at the corners, fold pastry over chops, envelope-style, overlapping slightly in center. (If rib bones are long, fold pastry around bone, leaving end portion of bone outside pastry bundle.) Press edges of pastry together to seal. Place pastry bundles seam-side-up 2 inches apart on clean baking sheets.

In small bowl, whisk together egg yolk and water. Brush over pastry. Gently press decorative cutouts over center where dough points come together. Brush with glaze again. Freeze pastry bundles 10 minutes. Preheat oven to 425 degrees. Bake pastry bundles at 425 degrees for 15 to 18 minutes until pastry is puffed and golden brown. Serve with Cranberry Almond Conserve. Serves 6.

Mock Venison Duck

1 venison forequarter or small hindquarter
bacon
salt
pepper
6 medium potatoes, peeled

parsley
small molds of mint or Cranberry Jelly
thick orange slices

Have the butcher tie up venison shoulder in mock duck form, making the shank the bill.

Preheat oven to 350 degrees. Lard the 'duck's body' with strips of bacon. Sprinkle meat with salt and pepper. Wrap duck's head and tail with strips of bacon to prevent bones from charring. Place on a rack in an open roasting pan and roast to 138 degrees on a meat thermometer inserted into the thickest place on the meat. Cooking time will be somewhere around 1 to 2 hours. About 30 minutes before the meat is done, put potatoes in the pan around the roast. To serve, remove bacon strips; place meat on a platter, surround with potatoes and parsley, and small molds of mint or Cranberry Jelly on thick orange slices. Serves 4 to 6.

Venison Steak Southern Style

¼ cup all-purpose flour
¾ tsp. salt
red pepper
⅛ tsp. thyme
⅛ tsp. ground nutmeg
⅛ tsp. ground cloves
3 lbs. venison round steak
2 Tbsp. melted beef fat or shortening
3 large white onions, sliced thin
2 cups tomatoes, peeled and quartered,
    or 2 cups stewed tomatoes

1½ Tbsp. Worcestershire sauce
Tabasco sauce, to taste
1½ cups red wine or ruby port
1 garlic clove
Bouquet Garni
salt
pepper
1 cup sautéed mushroom caps
wild rice
Currant Jelly

Mix and sift flour, salt, dash of red pepper, thyme, nutmeg and cloves. Pound the flour mixture into venison steak. Cut the steak into 1½" to 2" cubes. Heat the melted beef fat in a Dutch oven and brown the venison on all sides; add the onions to the Dutch oven and brown; add tomatoes, Worcestershire sauce, Tabasco sauce, red (or ruby port) wine, garlic and bouquet garni. Cover the pot and cook in a moderate oven for 2½ hours or until meat is tender. Remove from oven and add salt and pepper to taste and bring to a boil on stove top. Stir in sautéed mushroom caps; serve on wild rice and Currant Jelly. Serves 2 to 4.

Orange & Lime Venison Roast

1 leg of venison
peel of 1 orange
peel of 1 lime
garlic slivers
salt
pepper
4 smoked bacon strips
butter
2 ribs celery

Dark Roux
1 bell pepper, quartered
1 small onion, quartered
½ bunch red seedless grapes
1 mango, sliced
4 Tbsp. drippings
4 Tbsp. all-purpose flour
1 cup water
1 cup Burgundy

Pierce roast and stud with orange and lime peel and garlic slivers. Rub roast well with salt and pepper. Spread roast with butter and lay bacon strips on top of meat. Place in roasting pan and surround with cut-up pieces of celery, bell pepper, onions, grapes, and mango. Put a little water in bottom of pan. Roast at 350 degrees, 20 minutes per pound for rare; or 22 minutes for medium. After about ½ of the roasting time, remove roast and strain drippings. Return the roast to the oven and continue cooking until roast is cooked to desired degree of doneness. Make a Dark Roux using flour and strained drippings. Add water and wine slowly, stirring until thickened. Serve roast with Dark Roux as gravy. Serves 4 to 6.

Oven-Baked Chevreuil Bourguignonne

4 lbs. venison fore or hindquarter, deboned
  and tied
pork, beef fat, or thick cut bacon
3 Tbsp. safflower oil
2 whole white onions, each stuck with 2
  cloves
2 cloves garlic
1 tsp, thyme

½ bay leaf
4 cups dry red wine
1 Tbsp. salt
1 tsp. black pepper
2 large orange slices
2 Tbsp. butter
18 pearl onions, peeled

Pull the deboned roast quarter together and tie with cotton twine. Tie pieces of pork, beef fat, or bacon on all the outside of the tied roast. Heat a large Dutch oven over medium-high heat. Add safflower oil and brown venison roast thoroughly on all sides. Pour cognac over the roast and ignite with a match. Allow flames to burn out. Heat oven to 300 degrees. Add the two cloves onions, garlic, bay leaf, dry red wine, salt, pepper and orange slices. Bring to a boil on top of the stove. Cover Dutch oven and bake for about 2 to 2½ hours. Turn roast twice during the baking period. Melt butter in a skillet. Add pearl onions and brown on all sides. Add onions to venison in the Dutch oven and cook 30 minutes more or until venison is tender. Remove venison and onions to a hot serving platter. Reduce the liquid in the Dutch oven. Strain and serve with slices of the venison roast. Serves 8 to 10.

Roast Leg of Venison with Spinach-Shiitake Mushroom Stuffing and Baked Polenta

butter
3 cups canned chicken broth
1 cup yellow cornmeal
¾ cup Parmesan cheese, grated, divided
pepper

2 Tbsp. homemade butter
1 large green bell pepper
4 oz. green beans, cut into 2" long
  pieces
1 large carrot, peeled, cut julienne

Make polenta by first buttering a small cookie sheet. Bring broth to boil in a large saucepan over medium-high heat; gradually whisk in cornmeal. Continue cooking until cornmeal mixture is very thick; stir constantly for about 6 minutes. Mix in ½ cups of Parmesan cheese. Season with pepper. Pour cornmeal mixture out onto the buttered cookie sheet; spread ½" thick. Allow to completely cool. Cut the polenta into 2" circles using a cookie cutter. Place circles on large cookie sheet and space evenly. Sprinkle the polenta circles with the remaining Parmesan cheese. Place a small piece of homemade butter on top of each circle. Char bell pepper over gas flame until blackened on all sides. Wrap the charred pepper in a small brown paper bag and let steam for 10 minutes. Remove the pepper; peel and seed. Cut the pepper into julienne strips. Cook the green beans in boiling salted water 1 minute. Add the carrots and cook until they are just tender, about 2 minutes. Drain the vegetables and pat dry. Combine vegetables with the bell pepper strips. Cover the polenta circles with beans and pepper strips. If prepared in advance, refrigerate polenta and vegetables in separate containers.

1¾ oz. dried shiitake mushrooms
1¾ cups boiling water
¼ cup unsalted butter
⅓ cup green onions, chopped
1 (10-oz.) pkg. frozen spinach, thawed,
  squeezed dry

4 oz. cream cheese, cut into pieces
2 tsp. Dijon mustard
¼ tsp. nutmeg, fresh grated
  salt
pepper

Make filling by covering dried mushrooms with boiling water; let stand for 20 minutes. Drain mushrooms and save the soaking liquid for use in the sauce. Cut off and discard mushroom stems. Cut the mushroom caps into ¼"-wide strips; set aside. Melt butter in a large skillet over medium-high heat. Add green onions and sauté for 3 minutes; add ½ cup mushrooms and sauté for 2 minutes (save the remaining mushrooms for use in the sauce). Add the squeezed spinach, cream cheese, Dijon mustard and nutmeg and stir until well blended; about 4 minutes. Season to taste with salt and pepper. Remove from heat and allow to cool completely. If filling is prepared in advance, cover and refrigerate reserved soaking liquid, reserved mushrooms, and filling separately. Bring ingredients to room temperature before continuing with the recipe.

1 (5 lb. to 6 lb.) quarter of venison, trimmed,
  deboned and butterflied
salt
black pepper

1 lb. very thick cut bacon
⅓ cup safflower oil
½ cup Burgundy
½ cup canned beef broth

Prepare venison by boning venison. Cut ½" slits across the grain. Cover venison with plastic wrap. Using a heavy meat mallet, pound venison into a 1½" thick rectangle. Season generously with salt and pepper. Spread prepared filling over surface, leaving a 1" clear border around the edges of the venison. Begin rolling from a long side; roll venison jelly-roll style. Tie roast with string at 1" intervals. Wrap string several times lengthwise around roast. The roast can be prepared 3 hours in advance. Slice very thick cut bacon in long strips. With a larding needle, liberally lard the roast very deep; and on all sides with bacon strips. Leave a small end of each piece of bacon larding sticking out. Cover roast with plastic wrap and refrigerate.

Remove roast from the refrigerator and allow it to return to room temperature before placing in the oven. Preheat to 350 degrees and position rack in center of oven. Heat safflower oil in a large roasting pan over medium-high heat. Add venison roast and brown on all sides. Remove the venison roast from the pan. Place a rack in same roasting pan; place the venison roast, seam-side-down, on the rack. Roast until meat thermometer inserted in the center of the roast registers 135 degrees for medium-rare. Mix wine and beef broth. Pour ¼ cup of the wine mixture into the bottom of the roasting pan. Baste every 15 minutes with wine-stock mixture. Remove roast from the oven. Maintain oven temperature. Place the roast on a platter and tent with aluminum foil and let stand for 30 minutes. Do not clean roasting pan. Place the pan juices in cup; degrease the pan and save for use in the sauce.

7 Tbsp. unsalted butter	½ cup canned beef broth, divided
1 Tbsp, green onions, chopped	salt
½ cup dry red wine	white pepper

Make sauce by heating a roasting pan over medium heat. Add 1 Tbsp. unsalted butter and stir until melted. Add the reserved mushrooms and green onions and sauté for 3 minutes. Add the reserved degreased pan juices, reserved mushroom soaking liquid, wine and beef broth, and bring to boil; scrape up any browned bits. Pour into a saucepan and cook over medium high heat until sauce is reduced to about 1⅛ cups; stir frequently for about 10 minutes. Add the remaining 6 Tbsp. butter in small amounts, and whisk until it is smooth. Mix in the reserved mushrooms. Season with salt and pepper. Serve separately with the roast.

1 Tbsp. butter	fresh spinach leaves
salt	stuffed green olives, sliced
black pepper	

Assemble by uncovering baking the polenta until it is heated through; about 10 minutes. Melt the butter in large skillet over medium-high heat. Add the bell peppers, beans and carrots and sauté until heated through. Season with salt and pepper. Carefully cut the strings off the roast. Gently cut the roast into ½" thick slices. On a serving plate, make a bed out of the spinach leaves. Arrange the slices in a overlapping arrangement on a serving platter. Spoon some of the sauce over venison. Arrange the polenta around venison. Arrange the vegetables on the polenta. Garnish around the edges with the sliced green olives. Pass sauce separately. Serves 6 to 8.

Roast Hindquarter of Venison with Currant Sauce

6 Tbsp. butter
1 large yellow onion, chopped
3 Tbsp. green onions, chopped
1 large carrot, chopped
6 whole cloves
½ tsp. dried thyme
¾ tsp. dried marjoram
¼ tsp. dried tarragon
½ tsp. dried basil

½ tsp. dried rosemary
⅛ tsp. sugar
1 cup Burgundy wine
1 hindquarter of venison, with bones
olive oil
black pepper
cayenne pepper
½ lb. salt pork, cut into thin strips
4 cloves garlic, sliced

Make Red Wine and Spice Marinade by melting the butter and sautéing the onion, green onions, and carrots over low heat until they are tender; add the cloves, thyme, marjoram, tarragon, basil, and rosemary; mix well; add the Burgundy; mix well and remove from heat. Brush the venison with olive oil and sprinkle generously with salt, black pepper, and cayenne pepper. Place venison in a large glass bowl and pour the marinade over. Cover the bowl and refrigerate for 6 to 8 hours.

pan drippings
¾ cup dry red wine
¼ tsp. ginger
¼ tsp. cloves

1½ tsp. fresh lemon juice
½ cup Currant Jelly
3 Tbsp. flour
1½ Tbsp. brandy

Make Brandy and Lemon Sauce by removing the roast from the marinade and allowing to drain. Strain and reserve the marinade. Make deep cup all around the roast and place a piece of salt pork and a slice of garlic into each cut. Preheat oven to 450 degrees. Insert a meat thermometer into the thickest part of the roast. Do not touch the bone. Place roast in a roasting pan and pour ¾ cup of the marinade over the roast; cook for 30 minutes. Reduce heat to 325 degrees and roast until less than medium done (138 degrees). Baste frequently with pan drippings. When the roast is done, reduce oven to 200 degrees; remove roast to a platter and let set in the oven until the sauce is made. Pour the pan drippings into a large saucepan; add sauce ingredients and cook over low heat until Currant Jelly is melted. Reduce sauce by ⅓. Slice roast and spoon the sauce over each serving. Serves 10 to 12.

Roast Venison Tenderloin with Blackberry Sauce

1 lb. venison loin
½ tsp. ground thyme
¼ tsp. ground nutmeg
1 tsp. black pepper
½ cup soy sauce
1 cup hickory chips

5 lbs. of charcoal
Blackberry Sauce with Bourbon
parsley sprigs
radish rosettes
yellow squash slices

Mix thyme, nutmeg, pepper and soy sauce, and marinate venison loin overnight in the refrigerator. Soak 1 cup of hickory chips in a bucket of water overnight. Build a fire in a covered barbecue grill using 5 lbs of charcoal. Allow the coals to burn for 30 minutes. If using a gas grill, preheat for 30 minutes. Scatter the soaked chips over the coals and close the lid for 10 minutes. Place the loin on the grill and baste with the marinade; close the lid and cook for 10 minutes. Turn the loin and baste again. Close the lid and cook for another 10 minutes. The meat should be slightly pink in the center and quite moist. Serve on a platter with Blackberry Sauce. Garnish with parsley sprigs, radish rosettes and yellow squash slices. Serves 2 to 4.

Roasted Loin of Venison with Baby Greens, Orange-Ginger Vinaigrette and Sweet Potatoes

8 (1"-thick) medallions of venison loin
½ cup walnut oil
2 Tbsp. raspberry vinegar
2 Tbsp. apple cider
1½ tsp. green onions, minced
6 dried juniper berries
4 cracked black peppercorns
1 cup fresh orange juice
3 large oranges (juice of 2; 1 cut into 8 wedges)
¼ cup rice wine vinegar
¼ cup olive oil
1 tsp. fresh ginger, minced
½ tsp. garlic, minced
½ tsp. red and green peppercorns
1 sweet potato, peeled and cut into small julienne cut
safflower oil for deep frying
4 slices Rapid Mix French Bread with centers removed
basil-flavored olive oil
½ lb. assorted baby greens (red and green oak leaf, frisee, red leaf lettuce
4 baby Belgian endives, cut in half and grilled or sautéed in herb oil
edible flowers for garnish

Place the venison medallions in a flat glass dish. Combine walnut oil, raspberry vinegar, apple cider, 1 tsp. of green onions, juniper berries, and black peppercorns. Pour mixture over the venison, cover, and marinate in refrigerator overnight. Make vinaigrette by whisking together orange juice, juice of 2 oranges, rice vinegar, olive oil, ginger, garlic, green onions, and red and green peppercorns. Set aside. Preheat oven to 350 degrees. Remove venison from the marinade and sear each piece in a hot skillet until they are browned on all sides. Transfer skillet to hot oven and cook until meat is cooked to no more than medium rare. Remove and let stand covered. Leave oven on. Pour oil to a depth of about 2" into a skillet and fry sweet potatoes until crisp, then drain well. Brush Rapid Mix French Bread lightly with flavored oil. Toast in a hot oven until lightly browned, then cool to room temperature. Place toast on serving plates and fill centers with assorted greens. Place 2 grilled halves of Belgian endive on each plate. Place 2 venison tenderloins on each plate. Drizzle with vinaigrette and garnish with fried sweet potato, orange wedges, and edible flowers. Serves 4.

Venison Backstrap Steaks
with Stilton Cheese Mousseline

Stilton Cheese Mousseline:
½ lb. chicken breasts, skinned and boned
1 egg white
½ cup cream
⅓ cup walnuts, finely chopped
2½ oz. Stilton cheese, crumbled
4 fresh basil leaves, minced
¼ tsp. dried marjoram, crumbled
⅛ tsp. dried rosemary, crumbled
⅛ tsp. freshly ground pepper
pinch of dried thyme, crumbled

Port Wine Sauce:
2 cups canned beef broth
1 Tbsp. unsalted butter
1 Tbsp. all-purpose flour
black pepper
2 Tbsp. Ruby Port

Venison Backstrap Steaks:
4 (8-oz.) venison backstrap, cut
    1½" thick
½ tsp. salt
¼ tsp. black pepper
2 Tbsp. safflower oil

Make Stilton Cheese Mousseline by cutting chicken into 1" pieces. Grind chicken into a paste; add egg white and blend; add cream and blend; add walnuts, cheese, basil, marjoram, rosemary, pepper and thyme. Blend until mixture is fluffy. Remove to a small bowl; cover and refrigerate at least 2 hours.

Make Port Wine Sauce by reducing beef broth to 1 cup. In another saucepan, melt butter; add flour and pepper and stir 3 minutes. Whisk in reduced broth and simmer until sauce is thick and smooth. Reduce heat to low; stir in port and cook for 10 minutes.

Make Venison Backstrap Steaks by preheating the oven to 375 degrees. Sprinkle all sides lightly with salt and pepper. Heat safflower oil in large skillet over medium-high heat. Add steaks and brown on one side for 3 minutes. Remove and arrange, browned-side-down, in large shallow roasting pan. Place a portion of the Stilton Cheese Mousseline on top of each steak and shape it into smooth flattened domes. Roast the steaks for about 5 to 15 minutes for medium rare. Reheat Port Wine Sauce. Place steaks on individual serving plates and spoon some of the wine sauce on top of the steaks. Serve immediately. Pass remaining sauce separately. Serves 4.

The Hanson Buck—The Official World Record White-tailed Deer: Shot Nov. 23, 1993 near Biggar, Saskatchewan, Canada. Official Boone and Crockett score is 213⅝. This replaces the Jordan Buck, shot in 1914. The Hanson Buck was shot on land belonging to Milo Hanson. Shot with .308 Winchester 150 grain factory ammo - three shots hit the buck. The rifle was a Winchester model 88 with a Weaver K4 scope. The distance was about 100 yards. The buck was an estimated 3½ years old. The estimated body weight was 200 pounds.

Roulade of Venison with Oysters and Green Onions

½ cup butter
1 cup green onions, minced
½ cup celery, minced
18 oysters, chopped
2 cups bread cubes, dampened with oyster
    water
1 egg, beaten
pinch of thyme
salt and pepper to taste

1 tsp. parsley, chopped
4 venison loin steaks, cut ¾" thick
1 dill pickle, quartered
salt
pepper
all-purpose flour
3 cups canned tomato sauce
Spanish Rice

Melt butter in a skillet and sauté green onions and celery until just tender. Add oysters and cook for no more than 5 minutes, stirring constantly. Add bread cubes and heat through. Remove from heat and mix thoroughly with egg, thyme, salt and pepper. Add parsley. Pound loin thin. On the center of the venison chop, fill with oyster dressing and ¼ dill pickle and roll up to form a 'jelly roll.' Secure with tooth-picks. Sprinkle with salt and pepper and roll in flour. Place roulades in a pan and bake in 350 degree preheated oven 15 to 20 minutes, or until brown; *Do not over-cook.* Remove from oven. Cover with tomato sauce and simmer 20 minutes; *Do not overcook.* Serve with Spanish Rice. Serves 4.

Venison Roulades with Green Onions and Anchovies

2 lbs. venison round steak
4 Tbsp. butter
4 Tbsp. canola oil
2 cups green onion, minced
2 Tbsp. all-purpose flour
1 tsp. salt

½ tsp. black pepper
20 flat anchovies
½ cup water
1 cup Burgundy wine
sour cream
green onions, finely chopped

Cut venison into 1"-thick slices and pound to ¼" thin. Trim into 6" rounds. Heat 1 Tbsp. butter and 2 Tbsp. canola oil in a large skillet. Add onions and sauté until the onions are tender. Remove from heat and stir in the flour. Return the pan to the heat and cook for 4 to 5 minutes. Reserve 3 Tbsp. of this mixture for the sauce. Sprinkle each slice of venison with salt and pepper and spread the butter and flour mixture evenly over the meat. Place 3 anchovy fillets on each slice of venison and roll the slices up jelly-roll fashion. Tie each with cotton kitchen string around each end. Heat the remaining butter and oil in a 2-qt. casserole dish over moderate heat on top of the stove. Add all venison roulades and cook them for 8 minutes; quickly brown on all sides. Preheat the oven to 325 degrees. Pour the water and wine into the casserole and add the reserved butter and flour mixture. Cover tightly and bake for 1 hour. Mix green onion into sour cream. Serve venison with sour cream sauce. Serves 2.

Rounsaville Camp Leg of Venison Mosaic

Cooked and served for the first time to friends, family and guests at Rounsaville's Camp at Coakers Bend on the Chickasawhay River in Greene County, Mississippi, on Thanksgiving Day 1995. This land has been in the Rounsaville family for over 100 years.

Roast:
1 (5-lb.) leg of venison, boned and butterflied
1 Tbsp. fresh rosemary, minced or 1 tsp. dried, crumbled
2 tsp. garlic, minced
¼ lb. spinach leaves, stemmed, divided
4 medium carrots, steamed, sliced once
4 whole pimientos, sliced into thin strips
½ medium onion, thinly sliced, and halved
¼ cup fresh parsley, minced
2 tsp. salt
¾ tsp. black pepper
¼ tsp. cayenne pepper
6 to 10 bacon strips
salt
pepper

Sauce;
⅓ cup dry vermouth
2 medium celery stalks, chopped
2 medium carrots, chopped
1 medium onion, chopped
½ cup water, if needed
1 cup canned chicken broth

Garnish:
20 to 25 fresh spinach leaves
long, thin carrots, steamed or boiled and cut in 4" lengths, or baby carrots, 6 to 12 pieces
6 to 12 pearl onions, steamed or boiled
6 to 12 cherry tomatoes
6 to 12 kumquats
6 to 12 fresh rosemary sprigs

Place rack in center of oven and preheat to 325 degrees. Pat venison dry. Place venison on work surface, outside down, with long edge toward you. If venison is too thick to roll, you may need to slice it a bit thinner. If needed, gently and carefully pound roast to spread. Sprinkle inside of butterfly with minced rosemary and garlic. Then cover with ½ of spinach leaves. Slice steamed carrots once lengthwise and lay evenly-spaced out across meat. Lay long pimento slices alongside the carrots. Lay halved onion slices across roast on top of carrots. Sprinkle with minced parsley, salt, black pepper and cayenne pepper. Cover with the remaining ½ of spinach leaves. Starting at short end, roll the meat very tightly. Tie the rolled roast securely with kitchen twine at 2" intervals along the roast and from end to end. Completely cover the outside and ends of roast with bacon strips secured with tooth picks. Finished roast will weigh between 5 lb. and 7 lb.

Place the rolled roast in a roasting pan. Season roast with salt and pepper. Add celery pieces, chopped carrots and onions to pan. Pour dry vermouth over roast. Insert a meat thermometer into thickest part of meat. Roast until the thermometer registers 150 degrees for a little less than medium, about 2½ hours, add up to ½ cup of water to pan if necessary to keep vegetables from sticking.

Transfer the meat to a cutting board; let roast stand for 15 minutes. In the meantime, pour off juices from pan. Stir chicken stock into pan, scraping up browned bits and mashing vegetables into liquid. Bring to a boil. Strain sauce, pressing on vegetables to extract all liquid. Boil liquid to reduce sauce.

Gently remove strings from meat. Carefully, cut a thin slice off both ends of the roast and discard. Slice the remaining venison roast into ¼" to ½" rounds.

If serving on individual plates: spoon sauce onto plate; lay a small spinach leaf on one edge; lay slice of roast on the center of the plate; spoon a line of sauce across roast; garnish with pearl onion, cherry tomato, baby carrot, kumquats; lay a sprig of rosemary atop slice of roast.

If serving on a platter: arrange fresh spinach leaves on a serving plate. Arrange venison slices on top of fresh spinach; spoon just enough sauce on top of rounds to coat the top surface. Serve remaining sauce separately. Alternate carrots, pearl onions and cherry tomatoes and kumquats around the edge of the roast. Insert sprigs of rosemary in two rows, alternating right and left, between the roast slices.

Depending on the size of the venison hindquarter and the thickness of the cuts, serves 6 to 12.

Sausage-Stuffed Venison Roast

1 venison hindquarter, deboned
3 long Polish sausages
salt
pepper

garlic powder
6 strips smoked bacon
2 cups dry red table wine
1 turkey-cooking bag

Debone the venison hindquarter. Place Polish sausages in cavity. Season with salt, pepper and garlic powder. Roll roast and tie with string. Place strips of bacon over roast. Place roast and red wine in cooking bag. Close bag, punch 6 holes in top of bag and place in covered roasting pan. Insert a meat thermometer and roast at 350 degrees until internal temperature reaches 138 degrees. Make gravy with drippings in bag. Serves 8 to 10.

Venison Wellington with Madeira Sauce

1 recipe French Venison Wellington
  Pastry
1 venison backstrap, large end, 16" long
1 clove garlic, pressed
salt
pepper
6 strips bacon

Venison Forcemeat Filling or
  Venison Liver Pâté
3 truffles
1 egg, lightly beaten
Madeira Wine and Green Onion Sauce

Prepare French Venison Wellington Pastry. Heat oven to 450 degrees. Rub the venison with the garlic. Season with salt and pepper. Cover venison with the bacon strips and secure with toothpicks or string. Place backstrap on a rack in a roasting pan and insert a meat thermometer into the thickest part of the backstrap. Roast until the thermometer registers 138 degrees. Remove the backstrap from the oven and allow to slightly cool. Remove the bacon strips and place the backstrap in the refrigerator until ready for final baking. Heat oven to 425 degrees. Roll pastry into a 18"x18" square or large enough to completely enclose the backstrap. Lay venison along one side of the pastry. Cover venison with the Venison Forcemeat Filling or Venison Liver Pâté. Cut truffles in halves and place in a line along the top of the filling. Lay pastry on top of the venison and wrap the edges underneath the venison; seal the edges. Brush pastry with beaten egg to seal edges. Garnish top with decorative cutouts from surplus pastry. Place venison, sealed-side-down, on a baking sheet. Brush again with the beaten egg. Bake about 30 minutes or until the pastry is lightly browned. Carefully remove to a serving platter. Serve fairly thick slices with Madeira Wine and Green Onion Sauce. Serves 10 to 12.

Sautéed Venison Crepes

1 lb. venison roast, cut in ¼" thick x1½"
    long ¼" wide strips
¼ cup bell pepper, chopped
¼ cup green onion, chopped
2 Tbsp. celery, minced
1 clove garlic, minced
¼ cup butter
1 (2-oz.) jar chopped pimiento, drained
2 Tbsp. Burgundy wine
1 tsp. fresh parsley, chopped

1 tsp. Italian seasoning
¼ tsp. salt
¼ tsp. dry mustard
dash of Tabasco sauce
1 egg, beaten
3 Tbsp. Mayonnaise
8 (8") Basic Crepes
Mushroom-Red Wine Venison Sauce
fresh parsley, chopped

Sauté venison, bell pepper, green onions, celery, and garlic in butter. Remove from heat. Stir in pimiento, Burgundy, parsley, Italian seasoning, salt, dry mustard, and Tabasco sauce. Combine egg and Mayonnaise in a bowl; stir in venison mixture. Fill each Basic Crepe with a heaping ¼ cup of the venison mixture. Roll up, and place seam-side-down in a lightly greased 13"x9"x2" baking dish; spoon Mushroom-Red Wine Sauce over crepes. Cover and bake at 350 degrees for 15 to 20 minutes. Garnish with chopped fresh parsley. Serves 4.

Spinach-Stuffed Smoked Venison Backstrap

1 whole head of elephant garlic
olive oil
2 Tbsp. butter
4 cups spinach, stemmed, washed and
    drained
2 to 3 Tbsp. flour
½ cup cream
salt

pepper
2 (1 to 1½ lbs.) venison backstraps
Bourbon & Balsamic Vinegar Marinade
1 cup mesquite wood chips
    soaked in water
Molasses & Bourbon Sauce For
    Smoked Vegetables
Mashed Potatoes & Turnips

Cut the head of garlic in half across cloves. Brush with olive oil; wrap in foil and place on grill over medium heat; cook for 30 minutes or until very tender. Remove from grill. Squeeze the soft garlic out of the halves; discard skins. In a sauté pan, melt butter, add spinach and toss until wilted. Sprinkle with flour; stir; slowly add cream. Cook 2 to 3 minutes or until the mixture thickens. Season to taste with salt and pepper. Stir in the roasted garlic. Transfer mixture to a bowl, cover and chill. Make a hole through the center of the venison backstraps with a long slender knife. Expand the 'tube' with your fingers. Stuff the stuffing into the hole from both ends until filled. Sew the ends shut with skewers and wraps of cotton twine. Place stuffed backstraps in Bourbon & Balsamic Vinegar Marinade and refrigerate for 4 hours. Remove venison from the marinade and season with salt and pepper. Sear stuffed backstraps on all sides on the grill. Place wet mesquite chips on coals, lower lid and smoke the backstraps for about 20 to 30 minutes, turning once. Remove backstraps from the grill and let rest before slicing. Serve 2 slices of the stuffed backstrap with Molasses & Bourbon Sauce with Vegetables on top and ⅔ cup of the Mashed Potatoes & Turnips on the side. Serves 4 to 6.

Chevreuil Stew

1 venison forequarter, deboned
vegetable oil
2 Tbsp. all-purpose flour
1 onion, minced
3 Tbsp. semi-thick tomato paste
1 bay leaf
1 sprig fresh thyme

1 Tbsp. garlic, minced
1 qt. canned beef broth
1 hot red pepper
salt
black pepper
½ glass Burgundy
Potato Croquettes

Cut the venison into 2" pieces and marinate in the refrigerator overnight. (Make a marinade by mixing together apple cider vinegar, sliced yellow onions, bay leaf, fresh thyme, fresh parsley, whole spice, salt and pepper, and hot pepper.)

Remove venison and allow to drip dry. Brown venison in oil; add flour and onion and tomato paste. Let come to a boil and add all other seasonings. Cover and simmer for one hour. Pour in wine 10 minutes before serving. Serve with Potato Croquettes.

Nevada Roasted Venison Backstrap
with Garlic Potatoes

2 lb. venison backstrap
1 cup red wine vinegar
1½ cups teriyaki sauce
¼ cup green onions, chopped
¼ cup garlic chopped
1 white onion, sliced thin
1 cup honey
3 Tbsp. olive oil plus extra for
  browning

1 small white onion, chopped fine
2 cloves garlic, minced
½ lb. fresh spinach leaves, stemmed
2 Tbsp. Maggi seasoning
2 Tbsp. balsamic vinegar
salt
pepper
1 cup pinion pine nuts, lightly toasted
Garlic Potatoes

Make marinade by mixing red wine vinegar, teriyaki sauce, green onions, garlic, onion, and honey. Place venison in a large flat glass dish. Pour marinade over the venison; cover and refrigerate for 24 hours. Preheat the oven to 350 degrees; butterfly steaks by slitting horizontally in the direction of the grain. Heat olive oil over medium heat; add onion, and cook until just tender. Add garlic and sauté. Mix in fresh spinach, Maggi seasoning and balsamic vinegar. Remove the pan from heat and stir until spinach is limp. Season with salt and pepper to taste and set spinach aside to cool; stir in toasted pinion pine nuts. Spread steak out and thinly spread with spinach mixture. Roll steak up and tie at 2" intervals with cotton butcher's twine. Heat a few tbsp. olive oil in a large skillet; add venison and brown evenly on all sides. Insert a meat thermometer into the thickest part of the venison roll. Place venison roll on a roasting rack and roast about 30 minutes or until the meat thermometer registers 138 degrees. Remove venison roll from the oven and let rest for 10 minutes. Slice and serve with Garlic Potatoes. Serves 4.

Tenderloin of Venison Braised in Oyster Sauce

1 lb. tenderloin of venison
1 garlic clove, minced
1 small onion, sliced thin
1 Tbsp. teriyaki sauce
2 Tbsp. Chinese oyster sauce
1 tsp. sugar

1 tsp. Accent
3 Tbsp. rice wine
1 tsp. fresh ginger root, minced
½ cup canned beef broth
¼ tsp. cornstarch
2 Tbsp. cold water

Cut venison into small, very thin slices. Sauté the garlic and onion, teriyaki sauce, oyster sauce, sugar, Accent, wine, and ginger; season with salt and pepper, Stir well. Add beef broth and simmer for just a minute. Mix cornstarch into cold water. Add cornstarch liquid a small amount at a time until broth reaches the desired thickness. Serves 2.

Tenderloin of Venison Braised with Green Olives

1 lb. tenderloin of venison
1 Tbsp. teriyaki sauce
1 tsp. Accent
¼ cup rice wine or sherry

salt
10 green olives, pitted
¼ cup canned beef broth

Cut the venison tenderloin into ½" cubes and sauté until lightly browned. Add the teriyaki sauce, Accent, and wine; season with salt. Cover and braise until the venison is nearly done. Score the skin of the green olives with a knife to the beef broth. Cover and simmer 10 minutes longer. Serves 2.

Siamese Venison Backstrap with New Potato Salad

1 (1 lb.) venison backstrap
1 cup corn oil
1 cup sesame oil
3 Tbsp. chili paste
1½ Tbsp. garlic, minced

1 cup terriaki soy sauce
¼ cup fresh cilantro, chopped fine
½ cup dark brown sugar
juice of 2 limes
New Potato Salad

Place venison in a glass dish. Combine oil, sesame oil, chili paste, garlic, soy sauce, cilantro, brown sugar, and lime juice and pour over meat. Cover and marinate in refrigerator at least 8 hours. Make New Potato Salad. Grill marinated venison over charcoal, 5 minutes on the first side and 2 on the second for medium rare. Serve with New Potato Salad. Serves 2.

The white-tailed deer has existed essentially unchanged for perhaps as much as 20 million years and is thought to be the ancestral form from which today's mule deer and black-tailed deer evolved.

Succulent Venison Steak Roll

1 lb. venison top round steak,
   cut in 5 thin slices
garlic
salt
pepper
3 Tbsp. tomato catsup
1 Tbsp. prepared mustard

5 slices smoked bacon
5 olives
1 dill pickle, cut in 5 thick slices
1 onion minced
2 Tbsp. safflower or canola oil
water
½ cup red wine

Rub slices of venison top round steak with garlic, and season with salt and pepper. Add tomato catsup and mustard to each slice. On each slice put 1 slice of smoked bacon, 1 olive, 1 slice of pickle, and sprinkle with minced onion. Roll up and tie with butcher string or fasten with bamboo skewers. Heat safflower oil in skillet. Add steak rolls and sauté for about 10 minutes, turning venison rolls to brown each side. Reduce heat. Add water to half cover venison steak rolls; cover and simmer for about 20 minutes. Add wine and simmer for an additional 5 minutes. Serves 5.

Tournedos Venison Haroldo

¼ cup butter
1½ Tbsp. all-purpose flour
1 cup canned beef broth
5 peppercorns, crushed
1 bay leaf
1 allspice
1 clove

2 Tbsp. brandy
2 Tbsp. Burgundy
2 Tbsp. safflower or canola oil
8 venison backstrap filets, cut 1" thick
½ lb. pork liver pâté
truffles, sliced (optional)
Fresh Lemon and Orange Sauce

In a small saucepan melt butter and stir in flour. Brown flour, stirring constantly. Stir in beef broth until smooth. Add peppercorns, bay leaf, allspice, clove, brandy, and safflower oil; simmer for 5 minutes. Remove bay leaf, allspice and clove. Grill backstrap filets to no more than medium rare. *Do not overcook filets.* Spread a thin layer of Fresh Orange Sauce on each serving plate. Arrange 2 filets on each serving plate, arrange a large slice of pâté on top. Garnish with slices of truffle. Serves 4.

Tournedos Venison Royal

¼ cup butter
½ cup onion, chopped
¼ cup bread crumbs
1 tsp. paprika
1 tsp. capers
1 tsp. truffles, chopped
pinch powdered thyme

1 cup beef sweetbreads, parboiled,
   chopped fine
4 artichoke cups
8 venison backstrap filets, cut 1" thick
salt and pepper
¼ cup Bearnaise Sauce

In a small skillet melt butter and sauté onion, bread crumbs, paprika, capers, truffles and thyme until done. Add sweetbreads and heat through. Remove pan from the heat. Divide the mixture into 4 equal portions and roll it into balls. Place each ball in an artichoke heart. While cooking onion mixture, season the backstrap filets and grill them to medium rare; *Do not overcook.* Place 2 filets on a serving plate. Place stuffed artichoke heart on the plate and pour about 1½ tbsp. Bearnaise Sauce over filets. Serves 4.

Venison and Ham Mousse

pimento stuffed green olives, sliced thin
1 envelope unflavored gelatin
¼ cup cold water
½ cup boiling water
1 (10½-oz.) can condensed beef
  consommé
½ cup mayonnaise
¾ tsp. salt
¼ tsp. nutmeg

1 Tbsp. lemon peel, grated
1 Tbsp. onion, minced
½ cup celery, finely minced
2½ cups cooked venison, ground fine
1 cup cooked smoked ham, ground fine
½ cup onion cracker crumbs, finely
  rolled
1 cup heavy cream, whipped
1 can pressurized processed cheese
  spread

Lightly oil a 9" loaf pan. Lay sliced olives in circular/flower patterns in the bottom of the pan. Soften gelatin in cold water. Add the boiling water and stir until the gelatin is dissolved. Add consommé. Measure out ¾ cup of the consommé mixture and pour it into the loaf pan. Chill until just set. In a large bowl combine mayonnaise, salt, nutmeg, lemon peel, onion and celery. Stir in remaining consommé mixture. Fold in ground venison, ham and cracker crumbs. Fold in whipped cream. Pour mixture over set aspic in bottom of loaf pan. Chill 5 to 6 hours or overnight in the refrigerator. Unmold on a large serving plate. Garnish top with pasteurized processed cheese spread from a pressure can. Serve as a buffet dish or makes 10 to 12 first course servings.

Venison Backstrap Steaks with Sherry Sauce

½ cup white onion, chopped fine
½ cup watercress, chopped fine
½ tsp. ground mustard
1 cup very dry sherry

4 venison backstrap steaks, cut 2" thick
olive oil
English peas
small boiled potatoes

Mix together onion, watercress, mustard and sherry. Preheat a large skillet over high heat. Quickly brown backstrap steaks on one side; turn and quickly brown other side. The venison should be very rare in the center. Pour the sherry mixture over the steaks. Keep heat on high and let sherry sizzle for 1 to 2 minutes. Place the steaks on individual serving plates. Spoon sauce over the steaks. Serves 4.

Venison Loin Chops with Muscadine Sauce

8 (4-oz.) venison loin chops, cut ¾" thick
¼ tsp. salt
1¼ tsp. Tabasco sauce, divided
¼ lb. butter, softened
1 Tbsp. canola oil

½ cup shallots, sliced
1 cup Burgundy wine
½ cup muscadine jelly
¼ tsp. salt
fresh parsley, chopped

Mix salt and Tabasco sauce and spread over chops. Melt 1 Tbsp. butter and the canola oil in a large cast iron skillet over medium-high heat. Do not crowd; cook chops to medium in several batches; turn once; remove chops to a large serving platter. Melt 2 Tbsp. of the butter in the same skillet. Add the scallions and cook until just tender. Stir in the Burgundy. Bring to a boil and reduce to about ½ cup. Stir in and melt the muscadine jelly; add the remaining ¼ tsp. of Tabasco sauce;

salt to taste. Remove the sauce from the heat and stir in the remaining 5 Tbsp. of butter, a small amount at a time, allowing the sauce to thicken slightly. Spoon the sauce over the chops. Garnish with the chopped parsley. Serves 4 to 6.

Brandy Flamed Venison Kidneys

2 venison kidneys
butter
2 jiggers brandy, warmed
⅓ cup dry sherry
½ cup fresh mushrooms, sliced
1 Tbsp. white onions, chopped
½ cup whipping cream

1 Tbsp. lime juice
1 tsp. Homemade Horseradish
salt
white pepper
crisp toast
butter, melted

Clean and remove membrane covering on kidneys. Cut the kidneys into ½" to 1" size pieces. Melt the butter in a skillet and brown the venison pieces for 3 minutes. Pour brandy over the kidneys; light and allow the flames to die out. Add sherry, mushrooms and onions. Heat to simmering. When the mushrooms are just tender; add cream, lime juice, and Homemade Horseradish. Season with salt and white pepper. Bring to a simmer. Serve at once on toast and spoon on melted butter. Serves 2 to 4.

Venison Liver Pâté

½ envelope (1½ tsp.) unflavored gelatin
½ cup bouillon or consommé
pimiento
capers
truffles or ripe olives
1 lb. venison liver
½ tsp. MSG

6 Tbsp. butter
2 Tbsp. onion, minced
½ tsp. salt
1 tsp. dry mustard
¼ tsp. cloves, ground
½ tsp. nutmeg, ground
2 Tbsp. brandy

Sprinkle the gelatin over the bouillon in a small saucepan to soften. Place the saucepan over low heat; stirring constantly and until gelatin is dissolved. Pour a thin layer of the bouillon mixture in the bottom of an 8"x4"x2½" loaf pan. Let the mixture thicken slightly. Press a design of pimiento, capers and truffles or ripe olives into thickened bouillon mixture. Pour the remaining bouillon mixture carefully over the design and chill while preparing the pâté mixture. Sprinkle the venison liver with MSG. Melt 2 Tbsp. of the butter in a sauté pan. Sauté the venison liver and the onion in the butter for 6 to 7 minutes. Remove liver from the heat. Scrape the venison and onions into a blender bowl. Add salt, dry mustard, cloves and nutmeg. Turn on the blender and blend until smooth. Add the remaining 4 Tbsp. butter and brandy. Blend until smooth. Turn the mixture into the loaf pan and chill. Unmold by quickly dipping the pan into hot water up to the top. Loosen around the edges with a sharp knife. Lay serving platter on top of the loaf pan and turn over together. Lift off loaf pan. Serves 24.

Venison Liver Pâté with Madeira and Diced Ham

6 Tbsp. butter
¼ cup green onions, chopped
2 cloves garlic, chopped fine
1 lb. venison liver, cut 1" thick

¼ cup Madeira or wine
4 thin slices ham, diced
salt
pepper

Melt the butter in a heavy skillet over medium heat. Add green onions and garlic and cook until just tender, not browned. Turn to high heat. Add venison liver and cook quickly until browned on all sides. Add the Madeira and stir to scrape up browned bits from the bottom of the skillet. Add diced ham and simmer for 2 minutes and cool. Add salt and pepper. Put the mixture through a food grinder twice. Mold into a loaf. Refrigerate. Serve at air temperature with crackers.

Mississippi Venison Roast with Red Wine & Mushroom Sauce

1 (3 lb. to 4 lb.) venison hindquarter roast
Homemade Non-Cultured Buttermilk
½ cup all-purpose flour
1 tsp. salt
1 tsp. pepper
1 tsp. garlic powder
1 tsp. paprika
¼ cup olive oil

¼ cup bacon drippings
½ cup tomato juice
juice of 2 limes
juice of 1 orange
2 bay leaves
2 Tbsp, red plum jelly
½ cup Burgundy wine
1 (8-oz,) can mushrooms, drained

In a large glass container, soak venison overnight in the buttermilk; turn frequently. Remove venison and allow to drain. Mix and sift flour, salt, pepper, garlic powder, and paprika. Roll roast in the flour mixture, reserve flour for sauce. In a large Dutch oven or heavy roaster, quickly brown the roast in the olive oil. Combine wine, juices, bay leaves, and jelly and mix well. Pour the wine and jelly mixture over the roast. Preheat oven to 300 degrees. Cover roast and bake for 1 to 2 hours or until tender. Add the mushrooms. Thicken pan drippings by adding a little of the flour mixture which was left over from coating roast. Serves 8.

Venison Pâté De Grand Marnier

2 pkgs. pie crust mix
1 cup Bonbel or Port Salut cheese, grated
5 eggs, divided
¼ cup water
2 Tbsp, butter
1 large onion, minced
1 clove garlic, mashed
1½ lbs. venison, ground
1½ lbs. lean pork, ground

1 lb. Mississippi Country Venison
    Sausage
1 Tbsp. salt
½ tsp. pepper
½ tsp. marjoram
4 to 6 eggs, beaten
6 hard-boiled eggs, halved
Grand Marnier Cream Sauce for
Venison Roasts

Mix together pie crust mix with ½ cup of the grated cheese. Beat 2 eggs well with

¼ cup water. Stir egg mixture into the pie crust mix and stir until dough makes a ball in the middle of the bowl. Turn dough out on a lightly floured board and knead it until it is smooth and elastic. Line a greased 13" by 4" by 2½" loaf pan with heavy-duty aluminum foil, with the foil extending over edges of pan. Roll out ⅔ of the pastry on a lightly floured board into a 20" by 11" oblong. Line bottom and sides of the pan with the pastry; allow an excess of pastry to extend over the edges of the pan. Place pan in a refrigerator and allow to chill. Reserve the remainder of the pastry in the work area. Heat oven to 350 degrees. Melt butter in a small skillet. Add onions and garlic and cook until just tender. Scrape the onion and garlic mixture into a large mixing bowl. Add venison, pork, sausage meat, salt, pepper and marjoram. Beat eggs; reserve ¼ cup of the beaten eggs for later use. Add the beaten eggs to the meat mixture and mix until it is smooth and well blended. Spoon ½ of the mixture into the pastry-lined pan. Top mixture with the halved eggs. Sprinkle with remaining ½ cup grated cheese. Spread evenly with remaining meat mixture. Turn pastry extending over sides of pan and over the meat. Brush pastry with reserved beaten egg. Roll out remaining pastry on a lightly floured board and cut into a 13' by 4" oblong to fit top of pan. Place pastry on top; trim and seal edges firmly. Brush the top with reserved beaten egg and decorate top with small seasonal cutouts from the pastry scraps. Brush again with reserved beaten egg. Bake for 2 hours or until pastry is richly browned. Remove the pan from the oven and cool for 20 minutes. Remove pâté from the pan by pulling up on the foil overhang. Place the pâté on a serving platter and remove foil. For a dinner first course or buffet serve sliced and hot with Grand Marnier Cream Sauce for Venison Roasts. For a luncheon dish serve cold. Leave pâté in the pan and chill for several hours. Remove from pan and slice thin. Serves 4 to 6.

Venison Steak Tartare with Eggs and Anchovy

½ lb. venison tenderloin, fine ground 3 times
2 x-small chicken, 4 quail, 2 turtle egg yolks or 2 Tbsp. sea urchin roe
2 Tbsp. salt
2 Tbsp. pepper

2 Tbsp. capers, drained
2 Tbsp, onions, finely chopped
2 Tbsp. fresh parsley, chopped
8 flat anchovy filets, drained
dark bread
butter

Traditionally, the meat for Venison Steak Tartare is ground very fine and served at room temperature and as soon as possible. Shape the venison into 2 mounds and place then in the center of separate serving plates. Make a well in the middle of each mound and carefully drop an egg yolk or urchin roe in each well. Serve the salt, black pepper, capers, chopped onions, parsley and anchovy fillets in small separate saucers on the side. The venison and other ingredients are combined at the table by the diner. Serve with dark bread and butter. Serves 2.

Venison Steak with Wine Sauce

This is a 1758 venison recipe from Fredericksburg, Virginia.

6 venison steaks, cut ¾" thick
6 slices bacon
2 Tbsp, all-purpose flour
1 tsp, sage
1 tsp. celery salt

½ tsp. thyme
⅛ tsp. cayenne pepper
2 Tbsp. butter
1 cup Burgundy wine

Trim steaks and remove all fat. Wrap each steak with bacon around the outside and secure bacon strip with a toothpick. Mix and sift together flour, sage, celery salt, thyme, and cayenne pepper. Sprinkle the flour mixture over both sides of the steaks. Melt the butter in a heavy skillet and quickly fry the steaks on each side. Remove the steaks from the frying pan to a serving platter. Place the steaks in a warming oven. Add Burgundy to the frying pan and scrape the bottom to dislodge bits. Simmer until the sauce is slightly thickened. Pour the sauce over the steaks. Serves 6.

Venison Tournedos à La Anna

4 small backs trap steaks, about 1½" thick
salt
pepper
4 thin slices tomato
4 large fresh mushroom crowns

butter
4 slices canned truffles
Marchand de Vin Sauce for Venison
parsley sprigs

Sear venison backstrap steaks on each side in a very hot iron skillet so they are just browned to the rare stage; *do not overcook*. Arrange steaks in oven proof serving dish and sprinkle with salt and pepper. Place a thin slice of tomato and a large mushroom crown which has been previously browned in butter on top of each steak. Top each steak with a slice of truffle. Pour Instant Marchand de Vin Sauce over steaks and place in a 350 degree oven for about 10 minutes. Steaks should be cooked to no more than medium when removed from the oven. Garnish with parsley snips. Serves 4.

Venison Sausage and Sweet Potato Stuffing

½ lb. venison breakfast sausage
½ cup minced onion
½ cup chopped celery
¼ tsp. commercial poultry seasoning

½ tsp. salt
⅛ tsp. ground white pepper
1½ cups soft,dry bread crumbs
2 cups mashed, cooked sweet potatoes

Cook sausage and break into small pieces. Mix in onion, celery, poultry seasoning, salt, and pepper. Cook in a skillet until meat is almost done. Drain off fat and mix in bread crumbs and sweet potatoes.

Crown Roast of Venison; with Sausage & Sweet Potato Stuffing and Fruit Sauce

Note: This is the most elegant and challenging recipe in this book. The assembly of the crown is tricky, if not difficult. I recommend that you take two whole rib sections, with backstraps, to a butcher who has experience assembling crown roasts and have them to make the crown roast for you. Because of the difference in the sizes of deer, I recommend that you have two matched rib sides available and that you should be prepared to adjust the amount of stuffing as required.

2 whole venison rib sections with backstraps
Sausage and Sweet Potato Stuffing for
   Venison Crown Roast
½ tsp, garlic salt

⅛ tsp. black pepper
Blackberry Sauce with Bourbon
decorative frills for rib tips

If you would like to assemble your own crown roast, I recommend that you think the process completely through. The cuts of venison that you will be using are the more difficult pieces to obtain in matched sections. Cut off rib tips where they join the sternum. Crack open and gently separate the backbone joints between each rib. Cut off the connecting tissue between each rib ⅓ way down the rib. Scrape the upper crown bones clean. Place the two rib roasts end to end on meat board. Cut two small slits behind the adjoining ribs and tie together with cotton twine. Cut two small slits on the end ribs; pull together, meat side toward center, and tie, forming a crown roast. Or, pull both ends of 13 rib roast in to a circle and tie forming a small crown. You may need to adjust the lengths of the ribs and the scraped area to make an even presentation. Make the Sausage and Sweet Potato Stuffing for Venison Crown Roast. Mix garlic salt and pepper together; rub mixture into all sides of roast. Place seasoned roast, bone ends up, in a shallow roasting pan. Fill the center of crown roast with stuffing mixture; cover with aluminum foil. Insert meat thermometer into center of roast. Bake at 325 degrees for 2 or 3 hours or until meat thermometer reads 135 degrees to 140 degrees. (Time varies according to size and age of animal.) Add decorative frills for the top of each crown point (available at local butcher shop.) Serve with Blackberry Sauce with Bourbon on the side. Serves 10 to 14.

Deer were originally brought to New Zealand by European settlers, and the deer population rose rapidly. This caused great environmental damage and was controlled by hunting and poisoning until the concept of deer farming developed in the 1960s. Deer farming has advanced into a significant economic activity in New Zealand with more than 3,000 farms running over 1 million deer in total. Deer products are exported to over 50 countries around the world, with New Zealand becoming well recognized as a source of quality venison and co-products.

Raisin, Apricot & Onion Stuffed Venison Crown Roast

2 whole venison rib sections with backstraps attached
Raisin, Apricot & Onion Stuffing for Venison Crown Roast
½ tsp, garlic salt
⅛ tsp. black pepper
Cumberland Sauce
decorative frills for rib tips

If you would like to assemble your own crown roast, I recommend that you think the process completely through. The cuts of venison that you will be using are the more difficult pieces to obtain in matched sections. Cut off rib tips where they join the sternum. Crack open and gently separate the backbone joints between each rib. Cut off the connecting tissue between each rib ⅓ way down the rib. Scrape the upper crown bones clean. Place the two rib roasts end to end on meat board. Cut two small slits behind the adjoining ribs and tie together with cotton twine. Cut two small slits on the end ribs; pull together, meat side toward center, and tie, forming a crown roast. Or, pull both ends of 13 rib roast into a circle and tie forming a small crown. You may need to adjust the lengths of the ribs and the scraped area to make an even presentation. Make the Raisin, Apricot & Onion Stuffing for Venison Roast. Mix garlic salt and pepper together; rub mixture into all sides of roast. Place seasoned roast, bone ends up, in a shallow roasting pan. Fill the center of crown roast with stuffing mixture; cover with aluminum foil. Insert meat thermometer into center of roast. Bake at 325 degrees for 2 or 3 hours or until meat thermometer reads 135 degrees to 140 degrees. (Time varies according to size and age of animal.) Add decorative frills for the top of each crown point, (available at local butcher shop.) Serve with Cumberland Sauce on the side. Serves 10 to 14.

Classic Venison Soufflé

The baked soufflé must always be kept away from drafts and served at once in the straight-sided dish in which it is cooked. If your soufflé is well made, you may be able to count on no more than about 10 minutes in a warm holding oven.

Butter
all-purpose flour
1 cup Venison Soufflé Cream Sauce
¾ to 1 cup cooked venison, finely chopped
¼ cup carrots, finely chopped
¼ cup celery, finely chopped
¼ cup parsley, finely chopped
3 egg yolks, beaten
salt
nutmeg
lemon juice
⅓ cup sliced olives
3 to 4 egg whites
Venison Soufflé Tomato Sauce

Preheat oven to 325 degrees. Grease the bottom and sides of a 7" straight-side soufflé dish with butter and dust with flour. Make Cream Sauce and when it is smooth and hot stir in venison, carrots, celery and parsley. Heat, then stir in egg yolks and season with salt, paprika, nutmeg and lemon juice. Add sliced olives. Let mixture cool slightly. Whip egg whites until stiff, but not dry. Fold whipped egg whites very lightly into mixture. Gently pour into greased and floured soufflé dish. Place soufflé on the center of the center shelf. Bake until firm, for about 40 minutes. Handle soufflé gently and serve immediately with Tomato Sauce.

Venison and Spinach Ravioli

½ cup cooked venison, ground
3 Tbsp. cooked ham, ground
½ cup cooked spinach, squeezed dry and
   chopped fine
2 Tbsp, grated Parmesan cheese
1 tsp. parsley, minced

dash nutmeg
salt
pepper
1 egg, beaten
Basic Homemade Pasta Dough

Mix venison, ham, spinach, Parmesan cheese, parsley, nutmeg, salt, and pepper. Add just enough egg to bind the mixture together. Make Basic Pasta Dough. Divide dough into 4 equal portions. Roll each portion into ⅛" thin sheets. On one sheet place a tsp. of filling every 2". Cover the filling with a second sheet of dough and, with your fingertips, press gently around each mound of filling. Cut the dough into 2" squares with a small pastry wheel. Make sure that the ravioli is firmly sealed around the filling. Let the ravioli stand for about an hour to dry. Cook in a large pot of rapidly boiling water or beef stock for 6 to 7 minutes. Drain and serve with any tomato or meat sauce. Makes about 24 ravioli.

Cacciagione Gwen

Created especially for Signora Gwen McKee 1996.

4 oz. Portobello mushrooms
1 Tbsp. Homemade Butter
8 oz. raisins
1 cup Cognac
2 Tbsp. Homemade Butter
2 Tbsp. chopped green onions

2 Tbsp. fresh sage
2 Tbsp. tarragon
1 Tbsp. whole peppercorns
2 cups Burgundy
1 cup demi-glaze
4 (6-oz.) venison loin steaks

Chop mushrooms and sauté 1 Tbsp. of butter; set aside. Soak raisins in Cognac for 1 hour. Sauté green onions, herbs, peppercorns in 2 Tbsp. butter; add red wine, demi-glaze, raisins, and Cognac. Slow simmer for at least ½ hour; reduce sauce to desired consistency, strain and add reserved mushrooms. Sauté venison steaks rare to medium-rare and serve on sauce. Serves 4.

3

Venison Steaks

Venison steaks are cut from the hind, forequarters, and backstraps. On the average 120 lb. white tail buck, the hindquarters weigh 10 lbs. each and the forequarters weigh 5 lbs. each. The number of steaks which can be cut from a quarter is determined by how thick you make the steaks.

For many cooks, the only way to cook venison steaks is to slice them thin and fry them until they are very well done. Unfortunately, this is the way most of us were served our first taste of venison. There are some recipes which call for thin cuts. Thin-cut hard-fried venison will leave you wanting. Venison steaks taste best when the cuts are thicker. Thick cuts can be sautéed and broiled. Thin cuts can be fried, but moist cooking may serve the purpose better.

Frying and broiling steaks can be tricky. Unlike marbled beef, venison is a fat-free meat, and it needs a lot of help to provide internal and external moisture during cooking.

Venison should not be fried or broiled to the well-done stage. In a slow-cooking stew, this works fine. But in dry heat, you will end up with a very tough piece of meat. Fry or broil your venison to less than medium done (138 degrees). If your conscience or eating habits won't let you do this, then you can enjoy exploring the moist soup, stew, stroganoff, chili, meatloaf and meatball recipes.

Quick Fried Venison Round Steaks

2 venison round steaks, cut ½" or less	4 Tbsp. Wesson oil
Worcestershire sauce	pan drippings
salt	1 Tbsp. all-purpose flour
pepper	½ cup finely chopped onions
all-purpose flour	1 cup whole milk
	salt and pepper to taste

Tenderize venison round steaks by beating/chopping both sides of the steaks with the sharp edge of a knife. Season the steaks with Worcestershire sauce and salt and pepper. Dredge the steaks in flour. Heat the Wesson oil in a heavy skillet and quickly fry steaks on both sides. *Do not overcook.* Remove the steaks to a warm serving platter. Brown the onions in the pan drippings. Mix flour with milk and add to onions and make a gravy. Add more milk to achieve the desired consistency. Salt and pepper to taste. Pour the gravy over the steaks and serve. Serves 2 to 4.

Mrs. Mary Sue Rounsaville

Coca-Cola Marinated Venison

¾" thick venison round steaks cut
   in ¾" wide strips
Coca-Cola
all-purpose flour

salt
pepper
Criseo

Cover the venison strips with Coca-Cola and marinate in the refrigerator overnight. Remove venison from the marinade and allow to drain. Season flour with salt and papper and dredge the venison in the seasoned flour. Melt the Crisco in a deep fat cooker. Quickly fry the venison to just a little more than rare or until it is just brown. *Do not overcook.*

Miss Jo Leslie

Barbecued Venison Flank Steak in Honey-Ginger Marinade

¾ cup safflower oil
⅓ cup teriyaki sauce
3 Tbsp. honey
3 Tbsp. red wine vinegar

2 tsp. ginger, ground
1 green onion, chopped
1 large clove garlic, crushed
1 (1½ lb.) venison flank or brisket
   steak

Make marinade by combining safflower oil, teriyaki sauce, honey, red wine vinegar, ginger, green onion and garlic. Place venison flank steak in a large glass baking dish and pour marinade over. Cover and refrigerate overnight, turning twice. Grill steak to desired doneness, 4 to 5 minutes for rare. Baste with marinade while cooking. Slice across the grain into thin slices. Serves 4 to 6.

Venison Steaks with Mixed Vegetables and Apples

2 venison round steaks, cut ¾" thick
all-purpose flour
Crisco
1 Tbsp. apple cider vinegar

½ cup celery, chopped
½ cup apple, chopped
½ cup carrot, chopped
¼ cup onion, chopped

Dredge steaks in flour. Melt Crisco in a heavy skillet and quickly brown the steaks on all sides. Place steaks in glass baking dish; add vinegar. Cover tightly and cook very slowly in 300-degree oven for 2 hours. If necessary add more liquid. About 30 minutes before meat is tender, add celery, apple, carrot, and onion. Serves 4 to 6.

In 2009, bow hunters harvested a total of 91,546 deer during the four-month Ohio archery season. Approximately 345,000 bow hunters participated. The Ohio statewide deer population was estimated to be 750,000 in early October 2010.

Carpetbagger Venison Steaks

4 eye-of-round venison steaks, cut about
   1½" thick
½ pt. oysters (8 to 12)
2 cups sherry

¼ lb, butter
salt and pepper to taste
paprika

Cut pockets into each of the steaks. Marinate the oysters in 1 cup of sherry for 1 hour. Place 2 or 3 oysters into each steak pocket with a little sherry; seal with a tooth pick. Place butter into a large skillet and melt. Add 1 cup of sherry to butter. Place the steaks in wine-butter sauce and steam on each side for 1 minute. Remove steaks from skillet, and salt and pepper to taste. Sprinkle paprika on steaks and place in a preheated broiler. Broil desired amount of time, then baste with wine and butter sauce. Serves 4.

Chicken-Fried Venison Round Steak

venison round steaks, cut into serving sizes
all-purpose flour
salt

black pepper
shortening
1½ cups whole milk

Cut round steaks into serving size pieces. Tenderize each steak by pounding with a heavy steak tenderizing mallet. Mix and sift flour, salt and pepper. Dredge the steaks in flour mixture. Melt ¼" of Crisco in a hot skillet and brown steaks on both sides until less than medium. Remove and drain steaks; keep warm. Pour off all but 3 Tbsp. of the pan drippings. Whisk the flour into the milk and add to the pan drippings. Stir constantly until thickened. If too thick, add more milk. Season to taste with salt and pepper

Country-Fried Venison Steak
with Buttermilk Marinade

venison round steaks, cut ¾" thick
cultured buttermilk
safllower oil
all-purpose flour
salt

pepper
1 Tbsp. flour
3 Tbsp. cold water
1½ cups whole milk
salt and pepper to taste

Cut venison round steaks into serving-size pieces. Pound each piece with heavy steak tenderizer. Place steaks in a dish and completely cover them with buttermilk. Refrigerate 6 to 12 hours. Wipe off excess buttermilk; dredge steaks in flour seasoned with salt and pepper. Fry steaks in a heavy skillet in ¼ inch of fairly hot safflower oil, browning steaks well on both sides; cook to more than medium. Place steaks aside to drain on paper towels. Pour off all but 3 Tbsp. of oil. Add 1½ cups whole milk to the skillet and heat until it begins to bubble. Mix flour with water and slowly add, a small amount at a time, to the milk; stirring constantly. If too thick, add more milk. If too thin add a very little more flour. Season to taste.

Southern Fried Venison Steak with Baked Grits

2 venison round steaks, cut ½" thick
1 tsp. salt
½ tsp. black pepper
½ tsp. garlic or onion salt
½ tsp. MSG
1 tsp. ground allspice

½ cup all-purpose flour
2 Tbsp. margarine
2 medium yellow onions, chopped
1 cup water
Mashed Potatoes
Baked Cheese Grits

Pound venison steaks to tenderize. Mix salt, black pepper, garlic or onion salt, MSG and allspice. Rub mixed spices on all sides of steak. Sprinkle with flour. Melt margarine in a skillet and quickly brown venison on both sides. Add more margarine if necessary. Remove venison and onions. Return venison to skillet. Add water; cover, and cook over low heat 1 to 1½ hours or until tender. Adjust seasonings to taste. Serve with Mashed Potatoes or Baked Cheese Grits. Serves 5.

Filet of Venison with Mustard Cream Sauce

2 Tbsp. butter
2 (8 oz.) venison round steaks, cut 1¼" thick
2 Tbsp. Dijon mustard
1 tsp. Worcestershire sauce

pepper
¼ cup brandy
½ cup heavy cream

Melt butter in large skillet over medium-high heat. Add venison steaks and cook to desired degree of doneness, about 4 minutes per side for rare. Add Dijon mustard and Worcestershire to skillet. Season with pepper. Stir to combine. Remove the pan from the heat. Add brandy and ignite with match. When flames subside, return venison to the skillet to warm. Place steaks on warm serving plates. Add cream to the skillet and boil until reduced to thin sauce consistency. Pour sauce over steaks and serve. Serves 2.

French Quarter Venison Steaks

½ cup all-purpose flour
2 tsp. salt
½ tsp. pepper
2 tsp. paprika
1 lb. venison round steaks
1 cup chopped onions

⅓ cup bell pepper, chopped
Crisco
½ cup rice
1½ cups canned tomatoes
2 cups hot water

Combine flour, salt, pepper and paprika. Coat venison steak well, reserving remaining flour mixture. onion and bell pepper in a small amount of Crisco in skillet. When just tender, remove vegetables and set aside. Brown the round steaks on both sides. Return the onion and pepper to skillet; sprinkle rice over the steak mixture. Pour tomatoes on top. Pour hot water over tomatoes, then sprinkle with reserved flour mixture and stir. Cover tightly and simmer 1 hour. Serves 2.

Garlic and Pepper Venison Steak with Onion Sauce

1 (1½-lb.) trimmed lean venison round
  steak, cut 1" thick
1 large garlic clove, minced
2 tsp. ground pepper
1½ lbs. onions, thinly sliced and halved
3 bay leaves
1 cup dry red wine

1 Tbsp. safflower oil
2 garlic cloves, minced
1 Tbsp. sugar
1+ Tbsp. red wine vinegar
salt
pepper

Place venison steak in a large glass baking dish. Combine 1 garlic clove and pepper. Rub each side of the steak with ½ the spice mixture. Sprinkle with onions and bay leaves. Pour wine over steaks. Refrigerate overnight. Remove steak from marinade and reserve marinade. Heat safflower oil in heavy skillet over medium heat. Add marinade and remaining 2 garlic cloves. Cook until onions are just tender and all of the liquid is absorbed, stirring frequently, about 35 minutes. Stir in sugar and cook 5 minutes. Add 1 Tbsp. red wine vinegar. Taste and add more vinegar if desired. Season onion marinade with salt and pepper. Remove the bay leaves. Heat a heavy skillet over medium-high heat or preheat the broiler. Add the venison steak and cook to desired doneness, 8 to 10 minutes per side for medium-rare. Remove steak from skillet. Let stand 5 minutes. Cut diagonally into thin slices. Serve immediately with onion marinade. Serves 6.

Mrs. Kathryn Breland

Fried Venison Finger Steaks

1 lb. boneless venison steaks cut from the round or backstrap, cut ½" thick
1 tsp. lemon-pepper seasoning
½ tsp. salt

½ cup buttermilk
1 egg, whipped
1 cup all-purpose flour
¾ cup vegetable oil or shortening

Pound venison steaks to ½" thickness. Sprinkle steaks with lemon-pepper seasoning and salt. Cut pounded steaks into strips. Mix buttermilk and egg in a small bowl. Dip strips into mixture and dredge in flour. Preheat iron skillet, add vegetable oil and brown steaks on both sides. Cook until done, remembering that medium-rare to medium-done steaks are tender and juicy. Serves 3 to 4.

Pan Fried Venison with Potatoes and Onions

venison round or back steaks, cut ½" thick
corn oil
potatoes, sliced
white onions, sliced

water
salt
black pepper
all-purpose flour

Fry venison in corn oil until it is about half-done. Pour off drippings, leaving just enough to make gravy. Add potatoes, onions and water. Cook slowly over very low heat until the venison is tender. Season with salt and pepper. Mix flour with water and add, a small amount at a time, to thicken gravy.

The white-tail deer was well on its way to extinction at the turn of the nineteenth century; there are now 52 times as many deer as there were in 1900.

Grilled Italian Steaks with Vegetables

5 med. garlic cloves, crushed
1½ tsp. dried basil leaves
¾ tsp. pepper
¼ cup Parmesan cheese, grated
1 Tbsp. olive oil
1 Tbsp. red wine vinegar
1 large red onion, sliced ½" thick

2 to 3 lbs. of venison backstrap or
    round steaks cut 1"+ thick
2 yellow bell peppers, quartered
½ tsp. salt
salt
pepper
fresh basil sprigs

Combine garlic, basil and pepper; reserve 2 teaspoons for the steaks. Add cheese, oil, and red wine vinegar to the remaining seasonings; brush seasonings onto bell peppers and onion slices. Place onion slices on medium grill. Cook onion for 15 to 20 minutes, turning once. Press the reserved seasonings mixture evenly into both sides of the steaks. Place bell peppers and steaks on grill with onion. Grill peppers 12 to 15 minutes or until just tender; cook steaks 10 to 14 minutes for medium rare to medium; turning both once. Season steaks with salt and pepper. Serve with vegetables and garnish with fresh basil sprigs. Serves 2.

Grilled Venison Top Round Steak Thai Style

3 large garlic cloves
3 serrano chilies, stemmed
4 large green onions, trimmed, cut into 1"
    pieces
1 bunch (½ cup) cilantro leaves
4 ½ Tbsp. fresh lime juice

¼ cup fish stock
2 Tbsp. sugar
¼ tsp. salt
1 (3½-lb.) venison top round, cut
    1¼" thick, fat trimmed
salt

Process cloves and chilies in a food processor until finely chopped. Add green onions and cilantro leaves and process until minced. Add lime juice, fish stock, sugar and ¼ tsp. salt and blend. Transfer marinade to a 1 gal. Zip Lock bag. Add steak. Seal bag. Turn over several times to coat steak. Refrigerate overnight, turning occasionally. Heat barbeque grill to high heat. Drain steak, reserving marinade. Season both sides of steak with salt. Grill to desired degree of doneness, about 4 minutes per side for medium-rare. Meanwhile, gently warm the marinade in a saucepan over medium heat, Remove steak from the grill. Cut across the grain into ¼" thick slices. Place slices on a warm platter. Brush with marinade and serve. Serves 6 to 8.

Grilled Marinated Forequarter Steak

1 cup cider vinegar
1 cup Worcestershire sauce
¼ cup Tabasco sauce
2 Tbsp. butter
1 tsp. dark brown sugar

1 (3½-lb) venison forequarter,
 deboned and butterflied
fresh rosemary sprigs
Greek olives

Make marinade by combining cider vinegar, Worcestershire sauce, Tabasco sauce butter, and brown sugar and bring to a boil, stirring until the brown sugar is dissolved. Cool. Place venison in a glass pan. Pour marinade over venison. Cover with plastic wrap and refrigerate at least 3 to a maximum of 8 hours, turning occasionally. Heat barbeque grill to high. Drain venison, reserving the marinade. Grill venison about 4 minutes per side for medium-rare, basting occasionally with marinade. Thinly slice venison across the grain. Arrange slices on a serving platter. Garnish with rosemary sprigs and Greek olives. Serves 6 to 8.

Polynesian Venison Steak

1 lb. venison round or back steaks
¼ cup all-purpose flour
¼ cup corn oil
½ cup boiling water
1 tsp. salt

2 or 3 green bell peppers, cut in 1"
 squares
½ cup pineapple chunks
Hawaiian Pineapple Sauce
Boiled Rice

Cut venison steaks into 1" to 2" cubes; sprinkle with flour. Brown in hot oil. Add water and salt; simmer over low heat until tender. Boil pepper pieces for 10 minutes and drain. Add pepper squares and pineapple chunks to browned venison. Pour Hawaiian Pineapple Sauce over venison and simmer for 5 minutes. Serve over Boiled Rice. Serves 4 to 6.

Herb and Wine-Marinated Venison Round Steak

1⅔ cups Burgundy wine
½ cup safflower oil
2 Tbsp. dehydrated onion bits
2 tsp. thyme leaves
2 tsp. salt
¾ tsp. dehydrated garlic bits
¼ tsp. pepper

3 lbs. venison round steak, cut 2½"
 thick
1 cup water
1 (⅞-oz.) pkg. brown gravy mix
canned peach halves
whole cloves

Combine the Burgundy, safflower oil, onion, thyme, salt, garlic and pepper and mix well. Place the steak in a pan and pour Burgundy mixture over steak. Marinate for at least 18 hours in refrigerator, turning occasionally. Drain steak and reserve marinade. Grill steak over hot coals for 15 to 20 minutes on each side or to desired doneness. Strain reserved marinade and combine with 1 cup water and gravy mix in a saucepan. Bring to boiling point, stirring constantly, and cook until slightly thickened. Serve with steak. Garnish steak with canned peach halves pierced with whole cloves. Serves 6.

Holiday Venison Steaks

1 cup Burgundy wine
2 Tbsp. safflower oil
1 white onion, sliced
2 bay leaves

½ tsp. salt
venison steaks, cut ¾" thick
butter, melted
½ cup hot water

Mix together Burgundy, oil, onion, bay leaves and salt. Heat, in a saucepan, to just a boil. Remove from heat and allow to cool. Brush venison steaks with butter and quickly brown in a skillet. Add wine mixture. Reduce heat and cook over a very low heat until tender. Before done, add hot water. Cover skillet and allow meat to steam. Juices can be reduced or thickened with flour for gravy.

Italian Venison Spaghetti

1½ lbs. venison round steak
2 Tbsp. bacon grease
1 Tbsp. all-purpose flour
1 large can tomatoes
1 small can tomato sauce
2 large onions
4 or 5 pieces celery (with green leaves)
6 sprigs parsley
salt and black pepper

Cayenne pepper
onion salt
celery salt
garlic salt
tomato catsup
Worcestershire sauce
water
1 (14-oz.) pkg. spaghetti
Parmesan cheese

Boil venison round steak for about 15 minutes in a Dutch oven. Put bacon grease in a skillet and heat. Blend in flour and brown only slightly. Pour in can of tomatoes and stir, chop larger pieces, then add tomato sauce. Medium chop boiled venison, onions, celery, and parsley and add to tomato mixture. Add to venison mixture: salt, black pepper, Cayenne pepper, onion salt, celery salt, garlic salt, tomato catsup and Worcestershire sauce to taste. Cover tightly and let simmer at least 2 or 3 hours. Add a little water if necessary. Serve over spaghetti, topped with Parmesan cheese. Serves 4.

Lemon-Venison Round Steak with Gratin of Ratatouille and Zucchini

Gratin:
7 Tbsp. extra-virgin olive oil
1 medium red bell pepper, seeded and
   cut ⅜"
1 large zucchini, peeled and cut ⅜"
1 (1-lb.) eggplant, peeled and cut ⅜"
3 small onions, cut ⅜"
3 med. tomatoes, peeled, seeded and cut ⅜"
3 garlic cloves, minced
1 fresh thyme sprig
salt
black pepper
¼ cup cream
1 medium zucchini, cut into fine julienne

¼ cup parmesan cheese, grated

Steaks:
1 large lemon
2 venison round steaks, 1" thick
extra-virgin olive oil
2 Tbsp. butter
2 Tbsp. extra-virgin olive oil
salt
black pepper
1 cup dry white wine
⅓ cup cream
4 cherry tomatoes, halved
fresh basil leaves

To make gratin heat 2 Tbsp. olive oil in a medium skillet over medium-high heat. Add bell pepper and stir until crisp-tender. Transfer bell pepper to a strainer. Repeat with 2 Tbsp. olive oil and zucchini. Repeat with 2 Tbsp. olive oil and eggplant, cooking until eggplant begins to brown and adding more oil if necessary. Transfer to strainer. Heat 1 Tbsp. olive oil in Dutch oven over medium-low heat. Add onions and cook until tender, stirring occasionally. Mix in tomatoes, bell pepper, zucchini, eggplant, garlic and thyme. Season with salt and pepper. Reduce heat to low, cover and cook until vegetables are very tender, stirring occasionally. Discard thyme, spoon mixture into a 6-cup gratin or other shallow pan. Heat cream in small saucepan over medium heat. Add zucchini julienne and simmer until just crisp-tender, stirring occasionally. Drain. Spread zucchini over eggplant mixture. Sprinkle with cheese. To make venison steaks remove yellow peel from lemon; reserve lemon. Mince peel. Add peel to small pan of boiling water and return to boil. Drain. Rinse with cold water and drain well.

Remove white covering from the lemon. Halve lemon lengthwise. Cut between membranes of one half, removing the sections. Squeeze the juice from other half, and reserve. Preheat broiler. Brush one side of each venison steak with olive oil. Melt butter with 2 Tbsp. olive oil in a large skillet over medium-high heat. Add steaks, oiled side down. Cook until beads of red juice appear on top, about 4 minutes. Brush top of steak with olive oil; turn venison over. Cook 3 more minutes for rare. Meanwhile broil gratin until golden brown, 3 to 4 minutes. Season steaks with salt and generous amount of pepper. Transfer steaks to a plate and cover with aluminum foil to keep warm. Add wine to the skillet and bring to a boil, scraping up any browned bits. Boil for 2 minutes. Stir in cream and return to a boil. Add 1½ tsp. of the lemon peel. Arrange steaks on heated serving plates. Garnish with lemon sections. Spoon sauce over steaks. Slice gratin into serving squares and place beside steak. Garnish with a cherry tomato and basil leaves. Serve immediately. Serves 4 to 6.

Mary McCall's Best Deer Steak

This recipe was given to Mrs. June Corley by her cousin, Mary McCall, who lives on the Trinity River in East Texas. Mrs. McCall's husband, Homer, keeps two big freezers filled with fish from the Trinity River and wild hog and venison from their hunting camp.

deer steak	garlic powder
salt	flour
pepper	oil or shortening

Partially freeze venison, then slice ½" thick. Tenderize steaks with a mallet or the edge of a saucer. Put garlic powder in flour (go lightly). Flour both sides of steak and fry in hot oil on medium heat. Venison will toughen if overcooked.

Country-Style Venison Steak with Wine Sauce

2 Tbsp. all-purpose flour
2 tsp. Seasoning Salt
¼ tsp. black pepper
⅛ tsp. Accent
dash nutmeg
2 lbs. venison round steak, cut ½" thick

3 Tbsp. corn oil
2 Tbsp. dehydrated onions, chopped
2 carrots, sliced
1 tsp. canned beef broth
¾ cup hot water
¾ cup red wine

Mix and sift together flour, Seasoning Salt, pepper, Accent and nutmeg. Pound this mixture into all sides of the venison steak. Heat oil in a heavy skillet and quickly brown the steak on both sides. Add onions, carrots, beef broth, water, and wine. Cover and cook over very low heat for 1½ hours or until the venison is tender. Serves 4.

Mushroom Venison Round Steak

6 Tbsp. butter
1 medium onion, sliced
½ lb. mushrooms, sliced
2 lbs. venison round steak cut into thin strips
1 cup heavy cream

⅛ tsp. ground ginger
salt
pepper
fresh parsley, chopped
Boiled Rice

Melt 4 Tbsp. butter in a large skillet over medium heat. Add onions and cook until soft, stirring occasionally. Reduce heat to low. Add mushrooms and cook until just tender. Increase heat to high. Push vegetables to side. Add remaining 2 Tbsp. butter to the skillet and melt. Add venison and stir-fry until just browned. Mix vegetables. Stir in cream and ginger and heat through. Season with salt and pepper. Transfer to serving platter. Garnish with parsley. Serve immediately with Boiled Rice. Serves 4.

Mushroom Venison in a Skillet

2 lbs. venison flank or brisket steak
2 cups canned beef broth
1 cup onion, chopped
1 lb. fresh mushrooms, chopped
¼ cup cold water
2 Tbsp. all-purpose flour
2 Tbsp. cornstarch

½ cup plain yogurt
1 tsp. paprika
1 tsp. prepared mustard
½ tsp. garlic powder
salt
pepper
hot cooked noodles

Broil the venison steak until it is rare, about 5 minutes on each side. Cut steaks diagonally into thin strips; set aside and keep warm. In a large skillet, bring beef broth to a boil. Add onion and mushrooms; cover and simmer until tender, about 5 minutes. In a small bowl, mix cold water, flour and cornstarch until smooth. Whisk flour/cornstarch mixture into broth; cook and stir over low heat until thickened and bubbly. Remove from heat. In a bowl, combine yogurt, paprika, mustard and garlic powder; add to broth and stir until smooth. Add the venison; cook over low heat, stirring constantly, until thoroughly heated, about 5 minutes. Salt and pepper to taste. Serve over noodles. Serves 6.

Pan-Fried Venison Sandwich Steaks

3 Tbsp. butter
4 medium onions, sliced thin
4 green peppers, sliced thin
2 Tbsp. Parmesan cheese
1 cup Mozzarella cheese, grated

½ tsp. garlic salt
¼ tsp. black pepper
4 venison steaks from the top of round,
    cut ¼" thick
fresh bread

Place butter in a large heavy skillet, turn heat to medium. Add onions, green peppers; sauté until tender, being careful not to overcook. While onion mixture is cooking, combine remaining ingredients in a small bowl. Remove cooked onion mixture from skillet and set aside. Add steaks to skillet. Fry one minute on each side; turn heat to medium low. Spread onion and cheese mixture evenly over steaks. Cover and cook until cheese is melted. Serve hot on fresh bread. Serves 4.

Mrs. Kathryn Breland

Italian-Style Thin Cut Venison Round Steaks

1 lb. venison round steak, cut ¼" thick
salt
black pepper
1 egg
2 tsp. water
⅓ cup Parmesan cheese
⅓ cup dried bread crumbs
¼ cup extra-virgin olive oil

2 Tbsp. butter
1 white onion, chopped fine
1 (6-oz.) can tomato paste
2 cups hot water
1 tsp. salt
½ tsp. ground marjoram
⅛ tsp. garlic powder
½ lb. Mozzarella cheese

Clean and trim all fat and connecting tissues from steaks. Cut steaks into serving-size pieces and season with salt and pepper. Mix egg and water and lightly beat. Mix Parmesan cheese and bread crumbs. Dip venison in the egg mixture and then roll venison in cheese mixture. Heat olive oil in large skillet and quickly fry the venison, a few pieces at a time. *Do not overcook.* Lay the venison in wide glass baking dish. In same skillet cook onions in butter until just tender. Mix tomato paste, hot water, salt and marjoram and add to onions. Boil a few minutes, scraping all of the brown bits from the bottom. Pour most of the sauce over the venison steaks. Lay thin slices of Mozzarella cheese on top of each steak. Pour the remaining sauce over the steaks. Bake steaks in moderate oven, 350 degrees, for about 30 minutes. Serves 2.

Quick Pan-Fried Venison Round Steaks

2 lbs. venison round steaks, cut ½" thick
¼ cup cream
¼ cup all-purpose flour
3 Tbsp. butter

salt
white pepper
garlic or onion powder

Tenderize venison steaks by pounding with a steak tenderizing mallet. Cut steaks into serving pieces. Dip steaks into cream and then roll in flour. Melt butter in a hot skillet and quickly brown steaks on one side. Turn steaks and season with salt, pepper and garlic or onion powder to taste. Cover and continue cooking till second side is well browned. Cook to the rare to medium stage. Serve hot. Serves 4.

Pizza-Swiss Venison Steak

¼ cup all-purpose flour
2 tsp. salt
¼ tsp. pepper
2 lbs. venison round steak, cut 1" thick
3 Tbsp. bacon grease
1 (8-oz.) can seasoned tomato sauce

1 (5-oz.) can pizza sauce
½ cup water
½ tsp. sugar
1 bay leaf
1 medium onion, sliced

Combine flour, salt and pepper. Pound venison round steak. Brown steak slowly on both sides in fat. Combine tomato sauce, pizza sauce, water, sugar, bay leaf and onion; pour over venison. Simmer uncovered for 10 minutes then cover and bake at 350 degrees for 1 hour or until tender. Add more liquid if necessary to keep steak from drying out. Serves 6.

Ruby Port-Marinated Venison Round Steaks

venison round steaks
1 lb. dark brown sugar

ruby or tawny port wine

Lay venison steaks in a stone crock. Layer brown sugar between and around all steaks. Completely cover the steaks with ruby or tawny port. Weigh steaks down with a large weighted plate. Let stand and marinate in a cool place for no more than 24 hours. Cook steaks as you wish.

Quick French Venison and Wine Steaks

1 (1-oz.) pkg. beef gravy mix
1 cup beef broth
1 cup dry red wine
1 Tbsp. red currant jelly
6 thin, tender venison steaks, cut just less than ½" thick

1 tsp. salt
¼ tsp. pepper
¼ cup butter

NOTE: This is a quick high-heat recipe. Use a very tender cut of venison. Even with a tender cut; if steak is cooked over medium it will have a tendency to toughen. If you have the time, cook steaks in wine sauce very slowly over low heat. Make beef gravy according to directions on the box, using beef broth. Stir in wine and currant jelly. Heat and stir until jelly is dissolved. Sprinkle steaks with salt and pepper. Heat butter in a large skillet. Brown steaks very quickly. Pour wine sauce over the steaks and cook over high heat until steaks are less than medium. Serves 6.

Venison Steak Rehrbraten

4 venison round steaks, cut ½ to 1" thick
1 box (1½ oz.) pickling spices
1 bottle (8 oz.) Italian dressing
1½ cups Burgundy

meat tenderizer
all-purpose flour
butter

Cut venison round steaks into "teriyaki" strips. Make the marinade by mixing pickling spices, Italian dressing and Burgundy. Lay venison strips in a shallow glass dish and pour enough marinade over venison to completely cover. Cover the dish and refrigerate for 3 days. Remove the venison from the marinade, drain and dry well. Sprinkle meat tenderizer on both sides of the venison. Sprinkle flour on both sides of the meat. Brown in butter heavy skillet or Dutch oven. Strain the marinade. Add to meat, cover and continue cooking over very low heat until meat is tender, about 3 hours. Check occasionally; if the gravy cooks down, add more wine. The venison should be completely covered at all times. Serve with steamed vegetable such as broccoli, cauliflower, asparagus, or Brussels sprouts. Serve vegetables with Hollandaise Sauce or Hot Slaw Dressing . Serves 6 to 8.

Rolled Venison Steak Fleisch

1 or 2 thin venison round steaks,
   cut ¼"+ thick
salt and pepper to taste
½ cup chopped onions
½ cup chopped bacon

all-purpose flour
¼ cup water
Mustard and Lemon Hollandaise Sauce
pickled red apple rings
fresh basil leaves

Trim steak and sprinkle with salt and pepper. Mix the onions and bacon and spread on steak(s). Roll as for jelly roll and tie with string. Flour lightly and brown very quickly in a small amount of fat in a large skillet. Add water and cover tightly. Simmer over very low heat for 1½ to 2 hours, adding water, if needed. Carefully remove string and slice in ¾" pieces. Spoon Mustard and Lemon Hollandaise Sauce on medium dinner plate and place sliced fleish in center. Garnish with apple ring and basil leaves. Serves 2 to 4.

Rosemary-Mustard Venison Eye of Round

4 (6 oz. ea.) venison round steaks cut 1½"
    thick
salt
pepper
1½ cups fresh Basic White Bread
    Crumbs
2 Tbsp. fresh rosemary, finely chopped

1¾ Tbsp. fresh lime or lemon juice
1½ Tbsp. unsalted butter
4 tsp. onion, chopped
1 tsp. garlic, finely chopped
2 Tbsp. hot English mustard

Pat venison dry. Season with salt and pepper. Mix breadcrumbs, rosemary, parsley and lime juice in a shallow pan. Melt 1 Tbsp. butter in large skillet over medium-low heat. Add onion and garlic and cook until golden brown, stirring frequently. Add to crumbs and increase heat to medium-high. Melt remaining butter in skillet. Add venison and cook until brown, about 2½ minutes per side. Preheat broiler. Brush meat on both sides with mustard. Dip in flavored crumbs, coating completely. Broil until crumbs are golden brown, about 2 minutes per side. Serve immediately. Serves 4.

Sautéed Venison Steak with Hot Cumberland Sauce

venison round steaks, cut ½" thick
whole garlic, sliced
1 Tbsp. butter

2 Tbsp. canola oil
Hot Cumberland Sauce

Rub venison steaks on sides with sliced garlic. Sauté steaks in butter and canola oil for 5 to 6 minutes on each side until outside is crisp and brown. Serve with Hot Cumberland Sauce,

Spanish Venison Round Steak

4 lbs. venison round steak, 2" thick
salt
pepper
flour
cooking fat
3 carrots, diced
1 Mexican pepper, chopped
1 green pepper, chopped

2 onions, diced
2 canned pimientos, chopped
2 cups tomatoes
½ cup cooking fat
1 cup raw English peas
3 stems celery, chopped
½ cup salt pork, finely diced

Rub venison with salt and pepper. Pound all the flour possible into the steak. Sear steak in hot fat. Add all remaining ingredients. Cover and simmer slowly for about 3 hours, or until venison is tender. Serves 8 to 10.

Star Anise Venison with Leek and Hoisin-Chili Sauce

wok-type stir-cooking skillet
10 oz. venison round steak, cut ⅛"x 2" shreds
4 Tbsp. safflower oil
1 Tbsp. soy sauce
¾ tsp. cornstarch
⅛ tsp. white pepper
1 star anise (available at Oriental market)
1 Tbsp. fresh ginger, minced
2 large garlic cloves, very thinly sliced
¼ tsp. salt

2 Tbsp. plus 1 tsp. hoisin sauce (available at Oriental markets)
½ tsp. hot chili sauce (available at Oriental markets)
1 large leek cut ⅛"x1½" pieces
1 large red bell pepper cut ⅛"x1½" pieces
1 small fresh red chili, seeded and cut ⅛"x1½" pieces
Boiled Rice

Combine venison steak, 1 Tbsp. safflower oil, soy sauce, cornstarch and white pepper in a glass or stainless steel bowl. Cover and refrigerate for 2 hours. Heat wok over high heat 30 seconds. Reduce heat to medium. Add 2 Tbsp. safflower oil and star anise and stir 2 minutes. Remove star anise. Increase heat to high and cook oil 30 seconds. Add ginger and garlic and stir-fry 45 seconds. Add venison and stir-fry 1 minute. Mix salt, hoisin sauce and hot chili sauce. Add hoisin sauce mixture and stir-fry 30 seconds. Add vegetables and stir-fry 45 seconds. Serve immediately with Boiled Rice. Serves 2 to 4.

Milk Marinated Venison Steaks

2 lbs. venison round steaks, cut ½" thick
1 cup whole milk
4 Tbsp. flour seasoned with salt and pepper

2 Tbsp. shortening
1 cup water

Soak the venison steaks in milk for several hours. Drain and dredge with the seasoned flour. Brown in shortening in a 10" skillet. Add water and bring to a boil. Reduce the heat and cover. Simmer for 2 hours or until tender. Serves 2 to 4.

Stuffed Venison Steak

4 large venison round steaks, cut ½"
½ tsp. salt
⅛ tsp. pepper
¼ cup flower
3 cups breadcrumbs
¾ cup onions, chopped fine
¾ cup celery, chopped fine

½ cup butter
½ tsp. paprika
1 green pepper, chopped fine
salt
pepper
8 slices smoked bacon

Season steaks with salt and pepper, dredge in flower and pound well on both sides. Mix breadcrumbs, onions, celery, butter, paprika and green pepper; place mixture on steaks. Roll up and wrap each steak with 2 pieces of bacon secured with toothpicks. Set rolled steaks in roasting pan. Roast until tender in a 325-degree oven. Serves 8.

Sweet and Sour Venison Steaks

2 venison round steaks, cut ¾" thick
6 Tbsp. olive oil
1½ tsp. salt
pinch of cayenne pepper

1½ cups brown sugar
2 tsp. mustard
2 Tbsp. vinegar

Place steaks in a Dutch oven and brown steaks in oil. Combine remaining ingredients to make sauce. Layer steak with sauce. Bake in a 350-degree oven 20 minutes per pound.

Swiss Venison Steak with Onion Soup

2 lbs, venison round steaks, cut ¾"
flour
shortening
1 pkg. dry onion soup mix

water
salt
pepper

Dredge venison steaks in flour. Melt shortening and brown venison steaks on both sides. Add dry onion soup mix and cover with water. Cover tightly and simmer on the top of the stove for 1½ hours or until tender. Make gravy from drippings. Serves 2 to 4.

Swiss Venison Steak with Vegetables

3 lbs. venison round steak
2 tsp. salt
½ tsp. black pepper
1 cup all-purpose flour
5 Tbsp. bacon drippings

1 cup onion, diced
1 cup carrot, diced
1 can tomatoes
8 new potatoes, peeled

Slit the steak vertically along the edges to keep the edges from curling. Mix salt and pepper and season one side of the steak with ½ of the mixture. Pound in as much flour as you can. Turn the steak over and repeat seasoning and pounding. Brown steak in bacon dripping on both sides. Spread onion and carrots over the steak. Add tomatoes. Cover and simmer over low heat 1½ hours. Add potatoes, cook for an additional half hour or until potatoes are tender. Serves 3 to 4.

White-tailed deer are territorial and have a relatively small home range. Normally, when food conditions are adequate, the deer tend to stay in one locality for long periods.

Thin Venison Steaks with Vegetables

2 lbs. venison round steak
¼ cup safflower oil
¾ cup teriyaki sauce
4 cloves garlic, sliced
¼ tsp. ground ginger
5 green onions, chopped
water
yellow squash
Boiled Rice

celery
cauliflower
zucchini
broccoli
onion
1½ Tbsp. cornstarch
1½ tsp. baking soda

Cut steaks at an angle across the grain into very thin slices. Place venison, safflower oil, teriyaki sauce, garlic, ginger and onions in a non-metallic container and refrigerate. Chop or slice vegetables and place them in another container and refrigerate. Just prior to preparation, add cornstarch and baking soda to meat mixture. Quickly stir-fry vegetables with a little water to prevent vegetables from sticking. Remove the vegetables and quickly fry venison with a little water to prevent venison from sticking. Mix cooked vegetables into the cooked venison and warm. Serve with Boiled Rice or egg noodles. Serves 2 to 4.

Simmered Venison with Tomatoes and Mushrooms

3 Tbsp. butter
1 tsp. ground mustard
1 tsp. light brown sugar
2 onions, chopped
2 lbs. venison round steak
¼ cup all-purpose flour

1 tsp. salt
¼ tsp. black pepper
4 medium tomatoes, sliced
1 cup fresh whole mushrooms, sliced
1 tsp. apple cider vinegar

Melt the butter in a large 2 to 3-qt. saucepan. Add the mustard, sugar and onions and cook until the onions are just tender. Trim all fat and connecting tissue from the venison. Cut the venison into 1" pieces. Mix and sift together the flour, salt and pepper. Dredge the venison with the flour mixture. Add venison, tomatoes and mushrooms to the onion mixture. Add the vinegar. Simmer over very low heat for 3 hours. Stir occasionally. Serves 2 to 4.

Venison Cutlets in Sour Cream

2 lbs, venison round steak
flour seasoned with salt and pepper
butter
½ cup sour cream
salt

pepper
Worcestershire sauce
celery salt
1 bay leaf

Cut venison into individual cutlets and roll them in well-seasoned flour. Melt butter in a heavy skillet, over medium heat, and brown cutlets on both sides. When browned, pour sour cream over cutlets and season with salt and pepper, Worcestershire sauce, celery salt, and bay leaf. Cover skillet and cook about an hour on low heat or until tender. Remove bay leaf. Serves 6 to 8.

Venison Oriental Stir Fry with Rice

This is one of Anne's favorite recipes.

1 Tbsp. House of Tsang Mongolian Fire Oil
4 Tbsp. House of Tsang Wok Oil, divided
2 cloves of garlic, slivered
1½ cups venison round steak cut less the
    ½" thick, cut into long thin strips
1 cup potato, sliced thick and halved
2 medium carrots, cut 2"; then sliced thin
½ cup zucchini, chopped

1 cup broccoli, thick stems peeled and
    sliced thin; can be used with heads.
1 apple, peeled and sliced thin
1 cup yellow squash, sliced thin
4 large mushrooms, sliced
¼ cup water
salt
pepper
Boiled Rice

Mix 1 tbsp. Tsang Mongolian Fire Oil with venison strips; set aside. Add and heat 2 tbsp. Tsang Wok Oil in a skillet; add and brown garlic slivers. Add venison strips to skillet; stir quickly; cook to rare for only a moment, quickly remove venison strips and set aside. Scrape skillet and add 2 tbsp. Tsang Wok Oil to skillet and heat. Add potatoes, carrots to skillet; cover and cook until almost tender. Add remainder of vegetables and water to skillet. Salt and pepper to taste. Cover and simmer until tender; stirring occasionally. Season with salt and pepper to taste. Serve with teriyaki sauce over Boiled Rice. Serves 4 to 6.

Venison Peperonata

Venison:
½ cup olive oil
¼ cup red wine vinegar
1 Tbsp. fresh lime or lemon juice
¾ lb. venison round steak

Peperonata:
¼ cup olive oil
1 large red bell pepper, cut julienne
1 large yellow bell pepper, cut julienne

1 small onion, thinly sliced
3 Tbsp. capers with juice
salt
pepper
1 Tbsp. red wine vinegar
1½ tsp. Cajun blackened meat
    seasoning mix
¼ tsp. salt
¼ tsp. pepper
1 tsp. fresh parsley, minced

Make marinade by mixing oil, vinegar and lime juice in small bowl. Place venison in a large shallow baking dish, pour marinade over. Cover with plastic wrap and refrigerate at least 4 hours or overnight. Make peperonata by heating oil in large deep skillet over medium-high heat. Add peppers, onion and capers with juices. Season with salt and pepper. Cook until vegetables are just tender, stirring frequently. Add red wine vinegar and bring to boil. Remove skillet from heat.
Cook venison by heating barbecue grill to medium-high heat. Remove venison from marinade; reserve marinade. Mix Cajun seasoning, ¼ tsp. salt and ¼ tsp. pepper and sprinkle over venison. Grill for about 4 minutes per side for medium-rare, brushing occasionally with marinade. Transfer to a cutting board and let stand for 5 minutes. Cut meat across the grain into thin diagonal slices.
Cut and fan venison slices on plates. Rewarm peperonata over medium heat. Mix in parsley. Spoon peperonata onto venison slices. Serves 4.

Venison Pepper Steak

1 medium onion, sliced
1 green pepper, sliced
½ lb. mushrooms, sliced
2 Tbsp. butter
1½ lbs. venison steak, cut ½"+ thick
½ tsp. garlic powder
2 Tbsp. butter

¼ cup soy sauce
½ cup Venison Soup Stock or
    canned beef broth
1 tsp. tomato purée
⅓ cup cold water
1½ tsp. cornstarch
Boiled Rice

Sauté onion, green pepper, mushrooms in butter and remove from pan. Sauté venison and garlic in butter until meat is medium rare. Mix soy sauce, Venison Soup Stock, and tomato purée in a saucepan and bring to a boil. Thoroughly mix cornstarch with cold water and slowly stir into boiling liquid. Add cooked vegetables to meat. Pour sauce over vegetables and meat. Simmer until tender. Serve over Boiled Rice. Serves 2 to 4.

Venison Steak Tartare with Mustard & Wine Vinegar

3 Tbsp. olive oil
1 Tbsp, red wine vinegar
1 tsp. Dijon Mustard
2 egg yolks
¼ cup onion, finely minced
salt
pepper

1 lb. thrice-ground venison round steak
capers
parsley
pimento, sliced
French Bread Pizza Style
butter
1 clove garlic, minced

Mix olive oil, red wine vinegar, Dijon mustard, and egg yolks into thick sauce. Add onion and salt and pepper and blend with the venison. Press into separate copper Jell-O molds, with seasonal relief designs. Chill thoroughly and remove from the molds before serving. Garnish with capers, parsley and pimento slices. Serve each serving with ½ loaf of French Bread Pizza Style toasted with butter and minced garlic. Serves 2 to 4.

Venison Steak with Lemon and Hot Wine Sauce

1 venison round steak, cut ¾" thick
Seasoning Salt
lemon pepper
dash Accent

1½ lemons, juice only
½ cup butter
Hot Wine Sauce

Season both sides of venison steak with Seasoning Salt, lemon pepper and Accent. Rub in and allow steak to rest for 10 minutes. Squeeze lemon juice on both sides of the steak and let stand for one hour. Broil steak in a heavy skillet to between rare and medium. When steak is done, remove it to a hot platter and keep in a warm oven. Serve with Hot Wine Sauce, Serves 2 to 4.

Venison Steak with Mushrooms & Onions

4 lbs. venison round steaks
butter
1 cup mushrooms, chopped fine
1 cup onions, chopped fine

butter
salt
pepper

Cut venison round steak into thin steaks and very quickly sear in butter. Mix mushrooms and onions and quickly sear in butter. In a baking dish, put alternating layers of venison, mushrooms and onions. Salt and pepper to taste. Bake in a 300-degree oven for about 2 hours. Serves 4 to 6.

Baked Venison Steaks with Mushrooms and Chianti

2 lbs. venison round steaks
salt
black pepper
all-purpose flour
olive oil

½ green bell pepper, sliced thin
1 medium white onion, sliced thin
1 can sliced mushrooms
1 can mushroom gravy
¼ cup Chianti wine

Cut venison into serving-size pieces and season with salt and pepper. Dust venison with flour and brown venison in olive oil. Drain off all excess grease. Layer venison, green bell pepper, onions and mushrooms in a shallow baking dish. Cover venison with mushroom gravy and Chianti. Bake at 300 degrees for 2 or 3 hours or until meat is tender. Serves 6.

Venison Steaks with Burgundy & Honey

½ cup beef consommé
½ cup Burgundy
⅓ cup teriyaki sauce
1½ tsp. Lawery's seasoned salt
¼ cup onion, chopped

¼ cup parsley, chopped
1 Tbsp. lime juice
2 Tbsp. honey
2 venison round steaks, cut ¾" thick

Mix all ingredients together and marinate steaks in the refrigerator for 4 to 8 hours. Turn frequently. Cook to no more than medium on a grill. *Do not overcook* the steaks. Venison steaks are best cooked to no more than medium done. Serves 4 to 6.

4

Venison Chops

Chops are made from the back area that contains the backstrap and tenderloin. Because of this, chops can be the tenderest little cuts you can serve. Venison chops are cut the same way as lamb or pork chops or T-bone and Porterhouse steaks in beef.

Separate the deer into two halves by sawing the backbone down the middle. Remove the forequarter, being careful not to damage the front section of the backstrap. On the hindquarter, work your fingers around the backstrap and under the hindquarter, and gently separating the hindquarter muscles from the backstrap, saw off the hindquarter.

Carefully remove the white membrane covering the backstrap. This covering is very tough and is easier to remove whole than from each chop after they are cut. Saw the ribs off the ½ backbone, leaving the backstrap and tenderloin in place.

On a 120-lb. deer, the chop area of the backbone is about 18 to 20 inches long. This piece provides two distinct areas to cut from—the front rib section and the area back of the ribs which contains the tenderloin. The front area makes chops with meat on one side of the bone. The back area, with the tenderloin, is where the T-bone and Porterhouse steaks come from on beef.

How many chops you can cut from each side depends on the size of your deer and how thick you saw your chops. Although there are many people who prefer their chops cut ¼ to ½ inch, these cuts are best left for slow and moist cooking methods rather than roasting or frying. The thin cuts have a tendency to become tough if cooked too well done or too quickly. Thicker (¾ to 1 inch) cuts can be sautéed, stuffed, and broiled. Cook these cuts to less than medium.

Anglo-Indian Venison Chop Curry with Onions and Potatoes

6 (7-oz.) venison chops, cut ¾" thick
1½ Tbsp. Apple Cider Vinegar
1 Tbsp. fresh garlic, minced
1 Tbsp. fresh ginger, peeled and minced
1 tsp. salt
½ tsp. cayenne pepper
½ cup water

¼ cup prepared chili sauce
¾ lb. red potatoes, unpeeled, cut into
  ¼" thick sliced
1 medium onion, cut into ¼" thick
  slices
1 large tomato, cut into ¼" thick slices
1 Tbsp. green onion tops

Arrange venison chops in single layer in shallow dish. Mix vinegar, garlic, ginger, salt and cayenne pepper. Rub spice mixture into venison. Cover venison and refrigerate for 2 to 4 hours. Transfer venison to large cast-iron skillet. Add ½ cup water and bring to a boil. Reduce heat to medium and cook until venison is tender and cooked through, turning venison over occasionally, about 20 minutes. Pour chili sauce around venison. Arrange potato slices over venison in single layer. Cover with onion and tomato slices. Cover and cook over medium heat until potatoes are tender. Divide venison, potato, onion and tomato slices onto serving plates. Pour sauce over. Sprinkle with green onion tops and serve. Serves 6.

Baked Venison Chops

4 venison chops, cut ¾" thick
1 cup canned tomato
1 onion, sliced
1 clove garlic, chopped
½ tsp. chopped black olives

1 cup water
salt
pepper
Mashed Potatoes

Arrange chops in an open baking pan. Pour tomatoes, onions, garlic, black olives and water over chops. Salt and pepper to taste. Bake in a 350-degree oven for 45 minutes. Turn chops once. Bake another 30 minutes. Serve with Mashed Potatoes topped with a spoonful of the baking juice. Serves 2 to 4.

Jelly-Glazed Venison Chops

½ cup Mayhaw Jelly
2½ Tbsp. coarse-grained mustard
8 venison chops

Boiled Rice
spinach leaves
4 cherry tomatoes, halved

Combine Mayhaw Jelly and mustard in a small bowl. Taste and adjust mustard and jelly to taste. Place venison chops on broiler rack. Brush lightly with glaze. Broil until browned. Turn and brush other side with glaze. Broil to desired degree of doneness. *Do not overcook.* Place chops on a bed of Boiled Rice and spoon glaze across chops. Garnish with spinach leaves and cherry tomato halves. Serves 4.

Venison Chops with Mushroom Gravy

venison chops, cut ½" thick
all-purpose flour
salt
black pepper

Crisco or other shortening
½ cup water
1 cup dry red wine
1 small can mushroom pieces and
    liquid

Mix and sift the flour, salt and pepper. Quickly brown venison in Crisco. Add water and simmer over very low heat until tender. Pour wine over chops and cook over low heat until almost dry. Remove chops and make a gravy by adding mushrooms and liquid. Simmer 3 minutes. Pour gravy over chops before serving.

Chevreuil Cutlets à la Janelle

2 or 3 Tbsp. canola oil
8 small venison back steaks
salt
pepper
½ tsp. paprika
1 green onion, chopped
pinch of oregano
2 Tbsp. white onion, chopped

2 Tbsp. parsley, chopped, divided
1 clove garlic, mashed
water
½ cup heavy cream
3 Tbsp. brandy
3 Tbsp. Madeira
2 egg yolks, well beaten

Heat oil in a large skillet over medium high heat. Sprinkle venison with salt, pepper and paprika. Sauté in oil until golden brown on both sides. Add green onion, oregano, onion, 1 Tbsp. parsley and garlic. Cover and simmer about 10 minutes, or until venison is tender. Add a little water if mixture looks dry. remove venison to a warm serving platter. Combine cream, brandy, Madeira and egg yolks. Stir into skillet. Place over very low heat and cook, stirring constantly, until slightly thickened and heated through. Pour over venison and sprinkle with remaining Tbsp. parsley. Serves 5 to 6.

Venison Chops with White Cream Gravy

4 venison chops, cut ½" thick
¾ cup cream
Seasoning Salt
2 Tbsp. olive oil

safflower oil for frying
White Cream Gravy
Boiled Rice

Marinate venison chops 12 hours in the cream. . Remove chops from cream and wipe dry. Rub steaks with olive oil. Season chops with Seasoning Salt. Dust chops with flour and fry until done. *Do not overcook.* Serve with White Cream Gravy and Boiled Rice. Serves 4.

German Style Venison Chops

6 venison chops, cut ¾" thick
2 Tbsp. safflower oil
salt
pepper

½ tsp. caraway seeds
water
1 tsp. all-purpose flour
Mashed Potatoes

Heat safflower oil in frying pan and put chops in. Sprinkle with salt, pepper and caraway seeds. As soon as the chops are brown, turn them. When the second side is brown pour in just enough water to cover the chops and cook until the water has boiled away. Then add another half cup of water in which flour has been added blended, and cook very slowly until the chops are tender, about 20 to 40 minutes. Serve with Mashed Potatoes. Serves 3 to 4.

Pan-Broiled Venison Chops with Onions and Mushrooms

6 venison rib chops, cut 1 to 1½" thick
2 Tbsp. bacon fat
3 medium onions, sliced
1½ lbs. fresh mushrooms, sliced
⅓ cup all-purpose flour

1 cup beef broth
1 cup whole milk
½ tsp. salt
¼ tsp. black pepper

In an iron skillet, over moderately high heat, lightly brown chops on both sides in bacon fat. Transfer chops to a shallow pan; retain drippings in skillet. Broil chops at high heat, five inches below heating element. Turn once and broil until medium-rare. In the drippings in the skillet, gently cook onions and mushrooms until lightly browned. Blend all-purpose flour, broth, milk, salt and pepper. Add to pan. Cook, stirring constantly until thickened and bubbly; about 4 minutes. Serve onion and mushroom sauce over chops while both are hot. Serves 6.

Mrs. Kathryn Breland

Spanish Venison Chops

4 venison chops, cut ¾" to 1" thick
2 Tbsp. safflower oil
salt and pepper
1 tsp. dry mustard

4 tsp. tomato catsup
¾ cup juice from bottled sweet pickles
Boiled Rice or Mashed Potatoes

Heat safflower oil in a cast iron skillet; sear chops on both sides. Season chops with salt and pepper. On each chop spread ¼ tsp. dry mustard and 1 tsp. tomato catsup. Pour sweet pickle juice around chops. Cover and cook slowly, over low heat, for 45 minutes or until tender. Serve over Boiled Rice or with Mashed Potatoes. Serves 4.

Venison Braised with Fried Almonds and Black Pepper

4 Tbsp. Clarified Butter
½ cup (about 2 oz.) sliced almonds
¼ cup water
8 large garlic cloves
12 whole green cardamom pods, husked
1 (2" long) piece fresh ginger, cut into pieces
1 Tbsp. whole black peppercorns
1 tsp. salt
1 tsp. fennel seeds

¼ tsp. ground mace
¼ tsp. ground cloves
4 (4-oz.) venison chops, cut ¾"
   thick, trimmed
⅔ lb. long green beans
½ cup water
¼ cup fresh cilantro, minced
1 tsp. cracked black peppercorns

Heat 2 Tbsp. Clarified Butter in large skillet over medium heat. Add almonds and stir until light golden, about 3 minutes. Transfer almonds to paper towel using slotted spoon. Process next 9 ingredients in blender until paste forms, stopping occasionally to scrape down sides of container. Arrange venison in large shallow dish. Spread paste over both sides of the venison. Cover and chill for 30 minutes. Add remaining 2 Tbsp. of Clarified Butter to skillet just large enough to accommodate venison chops in single layer. Heat for 1 minute over a medium-high heat. Add venison and brown well on all sides. Add beans and ¼ cup water and bring to boil. Reduce heat, cover and simmer until almost no liquid remains in skillet. Add remaining ¼ cup water. Cover and cook until venison is tender, about 10 minutes; do not turn chops over. Sauce should be very thick. If not, uncover and simmer until thickened. Transfer venison to platter. Spoon beans around sides. Top with almonds, cilantro and cracked peppercorns. Serves 2.

Rum Marinated Venison Chops

1 cup apple juice
¾ cup teriyaki sauce
½ cup honey
3 medium garlic cloves, crushed
2 Tbsp. ginger root, minced finely
1 Tbsp. dry mustard

1 tsp. Worcestershire sauce
½ cup dark rum
8 full venison chops, cut 1" thick
1⅛ cups apple jelly
3 Tbsp. lime or lemon juice
⅛ tsp, nutmeg

Combine apple juice, ½ cup teriyaki sauce, honey, garlic, ginger root, mustard Worcestershire sauce, and rum. Place venison chops in a shallow pan and cover with marinade, refrigerate overnight and turn occasionally. Drain marinade into a saucepan and add the jelly and remaining teriyaki sauce. Bring the sauce to a boil and reduce it to 1½ cups and then stir in lime juice and nutmeg. Grill chops for 20 minutes or until they are cooked to less than medium. While cooking, turn every 5 minutes and baste frequently with the sauce. Serve the chops with the sauce. Serves 4.

Stuffed Venison Chops with Mushroom & Onion

2 Tbsp. butter
5 oz. mushrooms, sliced
2 large green onions, minced
3 Tbsp. Burgundy
salt
pepper
2 oz. Gruyère cheese, grated
4 venison chops, cut 1¼" to 1½" thick
4 Tbsp. Clarified Butter
1 cup onion, minced
½ cup carrots, minced
½ cup celery, minced

1 cup dry Riesling wine
1 Tbsp. tomato paste
8 bay leaves, broken
1 large garlic clove, minced
⅛ tsp. dried thyme, crumbled
2 cups canned beef broth
½ cup heavy cream
4 Tbsp. fresh chives, snipped
2½ tsp. fresh lime juice
salt
pepper

Melt 2 Tbsp. butter in medium skillet over medium-high heat. Add mushrooms and sauté until light brown. Add green onions and sauté 30 seconds. Pour in Burgundy and boil until reduced to glaze. Season with salt and pepper. Cool to room temperature. Blend in cheese. Make 1½" long slit in edge of each chop opposite rib bone. With knife inserted in slit, and in an arc, cut a wide pocket inside the chop with as small an opening as possible. Stuff mushroom mixture into the pockets. Press to close and seal closed with a toothpick.

Preheat oven to 325 degrees. Heat Clarified Butter in large skillet over medium-high heat. Pat chops dry and brown on both sides. Transfer to shallow baking dish. Pour off all but 3 Tbsp. fat from skillet. Sauté onion, carrot and celery in same skillet over medium heat until golden, about 5 minutes. Add Burgundy, tomato paste, bay leaves, garlic, and thyme. Boil until liquid is reduced to glaze, scraping up browned bits, about 12 minutes. Pour in beef broth and boil until reduced by half. Spoon over chops. Cover lightly with foil. Bake until chops are tender, about 1¼ hours. Strain sauce into the skillet, pressing on solids to extract as much juice as possible; degrease. Cover the chops with foil. Boil sauce until reduced by ⅓. Add cream and boil until sauce thickens enough to coat spoon. Add 3 Tbsp. green onions, lime juice to taste, salt and pepper. Place chops on warmed serving plates. Spoon some sauce on top of chops. Sprinkle with green onions. Serve immediately. Serve sauce separately. Serves 4.

Since ancient times, deer have been important in the economy of man. Red deer became the basis of specialized Mesolithic economies throughout Eurasia. (This was the period between the Paleolithic and Neolithic eras, marked by the appearance of the bow and of cutting tools.)

Venison Chops and Black Jack

2 Tbsp. safflower oil
6 venison chops cut ¾" thick
1 large onion, sliced
1 lemon, sliced
½ cup firmly packed dark
   brown sugar

salt and pepper
6 Tbsp. tomato catsup
4 Tbsp. Jack Daniel's Black
   Label Whiskey

In a large skillet, heat safflower oil and brown chops over medium heat. Season with salt and pepper generously. When browned, place the chops in a shallow baking dish. Place one onion slice and one lemon slice on top of each chop. Combine remaining ingredients and spoon over the top of each chop. Cover and bake at 350 degrees for 30 minutes. Remove the cover and bake 25 minutes or until done. Spoon basting sauce over chops occasionally. Serves 6.

Harold W. Webster, Sr.

Simmered Venison Chops in White Wine with Ginger

4 large venison chops, cut 1" thick
2 Tbsp. corn oil
1 cup honey
1 cup dry white wine

2 Tbsp. Worcestershire sauce
1 large garlic clove, crushed
¼ tsp. fresh ginger, chopped fine
dash Tabasco sauce

Brown venison chops very slowly on both sides in corn oil. Mix well honey, white wine, Worcestershire sauce, garlic, ginger and Tabasco sauce. Simmer over very low heat for about 45 minutes or until tender. Serve chops and sauce over hot, buttered pasta. Serves 4,

Venison Chops in Italian Sauce

20 thin-cut venison chops
safflower oil
1 green pepper, sliced
celery chunks and leaves
olive oil
1 large can tomato paste
3 cups water

salt
pepper
rosemary
garlic salt
oregano
onion salt
1 cup Romano cheese, grated

Brown venison chops in safflower oil and drain. Place chops in roaster or large casserole dish. Sauté green pepper, celery chunks and leaves in olive oil. When vegetables are done, add tomato paste, water, salt, pepper, rosemary, garlic salt, oregano, and onion salt. Add Romano cheese. Simmer sauce about 15 minutes. Cover chops with sauce and bake for about 1½ hours at 350 degrees. Serves 10 to 12.

Venison Chops with Onions, Bacon and Mushrooms

butter
2 Tbsp. butter
6 (5 oz. ea.) venison chops cut ¾" thick
salt
pepper
2 cups mushrooms, quartered
2 medium onions, chopped

¼ lb. bacon, diced
2 Tbsp. all-purpose flour
1½ tsp. paprika
1 cup heavy cream
1 cup canned beef broth
2 Tbsp. tomato sauce
Boiled Rice

Preheat oven to 375 degrees. Butter a 9"x16" glass baking dish. Melt 2 Tbsp. butter in a large skillet over high heat. Season venison chops with salt and pepper. Add to skillet (in batches if necessary) and sear until brown, about 2 minutes per side. Transfer chops to buttered baking dish. Top with mushrooms. Add onions and bacon to same skillet and cook over medium heat until onions are translucent and bacon is crisp, stirring frequently, about 10 minutes. Mix in flour and paprika. Increase heat to medium-high. Stir in cream and broth and bring to boil, stirring constantly. Mix in tomato sauce. Season with salt and pepper. Pour sauce over mushrooms and venison chops. Transfer to oven and bake until chops are tender; about 20 to 25 minutes. Serve with Boiled Rice. Serves 6.

Venison Chops with Raisin Sauce

8 venison chops, cut ½" thick
2 Tbsp. shortening
½ tsp. salt
3 tart red apples
3 cups toasted bread cubes
1½ cups chopped, unpared apples
½ cup seedless raisins

½ cup chopped celery
½ cup chopped onion
1 tsp. salt
1 tsp. poultry seasoning
¼ tsp. pepper
1 beef bouillon cube dissolved in ½
    cup water

Brown venison chops on both sides in shortening. Season with salt. While chops are browning, core and halve apples and make the raisin stuffing by mixing together the bread cubes, chopped apple, raisins, celery, onion, salt, poultry seasoning, pepper and beef bouillon broth. Place browned chops in baking dish. Cover with a layer of raisin stuffing and top with an apple half. Sprinkle with sugar. Cover dish tightly with foil. Bake in 350-degree oven for 1 hour. Serves 4 to 6.

Venison Chops with Roasted Pepper Compote

¾ cup (about 7 oz.) drained, chopped
    roasted red peppers packed in jars
3 Tbsp. olive oil
1 green onion, minced
1 garlic clove, minced
1 Tbsp. fresh parsley, minced

1½ tsp. balsamic vinegar
1½ tsp. capers, drained
⅛ tsp. red pepper flakes
4 (about 8 oz. ea.) venison chops cut 1"
    thick
salt and pepper

In a small bowl mix together red peppers, 2 Tbsp. olive oil, green onion, garlic, parsley, vinegar, capers and dried red pepper. Set compote aside. Preheat broiler. Brush venison chops with remaining 1 Tbsp. olive oil and season with salt and pepper. Broil to desired degree of doneness, about 6 minutes per side for medium. Transfer chops to serving platter. Spoon pepper compote over. Serve immediately. Serves 4.

Venison Chops with Spiced Peaches

4 to 6 venison chops cut ½" to ¾" thick
¼ cup chili sauce
3 Tbsp. lime or lemon juice
1½ Tbsp. dark brown sugar
1 Tbsp. white onion, chopped
1 tsp. yellow mustard

½ tsp. Worcestershire sauce
¼ tsp. chili powder
⅓ cup juice from peaches
4 to 6 canned peach halves
8 to 12 whole cloves

Brown venison chops; drain excess fat. Combine remaining ingredients except peach halves and cloves. Pour over chops. Cover and cook over very low heat for 45 minutes, turning chops once. When chops have cooked for 45 minutes, stud each peach half with 2 cloves. Place peaches around chops; spoon sauce over and cover. Cook 5 minutes more. Serve with sauce poured over all. Serves 2 to 4.

Venison Chops with Warm Garlic-Mint and Balsamic Vinaigrette

1 cup canned chicken broth
1 Tbsp. olive oil
½ Tbsp. garlic, minced
¼ cup Balsamic vinegar
1 Tbsp. fresh mint leaves, minced

1 Tbsp. fresh parsley, minced
salt
pepper
6 (4-oz.) venison chops

Boil broth in a saucepan until it is reduced by half. Heat oil in a medium skillet over medium heat. Add garlic and sauté until golden brown. Add reduced stock and vinegar and boil until liquid is reduced by half. Mix in mint and parsley. Season with salt and pepper. Heat barbeque grill to medium-high. Season venison chops with salt and pepper. Grill for about 3 minutes per side for medium rare. Transfer to serving plates. Spoon warm vinaigrette over venison chops and serve. Serves 4.

Venison Cutlets

3 lbs. venison roast
1 egg
½ cup whole milk
1 (4-oz.) pkg. Saltine crackers, crushed
½ cup all-purpose flour

canola or corn oil
1 lemon or 2 limes
salt
black pepper

Slice venison roast into ¼" pieces and cut each piece into a 4" diameter roundel. Pound the roundels with a tenderizing mallet. In a bowl lightly beat egg and milk. Dip venison into egg milk mixture and then dredge in cracker crumbs. Slowly fry venison in oil. . Remove the venison and allow to drain. Squeeze lemon juice on venison immediately after removing from skillet. Salt and pepper to taste and serve.

Venison Cutlets Simmered in Sour Cream

2 lbs. venison chops, cut ½" to ¾" thick
flour
cooking oil

celery salt
½ cup sour cream
1 tsp. Worcestershire sauce

Cut venison into serving pieces; roll in flour. Brown in cooking oil on moderate heat. Add sour cream, Worcestershire sauce and celery salt. Cover skillet; simmer over low heat for 1 hour or until tender. Serves 6.

Venison Cutlets with Pears and Cognac

1 lb. venison chops
salt
white pepper
1½ Tbsp. unsalted butter
1½ Tbsp. safflower oil
1 large firm ripe pear, cored and thinly
   sliced

1 tsp. dried thyme, crumbled
2 garlic cloves, minced
3 Tbsp. red wine vinegar
¾ cup canned chicken broth
1 Tbsp. Cognac
2 Tbsp. unsalted butter
fresh thyme sprigs

Flatten venison between sheets of waxed paper to thickness of ¼" using meat mallet or rolling pin. Season venison with salt and pepper. Melt butter with safflower oil in a large skillet over medium-high heat. Add venison and cook until browned. Remove venison and tent with aluminum foil. Add pear slices to skillet. Sauté over medium-high heat until light brown, about 3 minutes. Add minced thyme and garlic. Cook 1 minute. Add vinegar and cook 30 seconds, scraping bottom of pan. Mix stock and Cognac. Simmer until sauce is slightly reduced and pears are tender, about 3 minutes. Whisk in butter. Return cutlets and any accumulated juices to skillet. Cook mixture until heated through. Arrange cutlets on serving platter. Pour sauce over. Garnish with thyme sprigs and serve immediately. Serves 4.

5

Venison Backstraps and Tenderloins

These are the two choicest cuts of venison. Many people confuse the venison backstrap (loin) with the tenderloin. When I serve people venison for the first time, I try to serve them recipes containing the backstrap or tenderloin.

On a 120 lb. deer, each backstrap is about 25" long x 3½" wide x 1¾" thick and weighs about 3¾ lbs. Backstraps are located on the outside of the back and they run along each side of the backbone from the neck down to where the hindquarters join the rump area. Remove the forequarter; being careful not to damage the front section of the backstrap. On the hindquarter, work your fingers around the backstrap and under the hindquarter gently separating the hindquarter muscles from the backstrap. With your fingers carefully separate the backstrap from the backbone all the way from the neck area to where the backstrap ends under the hindquarter.

The backstrap has a tough white membrane covering. Remove this covering by making a small cut between the membrane and the red meat of the backstrap. Lay the backstrap, membrane-side-down, on the work area; grasp the membrane end with a pair of pliers; lay a sharp knife flat on the membrane; pull the membrane with the pliers and work the knife to separate the membrane from the backstrap.

The little tenderloins are the tenderest cut of venison. They are located on the inside of the ribcage; at the rear; on each side of the backbone; and under the area where the hindquarters join the backbone. Many home butchers forget about this small and delicate piece of meat. Each tenderloin is about 10" to 13" long x 3" wide x 1" thick and weighs about ¾ lb.

BACKSTRAPS

Backstrap of Venison with Walnut-Port Stuffing

Filling:
2 Tbsp. butter
½ cup onions, minced
¼ cup port wine
1 cup fresh parsley, chopped
½ cup fine fresh Basic White Breadcrumbs
½ cup (2 oz.) toasted walnuts, finely
   chopped
2 tsp. fresh thyme, minced

2 tsp. orange peel, grated
1 large egg, beaten

Backstrap:
1 (3-lb.) venison backstrap
3 Tbsp. Dijon mustard
salt
pepper
¼ cup butter, melted

To make filling melt butter in a medium skillet over medium heat. Add onion and sauté until soft. Mix in port and cook until liquid evaporates, stirring occasionally, about 5 minutes. Transfer onion mixture to medium bowl. Add parsley, bread-crumbs, walnuts, thyme and orange peel to mixture. Mix in egg.

Place venison on work surface and butterfly by cutting ⅔ through backstrap down length of meat. Open meat along the slice. Make another lengthwise cut down the center of each cut side, cutting ⅓ through. Flatten out backstrap. Rub mustard over both sides of venison. Season with salt and pepper. Arrange venison, cup side up. Spread filling over meat leaving 1" border on all sides. Fold in half lengthwise, enclosing filing. Tie string around backstrap at 1" intervals. Roast can be prepared 6 hours ahead. Cover with plastic wrap and refrigerate. Preheat oven to 400 degrees. Place backstrap in a roasting pan and brush with butter. Roast until ther-mometer, inserted in thickest part of meat, registers 120 degrees for rare, basting occasionally with butter. Let stand for 10 minutes. Carefully remove the string and cut backstrap into ¾" thick slices. Serves 6.

Blue Cheese Venison Backstrap Steaks

2 lbs. venison backstrap cut from large end
1 oz. cream cheese
⅔ oz. blue cheese
4 tsp. plain yogurt
2 tsp. onion, minced

⅛ tsp. white pepper
1 medium garlic clove, crushed
½ tsp. salt, divided
2 tsp. dried parsley

Combine cheeses, yogurt, onion and pepper; set aside. Cut backstrap into four 1" thick pieces. Rub sides of steaks with garlic, Place steaks on a broiler pan 2" from heat. Broil 2 to 4 minutes. Season with ¼ tsp. salt. Turn; broil for 3 to 4 minutes. Season with remaining salt. Top each steak with an equal amount of cheese mix-ture. Broil an additional 1 to 2 minutes. Garnish with parsley. Serves 4.

Broiled Venison Backstrap

3 lbs. venison backstrap
3 tsp. garlic salt

1½ tsp. black pepper
1 stick butter

To prevent meat from curling, diagonally score topside of backstrap with sharp knife. Vigorously rub all sides and ends of meat with garlic salt and pepper. Lay bacon strips on meat, place in broiling pan. Preheat broiler and position meat five to six inches below heating element. Sear both sides of meat. Place butter on top of backstrap so that it melts and bastes the meat. Continue broiling until desired doneness is obtained. Loin sizes vary so you may want to use a meat thermometer to ensure doneness. Serves 4 to 6.

Mrs. Kathryn Breland

Egg and Venison Benedict

2 English muffin halves
butter
olive oil
4 slices venison backstrap, cut ¼" thick
2 eggs, soft poached

Hollandaise Sauce
2 slices truffle
paprika
2 sprigs parsley

Split, butter and toast English muffin halves. Briefly sear both sides of venison backstrap in a hot skillet containing olive oil and place 2 slices on top of each toasted muffin half. Soft-poach eggs and place on top of venison. Spoon ¼ cup of Hollandaise Sauce on top of each egg. Place a small slice of truffle on top of Hollandaise Sauce. Garnish with a sprinkle of paprika on top and a sprig of parsley on the side. Serve immediately. Serves 2.

Fettucine Béarnaise Venison Backstrap

4 slices backstrap, cut 1½" thick
¼ cup Worcestershire sauce
salt

pepper
Béarnaise Sauce
paprika

Place backstraps slices and Worcestershire sauce in a ziplock bag; mix well. Place backstrap slices in the refrigerator for 1 hour. Cook to medium rare to medium on Bar-B-Q grill. *Do not overcook.* Serve over Fettucine. Spoon Béarnaise Sauce on top of steak. Sprinkle with a small amount of paprika. Serves 4.

Mule deer are most active during dawn and dusk. They venture from protective cover when it is time to feed.

Medallions of Venison
with Black Currant Sauce

3 Tbsp. butter
¼ cup carrots, finely diced
¼ cup celery, finely diced
¼ cup onion, finely diced
¼ cup fresh parsley, minced
1 tsp. dried thyme, crumbled
salt
pepper
½ venison backstrap, trimmed and
    cut into twelve 1" thick medallions

all-purpose flour
3 Tbsp. (or more) peanut oil
2 cups canned veal or beef stock
3 Tbsp. cassis
1 cup imported canned black currants.
    If unavailable, substitute ⅓ cup
    dried currants. Soak in 3 Tbsp. cassis
    overnight. Drain currants, reserving
    cassis for sauce,

Melt butter in small skillet over low heat. Add carrot, celery, onion, parsley and thyme. Cover and cook until tender, stirring occasionally, about 15 minutes. Season with salt and pepper. Cool completely. Make horizontal slit in each medallion, cutting ⅔ through to form pocket. Flatten each slightly with a mallet. Season pockets with salt and pepper. Fill each with some of cooled vegetable mixture. Season flour with salt and pepper. Dredge medallions lightly in flour, shaking off excess, heat 3 Tbsp. oil in large skillet over medium-high heat. Add medallions to skillet in batches and cook until meat thermometer inserted into venison registers 170 degrees, about 5 minutes per side, adding more oil to skillet if necessary. Remove medallions and keep warm. Pour off oil in skillet. Stir in stock and cassis and cook over high heat until thick and reduced by about half, 10 to 12 minutes. Mix in currants and heat through. Arrange 2 medallions on each plate. Spoon sauce over each and serve immediately. Serves 6.

Medallions of Venison with Prunes

1 cup pitted prunes
¾ cup Burgundy
4 Tbsp. unsalted butter
12 (2-oz.) venison backstrap medallions,
    flattened to ½" thickness

1 cup canned beef broth, reduced
    to ½ cup
salt
pepper

Place prunes in a bowl. Pour the Burgundy over. Cover and let stand overnight. Drain, reserving wine. Melt 2 Tbsp. butter in a large skillet over medium-high heat. Add venison in batches (do not crowd) and cook until browned, about 4 minutes per side. Transfer to plate. Cover with aluminum foil. Pour reserved wine into skillet and boil until liquid is reduced by half. Add reduced beef broth until reduced by half. Reduce heat, add prunes and simmer until heated through, about 2 minutes. Remove from heat. Swirl in remaining 2 Tbsp. butter, 1 Tbsp. at a time. Season with salt and pepper. Pour over medallions and serve immediately. Serves 4.

Mexican Venison Filet with Tomato-Orange Cumin Sauce

1 tsp. olive oil
3 medium garlic cloves, minced
1 tsp. ground cumin
½ tsp. ground coriander
¼ tsp. dried red pepper flakes
2 cups canned chicken broth
1 cup water (or more)

1 tsp. vinegar
1 bay leaf
¾ tsp. coarse salt
1 (2½-Ib.) venison backstrap, cut and
    tied lengthwise and crosswise
Tomato-Orange Cumin Sauce

Heat oil in a Dutch oven (wide enough just to hold backstrap) over high heat. Add garlic, cumin, coriander and pepper flakes and stir 30 seconds. Add 2 cups chicken broth, 1 cup water, vinegar, bay leaf and salt and bring to a boil. Add backstrap and reduce heat so liquid simmers (if venison is not covered by liquid, add more broth). Simmer gently 20 to 25 minutes (for rare). Remove meat from pan. Let stand 5 minutes. Skim fat from surface of liquid. Cut venison diagonally ¼" thick. Spoon ⅓ cup over each serving. Serves 6.

Salt and Pepper Crusted Venison Backstrap

2 tsp. pepper
1 tsp. salt
1 tsp. dried rosemary

1 large garlic clove, minced
¼ (16-oz.) venison backstrap
1 Tbsp. olive oil

Cut venison backstrap in two pieces and tie together at 2" intervals with kitchen twine. Combine pepper, salt, rosemary and garlic in a small bowl. Rub over venison. Let venison stand at least 15 minutes. Preheat oven to 400 degrees. Heat oil in heavy medium ovenproof skillet over high heat. Add tied venison and brown on all sides and ends. Transfer skillet with venison to oven and roast until venison is cooked to medium rare. Turn occasionally, about 20 minutes. Slice and serve. Serves 2 to 4.

Stuffed Venison Backstrap with Balsamic Vinegar Sauce

Sauce:
3 lbs. meaty veal bones
2 Tbsp. safflower oil
2 celery stalks, chopped
1 carrot, chopped
1 onion, chopped
1 garlic head, halved
2 smoked bacon slices, chopped
2 cups Burgundy
2 cups balsamic vinegar
6 cups canned chicken broth
salt
pepper

Venison:
1 red bell pepper
½ (2 lb.) venison backstrap
3 Tbsp. olive paste (olivada) available at Italian markets or specialty stores
6 anchovy fillets
24 asparagus spears, tips only
Pressed and Baked Shiitake Mushroom and Potato Roundel

To make the sauce preheat the oven to 400 degrees. Place bones in baking pan. Roast until bones are well browned, about 1 hour. Heat oil in heavy large stockpot over medium-high heat. Add celery, carrot, onion, garlic and bacon and sauté until light brown. Add roasted bones and Burgundy. Bring to boil, scraping up any browned bits. Boil until reduced to glaze. Add vinegar and boil until reduced to ½ cup. Add chicken broth and simmer until liquid is reduced to 2 cups, about 1½ hours. Strain sauce and degrease. Season to taste with salt and pepper. The sauce can be prepared 1 day ahead. Cover with plastic wrap and refrigerate.

To cook the venison char bell pepper over gas until blackened on all sides. Place in a small brown paper bag and let stand 10 minutes. Peel and seed. Rinse; pat dry and cut julienne. Slice venison lengthwise down center, cutting ⅔ of the way through. Open venison flat; cut-side-up. Using meat pounder, flatten to about 1½". Spread venison with olive paste. Arrange alternating rows of roasted pepper strips and anchovies on top of the olive paste. Fold sides of backstrap closed. Tie with string. Preheat oven to 500 degrees. Roast venison until thermometer registers 125 degrees for medium-rare, about 40 minutes. Remove from the oven and let rest for 10 minutes. Meanwhile, rewarm the sauce over medium heat, stirring frequently. Blanch asparagus tips in boiling salted water until just tender. Drain asparagus. Slice tenderloin into 12 pieces. Place venison in center of each plate. Surround with sauce and blanched asparagus tips. Serve with Stuffed Venison Backstrap with Balsamic Vinegar Sauce. Serve immediately. Serves 6.

The Lieber State Recreation Area in west-central Indiana offers three dates in November and December for deer gun hunts for wheelchair users.

Tender Backstrap Kebabs with Spicy Peanut Sauce and Grilled Chapati

Venison:
¼ cup coconut milk
¼ tsp. dried red pepper flakes
¼ cup safflower oil
¼ cup fresh cilantro, chopped
2 Tbsp, fresh lime juice
2 Tbsp. fresh lemon juice
1 Tbsp. sugar
2 tsp. cumin seeds, crushed
2 tsp. aniseed, crushed
2 tsp. salt
1 tsp. turmeric
1 tsp. peeled fresh ginger, minced
3½ lbs. venison backstrap, cut 1" pieces
2 large onions, cut 1" pieces

Sauce:
1 Tbsp. peanut oil
½ cup onion, minced
3 garlic cloves, minced
1 tsp. ground cumin
½ tsp. dried red pepper flakes
¼ tsp. aniseed, crushed
1 cup (or more) coconut milk
1 cup chunky peanut butter
3 Tbsp. fresh lime or lemon juice
salt
green onions, minced
Grilled Chapati

Marinate the venison in a large bowl, combine first 12 ingredients. Add venison backstrap and onions; toss to coat. Cover and marinate in the refrigerator for at least 6 hours. Can be prepared 24 hours in advance. Allow to return to room temperature before cooking. Make the sauce by heating the peanut oil in medium skillet over medium heat. Add onion, garlic, cumin, red pepper flakes and aniseed. Sauté until the onion is just tender, stirring frequently. Add 1 cup coconut milk and bring to simmer. Remove from heat. Add peanut butter and whisk until smooth. Stir in lime juice. If needed, thin sauce with additional coconut milk. Season with salt. Cool sauce to room temperature. Transfer to serving bowl. The sauce can be prepared 3 hours ahead. Cover and store at room temperature.

To cook the venison heat grill to medium-high heat. Remove venison and onions from marinade, Alternate venison and onion pieces on skewers. Arrange skewers on grill. Cook until venison until it is slightly charred on outside and pink on the inside, turning occasionally. Do not over-cook. Arrange skewers on platter. Cover with aluminum foil to keep warm. Serve venison with peanut sauce and Grilled Chapati. Serves 8.

Pounded Venison Backstrap with Brown Gravy

1 venison backstrap, rib section
salt
black pepper

all-purpose flour
butter

Partially freeze venison backstrap and cut, across the grain in very thin slices. Mix and sift flour, salt and pepper. Sprinkle venison with flour mixture. Tenderize with a pounding mallet. Brown the venison very quickly in butter. Remove venison and allow to drain. Make a brown gravy in skillet and put meat in gravy. Cover venison and simmer over very low heat for 30 minutes to an hour. Serve the venison and gravy over biscuits or toasted hamburger buns. Serves 4 to 8.

Venison Backstrap Sauté
with Gratin of Turnips

Gratin of Turnips:
3 Tbsp. Clarified Butter
2½ lbs. young turnips, peeled and
    cut ¼" rounds
2 medium onions, chopped
2 Tbsp. fresh parsley, chopped
salt
pepper
1 cup dry vermouth
3 cups canned beef broth
¼ tsp. sugar
pinch of cinnamon

Venison Backstrap Sauté:
2 (1½-lb.) venison backstrap
3 Tbsp. Clarified Butter
4½ Tbsp. green onions, minced
¼ cup Cognac
1⅓ cups dry red wine, divided
1 tsp. fresh tarragon, minced or ⅓
    tsp. dried, crushed
pinch of dried thyme, crushed
1½ tsp. red wine vinegar
1½ tsp. tomato paste
1½ tsp. cornichons, minced
1½ tsp. water-packed green
    peppercorns, rinsed, drained and
    crushed
2 Tbsp. fresh parsley, minced

To cook the turnips grease 12" gratin dish. Heat Clarified Butter in a large skillet over medium-high heat. Sauté turnip slices 3 minutes; add onions and sauté until golden, about 7 minutes. Mix in parsley and sauté 30 seconds. Sprinkle with salt and pepper. Add vermouth and boil until liquid is reduced to glaze, scraping up any browned bits, about 4 minutes. Add chicken broth and boil until reduced by half. Reduce heat and simmer until turnips are just tender, about 15 minutes. Increase heat and boil until liquid is reduced to ½ cup, about 12 minutes. Transfer to gratin dish. Cool to room temperature. Preheat oven to 375 degrees. Bake turnips 10 minutes. Sprinkle with sugar and cinnamon and continue baking 15 minutes. Can be kept warm in oven on lowest setting for 20 minutes.

Cut each venison backstrap into 5 slices, 1½" thick at the wide end of the backstrap and slightly thicker as meat narrows. Flatten each to 1" thickness; using heel of hand. Shape into rounds and pat dry. Heat Clarified Butter in a large skillet over medium-high heat. Brown backstrap on all sides, including edges, reduce heat to medium-low. Cook venison for about 5 minutes. Turn and cook second side until medium rare. Transfer venison to a heated platter and sprinkle with salt and pepper. Cover with aluminum foil. Pour off all but 3 Tbsp. fat from skillet. Add shallots and stir over medium-high heat 1 minute. Add Cognac and boil until reduced to a glaze. Stir in ⅔ cup wine, tarragon and thyme. Boil until reduced to a glaze, scraping up any browned bits. Add remaining ⅔ cup wine and boil until reduced to glaze. Mix in stock, vinegar and tomato paste. Boil, stirring occasionally, until sauce is thickened and is reduced by ¾, about 15 minutes. Stir in cornichons, green peppercorns, salt and pepper. Divide venison and turnips among heated dinner plates. Spoon the sauce on venison. Sprinkle with parsley and serve immediately. Serves 4.

Venison Backstrap with Creamy Mustard Sauce

1 (3½-lb.) venison backstrap, halved & tied
1½ cups Burgundy wine
¼ cup Dijon mustard
1 Tbsp. plus 1½ tsp. mustard seeds
2 large garlic cloves, pressed
pepper

¼ cup mashed soft silken tofu
1 tsp. fresh rosemary, minced
½ tsp. potato starch, dissolved in 1
   Tbsp. water
8 green onions
fresh rosemary

Preheat oven to 325 degrees and preheat broiler. Place venison on broiler rack and broil until brown on all sides. Pat venison with paper towels to remove fat. Mix mustard, mustard seeds and garlic in a small bowl. Season with pepper. Rub all but 1½ Tbsp. mustard mixture over venison. Transfer venison to heavy Dutch oven. Add Burgundy. Partially cover and bake for 1¼ hours, basting occasionally with pan juices. Uncover, baste and cook about 30 minutes longer for medium. Move venison to platter. Cover loosely with aluminum foil to keep warm. Degrease pan juices. Mix tofu and remaining 1½ Tbsp. mustard mixture in medium saucepan. Using electric mixer, gradually add pan juices, beating until sauce is smooth. Add rosemary add potato starch mixture. Stir constantly over low heat until sauce thickens, about 2 minutes. Meanwhile, blanch onions in pot of boiling water until tender, about 3 minutes. Drain well. Carefully cut strings off venison. Spread a thin layer of sauce on serving plates. Slice venison and arrange on plates. Spoon a small amount of the sauce over the venison. Sprinkle with rosemary. Garnish plate with onions. Serves 8.

Venison in Olive Sauce

1 (3-lb.) venison backstrap
3 Tbsp. Worcestershire sauce
3 garlic cloves, minced
salt
pepper
7 Tbsp. butter
1 Tbsp. peanut oil
all-purpose four

1½ cups Venison Soup Stock or
   canned beef broth
½ cup pimiento-stuffed green olives,
   sliced
1 tsp. Dijon mustard
1 small onion, minced
¼ cup dry sherry
2 hard-cooked eggs, minced
lettuce leaves

Set venison in non-aluminum pan. Combine Worcestershire sauce, garlic and salt and pepper. Rub over venison. Cover and refrigerate overnight, turning occasionally. Melt 6 Tbsp. butter with oil in heavy skillet over medium-high heat. Dredge venison in flour; shake off excess flour. Add venison to large skillet and brown well on all sides. Add broth, olives and mustard. Simmer to desired doneness, 30 minutes for medium-rare (130 degrees). Meanwhile, melt remaining 1 Tbsp. butter in small skillet over medium-low heat. Add onion and cook until translucent, stirring occasionally. Set aside. Add sherry to venison. Simmer 5 minutes. Stir in onion. Taste sauce and adjust seasoning with salt and pepper. To serve, slice venison thinly. Arrange on platter. Sprinkle with eggs. Garnish with lettuce. Serve sauce separately. Serves 8 to 10.

Venison Backstrap with Plantain Stuffing

Marinade:

½ red onion, peeled and thinly sliced
1 head garlic, cut in half crosswise
2 oranges, cut in half
1 lime, cut in half
1 Scotch bonnet or habanero chili, cut in half
12 black peppercorns, toasted and slightly crushed
1 bay leaf, broken
½ bunch cilantro, roughly chopped
1 cup olive oil
2 (about 10 oz. ea.) venison backstraps, trimmed

Stuffing:

2 Tbsp. canola oil
2 ripe plantains, peeled and cut into ½" thick slices
salt and pepper to taste
2 tsp. toasted and ground cumin
2 tsp. toasted and ground black peppercorns
1 tsp. sugar
1 tsp. salt
2 Tbsp. canola oil
Brown Sugar and Lemon Sauce for Venison

Mix all marinade ingredients in a bowl. Squeeze the fruit and add with juice to the marinade. Cut backstraps in half to yield 4 portions, and place in marinade. Cover and refrigerate from 2 to 8 hours, turning occasionally. To prepare the stuffing, heat oil in a sauté pan. Sauté plantain slices until dark on both sides. Drain on a paper towel and let cool. Transfer to a bowl and cover with butter. Season with salt and pepper and set aside. Preheat oven to 400 degrees. Remove venison from marinade and pat dry. Make a narrow deep slit in the inside of each piece of venison to form a pocket. Do not cut all the way through and only to a half inch from each end. Pack the plantain stuffing in the center of each backstrap portion and press meat together to close the pocket. Tie venison with butcher's twine at 2" intervals. Combine cumin, pepper, sugar and salt in a bowl and sprinkle over meat. Heat oil in a cast iron skillet or ovenproof sauté pan and sear venison on all sides for 2 minutes over medium-high heat. Drain excess oil from skillet and place skillet in oven for 7 to 8 minutes. Remove venison from oven and let portions rest for a few minutes. Gently remove twine and slice meat. Arrange on serving plates. Serve with Brown Sugar and Lemon Sauce for Venison. Serves 4.

Venison Roll Veracruzana

Chorizo:
8 dried ancho chilies
3 dried pasilla chilies
½ lb. venison backstrap, ground
6 oz. pork fat
½ cup rice wine vinegar
½ medium white onion, minced
3 garlic cloves, mashed
1 Tbsp. paprika
1½ tsp. salt
1 tsp. pepper
⅛ tsp. ground cloves
⅛ tsp. ground cinnamon
⅛ tsp. ground cumin
⅛ tsp. dried oregano, crumbled
⅛ tsp. ground coriander
   safflower oil

Salsa Veracruzana:
4 oz. dried mulato chilies
1 cup fresh orange juice
1 small white onion, chopped
⅓ banana
2 garlic cloves

Venison Backstrap Roll:
6 green onions, green part only
¼ cup white onion, minced
¼ cup fresh parsley, minced
¼ cup canned chicken broth
1 egg, beaten
1 (4-lb.) venison backstrap, split in half
salt
pepper

To make the chorizo, roast ancho and pasilla chilies over gas flame just long enough to soften; do not char. Core, seed and devein. Break into small pieces. Grind to powder in a blender; you should have about 6 Tbsp. Mix ground venison with powdered chilies and remaining ingredients in a large bowl. Cover with plastic wrap and refrigerate until ready to use.

To make the salsa, soak chilies in hot water until soft, about 30 minutes. Drain. Core, seed and devein. Purée in a blender with remaining ingredients until smooth.

Venison Roll: Combine chorizo, onions and parsley. Blend in chicken broth and egg; mixture will be thin. Season with salt and pepper. Spread chorizo mixture on one side of venison backstrap. Tie both sections of backstrap together at 2" intervals. Sprinkle salt and pepper on all sides. Heat oil in a large skillet over medium heat. Pat venison dry. Brown venison well on all sides. Wrap loosely in banana leaves. Preheat oven to 325 degrees. Lightly oil a heavy baking dish. Spoon half of prepared salsa into dish. Set venison in the center. Top with the remaining salsa. Cover and bake 25 minutes per pound, basting often. Transfer venison to carving board. Carefully remove banana leaves. Gently remove strings. Add enough water to sauce to thin slightly. Strain into small saucepan; degrease. Re-warm over low heat. Slice venison ½" thick. Place fresh banana leaves on serving plate. Arrange on platter. Ladle some sauce over and serve. Pass remaining sauce separately. Serves 6 to 8.

Over one billion dollars is spent on sport hunting in the United States each year.

Venison Scallops
with Greek Eggplant and Peppers

1 eggplant (1 lb.) peeled and cut into
   1½"x⅛"x⅛" strips
1 Tbsp. salt
1 lb. venison backstrap, trimmed and cut
   across the grain into about twelve ⅜"
   thick slices
3 Tbsp. olive oil
3 large red bell peppers, seeded and cut into
   ⅛" wide strips
1 large onion, halved and sliced ⅛" thick

1 large garlic clove, minced
pinch of ground allspice
pinch of cinnamon
4 to 5 Tbsp. fresh lime or lemon juice
1 cup all-purpose flour
2 Tbsp. Clarified Butter
3 Tbsp. butter
1 medium garlic clove, minced
1 tsp. fresh oregano or ⅓ tsp. dried,
   crushed

Toss eggplant and 1 Tbsp. salt in colander; let drain 30 minutes. Pound venison slices between sheets of waxed paper to ⅛" thickness. Rinse eggplant and pat dry. Heat 2 Tbsp. olive oil in large skillet over medium-high heat. Add pepper strips and onion and sauté until onion begins to soften. Add eggplant and sauté until tender, about 5 minutes. Mix 1 garlic clove, allspice and cinnamon and sauté 2 minutes. Sprinkle with 2 Tbsp. lime juice, salt and pepper. Divide mixture among 4 heated dinner plates. Place in oven on lowest setting. Wipe skillet clean. Pat venison dry and lightly sprinkle with flour, shaking off excess. Heat 1 Tbsp. olive oil with Clarified Butter in skillet over medium-high heat. Cook venison in batches, do not crowd, until just cooked through, about 10 seconds per side. Sprinkle with salt and pepper. Divide among plates and return to oven. Pour off fat from skillet. Wipe clean with paper towels. Add 3 Tbsp. butter and melt over medium-low heat. Add 1 garlic clove and sauté until soft, 3 to 4 minutes. Stir in oregano and cook until aromatic, about 1 minute. Add 2 to 3 Tbsp. lime juice. Taste and adjust seasoning. Drizzle sauce over venison. Serve immediately. Serves 4 to 6.

Venison with Raisin and Black Peppercorn Sauce

2 cups canned beef broth
1 Tbsp. butter
1 Tbsp. walnut or safflower oil
1½ lbs. venison backstrap, cut into four
   1" thick pieces

¾ cup dry sherry
⅔ cup seedless raisins
1 Tbsp. black peppercorns, cracked
1 cup heavy cream
rosemary sprigs

Boil broth in small saucepan until reduced to ½ cup, about 15 minutes. Set aside. Melt butter with oil in large skillet over medium-high heat. Add venison and cook to desired degree of doneness, about 4 minutes per side for medium rare. Transfer venison to individual serving plates. Cover with aluminum foil to keep warm. Add sherry, raisins and peppercorns to same skillet and boil until liquid is reduced by half, stirring occasionally; about 5 minutes. Add stock and cream and boil until thickened to sauce consistently, stirring occasionally, about 8 minutes. Spoon sauce over steaks. Garnish with a rosemary sprig. Serves 4.

Venison Backstrap Steaks with Blackberry Sauce with Nutmeg and Cloves

½ venison backstrap, begin cutting from
   large end
bacon strips
1 oz. cream cheese
⅔ oz. blue cheese
4 tsp. plain yogurt
2 tsp. onion, minced very fine
⅛ tsp. white pepper

2 large garlic cloves, crushed
½ tsp. salt, divided
2 tsp. fresh parsley, chopped
Blackberry Sauce with Nutmeg and
   Cloves
Mashed Potatoes
hair-thin strips of green scallion stems

Combine cream cheese, blue cheese, yogurt, onion and white pepper and set aside. Cut backstrap into eight 1+" thick pieces. Wrap each piece of backstrap with a strip of bacon and secure with a toothpick. Rub steaks with crushed garlic. Place steaks on a wire broiler pan 2" from heat. Broil for 2 to 4 minutes. Season broiled sides with ¼ tsp. salt. Turn and broil for 3 to 4 minutes. Season second broiled side with the remaining salt. Top each steak with an equal amount of cheese mixture. Broil steaks an additional 1 to 2 minutes until cheese mixture shows a toasted spot. Spoon or squeeze Mashed Potatoes on hot serving plate; garnish with green scallion strips. Drizzle Blackberry Sauce with Nutmeg and Cloves on the serving plates where the steaks will sit. Remove toothpicks from steaks and set steaks on top of the sauce. Garnish steaks with fresh parsley. Serves 4.

Coiled and Roasted Venison Backstrap

½ tsp, garlic salt
⅛ tsp. black pepper
1 whole venison backstrap

Crisco, for browning
bacon strips

Rub backstrap with garlic salt and pepper. Coil venison backstrap as one would coil a rope and tie with cotton butcher twine to hold shape. In a large skillet brown coiled backstrap on both sides. Cover backstrap completely with bacon strips. Insert a meat thermometer in the thickest part of the meat. Cook in a 250 degree oven until thermometer registers less than medium. When done remove backstrap from oven and place on a cutting board. Allow to rest for 5 minutes. Gently remove the butcher twine. Cut backstrap in 1"+ rounds. Serve with a sauce. Serves 8 to 10.

Marinated Venison Backstrap Medallions
on Béarnaise Sauce

Bourbon & Balsamic Vinegar Venison
  Marinade
8 venison backstrap pieces cut across
  the grain in 1" pieces
Very thin strips of red and yellow bell
  peppers

1½ Tbsp. pine nuts, roasted
Béarnaise Sauce
fresh ground nutmeg
parsley sprigs

Make a double batch of Bourbon & Balsamic Vinegar Venison Marinade. Place venison backstrap pieces in a 1 gal. ziplock bag and pour the marinade over. Exhaust all air from the bag and refrigerate for 24 hours. Cut very thin strips of red and yellow bell peppers; place in water and refrigerate. Under a hot broiler or toaster oven, toast the pine nuts until they are deep golden. Preheat the broiler to hot. Make the Béarnaise Sauce and remove from the heat, but keep warm. Remove the venison backstrap pieces from the marinade and quickly grill on both sides to just a little more than rare. Spoon the Béarnaise Sauce onto the serving plates; place two venison backstrap medallions on each plate; garnish sauce with thin strips of peppers and a sprig of parsley; sprinkle venison with toasted pine nuts, and dust venison and sauce with a little fresh-grated nutmeg. Serves 4. Also delicious using thick-cut chops in place of backstrap pieces.

TENDERLOINS

Basil Venison Tenderloin and Broccoli Stir-Fry

1 Tbsp. canola oil
¾ lb. venison tenderloin cut in ½" thick
  medallions
2 cups frozen broccoli pieces
1 medium red bell pepper, cut in thin 2"
  strips
½ cup snow peas
½ cup fresh mushrooms
¼ cup water chestnuts

½ cup boiling water
2 tsp. chicken-flavored instant bouillon
  granules or 2 cubes
¼ cup cold water
1 Tbsp, cornstarch
1 tsp. dried basil leaves
1 tsp. lime juice
½ cup sliced green onions

Cut venison tenderloin into ½"-thick medallions. Heat cooking oil in a large skillet on medium heat. Add venison. Stir fry until venison is medium rare. *Do not overcook.* Remove venison to a serving dish. Add all vegetables except green onions. Stir fry until crisp and just tender. Combine boiling water and bouillon. Stir to dissolve. Combine cold water, cornstarch, basil and lime juice. Stir well. Add to vegetables in skillet. Cook and stir until sauce is thickened. Add green onions to venison. Heat until venison is warm. Serves 2 to 4.

Broiled Venison Tenderloin

2 whole venison tenderloins, about
  1½ lbs. each
1¼ tsp. garlic salt
½ tsp. black pepper

2 Tbsp. soy sauce
1 Tbsp. catsup
1 Tbsp. vegetable oil
¼ tsp. oregano, crushed

Mix all ingredients except tenderloins in large shallow container. Add meat, cover and marinate 4 hours in refrigerator. Remove tenderloins from marinade. Briefly sear both sides of tenderloin over hot coals or under broiler element. Continue broiling until desired doneness is obtained. Remove from heat, slice thinly and serve while hot. Serves 4 to 6.

Mrs. Kathryn Breland

Cider-Sauced Venison Tenderloin

1 venison tenderloin
½ tsp. black pepper
½ tsp. sage
½ tsp. thyme
½ tsp. ginger
½ tsp. cinnamon

½ tsp. salt
1 Tbsp. canola oil
1 onion, minced
1 large apple, peeled and chopped
½ cup apple cider
Boiled Rice

Slice the venison tenderloin crosswise into 8 medallions. Mix the seasonings together and use all to coat the venison slices. In a skillet heat the oil and briefly sear the venison on both sides until brown. Remove the venison to a platter and cover to keep warm. To the oil in the skillet, add the onions and sauté until ½ cooked; add chopped apples and cook until onions are clear; add apple cider to the skillet and heat to simmer. Place the venison slices in simmering liquid, cover and simmer very slowly for 20 to 30 minutes. Serve over Boiled Rice. Serves 2.

Japanese Venison Tenderloin

2 or 3 venison tenderloins
½ cup Brazil nuts
1 cup onion, minced
2 med. garlic cloves, minced
¼ cup lime juice
¼ cup teriyaki sauce

2 Tbsp. light brown sugar
2 Tbsp. coriander, ground
¼ tsp. cayenne pepper
¼ cup olive oil
Boiled Rice

Grate Brazil nuts. Cut venison tenderloin into 1" cubes. Combine nuts, onion, garlic, lime juice, teriyaki sauce, sugar, coriander, pepper and olive oil. Add venison cubes and marinate for 10 minutes. Reserve marinade. Place venison on skewers and grill or broil for about 5 to 10 minutes on each side. Brush once with reserved marinade. Serve venison on skewers with Boiled Rice. Serves 4.

Molded Venison Tenderloin

2 envelopes unflavored gelatin
1½ cups water
2 (10½-oz.) cans condensed beef
  consommé
2 Tbsp. lemon juice
1 (2-oz.) jar pimientos, sliced, drained

2½ cups cooked venison tenderloin,
  cut into bite-size pieces
¾ cup celery, thinly sliced
1 (11-oz.) jar mixed pickles, drained
2 eggs, hard-boiled, sliced

Soften gelatin in ½ cup of cold water. Heat remaining water with 1 can of beef consommé. Add gelatin and stir until dissolved. Add lemon juice and remaining consommé. Measure out ⅓ cup of the consommé mixture and put it into a blender. Add pimientos and blend until smooth. Pour into a 1½-qt. mold. Refrigerate until set. Chill remaining consommé mixture until it mounds slightly when dropped from a spoon. Stir in venison, celery and ¾ cup of the chopped pickles. Spoon into the mold on top of the pimiento mixture. Chill until thoroughly set. At serving time, unmold onto serving dish. Garnish with egg slices and remaining pickles. Makes 8 to 10 first-course servings.

Portuguese Venison Tenderloin Steak

1 Tbsp. red wine vinegar
1 garlic clove, minced
1 venison tenderloin, cut into 1" thick pieces
salt and pepper
1 Tbsp. butter
1 Tbsp. olive oil
½ cup dry red wine

1½ tsp. tomato paste
2 Tbsp. butter, cut
  into pieces, room temperature
2 thin slices presunto or proscuitto,
  chopped (available at Italian markets
  or specialty meat markets)
2 Tbsp. fresh parsley, chopped

Combine vinegar and garlic in glass or stainless steel bowl. Let stand 10 minutes. Sprinkle venison steaks with salt and pepper on both sides. Rub vinegar mixture into steaks on both sides. Let stand at room temperature 10 minutes; or cover with plastic wrap and refrigerate for up to 1 hour. Melt 1 Tbsp. butter with oil in medium skillet over medium heat. Add steaks and cook to desired doneness. Transfer steaks to plates and cover with foil. Pour off liquid in skillet. Stir in wine over high heat, scraping up any browned bits. Boil until liquid is syrupy, about 3 minutes. Whisk in tomato paste. Remove from heat. Whisk in remaining 2 Tbsp, butter in small amounts, incorporating each piece before adding the next. Stir in presunto and parsley. Spoon sauce over steaks and serve. Serves 2.

Sautéed Venison Tenderloin with Cream of Shallot Sauce

8 venison marrow bones

Sauce:
2 lbs. veal bones (preferably shank end, cut up)
3 cups canned chicken broth
1 cup canned beef broth
1 Tbsp. butter
4 large green onions, minced
½ cup dry white wine
6 Tbsp. butter
salt
pepper

Venison:
4 (8-oz.) venison tenderloins
coarse salt
3 Tbsp. butter
1 Tbsp. olive oil
fresh parsley, minced

Crack each marrow bone. Remove as large a piece of marrow as possible. Transfer marrow to colander. Run under cold water. Transfer to a bowl. Cover with cold water. Refrigerate marrow overnight. To make the sauce preheat oven to 450 degrees. Place veal bones in roasting pan and roast until well browned, turning occasionally, about 45 minutes. Transfer bones to large roasting pan. Set roasting pan over high heat. Add both broths and bring to a boil, scraping up browned bits. Pour into pan with bones. Simmer until reduced to 1 cup, about 2 hours. Melt 1 Tbsp. butter in medium skillet. Add green onions and sauté until golden brown. Add wine and boil until almost completely evaporated, about 4 minutes. Add reduced broth and boil until reduced to ⅔ cup, about 6 minutes. Whisk in 6 Tbsp. butter 1 piece at a time. Season with salt and pepper. Remove from heat.

Pat the venison dry and sprinkle with coarse salt. Melt 3 Tbsp. butter with oil in large skillet over medium-high heat. Add venison and cook to desired doneness. Meanwhile, drain marrow and cut into ⅜" thick pieces. Bring pot of salted water to boil. Reduce heat, add marrow and simmer until opaque, 5 minutes. Remove using slotted spoon. Set venison tenderloin on each plate. Trail sauce over tenderloin. Sprinkle with parsley. Garnish with marrow slices. Serves 4.

In Tennessee, venison from Hunters for the Hungry (HFH) is the major source of meat being provided to the food banks, coming in the winter when people really need it. In Pennsylvania, Hunters Sharing the Harvest (HSH) provides 750,000 meals annually to needy recipients across the state. Nearly every state has a venison donation program, and donations nationwide go as high as five to six million pounds yearly. Hunters can help the needy and also deduct the processing fees from their taxes.

Venison Tenderloin with Herbed Cream Sauce

3 Tbsp. unsalted butter
½ cup loosely packed fresh tarragon
  leaves
¼ cup green onions, green parts only,
  chopped
8 baby carrots, peeled
8 turnips, peeled, quartered
8 pearl onions, peeled
4 baby zucchini, trimmed
1 Tbsp. Unsalted butter

2 Tbsp. green onions, finely chopped
1 Tbsp. garlic, minced
2 Tbsp. Cognac
⅓ cup plus 2 Tbsp. heavy cream
salt
pepper
2 Tbsp. fresh mint, chopped
1 Tbsp. water
1 Tbsp. olive oil
2 (8-oz.) venison tenderloins, each
  halved crosswise

Purée 3 Tbsp. butter with tarragon and green onions in a food processor until smooth. Transfer to bowl. Cover and refrigerate until well chilled. Bring large saucepan of salted water to boil. Add carrots and cook until crisp-tender. Using slotted spoon, transfer carrots to a bowl filled with ice and water. Add turnips and pearl onions to the saucepan and cook until crisp-tender. Transfer to same bowl as carrots using slotted spoon. Add zucchini to saucepan and cook until crisp-tender. Transfer to same bowl using slotted spoon. Drain vegetables and pat dry with paper towels.

Melt 1 Tbsp. butter in large skillet over medium heat. Add green onions and garlic and sauté 3 minutes. Mix in Cognac and bring to boil. Add ⅓ cup cream and boil until reduced to a thin sauce. Season with salt and pepper. Set aside. Heat vegetables with remaining 2 Tbsp. cream, mint and 1 Tbsp. water in medium skillet over medium heat. Cook until cream coats vegetables, stirring occasionally, about 5 minutes. Add salt and pepper. Heat oil in large skillet over medium-high heat; add venison and cook to medium-rare. Transfer to warm plates. Bring sauce to simmer. Add 3 Tbsp. herb butter and whisk until melted. Pour sauce over steaks. Surround with vegetables and serve. Serves 2.

6

Venison Oven Roasts

Oven roasts provide you with one of you biggest challenges and an opportunity to serve your guests a truly American dish. Your efforts will be rewarded with outstanding cuisine. Try serving your venison roast slices with the sauce recipes in the chapter Sauces and Gravy. The fruit based sauces are especially good with leftover and warmed roast slices.

Oven roasting cooks by using dry heat. Venison tends to dry out during roasting. Since venison contains no or very little fat, your challenge is to keep the roast moist throughout the cooking process.

Keeping the roast moist can be accomplished in one of three ways; (1) frequent basting during cooking, (2) larding the roast, using a larding needle, with another moist meat such as salt pork, bacon, beef or pork fat, and (3) wrapping the outside of the roast with a moist meat such as bacon or slabs of pork or beef fat.

The prudent cook may wish to utilize ALL THREE *moistening methods at the same time.*

Venison roasts should be cooked at 350 degress to no more than 138 degrees of internal temperature. The use of a meat thermometer inserted to the center of the thickest part of the roast is a must. For accurate reading, Do not let the meat thermometer touch the bone. If you are ever in doubt about whether you have cooked the roast too much, it is better to err on the rarer side. You can always check the meat by cutting it. If the roast is not cooked to your likeness you can always put it back in the oven and cook it some more. You cannot un-cook it.

Whole venison hindquarters are easier to obtain than the more specialized cuts such as tenderloins, thick cut chops, eye of round roasts or crown roasts. The reason for this is that most venison is butchered on site and most of us are not as educated as we would like when it comes to identifying specific cuts of meat. The professional game processing firm is well worth the small fee charged. These firms can butcher your venison to your exact specifications.

Most venison roasts come from whole or large cuts of fore and hindquarters. Neck roasts are best saved for slow-cooking pot roasts.

WEIGHTS FOR TYPICAL VENISON ROASTS

(Weights are for an average 120-lb. white tail buck)

Hindquarter with bones	10¾ lbs.
Hindquarter without bones	8½ lbs.
Forequarter with bones	5 lbs.
Forequarter without bones	3 lbs.
2" Top Round Roast	2¾ lbs.
4" Top Round Roast	5 lbs.
Backstrap Roast (25"x3½"x1¾")	3¾ lbs.
Neck Roast (8½"x5"x5")	3 lbs.

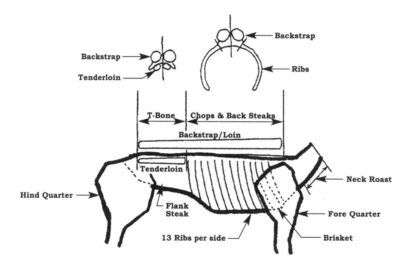

Listed here are several cuts of meat and their percentage of total calories from fat. All figures are for raw cuts, trimmed of visible fat: Buffalo top sirloin 15%; venison 18%; veal cutlets 24%; pork tenderloin 27%; beef top round 29%; beef eye of round 32%; leg of lamb 34%; beef round tip 35%; rabbit, domestic 37%; beef sirloin 38%.

Old Tavern Venison Roast

This circa 1800 recipe was served at an old river tavern. Most of the meat served at this tavern was wild game harvested from the nearby forest.

large center cut roast from aged venison
   hindquarter, cut at least 2" thick
mild vinegar
salt
water
bay leaves
sage leaves
onion slices

garlic slivers
ground allspice
coarse black pepper
celery salt
slices, smoked bacon
all-purpose flour
canned beef broth
tawny port

Mix vinegar, salt and water and marinate the venison for 1 hour. Remove venison and pat dry. Trim off all fat and connecting tissue. Cut slits in venison using a sharp knife. Insert bay leaf, sage leaf, onion slices and garlic slivers into slits. Make a mixture of salt, allspice, black pepper and celery salt. Use ¼ teaspoon for each pound of meat. Rub spice mixture into venison. Wrap roast completely in smoked bacon slices; secure with toothpicks. Insert a meat thermometer into the deepest part of the roast. Preheat oven to 300 degrees. Place venison in a covered roaster. Venison is excellent rare (15 minutes per pound). For gravy, pour off grease in drippings, add flour and a little beef broth. Add port before serving. Slice thin. This roast is also excellent when served chilled. Serves 6 to 10.

Venison Roast Marinated in Apple Vinegar with Sour Cream Gravy

1 venison fore or hindquarter roast
salt
1½ cups apple cider vinegar
3 cups water
1 large onion, sliced
6 whole cloves
10 whole allspice

10 black peppercorns
1 bay leaf
lemon rind
1⅓ cups sour cream
1 tsp. all-purpose flour
1 egg yolk, beaten
Mashed Potatoes

Rub salt into all sides of venison roast. Mix vinegar, 2 cups water, onion, cloves, allspice, peppercorns, and bay leaf. Cover and boil for 10 to 15 minutes. Let mixture cool and pour over venison roast. Let venison marinate for 2 or 3 days, turning once or twice each day. Remove roast from marinade and allow to drain. Place the roast in a baking pan and add ½ of the marinade, remaining cup of water, and a piece of lemon rind. Insert a meat thermometer into the thickest part of the meat. Bake in 350 degree oven for 25 to 35 minutes per pound or to between rare and medium (138 degrees) on the meat thermometer. When half done, baste with ⅓ cup sour cream. Turn roast over once while baking. Baste with pan juices frequently. When done, remove roast from baking pan. Mix remaining cup of sour cream into the pan liquid. Thicken pan liquid with flour and beaten egg yolk. Strain sauce and serve with Mashed Potatoes. Serves 6 to 10.

Braised Stuffed Shoulder of Venison

1 deboned venison forequarter
3 Tbsp. canola oil, divided
¼ cup white onion, finely chopped
12 saltine crackers, finely rolled
2 tsp. lemon rind, grated
1 tsp. mint leaves, crushed
½ tsp. salt
¼ tsp. black pepper

1 egg, lightly beaten
4 oz. smoked ham, cut in julienne strips
smoked pork fat
½ cup apple juice
1 (10½-oz.) can condensed beef
   consommé
2 cups cherry tomatoes
2 Tbsp. all-purpose flour
cold water

Unroll venison and wipe with a damp cloth. Heat 2 Tbsp. canola oil in a large Dutch oven. Add onion and cook until just soft. Scrape the onion and the oil into a mixing bowl. Add crackers, lemon rind, mint, salt, pepper and egg. Blend lightly. Spread the stuffing mixture onto the meat. Lay strips of the ham on top of the stuffing. Roll roast and tie with cotton butcher's twine. Heat the remaining canola oil in the Dutch oven. Brown the venison slowly on all sides. Remove roast and tie pork fat on all sides. Place venison back in the Dutch oven and add apple juice and ½ of the beef consommé. Refrigerate the remaining consommé for use in another recipe. Heat oven to 325 degrees. Cover the Dutch oven and cook for 1½ to 2 hours or until venison is done. Add cherry tomatoes the last 10 minutes of the cooking time. Remove the roast and the tomatoes to a heated serving platter. Remove the bacon and the strings from the roast. Blend the flour with enough water to make a fluid paste. Add flour to the venison juices in the Dutch oven. Cook, stirring constantly, until the mixture comes to a boil; simmer 2 minutes. Slice venison and serve gravy on the side. Serves 8 to 10.

Venison Roast Marinated in Spices with Brandy and Burgundy

1 Tbsp. peppercorns, crushed
3 bay leaves
½ tsp. allspice
3 to 6 cloves
1 cup brandy
1 cup Burgundy wine
1 cup canola oil
1 venison fore or hindquarter

8 carrots, washed and scraped
8 small white onions, peeled
¼ cup butter
1 cup marinade, reserved
¼ cup flour
2 cups beef stock
salt
pepper

Mix together peppercorns, bay leaves, allspice, cloves, brandy, Burgundy and canola oil. Marinate venison for 24 hours or more. Reserve marinade. Preheat oven to 375 degrees. Remove venison from marinade and drain. Place venison in shallow baking pan, arrange carrots and onions around the venison. Dot meat with butter and baste with marinade. Bake 15 minutes per pound. Baste every 10 minutes and turn meat occasionally to keep meat from drying out. When done remove meat and vegetables to serving dish and make a sauce with the drippings by adding flour, beef stock, marinade and salt and pepper to taste. Simmer until reduced to gravy consistency. Serves 6 to 10.

Burgundy Wine-Roasted Venison Roast

6 lb. to 7 lb. quarter of venison, deboned
2 cups Burgundy
1 cup canned beef broth
1 large white onion, sliced
2 med. garlic cloves, chopped fine

1 bay leaf
6 dried juniper berries
1 tsp. salt
6 to 10 slices salt pork

Make marinade by combining Burgundy, beef broth, onion, garlic, bay leaf, juniper berries and salt. Place venison roast in a large glass bowl and completely cover with marinade. Refrigerate for 24 hours. Remove venison and allow to drain. Tie with cotton butcher twine to retain shape. Strain marinade and reserve. Place venison in a uncovered roasting pan. Preheat oven to 350 degrees. Place slices of salt pork over roast. Insert a meat thermometer into the thickest part of the roast. Roast for 10 minutes. Reduce oven temperature to 325 degrees and roast 15 to 18 minutes per lb. or to 138 degrees on the meat thermometer. Baste venison occasionally with reserved marinade. When done, remove roast; strain drippings; pour off fat and serve as a sauce for the roast. Serves 8 to 10.

Venison Roast with Buttermilk

3 lb. to 5 lb. venison quarter roast
salt
garlic powder

black pepper
fresh onion, sliced into rings
1 qt. Non-Cultured Buttermilk

Trim all fat from roast. Mix salt, garlic powder and black pepper. Rub seasoning into roast. Brown roast on all sides. Insert toothpicks all over roast and hang onion rings on toothpicks. Pour Non-Cultured Buttermilk over roast and bake in a 375 degree oven to 138 degrees internal temperature. Allow to rest 10 minutes before slicing. Remove toothpicks and serve onion rings with sliced roast.

Ginger Flavored Venison Roast

1 (3 lb. to 4 lb.) venison quarter roast
1 bay leaf, ground
1 medium white onion, diced
salt

black pepper
8 whole allspice
30 Gingersnap Cookies about
    1½" wide

Mix ground bay leaf, onions, salt, and pepper. Rub venison with mixed spices. Insert allspice deep into venison. Place venison in a roasting pan. Lay Gingersnap Cookies on the roast. Place roast in a 350 degree oven and cook until internal temperature reaches 138 degrees. Remove Gingersnap Cookies. Make a gravy with pan juices. Serves 6 to 8.

Forequarter Venison Roast
with White Beans

1 lb. dried pea beans
water
¼ cup butter
2 cloves garlic
2 lbs. white onions, sliced thin
Seasoned Salt

½ tsp. salt
¼ tsp. black pepper
1 tsp. rosemary, divided
2 (16-oz.) cans Italian plum tomatoes
1 venison forequarter, with bones
several strips of bacon

Place the pea beans in a large pot, cover with water and bring to a boil over high heat and simmer for 2 minutes. Remove the beans from the heat, cover and let stand for about 1 hour. Return the beans to the heat and bring to a boil. Reduce the heat and simmer covered for about 1 hour or until the beans are tender. Check the liquid level during cooking and add more water if required. After cooking, drain the beans. Heat the oven to 350 degrees. Heat the butter in a large skillet; crush 1 clove of garlic and add with onions; cook until just browned. In the bottom of a shallow roasting pan, combine the cooked beans, onion mixture, 2 tsp. Seasoned Salt, salt, pepper, ½ tsp. rosemary and tomatoes. Gently blend. Split the remaining clove of garlic and rub over the outside of the venison. Sprinkle the roast with seasoned salt and remaining rosemary. Lay several strips of bacon on top of the roast. Insert a meat thermometer into the thickest part of the roast, being careful not to let it touch the bone. Roast uncovered until a meat thermometer registers 138 degrees. Remove the roast to a carving board. Place beans in a large serving dish. Serve slices of the venison with the beans. Serves 8 to 10.

Glazed and Stuffed Venison of Cremona

1 (3 lb, to 3½ lb.) venison round roast
Marinade:
⅓ cup light rum
⅓ cup lime juice
1 medium onion, quartered
3 large cloves of garlic
1 Tbsp. canola oil
½ tsp. dry mustard
½ tsp, ground ginger
½ tsp. pepper
⅛ tsp. ground cloves
pinch of ground red pepper
Fresh watercress sprigs
Stuffing:
1 (14-oz.) jar fruits in mustard flavored syrup
(Mostarda di Frutta) drained (syrup

reserved) Available at Italian
groceries and specialty shops
2 Tbsp, butter
½ cup onion, minced
1 large clove garlic, minced
½ cup blanched almonds, well toasted
and coarsely chopped
2 Tbsp. red wine vinegar
salt
pepper
1 Tbsp. canola oil
¼ cup canned beef broth
3 Tbsp. lime juice
1 cup canned beef broth

Cut venison into 1 long flat piece of meat 1" thick. Cut along bottom of roast down full length parallel to work surface, leaving 'hinge' at far long side. Pull back on top of roast to uncover the bottom strip of meat. Place flat in non-aluminum pan.

For Marinade: Mix all ingredients in processor until onion is minced. Pour over venison. Chill 6 to 8 hours, turning occasionally.

For stuffing: Coarsely chop 1 jar of mustard fruits, reserve syrup. Melt butter in medium skillet over medium-high heat. Add onion and sauté until brown. Remove from heat. Stir in garlic, chopped fruits, almonds and vinegar. Add salt and pepper to taste. Preheat oven to 425 degrees. Remove meat from marinade and pat dry. Strain marinade and reserve ⅓ cup. Spread stuffing over cut side of meat, leaving a 1" border all around. Roll meat up with grain, jelly-roll fashion. Tie with heavy string at 1" intervals. Tie around ends. Rub surface with oil. Sprinkle with salt and pepper. Set roast in dry roasting pan. Roast 20 minutes, turning once. Reduce oven temperature to 325 degrees and continue roasting 40 minutes, basting frequently with pan juices; if juices evaporate, add ¼ cup broth. Combine ⅓ cup reserved marinade with 6 Tbsp. syrup from mustard fruits and lime juice. Insert meat thermometer into thickest part of meat. When thermometer reaches 120 degrees, baste roast with marinade. Roast until thermometer registers 138 degrees, basting frequently, about every 30 minutes. Transfer roast to another pan. Let venison rest for about 10 minutes before carving. Meanwhile, degrease pan juices. Add the remaining 1 cup of broth and boil, scraping up any brown bits, until reduced and thickened to a sauce-like consistency. Taste and adjust seasonings. Pour sauce into a sauceboat. Cut the roast into ¼" slices. Arrange on heated platter. Garnish with clusters of remaining mustard fruits nested in bouquets of mint. Serve immediately. Pass sauce separately. Serves 6 to 8.

Hindquarter Roast with Dates and Figs

1 (8 lb. to 10 lb.) butterflied venison
   hindquarter roast
2 tsp. salt
1 tsp. white pepper
1 tsp. cayenne pepper
1 tsp. paprika

1 tsp. thyme
1 tsp. dry mustard
½ lb. dried figs
½ lb. dried dates
5 sprigs fresh rosemary, divided
canola oil

Mix together, salt, white pepper, cayenne pepper, paprika, thyme and mustard. Apply spices over entire venison roast, inside and out. Chop the dates, figs and rosemary. Spread dates, figs and rosemary over the inside of the roast. Roll up roast and tie at 2" intervals with butcher's twine. Tie around ends. Rub roast with canola oil. Put a spit through the center and let turn about 1½" above heat. When the roast is cooked, the outside should be brown and crusty. Check doneness by inserting and removing a meat thermometer and cook until thermometer registers 138 degrees in the center. For cooking in an oven; Preheat oven to 400 degrees; place roast in a roasting pan; add ¼ cup red wine; insert meat thermometer and cook until thermometer registers 140 degrees. Serves 6 to 10.

German Venison Roast with Brussel Sprouts and Chopped Walnuts

(6 lb. to 7 lb.) hindquarter of venison	7 strips of salt pork
salt	¾ cup butter, melted
2 cups Burgundy wine	2 Tbsp. all-purpose flour
2 medium white onions, quartered	1 cup canned beef broth
2 medium carrots, sliced	3 lbs. small potatoes
4 sprigs parsley	white pepper
2 bay leaves	snipped parsley
10 peppercorns	1 (10-oz.) pkg. thawed Brussels sprouts
4 whole cloves	¼ cup chopped walnuts
dash of thyme	

Rub salt into the venison. Place venison in a shallow roasting pan. Make marinade by mixing wine, onions, carrots, parsley, bay leaves, peppercorns, cloves and thyme. Pour marinade over venison and refrigerate for 24 hours. Turn roast over several times during the marinating process. Remove venison from marinade and strain and reserve marinade. Place the venison on rack in a shallow baking pan and place salt pork across venison. Roast in 450 degree oven for 25 minutes. Reduce temperature to 325 degrees and roast for about 2 hours longer or until internal temperature reaches 140 degrees. Baste frequently with half the reserved marinade. Remove the venison to a hot serving platter. Combine remaining marinade with pan drippings in a saucepan and bring to a boil. Blend 2 tbsp. butter with flour and stir into boiling marinade. Stir beef broth in slowly and cook, stirring constantly, until mixture comes to a boil. Cook for 1 minute longer. Peel potatoes and cut in half. Cook potatoes in boiling, salted water for 15 to 20 minutes or until tender. Drain potatoes and toss with 6 tbsp. butter, white pepper, salt and parsley. Sauté the Brussel sprouts in remaining butter for 10 minutes. Add the chopped walnuts and cook for 5 minutes. Arrange potatoes and Brussels sprouts around venison on the serving plate and serve with gravy. Serves 6 to 8.

Spice-Flavored Venison Roast

This is an 1800 Native American recipe.

1 (4 lb. to 6 lb.) boneless roast	ground cloves
1 onion, chopped	allspice
1 bay leaf	vinegar
salt	lard
pepper	flour

Slit the sides and the top of the roast at 3" intervals and stuff the slits with pieces of onion, bay leaf, salt and pepper, ground cloves and all spice. Place the roast in a large glass bowl. Pour enough vinegar over the roast to completely cover it. Cover and let marinate for 12 hours or more. Lift venison out of the marinade; coat with lard and flour and quickly brown on both sides. Pour over with the same vinegar, cover and cook 20 minutes to the pound or until the internal temperature reaches 140 degrees. Slice and serve either hot or cold. Serves 4 to 8.

Grilled Venison Roast with Blackberry Sauce

1 bone-in venison hindquarter, trimmed
2 cloves garlic, halved
½ cup Worcestershire sauce
2 Tbsp. teriyaki sauce
2 tsp. garlic powder
2 tsp. lemon-pepper seasoning

hickory chips
Blackberry Sauce (II)
fresh bay leaves
kumquats
fresh or frozen blackberries

Place venison roast in a roasting pan. Cut 4 slits in venison and insert garlic halves. Combine Worcestershire sauce and teriyaki sauce, and pour over venison; sprinkle all sides with garlic powder and lemon-pepper seasoning. Cover and refrigerate 2 to 6 hours. Soak hickory chips in water 30 minutes. Prepare charcoal fire and let burn 30 minutes. Place venison on grill rack over drip pan. Cook covered, over low coals (250 degrees) 3 hours or until meat thermometer inserted in thickest portion of meat registers 140 degrees or desired doneness. Carefully remove drip pan, and reserve 2 Tbsp. of drippings to use in Blackberry Sauce. Serve venison with Blackberry Sauce, and garnish with bay leaves, kumquats and blackberries. Serves 12.

Venison Roast Marinated in Spirits and Spices

1 cup beer
1 cup sour mash bourbon
1 cup Wesson oil
1 medium white onion, sliced
½ tsp. black pepper

½ tsp. onion powder
½ tsp. garlic salt
1 tsp. salt
1 (4 lb. to 6 lb.) venison roast
2 Tbsp. cornstarch

Make marinade by mixing together, beer, bourbon, Wesson Oil, onion, pepper, onion powder, garlic salt, and salt. Place venison roast in a large glass bowl. Pour marinade over the roast. Completely cover and marinate for 2 weeks. Turn venison once each day. Remove venison and marinade to a covered roasting pan. Preheat oven to 300 degrees and cook for about 5 hours or until a meat thermometer reaches 140 degrees. Remove venison and thicken juices with cornstarch. Serves 6 to 8.

Amite River County Venison Roast

1 large venison roast
1 cup water

garnish with mint, watercress or parsley

Place venison in a roasting pan; pour water over. Preheat oven to 350 degrees. Cook 20 minutes per lb. for rare or 25 minutes per lb. for medium. Insert a meat thermometer into the thickest part of the roast and cook until meat thermometer reaches between 140 degrees (medium). Serve with pan gravy and garnish with wild fruit relish or wild fruit jelly. Serve with hearty vegetable side dishes and traditional desserts.

Roast Forequarter of Venison with Stewed Tomatoes and Spicy Wine Sauce

1 cup dry red wine
¼ cup canola oil
1 med. white onion, coarsely chopped
2 cloves garlic, minced
½ tsp. Tabasco sauce

salt
1 venison forequarter, with bone
bacon strips
Stewed Plum Tomatoes
parsley for garnish

Combine wine, canola oil, onion, garlic, Tabasco sauce and salt to taste. Place venison in a glass dish and pour wine over roast. Cover and let stand in the refrigerator overnight. Turn venison occasionally. Heat oven to 350 degrees, remove lamb and place on a roasting rack in a shallow roasting pan. Lay strips of bacon over roast. Insert a meat thermometer into the thickest part of the roast; being careful not to touch the bone. Roast until thermometer registers 140 degrees. Venison should be slightly pink in the center. Baste venison occasionally with the wine marinade. Place roast in an oval serving bowl; pour Stewed Tomatoes around the edges. Garnish with a large sprig of parsley and sprinkle with parsley flakes. Serves 8 to 10.

Venison Leg Roast with Madeira Sauce

1 (6 lb. to 8 lb.) fore or hindquarter of venison
3 cloves garlic, chopped fine
1 tsp. dried rosemary
¼ tsp. thyme
1 tsp. salt

½ tsp. black pepper
4 Tbsp. butter
1½ Tbsp. all-purpose flour
1 cup canned beef broth
½ cup Madeira

Mix together garlic, rosemary, thyme, salt and pepper. Rub spice mixture into all sides of the roast; let stand for 2 hours; rub in homemade butter. Place the venison on a rack in a shallow roasting pan. Insert a meat thermometer into the thickest part of the venison but not touching the bone. Roast 15 minutes at 450 degrees, lower the heat to 350 degrees and continue to roast until the thermometer registers 140 degrees for medium. Baste the roast every 20 minutes with the pan drippings. Remove the venison to a warm serving platter and let rest 10 minutes. To prepare the sauce: remove all but 1 Tbsp. of fat from the pan; place the pan over low heat. Add the flour and cook, stirring one minute. Remove the pan from the heat and gradually add the beef broth and Madeira, stirring constantly to remove all the bits in the bottom of the pan. Return pan to the heat and cook until the sauce thickens. Salt and pepper to taste. Serve the sauce on the side. Serves 10 to 12.

Roast Rack of Venison with Puréed Chestnuts

1 (6 lb. to 8 lb.) venison hindquarter roast
butter
salt pork, sliced
salt

pepper
Cumberland Sauce
Puréed Chestnuts

Bring venison to room temperature before roasting. Place in a roasting pan, rub with butter and cover with slices of salt pork, secured with string. Baste occasionally during roasting. Place in a preheated 325-degree oven and roast 18 minutes per pound. *Do not overcook*. Venison should be rare, not well done. Let roast stand on a warm platter before carving to allow the juices to settle. Salt and pepper to taste. Then serve with Cumberland Sauce. Puréed Chestnuts, potatoes, squash, or wild rice are all excellent accompaniments. Serves 4 to 6.

Roast Venison with Apple Filling & Topping

1 venison forequarter, butterflied
4 medium sized sweet apples
3 cups applesauce
1 cup dark brown sugar
½ tsp. mace
1¾ tsp. salt, divided
1 tsp. dry mustard

1 tsp. caraway seed
½ tsp. sugar
½ tsp. pepper
¼ tsp. rubbed sage
spinach leaves
very small red apples or cherry
    tomatoes

Clean and butterfly venison. Lay on work area outside down. Peel, core and cut apples in thin slices and lay on venison. Mix applesauce, brown sugar and mace. Divide in half and spread ½ apples over roast leaving a 1" border. Reserve the other half. Roll the venison up jelly-roll fashion tie with cotton twine at 2" intervals and around ends. Combine 1½ tsp. salt, mustard caraway seeds, sugar, pepper and sage and rub over roast. Lay roast on a greased baking rack, stitched side down, in a roasting pan. Bake uncovered at 325 degrees for 1 hour. Add remaining salt to applesauce mixture and spread over roast. Roast 1 hour longer or until meat thermometer reaches 140 degrees. Very carefully remove stitching and place roast on large serving plate; garnish with spinach leaves and very small apples or cherry tomatoes. Let stand 15 minutes before slicing. Serves 8 to 10.

Roast Venison with Poivrade Sauce

1 (4½-lb.) boneless venison roast
salt
black pepper
8 dried juniper berries, powdered

1 tsp. grated lemon rind
4 Tbsp. butter
½ cup cognac
Poivrade Sauce

Mix together, salt, pepper, powdered juniper berries, and lemon rind. Let rest for 1 hour. Melt butter and gently pour over all sides of the roast. Bake roast uncovered at 450 degrees, basting and turning the meat frequently, for 30 minutes. Reduce heat to 400 degrees. Continue basting and roasting 15 minutes for medium rare or longer for well done. Remove meat and keep warm. Add cognac to skillet and ignite it. Stir. Save this liquid for making the Poivrade Sauce. Slice meat and serve with sauce spooned over. Serves 8 to 10.

Roast Venison
with Sweet Potatoes and Apples

1 (5-lb.) venison loin
1 cup water
1 tsp. salt
½ tsp. pepper
2 lbs. sweet potatoes, peeled and cut into
   ½" slices
1½ lbs. apples, peeled, cored, and cut into
   ¼" rings

⅓ cup packed, light brown sugar
1 tsp. ground cinnamon
¼ tsp. ground nutmeg
1 Tbsp. all-purpose flour
1 cup canned beef broth
basil leaves

Saw lengthwise through the backbone of the loin and tie the backbone on the roast in several places. The bone will add flavor to the meat, and the meat will be easier to cut when the bones are removed before serving. Preheat the oven to 350 degrees. Rub the meat all over with the salt and pepper. Insert a meat thermometer in the thickest part of the meat but not touching the bone. Add water to bottom of roasting pan. Roast about 30 minutes per pound or until the thermometer reaches 140 degrees. While the venison is roasting, boil the sliced sweet potatoes in salted water until tender, but not falling apart. Drain. Remove the venison from the oven 30 minutes before it is done, and skim off most of the fat from the roasting pan, leaving the venison drippings behind. Place the cooked sweet potatoes and the raw apple rings around the venison. Mix the brown sugar and spices, and sprinkle them over the apples and sweet potatoes. Spoon the reserve drippings over the apples and sweet potatoes. Return the venison to the oven and bake about 30 minutes until the apples are tender. Place the venison on a platter and surround with the sweet potatoes and apples. Keep warm. Again skim off most of the fat from the roasting pan, leaving the venison drippings behind. Add the flour to the contents of the pan. Cook over low heat on top of the stove for 2 minutes, stirring constantly until the gravy is well blended. Return gravy to the heat and cook, stirring until it thickens. Serve gravy separately. Serves 8 to 10.

Rump Roast of Venison

1 rump or backstrap roast
salt pork, sliced
onion

celery
garlic
bacon

When ready to cook, wipe venison off with clean cloth. With a sharp knife, punch holes deep into roast and insert pieces of salt meat, onion, celery and garlic into each hole. Lay bacon strips across roast. Place on roasting rack. Preheat oven to 350 degrees. Cook 20 to 25 minutes per pound. Serves 6 to 8.

Roast of Venison
with Wild Rice and Currant Jelly

1 (4-lb.) boneless venison forequarter
1 tsp, salt
½ tsp. black pepper
1 Tbsp. melted lard

2 Tbsp. water
Currant Jelly
Wild Rice

Wipe venison with a damp cloth. Rub salt and pepper into meat, Roll roast up and tie with cotton butcher twine. Lay venison in a roasting pan. Pour melted lard over the roast. Add water. Roast in a 425-degree oven for 45 minutes. Turn and baste frequently with broth. Remove from oven. Place on a warm serving platter. Mound wild rice around roast. Skin fat from broth and strain. Pour over venison and wild rice. Serve with Currant Jelly. Serves 6 to 8.

Aged and Larded Stag
with Wine and Fruit Sauce

1 hindquarter of venison
½ lb.± pork fat
1½ tsp. salt
¼ tsp. black pepper
½ Tbsp. ground ginger
½ tsp. oregano
½ tsp. marjoram leaves
2 Tbsp. olive oil
1 cup melted lard or butter

2 cups canned beef broth
1 cup dry sherry
⅓ cup all-purpose flour
2 Tbsp. butter
5 tsp. Chianti wine or Apple Cider
   Vinegar
¼ Tbsp. orange rind, grated
2 Tbsp. Currant Jelly
bits of Currant Jelly

Age venison 3 or 4 days (see directions in chapter on Processing Venison.) Remove all skin, membrane, and sinews. Cut pork fat into long and thin strips. Mix salt, pepper, ginger, oregano and marjoram leaves. Roll larding strips in the spices. With a larding needle insert the strips deeply into the roast at regular intervals. Allow a portion of the pork to remain outside of the roast. Roll the roast in the olive oil. Lay the roast in an uncovered roasting pan and pour melted lard or butter over the whole roast. Insert a meat thermometer in center of the roast. Preheat oven to 325 degrees and roast until internal temperature reaches 140 degrees. Mix beef broth and ½ cup sherry and baste every 10 to 15 minutes. Remove the roast from the pan, and skim off the fat from pan juices. Make a smooth paste from the flour, butter and the pan juices; add Chianti wine or apple vinegar and orange rind and stir to make a gravy in the pan. Cook the gravy for about 10 minutes on low heat and add the remainder of the sherry and Currant Jelly. Stir until jelly is dissolved. Place roast in a low-heated oven and frequently baste with gravy for 30 minutes to 1 hour. Serve gravy on the side and garnish or serve the venison with Currant Jelly. Serves 6 to 8.

Vegetable Stuffed Venison Roast

1 (10-lb.) whole venison hindquarter
Seasoning Salt
1 green bell pepper, chopped
1 white onion, chopped
2 stalks celery, chopped
4 cloves garlic, minced
2 sticks butter

1 cup dry red wine
6 strips smoked bacon
1 Tbsp. all-purpose flour
1 can (8-oz.) mushrooms, with juice
1 Tbsp. green onion tops, minced
1 Tbsp. parsley, minced
3 Tbsp. Currant Jelly

Lay venison hindquarter on a cutting board and cut a long pocket from the large end to the small end. Season and rub all sides with Seasoning Salt. Mix together green bell pepper, onion, celery, garlic and butter. Pour wine over roast. Lay bacon strip on tip of the roast. Preheat the oven to 300 degrees. Place roast in covered roasting pan and cook until tender. Remove roast from the pan. Add flour to juice from mushrooms and mix well. Add mushrooms, onion tops, parsley and Currant Jelly to pan juices. Place sauce over high heat and cook until gravy thickens. Put roast back into gravy and cook, uncovered, for 5 minutes to brown. Slice roast and serve with gravy on the side. Serves 6 to 8.

Greene County Style Venison Roast

1 qt. cider vinegar
1 qt. water
1 Tbsp. red pepper
1 Tbsp, black pepper
1 Tbsp. salt
3 cloves garlic, chopped
3 bay leaves
1 tsp. cloves
1 tsp. allspice

1 tsp. mustard seed
1 tsp. thyme
1 venison fore or hindquarter roast
½ lb. salt pork, cut into strips
1 medium yellow onion cut in strips
12 strips celery
½ cup sour cream
½ cup Currant Jelly
1 Tbsp. inexpensive brandy

Make marinade by mixing vinegar, water and spices. Place venison roast in a large glass bowl and completely cover with marinade. Refrigerate for 12 to 24 hours; turn 3 or 4 times. With a long and thin knife punch 10 to 20 holes deep into the roast. Insert the salt pork strips, onion strips and celery strips. Insert a meat thermometer into the thickest part of the roast. Preheat oven to 325 degrees. Baste frequently with the remaining marinade and meat drippings. Roast is done when thermometer registers 140 degrees. Remove roast. Skim fat from pan juices and add sour cream, Currant Jelly, and brandy. Mix well and warm. Slice roast and spoon gravy over the roast slices. Serves 6 to 8.

Venison Forgotten Rib Roast

1 (4 lb. to 6 lb.) standing venison rib roast   salt and pepper

Preheat oven to 400 degrees. Rub salt and pepper on all sides of the roast. Cook for 5 minutes per pound for very rare. For medium-rare meat, add 5 minutes to the rare cooking time. For medium meat, add 10 minutes to the rare cooking time. After cooking, turn the oven off; *do not open the door*, and let the roast rest in the oven for 2 to 4 hours. Serves 4 to 6.

Butterflied Venison
With Apricot-Wild Rice Stuffing

Wild Rice Stuffing:
½ cup dried apricots, diced
3 Tbsp. unsalted butter
2 medium onions, chopped
2 cups wild rice, rinsed and drained
5 cups canned chicken broth
½ cup almonds, chopped and toasted
¼ cup fresh parsley, minced steamed
salt
pepper
(7-lb.) leg of venison, butterflied & trimmed
2 Tbsp. Cognac

Glaze:
¼ cup Dijon mustard
2 Tbsp. vegetable oil
2 medium garlic cloves, minced
1 tsp. dried rosemary, crumbled
¼ tsp. pepper
bacon strips
broccoli florets
cherry tomatoes

To make the stuffing: Soak apricots in water for 2½ hours, turning occasionally. Melt butter in a large saucepan over medium-low heat. Add onions, cover and cook until clear, stirring occasionally. Mix in wild rice and coat with butter. Add broth, drained apricots, almonds and parsley. Bring to boil. Reduce heat, cover and simmer until rice is tender and slightly puffed, about 50 minutes. Season with salt and pepper. Place venison on work surface outside down. Score with a knife if necessary to open out flat. Sprinkle with Cognac, salt and pepper. Pat ½" layer of stuffing over meat and into scoremarks, leaving 1" border. Spoon remaining stuffing into buttered 2 qt. baking dish. Cover with buttered parchment paper. Thread trussing needle with 3 feet of kitchen twine. Stitch loosely around circumference of venison. Pull ends of twine to gather venison into a ball; tie securely wrap ends of twine around ball to secure shape.

To make the glaze: Combine mustard, oil, garlic, rosemary and pepper in small bowl. Oil rack and set in roasting pan. Place pan in center of oven and preheat to 435 degrees. Pat venison dry, then rub glaze over. Cover with strips of bacon secured with toothpicks. Place venison seam side down on rack. Roast 20 minutes. Reduce oven temperature to 350 degrees. Continue cooking until thermometer inserted in thickest portion of meat registers 140 degrees. Bake rice stuffing in dish during last 30 minutes of roasting time. Let venison rest 10 minutes. Carefully remove string. Place venison on a round serving platter and surround with broccoli and tomatoes. Cut venison into wedges. Serve additional stuffing alongside. Serves 8 to 10.

Venison Ham

From an 1850 recipe, Providence, Rhode Island.

1 fresh venison ham	bacon fat
Marinade for Game	1 to 1½ Tbsp. cornstarch
salt	

Marinate venison in Marinade for Game in an enamelware or glass dish in refrigerator for about 2 days, turning every 12 hours. Remove from marinade, wipe dry, season with salt, and brown well on all sides in bacon fat. Pour off excess fat and deglaze pan with ½ cup of marinade, strained. Return venison to pan, cover tightly, and bake in 350-degree until medium. Time will vary according to size and age of animal. If necessary, add more marinade with equal amount of water during cooking, maintaining 1 to 1½ inches of liquid in bottom of pan. When done, remove meat to a hot platter. Thicken pan juices with cornstarch to serve with meat. Cranberry-Rice Stuffing or Brown Rice Pilau go well with this hearty meat. Serves 6 to 8.

Italian Flavored Venison Roast

1 large venison roast	Seasoning Salt
1 btl. Italian salad dressing	red pepper
¼ lb. butter	garlic powder
½ cup fresh lime juice	onion powder
½ cup Worcestershire sauce	Heinz 57 steak sauce
½ cup teriyaki sauce	6 bay leaves, crumbled
black pepper	⅓ cup ruby port or sherry

Place venison roast in a large glass bowl and pour salad dressing over the roast; rub in and let marinate for 2 hours. Remove venison. Mix butter, lime juice, Worcestershire sauce, teriyaki sauce, black pepper, Seasoning Salt, red pepper, garlic powder, onion powder, and Heinz 57 sauce to taste; add crumbled bay leaves. Rub spice mixture into the roast. Place roast in a covered roaster. Preheat oven to 275 degrees. Cover the roaster and roast for 1 hour. Remove roast from oven and add port or sherry to the pan juices. Cut the roast into slices about ⅓ of the way through the meat and spoon the gravy mixture between the slices. Cover roast and return to the oven. If needed, add a little water as the venison cooks. Roast the venison for about 4 to 5 hours or until tender.

Venison Roast with Turnips and Smoked Sausage

1 turkey-cooking bag	1 lb. smoked hot pork sausage links
1 Tbsp. all-purpose flour	½ tsp. dried mint
3 lb. to 4 lb. venison hindquarter roast	2 Tbsp. dried parsley
cayenne pepper to taste	½ tsp. garlic powder
salt to taste	2 cups dry white wine
2 med. turnips, peeled and cut into 1" pieces	1 Tbsp. Worcestershire sauce
10 large white pearl onions, peeled	4 drops Peychaud's bitters

Dust the inside of the roasting bag with the flour. Season venison roast to taste with cayenne pepper, salt, and pepper. Place the roast inside of the roasting bag. Place the turnips, onion, and sausage around the roast. Mix mint and parsley and sprinkle over roast. Mix garlic powder, white wine, Worcestershire sauce and bitters. Pour wine mixture into the bottom of the bag. Seal the roasting bag and prick numerous small holes in the top of the bag. Preheat oven to 325 degrees and cook venison roast for 2 hours. Remove the roast to a serving plate and slice. Place vegetables around plate. Serves 6 to 8.

Venison Roast Chieti Style

3 Tbsp. smoked bacon, chopped
2 sprigs parsley, chopped
1 large garlic clove, minced
1 Tbsp. fresh rosemary leaves or 1 tsp. dried leaves, crumbled
1 (5-lb.) venison forequarter with bone
¼ cup canola oil

black pepper
salt
¼ cup red wine vinegar
¾ cup very fine dry breadcrumbs
½ cup fresh parsley, minced
1 Tbsp. fresh mint, minced

Preheat oven to 400 degrees. Combine smoked bacon, parsley, garlic and rosemary. Freeze briefly. Make several long thin holes in venison with sharp knife. Widen and lengthen holes slightly by piercing with handle of wooden spoon. Pack, parsley mixture into each hole. Pour canola oil into roasting pan. Roll venison in oil so meat is evenly coated. Sprinkle with pepper. Roast 15 minutes. Reduce oven to 350 degrees and continue roasting until thermometer registers 125 degrees. Sprinkle meat with salt once, basting with vinegar several times, about 50 minutes for rare. Remove roast from oven and set roast aside. Retain oven temperature. Mix breadcrumbs, parsley and mint on baking sheet. Hold venison leg bone and roll venison evenly in breadcrumb mixture. Return venison to the roasting pan. Baste with pan juices. Continue roasting until coating is brown, 15 to 20 minutes. Cool roast 15 minutes before carving. Serves 6 to 8.

Mustard Plastered Venison Roast

1 venison quarter roast
salt
black pepper
garlic powder
4 large garlic cloves, sliced
all-purpose flour
dry mustard powder

Apple Cider Vinegar
2 cans Italian tomatoes
3 stalks celery, without leaves
½ large white onion
1 bay leaf
water

Mix equal parts of salt, pepper and garlic powder and rub into all sides of the venison roast. Make small cuts in the roast and insert the garlic slices. Mix equal parts of flour and mustard; add just enough vinegar to make a paste. Completely cover the roast with the paste. Place the roast in a shallow roasting pan. Preheat oven to 500 degrees and roast, uncovered, for 15 minutes. Lower the temperature to 300 degrees and add tomatoes, celery, onion and bay leaf. Roast until venison is tender. Baste often. If needed, add a little water to the pan to keep vegetables from drying out.

Venison Roast
with Salami, Pistaschio Nuts and Garlic

1 (3¼-lb.) venison round roast, trimmed
2 thin slices hard salami, cut julienne
3 large parsley sprigs, stemmed and coarsely
   chopped
2 Tbsp, shelled raw unsalted pistaschio nuts

2 cloves garlic, slivered
canola oil
¾ tsp. salt
½ tsp. pepper

Preheat oven to 375 degrees. Pat meat dry. Make four 4" deep and ¾" wide slits in one end of roast, using sharp knife. Stuff one slit with half of salami, one with half of parsley, one with half of nuts and one with a third of garlic, using handle of wooden spoon as a stuffing aid. Wrap roast with string at ½" intervals to hold shape. Tuck remaining garlic under string. Rub roast generously with oil; sprinkle with salt and pepper. Place on rack in roasting pan. Insert a meat thermometer into thickest part of meat and cook until thermometer registers 140 degrees for medium, about 1 hour. Let rest for 10 minutes; slice roast thinly. Serves 8.

Wishbone Italian Slow Cooked Venison Roast

Mr. J.A. Huff, Sr. stated that this recipe was given to him by his son Jackson A. Huff, Jr., Jackson was the Chief Executive Officer of the Bank of Laurel, Mississippi and is now a senior Executive Officer with Union Planters Bank.

1 venison ham
heavy aluminum foil

1 btl. Wishbone Italian salad dressing

Roll out a large piece of heavy aluminum foil. Place the venison roast on the foil and pull up the sides. Pour the salad dressing over the roast and fold and seal the roast in the aluminum foil. Place the roast in an uncovered roasting pan. Place the roast in a 200 degree oven and cook for 12 hours. Mr. Huff states that he puts his roast in the oven at 7:00 am and takes it out at 7:00 pm. This roast will melt in your mouth. Serves 6 to 8.

Venison Roast in Tomatoes, Spice
and Gingersnap Gravy

1 (3 lb. to 5 lb.) venison shoulder roast
1 cup cider vinegar
1 large tomato, peeled and diced
2 bay leaves
¼ tsp. whole cloves
¼ tsp. peppercorns
¼ cup all-purpose flour

½ tsp. black pepper
1 tsp. salt
½ tsp. allspice
4 Tbsp. margarine
1 large white onion, chopped
8 Gingersnap cookies, crushed

Make marinade by mixing vinegar, tomato, bay leaves, whole cloves and peppercorns. Place venison in a large glass bowl and cover with marinade. Refrigerate 6 to 12 hours. Remove venison and allow to drain. Mix flour, pepper, salt and allspice. Rub venison with the flour and spice mixture. Melt margarine in a skillet and brown venison and onions. Place venison and onions in a covered roaster and add 1½ cups of the marinating liquid and water to almost cover the roast. Preheat the oven to 300 degrees and cook 2½ to 3 hours or until venison is tender. Add Gingersnaps to the gravy; season to taste with salt and pepper. Remove roast to a serving dish and slice. Spoon gravy over slices. Serves 4 to 6.

Rolled Venison Forequarter Roast with Bacon

1 venison forequarter
thin cut bacon, smoked if possible

2 cups tawny or ruby port
¼ cup butter, pieces

Debone a venison forequarter. Lay the meat open and make long slits inside if needed to make venison lay flat. Place a layer of bacon over the inside. Roll the roast longways to make a log roll. Tie at 2" intervals with cotton butcher twine. Trim ends flat. Place roast in an open roasting pan and cover outside with strips of bacon secured with toothpicks. Insert a meat thermometer into the center of the roast. Pour port wine over the roast. Add butter pieces to wine. Roast at 350 degrees until meat thermometer registers 140 degrees. Baste with wine multiple times during the cooking process. Add more port to roasting pan if needed. When done, remove roast to a cutting board and allow roast to rest for 10 minutes. Save wine and dripping as a base for a sauce. Gently remove and reserve bacon strips. Remove cotton twine and cut into ½" slices. Serve slices of roast with strips of reserved bacon. Serves 8 to 10.

Herbed Venison Round Roast in a Salt Crust

⅓ cup olive oil
¼ cup grated onion
1 tsp. garlic salt
1 tsp. dried basil leaves
½ tsp. dried marjoram leaves

½ tsp. dried thyme leaves
¼ tsp. black pepper
1 (2½ to 3 lb.) venison round roast
1 (3-lb.) box Morton Coarse Kosher Salt
1¼ cups water

Combine olive oil, onion, garlic salt, basil leaves, marjoram leaves, thyme leaves and black pepper in a heavy 1 gal. plastic bag and mix well. Add venison roast and marinate in a refrigerator overnight. Line a roasting pan with aluminum foil. Combine salt and water to make a thick paste. Pat 1 cup salt paste into a ½" thick rectangle in the bottom of the pan. Pat roast dry and insert a meat thermometer. Place roast on the salt layer; pack the remaining salt paste around the meat to seal well. Roast at 350 degrees until meat thermometer registers 140 degrees: 1½ to 2 hours. Steam may cause salt crust to crack slightly during the roasting. Remove the roast from the oven; let stand for 10 minutes. Remove and discard the salt crust. Serves 8 to 10.

7

Venison Pot Roasts

Contrary to oven roasting, which cooks with dry heat, pot roasting will provide a moist cooking environment. For the beginning venison chef, pot roasts are an excellent way to begin learning to cook venison roasts and for cooking the tougher cuts such as neck roasts. Slow cooking pot roasts provide a large margin for error.

Dutch ovens and crock pots are the usual cooking containers. Slow-cooking roasts will take anywhere between 4 and 9 hours. The lower the temperature and the longer the cooking time, the better. Long-and low-cooked pot roasts will melt in your mouth.

If there is any doubt in your mind that your pot roast may dry out during cooking, use the moistening methods recommended in Chapter 6, Venison Oven Roasts.

Braised Venison Shoulder Roast

1 (4½-lb.) deboned venison shoulder roast
6 strips uncooked bacon
½ cup all-purpose flour
½ cup vegetable oil
2 cloves garlic, minced
1 qt. tomatoes

1 large onion
½ cup green pepper, chopped
2 tsp. ground cumin
½ tsp. salt
½ tsp. black pepper

Insert bacon strips where bones were removed from roast; close and bind with cotton twine. Dredge tied meat in flour. Brown in hot oil in a large Dutch oven. Add remaining ingredients, cover tightly and bring to a quick boil. Reduce the heat immediately; simmer 3 hours or until meat is tender. Serves 4 to 6.

Mrs. Kathryn Breland

Caribbean Venison Pot Roast

1 (7-lb. to 8-lb.) venison roast
3 Tbsp. Crisco
1½ Tbsp. red wine vinegar
1 Tbsp. cinnamon
1 Tbsp. ginger
1 tsp. nutmeg
1 Tbsp. salt

¼ tsp. pepper
1½ cups water
3 cups apple juice
1 can condensed tomato soup
1 cup onion, chopped
1 tsp. garlic, chopped
flour

Melt Crisco in the bottom of a Dutch oven and brown the meat on top of the stove.

Blend the vinegar, cinnamon, ginger, nutmeg, salt, and pepper. Add the water and apple juice. Pour over roast. Spoon the tomato soup, onion and garlic on top of the roast. Cover and cook in enough heat to keep the pot simmering for 4 hours or until the roast is tender. Thicken the gravy with flour. Serves 4 to 6.

Spiced Venison Crock Pot Roast

Marinade:
⅓ cup soy sauce
⅓ cup Worcestershire sauce
⅓ cup lemon juice

Venison Roast:
1 venison roast
natural meat tenderizer
cumin seed
fennel seed
fresh rosemary

Soak venison roast in cold water in the refrigerator for 24 hours. Prepare a marinade using equal parts of soy sauce, Worcestershire sauce, and lemon juice. Sprinkle venison roast generously with tenderizer. Puncture meat with a fork on all sides. Using a bulb baster equipped with an injecting needle, inject the marinade into the roast at close intervals on all sides. Place roast in a non-reactive pan, pour remaining marinade over, cover and refrigerate for 24 hours. Sprinkle roast with cumin seed, fennel seed, fresh rosemary or other spice over roast (for variety add cloves or bay leaves). Place roast and the marinade in a crock pot and cook over low heat for 5 to 6 hours.

Mr. Gray Wiggers, Jackson, Mississippi

Crock Pot Venison Roast Citrusbraten

1 (5-lb.) boneless venison roast
1 (6-oz.) can frozen grapefruit juice
1 cup dry red wine
¼ packed cup light brown sugar
1 Tbsp. mixed pickling spices
2 tsp. salt
¼ tsp. peppercorns

2 bay leaves
1 medium onion, sliced
¾ cup gingersnap crumbs
4 Tbsp. light brown sugar
½ cup raisins
½ cup dairy sour cream
1 grapefruit, peeled and sectioned

Put meat in non-aluminum bowl. Combine grapefruit juice, wine, brown sugar, pickling spices, salt, peppercorns, bay leaves and onion in a saucepan and bring to boil. Pour over meat and allow to cool. Cover and marinate in the refrigerator for 2 to 4 days, turning twice a day. When ready to cook, remove the meat from the marinade and put in crock pot cooker. Add marinade; cover and cook on low for 8 to 9 hours, or until meat is tender. Remove to a heated platter and keep warm. Strain marinade and put 4 cups in a saucepan; discard remainder. Stir in gingersnap crumbs, brown sugar and raisins. Reduce, stirring occasionally, until thickened. Stir in sour cream and pour sauce into a heated gravy boat. Slice meat, garnish with grapefruit sections and serve with the gravy. Serves 8 to 10.

Burgundy and Spice Crock Pot Venison Roast

1 cup Burgundy	6 whole allspice
1 cup water	2 chili peppers
1½ tsp. salt	1 large white onion, sliced
2 or 3 bay leaves	1 (5-lb. to 6-lb.) venison roast
10 whole cloves	2 Tbsp. cooking oil

Make marinade by mixing Burgundy, water, salt, bay leaves, cloves, allspice, chili peppers and onions. Place venison roast in a large glass bowl and cover with marinade. Cover the bowl and refrigerate for 2 days. Remove roast and allow to drain; pat dry. Strain and reserve the marinade. Brown meat on all sides in the cooking oil and put in crock pot cooker. Add 2¼ cups of the strained marinade. Cover and cook on high for 2 hours. Turn to low and cook 8 to 10 hours or until the venison is tender. Remove venison and thicken liquid with a flour-water paste. Serve with Boiled Rice or egg noodles. Serves 6 to 8.

Crock Pot Venison Roast with Vegetables

1 (2-lb. to 4-lb.) venison roast	pepper
2 cans French onion soup	Tabasco sauce
2 med. potatoes quartered	2 dps. liquid smoke
2 med. onions, quartered	½ cup cooking liquid
3 carrots, cut 2" pieces	¼ cup flour
1 bay leaf	skim milk
10 fresh mushrooms, coarsely sliced	Boiled Rice
salt	

Place all ingredients in a large crock pot; add salt, pepper, liquid smoke and Tabasco sauce to taste. Cook on low setting for 8 to 12 hours. Make a gravy in a skillet by adding flour, cooking liquid and skim milk as needed to keep gravy from thickening too much as the flour browns. Stir frequently to keep from burning. Salt and pepper to taste. Serve gravy over Boiled Rice. Serves 4 to 6.

Deviled Venison Pot Roast

1 (4-lb, to 5-lb.) venison roast	5 Tbsp. safflower oil, divided
½ cup stuffed olives	1 large onion, chopped
salt	⅛ tsp. thyme
pepper	⅛ tsp. marjoram
all-purpose flour	1 can (1 lb.) tomatoes, undrained

Cut slits about 1½" deep in venison roast, and into each of these push an olive. Tie with cotton string if needed. Season roast with salt and pepper; dredge with flour. Heat 3 Tbsp. oil in a heavy skillet and brown meat on all sides. Sauté onion in 2 Tbsp. of oil in a Dutch oven large enough to accommodate the roast. Transfer browned roast to Dutch oven; sprinkle with additional salt, pepper, thyme and marjoram. Spoon tomatoes slowly over roast so as not to disturb seasonings; cover tightly. Bake at 300 degrees about 3½ hours or until meat is tender. Baste the roast occasionally. When venison is done, remove from the pot. Pour off gravy and chill so fat may be lifted from the top. Reheat whole or sliced roast in the gravy. Roast is good served either hot or cold. Serves 4 to 6.

French Onion Venison Roast

1 (3-lb.) boneless venison roast
6 small potatoes, halved
6 med. onions, halved
2 cloves garlic, chopped
2 bay leaves

⅛ tsp. Tabasco sauce
¼ tsp. pepper
2 cans French onion soup
Boiled Rice

In a 6-qt. crock pot, add venison roast, potatoes, onions, garlic, bay leaves, Tabasco sauce, pepper and French onion soup. Set heat control on low. Cook for 8 to 10 hours. Serve over Boiled Rice. Serves 4 to 6.

Poppy Seed Venison Pot Roast with Sour Cream Gravy

1 tsp. canola oil
1 (4-lb. to 5-lb.) venison roast
2 cups water
2½ tsp. salt, divided
¼ tsp. pepper
2 tsp. poppy seed

1 lb. carrots, cut into pieces
1 can peas, drained
1 Tbsp, all-purpose flour
4 Tbsp. cold water
1 tsp. paprika
½ cup sour cream

Heat the oil In a Dutch oven and brown the venison roast well on all sides. Add the water, 1½ tsp. salt, pepper and poppy seeds and cover Dutch oven. Simmer for 3 to 4 hours and remove. Place the carrots in a saucepan and drain enough of the liquid from the Dutch oven to cover carrots and bring to a boil. Simmer until carrots are done and place them into the Dutch oven. Add the peas to the Dutch oven. Heat liquid to boiling point. Thicken with flour mixed with water and season with the remaining salt and paprika. Remove from heat, add sour cream and mix well. Remove roast and allow to rest 10 minutes before slicing. Serve sauce with roast. Serves 2 to 4.

Pot Roast of Venison with Vegetables and Burgundy

1 venison haunch or backstrap
salt pork
3 med. yellow onions
4 carrots
2 small turnips
4 stalks of celery
parsley
⅛ tsp. rosemary

⅛ tsp. thyme
2 bay leaves
2 strips lemon peel
salt
10 peppercorns
2 cups Burgundy
2 cups water
½ cup sour cream

Cut away all fat and connecting tissues from venison. Generously lard venison with salt pork. Place the vegetables, spices, Burgundy and water in a large Dutch oven, bring to a boil and simmer for 30 minutes. Add venison and simmer for 2 hours. Remove the venison, strain and reserve the pan liquid. Place the venison in a covered roasting pan. Pour the reserved pan liquid over the roast; add sour cream. Cook slowly 2 to 4 hours or until tender. Serves 6 to 8.

Potato-Prune Venison Roast

4 Tbsp. canola oil
1 (3-lb.) venison top round roast
1 tsp. salt
2 med. lemons, juiced
3 Tbsp. honey

1 bay leaf
2 cups dried seedless prunes
5 med. potatoes, peeled and halved
7 med. carrots, peeled and halved

Heat oil in a Dutch oven and brown venison roast on all sides. Pour off oil. Lightly salt roast. Mix lemon juice and honey and pour over roast. Add enough water to cover ½ of the roast. Add bay leaf and prunes and simmer for 3 to 4 hours, or until roast is tender. Remove meat from the Dutch oven and add potatoes and carrots to the juice. Salt lightly, then lay roast on top of the vegetables. Cover and put in a 325-degree oven for 1 hour or until vegetables are tender. Add water as needed to maintain stew-like consistency of juice. Serves 6 to 8.

Sour Venison Pot Roast

1 large onion, sliced
6 peppercorns
2 bay leaves
1 tsp. salt
¾ cup cider vinegar

1 cup water
1 (3-lb.) venison roast
2 Tbsp. butter
Potato Dumplings or Mashed
    Potatoes

Make marinade by combining onion, peppercorns, bay leaves, salt, cider vinegar and water in a large glass container. Add the venison roast and refrigerate for 1 to 3 days. Drain roast. Remove onion from marinade and reserve. Strain and reserve marinade. Melt butter in a Dutch oven. Add the roast and brown on all sides. Add reserved onion and ½ cup reserved marinade. Simmer for 4 to 6 hours or until tender, adding remaining marinade as needed. Thicken the gravy. Serve venison and gravy with Potato Dumplings or Mashed Potatoes. Serves 2.

Venison Steak Pot Roast

2 Tbsp. oleo
3 large onions, coarsely chopped
3 large garlic cloves, coarsely chopped
1 Tbsp. paprika

pinch of dried thyme, crumbled
4-lb. venison steak
salt
freshly ground pepper

Melt oleo in large Dutch oven over low heat. Add onions and garlic and cook until onions are very soft, stirring frequently. Add paprika and thyme and cook 4 minutes, stirring mixture frequently. Remove Dutch oven from heat. Preheat oven to 375 degrees. Set venison brisket, fat side up, on a large baking sheet. Season with salt and pepper. Roast until outside skin is no longer pink. Set brisket on top of onions in the Dutch oven. Pour any of the pan juices over the brisket. Add enough water to almost cover brisket. Cover and simmer over very low heat, basting every 30 minutes until a knife inserted in center of meat goes through easily, 2½ to 3 hours. Cool brisket in juices. Refrigerate overnight. Preheat oven to 350 degrees. Lift fat from the surface of the meat and liquid. Cut brisket diagonally into thin slices. Transfer slices to a large ovenproof dish. Boil liquid until it is reduced to 2½ cups. Pour reduced liquid over brisket. Cover brisket with aluminum foil and bake until heated through, about 20 minutes. Serve hot. Serves 8.

Venison Pot Roast with Tomato Gravy

1 (4-lb. to 5-lb.) venison shoulder roast
4 Tbsp. liquid bacon fat
1 clove of garlic
½ tsp. thyme
½ cup red wine vinegar
  cooked noodles

salt and pepper to taste
⅓ cup water
1 can tomatoes
4 Tbsp. all-purpose flour
¼ cup water

Brown the venison pot roast in fat in a Dutch oven. Add the garlic, thyme, vinegar, salt, pepper and water and cover. Cook over low heat for 3 hours. Add tomatoes and simmer for about 1 hour longer or until roast is tender. Remove roast to hot platter. Remove garlic and discard, Mix the flour with water and stir into tomato mixture. Cook until thick, stirring constantly and pour over noodles. Serve noodles and sauce with sliced roast. Serves 4 to 6.

Basic Venison Round Roast

1 (5-lb. to 6-lb.) venison round roast
½ cup all-purpose flour
2 tsp. salt
black pepper

cooking oil
1 cup hot water
1 clove garlic, chopped
1 large white onion, chopped

Mix and sift flour, salt and pepper. Dredge venison in seasoned flour. Brown venison quickly on both sides in small amount of cooking oil. Place venison in a heavy Dutch oven. Add water, garlic and onion. Cover and simmer for 4 to 6 hours or until tender. Remove venison and allow to cool. Slice roast and place slices on a serving platter. Spoon hot pot gravy on all slices. If necessary, add hot water to pot gravy while cooking. Serves 2 to 4.

Sauerbraten-Style Venison Roast

4 lb.± venison round roast, 3" or 4" thick
2 cups cider vinegar
2 cups water
2 cups yellow onions, sliced
4 bay leaves
16 whole cloves

1 Tbsp. salt
¼ tsp. black pepper
4 Tbsp. dark brown sugar
5 Tbsp. cooking oil
12 Gingersnap Cookies, crumbled

Make marinade by mixing vinegar, water, onions, bay leaves, cloves, salt, pepper and brown sugar. Place venison in a large glass container and pour over with marinade. Place venison in refrigerator for 24 hours to marinate. Remove venison from marinade and wipe dry. Reserve and strain the marinade. Brown the venison in hot cooking oil. Place venison in heavy 4-quart skillet or Dutch oven. Add 3 cups of the reserved marinade to the Dutch oven; cover and simmer slowly about 2½ to 3½ hours. Thicken the pot gravy with Gingersnaps. Serves 6 to 8.

Downeast Venison Pot Roast

1 (5-lb.) venison round roast
2 cups apple cider vinegar
2 cups water
1 large white onion
2 tsp. salt
1 Tbsp. peppercorns

1 bay leaf
3 long red peppers
1 tsp. cloves
2 celery stalks, chopped
bacon drippings

Mix all ingredients. Place venison roast in a large glass or vitrified clay crock and pour ingredients over the venison roast so that meat is submerged to a little over half way. Allow venison roast to remain in marinade in a cool area of the house for 24 hrs.; turn several times. Remove venison from the marinade; pat dry. Reserve the marinade. Quickly brown all sides of the venison in bacon drippings in a Dutch oven. Add 1 cup or more of the reserved marinade; reduce heat to a simmer and cook very slowly until tender. Serves 2 to 4.

Burgundy and Spice Venison Pot Roast

1 (3-lb. or 4-lb.) venison round roast
2 cloves of garlic, sliced
salt
black pepper
all-purpose flour
1 small yellow onion, minced

¼ cup safflower oil
2 Tbsp. butter
allspice
ground cloves
cinnamon
2 cups Burgundy

Make deep cuts in venison and place a slice of garlic in each cut. Rub the roast with salt and pepper. Dredge the venison in flour. Flour the roast after salting and peppering it. Brown venison on all sides in Dutch oven. Brown minced onion in small amount of safflower oil. Place browned onions on top of browned roast. Sprinkle roast with dash of allspice, cloves and cinnamon. Pour Burgundy over the venison roast; cover, and simmer on top of stove for 4 to 6 hours or until tender. Add more wine if needed. Remove roast to a warm oven. Reduce pan liquids to make a gravy. Slice roast and spoon gravy over the slices.

Deer are most active just before sunset and again shortly after sunrise. During the middle part of the day, they are generally bedded down in some thicket or in some area where they are more or less protected. It is not uncommon for deer to feed well into the night, but there is usually a period of resting and cud chewing during the middle part of the night.

8

Venison Ribs

Unfortunately, this cut of venison has been of minimal interest to most venison cooks. Venison ribs, unlike other cuts of venison, need no special treatments such as larding or marinating.

Venison ribs are not as large as beef and they are not as greasy as pork. On a 120 lb. deer the average weight of one side of ribs is 3-lb. or 6 lb. With venison ribs you have the best of all worlds. Save those ribs for the freezer until you have enough sides to have a real outdoor feast.

You can freeze your ribs in whole sections or you can cut your ribs into short or serving-size portions. When you cook out for very large groups, you may be able to make arrangements with your favorite barbeque house for them to smoke/cook your ribs for you. I pay my barbeque house to smoke/cook my ribs and I also buy several quarts of their sauce, potato salad, baked beans and cole slaw. For the cookout, all I need to do is to keep the ribs warm on the outdoor grill and baste with the sauce.

Since venison fat, like mutton fat, solidifies at a lower temperature than does beef or pork fat, all fat must be removed from the ribs.

Bar-B-Q Venison Ribs

If you like tender ribs with barbecue sauce, this recipe is the one for you.

2 sides of venison ribs
2 qts. Barbecue Sauce
Boston Baked Beans

Potato Salad
Cole Slaw

Preheat outdoor grill to hot. Slice venison ribs through meat to make single ribs. Pour Barbecue Sauce in a pan or very large mixing bowl. Soak ribs in sauce for 20 minutes. *Do not overcook* ribs. Lay and nest ribs, meat-side-down on hot grill. Cook ribs until meat is cooked on first side. Remove ribs one at a time and dip in sauce. Re-lay and nest ribs back on hot grill with the other meat-side-down. Cook until second meat side is done. Remove ribs one at a time and dip in sauce. Lay ribs on grill, bone-side-down. Cook ribs until third side is done. Remove ribs one at a time and dip in sauce. Re-lay ribs back on grill with other bone side down. Cook ribs until fourth side is done. You may need to occasionally spray the grill with water because the dripping sauce may flare up and burn the ribs. Serve with baked beans, potato salad, and cole slaw. Serve immediately. Serves 4 to 6.

Barbecue of Venison Ribs

6 venison rib or back steaks
black pepper
1 med. white onion, sliced thin
1 lemon, sliced thin
1 cup tomato catsup
1 cup water

1 tsp. salt
1 tsp. chili powder
⅓ cup Worcestershire sauce
dash of Tabasco sauce
¼ cup apple cider vinegar

Arrange venison steaks in Dutch oven; sprinkle with pepper. Cover venison with onion; lay lemon slices on top of the onion. Bake, uncovered at 400 degrees for 10 minutes until browning begins. Mix remaining ingredients in saucepan; bring to boil. Pour this sauce over the venison rib steaks; reduce heat to 350 degrees. Cook for 1 hour or until tender. Spoon sauce over the venison several times during cooking. Add a little water if sauce becomes thick. Serves 6.

Barbecued Venison Short Ribs

venison short ribs (2 or 3 ribs per serving)
water
1 med. white onion, sliced
1 Tbsp. garlic, diced

1 Tbsp. Seasoning Salt
¼ tsp. black pepper
Barbecue Sauce

Cut ribs into 3" lengths. Place venison ribs in a roasting pan and cover with water. Add onion, garlic, Seasoning Salt, and pepper. Cover and simmer over very low heat for 1 hour. Drain ribs; reserve the pan liquid. Cover ribs with Barbeque Sauce. Add 1 cup of reserved pan liquid. Preheat oven to 350 degrees and bake until tender; adding more Barbecue Sauce and/or liquid if necessary.

Braised Short Ribs of Venison with Celery

3 lbs. venison ribs
4 Tbsp. all-purpose flour, divided
3 tsp. salt
2 Tbsp. Crisco
2 cups boiling water

6 medium white onions
5 stalks celery
½ tsp. pepper
½ tsp. thyme leaves
2 Tbsp. water

Trim excess fat from the venison ribs and discard. Cut ribs into 3" pieces. Mix 3 Tbsp. flour with salt and dredge ribs with the seasoned flour. Brown on all sides in Crisco in a deep skillet. Add the boiling water and cover skillet. Simmer for 2 hours or until venison is almost tender. Add the onions and cover. Cook for 10 minutes. Cut the celery into 2" pieces. Add celery, pepper and thyme to venison mixture and cover. Cook for about 25 minutes longer or until the vegetables are tender. Remove venison and vegetables to a heated platter. Blend remaining flour with water and stir into liquid in skillet. Cook for 1 minute and serve with venison ribs. Serves 6 to 8.

Braised Venison Spareribs in Tomato Sauce

3 lbs. venison spareribs
5 Tbsp. teriyaki sauce, divided
2 Tbsp. rice wine or sherry
1 tsp. Accent
2 eggs, beaten

fine cracker crumbs
1 large onion, sliced thin
2 tsp. sugar
¼ cup tomato catsup
1 cup canned beef broth

Cut the venison spareribs in 2" lengths. Combine 4 Tbsp. teriyaki sauce, wine and Accent. Marinate the spareribs in this mixture for one hour, turning occasionally. Remove the ribs and dip them in beaten egg, then roll in the cracker crumbs. Fry the ribs in deep fat, a few at a time, until golden brown. Drain and keep warm. Sauté the sliced onion until just soft, but do not brown. Add the 1 Tbsp. teriyaki sauce, sugar, and catsup. Add the beef broth and simmer for a moment. Add the spareribs and braise until they are tender. Serves 4 to 6.

Chicory-Glazed Venison Spareribs

Glaze:
3 Tbsp. ground chicory, divided
6 Tbsp. safflower oil
1 large onion, minced
2 garlic cloves, pressed
2 Tbsp. chili powder
1 Tbsp. light brown sugar
½ tsp. cinnamon
½ tsp. ground allspice
½ tsp. ground ginger
1½ cups bottled chili sauce
1 cup freshly brewed coffee
⅓ cup light molasses
3 Tbsp. Worcestershire sauce

½ tsp, liquid smoke
salt

Ribs:
1 Tbsp. salt
1 Tbsp. black pepper
1 tsp. sugar
1 tsp. cinnamon
1 tsp. ground allspice
3 venison sparerib racks (about 6 lbs.)
    cut into 3 rib sections
2 cups coffee
⅔ cup apple cider vinegar

To make glaze: Grind chicory to powder in a food processor. You may wish to have a coffee specialty shop grind it for you. Ask that they use a *Turkish Grind*. Heat oil in a large saucepan over medium-high heat. Add onion and sauté until lightly browned. Add garlic and sauté for 2 minutes. Add 1 Tbsp. chicory (reserve remainder for ribs), chili powder, sugar, cinnamon, allspice and ginger. Cook 3 minutes, stirring occasionally. Add chili sauce, coffee, molasses, Worcestershire and liquid smoke. Cook mixture over medium-low heat until thick and glossy, stirring occasionally, about 30 minutes. Season with salt.

To cook venison ribs: Combine salt, black pepper, sugar, cinnamon, and allspice in a bowl. Mix in chicory reserved from glaze. Sprinkle mixture over both sides of ribs. Cover and let stand for 1 hour at room temperature. Heat barbeque grill to medium-high heat. Mix coffee and vinegar in a small bowl. Place ribs on the grill and brown on each side. Brush ribs with some of coffee-vinegar mixture. Cover with grill lid and cook until ribs are almost tender, brushing occasionally with coffee-vinegar mixture and turning occasionally. Brush some of the glaze over ribs and grill until meat is tender. Arrange ribs on a platter. Serve with remaining glaze. Serves 6 to 8.

Deviled Herb and Mustard Venison Ribs

Glaze:
½ cup unsalted butter
¼ cup canola oil
6 green onions, white and green parts
   chopped separately
1 cup yellow onion, finely minced
3 large garlic cloves, pressed
¼ cup Worcestershire sauce
¼ cup dry sherry
2 Tbsp. firmly packed light brown sugar
2 Tbsp. fresh lime juice
⅔ cup Dijon mustard
1 tsp. cracked black peppercorns
¼ tsp. red pepper
2 Tbsp. fresh parsley, minced cherry tomatoes
2 Tbsp. fresh tarragon, dried, minced
   or 2 tsp. crumbled
2 Tbsp. fresh thyme, minced or 2 tsp. dried,
   crumbled
salt

Seasoning:
1½ Tbsp. hickory-smoked salt
1½ Tbsp. orange peel, grated
1 Tbsp. sugar
1 Tbsp. black pepper
1 Tbsp. lemon peel, grated
1½ tsp. ground allspice
1½ tsp. dry mustard
1½ tsp. ground ginger
1½ tsp. ground coriander
1½ tsp. paprika
3 venison rib racks (about 9 lbs.)
fresh parsley sprigs
fresh basil leaves

For Glaze: Melt butter with oil in large saucepan over medium-high heat. Add chopped white part of green onions and minced yellow onion and sauté until translucent. Add garlic and sauté for 2 minutes. Add Worcestershire, sherry, sugar and lime juice and cook until thick and bubbling, stirring constantly. Remove from heat. Whisk in mustard, peppercorns and red pepper. Add minced herbs and ¼ cup chopped green onion tops. Season with salt.

For Seasoning: Mix first 10 ingredients in small bowl to blend. Rub the venison ribs with cut sides of limes. Rub ribs with ½ cup of the mixed seasonings. Cover ribs and let stand for 1 hour. Heat barbeque grill to medium-high heat. Brush grill lightly with oil. Place marinated ribs on grill and sear both sides. Continue grilling until meat is tender and ribs are very lightly charred, turning occasionally and brushing with some of glaze shortly before removing. Transfer ribs to work surface. Cut into individual ribs. Arrange ribs on a serving platter. Garnish with parsley, basil and cherry tomatoes. Serve with remaining glaze. Serves 6 to 8.

Oven Barbecued Venison Long Ribs

3 lbs. venison long ribs
1 qt. water
⅓ tsp, soda

salt
black pepper
Barbecue Sauce

Dissolve soda in the water. Soak the venison ribs in soda water 15 minutes. Remove the venison and rinse thoroughly in clear water. Salt and pepper to taste. Place venison ribs in a shallow baking dish. Preheat oven to 250 degrees and bake ribs, uncovered, for 1¼ hours. Baste with sauce and bake for another ¼ hour. Serves 4.

Korean-Style Venison Short Ribs

4 lbs. venison short ribs
5 med. garlic cloves, minced
½ cup teriyaki sauce
3 Tbsp. sesame oil
2 tsp. gingerroot, minced

3 Tbsp. sugar
2 tsp. white wine vinegar
2 tsp. sesame seeds
1 tsp. pepper
18 pieces green onion, cut 2" to 4" long

Trim fat from venison short ribs. Cut the meat side of each rib to the bone at ½" intervals. Whisk together garlic, teriyaki sauce, sesame oil, gingerroot, sugar, vinegar, sesame seeds and pepper. Add this marinade with ribs and green onions to a plastic bag and marinate in the refrigerator overnight. Turn bag over occasionally. Remove ribs and green onions from the bag. Discard the marinade. Grill the ribs, meaty-side-down, for 8 minutes; turn them over and grill for another 6 minutes or until medium-rare. Grill the green onions, turning them occasionally, for 4 minutes, or until they are just browned. Serves 6.

Oven Barbecued Venison Short Ribs
with Chili Biscuits

3 lbs. venison short ribs, cut into 1" pieces
3 Tbsp. safflower oil
2 large onions, coarsely chopped
4 large garlic cloves, pressed
2 (16-oz.) cans tomatoes, undrained
2 cups canned beef broth
⅓ cup cider vinegar
¼ cup firmly packed light brown sugar
3 Tbsp. Worcestershire sauce
2 Tbsp. Dijon mustard
1½ tsp. salt

1½ tsp. red pepper
½ tsp. black pepper
½ tsp. paprika
½ tsp, ground turmeric
10 parsley sprigs, tied
2 (¼"-thick) lime slices
1 lb. med. boiling potatoes, peeled
  and cut into 1" cubes
1 lb. med. carrots, cut into 2" pieces
Chili Biscuits

Preheat broiler. Arrange venison ribs in a single layer in a large shallow roasting pan. Broil 4" from heat until brown, turning frequently. Preheat oven to 350 degrees. Heat oil in Dutch oven over medium-low heat. Add onions and garlic and cook until soft and lightly browned, stirring frequently. Add ribs and any drippings. Stir in tomatoes, broth, vinegar, sugar, Worcestershire sauce, mustard, salt, red pepper, black pepper, paprika, turmeric, parsley and lime. Increase heat and bring to a boil. Transfer to oven, cover and bake until short ribs are tender, about 2 hours. Stir potatoes and carrots into ribs. Cover and bake until vegetables are tender, about 30 minutes. Discard the parsley and lime. Degrease sauce. Season to taste. Bring to simmer. Increase oven temperature to 450 degrees. Arrange Chili Biscuits over ribs. Bake uncovered until biscuits are puffed and slightly browned, about 15 minutes. Serve short ribs and biscuits immediately. Serves 6 to 8.

Orange Marmalade and Chili-Glazed Venison Ribs

Marinade:
2 med. oranges, unpeeled, quartered and seeded
¼ cup canola oil
1 large red onion, minced
6 large garlic cloves, minced
1½ cups chili sauce
¾ cup orange marmalade
⅓ cup red wine vinegar
3 Tbsp. teriyaki sauce
1 (3" piece) fresh ginger, peeled, grated
1 tsp. black pepper

½ tsp. cinnamon
½ tsp. ground cloves
¼ tsp. red pepper
1 Tbsp. Oriental sesame oil
½ tsp. liquid smoke
salt

Ribs:
6 to 9 lb. thick venison short ribs, well trimmed
⅓ cup sesame seeds, toasted
⅓ cup green onions, minced

For Marinade: Grind oranges in processor. Heat oil in large saucepan over medium-high heat. Add onions and sauté until lightly browned. Add garlic and sauté. Add ground oranges, chili sauce, marmalade, vinegar, teriyaki sauce, ginger, pepper, cinnamon, cloves and red pepper. Bring mixture to a boil, stirring constantly. Reduce heat and simmer until sauce is thick and glossy, stirring frequently. Remove marinade from heat. Mix in sesame oil and liquid smoke. Season with salt to taste. Allow marinade to come to room temperature.

For Venison Ribs: Place ribs bone side down on work surface. Using small sharp knife, cut ¼"-deep slits down length of meat, spacing cuts about ½" apart. Repeat in opposite direction, forming X pattern. Divide ribs between 2 heavy, 1-gal. Zip Lock bags. Add half of marinade to each bag, remove air and seal. Refrigerate at least 24 hours and up to 48 hours, turning occasionally. Preheat oven to 350 degrees. Place ribs and marinade in large roasting pan. Cover and bake until the meat is tender, about 1¾ hours. Place ribs on a platter; reserve the marinade. Pour the marinade into medium saucepan. Cook marinade over medium heat until it is reduced to thick-sauce consistency, stirring occasionally. Heat barbeque grill to medium-high heat. Brush grill lightly with oil. Place ribs on grill and sear both sides. Brush ribs with the glaze and continue grilling until ribs are very tender and very slightly crusty, turning and basting occasionally with glaze. Arrange ribs on serving platter. Brush with more glaze. Sprinkle with sesame seeds and onions and serve. Serves 4 to 6.

Short Ribs of Venison with Parsley Dumplings

2 lbs. venison short ribs
1½ cups all-purpose flour, divided
1 Tbsp. salt
¼ tsp. black pepper
1 stick oleo
1 (1-lb.) can tomatoes
2 cloves of garlic, minced
1 Tbsp. Worcestershire sauce
4 carrots, sliced

2 onions, sliced
2 potatoes, cubed
2 tsp. baking powder
1 tsp. salt
2 Tbsp. parsley, chopped
2 Tbsp. canola oil
½ cup whole milk
2 cups water

For Venison Ribs: Cut the ribs into serving pieces. Combine ½ cup flour, 1 Tbsp. salt and pepper. Dredge ribs with the flour mixture and brown in oleo in a Dutch oven. Add tomatoes, garlic and Worcestershire sauce and cover. Simmer for 1½ hours. Add the carrots, onions and potatoes and simmer for ¾ hour longer.

    For Dumplings: Mix remaining flour, baking powder, 1 tsp. salt and parsley. Add the oil and milk and stir until mixed. Add water to the ribs mixture and bring to a boil. Drop flour mixture by serving spoonfuls into rib mixture. Reduce heat and simmer for 15 minutes or until dumplings are firm. Serves 4 to 6.

Short Ribs of Venison with Raisin Sauce

3 lbs. venison short ribs
salt and pepper to taste
3 Tbsp. bacon fat liquid
1 onion, chopped
½ cup dark brown sugar, firmly packed
1 tsp. dry mustard
½ cup raisins

1 Tbsp. all-purpose flour
2 Tbsp. vinegar
2 Tbsp. lemon or lime juice
¼ tsp. grated lemon or lime rind
1 bay leaf
1½ cups water

Cut the venison ribs into serving pieces and season with salt and pepper. Brown ribs in hot fat in a heavy skillet. Drain off excess fat; add the onion and cook until the onion is tender. Combine remaining ingredients in a saucepan and bring to a boil. Pour over the ribs and cover tightly. Cook over very low heat for about 2 hours or until the ribs are tender. If desired, the sauce may be thickened with additional flour. Serves 4 to 6.

In the 1st Century AD, the Roman Plinius Secundus wrote that antlers contained "some sort of healing drug" and described its use for treatment of epilepsy. Topsell (1607) described the use of powdered deer antler to treat baldness, pimples, lice, toothaches and snakebite. Use of deer for medicinal purposes dates to the Qing Dynasty (221–207 BC).

Spanish Venison Spareribs with Saffron and Potatoes

3 Tbsp. olive oil
3 lbs. venison spareribs, cut 1"x2" pieces
2 med. onions, chopped
1 small red bell pepper, seeded and cut into ½" squares
3 strips orange peel, cut 3"x1" strips
1 heaping Tbsp. fresh fennel fronds, minced
1 large garlic clove, minced
1 pinch of dried thyme, crumbled
2 bay leaves
½ cup dry vermouth
2 cups canned beef broth

3 Italian plum tomatoes, peeled, seeded and chopped
large pinch of crushed saffron threads dissolved in 1 Tbsp. warm water
1 lb. new potatoes, peeled and cut into 1" chunks
1½ tsp, olive oil
¼ lb. large green beans, cut into 1" lengths
1 (¼-lb.) fennel bulb, discard tough outer ribs, peel, trim and cut 1" chunks
⅓ cup pitted green olives, halved lengthwise
salt and pepper to taste

Heat 3 Tbsp. olive oil in large skillet over medium-high heat. Brown venison ribs in batches. Transfer ribs to a heavy 5-qt. pot. Discard all but 2 Tbsp. fat in skillet. Add onion and bell pepper and cook over medium-low heat until onion is soft and beginning to brown. Add orange peel, fennel fronds, garlic, thyme and bay leaves and stir until orange becomes aromatic. Pour in vermouth. Bring to a boil, scraping up any browned bits. Cook until the liquid is reduced to a glaze. Add beef broth, tomatoes and dissolved saffron and boil until reduced by ⅓. Pour over venison ribs and bring to simmer. Reduce heat, partially cover and simmer ¾ hour, turning venison occasionally. Stir in potatoes. Partially cover and simmer for 15 minutes, turning venison and potatoes occasionally.

Meanwhile, heat 1½ tsp. olive oil in a medium skillet over medium-high heat. Add green beans and fennel; sauté until beginning to brown. Stir into venison mixture. Partially cover and simmer until the venison is tender. Add olives, salt and pepper. Taste and adjust seasoning. Degrease sauce. Place ribs on a serving dish and serve immediately. Serves 4 to 6.

Spareribs of Venison Barbecued with Fragrant Spices

2 lbs. venison spareribs
2 Tbsp. sherry
1 Tbsp. sugar
2 garlic cloves, mashed
½ tsp. cinnamon

4 Tbsp. teriyaki sauce
½ tsp. powdered aniseed
½ tsp. cloves powder
1 tsp. salt
hot English mustard

Do not cut the venison ribs apart. Mix teriyaki sauce, wine, sugar, garlic, cinnamon, aniseed, cloves, and salt. Marinate the spare ribs in this mixture for 24 to 36 hours. Roast the spareribs on a rack in a 325-degree oven until tender, basting occasionally. Chop the ribs apart and serve with hot mustard. Serves 2 to 4.

Spiced Venison Short Ribs

3 lbs. venison short ribs
1½ tsp. salt
¼ cup all-purpose flour
2 Tbsp. Crisco
1¼ cups water
1 cup prunes

1 cup dried apricots
½ cup sugar
½ tsp. allspice
¼ tsp. ground cloves
½ tsp, cinnamon
3 Tbsp. rice wine vinegar

Cut the venison ribs into serving pieces and season with salt. Dredge with flour and brown in Crisco in a skillet. Add the water and cover. Simmer for 1 hour. Add prunes, apricots and remaining ingredients and simmer until venison is tender. Thicken the liquid for gravy. Serves 4 to 6.

Smothered Venison Ribs

venison ribs
liquid smoke
1½ cups celery, diced
½ cup onion, minced
1 tsp, salt
1 small can mushroom stems

¼ lb. butter
1 cup soft bread crumbs
1½ tsp. poultry seasonings
1 cup carrots, sliced
2 cups hot water
2 beef bouillon cubes

Cut venison ribs into serving-size portions and brush with liquid smoke. Lay ribs close together in a large roaster. Preheat oven to 450 degrees. Make dressing by mixing celery, onion, salt, mushrooms and butter. Sauté vegetables in butter for 15 minutes; remove from heat and stir in soft bread crumbs and poultry seasonings. Brown ribs in the oven for 10 minutes. Remove the ribs and spread carrots and celery over the bottom of roaster. Arrange the ribs tightly together on top, their more raw sides toward the top. Cover ribs with the dressing, smoothing it evenly down, and brown for another 10 minutes. Dissolve the bouillon cubes in the hot water then pour the bouillon over the dressing. Cover the roaster and return it to the oven. Turn the heat down to 300 degrees and bake ribs for 2 hours. Add more bouillon if necessary.

Sweet and Sour Venison Spareribs

3 lbs. venison spareribs, cut into 3" lengths
1½ cups water
4 Tbsp. teriyaki sauce

3 Tbsp. apple cider vinegar
4 Tbsp. light brown sugar
2 Tbsp. cornstarch

Cut venison ribs into 3" pieces. Place ribs, ½ cup water, teriyaki sauce and salt in large saucepan. Bring to boil; simmer for 1 hour. Remove ribs to a skillet. Mix apple cider vinegar, brown sugar, cornstarch and remaining 1 cup of water. Add to liquid from ribs; stir well. Cook until mixture is thickened and clear. Pour over ribs in the skillet; continue cooking for several minutes or until meat is tender. Serves 6 to 8.

Sweet and Sour Venison Spareribs on Peppery Pickled Cabbage

⅓ cup syrupy rice wine (mirin)
⅓ cup cider vinegar
¼ cup teriyakl sauce
2 Tbsp. roasted sesame seeds
2 Tbsp. light brown sugar, firmly packed
1 (1") cube fresh ginger, peeled
1 small clove garlic
4 cups firmly packed fresh sauerkraut, rinsed, drained and squeezed dry
¼ tsp. red pepper flakes

6 lbs. venison spareribs, cut into 2-rib widths
1½ cups firmly packed light brown sugar
½ cup fresh orange juice
1 cup teriyaki sauce
¼ cup medium-dry sherry
¼ cup rice wine vinegar
2 Tbsp. tomato sauce
2 Tbsp. fresh ginger, minced
8 large garlic cloves, halved
½ cup green onions, minced

Blend first 7 ingredients in processor 30 seconds, scraping down sides of bowl. Pour into large non-aluminum bowl. Add sauerkraut and pepper flakes.; Cover and refrigerate for at least 3 hours, stirring occasionally. Remove from refrigerator and let stand at room temperature for at least 1 hour. Preheat oven to 375 degrees. Arrange venison spareribs in single layer in a large shallow roasting pan. Cover ribs with cold water. Cover roasting pan with aluminum foil and bake until ribs are tender, about 1½ hours or less. Pour off cooking liquid; degrease and reserve 1 cup of the liquid, Reduce oven temperature to 350 degrees. Combine reserved cooking liquid, sugar, teriyaki sauce, orange juice, sherry, vinegar, tomato paste, ginger and garlic in a medium saucepan and stir over low heat until sugar dissolves. Pour mixture over the ribs. Bake uncovered for 1 hour, basting every 15 minutes. Strain pan juices back into a saucepan. Cover ribs with aluminum foil and keep ribs warm. Boil juices over medium heat until it is reduced to 1½ cups. Mound sauerkraut on a deep serving platter. Arrange ribs on top of sauerkraut. Pour sauce over. Sprinkle with green onion and serve. Serves 4 to 6.

Sweet and Sour Venison Spareribs with Vegetables

2 lbs. venison ribs
3 Tbsp. safflower oil
½ cup water
¼ cup raisins
½ tsp. salt
1 clove of garlic, minced
1 cup chopped mixed vegetables such as; celery, watercress, peas, cauliflower, broccoli etc.

1½ Tbsp. cornstarch
1¼ cups sugar
1¼ cups rice wine vinegar
1 cup water
teriyaki sauce
Boiled Rice

Saw venison ribs into serving portions. Brown in safflower oil over moderate heat for about 5 minutes on each side. Add water, garlic, raisins, and salt. Cover pan tightly and cook over very low heat for about 20 minutes. Add garlic and vegetables. Mix cornstarch, sugar, vinegar and water. Add this mixture to other ingredients in the pan. Re-cover and continue cooking over low heat for another 1½ hours. Stir occasionally and add more water to prevent drying. Sprinkle with teriyaki sauce. Serve with Boiled Rice. Serves 4 to 6.

Texas Smoky Venison Short Ribs

9 lbs, venison short ribs
3 large onions, chopped
2 bay leaves
salt
pepper
¼ cup canola oil
2 celery stalks, chopped
1 green bell pepper, chopped
4 garlic cloves, minced

2 cups tomato catsup
½ cup red wine vinegar
¼ cup chili powder
1 Tbsp. dark brown sugar
2 tsp. liquid smoke
1 tsp. dried basil, crumbled
1 tsp. dried oregano, crumbled
1 tsp. ground cumin
¼ tsp. red pepper

Divide venison ribs, 2 onions and bay leaves between 2 large pots. Season with salt and pepper. Add enough water to each pot to cover ribs. Boil 5 minutes. Skim the foam from surfaces. Reduce heat and simmer until ribs are tender, about 1½ hours. Drain, reserving 4 cups cooking liquid. Place reserved liquid in medium saucepan. Boil until reduced to 1 cup, about 25 minutes. Heat oil in large skillet. Add remaining onion, celery, bell pepper and garlic. Cook until vegetables are tender, stirring occasionally, about 10 minutes. Mix in reduced cooking liquid, tomato catsup, vinegar, chili powder, sugar, smoke flavoring, basil, oregano, cumin and red pepper. Simmer until sauce is thick, about 30 minutes. Preheat oven to 375 degrees. Arrange ribs in single layer in baking pans. Pour sauce over ribs. Cover pans with aluminum foil and bake ribs until they are heated through. Cut into individual ribs and serve. Serves 6 to 8.

Ruby Mountain Venison Short Ribs

3 lbs. venison ribs, cut into 3" lengths
1 Tbsp. salt
1 qt. warm water
1 tsp. paprika
1 large white onion, chopped

½ cup tomato catsup
¼ cup apple cider vinegar
2 Tbsp. water
2 tsp. chili powder
3 Tbsp. bacon drippings

Dissolve the salt in the water and soak venison ribs overnight. Remove the ribs and wash with fresh water. Parboil in a pressure cooker for 30 minutes at 10 lbs. pressure. Remove the ribs from the pressure cooker and place the ribs in a frying pan. Mix the remaining ingredients and pour over the ribs. Bake in a 375-degree oven for about 1 hour or until the ribs are tender and browned. Serves 4 to 6.

Animals have a very important place in all Native American cultures. They are considered with respect and understood to have certain powers. They are used as symbols for various family totems and are referred to as he/she rather than "it."

Venison Spareribs with Pineapple

2 lbs. venison spareribs
soy sauce
1 Tbsp. all-purpose flour
½ cup pineapple Juice
¼ cup sugar

¼ cup rice wine vinegar
½ cup water
1 cup pineapple chunks
cornstarch

Marinate the venison spareribs in soy sauce, drain, then sauté for 5 minutes. Stir in the flour, then add the pineapple juice, sugar, vinegar, and water. Stir, cover, and simmer for about one hour, or until ribs are tender. Season with salt. Add the pineapple chunks, heat the sauce and thicken with cornstarch binder. Serves 2.

Whiskey Glazed Venison Ribs

Glaze:
½ cup unsalted butter
⅓ cup canola oil
1 cup minced onion
⅔ cup tomato catsup
⅔ cup sour mash bourbon
½ cup apple cider vinegar
½ cup fresh orange Juice
½ cup pure maple syrup
⅓ cup molasses
2 Tbsp. Worcestershire sauce
½ tsp. black pepper, cracked

½ tsp. liquid smoke
½ cup salt
1 Tbsp. orange peel, finely grated
Venison Ribs:
3 venison sparerib racks (about 9 lb.)
    cut into 5 rib sections
4 tsp. sugar
1½ tsp. ground allspice
salt
pepper
green onions

For Glaze: Melt butter in large saucepan over medium heat. Add oil and heat 2 minutes. Add onion and sauté until pale golden. Add tomato catsup, bourbon, vinegar, orange juice, maple syrup, molasses, Worcestershire sauce, pepper, liquid smoke and salt. Bring to a simmer, stirring frequently. Reduce heat to medium-low and cook until the mixture is thick and glossy, stirring occasionally, about 1 hour. Add orange peel and cook 5 minutes, stirring occasionally.

For Venison Ribs: Season both sides of ribs with sugar, allspice, salt and pepper. Cover and let stand for 1 hour. Heat barbeque grill to medium-high. Oil the grill. Place ribs on the grill and sear both sides. Move ribs to outer edges of grill. Close grill lid and continue grilling until the meat is tender, turning ribs occasionally and brushing with glaze during the last 5 minutes. Arrange ribs on platter. Garnish with green onions. Serve with remaining glaze. Serves 4 to 6.

9

Venison Variety Meats

Variety meats are a mystery to most of us. This is because of our own personal preferences, their tendency to be the first meat to spoil, and our lack of knowledge regarding the appropriate preparation techniques.

These cuts of meat do not freeze well. They are best when cooled quickly, refrigerated and cooked within 48 hours of slaughtering.

Variety meats are nutritious and when properly prepared are a tasty variation to our menu. If you enjoy these particular cuts of meat or if you want to give them a try, these recipes will provide you with the opportunity to expand your recipes and to try interesting variations.

Growing up in Nelliesburg, Mississippi, my mother would prepare a delicious main dish consisting of fried liver and onions. The Venison Liver With Onions is a variation of this old family recipe. I hope that you enjoy it as much as I do.

Barbecued Venison Bones

¼ cup Blackberry Jelly or jam
¼ cup Dijon mustard
¼ cup wine or apple cider vinegar

1 large garlic clove, minced
pinch of cayenne pepper
4 lbs. meaty venison bones or ribs

Heat barbecue grill to medium. Make glaze by mixing Blackberry Jelly or jam, mustard, vinegar, garlic and cayenne pepper in a small bowl. Set aside. Grill venison bones 45 minutes, turning occasionally. Brush with glaze. Continue cooking until bones are crisp and brown, brushing with glaze every 10 minutes and turning occasionally, about 35 minutes. Serve hot or warm. Serves 4.

Buttered and Broiled Venison Liver

1 venison liver
butter, melted

salt
black pepper

Slice the venison liver about ¾" thick. Brush it with melted butter. Broil the liver on a greased rack, with the top of meat 2" from heat for about 2 minutes on each side or until the liver is well browned outside and still red and juicy within. Salt and pepper to taste. Serves 4 to 6.

New York-Style Venison Liver

½ lb. venison liver
1 cup whole milk
salt
black pepper
1 tsp. canola oil

¼ tsp. dried marjoram, crumbled
2 Tbsp. canola oil
1 med. Golden Delicious apple, sliced
1 med. white onion, thinly sliced

Soak venison liver in milk in shallow dish 15 minutes, turning once. Preheat broiler. Drain liver. Transfer to broiler pan. Season with salt and pepper. Brush with ½ tsp. oil. Broil until browned, about 4 minutes; turn and brush with ½ tsp. oil. Continue broiling until browned. Sprinkle with marjoram. Keep warm. Heat remaining oil in medium skillet over medium-high heat. Add apple and onion and sauté until soft. Transfer liver to platter. Top with apple mixture and serve. Serves 2.

Braised Venison Tongue with Capers and Herb Sauce

½ cup canola oil
2 lbs. venison tongues
1 lb. pearl onions, peeled
¼ cup red wine vinegar, divided
3 green onions (white plus 2" of green), minced
1 garlic clove
1 tsp. dried oregano, crumbled
1 tsp. dried thyme, crumbled
1 tsp. dried rosemary, crumbled

1 tsp. fresh parsley, minced
1 bay leaf
½ tsp. dried basil, crumbled
¼ tsp. dried dillweed
salt
pepper
2 Tbsp. red wine vinegar
2 Tbsp. capers
pickled peppers
watercress

Heat oil in Dutch oven over medium heat. Add venison tongue and brown lightly on all sides. Add all remaining ingredients except 2 Tbsp. vinegar, capers, pickles and watercress. Cover, reduce heat to very low and cook until tongues are tender when pierced with fork, about 1 hour. Remove tongues and onions from pan, using slotted spoon. Add 2 Tbsp. vinegar to pan. Strain cooking liquid through fine sieve, pressing to extract as much liquid as possible. Peel tongue and cut into ⅛" thick slices. Arrange slices on a serving platter with onions. Spoon sauce on top. Garnish with capers, peppers and watercress. Serve warm or at room temperature. Serves 6 to 8.

Broiled Venison Kidneys with Parsley Snips

4 venison kidneys
butter, melted
salt

black pepper
parsley or watercress snips

Remove all connecting tissues from the venison kidneys. Quarter each kidney longways and wash with clear water. Broil kidneys for 3 minutes on one side and 2 minutes on the other side. *Do not overcook.* Baste several times with butter. When the kidneys are done, season with salt and pepper. Garnish and serve with parsley or watercress snips. Serves 4.

Chevreuil Liver in a Tomato Roux

2 lbs. venison liver
ice
1 Tbsp. bacon drippings
1 large onion, minced
1 clove garlic, chopped
1 green bell pepper, chopped

1 tsp. thyme
salt
red pepper
1 Tbsp. flour
1 small can tomatoes
2 cups water

Put venison liver in a bowl; cover with ice and place in a refrigerator overnight. The next day, make a roux by heating bacon drippings in a deep saucepan into which stir onion, garlic, and when onion withers, add bell pepper, thyme, salt, red pepper and flour. Stir until the flour browns a little, add tomatoes and water. Keep hot. Take liver from the refrigerator, skin and remove fiber, and plunge it twice into boiling water. Add the liver to the saucepan with the roux. Cover tightly and let simmer until tender. When tender, put liver and other ingredients into an uncovered baking dish and slightly brown in the oven, basting frequently. Serves 2 to 4.

Cold Venison Tongue and Cheese Sandwich

1 cup cooked venison tongue, chopped
1 cup Swiss cheese, grated
1 Tbsp. prepared mustard
2 tsp. Horseradish
¼ cup Mayonnaise

lettuce
tomato
Armenian Bread
Potato Salad

Combine all ingredients and mix well. Serve on Armenian Bread with lettuce and tomato. Cut sandwich on the diagonal. Serve with Potato Salad on the side. Serves 2 to 4.

Mr. Harold W. Webster, Sr.

Creamed Venison Brains in Potato Shells

2 pr. venison brains
2 cups White Sauce
1 tsp. salt
dash Worcestershire sauce

1 tsp. celery salt
1 tsp. paprika
3 cups Mashed Potatoes
Parsley

Wash the venison brains and remove skin and veins. Soak in cold, salted water for 20 minutes, then drain. Place in a saucepan, cover with boiling water and simmer for 20 minutes, Drain, cool and cut into cubes. Mix with White Sauce and add seasonings. Heat to boiling point. Make nests of Mashed Potatoes on a large, buttered platter. Fill potato nests with brain mixture and garnish with parsley. Serves 2 to 4.

Liver Loaf

1 lb. venison liver
1 cup bread crumbs
2 eggs, beaten
2 tsp. onion, grated
2 tsp, parsley, chopped

1 Tbsp. celery, finely minced
salt
pepper
1 cup whole milk, approximately
3 slices smoked bacon

Pour boiling water over venison liver, let stand 5 minutes. Drain. Force liver through fine food grinder. Add bread crumbs, eggs, onion, salt, parsley, and celery. Salt and pepper to taste. Add enough milk to moisten well. Line a loaf pan with slices of smoked bacon; pack in liver mixture. Bake in a 300-degree oven until firm, about 1 hour. Serves 2 to 4.

Sautéed Kidneys with Burgundy Flavored Sauce

4 venison kidneys, thinly sliced
butter
salt
black pepper

1 Tbsp. yellow onion, diced
4 Tbsp. Burgundy
pinch of red pepper
pinch of garlic powder

Melt the butter in a medium-size skillet; add sliced venison kidneys and sauté them for 4 minutes; salt and pepper to taste. Remove kidneys from the skillet and hold them in a warm place. Stir onions into the skillet juices and cook until just soft but not browned. Add Burgundy and cook until it thickens. Add red pepper and garlic powder. Pour the sauce over the kidneys and serve. Serves 4.

Sautéed Watercress with Venison Liver
and New Potatoes

4 Tbsp. butter
½ cup white onions, minced
2 cups watercress, finely chopped
1 lb. venison liver
½ tsp. salt

½ tsp. black pepper
2 Tbsp. Burgundy
2 Tbsp. parsley, finely chopped
6 small new potatoes, peeled and boiled

Heat 2 Tbsp. butter over high heat. Reduce heat, add the onions, and cook until tender. Stir in the watercress and cook for another 4 minutes. Set aside. Cut the venison liver into ¼" strips crosswise. Pat the strips dry and season with salt and pepper. Heat the rest of the butter over high heat and drop in the liver and sauté, turning frequently. Cook liver until it is lightly browned; about 3 minutes. Liver should be cooked for a very short time over high heat; liver has a tendency to get tough if cooked over low heat for a long time. Stir in the watercress and onion and cook for another 3 minutes. Transfer liver, watercress and new potatoes to a heated platter. Immediately pour wine into the skillet, boil briskly for 2 minutes, scraping in any browned bits clinging to the pan. Stir in parsley and pour sauce over liver, watercress and new potatoes. Serve at once. Serves 2 to 4.

Simmered Venison Heart with White Cream Sauce

1 lb. venison heart, cubed
2 cups cold water
½ tsp. salt
2 Tbsp. butter
½ cup celery, chopped
2 Tbsp. all-purpose flour

evaporated milk
salt
black pepper
paprika
parsley flakes

Cube and wash the venison heart. Dissolve the salt in the cold water. Soak the venison heart in the cold salted water for 5 minutes. Transfer the heart and salt water to a pot and simmer until the heart is tender. Melt the butter in frying pan and sauté onions and celery until they are just tender. Gradually add flour, stirring until smooth and thick. Then slowly stir in the 2 cups of salted water and continue to cook over low heat, stirring constantly, until the gravy is smooth and thickened. Add the heart pieces. Stir over low heat. Add evaporated milk to make a white creamy sauce. Salt and pepper to taste. Garnish with paprika and parsley flakes. Serve hot. Serves 2 to 4.

New England Venison Heart in Wine and Mustard Sauce

1 venison heart
1 cup dry red wine
2 Tbsp. Balsamic vinegar
1 tsp. salt
2 peppercorns

1 tsp. Dijon mustard
1 med. white onion, sliced
1 bay leaf
all-purpose flour
2 Tbsp, butter

With a sharp knife split venison heart open from top to bottom and remove all vents and ducts. Make a marinade of wine, vinegar, salt, peppercorns, mustard, onion and bay leaf and marinate heart for 4 hours. Remove the heart from the marinade and dredge in flour and place in butter melted in a hot skillet. Sear heart on all sides. Reduce heat slightly and cook about 5 minutes. Serves 4.

In Vermont, the week that begins on November 11th is like the beginning of an unofficial holiday in the state. In many rural areas, boys old enough to attend a hunter safety course are taken into the woods to hunt. An estimated 18,000 deer are harvested annually.

Venison Brains in Brown Butter Sauce

An old Oak Ridge, Mississippi recipe of Harold W. Webster, Sr. This recipe could easily date to the 1790s or before.

2 venison brains	pinch of ground thyme
1 tsp. salt	4 peppercorns
1 onion	2 Tbsp. butter
3 whole cloves	2 Tbsp. rice wine vinegar
2 bay leaves	

Soak venison brains in cold water for 2 hours. Remove the thin outer skin, as gently as possible, without tearing flesh. Cover brains with cold water and soak for 3 hours. Drain. Place brains in a large saucepan. Cover with cold water. Add salt, onion with cloves stuck in, bay leaves, thyme and peppercorns. Cover and bring to a boil. Lower heat and simmer 20 minutes. Set aside and keep warm. In a small skillet melt butter and cook until butter is dark brown. Arrange brains on a heated serving dish and pour butter over. Put vinegar in skillet and cook briskly. Pour over brains. Serve at once. Serves 4.

Venison Kidneys and Mushroom Sauté

6 venison kidneys	2 cups hot canned beef broth
6 Tbsp. butter	¼ cup sherry
½ lb. small whole fresh mushrooms	salt
6 Tbsp. all-purpose flour	pepper
1 cup non-dairy creamer	

Trim venison kidneys by removing fat and the thin filament surrounding kidneys-Cut into slices. Melt butter in a skillet over very high heat. When foam from butter subsides a little, add kidneys and cook very quickly. Remove kidneys to a chafing dish. Reduce heat a little and cook mushrooms in the skillet until lightly browned on all sides. Remove to chafing dish. Add flour to the liquid in the skillet, blending with a wire whisk; cook and stir 1 minute, but do not brown. Remove skillet from heat and stir in creamer and hot beef broth all at once. Beat with wire whisk to blend. Cook over moderately high heat, stirring constantly, until the sauce comes to a boil and thickens. Blend in sherry, salt and pepper. Pour over kidneys and mushrooms and heat gently, but do not boil. Serve from chafing dish. Serves 6 to 8.

Mr. Harold W. Webster, Sr.

It is estimated that about 3 million white-tailed deer, 500,000 black-tailed deer, 85,000 wapiti, 54,000 moose and 50,000 caribou are harvested by licensed hunters in the United States each year.

Venison Kidneys in Burgundy Wine

4 venison kidneys
10 large fresh mushrooms
4 Tbsp. butter
4 green onions, cleaned and chopped

salt
pepper
½ cup Burgundy
buttered toast or fried bread

Slice venison kidneys in thin slices and remove hard core and excess fat. Clean and slice mushrooms. Melt butter in a heavy skillet over medium high heat. Add kidney slices and cook quickly until nicely browned on both sides. Add mushrooms and green onions and cook and stir for about 5 minutes. Sprinkle with salt and pepper and Burgundy. Cook 4 to 5 minutes or until kidneys are tender and ingredients blended. Taste and add more seasoning if necessary. Serve on buttered toast or fried bread. Serves 4 to 6.

Venison Liver and Thick Cut Smoked Bacon

6 thick cut slices smoked bacon
1 large white onion, sliced

salt
1 venison liver

Sauté bacon slowly. Drain the bacon on paper towels. Reserve a small amount of the bacon fat for the venison liver. When the bacon is done, sauté the onions until golden and just tender. Remove the onions from pan and season with salt. Keep onions and bacon warm until the liver is ready. Sauté liver about a minute on each side. Place the liver on a serving plate and cover with onions and bacon.

Venison Liver Julienne

1 lb. venison liver
all-purpose flour
salt
black pepper
paprika
2 Tbsp, olive oil

2 Tbsp. butter
1 clove garlic, minced
½ cup dry white wine
2 Tbsp. parsley, chopped
¾ cup sour cream
buttered noodles or Boiled Rice

Cut liver into thin strips about ½ inch thick. Dredge liver in flour seasoned with salt, pepper and a little paprika. Heat olive oil and butter in a large skillet just until foam from butter begins to subside. Add strips of liver and garlic and cook very quickly, turning so that all the liver strips become browned and cooked. This should take about 2 to 4 minutes. Remove liver to a hot platter and keep warm. Pour off most of fat from skillet. Add wine and parsley and cook, stirring, so that brown bits are stirred up from the bottom of the skillet. Add sour cream and heat but *do not boil.* Taste and add more seasoning if desired. Return liver strips to pan and stir well. Serve with buttered noodles or Boiled Rice. Serves 4.

Venison Liver Pâté

cooked venison liver

sweet pickles or bread and butter pickles

stuffed olives

smoked bacon and drippings

black pepper

salt

Tabasco sauce

salad dressing

Grind all ingredients except salt, Tabasco sauce and salad dressing in a food processor. Add the other ingredients and mix well. Make a pâté log by placing the mixture on a clean dish towel and rolling tightly into a log; tie off both ends; place in a refrigerator for 2 hours; unwrap and serve. Serves 4 to 6.

Venison Liver with Gin and Lime Juice

3 Tbsp. butter

1 medium onion, minced

1 Tbsp. arrowroot

1¾ cups canned beef broth

¼ cup fresh lime juice

2 Tbsp. gin

2 Tbsp. apricot jam

1 Tbsp. lime peel, grated

2 tsp. white wine vinegar

1 tsp. tomato sauce

½ tsp. Dijon mustard

dash of Worcestershire sauce

2 Tbsp. safflower oil

2 (¾" thick) slices venison liver

all-purpose flour seasoned with salt and
  pepper

Melt 1 Tbsp. butter in large saucepan over medium-low heat. Add onion and cook until translucent, stirring occasionally. Dissolve arrowroot in ¼ cup broth. Add dissolved arrowroot, remaining stock and next 8 ingredients to saucepan and simmer 35 minutes or until thickened to sauce-like consistency. Purée in a processor; keep warm. Melt remaining 2 Tbsp, butter with oil in large skillet over medium-high heat. Pat venison liver dry. Dredge the liver in seasoned flour, shaking off excess. Add liver to skillet and cook until the liver is crusty outside but still pink inside, about 2 or 3 minutes on first side and 1 minute on second side. To serve, slice and set 1 slice on each plate. Spoon a little sauce over the liver. Pass remaining sauce separately. Serves 4.

Venison Liver with Onions

An old Oak Ridge, Mississippi recipe of Harold W. Webster, Sr.—could easily date to the 1790s or before.

5 slices smoked bacon

3 cups boiling water

1 lb. venison liver, sliced thin

stone ground flour

salt

coarse-ground black pepper

2½ cups yellow onions, thinly sliced

½ tsp. salt (additional)

pepper (additional)

½ cup hot water

Fry the smoked bacon over a very low heat until it is very crisp; remove the bacon from the skillet. Leave the bacon fat in the skillet. Pour boiling water over the sliced venison liver; drain and allow to dry. Dredge the venison liver in flour seasoned with salt and pepper. Place the liver on a plate and let stand for a few minutes. Fry the liver in the hot bacon fat over moderate heat until the liver is lightly browned on both sides. Place the liver in a greased casserole dish and cover with sliced onions. Sprinkle the liver with salt and pepper; add hot water. Crumble the crisp bacon on top of the liver and onions. Cover the dish and bake in a 350-degree oven for 40 minutes. Serves 4 or 5.

Venison Liver with Rice

1 cup boiling water
½ cup long grain rice
1 onion, chopped
2 Tbsp. butter,
    melted

1 cup cooked venison liver, chopped
2 cups canned tomatoes
salt
pepper

Cook rice 5 minutes in boiling water. Drain. Rinse with cold water. Brown onion in butter. Remove onion. Brown venison liver. Place onion in casserole. Add liver. Cover with rice. Add tomatoes and boiling water. Season to taste. Bake in 400-degree oven until tender. Serves 6.

Venison Marrow on Toast

large venison upper leg bones
salt

pepper
toast

Saw the large upper venison marrow bones into 4 to 6-inch lengths. Roast bone pieces in a 350-degree oven for 30 minutes or until fork can easily penetrate the soft marrow portion on the bones. Scoop out the marrow and serve as is or season with salt and pepper. Serve on crisp toast.

Venison Mouffle with Brown Butter Sauce

2 lb. fresh venison mouffles
2 med. white onions, sliced
1 large carrot, chopped
4 celery ribs, with leaves, chopped
6 sprigs parsley

4 peppercorns
4 whole cloves
1 bay leaf
Beurre Noir Sauce

Venison mouffle is the loose covering around the nose and lips of deer. Remove and clean the mouffles. Place the mouffle vegetables and spices in boiling water. After 5 minutes remove any scum that rises to the top. Simmer the mouffle uncovered until tender, about 50 minutes per pound. Drain and reserve cooking liquid. Skin and trim the mouffle. Reheat the mouffle in the cooking liquid. Serve with Beurre Noir Sauce. Serves 2 to 4.

Spiced and Simmered Venison Tongue

3 venison tongues
boiling water
2 med. yellow onions, peeled
2 med. garlic cloves, peeled
½ tsp. basil
2 bay leaves
1 tsp, salt
1 small can of Italian tomatoes

1 large onion, sliced
1 cup tarragon vinegar
¼ lb. butter, melted
1 tsp. McCormicks Hickory Flavored
    Salt
½ tsp. ground nutmeg
¼ tsp. ground cinnamon
⅛ tsp. ground cloves
Mashed potatoes

Clean venison tongues by scrubbing with clear water. Place the tongues in boiling water; add onions, garlic, basil, bay leaves, and salt. Simmer the tongues until they can be easily pierced with a fork. Remove from heat and allow to cool in the cooking liquid until it can be handled easily enough to skin. Transfer the tongues to a shallow baking dish. Mix tomatoes, sliced onion, tarragon vinegar, melted butter, hickory flavored salt, nutmeg, cinnamon and cloves. Pour this mixture over the tongues and bake in a 300-degree oven for 2½ hours. Serve tongues with hot Mashed Potatoes or hot biscuits and butter. Serves 4 to 6.

Venison Tongue Salad Sandwich

1 venison tongue, cooked and ground
green onions, chopped
bean sprouts
celery, chopped

ranch salad dressing
paprika
salt
rye bread, thin-sliced

Combine venison tongue, green onions, bean sprouts and celery. Moisten with salad dressing. Season with paprika and salt. Spread on thin slices of rye bread. Serves 4 to 6.

10

Venison Stroganoffs

Venison Stroganoffs are among the easiest one pot dinners that you can prepare. Slow-cooking stroganoffs will provide you with venison that will melt in your mouth. These slow-cooking recipes are ideal when you have a tough piece of meat or you have stew meat made from scraps and miscellaneous cuts of meat. Very good results can be obtained by pre-cooking and re-warming.

To remove the grease from the top of your stroganoff, lay several layers of paper towel on top of the dish and set it aside to cool. When the dish cools the grease will have solidified on the paper towel and the grease can be easily lifted off with the paper towel.

Bermuda Venison Stroganoff

2 cups canned beef broth
1 lb. venison, cut 2"x1"x¼" thick
 slices
salt
pepper
2 Tbsp. unsalted butter
3 Tbsp. safflower oil
1 small onion, sliced
½ red bell pepper, thinly sliced
½ yellow bell pepper, thinly sliced
½ cup dill pickles, chopped

¼ cup brandy
2 cups heavy cream
5 tsp. paprika
12 oz. fettuccine
1 Tbsp. fresh lemon or lime juice
6 dps. Tabasco sauce
salt
black pepper
sour cream
2 Tbsp. fresh parsley, chopped

Boil beef broth in a medium saucepan until it is reduced to ½ cup. Set reduced broth aside. Season venison with salt and pepper. Melt butter in large skillet over high heat. Add venison and sauté to desired doneness. Transfer to bowl. Heat oil in large deep skillet over high heat. Add onion, bell peppers and pickles and sauté 3 minutes. Remove skillet from heat. Add brandy and ignite with match. When flames go out, add reduced stock, cream and paprika. Simmer until reduced to sauce consistency, stirring occasionally. Meanwhile, cook fettuccine in large pot of boiling salted water. Drain fettuccine thoroughly. Add venison, lemon juice and Tabasco sauce to cream sauce. Season with salt and pepper. Stir until heated. Divide fettuccine among serving plates. Spoon venison and sauce over. Garnish with sour cream and chopped parsley. Serves 4 to 6.

Chili and Tabasco Sauce Venison Stroganoff

2 lbs. venison backstrap or hindquarter steak	2 Tbsp. chili sauce
¼ lb. butter	1 can mushrooms
1 med. yellow onion, minced	dash Tabasco sauce
1 to 2 Tbsp. all-purpose flour	1 Tbsp. Worcestershire sauce
1 can consommé soup	2 tsp. soy sauce
1 garlic clove	cooked noodles
½ pt. sour cream	French fried onion rings

Cut venison into ½" by ¼" strips. Melt butter and briefly brown meat (*rare*). Remove meat and add onions. Cook onions until light brown. Add flour and make base for gravy. Add consommé and the rest of the seasonings. Add to meat and simmer for 1 to 1½ hours. Serve over cooked noodles. Top with French fried onion rings. Just before serving, add sour cream. Serves 2 to 4.

Light & Healthy Venison Stroganoff

2 Tbsp. canola oil	¼ tsp. black pepper
1½ cups white onions, sliced	1 bay leaf
10 mushrooms, sliced	1 cup water
½ lb. venison round steak, cut into ¼" slices or cubes	3 Roma tomatoes
1 Tbsp. all-purpose flour	½ tsp. light Worcestershire sauce
¾ tsp. salt substitute	½ cup fat-free sour cream
	3 cups cooked wide egg noodles

Heat oil over low heat in a 12" skillet. Cook onions slowly until they are brown, stirring occasionally. Add mushrooms and cook for 8 minutes, covered. Remove onions and mushrooms from the skillet, draining as much oil as possible back into the skillet. Add venison and brown slowly on all sides. Sprinkle flour, salt and pepper over meat, cooking about 1 minute longer to toast the flour. Add water and bay leaf and use wooden spatula to scrape brown bits of meat and onion off the bottom of the skillet. Bring the mixture to a boil and stir until liquid thickens slightly. Add chopped tomatoes and Worcestershire sauce. Reduce heat to a simmer; cover and cook for 30 minutes. While venison is cooking, boil noodles according to package directions. When ready to serve, turn off heat under the venison and stir in the fat-free sour cream into the sauce. Serve each portion of meat and sauce over ½ cup of noodles. Serves 4 to 6.

In medieval times, cattle eventually became more important than deer for feeding troops, because cattle provided a meat that is high in fat content which was essential to soldiers who needed to stay warm during cold winters. For the same reason, beef became the staple food for peasants, while the leaner venison became a "royal food" for the gentry who lived in warm protected facilities.

Venison Stroganoff Beef Consommé and Dijon Mustard

2 lbs. venison roast
2 cups onion, chopped
2 garlic cloves, minced
½ cup butter
3 Tbsp. all-purpose flour

¾ tsp. salt
1 can (10½-oz.) beef consommé
2 tsp. Dijon mustard
½ cup sour cream
Boiled Rice

Cut venison into ¼" to ½" pieces. Sauté the onion and garlic in ¼ cup of butter until tender and just brown, Stir in flour, salt, beef consommé, and Dijon mustard. Cook, stirring constantly, until thick. Quickly fry the venison in the remaining butter. *Do not overcook.* Salt and pepper the venison and put it into consommé mixture. Stir in the sour cream. Arrange stroganoff on Boiled Rice and serve. Serves 2 to 4.

Mushrooms and Sherry Stroganoff Venison

1 Tbsp. all-purpose flour
½ tsp. salt
1 Tbsp. butter
1 lb. venison stew meat
1 cup mushrooms
½ cup white onion, chopped
1 clove garlic, minced
2 Tbsp. butter

3 Tbsp. all-purpose flour
1 Tbsp. tomato paste
1 can condensed beef broth
1 cup sour cream
2 Tbsp. cooking sherry
cooked noodles or
Boiled Rice

Combine flour and the salt; dredge venison stew meat in the mixture. Heat skillet, then add butter. When melted, add venison and brown quickly on all sides. Add mushrooms, onion and garlic; cook 3 to 4 minutes, until onion is barely tender. Remove the meat and mushrooms from skillet. Add butter to pan drippings; when melted, blend in flour. Add tomato paste. Slowly pour in beef broth; cook slowly over low heat until meat is tender about 1½ hours. Before serving, stir in sour cream and sherry and heat briefly. Serve with rice or noodles. Serves 2 to 4.

Onion and Mushroom Stroganoff

1 large yellow onion, diced
½ stick butter
1 lb. venison, cut in 1" cubes
½ lb. fresh mushrooms, cut up
1 tsp. seasoning salt

2 tsp. beef bouillon granules
1 cup water
2 cans cream of mushroom soup
1 pkg. (8 oz.) French onion dip
1 lb. wide noodles, cooked

Sauté onions in butter until onions are clear. Add venison and mushrooms. Sprinkle with seasoning salt and brown lightly over medium heat. Dissolve bouillon granules in water and add to mixture. Add mushroom soup and onion dip. Cook over low heat until venison is cooked to less than medium. Serve over cooked noodles. Serves 2 to 4.

Ripe Olive Venison Stroganoff

2 lbs. venison round steak
2 onions, sliced
¼ cup safflower oil
1½ tsp. salt
¼ tsp. pepper

2 beef bouillon cubes
¼ tsp. nutmeg
1 cup pitted ripe olives
1 Tbsp. cornstarch
1 cup sour cream
Boiled Rice

Cut the venison steak diagonally into ⅛" thick strips. Brown the steak and onions in hot oil in a skillet, then add the salt, pepper, ½ cup water, bouillon cubes and nutmeg. Cover the skillet. Simmer for 10 minutes. Slice the olives. Mix the cornstarch with 2 Tbsp. water and stir into the steak mixture. Cook, stirring constantly, until thickened. Stir in the olives and sour cream and heat through, but do not boil. Serve with Boiled Rice. Serves 6 to 8.

Venison Stroganoff with Onions and Biscuit Sour Cream Topping

Stroganoff:
1 lb. venison, ground
1 can (4 oz.) mushroom stems and pieces, drained
1 can (3½-oz.) French-fried onions, reserve ½ cup
1 can (10½-oz.) condensed cream of mushroom soup
½ cup sour cream

1 can (9½ oz.) Pillsbury refrigerated Hungry Jack Flaky Biscuits

Topping:
½ cup sour cream
1 egg
1 tsp. celery seed
½ tsp. salt
1 tsp. green chives chopped

Brown ground venison; drain well. In an ungreased 2½ or 3-quart deep casserole, combine ground venison, mushrooms and French fried onions; toss lightly. Bring undiluted mushroom soup to a boil; stir in ½ cup sour cream. Separate biscuit dough into 10 biscuits. Cut each biscuit in half, forming 20 half circles. Pour warm soup mixture evenly over meat; immediately stand biscuits, cut side down, in a circle inward around the edge of the casserole. Sprinkle reserved onions between biscuits. Make topping by combining sour cream, egg, celery seed and salt in a small mixing bowl. Pour Topping over biscuits. Bake at 375 degrees for 25 to 30 minutes until golden brown. Add chopped green chives. Serves 6 to 8.

Venison Stroganoff with Tomato and Mushrooms

1 lb. venison steak cut in long, thin strips
3 Tbsp. all-purpose flour
salt
pepper
Crisco
1 white onion, coarsely chopped

1 cup tomato juice
1½ cups water
1 tsp. sugar
1 can mushrooms
½ cup sour cream

Dredge venison with flour seasoned with salt and pepper. Lightly brown meat and onion in Crisco. Add onion, tomato juice, water and sugar. Simmer until tender. Ten minutes before serving, add mushrooms and sour cream. Serves 4.

11

Venison Chilies

There are as many chili recipes as there are types of chili peppers in Old Mexico. Chilies have several things in common: meat, chili powder, tomatoes, garlic and onion. Other than that, anything goes.

If you like your chili with or without beans you will find a recipe here that you will like. If by chance you don't find a recipe you like, modify the recipe to your liking or substitute your favorite chili recipe with venison and a little ground beef or pork fat.

There is absolutely nothing short of the use of Truffles or Indian Curry Powder that will spoil your chili. When I make chili, I make it with whatever Anne has in the refrigerator, pantry, garden or root cellar.

When grinding venison for chili, an average mix for the ground meat is 66% venison to 33% (10# venison to 5# moist meat)l. Some additives are bacon or pork/beef fat. A good bacon additive is to purchase a slab of smoked bacon and remove and discard the skin.

Since venison is virtually fat free, with the substitution of mushrooms you can convert most any of these recipes to fat free. This procedure has not been tested on all of these recipes. You will need to experiment. Make your ground meat by beginning with 25% (by weight) of mushrooms to 75% (by weight) of venison; break off a small piece and fry it. If the ground meat is dry, add more mushrooms to the mixture and test it again.

Chili Con Carne

3 lbs. venison round steak, cut into ½" cubes
¼ cup bacon fat
2 cups yellow onions, finely chopped
3 cloves garlic, finely chopped
2 tsp. salt

4 Tbsp. chili powder
2 tsp. ground cumin
1 tsp. oregano
1 tsp. crushed red pepper flakes
1 can beef broth

Dry the venison with paper towels. Heat half of the bacon fat in a large skillet and brown the meat over high heat. Remove the meat from the skillet and set aside. Heat the remaining bacon fat in the same skillet, and cook the onions and garlic over moderate heat 5 minutes. Remove the skillet from the heat and add the salt, spices, and browned meat. Add enough beef stock to cover the beef. Stir thoroughly. Cover and simmer 1 to 1½ hours or until the meat is tender. Stir the chili occasionally to prevent sticking. Carefully skim off the fat. Serves 6 to 8.

Black Bean and Venison Chili

2 cups black beans
1 lb. ham hocks
3 tsp. salt, divided
2 Tbsp. safflower oil
1 lb. 60% ground venison
2 cups onion, chopped
1 med. carrot, chopped
1 med. red bell pepper, chopped

1 tsp. salt
2 Tbsp. chili powder
2 Tbsp. garlic, minced
2 tsp. cumin, ground
½ tsp. red pepper
diced tomato
cheddar cheese, shredded
sour cream

Cover black beans with 2" of water and soak overnight. Drain and transfer to a Dutch oven and add 7 cups of water and ham hocks. Bring to a boil; reduce heat and simmer for 30 minutes. Add 2 tsp. salt; cover and cook for 30 minutes or until beans are soft. Heat oil in a skillet over medium-high heat; add ground venison and brown, stirring to break up meat. Add chopped onions, carrot, red bell pepper, salt, chili powder, garlic, cumin and red pepper to venison and cook for 10 minutes more. Remove ham hocks. If beans are soupy, remove 1 cup of the liquid. Add venison to beans and simmer for 10 minutes. Serve with diced tomato, cheddar cheese and sour cream. Serves 6.

Chili Venison Tacos with Corn and Green Olives

¼ cup chili powder
6 garlic cloves, crushed
5 Tbsp. fresh lime juice, strained
3 Tbsp. safflower oil
1 Tbsp. ground cumin
2½ lbs. boneless venison stewing meat, cut
    1½" cubes
1 (28-oz.) can Italian plum tomatoes, drained
    and crushed
2 cups canned beef broth
1 (12-oz.) bottle dark beer
3 Tbsp. safflower oil
1 large onion, chopped
2 fresh jalapeño chilies, minced

1 (10-oz.) pkg. frozen corn, thawed and
    drained
25 pimiento-stuffed green olives, sliced
½ cup pimientos, drained and
    coarsely chopped
salt
pepper
20 taco shells
12 oz. sharp cheddar cheese, shredded
½ bunch romaine lettuce, finely
    shredded
chopped seeded tomatoes
hot salsa
sour cream

Mix chili powder, garlic, lime juice, 3 Tbsp. oil and cumin in large bowl to form paste. Add venison and mix until coated. Refrigerate 24 hours, stirring occasionally. Position rack in lower third of oven and preheat to 350 degrees. Combine marinated venison, canned tomatoes, broth and beer in Dutch oven. Bring to boil over high heat. Cover and transfer to oven and bake 45 minutes. Uncover and continue baking until venison is tender, about 45 minutes. Cool. Shred venison. Return to cooking liquid. Cover and refrigerate overnight. Heat 3 Tbsp. oil in large skillet over medium-low heat. Add onion and jalapeños. Cover and cook until onion is tender and lightly browned, stirring occasionally, about 15 minutes. Strain venison cooking liquid into skillet. Bring to boil. Reduce heat and simmer uncovered until sauce is thickened and reduced to ½ cup, stirring occasionally, about 50 minutes. Mix in venison. Add corn, olives and pimientos and stir over medium heat until just heated through, about 5 minutes. Season with salt and pepper to taste.

To assemble: Half-fill taco shells with venison mixture. Top with cheese, lettuce and chopped tomatoes. Serve immediately, passing salsa and sour cream separately. Serves 10 to 15.

Chili with Venison and Beans

5 lbs. ground venison
1 lb. ground pork
3 large yellow onions, chopped
4 cloves garlic, minced
3 chill peppers, minced
½ box cumin seeds
6 cups water

2 Tbsp. white vinegar
1 cup tomato catsup
1 cup tomato sauce
2½ Tbsp. chili powder
4 cans chill beans
salt to taste

Mix venison and pork in a large skillet and cook until brown, stirring frequently. Add the remaining ingredients and mix well. Simmer for 25 to 35 minutes or until most of the liquid has evaporated. Serves 12.

Chunky Venison Chili with Dumplings

2 cups venison, cut into ½" cubes
1 cup water
1 (15-oz.) can tomato sauce
1 (1¾-oz.) pkg. chill seasoning mix
1 (15-oz.) can black beans, undrained
1 (8-oz.) can kidney beans, undrained

1 (8-oz.) can whole kernel corn, undrained
Quick Dumplings
Tabasco sauce to taste
salt and pepper to taste
½ cup Cheddar cheese, shredded

Mix venison, water, tomato sauce and seasoning mix in a 4-qt. Dutch oven. Heat to boiling; reduce heat. Cover and simmer 10 minutes, stirring constantly. Stir in beans and corn. Prepare Quick Dumplings. Heat chili to boiling; reduce heat to low. Drop 12 spoonfuls dumplings into the hot chili. Cook uncovered 10 minutes. Cover and cook 10 minutes longer. Season to taste. Sprinkle with cheese. Cover and cook about 3 minutes or until cheese is melted. Serves 6.

2-Alarm Venison Chili

1 cup green bell pepper, minced
1 cup green onion, minced
Wesson oil
2 lbs. ground venison

1 (8-oz.) can tomato sauce
2 cups water
1 pkg. (all pks.) 2-Alarm chill mix
hamburger buns

Remove all white and connecting tissues from the venison and coarse-grind one time. Sauté green bell pepper and green onions in a little Wesson oil. Add the ground venison and quickly sear until just barely brown. Add the tomato sauce, water and all packets in one package of 2-Alarm chili mix. Cover and cook for 3 hours over very low heat. If needed add a little water. Serve open-faced on hamburger buns.

Nevada-Style Venison Chili

3 lbs, coarsely ground venison
1 cup onions, diced
1 cup chili powder
1 Tbsp. paprika
1 Tbsp. cayenne pepper
2 cloves garlic, minced
2 bay leaves

1 (20-oz.) can tomato purée
1 qt. water
2 Tbsp. cornstarch
salt
black pepper
canned kidney beans

Quickly sear venison. When just browned, add remaining ingredients except corn starch and salt and pepper. Simmer over very low heat for 2 hours. Add kidney beans and simmer for 1 hour more. Thicken with cornstarch. Season with salt and pepper. Serves 2 to 4.

Green Chili Venison
with Tomato and Acorn Squash

1 lb. tomatoes, peeled, seeded and cut into
   large chunks
1 tsp. coarse salt
½ large avocado, peeled and diced
1 Tbsp. fresh lime or lemon juice
2 Tbsp. safflower oil
1 lb. venison, cut 2"x½"x½", pat dry
1½ cups acorn squash, peeled, seeded and
   chopped
½ small onion, thinly sliced

2 Tbsp. fresh chilies, minced
1 large garlic clove, minced
1 tsp. ground cumin
1 tsp. ground coriander
¼ tsp. red pepper
⅓ cup canned chicken broth
3 Tbsp. dry white wine
1½ Tbsp. fresh cilantro or parsley,
   diced

Toss tomatoes with ¼ tsp. salt in colander. Let drain 30 minutes, shaking colander occasionally. Combine avocado with 1 tsp. juice in a small bowl. Set aside. Heat 1 tsp. oil in a skillet over high heat. Add venison and brown on both sides. Remove from skillet. Heat remaining oil in same skillet. Add squash, onion, chilies, garlic, cumin, coriander and red pepper and stir. Blend in broth and wine, scraping up browned bits, and cook 1 minute. Cover and cook until squash is almost tender, about 2 minutes. Add tomatoes, meat and any exuded juices and cook about 1½ minutes for medium rare. Add remaining salt, avocado, remaining lime juice and cilantro and toss well. Serves 2 to 4.

Minnesota Crock Pot Venison Chili

1 lb. small dried red chili beans, soaked
   overnight and drained
2 cups venison pieces
1 Tbsp. salt
6 cups water

1 large yellow onion, chopped
3 cloves garlic, minced
2 tsp. oregano leaves
2 tsp. ground cumin
1½ tsp. dried sage, crumbled

Put all ingredients in a crock pot, cover and cook on high heat for 1 hour. Turn crock pot heat to low and cook for 8 to 10 hours more. Chili may need to be thickened with a flour-water paste. Serves 6 to 8.

Hot Venison Chili, Low Sodium

2 lbs. venison, diced
1 Tbsp. safflower oil
1¾ cups onion, chopped
1 cup celery, diced
3 cloves garlic, crushed
3 cups water
3 (14½-oz.) cans no-salt-added tomatoes, undrained and chopped
2 (10-oz.) cans diced tomatoes with green chilies, undrained
1½ Tbsp. reduced-sodium Worcestershire sauce

2 Tbsp, chili powder
¼ tsp. dried whole thyme
¼ tsp. dried whole oregano
¼ tsp. ground cumin
¼ tsp, salt substitute
1 (16-oz.) can no-salt-added kidney beans, undrained
3 cups iceberg lettuce, finely shredded
¾ cup shredded reduced-fat sharp Cheddar cheese
¾ cup tomato, diced

Brown venison in hot oil in a Dutch oven, stirring until it crumbles. Stir in onion, celery, and garlic; cook until tender. Add water and next 8 ingredients; bring to a boil. Reduce heat, and simmer, uncovered, 2 hours, stirring occasionally. Add beans, and cook 30 minutes. Ladle chili into individual bowls. Top each serving with ¼ cup lettuce, 1 Tbsp. cheese, and 1 Tbsp. tomato. Serves 8 to 10.

Mexican Venison Soup

1 lb. ground venison
1 med. yellow onion, chopped
4 med. potatoes, cubed
2½ cups water, divided
1 (16-oz.) can stewed tomatoes, undrained

2 tsp. ground cumin
2 tsp. chili powder
¼ tsp. garlic salt
1 tsp. salt
⅛ tsp. black pepper

Cook ground venison and onion until venison begins to brown; stir to crumble meat; drain well. Combine potatoes and 1½ cups water in a large Dutch oven; bring to a boil. Reduce heat; cover, and simmer 15 minutes. Add tomatoes, remaining water, and seasonings; bring to a boil. Add meat mixture; reduce heat, cover and simmer 1 hour. Serves 6 to 8.

Spicy Venison Chili

1 lb. ground venison
⅛ lb. ground pork
2 Tbsp. canola oil
4 cloves garlic, minced
1 med. red bell pepper, chopped
1 med. green bell pepper, chopped
1 cup celery, chopped
2 (14½-oz.) cans diced tomatoes with liquid
1 (16-oz.) can kidney beans, rinsed and drained

1 (6-oz.) can tomato paste
¾ cup water
2 tsp. dark brown sugar
1 tsp. dried oregano
1 tsp. chili powder
¼ tsp. dried red pepper flakes
¼ tsp. red pepper
dash of Tabasco sauce

Mix ground venison and pork. In a Dutch oven, brown meat and onion in canola oil until meat is no longer pink; drain. Stir in garlic, peppers and celery; cook 5 minutes. Add remaining ingredients; bring to a boil. Reduce heat; cover and simmer over very low heat for 2 hours. Can be covered, cooled, refrigerated overnight and warmed and served the next day. Serves 6 to 8.

Indiana Venison Chili

2 lbs. course-ground venison
½ cup beef fat
2 cans kidney beans
2 (8-oz.) cans tomato sauce
3 Tbsp. chili powder
½ tsp. red pepper

½ tsp. garlic powder
½ tsp. oregano leaves, crushed
½ tsp. salt
½ cup dehydrated onions, minced
1 cup water

In a Dutch oven, sauté the coarse-ground venison with the beef fat until just brown. Add the remaining ingredients and simmer for 4 hours, stirring occasionally. Add water if chili is too thick. Add salt and red pepper to taste. Serves 2 to 4.

Venison Chili with Tomatoes and Kidney Beans

2 lbs. venison, coarsely ground
¼ cup canola oil
1 cup white onion, chopped
2 cloves garlic, minced
1 large green bell pepper, cut julienne
3 Tbsp. chili powder

2 Tsp. sugar
3½ cups whole tomatoes
1 cup tomato sauce
1 cup water
½ tsp. salt
2 cups cooked kidney beans

In a large heavy pot or Dutch oven, just barely brown the venison in the canola oil; add the onion, garlic and green bell pepper. Simmer 5 minutes, stirring constantly. Add chili powder, sugar, tomatoes, tomato sauce, water and salt. Simmer for 3 hours. Thirty minutes before serving, add the kidney beans. For thicker chili, mix 1 Tbsp. flour with 3 Tbsp. water and slowly add to chili before adding kidney beans.

Venison Chili for 70 to 80

21 lbs. ground venison, just browned and
    drained
3 lbs, ground beef suet
9 (16-oz.) cans pork and beans, undrained
9 (16-oz.) cans kidney beans, rinsed and
    drained
9 (28-oz.) cans tomatoes with liquid, cut up
9 (29-oz.) cans tomato sauce
3 lbs. white or yellow onions, chopped
7½ cups celery, chopped with leaves

9 large green bell peppers, finely
    chopped
9 bay leaves
2 Tbsp. salt
5 Tbsp. chili powder
1 Tbsp. paprika
1 Tbsp. black pepper
1 Tbsp. ground cumin
1 Tbsp. cayenne pepper

Combine all of the ingredients in three large Dutch ovens. Cover and cook over low heat for 4 to 5 hours. Add additional water if required. Chili can be cooked the day before, refrigerated and rewarmed the next day. Makes about 18 to 20 qts. Serves about 70 to 80.

Venison Chili with Bacon and Dried Red Chilies

1 lb. bacon, chopped
2 lbs. venison round steak, coarsely ground
½ cup chili powder
1 tsp. salt
4 large yellow onions, chopped
1 (16-oz.) can diced tomatoes, undrained
½ tsp. baking soda

2 (15-oz.) cans pinto beans, undrained
3 whole large red chilies
3 cloves garlic
1¼ Tbsp. cumin
1 Tbsp. Worcestershire sauce
Tabasco sauce to taste

Divide bacon between 2 heavy large skillets and fry over medium heat until crisp. Remove bacon and drain on paper towels. Do not clean skillets. Brown venison with chili powder and salt in 1 skillet over medium-high heat. Sauté onions in other skillet over medium heat until clear. Combine tomatoes with liquid and baking soda in Dutch oven and bring to boil over high heat. Add beans with liquid, red chilies, garlic, cumin and Worcestershire sauce. Stir in bacon, venison and onions. Reduce heat to low, cover and simmer 5 hours, stirring occasionally. Cool completely. Refrigerate, covered, at least 8 hours or overnight. After cooling, cover chili and simmer over low heat, stirring occasionally for 7 or more hours. Remove and discard dried chilies and garlic. Serve hot. Serves 10 to 12.

Unlike white tails that thrive in areas of dense cover with good concealment, mule deer are more apt to be found in open upland habitats. The classic mule deer habitat is rough, steep canyons, sparsely vegetated, with brushy pockets that carve their way down through open grasslands.

Venison Chili with Kidney Beans

½ lb. bulk hot pork sausage
2 lbs. venison, cubed
2 med. yellow onions, chopped
1 med. green bell pepper, chopped
2 cloves garlic, minced
3 Tbsp. chili powder

1 Tbsp. salt
2 (15-oz.) cans kidney beans
1 qt. water
⅛ tsp. cayenne pepper
1 tsp. paprika
Boiled Rice

Just brown venison and sausage in a Dutch oven. Remove sausage and venison from saucepan. Sauté onions and bell pepper. Return the sausage and venison to the Dutch oven; then add the remaining ingredients with enough water to cover the meats. Simmer over low heat for 3 to 4 hours, stirring occasionally. Add water as needed. Serve over rice. Serves 6 to 8.

Venison Chili with Lemon, Beans & Tomato Juice

2 lbs, ground venison
juice of 1 lemon
bacon drippings
1 large yellow onion, chopped
2 cloves garlic, minced
salt
black pepper

3 Tbsp, chili powder
1 tsp. comino seed
½ tsp. oregano
1 (46-oz.) can tomato juice
2 (#2) cans kidney beans
3 cups cold water
½ cup all-purpose flour

Pour lemon juice over the ground venison. Brown the venison in bacon drippings; add onion, garlic, salt and pepper. Cook until well browned. Add spices, tomato juice and beans. Thoroughly mix flour with cold water and add slowly to chili mixture. Simmer over low heat for 2 hours. Add water if needed. Serves 4 to 6.

Kentucky-Style Venison Chili with Pinto Beans

½ lb. dry pinto beans
2 Tbsp. salt
5 cups canned tomatoes
1½ lbs. yellow onions, chopped
3 green bell peppers, chopped
1½ tsp. safflower oil
½ cup parsley, chopped
2 cloves garlic, crushed

2½ lbs. coarse-ground venison
1 lb. ground pork
1½ tsp. Accent
butter
½ cup chili powder
1½ tsp. black pepper
1½ tsp. cumin seeds

Wash dry pinto beans and soak overnight in water. The next day, wash beans again and simmer in salted water until tender for about 4 hours. Simmer tomatoes in separate saucepan for 5 minutes. Sauté onions and green pepper in safflower oil; add onions and bell peppers to the tomatoes and cook until tender. Add parsley and garlic. Sprinkle meats with Accent. Melt butter in a Dutch oven and sauté meats until just brown. Drain off grease and add the tomato and onion mixture to the meats. Stir in the chili powder and cook 10 minutes; add beans, pepper, and cumin seeds. Cover and simmer over low heat for 2 hours. Uncover and simmer 30 minutes more. Serves 8-10.

Venison Chili with Toasted Caraway Seeds

1 lb. ground venison
1 (15-oz.) can red kidney beans, undrained
1 (14½-oz.) can stewed tomatoes, chopped
2 med. yellow onions, chopped
1 small green bell pepper, cored and
  chopped
1 Tbsp. chili powder

2 med. garlic cloves, minced
salt
black pepper
1 tsp. all-purpose flour
1 tsp. caraway seeds, toasted and
  ground

Cook venison in large saucepan over medium heat until browned, stirring frequently, about 15 minutes. Pour off drippings. Reduce heat to low. Add next 6 ingredients. Season with salt and pepper. Simmer 30 minutes, stirring occasionally. Cover and simmer 30 more minutes. Heat flour in heavy small skillet over low heat until light brown, about 10 minutes. Add ground caraway; stir into chili. Cook 5 more minutes. Serve hot. Serves 6.

Deer move most often and for the greatest distances during spring and fall. In late spring, does may travel in search of fawning sites, although adult females move less than other deer. Greater travels are made by yearlings, on their own for the first time. Travel increases in fall after the harvest, as deer leave croplands and begin mating activities. In some areas where cover is extensive and other requirements are met, a deer may live its entire life and die within one or a few square miles.

12

Venison Stews

Stew was made to order for venison. A slow and long-cooking stew will make the most difficult venison a gastronomic delight. There is just something about walking into the house and smelling slow-cooking venison stew.

To remove the grease from the top of your stew, lay several layers of paper towels on top of the dish and set it aside to cool. When the dish cools, the grease will have solidified on the paper towels and the grease can be easily lifted off with the paper towels. Re-warm and serve.

Basic Mulligan Venison Stew

3 lbs. venison stew meat
2 Tbsp. butter
2 qts. water
1 Tbsp. salt
1½ cups pasta

2 (15-oz.) cans chili con carne
salt
pepper
Crackling Bread

Cut venison stew meat into 1-inch squares. Brown in butter. Cover with water, salt and boil until the meat is done. Add water to bring back to its original level. Add 1½ cups macaroni, spaghetti, noodles, etc. When pasta is soft, add chili con carne. Salt and pepper to taste. Cook only long enough for the mulligan to thicken. Serve with Crackling Bread. Serves 2 to 4.

Braised Venison Stew

½ lb. salt pork, cubed
6 to 8 lbs. boned venison forequarter,
   butterflied
5 Tbsp. all-purpose flour
2 tsp. salt
1 tsp. black pepper
5 Tbsp. lard

1 cup water
2 Tbsp. vinegar
⅔ cup onion, chopped fine
1 cup carrots, diced
2 Tbsp. green bell pepper, chopped fine
1 cup stewed tomatoes
1 med. apple, pared and chopped

Place the pork cubes down the inside center of the butterflied venison forequarter. Roll and tie the venison with cotton butcher twine. Mix and sift the flour, salt and pepper. Dredge in the seasoned flour mixture. Quickly brown the venison on all sides in hot lard. Place venison in a Dutch oven; add water and vinegar; cover and simmer over very low heat for 2½ to 3 hours. Add the remaining ingredients and simmer for 1 hour more. Use the pot liquid as the sauce and serve with the venison. Serves 4 to 6.

Apple Cider Venison Stew

3 Tbsp. all-purpose flour
1 tsp. salt
½ tsp. pepper
1 lb. venison stew meat, cut in 1" pieces
2 Tbsp. safflower oil
1 cup apple cider
½ cup water

1 Tbsp. apple cider vinegar
½ tsp. dried thyme
2 large carrots, cut 1" pieces
1 celery rib, cut 1" pieces
1 large potato, peeled and cubed
1 medium yellow onion, sliced

Combine flour, salt and pepper; add venison and dredge. Brown venison in oil in a Dutch oven. Add apple cider, water, apple cider vinegar, and thyme; bring to a boil. Reduce heat; cover and simmer for 2 hours or until meat is tender. Add carrots, celery, potato and onion; return to a boil. Reduce heat; cover and simmer for 45 minutes or until vegetables are tender. Serves 4.

Venison and Red Wine Stew

2 to 3 lbs. venison meat, any cuts
bacon fat
2 large white onions, sliced
3 Tbsp. all-purpose flour
2 Tbsp. red wine vinegar

3 Tbsp. tomato catsup
1 Tbsp. sugar
salt
black pepper

Cut venison into 1" pieces and brown in bacon fat. Add onions and continue browning. When browned stir in flour, vinegar, tomato catsup, and sugar. Salt and pepper to taste. Cover venison with water and bake in 375-degree oven for 2 to 3 hours, or until tender, adding water as needed to keep meat covered. When done, thicken gravy and serve. Serves 4 to 6.

Montana Venison Stew with Vegetables

1½ cups flour
salt
black pepper
4 cups venison backstrap, diced
1 cup cooking oil
7 cups water

1 bay leaf
1 med. yellow onion, chopped
2 med. clove garlic, chopped
2 med. potatoes, cubed
2 med. carrots, cubed

Mix and sift flour, salt and black pepper. Dredge venison in seasoned flour and quickly brown in cooking oil. Reserve the remaining flour mixture. Place bay leaf in boiling water; place browned venison in water. Reduce heat to a simmer. Add remaining flour to hot grease in skillet, reduce the heat and make a roux; adding more oil if needed to achieve the desired thickness. Making the roux should take about 30 minutes. Stir to prevent burning the flour. After desired brownness is reached, add the chopped onion and garlic and sauté for about 2 minutes. Add vegetables to the venison mixture. Cover and simmer for about 4 hours. At the end of the third hour, add potatoes and carrots and continue to cook. Add salt and pepper to taste. Serves 6 to 8.

Manzo Stracotto-Style Venison

1¼ lbs. venison, any cut
1 tsp. salt
⅛ tsp. black pepper
2 Tbsp. all-purpose flour
2 Tbsp. Crisco
1 (15½-oz.) can spaghetti sauce with
   mushrooms

1 cup water
8 small yellow onions
8 small carrots, peeled
3 potatoes, peeled

Cut the venison into 1" pieces. Mix the salt, pepper and flour and dredge venison with seasoned flour. Melt the Crisco in a skillet. Add the venison and brown well on all sides. Add spaghetti sauce and water and bring to a boil. Cover and reduce heat. Simmer for about 1 hour and 30 minutes. Add the onions, carrots and potatoes and simmer about 1 hour longer or until vegetables are tender. Serves 4.

Mary Sims' Venison Stew

This recipe will make tough cuts of venison melt in your mouth. Mary Sims first cooked this for me in Leakesville, Mississippi. Thank you, Mary.

2 cups venison, cut 2" cubes
safflower or canola oil
flour
salt
pepper
water
5 carrots, cut 2" pieces

5 medium onions, quartered
5 medium potatoes, quartered
Tabasco sauce
salt
pepper
Boiled Rice

Remove all fat and tough fibers. Score with a sharp knife the white tissue on the outside of the muscle groups. Dredge venison in flour seasoned to taste with salt and pepper. If need be, work flour into venison with your fingers. Pour ½" of oil in a Dutch oven and heat. Place dredged venison, a few pieces at a time, in hot oil and quickly sear all sides; then remove to paper towels to drain. Pour off excess oil from Dutch oven. Place browned venison, carrots, onions and potatoes in Dutch oven. Add 1 cup of water and cover pot. Turn heat on lowest level. Simmer for 3 to 5 hours. As venison has a tendency to stick and burn, occasionally scrape bottom of Dutch oven with a metal spatula. Add water as needed to keep gravy from thickening too much. After 1 hour, season with salt, pepper and Tabasco sauce to taste. Recipe can be cooked one day, refrigerated and warmed and served the next day. Serve over Boiled Rice or egg noodles. Serves 4 to 6.

Lincoln's Second Inaugural dinner menu featured "Roast Venison with Herb Crust."

New Jersey-Style Venison Stew

3 to 4 lbs. venison, cubed
all-purpose flour
3 Tbsp. bacon fat
1½ cups hot water
1 cup Burgundy
½ tsp. thyme
½ tsp. marjoram

½ tsp. basil
1 tsp. parsley flakes
1 large yellow onion, sliced
1½ tsp. salt
½ tsp. black pepper
3 carrots, quartered
3 potatoes, peeled and quartered

Remove fat, bones and connective tissue from the venison and cut into bite-size pieces; dredge in flour. Quickly brown the venison in hot bacon fat in a Dutch oven. Add hot water, Burgundy, spices, onions, salt and pepper. Cover Dutch oven and bring to a boil. Lower heat and simmer for 2 hours. Add carrots and potatoes. Cover and simmer for 1 hour more; add more hot water if needed. Serve when venison is tender and vegetables done. Serve hot. Serves 4 to 6.

Mogul Venison Curry

½ cup safflower or canola oil
2 lbs. stewing venison, cut 1½" to 2" cubes, patted dry
1½ lbs. beef soup bones, cut into 2" pieces
1 (3"-long) cinnamon stick
10 whole cloves
8 whole cardamom pods
3 bay leaves
1 lb. yellow onions, coarsely chopped
2 Tbsp. ground coriander
2 Tbsp. paprika

1 Tbsp. ground cumin
2 tsp. salt
1½ tsp, ground turmeric
6 large garlic cloves, minced
6 Serrano chilies, minced with seeds
1 (2"-long) piece fresh ginger, peeled and minced
¾ lb. tomatoes, cored and puréed with skins
1½ cups minced fresh cilantro
Boiled Rice

Heat ¼ cup oil in large Dutch oven over high heat. Add venison and brown on all sides, about 2 minutes. Transfer to bowl using slotted spoon. Add bones to Dutch oven and brown on all sides, about 2 minutes. Add bones to venison using slotted spoon. Add remaining ¼ cup oil to Dutch oven and heat 1 minute over high heat; reduce heat to medium. Add next 4 ingredients and stir until spices sizzle, about 2 minutes. Add onions and cook until brown, stirring frequently, about 15 minutes.

Add coriander, paprika, 1 Tbsp. cumin, salt and turmeric, and stir 30 seconds. Add garlic, chilies and ginger and stir 2 minutes. Add tomato purée and cook 5 minutes, stirring frequently. Add venison, bones and 1½ cups water and bring to boil, stirring frequently. Reduce heat to medium-low. Cover; cook until venison is tender, stirring occasionally 1¾ hours. Uncover curry. Discard bones. Reduce heat to low and cook until liquid is reduced to glaze, stirring frequently, about 15 minutes. Mix in roasted ground cumin. Can be prepared 1 day ahead. Cool, cover and refrigerate. Rewarm over low heat before continuing, stirring constantly. Transfer curry to a heated bowl. Sprinkle with cilantro. Serve, passing rice separately. Serves 6.

Venison Stew with Onions and Carrots

2½ lbs. venison, cubed
2 celery stems
1 med. green bell pepper
½ lb. carrots
1 large white onion
1 bunch green onions

3 Tbsp. all-purpose flour
thyme
bay leaf
salt
pepper

Sauté venison in a Dutch oven until just brown; add celery, green pepper, carrots, white onions, and green onions. With a little of the pan drippings, make roux with flour. Add the roux to the Dutch oven. Then add water and mix thoroughly. Cook over very low heat until the venison is tender, about 3 hours. Serves 2 to 4.

Mushroom Venison Stew
with Hot Egg Noodles

3 med. onions, sliced
½ cup bacon drippings
2 lbs. venison stew meat, cut 1" squares
4 Tbsp. all-purpose flour
1 cup ruby port
10½ oz. condensed beef broth

1 large pinch of thyme
1 large pinch of marjoram
salt and pepper to taste
1 lb. fresh mushrooms, sliced
hot egg noodles

In a large cast iron Dutch oven, sauté the onions in one half of the bacon drippings until golden. Remove onions to a bowl. Add the remaining bacon fat to the Dutch oven and quickly brown the venison cubes. When all is just browned, return it to the pan and stir in the flour. Add the port and about three-quarters of the broth, thyme, and marjoram, salt and pepper. Cover and simmer very gently for about 3 hours. Add onions and mushrooms and cook for another hour. Serve the stew over hot noodles. Serves 8 to 10.

Ragout of Venison Catalan

5 lbs. venison forequarter, cut 1½" cubes
1½ cups pitted prunes
1 cup Greek olives packed in brine, drained
1 (7-oz.) jar roasted red peppers, drained and chopped
⅓ cup red wine vinegar
⅓ cup safflower oil
1 (3½-oz.) jar capers with 4½ tsp. liquid
3 Tbsp. garlic, minced
3 Tbsp. dried oregano, minced
1 Tbsp. pure ground hot chili powder
2 tomatoes, peeled and diced
1 cup dry white wine
½ cup dark brown sugar, firmly packed
½ cup (or more) concentrated beef broth
2 Tbsp. red wine vinegar
2 Tbsp. water
2 Tbsp. all-purpose flour
fresh cilantro or parsley, chopped
saffron rice

Mix first 10 ingredients in large non-aluminum bowl. Cover and refrigerate overnight, turning occasionally. Preheat oven to 325 degrees. Transfer venison mixture to large Dutch oven. Mix in tomatoes, wine, sugar and ½ cup broth. Bring to a boil over high heat. Cover and bake for 45 minutes, adding more broth if necessary to keep venison just covered. Uncover pan and cook until venison is tender, about 15 minutes. Cool to room temperature. Cover and refrigerate overnight. Lift grease from the top of the cold stew. Bring stew to a boil over medium heat. Gradually add 2 Tbsp. vinegar and 2 Tbsp. water to flour in a small bowl to form a paste. Gradually stir flour paste into stew. Reduce heat and simmer until sauce thickens slightly, stirring frequently, about 5 minutes. Top with cilantro and serve with saffron rice. Serves 12.

Savory Venison Stew

2 lbs. venison, cubed
2 Tbsp. bacon fat
4 cups boiling water
1 tsp. lemon juice
1 tsp. Worcestershire sauce
1 clove of garlic
1 bay leaf
1 Tbsp. salt
½ tsp. pepper
½ tsp. paprika
dash of allspice or cloves
1 tsp. sugar
6 carrots, diced
1 lb. small yellow onions
2 cups potatoes diced

Cut the venison in 1½" cubes and brown in fat in a large cast iron skillet. Add the boiling water, lemon juice, Worcestershire sauce, garlic, bay leaves, salt, pepper, paprika, allspice and sugar, and simmer for 2 hours. Add the carrots, onions and potatoes and cook until the vegetables are done. Serves 4.

White-tailed doe and fawn(s) require only approximately .4 acres of pasture.

Red Venison Shank Stew

Carrots, onions and a generous amount of ginger highlight this fiery dish, traditionally spooned over thin egg noodles in clear broth.

Wok-type stir-cooking skillet
2 lbs. boneless venison shanks, cut 1½" x
   2" pieces
1 medium yellow onion, thinly sliced
10 large ⅛"-thick slices fresh ginger
5 cloves garlic, thinly sliced
4 small dried red chilies
1 star anise (available at Oriental markets)
2 Tbsp. teriyaki sauce
4 Tbsp. brown soy sauce
1 Tbsp. brown bean sauce

1 tsp. sugar
½ tsp. salt
7 tsp. hot chili oil (available at Oriental
   markets)
3 cups water
3 large carrots, cut on diagonal into
   ¾"x½" pieces
1 Tbsp. cornstarch
5 Tbsp. green onions, minced
thin egg noodles in clear broth

Bring large pot of water to boil. Add venison and boil 10 seconds. Drain; rinse under running water 1 minute. Combine onion, ginger, garlic, chilies and star anise in bowl. Blend soy sauces, brown bean sauce, sugar and salt in another bowl. Heat hot chili oil in wok over high heat 1 minute. Add onion mixture to wok and stir-fry 2 minutes. Add venison and stir-fry 3 minutes. Transfer to saucepan. Add 2¾ cups water and bring to boil. Reduce heat, cover and simmer until venison is tender but not falling apart, stirring constantly, about 1½ to 1¾ hours, adding more water if necessary. Add carrots to venison. Cover and simmer until tender, stirring occasionally, about 20 minutes. Remove chilies, ginger and star anise. Increase heat to high. Dissolve cornstarch in remaining ¼ cup water. Add to stew and stir for a little more than 1 minute. Transfer to platter. Garnish with green onions. Serve immediately.

Italian Flavored Venison Rehbraten

6 venison back steaks, cut ½" to 1"
1 box pickling spices
1 bottle (8-oz.) Wishbone Italian
   salad dressing

1½ cups Burgundy
powdered meat tenderizer
all-purpose flour
real butter

Cut venison into long and thin strips. Make marinade by mixing pickling spices, Wishbone Italian salad dressing, and Burgundy. Layer a flat shallow dish with venison strips and enough marinade to cover the venison. Cover the dish and place in the refrigerator for 4 days. Remove the venison, drain well, and wipe dry. Sprinkle both sides with the powdered meat tenderizer. Flour the meat on both sides and brown in margarine in a cast iron Dutch oven. Strain the marinade into a shallow baking dish. Add to venison and when it is simmering briskly, cover and continue cooking until venison is tender, about 3 hours. If needed, add more wine. The venison should be completely covered during the whole cooking process. Add onions, small potatoes, green onions, carrots and celery sticks. Serve with steamed or boiled vegetables such as broccoli, asparagus, cauliflower or Brussels sprouts. Serve Hollandaise Sauce or Hot Slaw Dressing on the side. Serves 6 to 8.

Spiced Indian Venison Stew with Yogurt

seeds from 6 cardamom pods
1 whole clove
⅛ tsp. freshly grated nutmeg
1½ cups plain yogurt
2½ lbs. venison, cut 1" pieces
1 Tbsp. whipped butter
2 cups yellow onion, finely chopped
1 Tbsp. ginger, peeled and grated

2 large garlic cloves, pressed
¾ tsp. coriander seeds
½ tsp. cumin seeds
¼ tsp. ground turmeric
¾ tsp. salt
pepper
1 cup plain yogurt, stirred until smooth
fresh cilantro, minced

Finely grind cardamom, cloves and nutmeg. Mix with 1 cup yogurt in large bowl. Dry venison cubes and add to spiced yogurt. Cover and refrigerate overnight. Melt butter in a skillet over medium-low heat. Add onion, ginger and garlic and cook until onion is just tender, stirring frequently. Set aside. Grind coriander, cumin and turmeric to powder. Sprinkle powder over meat mixture, and toss venison. Mix venison mixture into onion mixture. Add salt and season with pepper. Cover and cook 2 hours over very low heat, stirring frequently. Uncover and cook until venison is tender, stirring frequently and adding up to ½ cup additional yogurt if mixture becomes dry, about 30 minutes. Rub ice cubes over surface of sauce to solidify fat; remove fat. Rewarm venison if necessary. Divide venison between warmed serving plates. Drizzle 1 cup stirred yogurt over servings. Sprinkle with cilantro. Serves 6 to 8.

Stewed Venison with Ravioli Dumplings

2 lbs. boneless venison
3 Tbsp. all-purpose flour
1 tsp. salt
3 Tbsp. canola oil
1 cup beef broth

1 cup spaghetti sauce with mushrooms
⅛ tsp. basil
8 sm. white onions
1 (10-oz.) box frozen peas
1 (15½-oz.) can beef ravioli

Cut venison into 1½" cubes. Mix in flour and ½ teaspoon salt and dredge venison with seasoned flour. Heat the oil in a saucepan. Add venison and brown well on all sides. Add the broth, spaghetti sauce, and remaining salt, and cover. Cook over low heat for about 1 hour. Add the onions and simmer for 25 minutes. Break frozen peas into pieces and add to the venison mixture and cover. Cook for 10 minutes longer. Spoon beef ravioli on top and cover. Heat for 5 minutes. Serves 4 to 6.

According to the fossil record, the white-tailed deer as we know it today, has existed for perhaps as much as 20 million years. It has managed to colonize and habitat from the dense rainforests of South America to the subarctic tree lines of North America.

Stifago - Greek Venison Stew

⅓ cup olive oil
2 lbs. venison backstrap
3 cups white onion, sliced
5 garlic cloves
3 bay leaves

1 tsp. cloves, whole
⅓ cup red wine vinegar
½ cup dry red table wine
1⅔ cups tomato juice

Cut venison into 1½" pieces. Peel and crush the unpeeled garlic cloves. In a Dutch oven heat the oil over moderately high heat until it is hot but not smoking. Brown venison and remove pieces as they are browned. Reduce heat to simmer and return venison and add onions, garlic, bay leaves, cloves, vinegar, wine, tomato juice. Cover and simmer for 2 hours. Discard bay leaves. Salt and pepper to taste. Serves 4.

Syrian-Style Venison Stew

2 lbs. venison, cut in 1" cubes
⅓ cup flour seasoned with salt and pepper
2 Tbsp. beef fat drippings
2 medium yellow onions, sliced
4 medium tomatoes, peeled and quartered

2 cups boiling water
1 cup green beans, cut in ½" lengths
all-purpose flour
water

Dredge meat in seasoned flour. Heat drippings in a heavy Dutch oven; add onions and cook until yellow; add the meat and brown on all sides; add the tomatoes and boiling water. Cover and simmer gently over low heat about 1½ hours. Add green beans and continue cooking until venison and beans are tender. Remove venison and vegetables to a hot platter. Thicken gravy by mixing 2 Tbsp. flour in a small amount of water. Pour flour paste gradually into the stew liquid, stirring briskly to prevent lumping. Bring to a boil, stirring constantly; cook until smooth and thickened. Spoon gravy over venison and vegetables. Serves 4 to 6.

Venison Goulash

2 lbs. small yellow onions
8 oz. safflower oil
3 lbs. venison stew meat
1 Tbsp. butter

1½ Tbsp. paprika
2 cans beef broth
cooked wide noodles

Fry onions in oil until onions are soft, but not quite done. Add venison and brown on all sides. Spoon and sprinkle butter and paprika over venison and add beef broth. Cover pot and simmer over low heat for 3 hours or until meat is tender. Stir often and add more warm beef broth if needed. Gravy should be thick. Serve over wide noodles. Serves 2 to 4.

Venison Mulligan Stew with Dumplings

2 lbs. venison, cut 1" cubes
flour
salt
pepper
1 cup white onions, chopped
1 clove garlic, minced
4 cups water
1 cup English peas

4 small potatoes, diced
4 small carrots, diced
2 Tbsp. parsley, chopped
all-purpose flour
salt
pepper
nutmeg
Traditional Dumplings

Mix and sift flour, salt and pepper. Roll the venison cubes in the seasoned flour. Sauté onions and garlic in a Dutch oven. Add venison and just brown. Add water, cover and simmer until venison is nearly tender. Add English peas, potatoes, carrots, and parsley. Cook until tender. Thicken the broth with a thin flour and water paste. Season with salt, pepper, and nutmeg to taste. Make Traditional Dumplings and serve on the side with gravy. Serves 2 to 4.

Venison, Porcini and Onion Stew

½ oz. fried porcini mushrooms
½ cup hot water
⅓ cup olive oil
3½ lbs. stewing venison, cut 1
2 (1½-lb) venison marrow bones, cracked
2 large yellow onions, chopped
1 cup Chianti wine

3 bay leaves
3 whole cloves
¼ tsp. salt
½" pieces 1½ Tbsp. tomato paste
4 cups canned chicken broth
potato gnocchi, cooked fusilli or
    macaroni tossed with olive oil and
    Parmesan cheese

Place porcini mushrooms in a small bowl. Pour in hot water. Let stand until soft, about 30 minutes. Drain mushrooms, reserving liquid. Strain liquid through fine sieve lined with a dampened paper towel. Combine liquid and mushrooms in a small bowl. Heat oil in a large Dutch oven over high heat. Add venison and bones in batches and brown well, turning frequently. Transfer venison and bones to a large bowl. Add onions to Dutch oven. Reduce heat to medium and sauté onions until transparent. Return venison and bones and any juices to the Dutch oven. Add Chianti, bay leaves, cloves and salt. Boil until wine is reduced by half. Mix in tomato paste and mushrooms and their liquid; simmer 5 minutes. Add chicken broth. Bring mixture to boil; reduce heat. Cover and simmer gently until venison is just tender, stirring occasionally, for about 1¾ to 2 hours. Uncover and simmer until sauce is thick and chunky, about 25 minutes. Remove cloves and bay leaves. Serve over potato gnocchi, fusilli or macaroni tossed with olive oil and Parmesan cheese. Serves 6 to 8.

Venison Ragout with Spaetzle

3 lbs. venison, cut 1" pieces
3 Tbsp. olive oil
¾ lb. mushrooms; whole if small, halved if
  larger
12 small white onions, diced chunks
½ cup beef bouillon or broth
5 Tbsp. tomato paste
3 Tbsp. brandy

1½ cups red wine
¼ cup ruby port
4 Tbsp. all-purpose flour
1 large clove garlic, mashed
¼ tsp. black pepper
2 bay leaves
Spaetzle

Brown venison in hot olive oil in deep skillet or Dutch oven. Remove meat and replace with mushrooms and onions, browning slightly while stirring. Remove mushrooms and onions from pan. Shut off heat in skillet and stir in beef bouillon and tomato paste. In a separate bowl mix liquors with flour; then add to skillet, heating just short of boiling. Now add venison, mushrooms, onions, garlic, black pepper and bay leaves. Cover tightly and bake in 350-degree oven for 1½ hours. Serve over Schwabische Spaetzle. Serves 4 to 6.

Mrs. Kathryn Breland

Venison Stew
with Mushrooms and Green Peppers

2 lbs. venison, cut 2" cubes
all-purpose flour
onion salt
garlic salt
safflower oil
2 Tbsp. granulated beef bouillon
6 to 8 cups water
4 medium potatoes, quartered
1 large white onion, halved and quartered

4 carrots, chopped
3 stalks celery, chopped
1 can mushrooms
1 green pepper, chopped
3 Tbsp. all-purpose flour
1 cup cold water
salt
pepper

Dredge venison in flour seasoned with pepper, onion salt and garlic salt. Brown venison in safflower oil. In a Dutch oven, add venison, water and bouillon and simmer for 2 hours. Add remaining ingredients and simmer for ½ hour more. Thicken stew by thoroughly mixing flour with cold water and stirring in a small amount at a time until desired thickness is obtained. Salt and pepper to taste. Serves 2 to 4.

Venison Sausage and Seafood Ragout

2 Tbsp. olive oil
1 white onion, diced
1 red bell pepper, diced
½ green bell pepper, diced
1 celery stalk, diced
3 garlic cloves, minced
1½ Tbsp. paprika
3 fresh thyme sprigs or 1 tsp. dried thyme, crumbled
½ tsp. red pepper
4 ripe tomatoes, peeled, seeded, diced
¾ cup dry white wine
¾ cup bottled clam juice
¾ cup heavy cream

1 medium eggplant, cut crosswise into ¼" thick rounds
olive oil
11 oz. red snapper fillets, cut into 1" pieces
16 uncooked medium shrimp, peeled
8 raw oysters
¼ lb. crabmeat
¾ lb. Old-Fashioned Venison and Pork Sausage, cooked, cut ¼" thick slices, or other link sausage
salt
pepper
Boiled Rice

Heat 2 Tbsp. oil in large skillet over medium heat. Add onion and sauté until golden, about 8 minutes. Add bell peppers, celery and garlic and sauté 1 minute. Mix in paprika, thyme and red pepper and sauté 1 minute. Add tomatoes, wine, stock and cream and boil until sauce thickens slightly, stirring occasionally, about 10 minutes. Preheat oven to 400 degrees. Dip eggplant rounds in olive oil. Place eggplant on baking sheet and bake until lightly brown, about 20 minutes. Add red snapper and shrimp to ragout. Reduce heat and simmer 3 minutes. Add oysters, crab and venison sausage and bring to simmer. Season with salt and pepper. Arrange eggplant slices in center of each plate. Spoon ragout over eggplant. Serve with Boiled Rice. Serves 4 to 6.

Venison Stew with Onions and Potatoes

8 to 10 lbs. venison
2 Tbsp. apple cider vinegar
salt
water
1 Tbsp. Worcestershire sauce

2 cans tomatoes
2 cans tomato paste
2 med. onions, chopped
3 potatoes, sliced
Poochies Spoon Bread

Cook the venison over very low heat in Dutch oven water, salt, and vinegar until meat falls to pieces. Remove from heat, remove the venison, strain liquid and add meat back to the liquid. Add Worcestershire sauce, tomatoes, tomato paste, onions and potatoes and cook over very low heat for 6 to 8 hours. If not thick enough, add 1 tablespoon flour dissolved in a little water and cook 5 minutes longer. Serve with Poochies Spoon Bread and a green salad. Serves 10 to 15.

Those orange hunting jackets do not give the hunter's presence away—deer are color blind.

Stewed Venison with Fresh Vegetables

2 lbs. venison roast, cubed
apple cider vinegar
water
6 cups salted water
1 (8-oz.) can tomato sauce
1 (6-oz.) can tomato paste
1 cup carrots, diced

1 cup celery, diced
2 cups potatoes, diced
1 large white onion, diced
1 large bell pepper, diced
salt
black pepper

Soak venison in 1 part vinegar and 3 parts water for 3 hours. Remove venison from vinegar soak and rinse with water. Cook in approximately 6 cups of salted water over very low heat until venison is very tender. Add tomato sauce and tomato paste and stir well. Add vegetables and season with salt and pepper to taste. Continue cooking over very low heat until done. Serves 4 to 6.

Stracotta Venison Alia Fiorentina

May be eaten as is or the meats may be used for fillings in ravioli and cannelloni. The juices can be used as sauces for pasta recipes.

2 Tbsp. butter
1 white onion, chopped fine
1 carrot, chopped fine
1 stalk celery, chopped fine
2 lbs. piece of venison
¼ lb. piece lean pork

½ cup white wine
1 Tbsp. tomato paste
2 tomatoes, peeled and chopped
¼ cup beef broth
salt
pepper

Melt butter in a large pot; add onion, carrot, and celery. Sauté the vegetables until they are lightly browned. Add venison and pork and brown on all sides. Add wine, tomato paste, tomatoes, and beef broth. Season with salt and pepper. Cover pot and cook in a 250-degree oven for 3 hours or more. Add more liquid, if necessary, during the cooking period. The venison should be quite soft and the juices thick. Serves 2 to 4.

Winter Sausage and Venison Stew

canola oil
1 lb. Homemade Red Wine Sausage,
  cut diagonally into ½" wide slices
2½ lbs. venison stew meat, trimmed, cut
  into 1½" cubes and patted dry
¼ cup plus 2 Tbsp. all-purpose flour
2 Tbsp. butter
1 Tbsp. canola oil
4 med. yellow onions, sliced
1 Tbsp. garlic, minced
3 cups dry red wine
2 cups canned beef broth
3 sprigs parsley
2 bay leaves

1½ tsp. dried thyme, crumbled
5 large carrots, peeled and cut
diagonally into ½" wide pieces
1½ cups water
2 tsp. sugar
½ tsp. salt
1 lb. parsnips, peeled and cut diagonally into ½" wide pieces
1 Tbsp. butter, room
  temperature
black pepper
6 Roquefort Gougeres
6 Tbsp. fresh parsley, minced

Position rack in center of oven and preheat to 325 degrees. Add enough oil just to coat bottom of Dutch oven. Heat 1 minute over medium-high heat. Add venison sausage and cook until lightly browned, stirring frequently. Transfer sausage to paper towels and drain. Add ¼ of venison and brown on all sides. Transfer to paper towels and drain. Repeat with remaining venison in batches, adding additional oil to pan as necessary to prevent sticking. Pour off fat from Dutch oven. Return venison to Dutch oven; mix in ¼ cup flour. Bake 10 minutes, stirring occasionally.

Melt 1 Tbsp. butter with 1 Tbsp. oil in a large skillet over medium high heat. Add onions and cook until light brown, stirring frequently. Add garlic and stir. Add wine, broth, parsley, bay leaves and thyme. Bring mixture to simmer over medium heat, stirring frequently. Cover and bake until venison is tender, about 2¼ hours. Melt 1 Tbsp. butter in medium skillet over medium heat. Add carrots and cook 3 minutes, stirring frequently. Add 1½ cups water, sugar and ½ tsp. salt and bring to boil. Reduce heat, cover and simmer until carrots are tender. Drain.

Cook parsnips in a large pot of boiling salted water until tender. Drain thoroughly. Blend 1 Tbsp. room-temperature butter with remaining 2 Tbsp. flour, forming a paste. Skim fat off stew. Remove bay leaves and parsley. Bring stew to a simmer over medium heat. Gradually whisk in paste 1 tsp. at a time. Simmer until thickened, stirring constantly. Add sausage, carrots and parsnips and cook until heated through, stirring occasionally. Season with salt and pepper. Place 1 Roquefort Gougere on each plate. Spoon stew over Roquefort Gougeres. Sprinkle with parsley and serve. Serves 6 to 8.

Today the white-tailed deer is the most sought-after hunting target of all the North American mammals.

13
Ground Venison

Ground venison provides culinary options which range from burgers, pies, meatloaves, meatballs, salads, appetizers, sausages, and other tasty recipes.

When grinding venison, an average mix for the ground meat is ⅔ venison to ⅓ moist meat (10# venison to 5# moist meat does very well). Some additives are bacon or pork/beef fat. A good bacon additive is to purchase a slab of smoked bacon and remove and discard the skin.

If you like ground venison, but are concerned about the fat content in your diet, I recommend that you try the recipes for Low-Fat Stuffed Venison Bell Peppers, Low-Fat Venison Dumplings with Tropical Spices, and Low-Fat Venison Lasagna. Feel free to experiment with substituting mushrooms for the fat in any of these ground venison recipes. Mushrooms provide water, which substitutes for fat, in preventing the ground venison from tasting dry. Since venison is virtually fat-free, with the substitution of mushrooms you can convert most any of these recipes to low fat or fat free.

This substitution procedure has not been tested on all of the ground venison recipes. You will need to experiment. Make your ground venison by beginning with 25% (by weight) of mushrooms to 75% (by weight) of venison; break off a small piece and fry it. If the ground venison is dry, add more mushrooms to the mixture and test it again.

For many chefs, ground venison is the easy and quick way to utilize cuts of venison that may otherwise go unused. For small batches of ground venison a hand meat grinder will serve you well. For larger batches, if you contemplate grinding your own venison for several years or if you plan on using a grinder for other purposes, you may wish to consider purchasing an electric grinder. I have been using my Oster® Heavy-Duty Food Grinder (see appendix) for years. If it ever wears out, I will be ordering another one. In addition to grinding venison for ground meat dishes, the Oster® has sausage-stuffing attachments.

Apple-Venison Burger Balls in Pastry

¾ lb. ground venison
1 egg, beaten
2 cups canned applesauce
1½ cups herb-seasoned stuffing mix
¾ tsp. salt
dash of pepper
½ tsp. sage

¼ cup Crisco
1½ cups sliced yellow onions
¼ cup butter
pastry for 2-crust pie
1 can cream of mushroom soup
1 soup can whole milk

Combine the ground venison, egg and 1 cup of applesauce. Add the stuffing mix, ½ teaspoon salt, pepper and sage and mix thoroughly. Form into 10 balls. Brown on all sides in Crisco in a skillet and remove from skillet. Melt butter in the skillet, add onions and sauté until light brown. Add remaining applesauce and salt. Roll out pastry on a floured surface and cut into 10 squares. Place an equal amount of applesauce mixture and 1 meatball on each square. Moisten edges of pastry squares with water and lift up corners over the meatball. Press the edges of pastry squares together to seal and place on a baking sheet. Bake at 400 degrees for 20 to 25 minutes or until brown. Mix the mushroom soup and milk in a saucepan and heat through, but do not boil. Pour mushroom soup over venison pastries. Serve with steamed English peas. Garnish each serving with a sprig of parsley. Serves 4 to 6.

Baked Eggplant with Venison

½ cup all-purpose flour
1¾ tsp. salt
¼ tsp. pepper
1 egg, slightly beaten
1 Tbsp. whole milk
1 medium eggplant, peeled
⅓ cup canola oil

1 lb. ground venison
¼ lb. mushrooms, chopped
1 Tbsp. white onion, finely chopped
½ cup soft breadcrumbs
3 Tbsp. grated Parmesan cheese
2 medium tomatoes

Mix flour, ¾ teaspoon salt and ⅛ teaspoon pepper. Combine egg and milk and mix well. Peel eggplant and cut into 6 crosswise slices and dip into flour mixture. Dip into egg and milk mixture, then dip into flour mixture again. Reserve remaining egg and milk mixture. Heat 3 tablespoons oil in a large skillet and brown eggplant on both sides. Place in a 9"x13" baking pan. Cook the venison, mushrooms and onion in remaining oil until brown. Remove from heat and mix in breadcrumbs, cheese, remaining salt and pepper and reserved egg mixture. Spoon over eggplant slices and cover baking pan with foil. Bake in 350-degree oven for 20 minutes and uncover. Cut each tomato into 3 slices and place over venison mixture. Bake for 15 minutes longer and garnish with parsley. Serves 6.

Baked Bean and Ground Venison Savory

4 Tbsp. safflower oil
½ cup white onion, sliced
1 cup celery diced
¾ lb. ground venison
1 tsp. Worcestershire sauce

½ tsp. salt
1 tsp. sage, powdered
½ cup tomato juice
4 cups baked beans

Heat oil in a heavy skillet. Add onions, celery and venison, and cook uncovered for about 10 minutes, stirring frequently. Add remaining ingredients and heat thoroughly. Serves 6.

Baked Venison Enchilada

2 lbs. venison, ground
½ lb. beef fat, ground
1 (⅔ cup) medium onion, finely chopped
2 cloves garlic, minced
½ cup self-rising flour
3 Tbsp. chili powder

1½ tsp. salt
1 tsp. leaf oregano
4 cups hot water
6 corn tortillas
1 cup pitted black olives, sliced
2 cups shredded Cheddar cheese

Mix ground venison and beef fat. In a large skillet, brown ground venison mixture, onion and garlic. If necessary, drain. Add flour, chili powder, salt and oregano; mix well. Stir in water. Simmer until mixture thickens slightly, about 5 minutes, stirring occasionally. Place 3 tortillas in ungreased 13" by 9" (3-qt.) baking dish. Cover with ¼ of the venison mixture (about 2 cups). Top with ¼ cup olives and ½ cup cheese. Repeat 3 more times. Bake at 300 degrees for 20 minutes until heated through. Serves 4 to 6.

Calcutta Venison

3 Tbsp. butter
2 onions, sliced
1½ lbs. ground venison
1 tsp. salt
1 cup tomatoes
1 tart apple, chopped
1 Tbsp. green pepper, chopped

1½ Tbsp. curry powder
1 Tbsp. all-purpose flour
2 cups canned chicken broth
½ can green peas
cooked rice
raisins
1 box shredded coconut

Melt the butter in a skillet. Add onions, venison and salt and cook until brown. Add the tomatoes, apple and green pepper. Mix the curry powder with flour and stir in the chicken stock. Stir into the venison mixture. Cook for several minutes and place in a casserole dish. Bake at 350 degrees for 30 minutes. Place peas on top and bake for 5 minutes longer. Serve raisins and coconut browned in additional butter in side dishes. Serves 2 to 4.

Chalupes

1 lb. ground venison
¼ cup ground beef fat
4 Tbsp. chili powder
2 Tbsp. oregano
2 Tbsp. garlic salt
2 cans refried beans

1 pkg. frozen tortillas
Salt to taste
2 tomatoes, sliced
1 head lettuce, sliced
2 cups grated Cheddar cheese

Cook the venison and beef fat in a sauté pan until browned. Add the chili powder, oregano and garlic salt and stir until well blended. Drain off the grease into a 10" skillet. Add beans to the venison mixture and cook over low heat for 20 minutes. Fry tortillas until crisp in grease in skillet and drain. Salt each tortilla. Place the venison mixture in serving dishes and top each serving with tomatoes, lettuce and cheese. Serve with tortillas. Serves 6 to 8.

Chinese Ground Venison Casserole

1 lb. ground venison
2 Tbsp. safflower oil
1 large white onion, chopped
1 can cream of mushroom soup
1 can cream of chicken soup

1½ cups warm water
½ cup uncooked long grain rice
2 Tbsp, teriyaki sauce
¼ tsp. black pepper
1 can chow mein noodles

Brown ground venison in hot safflower oil until slightly crumbly. Add chopped onion, mushroom and chicken soups. Rinse out soup cans with the warm water and add the water to mixture. Stir in rice, pepper and teriyaki sauce. Pour into lightly greased 1½-qt. casserole dish. Cover and bake in 350-degree oven for 30 minutes. Remove cover and continue baking for 30 minutes. Remove cover and continue baking for 30 minutes longer. Cover mixture with chow mein noodles and bake for another 15 minutes. Serves 6 to 8.

Chinese Venison

1½ lbs. ground venison
¼ cup onion, chopped
3 Tbsp. bacon fat
1 cup raw green peas
1 cup celery, finely chopped

½ cup long grain rice, uncooked
¼ cup soy sauce
1 can chicken noodle soup
1 can cream of mushroom soup
3 cups water

Brown the venison and onion in bacon fat in skillet. Add the remaining ingredients and pour into a large baking dish. Bake at 350 degrees for 1 hour, stirring every 15 minutes. Serves 8 to 10.

Enchiladas

1 lb. ground venison
salt and pepper to taste
safflower oil
chili sauce

2 pkgs. Tortillas
1 lb. cheese, grated
3 medium white onions, finely chopped

Cook the ground venison, salt and pepper in 1 tablespoon oil in a sauté pan for 10 minutes, stirring frequently. Add 1 cup chili sauce and set aside. Cook the tortillas in oil in a skillet until soft. Fill each tortilla with venison mixture, cheese and onions and roll as for jelly roll. Place tortillas close together in a shallow baking pan and cover with chili sauce and remaining cheese and onions. Bake at 350 degrees until bubbly. Serves 4 to 6.

Ground Venison Steak Lorraine

2 lbs. venison, chopped
½ lb. beef suet, chopped
Salt
pepper

⅔ cup Roquefort cheese, crumbled
¼ cup Homemade Butter
½ lb. mushrooms, chopped
1¼ cups dry red wine

Mix and grind venison and beef fat. Season venison lightly with salt and pepper. Lightly mix. Divide into 12 oval patties. Divide Roquefort cheese on top of six of the patties. Place the remaining patties on top of the cheese and seal the edges. Melt 2 Tbsp. butter in a skillet; add mushrooms and lightly brown. Remove the mushrooms. Add the remaining butter to the skillet. Brown the venison patties on both sides. Return the mushrooms to the skillet; add the wine and simmer uncovered for 5 minutes, basting the venison constantly. Serve immediately. Makes 6 servings.

Hash Brown and Venison Pie

1 egg, lightly beaten
¾ cup soft bread crumbs
⅓ cup whole milk
2 tsp. salt
¼ tsp. hickory smoked salt
1 tsp. Accent
pepper
½ cup white onion, minced
¼ cup parsley, minced
1½ lbs. ground venison

1 (12-oz.) pkg. frozen hash brown
    potatoes, thawed
2 Tbsp. Homemade Butter,
    melted
¾ cup grated Cheddar cheese
1 (8-oz.) can tomato sauce
½ tsp. chili powder
½ tsp. prepared mustard
¼ tsp. Worcestershire sauce
dash of Tabasco sauce

Combine the egg with bread crumbs, milk, 1¼ tsp. salt, hickory smoked salt, Accent, ⅛ tsp. pepper, onion and parsley and mix well. Add the venison and mix well. Spread the venison mixture on the bottom and sides of greased 9" pie plate. Mix the potatoes with remaining salt and dash of Tabasco. Spoon onto venison and drizzle with butter. Sprinkle the cheese over potatoes and broil until cheese is melted and browned. Let stand for 5 minutes before cutting. Combine remaining ingredients in a sauce pan and bring to a boil, stirring frequently. Serve with venison pie. Serves 6 to 8.

Hot Tamale Venison Pie

6 cups boiling water
2 cups cornmeal
2 Tbsp. bacon fat
1 lb. ground venison
4 pieces ground smoked bacon
1 white onion, chopped

½ green bell pepper, chopped
2 cups canned tomatoes
salt
black pepper
chili powder

Sift cornmeal slowly into rapidly boiling water, stirring constantly. Cook 15 minutes. Mix ground venison and bacon and brown with onion and green pepper in hot fat. Add tomatoes. Season to taste with salt and pepper. Simmer 10 minutes. Fill well-oiled baking pan with alternate layers of cornmeal mush and meat mixture. Bake in a 400-degree oven for 20 minutes. Serve hot. Serves 4 to 6.

Hot Venison Tamales

1 lb. ground venison
4 Tbsp. chili powder
½ lb. hot or extra hot pork sausage
cayenne pepper to taste

2 Tbsp. salt
6 cups cornmeal
1 cup Crisco

Pour boiling water over dried corn shucks and soak to make pliable. Combine the ground venison, chili powder, sausage, cayenne pepper and ½ tablespoon salt in a large bowl and set aside. Mix the cornmeal, remaining salt and Crisco in a mixing bowl and stir in enough boiling water to hold ingredients together. Place 1 heaping tablespoon cornmeal mixture on a soaked corn shuck and pat out to desired length. Place 1 tablespoon venison mixture in the center of the cornmeal patty and pull up shuck on both sides to shape. Press edges of cornmeal patty together and pinch ends to seal. Tie ends and center of shuck together with cotton twine. Repeat with remaining cornmeal mixture and meat mixture. Place tamales in a large saucepan and cover with water. Bring to a boil, reduce heat and simmer for 40 minutes. Tamales may be frozen. Makes 23 to 25 tamales. Serves 6 to 8.

Italian Venison Goulash

1 lb. ground venison
1 small white onion, chopped
1 (28-oz.) can tomato sauce
2 garlic cloves, minced
1 tsp. dried basil, crumbled

½ tsp. sugar
½ (16-oz.) pkg. macaroni, freshly
    cooked
½ cup freshly grated Parmesan cheese

Cook venison and onion in large saucepan over medium heat until venison is browned, stirring frequently. Pour off drippings. Add tomato purée, garlic, basil and sugar. Cover and simmer until thick, stirring occasionally, about 25 minutes. Mix in macaroni. Transfer to a serving dish and sprinkle with Parmesan cheese. Serve immediately. Serves 2 to 4.

Italian Venison Biscuit Roll-Ups

1 lb. ground venison, crumbled
1 (1½-oz.) pkg. spaghetti sauce mix
1 (8-oz.) can tomato sauce
2 cups sifted flour all-purpose
1 Tbsp. baking powder
1 tsp. salt

¼ cup Crisco
¼ cup white onion, chopped
½ to ¾ cup whole milk
1 cup water
1 cup shredded sharp Cheddar cheese

Cook the ground venison in a skillet until brown, stirring frequently, then stir in spaghetti sauce mix and tomato sauce. Simmer for about 10 minutes or until thickened. Sift the flour, baking powder and salt together into a bowl and cut in Crisco until mixture resembles coarse crumbs. Stir in onion and blend in enough milk to make a soft dough. Turn out onto lightly floured board or pastry cloth and knead gently for 30 seconds. Roll out to a 12"x 16" rectangle. Spread 1 cup venison mixture evenly over dough and roll as for jelly roll, starting at narrow edge. Seal edges securely and cut into 1" thick slices. Place on lightly greased baking sheet. Bake in 425-degree oven for 12 to 15 minutes or until golden brown. Blend the water into remaining venison mixture and heat through. Spoon venison sauce over Biscuit Roll-Ups and sprinkle cheese over venison sauce. Serves 4 to 6.

Low-Fat Stuffed Venison Bell Peppers

6 green bell peppers
½ cup margarine
½ cup green onions, chopped
½ cup onions, chopped
2 cloves garlic, chopped
½ lb. ground venison

½ cup chopped mushrooms
1 cup wet squeezed bread
3 eggs
salt substitute
pepper
bread crumbs

Grind together venison and mushrooms. Cut off tops of peppers, remove insides and boil 5 minutes. Sauté onions in margarine, add garlic, venison mixture and cook 5 to 10 minutes. Add bread, work in eggs, season with salt and pepper. Stuff peppers with mixture, sprinkle with bread crumbs, dot with butter and bake 5 minutes at 350 degrees. Serves 6.

 *Trails and beds of deer are usually scraped out places under the protection of overhanging boughs, or at the bases of trees. In regions heavily populated with deer, their trails and beds are readily seen, and give some clue to the density of the population.*

Low-Fat Venison Lasagna

3 (16-oz.) cans stewed tomatoes
2 cloves garlic, crushed and divided
1¾ tsp. salt substitute, divided
¾ tsp. black pepper, divided
1 lb. ground venison
½ lb. mushrooms, chopped
1 Tbsp. safflower oil
1 medium onion, chopped
2 tsp. seasoned salt
1 tsp. basil leaves
¼ tsp. ground oregano
¼ tsp. dill-seasoned salt
1 tsp. celery salt
1 Tbsp. honey

3 Tbsp. parsley flakes, divided
½ cup Burgundy
1 to 2½ jars sliced mushrooms, drained
1 (14-oz.) package spinach lasagna noodles
2 (12-oz.) cartons small-curd cottage cheese
1 cup grated Parmesan cheese, divided
1 tsp. oregano leaves
2 lbs. Mozzarella cheese, shredded
½ lb. mild Cheddar cheese, shredded
½ lb. Muenster cheese, shredded

Grind together venison and mushrooms. Combine tomatoes, 1 clove crushed garlic, 1 tsp. salt, and ¼ tsp. pepper in a saucepan; simmer over low heat 2½ to 3 hours. Brown venison and mushroom mixture in safflower oil in a large skillet: add remaining garlic, ½ tsp. pepper, onion, seasoned salt, basil, and oregano. Cook until onion is tender; drain off drippings. To meat add tomato mixture, dill-seasoned salt, celery salt, honey, 2 Tbsp. parsley flakes, Burgundy, and mushrooms; simmer over low heat 8 hours or longer. (The sauce will be thick.)

Cook lasagna noodles according to package directions; drain. Combine cottage cheese, ½ cup Parmesan cheese, 1 Tbsp. parsley flakes, ¾ tsp. salt, and oregano leaves. Reserve ¾ cup meat sauce; set aside. In a 13x9x2" baking dish, alternate layers of noodles, meat sauce, Mozzarella, Cheddar, Muenster, and the cottage cheese mixture; repeat layers three times. Spread reserved meat sauce on top; sprinkle with remaining ½ cup Parmesan cheese. Bake at 350 degrees for 45 minutes; allow to stand 15 minutes before serving. Serves 10 to 12.

Potatoes with Venison Stuffing

6 med. baked potatoes
1 lb. ground venison
½ cup white onion, chopped
1 stalk celery, chopped
1 tsp. salt

½ tsp. pepper
2 eggs, beaten
4 Tbsp. tomato catsup
2 slices mild cheese
dried parsley flakes

Cut the potatoes in half. Scoop out potato with spoon, place potato into a bowl and mash. Add the ground venison, onion, celery, salt, pepper, eggs and catsup and mix well. Fill the potato shells with venison mixture and place in a shallow baking pan. Bake at 400 degrees for 30 to 35 minutes. Cut the cheese in narrow strips and place on potato mixture in crisscross fashion. Sprinkle with parsley and bake until the cheese is lightly browned. Serves 6 to 12.

Mexican Venison Meat Pie

6 slices of smoked bacon
1 cup all-purpose flour
6 Tbsp. cornmeal
3 to 4 Tbsp. cold water
1 lb. ground venison
2 Tbsp. safflower oil
1 (8-oz.) can whole kernel corn
¼ cup green bell pepper, finely chopped
¼ cup white onion, chopped
½ tsp. oregano

½ tsp. chili powder
1 tsp. salt
⅛ tsp. black pepper
1 (8-oz.) can tomato sauce
1 egg, beaten
¼ cup whole milk
½ tsp. dry mustard
½ tsp. Worcestershire sauce
1½ cups grated Cheddar cheese
4 stuffed olives, sliced

Fry the bacon in a skillet until crisp, remove from skillet and break into large pieces. Pour bacon drippings from the skillet, reserve ⅓ cup and chill in the refrigerator until firm. Combine the flour and 2 Tbsp. cornmeal in a mixing bowl. Cut in reserved bacon drippings until mixture is the size of small peas. Stir in the water gradually until pastry is just moist enough to hold together. Form into a ball and roll out on a floured surface to a circle 1½ inches larger than an inverted 9" pie pan. Fit pastry into the pie pan, then fold edge under the edge. Brown the ground venison in a large skillet with oil and drain off excess oil. Drain corn and add to ground venison. Add the green pepper, onion, remaining cornmeal, oregano, chili powder, ½ tsp. salt, pepper and tomato sauce and mix well. Place in pastry-lined pie pan. Bake in 425-degree oven for 25 minutes. Combine the egg, milk, remaining salt, mustard, Worcestershire sauce and cheese and mix well. Spread on venison mixture. Top with bacon and olives and bake for 5 minutes longer or until cheese melts. Remove from oven and let stand for 10 minutes before serving. May be served with tomato sauce, if desired. Serves 6.

Salisbury Venison Steak with Mushrooms and Noodles

1 lb. ground venison
1 egg white, lightly beaten
⅓ cup onion, chopped
¼ cup saltine cracker crumbs
2 Tbsp. whole milk
1 Tbsp. horseradish

¼ tsp. salt
⅛ tsp. black pepper
1 (12-oz.) jar beef gravy
1½ cups fresh mushrooms, sliced
hot cooked noodles

In a bowl, combine venison, egg white, onion, cracker crumbs, milk, horseradish and pepper. Shape into four oval patties. Fry in a skillet over medium heat for 10 to 12 minutes or until cooked, turning once. Remove patties and keep warm. Add gravy, mushrooms and water to skillet; heat for 3 to 5 minutes. Serve gravy over patties and noodles. Serves 4.

Southern Venison Meat Pie

1¼ cups all-purpose flour
¾ cup cornmeal
1¾ tsp. salt
Crisco
evaporated milk.

3 Tbsp. water
1 lb, ground venison
½ onion, chopped
1½ tsp. chili powder
1 can vegetable soup

Sift flour, cornmeal and 1 tsp. salt together into a mixing bowl and cut in ½ cup Crisco. Combine 6 Tbsp. milk and water and stir into the flour mixture. Roll out ¾ of the pastry on a floured board and line a pie pan. Bake at 425 degrees for 10 minutes. Brown ground venison and onions over low heat in 3 Tbsp. of shortening. Add the chili powder, remaining salt and soup and mix thoroughly. Remove from heat. Add ¾ cup milk and pour into baked crust. Roll out remaining pastry, cut in strips and place over pie crisscross fashion. Bake for 15 minutes longer or until brown. Serves 4 to 6.

Spanish Rice, with Venison

3 Tbsp. butter
¼ cup white onion, chopped
½ lb. to 1 lb. ground venison
½ cup green bell pepper, chopped
1 cup uncooked long grain rice

1½ tsp. salt
dash pepper
2 cups tomato purée
3 cups boiling water
½ tsp. paprika

Place butter in a frying pan. Wash and drain raw rice. Separate venison into small particles. Melt butter over low heat, put in onions and cook until they are browned slightly. Next add venison and brown it well, stirring it during the cooking. Add green pepper, salt and pepper. Stir in rice, then tomato purée and water. Cover the pan and cook over low heat or in a 350-degree oven until rice and venison are tender; roast 30 to 45 minutes. Season well and serve piping hot. Serves 6 to 8.

Stuffed Venison Bell Peppers

6 green bell peppers
½ cup butter
½ cup green onions, chopped
½ cup yellow onions, chopped
2 cloves garlic, chopped
½ lb. ground venison

3 slices, bacon, ground
1 cup wet squeezed bread
3 eggs
salt
pepper
breadcrumbs

Cut off tops of peppers, remove insides and boil 5 minutes. Sauté onions in butter, add garlic, venison, bacon and cook 5 to 10 minutes. Add bread, work in eggs, season with salt and pepper. Stuff peppers with mixture, sprinkle with bread crumbs, dot with butter and bake 5 minutes at 350 degrees. Serves 6.

Stuffed Venison Tomatoes

6 large tomatoes
4 oz. butter
½ cup green onions, chopped
2 cloves garlic
¾ lb. ground venison
¼ lb. smoked ham slices, finely chopped

1 cup wet squeezed bread
salt
pepper
paprika
bread crumbs

Slice tops off tomatoes and scoop out. Chop meat of tomato. Sauté onions in butter with garlic, venison, ham, and tomato. Add wet bread. Season with salt and pepper, stuff into tomato shells, cover with bread crumbs and paprika, dot with butter and bake at 350 degrees for 10 minutes. Serves 6.

Tacos

½ lb. ground venison
1 tsp. Accent
½ tsp. salt
¼ tsp. chili powder
⅛ tsp. garlic powder

safflower oil
12 soft tortillas
shredded lettuce
chopped tomatoes

Season the venison with Accent, salt, chili powder and garlic powder. Cover bottom of a skillet with ½ inch of oil and heat. Place the venison mixture in center of tortillas and fold over. Place in a small amount of hot oil and fry for 1 minute and 30 seconds on each side. Remove and drain on paper towel. Stuff remaining open space of tortillas with lettuce and tomatoes. Serves 12.

Texas Venison Hash

3 large onions, sliced
1 large green bell pepper, minced
3 Tbsp. pork fat
1 lb. ground venison
1 cup uncooked long grain rice

2 cups cooked tomatoes
1 tsp. chili powder
1 tsp. salt
⅛ tsp. black pepper

Cook onion and green pepper in fat until yellow. Add ground venison and fry until mixture falls apart. Stir in rest of ingredients. Pour into a greased 2-qt. casserole dish. Cover and bake 1 hour at 350 degrees. Remove cover the last 15 minutes of cooking. Serves 8 to 10.

The mule deer's reproductive rate of 94 fawns per 100 does is low compared to the white tail's 140 fawns for every 100 does.

Venison and Bacon Patties with Gravy

1 lb. ground venison
⅛ lb. ground smoked bacon
1 tsp. garlic salt
1 tsp. lemon pepper
7 crackers, crumbled
1 egg
1 tsp. salt

1 medium white onion, diced
⅛ tsp. sage
salt and pepper to taste
1 small can mushroom pieces
Primo's Creamy Grits
Kentucky Biscuits
butter

Mix all ingredients well and form into patties. Brown and remove from heat to make gravy. In the fat left over from browning the patties, make the gravy (see Sauces & Gravy recipes, Chapter 22.) Salt and pepper to taste. Add small can drained mushrooms, and put the patties into the gravy. Simmer for a few minutes until gravy thickens and seasonings cook through the gravy. Serve with fried eggs, gravy, Primo's Creamy Grits, Kentucky Biscuits, butter, jelly and coffee. Serves 4.

Venison and Vegetable Casserole

1 lb. fine ground venison, backstrap
1 green bell pepper, chopped
1 med. white onion, chopped
1 pkg. egg noodles
salt and pepper to taste

1 Tbsp. chili powder
1 can tomato soup
1 can mushroom soup
1 can cream-style corn
1½ cups Cheddar cheese, grated

Mix together the ground venison, green bell pepper and onion in a skillet and cook until just brown. Cook and drain the egg noodles. Add egg noodles to the venison and vegetable mixture. Add the salt, pepper, chili powder, tomato soup, mushroom soup, corn and 1 cup of the grated Cheddar cheese and mix together well. Pour casserole mixture into a greased 2-quart casserole dish and sprinkle the remaining grated Cheddar cheese on top. Preheat oven to 275 degrees and bake until heated through and cheese melts. Serves 10 to 12.

Yearling bucks have bumps on their skulls where antlers will grow when they are older. Large bucks can have seven or more points on a side. Antler growth begins in April to early May. The new antlers are tender and velvet covered, and the velvet is typically shed in early September. Most bucks drop their racks in January and February, but some carry them longer. A typical white-tail buck's antler has a main beam that sweeps forward and each of the points rise from it. Contrary to some opinions, numbers of points are no indication of age, but are of some value in judging the animal's condition.

Venison Chili Pot Pie

3 Tbsp. onion flakes
3 Tbsp. warm water
1½ lbs. ground venison, crumbled
3 Tbsp, safflower oil
1 tsp. garlic salt
½ cup bell pepper, chopped
1 (8-oz.) can tomato sauce
1 (1-lb.) can tomatoes
1 (20-oz.) can ranch-style beans
1 Tbsp. chili powder

1½ tsp. salt
¾ cup cornmeal
¼ cup. all-purpose flour
1½ Tbsp. baking powder
1 egg, beaten
½ cup whole milk
¼ cup bacon drippings
1 Tbsp. parsley
¼ cup grated Cheddar cheese
paprika

Combine the onion flakes and warm water in a small bowl. Sauté the venison in the cooking oil until partially done. Add the onion, garlic salt and bell pepper and 1 teaspoon salt and simmer for 10 minutes. Sift the cornmeal, flour, remaining salt and baking powder together into a mixing bowl. Add the egg, milk and bacon drippings and stir until smooth. Stir in parsley. Pour the venison mixture into a shallow baking dish and sprinkle with cheese. Spoon cornmeal mixture around edge of baking dish and sprinkle with paprika. Bake at 400 degrees for 15 minutes. Serves 4 to 6.

Venison and Onion Dumplings

1 lb. ground venison
½ lb. beef fat
1 cup bread crumbs
canned beef broth
¼ cup yellow onions, grated

1 tsp. salt
¼ tsp. black pepper
3 egg yolks
all-purpose flour
Mazola oil

Coarse-grind venison and beef fat separately. Mix together and fine grind twice. Moisten bread crumbs little beef broth; mix with, onion, salt and black pepper; add to ground venison. Bind together with egg yolks. Mold into small balls and slightly flatten into patties. Roll patties in flour. Tightly cover and simmer in Mazola oil and beef broth. Serves 2 to 4.

Venison Dumplings with Tropical Spices

1 lb. ground venison
½ lb. ground beef fat
1 cup fresh bread crumbs
1 Tbsp. lime juice
⅛ tsp. cinnamon
⅛ tsp. allspice
beef bouillon, divided

¼ cup white onions, grated
1 tsp. salt
¼ tsp. black pepper
3 egg yolks
all-purpose flour
olive oil

Mix together ground venison and beef fat. Mix together bread crumbs, lime juice, cinnamon, allspice; moisten with a small amount of the beef bouillon. Add onion, salt and black pepper. Add egg yolks. Make into small balls. Roll in flour and simmer, tightly covered, in olive oil and enough bouillon to partly cover. Serves 2 to 4. Easy to make lower in fat by substituting ½ lb. mushrooms for beef fat, and safflower oil for olive oil.

Venison Lasagna

3 (16-oz.) cans stewed tomatoes
2 cloves garlic, crushed and divided
1¾ tsp. salt, divided
¾ tsp. pepper, divided
1 lb. ground venison
½ lb. pork sausage
1 Tbsp. olive oil
1 medium onion, chopped
2 tsp. seasoned salt
1 tsp. basil leaves
¼ tsp. ground oregano
¼ tsp. dill-seasoned salt
1 tsp. celery salt
1 Tbsp. honey

3 Tbsp. parsley flakes, divided
½ cup Burgundy
1 to 2½ jars sliced mushrooms, drained
1 (14-oz.) package spinach lasagna noodles
2 (12-oz.) cartons small-curd cottage cheese
1 cup grated Parmesan cheese, divided
1 tsp. oregano leaves
2 lbs. Mozzarella cheese, shredded
½ lb. mild Cheddar cheese, shredded
½ lb. muenster cheese, shredded

Combine tomatoes, 1 clove crushed garlic, 1 tsp. salt, and ¼ tsp. pepper in a saucepan; simmer over low heat 2½ to 3 hours. Brown round steak and pork sausage in olive oil in a large skillet: add remaining garlic, ½ teaspoon pepper, onion, seasoned salt, basil, and oregano. Cook until onion is tender; drain off drippings. To meat add tomato mixture, dill-seasoned salt, celery salt, honey, 2 Tbsp. parsley flakes, Burgundy, and mushrooms; simmer over low heat 8 hours or longer (the sauce will be thick). Cook lasagna noodles according to package directions; drain. Combine cottage cheese, ½ cup Parmesan cheese, 1 Tbsp. parsley flakes, ¾ tsp. salt, and oregano leaves. Reserve ¾ cup meat sauce; set aside. In a 13x9x2" baking dish, alternate layers of noodles, meat sauce, Mozzarella, Cheddar, Muenster, and the cottage cheese mixture; repeat layers three times. Spread reserved meat sauce on top; sprinkle with remaining ½ cup Parmesan cheese. Bake at 350 degrees for 45 minutes; allow to stand 15 minutes before serving. Serves 10 to 12.

Venison Meal-in-a-Mug

1 lb. ground venison
2 cups water
1 can pork and beans, undrained
1 can tomatoes with liquid, cut up

1 envelope sloppy joe mix
1 cup uncooked elbow macaroni
salt
black pepper

In a large saucepan, brown ground venison; drain. Add water, pork and beans, tomatoes and sloppy joe mix. Bring to a boil; simmer 10 minutes or until the macaroni is cooked. Serve in mugs with a spoon. Serves 6 to 8.

Venison and Egg Noodle Casserole

1 lb. ground venison
bacon drippings
1 large white onion, chopped
1 (No. 2) can green beans, drained

½ lb. egg noodles, cooked
1 can cream of mushroom soup
1 can tomato soup
¼ cup grated Cheddar cheese

Sauté venison with onion in small amount of bacon drippings. Place venison in a casserole dish. Add beans, egg noodles and soups in layers. Sprinkle the top with Cheddar cheese. Bake at 350 degrees for 45 minutes. Serves 8.

Venison Pastitsio

1 large yellow onion, chopped very fine
½ lb. butter
2 lbs. ground venison
⅛ lb. mild pork sausage
½ can tomato paste
½ cup water
½ tsp. ground cinnamon

½ tsp. ground nutmeg
salt and pepper to taste
½ cup white wine
1 lb. elbow macaroni
1 lb. shredded Kefaloteri cheese
2 eggs, well beaten
1 cup whole milk

Sauté onion in a little butter. Mix ground venison and sausage. Add ground venison to onions and stir until brown. Add tomato paste thinned with ½ cup water. Add seasonings and wine and simmer slowly until thick. Cook macaroni in boiling salted water, and drain. Melt the remaining butter and pour over drained macaroni, mixing carefully. Spread half of the macaroni in the bottom of a 13x9" pan and sprinkle generously with cheese. Spread meat sauce over the bottom layer of macaroni and cover with remaining macaroni. Top with cheese. Over this pour a sauce made of 2 eggs and 1 cup milk, mixed well. Bake at 350 degrees for 45 minutes. Allow to cool slightly and cut into squares to serve. Serves 10 to 12.

The mule deer is named for its large mule-like ears which are usually about one-quarter larger than those of the white-tailed deer.

Venison Scrapple

2 cups ground venison
2 cups ground beef
3 cups Venison Soup Stock or
   beef bouillon
2 tsp. salt

¼ tsp. pepper
1½ tsp. sage
1 cup cornmeal
red pepper

Combine meats and stock. Heat to boiling. Add seasonings. Sift in cornmeal slowly, stirring constantly. Cook 30 minutes. Add few grains of red pepper. Pour into mold. Chill until firm. Cut in thin slices. Fry until well browned. Serves 2 to 4.

One Pot Venison Spaghetti

1 lb. venison Italian sausage
¼ cup olive oil
2 Tbsp. minced parsley
1 cup yellow onion, chopped
2 cloves garlic, minced
2 (8-oz.) cans tomato purée

2 (6-oz.) cans tomato paste
1 Tbsp. Worcestershire sauce
salt
black pepper
1 (8-oz.) box spaghetti, cooked
Parmesan cheese

Just brown venison in hot olive oil; add parsley, onions and garlic. Cook over very low heat until tender; add remaining ingredients except spaghetti and Parmesan cheese. Simmer over low heat for 2 hours. Serve over cooked spaghetti. Sprinkle with Parmesan cheese. Serves 4 to 6.

Venison Spaghetti Pie

6 oz. spaghetti
2 Tbsp. butter
2 eggs, beaten
½ cup grated Parmesan cheese
1 cup cottage cheese
1 lb. ground venison
½ cup white onion, chopped
¼ cup red bell pepper, chopped

1 (8-oz.) can tomatoes, cut up,
   undrained
1 (6-oz.) can tomato paste
1 tsp. sugar
1 tsp. dried oregano
½ tsp. garlic salt
½ cup shredded Mozzarella cheese

Cook spaghetti according to package directions; drain and place in a bowl. Add butter, eggs and parmesan cheese; mix well. Spread over the bottom and up the sides of a 10" deep-dish pie plate. Spoon cottage cheese into crust; set aside. In a skillet, brown venison, onion and red pepper until venison is browned; drain. Stir in tomatoes, tomato paste, sugar, oregano and garlic salt. Spoon over cottage cheese. Bake, uncovered, at 350 degrees for 20 minutes. Sprinkle with Mozzarella cheese; return to the oven for 5 minutes or until cheese is melted. Cut into wedges. Serves 6.

Venison-Stuffed Cabbage Leaves

2 lbs. ground venison
5 Tbsp. chopped yellow onion
3 Tbsp. butter
2 cups Boiled Rice
1 Tbsp. fresh dill, chopped

black pepper, to taste
salt, to taste
12 large cabbage leaves
1 (8-oz.) can tomato sauce

Brown ground venison and onion in butter. Mix in rice, dill, and pepper. Add cabbage leaves in boiling water for 1 minute. Drain and dry cabbage leaves on paper towels. Divide venison mixture into 12 equal portions. Place the venison mixture in the center of each cabbage leaf. Fold up bottom then right, then left of cabbage leaf. Then roll up cabbage leaf and if needed seal with a toothpick. Lay the filled cabbage leaves in a buttered baking dish. Pour the tomato sauce over stuffed leaves and bake in 325-degree oven 45 to 60 minutes. Serves 4 to 6.

Venison Supernatural

2 lbs. ground venison
4 ozs. hot pork sausage
2 cans refried beans
3 cups yellow onions, chopped fine
1 pkg. dry taco powder
1 can chilies, chopped small

2 cups Cheddar cheese, shredded
2 large jars taco sauce
1 can black olives, pitted, sliced thin
2 large containers sour cream
2 small jars pimento, chopped
1 block Velveeta cheese

Thoroughly mix venison and pork sausage. Coat a casserole dish with the refried beans. Brown venison and sausage mixture, ½ cup onions and taco powder in skillet; place this mixture on top of the beans. Cover with chilies. Place two cups of shredded cheese on top of the chilies. Cover cheese with taco sauce. One hour before serving place casserole in the oven at 350 degrees for 30 minutes or until cheese browns. Remove from oven quickly and cover with 1½ cups onions, black olives, sour cream and pimentos on top. Melt Velveeta cheese in a double boiler and serve with any type of Mexican-style chips. Serves 2 to 4.

Mrs. Ann Lynch Webster

Venison Tallerine

1 large white onion, chopped
1½ lbs. ground venison
1 pkg. egg noodles
1 can whole kernel corn

1 (No. 2) can tomato juice
1 (10½-oz.) can cream of mushroom
  soup
½ lb. any soft white cheese, shredded

Brown onion in skillet, add ground venison, and cook until done. Cook egg noodles as directed on the package, then add to ground venison. Add remaining ingredients, reserving part of the cheese to sprinkle on top. Bake at 350 degrees for 30 minutes in a 8x8x2" baking dish.

Venison Tacos

Cheese Sauce:
1 jar (8-oz.) processed cheese spread
3 drops Tabasco sauce

1 medium tomato, chopped
½ tsp. salt
¼ tsp. chili powder

Tacos:
1 lb. venison, ground
½ cup yellow onion, chopped
½ cup Cheddar cheese, shredded

2 cans Pillsbury Buttermilk Biscuits
1 cup lettuce, shredded
¼ cup ripe olives, chopped

Combine cheese spread and Tabasco to make Cheese Sauce and heat over medium low heat, stirring constantly. In a large skillet, brown ground venison; drain. Add onion, cheese, tomato, salt, and chili powder; mix well. Separate biscuit dough into 20 biscuits. Roll out or press 10 biscuits to 5" circles on ungreased cookie sheets. Spoon about ⅓ cup venison mixture on each circle. Roll out or press remaining 10 biscuits to 5" circles. Place over filling; seal edges with fork. Bake at 400 degrees 12 to 15 minutes or until brown. Cut each into 3 pieces. Serve at once, topped with shredded lettuce, Cheese Sauce and chopped olives. Serves 2 to 4.

At birth, a white-tail female fawn weighs about 5½ pounds; and a male about 7½ pounds. When the fawn is two or three weeks old, it begins eating vegetation in addition to nursing. A fawn is normally weaned when it is about four months old, but is capable of surviving without milk at three months or less.

14

Venison Meat Loaves

Venison meat loaf is a real surprise. So you say, "I wonder why I never thought of that?" Why not? Venison makes great meat loaf. If you like your meat loaf dry, use your ground venison just as is in your favorite recipe. If you like your meat loaf moist and a little juicy, add some beef or pork fat or a little more liquid than your recipe calls for.

Since venison is virtually fat free, the meat has very little moisture content. The addition of fat is needed to provide the moisture for quality meat loaves. The general rule of thumb is to mix 70% venison with 30% moist meats (14# venison to 6# fat). Bacon and pork/beef fat are normally the meats added. My favorite additive is ground smoked bacon.

If you like venison meat loaf, but are concerned about the fat content in your diet, I recommend that you experiment with substituting mushrooms for the fat in any of these venison meat loaf recipes. Mushrooms provide water, which substitutes for fat, in preventing the meat loaf from tasting dry. Since venison is virtually fat free, with the substitution of mushrooms, you can convert most any of these recipes to low fat or fat free.

This substitution procedure has not been tested on all of these venison meat loaf recipes, so you will need to experiment. Make your ground venison by beginning with 25% (by weight) of mushrooms to 75% (by weight) of venison; break off a small piece and fry it. If the ground venison is dry, add more mushrooms to the mixture and test it again.

Louisiana Venison Meat Loaf

2 Tbsp. butter
½ large onion, chopped
½ cup green bell pepper, chopped
1 tsp. salt
¾ tsp. red pepper
½ tsp. dried thyme, crumbled
½ tsp. pepper

¼ tsp. ground cumin
1 lb. ground venison
1 egg, beaten
½ cup fine dry bread crumbs
½ cup tomato catsup
1 tsp. Worcestershire sauce

Preheat oven to 375 degrees. Melt butter in medium skillet over medium-low heat. Add next 7 ingredients and cook until vegetables are tender, stirring frequently, about 10 minutes. Combine meat, egg, bread crumbs, ¼ cup tomato catsup and Worcestershire sauce in medium bowl. Blend in sautéed vegetables. Form mixture into loaf 1¾" high and 5" wide in baking dish. Bake 20 minutes. Spread top with remaining ¼ cup tomato catsup and bake for 40 more minutes. Serves 2 to 4.

Applesauce-Venison Meat Loaf

2 lbs. ground venison
¼ lb. ground beef fat
3 eggs, beaten
2 tsp. salt
1 tsp. Seasoning Salt
1 Tbsp. garlic salt
1 Tbsp. A-1 steak sauce
1 Tbsp. Worcestershire sauce

¼ tsp. black pepper
1 cup tomato juice
¼ cup tomato catsup
½ cup onion, chopped
¼ cup green bell pepper, chopped
1 cup rolled wheat or Quaker Oats
¾ cup applesauce
⅓ cup tomato catsup

Mix ground meats and place in refrigerator to cool. Reserve ⅓ cup tomato catsup. Mix remaining ingredients, except applesauce. Remove the ground meat mixture from the refrigerator and mix thoroughly with the other mixture. Add applesauce last and mix gently. Divide the mixture into two equal parts and pack firmly into two foil-lined 3x5½x9½" loaf pans. Using the catsup dispenser, squeeze a design onto the top with the reserved tomato catsup. Bake in 350-degree oven for 1 hour. Remove from pans and peel away the foil and place onto platter, or platters, and garnish with apple rings or spiced crab apples. Serves 8 to 10.

Baked Venison Kibbeh

Kibbeh:
2 cups bulgur (cracked wheat)
2 lbs. venison (ground twice)
1 tsp. ground allspice
1 tsp. black pepper
4 tsp. salt
1 medium onion, chopped fine

Filling:
1 lb. venison, ground coarse

¼ cup beef fat, ground coarse
½ cup ground allspice
1½ tsp. salt
2 Tbsp. butter
1 very small onion, chopped

Topping:
1 cup butter, melted

Wash and soak bulgur in warm water for 20 minutes. While bulgur soaks, place all Kibbeh ingredients together. Drain bulgur to remove water; knead Kibbeh ingredients and bulgur together. Place ½ of Kibbeh ingredients into the bottom of a buttered 8x12" pan or dish; pat and press smooth. Place all Filling ingredients in a skillet and fry until about ½ done. Place Filling ingredients on top of ½ of Kibbeh; pat and press smooth. Place the other ½ of Kibbeh ingredients on top of filling and pat smooth. Cut layered mixture all the way through into diagonal diamond shapes. Pour melted butter over the top. Bake in a 400-degree oven for about 1 hour. Cut Kibbeh all the way through a second time. Cover Kibbeh with a double layer of wet paper towels. Seal with plastic wrap and refrigerate overnight. Prior to serving, remove Kibbeh from the refrigerator and cut through a third time. Remove several pieces so that pieces can be gently separated in pan. Warm pieces in a microwave oven. Can be cut into bite-sized pieces and used as hors d'oeuvres. Serves 6 to 8.

Cheese and Mushroom-Stuffed Venison Meat Loaf

2 Tbsp. canola oil
1 medium onion, chopped
2 garlic cloves, minced
8 oz. mushrooms, sliced
1½ lbs. ground venison
⅔ cup fresh breadcrumbs
½ cup fresh parsley, minced

¼ cup tomato catsup
1 egg, beaten
1 tsp. salt
½ tsp. pepper
½ tsp. dried thyme, crumbled
¼ tsp. dried, ground or rubbed sage
1½ cups Monterey Jack cheese, grated

Heat oil in medium skillet over medium heat. Add onion and sauté until translucent, about 4 minutes. Add garlic and mushrooms. Cook until mushrooms are golden brown and liquid evaporates, stirring occasionally, about 7 minutes. Cool. Preheat oven to 350 degrees. Mix venison and next 8 ingredients in a large bowl until well blended. Turn out onto large square of plastic wrap. Pat into 9x12" rectangle. Spread mushroom filling over rectangle leaving ½" border on all sides. Cover mushrooms with cheese. Starting at one short side, roll meat up jelly roll fashion. Arrange seam side down in 9x5" loaf pan. Bake until loaf shrinks from sides of pan and browns, about 1 hour. Pour off any drippings. Gently turn out loaf and let stand 10 minutes. Cut in slices and serve. Serves 6 to 8.

Cheese Ribbon Venison Loaf

5 slices white bread
1 cup whole milk
1 egg, beaten
1 lb. ground venison
¼ lb. ground pork
¼ cup white onion, chopped

1¼ tsp. salt
¼ tsp. black pepper
1 Tbsp. Worcestershire sauce
1 egg white, slightly beaten
1 Tbsp. water
¼ lb. Cheddar cheese, grated

Tear 3 slices of white bread into pieces. Add the milk, egg, meats, onion, salt, pepper and Worcestershire sauce and mix thoroughly. Press ½ of the mixture into a loaf pan. Combine the egg white and water. Tear remaining bread into pieces and mix with egg white mixture. Stir in the cheese and spread over meat mixture. Top with remaining meat mixture. Bake at 350 degrees for 1½ hours. Serves 8.

On the basis of food consumed, seven deer will eat about as much as one medium-sized cow.

Congealed Venison Loaf

1 lb. venison round steak
1 lb. pork, fat removed
salt to taste
1 env. unflavored gelatin
1 green bell pepper, chopped
1 small can green peas, drained
2 pimentos, chopped

1 Tbsp. Durkee's Dressing
1 Tbsp. Worcestershire sauce
1 Tbsp. cider vinegar
1 Tbsp. French dressing
1 Tbsp. Mayonnaise
chopped sweet pickle to taste

Place the venison steak and pork in a saucepan, add salt and cover with water. Bring to a boil and simmer until tender. Drain and reserve 1¾ cups liquid. Grind steak and pork together. Soften gelatin in ¼ cup water. Heat the reserved liquid to boiling point and stir in gelatin until dissolved. Stir in ground meats. Add remaining ingredients and mix well, pour into a mold and chill until set. Serves 4 to 6.

Country Venison Meat Loaf

2 eggs, beaten
1 (10¾-oz.) can condensed cream of celery
  soup, undiluted
½ tsp. pepper

1 (6-oz.) box corn bread stuffing mix
1½ lbs. ground venison
½ lb. ground veal
¼ lb. ground pork

Mix eggs, soup, pepper and stuffing mix. Combine venison, veal and pork and add to egg mixture and mix well. Press meat mixture into a 9x5x3" loaf pan. Bake at 350 degrees for 1½ hours or until no pink remains. Drain. Serves 6 to 8.

Cranberry Venison Loaf

¼ cup dark brown sugar
½ cup Cranberry Sauce
1½ lbs. ground venison
½ lb. ground ham
¾ cup whole milk

¾ cup saltine cracker crumbs
2 eggs, beaten
salt and pepper to taste
2 Tbsp, white onion, chopped
2 bay leaves

Spread brown sugar over bottom of a greased loaf pan. Spread Cranberry Sauce over sugar. Combine remaining ingredients except bay leaves. Shape into loaf and place on cranberry sauce. Place bay leaves on top. Bake at 350 degrees for 1 hour. Remove bay leaves and serve. Serves 8 to 10.

Creole Venison Meat Loaf

2 lbs. ground venison
½ lb. ground pork
1 tsp. salt
1 tsp. black pepper
3 tsp. parsley, chopped
1 cup celery, chopped
2 medium onions, minced
3 Tbsp. flour

2 Tbsp. hot lard or bacon grease
1 cup cold whole milk
1 cup bread crumbs
1 egg, beaten
dash Tabasco sauce
1 tsp. Worcestershire sauce
¼ lb. butter

Mix together meat, salt, pepper, parsley, celery, and onions. Make a sauce by stirring flour into grease. When browned slightly, add milk. When this boils put the seasoned meat in. Cook for a minute, then mix in bread crumbs. Remove from heat and stir in beaten egg; add Tabasco and Worcestershire sauce. Form into a loaf and lay in a well-greased pan. Dot the top with lumps of butter and cook about 1½ hours, basting several times. Serves 6 to 8.

Favorite Venison Meat Loaf

2 eggs
¼ cup whole milk
1 Tbsp. Worcestershire sauce
1 tsp. Seasoned Salt
1 tsp. onion powder
1 cup quick-cooking oats

1 carrot, shredded
2 Tbsp. fresh parsley, chopped
1½ lbs. ground venison
1 lb. ground pork
½ cup tomato catsup

In a large bowl, beat eggs. Add milk, Worcestershire sauce, seasoned salt and onion powder; mix well. Stir in oats, carrot and parsley. Combine venison and pork; add to egg mixture and mix well. Press into a 9x5x3" loaf pan. Top with tomato catsup. Bake at 350 degrees for 1½ hours or until no pink remains. Drain. Serves 6 to 8.

Italian Venison Meat Loaf

1 lb. ground venison
½ lb. ground lean pork
12 salted crackers, crushed
¼ cup tomato catsup
¼ cup chili sauce
1 small white onion, grated
salt
black pepper
1 Tbsp. green bell pepper, minced

⅛ tsp. Dijon mustard
⅛ tsp. celery seeds
⅛ tsp. garlic salt
2 tsp. Worcestershire sauce
⅛ tsp. savory leaf, crushed
dash curry powder
1 cup water
Parmesan cheese
3 beef bouillon cubes

Grease a meat loaf pan. Combine all ingredients, except Parmesan cheese and bouillon cubes. Pour in 1 cup of water; mix well. Form mixture into a loaf and place in greased pan. Sprinkle loaf with Parmesan cheese. Bake in 350-degree oven for 1¾ hours. Make gravy by using drippings and bouillon cubes. Serves 6.

Venison Meat Loaf with Tomato Catsup Meringue

1½ lbs. ground venison
½ lb. pork sausage
¾ cup quick-cooking oatmeal
1 cup cracker crumbs
1 cup white onion, finely chopped
1 clove garlic, mashed
2⅛ tsp. salt
¼ tsp. chili powder

¼ tsp. pepper
1 cup whole milk
2 eggs, separated
¼ tsp. cream of tartar
¼ cup tomato catsup
4 cherry tomatoes, halved
8 sprigs of parsley

Combine the meats with the oatmeal, crumbs, onion, garlic, 2 Tbsp. salt, chili powder and pepper and mix thoroughly. Add milk to slightly beaten egg yolks and blend with the meat mixture. Pack into a greased 9¼x5¼x2¾" loaf pan and chill. Unmold onto a shallow baking pan. Bake for 1½ hours in a 350-degree oven. Remove from oven and let stand for several minutes. Add the remaining salt and cream of tartar to egg whites and beat until stiff. Fold in tomato catsup carefully. Cover top and sides of loaf with meringue. Return to oven and bake for about 15 minutes or until golden brown. Garnish with cherry tomatoes and parsley. Serves 6 to 8.

Olive-Stuffed Venison Meat Loaf

1½ cups crushed saltine crackers
¼ cup white onions, minced
½ cup stuffed olives, sliced
2 eggs, slightly beaten

1½ lbs. ground venison
2 Tbsp. horseradish
¾ cup tomato juice

Preheat oven to 375 degrees. Combine crushed saltines, onions, olives, eggs, beef, horseradish and tomato juice in a bowl and mix well. Press into a greased 9x5" loaf pan. Arrange additional sliced olives on top. Bake for 1 hour and remove to a warm platter. Serves 4.

Pizza Venison Meat Loaf

2 eggs
1 (14-oz.) jar pizza sauce, divided
1 (4-oz.) cup Mozzarella cheese, shredded
1 cup Italian-seasoned bread crumbs
¼ tsp. garlic salt

⅛ tsp. pepper
2 lbs. ground venison
½ lb. Homemade Red Wine Sausage
   or any link sausage

In a large bowl, beat eggs. Add ¾ cup of pizza sauce, cheese, bread crumbs, garlic salt and pepper; mix well. Combine venison and Homemade Red Wine Sausage; add to egg mixture and mix well. Press into a 9x5x3" loaf pan. Bake at 350 degrees for 1¼ hours. Drain. Spoon remaining pizza sauce over meat loaf; bake 15 minutes longer or until no pink remains. Let stand for 10 minutes before slicing. Serves 6 to 8.

Potato-Venison Meat Loaf

4 medium potatoes, sliced
1 white onion, sliced
½ lb. ground venison
½ lb. medium hot pork sausage
1 egg, beaten

6 crackers, crumbled
1 tsp. chili powder
½ tsp. salt
¼ tsp. pepper
½ cup Cheddar cheese soup

Place the potatoes in a baking dish and place onion over potatoes. Combine the ground venison, sausage, egg, cracker, chili powder, salt and pepper and mix well. Press into baking dish over onion and spread the soup over venison mixture. Bake for 1 hour at 350 degrees. Serves 4 to 6.

Ripe Olive-Cabbage Venison Loaf

1 medium head cabbage
1 gal. boiling water
salt
1½ cups pitted ripe olives
1½ lbs. ground venison
¼ cup onion, finely chopped
1 egg, beaten
¼ tsp. black pepper
½ cup soft bread crumbs

¼ cup whole milk
½ tsp. caraway seeds
¼ tsp. thyme
1 Tbsp. all-purpose flour
1 Tbsp. butter,
   melted
1 bouillon cube
⅓ cup white wine

Preheat oven to 350 degrees. Cut core from cabbage and pull leaves apart. Cook in boiling water with 2 Tbsp. salt for about 10 minutes or until leaves are wilted, then drain. Reserve ¼ cup olives for sauce and cut remaining olives in large pieces. Combine 1¾ tsp. salt, olive pieces, venison, onion, egg, pepper, crumbs, milk, caraway seeds and thyme and mix well. Line a greased loaf pan with cabbage leaves and cover with half the venison mixture, smoothing top. Arrange layer of cabbage leaves over venison mixture. Cover with remaining venison mixture, then top with cabbage. Cover with foil and place on a baking sheet. Bake for 1 hour and 15 minutes and remove foil. Drain the venison loaf and reserve liquid. Turn loaf out onto a heated platter and keep warm. Blend the flour with butter in a saucepan. Add enough water to reserved liquid to make ⅔ cup liquid and stir into flour mixture. Add the bouillon cube and wine and cook, stirring, until sauce boils and thickens slightly. Slice reserved olives and add to sauce. Serve with venison loaf. Serves 6 to 8.

Sorghum Venison Meat Loaf

½ cup sorghum molasses
¼ cup red wine vinegar
¼ cup prepared mustard
1 cup tomato juice
2 eggs, beaten
3 cups soft bread crumbs

1 onion, finely chopped
½ cup parsley, chopped
1 Tbsp. salt
1 tsp. black pepper
3 lbs. ground venison

Combine ¼ cup molasses, vinegar, mustard, tomato juice and eggs and mix well. Stir in the bread crumbs, onion, parsley, salt and pepper. Add the ground venison and mix well. Shape into a loaf. Place in a shallow baking dish and brush with 1 Tbsp. molasses. Bake at 350 degrees for 1 hour and 30 minutes, brushing with remaining molasses occasionally. Serves 4 to 6.

Spiced Venison Meat Loaf

1½ lbs. ground venison
1 cup whole milk
1 egg, lightly beaten
¾ cup soft bread crumbs
1 medium white onion, chopped
1 Tbsp. green bell pepper, chopped

1 Tbsp. tomato catsup
1½ tsp. horseradish
1 tsp. sugar
1 tsp. ground allspice
1 tsp. dill weed
additional tomato catsup

In a large bowl, combine the first 11 ingredients; mix well. Press into an ungreased 8½x4½x2½" loaf pan. Bake at 350 degrees 1 hour. Drizzle top of loaf with tomato catsup; bake 15 minutes more or until no pink remains. Serves 6 to 8.

Tamale-Style Venison Loaf

1 cup celery, finely chopped
½ cup onion, finely chopped
1 green pepper, chopped
4 Tbsp. butter
1 lb. ground venison
2 cans tomato sauce
1 cup yellow cornmeal

1 (No. 2) can cream-style corn
2 eggs, well beaten
2 tsp. salt
½ tsp. black pepper
1 Tbsp. chili powder
1 small can pitted ripe olives

Cook the celery, onion and green pepper in butter in a saucepan until tender. Add the venison and cook until venison is light brown. Add the tomato sauce and mix well. Stir in cornmeal, corn, eggs, salt, pepper, chili powder and olives and mix well. Place in a greased loaf pan. Bake for 1 hour at 350 degrees. Serves 4 to 6.

Venison and Burgundy Meat Loaf

2 lbs. venison
½ lb. veal
½ lb pork
2 eggs
1 cup seasoned bread crumbs
4 Tbsp. Worcestershire sauce

1 (10-oz.) can tomato and green chilies
1 large white onion, chopped
1 Tbsp. dry mustard
1 tsp. fresh parsley, chopped
1 cup Burgundy wine

Grind venison, veal and pork together. Combine ground meats with the remaining ingredients. Form meat loaf mixture into a loaf and place it in an ungreased pan. Bake in a preheated 350-degree oven for 1 hour. Serves 6.

Venison and Sausage Meat Loaf

¾ lb. ground venison
¼ lb. ground venison or other sausage
1 egg yolk
2 Tbsp. parsley, chopped
1 Tbsp. soft butter
1 Tbsp. bread crumbs

1 tsp. lime juice
1 tsp. salt
¼ tsp. pepper
½ tsp. onion juice
½ cup boiling water
1 pkg. dried tomato soup mix

Preheat oven to 350 degrees. Combine venison, sausage, egg, parsley, butter, bread crumbs, lime juice, salt, pepper, and onion juice. Make into loaf and place in a lightly greased pan. Baste with sauce made from water and dried tomato soup mix. Bake about 45 minutes. Serves 4.

Venison and Sour Cream Meat Loaf

4 slices stale white bread
1 lb. ground venison
1 medium onion, chopped
1 egg, beaten
1 tsp. salt
dash of pepper

2 slices bacon
1 medium carrot
2 Tbsp. chervil (spice)
2 bay leaves
1 cup sour cream
Boiled Rice

Soak bread in cold water and squeeze out excess liquid; add to the venison with onion, egg, salt and pepper. Cut bacon into small cubes and fry until crisp. Remove bacon from pan and pour the fat into a baking pan. Shape meat mixture into a loaf and place in the baking pan with the fat. Cut carrot into fine strips and mix with the bacon cubes, chervil and bay leaves. Place on top of the meat loaf, cover baking pan and bake in a moderate oven (350 degrees) for 1 hour. Remove meat loaf from pan onto a hot platter. Strain gravy; add sour cream and heat for a few minutes. Pour gravy over meat loaf, serve with spaghetti or Boiled Rice. Serves 6.

15

Venison Meatballs

One of my joys in working on this section is the fond memories I have of Eldora Tedesco. Eldora was of Greek heritage and she is married to Ignatious Tedesco. Ted is of Italian descent and is a physician, from a family of physicians. Eldora's cooking is a wonderful mix of Greek, Italian and Cajun. As an 11-year old, I remember sitting in her New Orleans kitchen and watching her take all day to make her meatballs and spaghetti sauce.

I can remember that all of the meatballs were the same small size and they had little flecks of green woven throughout the meat. I never did ask Eldora for her recipe. But I have never forgotten watching her working her magic.

When dinner was served, it was Ted who taught me how to load up my spaghetti with heaps of Parmesan cheese. I always thought this was how real Italians ate spaghetti. It wasn't until Anne and I visited Italy in 1994 that I found out that Ted just liked the cheese.

I have tried to duplicate the recipe, as well as I can remember. Try Harold's Venison Meatballs and Spaghetti Sauce. I feel that Eldora would approve of my efforts.

Since venison is virtually fat free, the meat has very little moisture content. The addition of fat is needed to provide the moisture for quality meatballs. The general rule of thumb is to mix 70% venison with 30% moist meats (14# venison to 6# fat). Bacon and pork/beef fat are normally the meats added. My favorite additive is ground smoked bacon.

If you like venison meatballs, but are concerned about the fat content in your diet, I recommend that you experiment with substituting mushrooms for the fat in any of these venison meatball recipes. Mushrooms provide water, which substitutes for fat, in preventing the meatballs from tasting dry. Since venison is virtually fat free, with the substitution of mushrooms you can convert most any of these recipes to low fat or fat free. You will need to experiment. Make your ground venison by beginning with 25% (by weight) of mushrooms to 75% (by weight) of venison; break off a small piece and fry it. If the ground venison is dry, add more mushrooms to the mixture and test it again.

Harold's Venison Meatballs and Spaghetti Sauce

Harold's Favorite Venison Meatballs:

½ lb. venison, ground
½ lb. pork, ground
2 medium white onions, minced
1 garlic clove, minced
¼ cup parsley, chopped fine
½ cup fresh grated Parmesan cheese
½ cup fine dry bread crumbs
1 egg
2 tsp. salt
½ tsp. pepper
2 cups canola oil

Mix all ingredients except oil thoroughly, Add a little water if mixture seems dry. Shape into 24 balls and brown quickly in hot oil. The meatballs can be eaten as is or they can be frozen and used in other recipes.

Harold's Favorite Spaghetti Sauce:

2 medium white onions, chopped
2 cloves garlic, minced
2 Tbsp. canola oil
1 (28-oz.) can tomatoes
1 cup water
½ tsp. dried basil
¼ cup parsley, chopped
½ tsp. thyme, crumbled
2 tsp. salt
¼ tsp. black pepper
¼ tsp. red pepper flakes
1 (6-oz.) can tomato paste
Harold's Favorite Venison Meatballs
12 oz. spaghetti, cooked and hot

Sauté onion and garlic until golden in hot oil in large saucepan. Add tomatoes and bring to boil. Simmer, uncovered, 20 minutes, stirring occasionally. Put in crock pot cooker, add remaining sauce ingredients and the browned meatballs, cover and cook on low 6 to 8 hours. Add more seasoning, if desired. Serve on hot cooked spaghetti. Serves 6.

Meatballs in Burgundy Sauce

1 lb. ground venison round steak
⅛ lb. ground pork
½ cup cornflake crumbs
1 medium white onion, minced
¾ tsp. cornstarch
dash ground pepper
1 egg, beaten
1 Tbsp. Worcestershire sauce
¼ cup canned chili sauce
½ cup evaporated milk
1 tsp. salt
Burgundy and Bouillon Sauce

Combine all ingredients; mix well and shape into teaspoon-size balls. Place on cookie sheet with sides and bake at 400 degrees for 10 to 15 minutes. Serve with Burgundy and Bouillon Sauce. Serves 6.

Meatballs with Bread Crumbs and Onion Soup

1 lb. ground venison
½ cup stale bread crumbs
1 egg, beaten
2 Tbsp. dry onion soup mix
Crisco or other shortening
remainder of dry onion soup mix
water as needed
Boiled Rice

Mix ground venison, bread crumbs, egg, and 2 Tbsp. dry onion soup mix. Shape into balls. Brown balls in Crisco. Sprinkle browned meatballs with remainder of dry onion soup mix, cover with water and simmer 1 hour. Add more water if necessary. Serve over Boiled Rice. Serves 2 to 4.

German Venison Meatballs

Meatballs:
1 medium white onion, chopped
2 Tbsp. butter
½ lb. ground venison
½ lb. ground veal
½ lb. ground pork
4 anchovy fillets, mashed
1 egg, slightly beaten
1 cup soft, fresh bread crumbs
¼ cup whole milk
¼ tsp. salt
¼ tsp. pepper

Poaching Liquid:
2 qts. water
1 med. white onion, peeled and sliced
1 bay leaf
1 tsp. salt

Sauce:
4 Tbsp. butter
4 Tbsp. all-purpose flour
1½ Tbsp. lime juice
2 Tbsp. capers, drained
1 egg yolk, well beaten
1 Tbsp. cream

Cook the onion in the butter about 10 minutes until soft. Mix in the remaining meatball ingredients and gently shape the mixture into 1" balls. Bring the water, onion, bay leaf, and salt to a boil. Boil 10 minutes, then add the meatballs and simmer uncovered 20 minutes or until the balls rise to the surface. Remove the meatballs to a platter, cover them with aluminum foil, and keep warm in a 250-degree oven. Strain the liquid and reserve 2 cups for making the sauce. To make the sauce, heat the butter in the skillet, add the flour, and cook slowly 1 minute. Remove the skillet from the heat. Gradually stir in the reserved liquid and cook, stirring until the sauce thickens. Add the lime juice and capers. Cook slowly for 5 minutes. In a small bowl mix the egg yolk with the heavy cream. Stir a few tablespoons of the hot poaching liquid into the egg mixture; return this to the hot liquid. Add the meatballs, cover, and simmer about 5 minutes to cook the egg yolk. Do not boil. Serves 6 to 8.

Oriental Meatballs with Far Eastern Sauce

3 slices white bread, crust removed
1 egg
2 tsp. horseradish
½ tsp. salt
1 (5-oz.) can water chestnuts, chopped
1 lb. ground venison
¼ cup all-purpose flour

2 Tbsp. peanut or canola oil
¾ cup orange marmalade
1 clove of garlic, minced
3 Tbsp. soy sauce
2 Tbsp. lime juice
¼ cup peanut butter

Combine first 6 ingredients with ½ cup water and mix lightly. Form into 24 meatballs and dredge with flour. Brown in hot peanut oil in a skillet. Remove to a platter and keep warm. Drain excess fat from skillet and add remaining ingredients and 3 Tbsp. water to skillet, Heat, stirring, for about 2 minutes or until bubbly. Spoon over meatballs. Serves 4.

Persian Venison Meatballs

1½ lbs. ground venison, with 10% fat filler
¾ cup white onion, minced
1 tsp. salt, divided
½ tsp. black pepper
1¼ tsp. coriander, ground, divided

2 med. cloves garlic
13 oz. canned beef broth
1 Tbsp, lime juice
20 oz. canned chick-peas
10 cups fresh, deveined spinach leaves

Mix ground venison, onion, ¾ tsp. salt, pepper, and ¼ tsp. coriander. Shape into sixteen 1½" meatballs, approximately 3 Tbsp. of mixture to each ball. Sprinkle remaining ¼ tsp, of salt on the bottom of a Dutch oven and heat over moderately-high heat. Add meatballs and cook for 5 minutes, turning once, until browned. Cover pot and cook until meatballs are no longer pink in the center. Place a colander over a bowl; pour meatballs and liquid into the colander and allow to drain. Return meatballs to Dutch oven. Skim fat from liquid and return liquid to Dutch oven. Add the remaining 1 tsp. of coriander, peeled garlic, beef broth and lime juice. Cover and cook over moderately-low heat for 15 minutes. Discard garlic. Stir in chick-peas and arrange spinach on top. Cover and cook for 5 minutes or until the spinach has wilted. Serves 4.

Indonesian Venison Meatballs

1 lb. ground venison
½ lb. ground pork
½ cup fine dry bread crumbs
1 egg, lightly beaten
½ cup Mashed Potatoes
1 tsp. Seasoning Salt
½ tsp. brown sugar

¼ tsp. black pepper
¼ tsp. ground allspice
¼ tsp. ground nutmeg
⅛ tsp. ground cloves
⅛ tsp. ground ginger
3 Tbsp. butter

Coarse grind venison and pork. Mix coarse ground meats and regrind using a fine blade. Mix together all ingredients except the butter. Mix well and shape into 1"-diameter balls. Melt butter in skillet over low heat. Add venison meatballs and brown on all sides. Cover and cook over low heat for 15 minutes. Serve with wild rice and gravy, hash browned or Mashed Potatoes, or Boiled Rice. Serves 6 to 8.

Swedish Venison Meatballs

1 lb. ground venison
2 Tbsp. white onion, finely chopped
1 tsp. salt
⅛ tsp. black pepper

2¼ cups whole milk
2 eggs, slightly beaten
4 cups cornflakes

Place the ground venison in a bowl and add the onion, salt, pepper, 1¼ cups milk and eggs. Roll cornflakes into crumbs and add to ground venison mixture. Mix thoroughly and form into balls. Sauté in butter in a skillet over low heat until brown and remove from skillet. Add remaining milk to the skillet drippings and heat through. Pour over the meatballs. Serves 4 to 5.

Turkish Venison Meatballs

1 slice dry bread	2 eggs
1 medium white onion	1 Tbsp. dried mint leaves
1 cup parsley sprigs	1½ tsp. salt
1 lb. lamb shoulder	½ tsp. black pepper
1 lb. venison, any boneless cut	olive oil

Put bread, onion, and parsley through grinder using coarse disc. Put lamb and venison through food grinder using fine disc. Add remaining ingredients except olive oil and mix well. Form into 30 meatballs about the size of golf balls. Place on broiler rack and brush with olive oil. Broil about 4 inches from heat until meat is desired doneness, turning to brown on all sides. Serve on a bed of cooked, cracked wheat with yogurt or sour cream. Serves 6.

A white-tailed deer (Odocoileus virginianus) is a relatively small deer with short ears; all major points of the antlers come off the main beam; the tail is relatively long, and white underneath; females are usually antlerless; upperparts are reddish brown in summer, bright grayish fawn sprinkled with black; in winter, the face and tail usually lack blackish markings. Males weigh 70 to 200 pounds (30 to 70 kg.). They are also called Virginia deer.

16

Venison Sandwiches and Burgers

Sandwiches and burgers are not traditionally associated with venison. But the fine texture of venison makes it a natural for these recipes. Venison ground for burgers needs the help of a little fat to hold the meat together and to prevent sticking while cooking.

Hot sandwiches such as Hot Venison Sandwiches and Hot Venison Sausage and Apple Sandwiches make outstanding large open-face sandwiches for dinner at the Monday night football game for the gentlemen or a family dinner on the porch one summer evening. Another favorite open-face sandwich is the Venison and Bacon Patties with Gravy recipe.

SANDWICHES

Barbecue Venison Sandwiches

2 lbs. venison, cubed
2 (16-oz.) cans tomatoes
1 large onion, chopped
½ cup red wine vinegar
1 cup water
⅓ cup Worcestershire sauce

1 Tbsp. sugar
1 tsp. salt
1 tsp. black pepper
Thick sliced whole grain bread
Cole Slaw

Combine venison, tomatoes, onion, vinegar, water, Worcestershire sauce, sugar, salt and pepper in a 2-quart saucepan. Bring to a boil; reduce heat. Simmer for 3 to 4 hours or to desired consistency, stirring occasionally. Remove meat from pan and chop. Return meat to pan; mix well. Serve on whole grain bread with Cole Slaw. Serves 4 to 6

Deer prefer to live near forests and agricultural areas, such as crop fields, because these areas provide food and cover. Deer have hooved feet, slender bodies, and long, thin legs. Don't let their skinny legs fool you. Deer are able to run up to 40 miles per hour, jump 9-foot fences, and swim 13 miles per hour.

Grilled Venison Steak, Onion and Bell Pepper Sandwiches

3 cups dry red wine
3 cups Vidalia onions, chopped
2¼ cups teriyaki sauce
¾ cup olive oil
8 large garlic cloves, chopped
1 Tbsp. plus 1½ tsp. dry mustard

1 Tbsp. plus 1½ tsp. ground ginger
4½ lbs. venison steak
6 large bell peppers (red, yellow and/or green) cut into ¾" wide strips
3 large red onions, cut ½" thick rings
Grilled French Bread Rolls

Combine first 7 ingredients in a large bowl. Divide steaks, bell peppers and red onions among large shallow pans. Pour marinade over. Turn to coat. Cover and refrigerate 3 to 6 hours. Heat barbecue grill to high heat. Drain steaks and vegetables. Grill steaks to desired degree of doneness. Slice steaks thinly across the grain. Arrange steaks and vegetables on large platter. Serve with grilled rolls. Allow diners to assemble individual sandwiches. Serves 12.

Grilled Venison Liver Sandwich

1 cup cooked venison liver, chopped
¼ tsp. salt
4 Tbsp. Mayonnaise

4 tomatoes, sliced
8 bacon slices
4 thick slices of bread

Put venison liver through the food chopper; add salt and mayonnaise. Toast one side of bread. Spread liver on untoasted side of bread; top with slices of tomato and bacon; broil until bacon is crisp and tomato soft. Serves 2.

Hot Venison French-Style Sandwiches

1 (4-lb.) venison roast
1 small onion, diced
½ pt. tomato juice
1 can tomato sauce
salt

½ tsp. pepper
2 tsp. Worcestershire sauce
½ tsp. garlic salt
1 tsp. Tabasco sauce
4 Small Loaf French Bread, split

Place roast in roasting pan; add onion, tomato juice, tomato sauce, salt and pepper. Cover. Bake at 400 degrees for 2 hours. Remove roast from pan; cool. Add Worcestershire sauce, garlic salt and hot sauce to pan drippings; stir well. Slice meat; replace in drippings. Just before serving, heat; spoon juices and meat over buns. Serves 8 to 9.

Sautéed Venison Sandwich

leftover cooked venison roast
White Cream Gravy
butter

bread
Tomato Sauce

Coarse grind leftover cooked venison. Add hot well-seasoned White Cream Gravy to moisten venison. Put ground venison between slices of bread; brown on each side in butter. Serve with Tomato Sauce.

Hot Venison Sausage and Apple Sandwich

¾ lb. Venison Sausage with Lemon
   and Spices or other bulk sausage
3 sweet apples

Cole Slaw
butter
toast bacon

Shape venison sausage into round patties ½" thick; fry and remove from pan. Keep hot. Core and slice apples, leaving skins on, and sauté in a little sausage fat. Place sausage patty and a slice of apple on buttered toast. Garnish with bacon curls. Serve with Cole Slaw. Serves 2 to 4.

Mock Venison Filet Sandwich

1 lb. ground venison
¼ lb. ground beef fat
1 cup cracker crumbs
1 egg, beaten
⅓ cup tomato catsup
¼ cup lime juice

1 cup Swiss cheese, grated
¼ cup green bell pepper, chopped
2 Tbsp. onion, chopped
salt
pepper
smoked bacon slices

Combine all ingredients except bacon. Preheat oven to 300 degrees. Make into patties and wrap a slice of bacon around each patty. Secure bacon with toothpicks. Bake 15 to 20 minutes. Serve as an open face sandwich on thick-cut toast with onion, tomatoes and lettuce.

Scotch Venison Patties

¾ lb. ground venison
⅓ cup whole milk
¾ cup quick-cooking oats
1 tsp. salt
pepper
2 Tbsp. bacon fat

1 cup water
¼ cup celery, chopped
¼ cup green bell pepper, chopped
¼ med. white onion, chopped
1 tsp. Worcestershire sauce
1 Tbsp. all-purpose flour

Combine the venison, milk, oats, salt and pepper and shape into thin patties. Brown on both sides in fat in a frying pan. Add the water, vegetables, Worcestershire sauce, salt and pepper to taste, and cover. Cook over low heat for 30 minutes. Blend flour with 1 tablespoon cold water and stir into the celery mixture. Cook until thickened, stirring occasionally. Serves 2 to 4.

Fawns are protected by a lack of scent. Enemies cannot smell them. Fawns are able to stand and walk shortly after birth. The mother keeps them hidden in bushes and checks up on them about 6 times a day to feed them. Young deer stay with their mothers for 1–2 years.

Southwestern Venison Sloppy Joses

4 dried ancho chilies, stemmed and coarsely
  chopped
2 Tbsp. Mazola or canola oil
3 med. celery stalks, diced
2 med. yellow onion, thinly sliced
1 large green bell pepper, seeded and finely
  chopped
3 garlic cloves, minced
2 Tbsp. chili powder
1 (16-oz.) can whole peeled tomatoes,
  undrained

1 cup canned beef broth
1 (4-oz.) can green chilies, chopped
2 Tbsp. sorghum molasses
1 Tbsp. paprika
1 tsp. ground cumin
1 tsp. salt
1¼ lbs, cooked venison roast, cut in
  strips
8 toasted hamburger buns

Cover and soak chilies in hot water until softened. Heat Mazola oil in a skillet over low heat. Add celery, onion, bell pepper and garlic. Cover and cook until the vegetables are just tender, stirring occasionally. Reduce heat to low and mix in chili powder. Cover and cook for 10 minutes. Drain chilies and reserve the liquid. Puree chilies, 3 Tbsp. soaking liquid and tomatoes with their liquid in a blender or food processor. Strain puree into the vegetable mixture. Add beef broth, green chilies, sorghum molasses, paprika, cumin and salt. Mix all ingredients well. Add venison and simmer until the sauce thickens. If needed add more of the chili soaking liquid. Toast hamburger buns. Spoon the venison mixture over the buns and serve hot. Serves 8.

Venison Muffuletta Sandwich

1⅔ cups pimento-stuffed olives, chopped
1½ cups black olives, pitted and chopped
⅔ cup olive oil
1 (4-oz.) jar pimientos, drained and chopped
⅓ cup fresh parsley, chopped
3 anchovy fillets, minced
2 Tbsp. capers, drained
1 Tbsp. garlic, minced
1 Tbsp. fresh oregano, minced or 1 tsp.
  dried, crumbled

salt
pepper
1 (8" round loaf.) Italian-Style Bread
  (about 1 lb.)
4 oz. Venison Pastrami, thinly
  sliced
4 oz. Provolone cheese, thinly sliced
4 oz. Mortadella cheese, thinly sliced

Combine the first 9 ingredients in medium bowl. Season with salt and pepper. Cover and refrigerate olive salad overnight to mellow flavors. Drain olive salad and reserve liquid. Using long serrated knife, cut bread in half, forming top and bottom. Remove centers of each half leaving 1" thick shell. Brush inside of bread shells with reserved olive salad liquid. Press half of salad in bottom shell. Layer Venison Pastrami, provolone and mortadella over. Press on remaining salad. Cover with top half of bread and press. Wrap in foil. Cover with 3 to 5 lbs. weight such as cutting board topped with cans or bricks and refrigerate at least 30 minutes. Can be prepared 6 hours ahead. Cut sandwich into wedges. Pierce each wedge with long toothpick or thin wooden skewer and serve. Serves 6.

BURGERS

Since venison is virtually fat free, the meat has very little moisture content. The addition of fat is needed to provide the moisture for quality venison burgers. The general rule of thumb is to mix 75% venison with 25% moist meats (15# venison to 5# fat). Bacon and pork/beef fat are normally the meats added. My favorite additive is ground smoked bacon.

If you like venison burgers, but are concerned about the fat content in your diet, I recommend that you experiment with substituting mushrooms for the fat in any of these venison burger recipes. Mushrooms provide water, which substitutes for fat, in preventing the burgers from tasting dry. Since venison is virtually fat free, with the substitution of mushrooms you can convert most any of these recipes to low fat or fat free. You will need to experiment. Make your ground venison by beginning with 25% (by weight) of mushrooms to 75% (by weight) of venison; break off a small piece and fry it. If the ground venison is dry, add more mushrooms to the mixture and test it again.

Basic Venison Burger Patties

1 lb. venison, ground	1/8 tsp. marjoram
1/4 lb. bacon, ground	1 egg
onions, minced	bread crumbs
1/2 tsp. lemon peel, grated	salt
1/8 tsp. thyme	black pepper

Mix all ingredients together by hand. Roll into a 3" roll and cut into slices. Fry in a skillet or broil in oven/outdoor cooker. Serves 4.

Campfire Venison Burgers

2 lbs. venison, chopped	10 to 15 toothpicks
1/2 cup beef fat, ground	3 large tomatoes
2 Tbsp. onion, chopped	Mayonnaise
1 tsp. salt	tomato catsup
1/8 tsp. pepper	lettuce
10 strips bacon	10 dinner rolls or hamburger buns

Combine venison, beef fat, onion, salt and pepper. Form into 10 fiat patties. Wrap each patty with a strip of bacon and secure with toothpicks. Broil or sauté. Serve between rolls with tomatoes, mayonnaise, catsup, and lettuce. Serves 4 to 6.

Texas-Style Chili and Onion Venison Patties

2 lbs. venison, fine ground twice
3 Tbsp. very fine bread crumbs
2 Tbsp. white onion, grated
2 tsp. salt
1 egg, slightly beaten
½ tsp. turmeric

¼ tsp. chili powder
¼ tsp. garlic salt
⅛ tsp. black pepper
½ cup butter
⅓ cup water
hamburger buns

Thoroughly mix together the first 9 ingredients. (Use the Can Method of making patties as detailed in the chapter on sausage.) Brown the patties in butter. When browned, add water and cover. Simmer over very low heat for 1½ hours. Serves 4 to 6.

Ed's Burgers

2½ lbs. venison, ground
½ cup onion, minced
1 clove minced, garlic
4 Tbsp. parsley, chopped
⅔ cup dry red wine
2 Tbsp. soy sauce

salt
pepper
Barbecue Sauce
tomato catsup
8 to 10 hamburger buns

Mix all ingredients; form into thick patties. Cook on grill or broil in oven, 10 minutes on each side. Serve on buns. Serves 8 to 10.

Mrs. Edwin S. Cook

Egg Noodles and Venison Burgers

1 egg, beaten
1 Tbsp. cold water
2 Tbsp. prepared mustard
2 tsp. salt, divided
⅛ tsp. pepper
1 lb. ground venison
½ cup beef fat, ground
¼ cup Parmesan cheese, grated

¾ cup green onions, finely chopped
¼ cup parsley, finely chopped
¼ cup butter
2 cups green peppers, diced
¼ cup pimentos, diced
3 qts. boiling water
4 cups wide egg noodles
4 toasted hamburger buns

Combine the egg, cold water, mustard, salt and pepper in a large bowl. Add the ground venison and beef fat, Parmesan cheese ¼ cup scallions and parsley and toss lightly until combined. Shape into patties and place in a shallow baking pan. Broil until brown on both sides and keep warm. Melt the butter in a large skillet over medium heat; add the green pepper and remaining scallions and sauté for 6 to 8 minutes or until tender. Stir in the pimentos. Add 1 Tbsp. salt to boiling water in a saucepan and add noodles gradually so that water continues to boil. Cook, stirring occasionally, until tender and drain. Toss noodles with vegetable mixture and season to taste with salt and pepper. Turn into a serving dish and top with venison burgers. Serves 4.

French Venison Burgers

1½ lbs. venison, chopped
½ lb. bacon, chopped
butter
¼ cup white onion, minced fine
1½ tsp. salt
⅛ tsp. pepper

⅛ tsp. thyme
1 egg, lightly beaten
all-purpose flour
1 tsp. safflower oil
½ cup dry red wine

Mix and grind venison and bacon. Cook onion in about 2 Tbsp. butter until just tender. Scrape onion and butter into a bowl. Add venison, salt, pepper, thyme and egg. Mix lightly to thoroughly blend. Form venison into patties about ¾ " thick. Dust patties lightly with flour. Place 1 Tbsp. butter and safflower oil in a skillet over high heat. When foam begins to subside, add patties and fry on each side. Remove patties and place on a warm serving platter. Keep warm. Pour off all fat from the skillet. Add wine and boil rapidly, scraping brown bits from the bottom of the skillet. When liquid is reduced to almost the consistency of syrup remove it from the heat. Stir in about 2 Tbsp. softened butter. Pour sauce over venison burgers. Makes 4 to 6.

Vermont-Style Venison Burgers

1¼ lbs. venison
¼ lb. beef fat
½ cup packaged seasoned dry stuffing mix
2 Tbsp. canned beef broth
½ medium white onion, chopped
1 garlic clove, minced
½ tsp. Worcestershire sauce
2 Tbsp. beaten egg

3 Tbsp. butter
4 oz. Mozzarella cheese, thinly chopped
8 rye bread slices, toasted
mustard
tomato catsup
white bread, cut in ¾"
   thick slices

Grind venison and beef fat together, Mix first 8 ingredients in a bowl. Chill 30 minutes. Form venison mixture into l"-thick patties. Melt butter in a large skillet over medium-high heat. Add patties and cook 5 minutes. Turn; top with cheese. Cook to desired degree of doneness. Place one thick slice of bread on each plate and top with burger. Spread with mustard and tomato catsup. Serves 6.

Does bred when they are less than a year of age normally produce a single fawn, with 10 percent of them bearing twins. Older does average almost two fawns—67 percent have twins, 21 percent have single fawns and 12 percent have triplets.

Pizza Venison Burgers

2 lbs. ground venison
¼ lb, ground beef suet
⅓ cup onion, minced
1 tsp. salt
½ tsp. leaf oregano
¼ tsp. black pepper

1 (8-oz.) can pizza sauce
6 slices Mozzarella cheese
3 large English muffins, split
butter, softened
6 slices Cheddar cheese

Mix and grind together venison and beef suet. In a bowl, lightly mix ground meat, onion, salt, oregano, pepper and ½ cup pizza sauce. Shape into 6 patties, about 4½" to 5" in diameter. Broil one side; turn and broil other side to desired degree of doneness. Spoon remaining pizza sauce over patties. Top patties with slices of Mozzarella cheese; return to broiler just until cheese begins to melt. Meanwhile, toast and butter muffins. Place a slice of Cheddar cheese on each half-muffin. Top each muffin with a venison patty. Serves 6.

Homemade Pizza with Venison Toppings

½ cup warm water
1 pkg. rapid rise yeast
½ cup rye flour
1 cup warm water
1 Tbsp. whole milk
2 Tbsp. olive oil
½ tsp. salt

3½ cups all-purpose flour
½ cup herbed tomato sauce
¼ - ½ lb. venison
1 cup onion, Julienne in thin cuts
¾ cup sliced mushrooms
2 Tbsp. Parmesan cheese
¾ cup Mozzarella cheese

For the venison topping, choose your favorite recipe for link or bulk venison sausage, smoked or hard venison sausage or ground venison hamburger.

In a large bowl, mix together and stir well the ½ cup water, yeast and rye flour. Cover and set aside in a warm place for 30 minutes. The dough may be sticky, grease a large bowl with olive oil, salt and all-purpose flour. Knead for 15 minutes. The dough may be sticky. Grease a large bowl with olive oil, add dough ball, and lightly oil the surface of the dough ball. Cover with aluminum foil or plastic wrap; set in a warm place and let rise for 2 hours. Punch down the dough and divide it into two pieces. Shape the dough into 12" to 14" pizzas and place on greased baking sheets (you may wish to sprinkle a little corn meal on the baking sheet to help keep the pizza from sticking). Preheat the oven to 450 degrees. Divide the tomato sauce, venison, onion, mushrooms, Parmesan cheese and Mozzarella cheese into halves. Spread the tomato sauce over the dough, cover with venison, add the Parmesan and Mozzarella cheeses. Place the pizzas into the preheated oven and bake for about 15 minutes or until the crust is browned and the cheeses begin to bubble. Makes 2 medium to large pizzas.

Swiss Cheese and Tomato Venison Burger

1¼ lbs, lean venison, ground
½ cup beef suet, ground
butter
6 hamburger buns
lettuce

Mayonnaise
6 slices Swiss cheese
sweet pickle relish
6 slices tomatoes
6 thin slices white onion

Combine ground venison and beef suet. Form into patties ½" thick. Store in refrigerator between sheets of waxed paper until ready to use. Brush pan lightly with fat and cook meat a very few minutes, just long enough to melt suet. Split buns, butter and toast lightly. On bottom half arrange a leaf of lettuce, mayonnaise and a slice of cheese. Top with venison burger patty, spread with sweet pickle relish, slice of tomato, slice of onion. Serves 4 to 6.

Pepper Venison Burger with Stale Beer Sauce

1 cup stale beer
½ cup Worcestershire or A-1 Sauce
½ cup sugar cane or other vinegar
½ cup brown sugar
tomato catsup or tomato paste to taste

2 Tbsp. butter
ground venison burgers, ½ lb. each
fresh or canned mushrooms
hamburger buns, toasted
green bell peppers, sliced

To make the sauce, combine and mix well the stale beer, Worcestershire sauce, vinegar, brown sugar, and tomato catsup. Parboil the green bell pepper slices. In a skillet, melt butter and just sear burgers on each side. Pour sauce over and cook over low heat until just less than medium. Toast the hamburger buns and pour a little sauce on the buns. Lay venison on the buns and pour the sauce over. Garnish with green bell pepper slices.

   This is equally good using sausage or tenderloin or roast slices in place of the ground venison.

Will Campbell, author
Mt. Juliet, Tennessee

Venison and Bacon Burgers

75% venison meat (15 lbs.)
   and 25% smoked bacon (5 lbs.)

OR 70% venison meat (14 lbs.)
   and 30% smoked bacon (6 lbs.)

Cut venison and bacon in small chunks, mix and grind together. Cook as you would any beef burger. The smoked bacon gives this recipe a delightful and different flavor.

Venison and Hot Pork Sausage Burger

2 parts venison, ground   1 part fresh hot pork sausage

Mix and ground venison and pork sausage together. Shape into ¾-inch thick patties. Place venison patties on a broiler rack, no more than 4 inches from the heat, or grill each side 5 to 6 minutes for a medium rare to medium-cooked burger.

Venison Burgers with Burgundy and Teriyaki Sauce

2½ lbs. venison, ground   2 Tbsp. teriyaki sauce
½ cup onion, minced   salt
1 clove garlic, minced   pepper
4 Tbsp. parsley, chopped   hamburger buns, toasted
⅔ cup Burgundy

Using a fine blade, grind venison twice. Mix all ingredients and form into ¾-inch thick patties. Cook on barbecue grill or broil in oven. Broil to no more than medium. Serve on toasted hamburger buns. Serves 8 to 10.

Venison Burgers with Spanish Olive Relish

2 Tbsp. olive oil   ½ tsp. basil leaves
1 cup onion, coarsely chopped   1 lb. ground venison
1 cup green bell pepper, diced   ¼ cup ground beef fat
1 small clove of garlic, crushed   1 tsp. salt
½ tsp. paprika   ⅛ tsp. black pepper
½ cup stuffed olives, sliced   6 toasted hamburger buns

Heat the olive oil in a large skillet. Add the onion, green pepper, garlic and paprika and sauté over medium heat until green pepper is tender. Stir in the olives and basil leaves, remove from skillet and keep warm. Mix the ground venison, ground beef fat with salt and pepper and shape into 6 patties. Fry patties in same skillet until browned. Spoon the olive mixture on venison burgers and heat through. Serve on hamburger buns. Serves 6.

Deer can live up to about 11 years in the wild. Just two deer, free of predators, can produce a herd of up to 35 deer in just seven years.

Venison Chili Burger

3 lbs. ground venison
½ lb. ground beef fat
3 med. white onions, chopped
1 cloves garlic
½ bunch celery
½ can tomato sauce

salt
black pepper
2 Tbsp. tomato catsup
2 (No. 2) can tomato
2 tsp. Worcestershire sauce
3 tsp. chili powder

Mix ground meats and fry in a skillet until brown or done. In another bowl, combine remaining ingredients. Cook until done, about 30 minutes. Add to meat mixture and cook a little longer, or to right consistency to spread between buns. This is better if cooked ahead of time and heated to serve. Makes enough for 36 buns.

Venison Kibbeburgers

3 slices Basic White Bread or other bread
¼ cup whole milk
1 lb. ground venison
1 egg, beaten
½ cup white onions, minced
¼ cup fresh parsley, minced

¼ cup pine nuts, toasted
½ tsp. dried oregano, crumbled
½ tsp. salt
¼ tsp. cinnamon
freshly ground pepper

Soak bread in milk in a large bowl until milk is absorbed. Mix in remaining ingredients. Shape into eight 1" thick ovals. Can be prepared 8 hours ahead and refrigerated. Let stand at room temperature for 30 minutes before cooking. Heat barbecue pit. Grill burgers to desired doneness, 4 minutes on each side for medium-rare. Serve immediately. Serves 6.

Venison and Bacon Breakfast Patties

1 lb. ground venison
⅛ lb. ground smoked bacon
1 tsp. garlic salt
1 tsp. lemon pepper
7 crackers, crumbled
1 egg
1 tsp. salt

1 medium onion, diced
⅛ tsp. sage
salt and pepper to taste
1 small can mushroom pieces
Primo's Creamy Grits
Kentucky Biscuits
butter

Mix all ingredients well and form into patties. Brown and remove from heat to make gravy. In the fat left over from browning the patties, make the gravy (see Sauces & Gravy). Salt and pepper to taste. Add small can drained mushrooms, and put the patties into the gravy. Simmer for a few minutes until gravy thickens and seasonings cook through the gravy. Serve with fried eggs, gravy, Primo's Creamy Grits, Kentucky Biscuits, butter, jelly and coffee. Serves 4.

Red Wine Venison Burgers

1 lb. venison, chopped
⅓ lb. bacon, chopped
½ cup dry red wine, divided
1 tsp. salt

⅛ tsp. pepper
butter
2 Tbsp. parsley, chopped fine
2 Tbsp. green onions, chopped fine

Mix and grind venison and bacon. Combine venison, ¼ cup wine, salt and pepper. Lightly mix. Shape into 4 patties. Heat butter in a skillet over medium-high heat. Fry patties on both sides. Remove patties and place them on a heated serving dish. Pour off fat from the skillet. Add remaining wine, parsley and chives. Cook over high heat about 1 minute, stirring up browned bits from the bottom of the pan. Pour sauce over patties. Makes 4 patties.

A mule deer (Odocoileus hemionus) is a moderately large deer with large ears; antlers are typically branched and are restricted almost entirely to males; the upperparts are cinnamon buff suffused with blackish in the winter, more reddish in summer; the brow patch is whitish; the ears are grayish on outside, whitish on inside. Weight is 100 to 225 pounds.

17

Venison Soups and Salads

Venison Soups & Salads provide a refreshing change of pace from our normal regime. These recipes are real treats. Have you ever wondered what you could do with that leftover roast? How about the bones?

Salads and soups are an excellent way to use leftover venison. Venison that been dry roasted is a better candidate for soups and salads than venison that has been fried.

SOUPS

Black Bean Soup with Venison

1 pint dry black beans
3 qts. water
¼ lb. salt pork
½ lb. venison stew meat
1 carrot, sliced
2 onions, chopped
1 Tbsp. salt

3 cloves
⅛ tsp. mace
¼ tsp. red pepper
3 hard-boiled eggs, sliced
1 lemon, thinly sliced and seeded
½ cup sherry

Soak the beans overnight in 1 quart of the water. The next morning, pour the water and beans into a large soup kettle and add 2 quarts water, salt pork, venison, carrots, onions, salt, and spices. Cover and simmer for 3 to 4 hours. Remove the meat and put the soup through a sieve, or blend in a blender until smooth. Serve piping hot in a tureen garnished with hard-boiled eggs and lemon slices. Add the sherry just before serving. Serves 20.

Peasant Venison Soup

3 Tbsp. butter
½ cup carrots, diced
½ cup turnips, diced
⅓ cup leeks, sliced
⅓ cup celery, sliced

⅓ cup white onion, sliced
½ cup cabbage, shredded
1 qt. Venison Soup Stock or beef broth
1 cup potatoes, diced
½ cup white cheese, grated

Heat butter in a Dutch oven; add all vegetables except potatoes; simmer about 5 minutes or until soft but not browned. Add soup stock and bring to boil; add potatoes; boil gently about 20 minutes or until vegetables are tender. Just before serving add grated cheese; stir over low heat until cheese is melted. Serves 6.

Hearty Fresh Venison and Vegetable Soup

4 lbs. venison soup bones with meat
2 qts. cold water
2 Tbsp. salt
6 peppercorns
2 medium white onions, quartered
2 sprigs parsley
2 stalks celery with leaves

2 carrots, quartered
4 cups potatoes, diced
1½ cups carrots, sliced
⅔ cup celery, sliced
1 cup snap beans, cut in pieces
6 cups canned tomatoes

Combine first 8 ingredients in a kettle and cover. Simmer for 2 hours. Remove the bones, trim of meat and set aside. Strain the stock and pour into kettle. Add remaining ingredients and cover. Cook until vegetables are tender. Add the meat and heat through. Serves 10 to 12.

Spring Venison Soup

1 Tbsp. butter
3 Tbsp. green onions, finely chopped
1½ qts. lettuce, outside leaves chopped
½ bunch water cress, chopped
½ cucumber, chopped

2 cups Venison Soup Stock or beef broth
1 cup whole milk
salt
black pepper

Heat butter in a Dutch oven; add green onions and simmer about 5 minutes or until soft but not browned. Add chopped vegetables and venison stock; simmer gently for 30 to 40 minutes. Strain; press vegetables through coarse sieve and add to stock; add milk and heat. Season to taste. Serves 4.

Valencia Venison Soup

2 qts. Venison Soup Stock or
   canned beef broth
2 Tbsp. rice
½ cup macaroni, broken in very small pieces
½ cup carrots, diced
½ cup English peas
1⅓ cups condensed tomato soup

¼ lb. venison round steak, ground
1 egg, slightly beaten
¼ tsp. salt
pepper
nutmeg
1 Tbsp. beef fat

Bring Venison Soup Stock or beef bouillon to boil in a large pot; add rice and boil gently about 15 minutes. Add macaroni, carrots, English peas and tomato soup; boil gently about 10 minutes or until macaroni is tender. Combine ground round venison steak and slightly beaten egg; add ¼ tsp. salt, pepper and a dash of nutmeg; mix thoroughly, shape into tiny balls and brown in fat. Add venison balls to soup and poach about 20 to 30 minutes or until cooked through. Serves 8.

Vegetable and Venison Soup

2½ lbs. venison and marrow bone
4 qts. water
6 sprigs parsley
2 red onions, sliced
15 peppercorns
1½ Tbsp. salt

2 cups celery, diced
3 cups tomatoes, cooked
4 carrots, sliced
2 turnips, sliced
4 potatoes

Wipe venison and bone with a damp cloth. Cut meat in cubes. Place half the cubes in soup kettle, cover with cold water and heat slowly to the simmering point. Scrape the marrow from the bone, putting it into a large frying pan. Melt over low heat. Add remaining half of meat and brown on all sides. Put venison with bone in soup kettle. Cover and simmer for 4 to 6 hours. Add all the vegetables and seasoning, cover and cook for 1 hour longer. Season to taste. Serves 8 to 10.

Venison and Corn Chowder

3 ears fresh corn
4 cups heavy cream
2 cups canned chicken broth
4 garlic cloves, minced
10 fresh thyme sprigs
1 bay leaf
1½ onions, finely chopped
½ lb. Indiana Farm Venison Sausage

2 Tbsp. unsalted butter
2 Tsp. jalapeño chilies, seeded, minced
½ tsp. ground cumin
2 Tbsp. all-purpose flour
2 medium baking potatoes, peeled, cut 1" cubes
1½ tsp. green onions, chopped

Cut corn from cob. Place cobs in large saucepan; set kernels aside. Add cream, stock, garlic, thyme, bay leaf and ⅓ of onions to pan. Simmer 1 hour, stirring occasionally. Strain through sieve set over large bowl, pressing on solids with back of spoon. Set corn stock aside. Cook sausage in large skillet over medium heat until cooked through, turning occasionally. Cool sausage and cut into 1" pieces. Melt butter in large saucepan over medium heat. Add remaining ⅔ of onions, chilies and cumin and sauté 5 minutes. Add flour and stir 2 minutes. Gradually whisk in corn stock. Add sausage and potatoes. Cover and cook until potatoes are tender, about 5 minutes. Season to taste with salt and pepper. Ladle chowder into bowls. Sprinkle with chopped green onions and serve. Serves 6.

Venison and Vegetable Soup

1 lb. boneless venison, cut 1½ " cubes
1 Tbsp. safflower or canola oil
1 onion, chopped
1 medium turnip, diced
1 cup canned Italian-style tomatoes
¼ cup tomato catsup
1½ tsp. salt

¼ tsp. pepper
3 cups Venison Soup Stock
   or beef broth
2 cups potatoes, peeled and cubed
2 cups carrots, peeled and sliced
6 small whole onions, peeled

In a Dutch oven, brown venison cubes on all sides in safflower oil. Add onion, turnip, tomatoes, catsup, salt, pepper and broth. Cover and simmer until meat is tender, about 1½ hours. Add potatoes, carrots and whole onions and more water if necessary. Cover and simmer until vegetables are tender. Add more salt and pepper to taste. Serves 6 to 8.

Venison Ball Soup

1½ lbs. ground venison
1 green pepper, minced
1 egg
1½ tsp. salt
⅔ cup cornflake crumbs
4 carrots, sliced
4 potatoes, quartered

1 large white onion, minced
1 cup frozen English peas
2 Tbsp. sugar
½ tsp. black pepper
2 cup water
2 (No. 303) cans tomatoes

Combine the ground venison, green pepper, egg, ½ teaspoon salt and cornflake crumbs in a large bowl and mix thoroughly. Shape into 1" balls. Place the vegetables in a 4-quart Dutch oven and sprinkle the remaining salt, sugar and pepper. Place meatballs over vegetables and pour water and tomatoes over meatballs. Bring to a boil and reduce heat. Simmer for 1 hour and 15 minutes. Serves 6.

Venison Neck Soup with Thick-Cut Toast

2 meaty venison necks
5 cups water
1¼ tsp. salt, divided
2 eggs, beaten

dash of white pepper
dash of fresh ground nutmeg
3 Tbsp. parsley, chopped

Place venison necks, water and 1 tsp. of salt in a large kettle or stock pot. Bring to a boil; reduce heat, and simmer for 1½ to 2 hours. Remove the neck bones; strain the liquid. Return the broth to the cooking pot and bring to simmer. Combine the remaining ingredients and gradually pour into the broth. Stir constantly. Serve hot with toasted thick crust bread. Serves 4.

Venison Sausage Gumbo

Dark Roux

Gumbo Ingredients:
1½ cups yellow onion, chopped
1 cup okra, chopped
½ cup celery, chopped
½ cup parsley, chopped
½ cup green bell pepper, chopped
2 tsp. garlic, chopped
2 Tbsp. Worcestershire sauce
4 cups dry red wine

4 cups water
2 lbs. venison, cubed
1 lb. Mississippi Country Venison
   Sausage or other link sausage
salt
pepper
Tabasco sauce
1 lb. peeled shrimp
24 oysters, with juice
File Powder
Boiled Rice

First make a Dark Roux by browning equal parts of flour and oil (or fat or shortening). Add onion, okra, celery and bell pepper to roux stirring constantly until onions are clear. Transfer vegetables and roux mixture to a large stock pot or large Dutch oven. Add parsley, garlic, Worcestershire sauce, red wine, water, venison and sausage. Let cook over low heat for 3 to 6 hours. Stir and scrape bottom of pot occasionally. Add additional water if needed. Season to taste with salt, pepper and Tabasco sauce. Add shrimp shortly before removing from fire. Add oysters no more than 5 minutes before removing from fire. Serve over boiled rice with file powder on the side. File powder is sprinkled over gumbo to act as a flavoring and thickening agent. Serve with buttered garlic bread. Serves 6 to 8.

Venison Petite Marmite

3 Tbsp. beef fat
1½ lbs. venison, cut in small cubes
1 venison marrow bone (optional)
3 quail or cornish hens, quartered
3½ qts. cold water
2 bay leaves
2 cloves
4 peppercorns

¼ tsp. thyme
1 cup carrots, diced
1 cup turnips, diced
¾ cup white onion, chopped
1-2 leeks, white portions, chopped
1 cup cabbage, shredded
1 Tbsp. salt
hot toast

Heat fat in skillet; add venison and cook until browned. Place venison and marrow bone (tied in a cheesecloth bag), and quail in kettle; add cold water and seasonings; bring slowly to boil; remove scum. Cover and simmer gently about 3 hours; strain, reserving meat and bones; return stock to kettle. Add vegetables and salt; boil gently about 20 minutes or until vegetables are tender. Remove meat from quail; dice and return with reserved venison to the hot soup stock. Serve in soup bowls. For an accompaniment spread hot toast rounds with marrow scraped from the cooked marrow bone. Serves 6.

Southern-Style Venison Soup with Turnips and Onions

1 lb. venison cut in 2" cubes
1½ cups turnips, diced
½ cup parsley, chopped
1 cup onion, minced
2 cups celery, diced
3 qts. canned beef broth

3 bay leaves
½ tsp. thyme
1 can tomato paste
3 tsp. sugar
salt
pepper

Combine all ingredients in a large stock pot. Cook over low heat for 3 hours. Add water if soup thickens. Serves 4 to 6.

SALADS

Retried Beans and Venison Salad

1 lb. ground venison
3 Tbsp. safflower or canola oil
1 can tomatoes, drained
1 cup Velveeta cheese, shredded
2 heads lettuce, shredded

½ cup green onions, chopped
½ tsp. Tabasco sauce
½ (15-oz.) can refried beans
6 oz. corn chips
salt and pepper to taste

Cook the ground venison in a skillet until brown. Drain and reserve cooking oil. Place the venison in a salad bowl. Drain the tomatoes and reserve juice. Chop tomatoes and add to venison. Add the cheese, lettuce and onion and toss lightly. Place the reserved cooking oil, tomato juice, Tabasco sauce and refried beans in a saucepan and heat through. Add to venison mixture and toss. Add corn chips and season with salt and pepper. Serves 12.

Blender Venison Salad

1 lb. venison stew meat
3 hard-boiled eggs
1 onion
1 clove of garlic
½ cup celery, chopped

¼ tsp. pepper
salt to taste
½ cup mayonnaise
6 lettuce leaves

Cook the venison stew meat in salted water in a crock pot until tender, drain and cool. Place the venison in a blender container, a small amount at time, and blend until ground. Blend the eggs, onion, garlic and celery in the blender and add to venison. Add the pepper, salt and mayonnaise and mix well. Serve on lettuce. Serves 6.

Greek-Style Venison Platter

2 cans red kidney beans
1 can whole mushrooms
1 can whole kernel corn
1 can pimentos
1½ cups diagonally sliced celery
2 Tbsp. onion, finely chopped
¼ cup parsley, finely chopped

2 Tbsp. capers
½ tsp. salt substitute
¼ tsp. black pepper
⅔ cup Cheddar and Wine Dressing
12 slices cold venison roast
mixed salad greens

Drain the kidney beans, mushrooms, corn, and pimentos and cut the pimentos in strips. Combine the celery, kidney beans, mushrooms, corn, onion, half the pimento strips, 2 tbsp. parsley and 1 tbsp. capers in a mixing bowl and sprinkle with salt substitute and pepper. Add the dressing and toss to mix well. Chill. Fold slices of roast venison and arrange along sides of a serving platter. Place salad greens at the ends of platter and spoon the corn, bean and vegetable mixture in mound in center. Garnish with remaining pimento strips, parsley and capers. Serves 6.

Cold Venison Salad

2 cups cooked venison, chopped
1 cup celery, thinly sliced
¼ cup pickle, chopped
2 Tbsp. white onion, chopped
3½ Tbsp. French dressing
salt

white pepper
½ cup Russian dressing
mixed salad greens
parsley
stuffed olives

Combine venison, celery, pickle, onion and French dressing. Chill. Drain and season with salt and pepper. Mix Russian dressing and serve on a bed of salad greens. Garnish with parsley and stuffed olives. Serves 4 to 6.

Dinner Venison Salad

3 cups cooked venison, diced
½ cups celery, thinly sliced
⅓ cup green pepper, minced
4 Tbsp. French dressing
salt and pepper to taste

1 cup mayonnaise
3 Tbsp. green onions, chopped
3 tomatoes
2 eggs, hard boiled
lettuce

Combine cooked venison, celery, green pepper and French dressing. Chill for 2 hours. Drain and season to taste with salt and pepper. Mix mayonnaise and chopped green onions. Add mayonnaise mixture to venison mixture. Serve in lettuce cups and garnish with tomato wedges and sliced hard-boiled eggs. Serves 6 to 8.

Old World Venison Salad Bowl

1 head romaine lettuce
1 bunch chicory
1 bunch escarole
thin smoked ham strips
thin roast venison strips
Swiss cheese strips
1 cup olive oil
1 cup wine vinegar
1 cup tomato catsup
1 cup chili sauce

1 Tbsp. white onion, grated
½ dill pickle, diced
1 clove garlic, minced
1 Tbsp. parsley, coarsely chopped
½ tsp. salt
½ tsp. sugar
tomatoes, peeled and quartered
hard-boiled eggs
black pepper to taste

Tear the romaine, chicory and escarole into bite-sized pieces and place in a large salad bowl. Add desired amounts of ham, roast venison and Swiss cheese. Combine remaining ingredients and mix well. Pour over the romaine mixture and toss well. Garnish with peeled and quartered tomatoes and hard boiled eggs. Season to taste with fresh ground pepper. Serves 6 to 8.

Main Dish Venison Salad

2 cups cooked venison, cut in strips
1 can kidney beans, drained
1 cup celery, chopped
¼ cup onion, chopped
2 hard-boiled eggs, chopped

2 Tbsp. sweet pickle, sliced
¼ cup mayonnaise
1 Tbsp. chili sauce
1 tsp. salt
1 head lettuce

Combine the venison, beans, celery, onion, eggs, pickle, mayonnaise, chili sauce and salt in a bowl and toss lightly. Cover and chill for 30 minutes. Serve in lettuce cups. Serves 4 to 6.

Pasta-Venison Salad with Snow Peas and Cauliflower

¼ lb. snow peas, strings removed
1 small cauliflower (1 lb.) broken into small
    florets
⅔ cup fresh parsley, minced
1 large garlic clove, minced
⅔ cup canola oil
¼ cup red wine vinegar
¼ cup fresh basil, minced
1½ Tbsp. Dijon mustard
2 tsp. sugar

2 tsp. salt
black pepper
1 large red bell pepper, sliced thick
2 large carrots, peeled, Julienne cut
2 medium zucchini, French fried cut
1 medium red onion, coarsely chopped
½ lb. cooked pasta; fettuccini, ravioli
    circles or lasagna noodles
1¼ lbs. cooked venison, cut 2" strips

Steam snow peas and cauliflower. Mince parsley, garlic and basil. To parsley, garlic and basil, add oil, vinegar, mustard, sugar, salt and pepper and blend in a food processor for 5 seconds. Gently mix in snow peas, cauliflower, bell pepper, carrots, zucchini and red onion. Blend in pasta and venison. Serves 6.

Salcom with Venison

3 lbs. venison round steak or backstrap
1 large green bell pepper
4 stalks celery
1 large white onion

1 can tomatoes, drained
dash of cayenne pepper
mayonnaise
green pepper or onion rings

Cook the venison steak in boiling, salted water until tender, drain and cool. Reserve ½ cup of venison stock. Grind steak fine. Grind the bell pepper, celery and onion and add to steak. Chop tomatoes and add to steak mixture. Add the cayenne pepper and reserved venison stock and mix well. Add enough mayonnaise to moisten. Place in salad bowl and garnish with green pepper or onion rings. Serves 4 to 6.

Sesame Venison and Snow Pea-Sesame Seed Salad

Dressing:
5 Tbsp. canola oil
3 Tbsp. plus 2¼ tsp. rice vinegar
5 tsp. Oriental sesame oil
5 tsp. teriyaki sauce
1½ garlic cloves, minced
¼ heaping tsp. red pepper flakes (optional)
salt
pepper

Salad:
4 oz. snow peas, strings removed
16 oz. thinly sliced roast venison, cut
   1½"x¼" strips
4 oz. mushrooms, thinly sliced
4 Tbsp. toasted sesame seeds
3 bunches arugula, stems removed
1 small head radicchio, leaves torn
tomato wedges

Make dressing by whisking all ingredients together. Make the salad by placing the snow peas in a shallow microwave-safe dish. Add ¼ " water. Cover and cook on high until just tender, about 1 minute. Drain and rinse under cold water. Dry thoroughly. Add snow peas, venison, pepper strips, mushrooms and 3 Tbsp. sesame seeds to dressing in bowl. Toss. Line 4 plates with arugula and radicchio. Divide venison salad among the plates. Sprinkle with remaining 1 Tbsp. sesame seeds. Garnish with tomato. Serves 4.

Tenderloin of Venison Salad

1 lb. venison tenderloin, sliced
1 lb. lean veal, ground
1 cup celery, diced

¼ cup olives, diced
¾ lb. brick cheese, diced
mayonnaise

Place the venison and veal in a saucepan and cover with water. Bring to boiling point, then simmer until tender. Drain, cool and dice meats. Add the celery, olives and cheese and mix well. Add enough mayonnaise to moisten, then chill. Serve on lettuce. Serves 12.

Venison Salad Con Came

1 lb. ground venison
3 Tbsp. canola oil
¼ cup red onion, chopped
1 Tbsp. beef gravy base
6 drops Tabasco sauce
1 tsp. cornstarch
1 med. head lettuce

1 large tomato, cut in wedges
½ small onion, sliced into rings
¼ cup green bell pepper, cut in strips
½ cup ripe olives, sliced
¼ lb. shredded sharp Cheddar cheese
1 (6-oz.) pkg. corn chips, crushed

Brown the venison in cooking oil in a skillet and add the chopped onion, gravy base and pepper sauce. Stir in ¾ cup water and mix well. Simmer 10 minutes, stirring frequently. Combine the cornstarch and 1 tbsp. water and stir into venison mixture. Cook, stirring, until thickened. Tear the lettuce into bite-sized pieces and place in a salad bowl. Add the tomato, sliced onion, green pepper, olives and cheese and toss well. Spoon beef mixture on top and sprinkle with corn chips. Serves 4 to 6.

Venison Stroganoff Salad

2 cups coarsely ground roast venison
1 cup sour cream
6 Tbsp. pickle relish
½ cup onion, minced

2 tsp. horseradish
2 Tbsp. chili sauce
1½ tsp. salt
lettuce

Combine all ingredients in a mixing bowl and mix well. Refrigerate until chilled. Serve on lettuce. Serves 4.

Venison Tongue Salad

2 cups venison tongue, cooked in strips
¼ cup white onions, minced
1 cup English peas, steamed
1 cup celery, thinly sliced
2 tomatoes, cut in chunks
4 Tbsp. French dressing

½ cup mayonnaise
mustard
chicory
lettuce
parsley
pickle

Combine all ingredients except mayonnaise and mustard. Chill. Add mustard to mayonnaise to taste. Drain tongue and vegetable mixture. Mix in mayonnaise mustard mixture and serve on a bed of chicory and lettuce. Garnish with parsley and pickle. Serves 4 to 6.

In Mississippi, it takes an archery hunter 21 man-days of hunting to take a deer. A man-day is defined as one hunter spending an entire day in the field. There are roughly 49,500 crossbow and vertical bow hunters in the state. They harvest on average about 42,800 deer a year for an 86.5 percent success rate.

Ziti Pasta Salad with Venison Sausage

⅓ cup red wine
½ tsp. salt
¼ tsp. black pepper
¼ tsp. dried rosemary, crumbled
¼ tsp. dried oregano, crumbled
¼ tsp. dried basil, crumbled
1⅓ cup olive oil
¼ cup Parmesan cheese
12 oz. ziti pasta

2 lbs. Garlic Venison Sausage
    thinly sliced and fried
1 lb. zucchini, thinly sliced
4 medium tomatoes, cut in wedges
1 medium green bell pepper, coarsely
    chopped
1 cup fresh parsley, chopped
3 oz. pimiento, chopped
Parmesan cheese

Combine vinegar, salt, pepper and herbs in small bowl. Whisk in oil in slow steady-stream until well blended. Mix in ¼ cup Parmesan. Set dressing aside. Cook ziti in 4 to 6 qts. boiling salted water until just firm but tender to the bite, about 7 minutes. Drain and rinse under cold water until cool. Drain again. Combine ziti and remaining ingredients, except Parmesan, in large bowl. Add half of dressing and toss. Add as much of the remaining dressing as necessary to coat salad thoroughly. Sprinkle with additional Parmesan if desired and serve. Serves 6 to 8.

18

Venison Appetizers

Venison appetizers are an excellent way to utilize smaller cuts of venison. Venison left over from making sausage, hamburger and cut off ends from backstraps, roasts and other tender cuts can be combined and made into appetizers. Instead of grilling venison ribs, they can be cut into smaller serving sizes and made into tasty appetizers.

When making sausage and hamburger, freeze a portion of the ground meat for future recipes. Packaging ground venison in 1-lb. packages makes for easy selection and preparation. Freeze ribs in large sections. When you are ready to cook you will have a choice of grilling or cutting the ribs for recipes that require smaller sections.

Appetizers are a good way to introduce friends to venison. A word of caution. As mentioned in other chapters, venison does not respond well to fast cooking such as frying in hot grease. For fondue and deep-frying appetizer recipes, venison should be cut in no less than ¾- to 1-inch pieces and your guests should be cautioned about overcooking. Well done venison has a tendency to become tough, for these recipes, tenderloin and backstrap work best. Small meatballs should also not be overcooked for the same reason.

The stuffed recipes are a good way to utilize leftover roasts. Raw venison should not be thawed and then re-frozen. But venison can be re-frozen after cooking. Freeze your leftover steak, chops, and roasts for use in stuffed and spread recipes.

Braised Venison Stuffed Cucumbers

6 small cucumbers
1 egg, beaten
½ tsp, cornstarch
1 tsp. teriyaki sauce

¾ cup canned beef broth
1 cup cooked venison, chopped
3 Tbsp. rice wine
cornstarch

Pare the cucumbers and cut them in half lengthwise. Scoop out the center, leaving a smooth cavity. Mince the venison well and mix the beaten egg and cornstarch. Season with salt. Fill each cucumber with 4 teaspoons of this mixture. Fry the stuffed cucumbers, filling-side-down, until light golden brown. Turn them over and add teriyaki sauce, beef broth, and wine. Cover pan and braise the cucumbers until tender, about 20 minutes. Remove the cucumbers to a serving dish. Thicken the broth with cornstarch binder and pour over the cucumbers. Serves 4.

Buffet Venison Meatballs

1 lb. ground venison
¼ cup onion, minced
1 cup dry bread crumbs
1 Tbsp. parsley flakes
¼ cup whole milk
1 tsp. salt

1 tsp. Worcestershire sauce
¼ tsp. pepper
2 Tbsp. butter
1 (10-oz.) jar grape jelly
1 (10-oz.) jar chili sauce

Combine ground venison, onion, bread crumbs, parsley flakes, milk, salt, Worcestershire sauce and pepper in bowl; mix well. Shape into 1" meatballs. Brown in butter in a skillet; drain. Combine jelly and chili sauce in 3-quart saucepan. Cook over medium heat until jelly is melted, stirring to mix well. Add meatballs. Simmer for 1 hour. Serve from a chafing dish. Serves 12.

Appetizer Venison Meatballs

Meatballs:
2 lbs. lean ground venison
2 eggs, lightly beaten
1 cup (4 oz.) shredded Mozzarella cheese
½ cup dry bread crumbs
¼ cup onion, finely chopped
2 Tbsp. Parmesan cheese, grated
1 Tbsp. tomato catsup
2 Tsp. Worcestershire sauce
1 tsp. Italian seasoning

1 tsp. dried basil
1 tsp. salt
¼ tsp. pepper

Sauce:
1 (14-oz.) btl. hot or tomato catsup
2 Tbsp. cornstarch
1 (12-oz.) jar apple jelly
1 (12-oz.) jar currant jelly

In a bowl, combine meatball ingredients; mix well. Shape into 1-inch balls. Place on rack in shallow roasting pan. Bake at 350 degrees 10 to 15 minutes. Remove meatballs and rack; drain. Combine tomato catsup and cornstarch in roasting pan. Stir in jellies; add meatballs. Cover and bake 30 minutes. Makes about 90 meatballs.

Braised Venison Sweet and Sour Ribs

3 to 4 lbs. venison ribs, cut 2" lengths
   to make small ribs
½ cup all-purpose flour
1 Tbsp. ground ginger
2 Tbsp. bacon grease
⅓ apple cider vinegar
⅓ cup sugar

¼ cup ketchup
1 Tbsp. Worcestershire sauce
2 Tbsp. soy sauce
2 Tbsp. cornstarch
1 (15-oz.) can pineapple chunks, with
   liquid

Cut away as much venison tallow from ribs as possible. Combine flour and ginger; dredge ribs in mixture. Over high heat in large Dutch oven, brown all sides of ribs in hot grease. Remove ribs and set aside. Reduce heat to low. Add remaining ingredients except pineapple chunks and juice to Dutch oven. Stir and cook 2 minutes. Place browned ribs into mixture; simmer 1 to 1½ hours or until tender; stir often. Add pineapple chunks just before turning off heat. Keep warm in chafing dish. Serves 4 to 6.

Mrs. Kathryn Breland

Cheeseburger Venison Bites

1 egg yolk, beaten
½ lb. venison, ground
2 Tbsp. white onion, grated
½ tsp. salt
dash pepper
6 slices bread

24 cubes cheddar cheese, cut ½"
tomato catsup
mustard
green onion stems, sliced ¼"
small dill pickles, sliced ¼"

In a bowl, combine egg yolk, ground venison, onion, salt and pepper. Shape mixture by teaspoonfuls into 24 balls. Remove crusts from bread; roll flat and cut into 1½" rounds. Place meatballs on bread rounds; make a depression in each ball and fill with a cube of cheese, making sure bread is covered with meat mixture. Place on baking sheet. Broil in preheated oven about 6" from heat for 3 to 5 minutes or until no pink remains. Garnish with tomato catsup, mustard, sliced green onions or sliced dill pickles if desired. Makes 24.

Cherry Tomatoes Stuffed with Venison

7 oz. venison backstrap, ground fine
butter
1 pt. (20 to 25) cherry tomatoes
¼ tsp. salt
½ tsp. curry powder

2½ Tbsp. mayonnaise
2 tsp. lemon juice
2 tsp. onion powder
parsley

Brown ground venison in butter; breaking up into small pieces as it cooks. Remove to a paper towel and allow to drain. With a sharp knife cut a circle in the top of each tomato and remove about ½ of the pulp. Turn tomatoes over and allow to drain. Break ground venison tenderloin into small pieces and add remaining ingredients. Mix until well blended. Stuff tomatoes with venison mixture. Refrigerate until serving time. Garnish with parsley. Makes enough stuffing for 20 to 25 cherry tomatoes.

Corned Venison Cream Cheese Logs

1 (8-oz.) pkg. cream cheese, softened
2 Tbsp. whole milk
3 cloves garlic, pressed
1 Tbsp. Worcestershire sauce

⅛ tsp. Tabasco sauce
12 oz. Corned Venison II
¾ cup parsley, minced
sesame crackers or melba-style crackers

Blend softened cream cheese with milk until mixture is smooth. Blend in garlic, Worcestershire sauce and pepper sauce. Flake unchilled corned venison with a fork. Blend into cheese mixture. Refrigerate 1 to 2 hours. Remove from refrigerator and divide mixture in half. Shape each portion into a log about 1½" in diameter and about 7" long. Sprinkle parsley on waxed paper. Roll logs in parsley to coat evenly. Wrap well in plastic wrap and chill thoroughly before serving. When ready to serve, remove plastic wrap, place on serving tray and surround with desired crackers. Makes 2 cheese logs.

Corned Venison Roll

12 oz. Corned Venison II
1 small onion, grated
1 Tbsp. Worcestershire Sauce

½ lb. mild cheese
2 Tbsp. mustard
½ cup mayonnaise

Mix all ingredients together thoroughly. Spread on trimmed slices of bread. Roll up, pin with toothpicks, and toast in moderate oven, 350 degrees. This may also be used as a sandwich. Makes approximately 24.

Deer Spread Appetizer

1 lb. venison, cut in 2" pieces
salt
pepper
4 stalks celery
4 green onions

8 oz. pecans or walnut pieces
1½ Tbsp. mayonnaise
1 (8-oz.) pkg. cream cheese, softened
Biscotti

Cover venison with water; season with salt and pepper; cook in a crock pot on low setting for 8 hours or until tender; drain; set cooked venison aside to cool. Strain liquid through cheesecloth and save as venison stock. Shred cold meat in a food processor using the finest blade; remove to mixing bowl. Shred celery, onions and nut pieces in a food processor using the finest blade; mix with shredded venison. Vegetable, nut and meat mixture can be refrigerated overnight. Add chopped vegetables and nuts to shredded venison; mix in mayonnaise and softened cream cheese. Re-process through food processor using finest blade. Serve cold with crackers or on thin sliced and toasted Biscotti. Serves 20.

Mr. Jack Clark

Country Fried Venison

venison backstrap
Pet evaporated milk
all-purpose flour

white pepper
salt

Trim and remove all fat and connective tissues. Cut the venison into 3"x¼"x½" strips. Soak the strips in evaporated milk for 1½ hours. Season flour with a generous amount of pepper. Dredge the venison in the seasoned flour. Deep fry venison in hot grease. *Do not overcook.* Remove venison and drain. Salt at this time. Serves 6 to 12.

Charlemagne (King of the Franks from 768 and Emperor of the Romans from 800 to his death in 814) originally suggested the concept that wildlife should be held in trust for the public by the state.

Indonesian Venison Spareribs

12 oz. dried tamarind pulp with seeds,
    available at Indian and Oriental markets
    and specialty food stores
2 cups boiling water
6 small dried chilies, stemmed and seeded
¾ cup dried unsweetened coconut
¾ cup water

3 Tbsp. sugar
3 Tbsp. teriyaki sauce
3 Tbsp. fresh lime juice
6 large cloves garlic, crushed
¾ tsp. ground coriander
3 lbs. venison spareribs, 3" long
salt

Combine tamarind and 2 cups boiling water in small bowl, breaking up pulp with fork. Soak 1 hour. Grind chilies in processor or blender. Add remaining ingredients except spareribs, salt and tamarind mixture. Pour tamarind through fine strainer into processor or blender, pressing through as much pulp as possible. Blend mixture 1 minute. Arrange spareribs in a shallow glass dish. Pour marinade over, turning ribs to coat evenly. Refrigerate 6 to 8 hours, turning ribs occasionally. Preheat oven to 325 degrees. Pat ribs dry (reserve marinade). Sprinkle ribs lightly with salt. Arrange on rack set over large shallow roasting pan containing 1 cup water. Roast 30 minutes. Turn ribs and brush with marinade. Continue cooking, brushing frequently with marinade and turning, until evenly browned, about 1 hour. Cut ribs apart. Serve hot. Serves 6.

Meatballs with Cranberry Sauce

2 lbs. ground venison
¼ cup ground pork
1 cup cornflake crumbs
Tbsp, parsley flakes
Tbsp. dry onion flakes
2 eggs

2 Tbsp. soy sauce
⅓ cup tomato catsup
1¼ tsp. salt
¼ tsp. black pepper
Cranberry Meatball Sauce

Combine the ingredients for the meatballs and shape into 1½-inch meatballs. Place meatballs in greased 9x13-inch baking dish. Pour Cranberry Meatball Sauce over meatballs. Bake at 350 degrees for 1 hour. Serve in a heated chaffing dish. Serves 8.

Olive and Venison Spread

1 tsp. dried minced onion
1 Tbsp. whole milk
1 pkg. cream cheese, softened
1 Tbsp. mayonnaise

¼ cup stuffed olives, chopped
2½ oz. smoked or cooked venison,
    chopped fine
Saltine crackers

In a small bowl, soften onion in milk. Stir in cream cheese and mayonnaise. Add olives and venison; mix well. Chill. Serve on crackers. Makes 1½ cups.

Medallions of Venison with Crabmeat Filling

6 venison tenderloins or 1 backstrap
cornstarch
½ cup canned crabmeat
¼ cup mushrooms, chopped
¼ cup bamboo shoots, chopped

½ tsp. lemon pepper
2 tsp. soy sauce
3 egg whites, beaten until frothy
parsley, chopped

Cook tenderloins to rare and set aside to cool. With a sharp knife, cut the cold venison roast into slices ¼" thick. Then cut the slices in half. Cut enough to yield 24 pieces. Dust venison wafers with cornstarch. Combine the crabmeat, mushrooms, and bamboo shoots. Chop very fine; add lemon pepper to taste, 1 teaspoon sifted cornstarch, and the soy sauce; season with salt. Spread 12 of the venison pieces with the crabmeat mixture. Top them with the remaining 12 pieces, sandwich-style. Press gently to make them stick. Cross-tie each sandwich with cotton twine. Dip each venison medallion in egg white, then fry in deep fat until golden brown. Remove twine. Serve medallions sprinkled with chopped parsley. Serves 6 to 12.

Sliced Venison Steamed with Tea Melon

3 venison tenderloins
2 tsp. cornstarch
1 Tbsp. soy sauce

½ tsp. sugar
¼ cup tea melon
green peppers, chopped

Slice the venison thin, then combine with the cornstarch, soy sauce, and sugar. Allow to stand a few minutes, then spread evenly in a dish. Wash and slice the tea melon; arrange over the venison. Sprinkle with chopped green peppers, then add a few drops of sesame oil or peanut oil. Steam 30 minutes. Serves 4 to 6.

Smoked Venison Finger Sandwiches

1½ cups smoked venison backstrap,
   chopped
8 oz. cream cheese
3 Tbsp. Dijon mustard
3 Tbsp. light brown sugar

½ tsp. cloves, ground
salt
pepper
white bread or crackers

Cut cream cheese into ½" cubes. Place smoked venison and cream cheese in a food processor and pulse until mixture is smooth. Add mustard, brown sugar and cloves and blend until well mixed. Salt and pepper to taste. Cover and refrigerate for 2 hours. Spread on white bread and make crustless finger sandwiches or on crackers. Garnish with a small piece of pimento and or a small piece of parsley or rosemary. Serves 10.

Steamed and Minced Venison in Whole Eggshells

6 eggs
¾ cup venison, cooked and chopped
¼ tsp. shortening
¾ cup onion, chopped
1 tsp. fresh ginger, minced

1 tsp. Accent or MSG
1 Tbsp. rice wine or sherry
teriyaki sauce
sesame oil

With a pin, carefully punch small holes at both ends of the eggs. Enlarge one of the holes of each eggshell to a diameter of ⅜". Blow out the contents and reserve for use elsewhere. Wash eggshells in hot water and drain. Combine venison shortening, onion, and ginger and mince well. Add 2 tbsp, of soy sauce, Accent, and wine; mix well. Stuff 4 tbsp. of this mixture carefully into each eggshell. Seal the holes by pasting tiny squares of white tissue paper over them. Place the stuffed eggshells on a dish and put in a steamer for about 30 minutes. Serve with a sauce made by heating equal amounts of teriyaki sauce and sesame oil. Serves 4 to 6.

Venison and Celery Appetizer

Deer Spread Appetizer

1 bunch celery

Make Deer Spread Appetizer. Clean and cut celery stalks in 2" pieces. Fill celery with spread. Refrigerate and serve cold.

Mrs. Anne Lipscomb Webster

Venison Fondue

fondue dish
fondue forks
peanut oil

venison tenderloin or backstrap
Red Fondue Sauce
1 or more other fondue sauces

Cut venison tenderloin into ¾ to 1-inch cubes and serve raw. In the center of the dining table, place a fondue dish over a hot alcohol flame, filled with peanut or other oil heated at a very high temperature. Provide each guest with a long fondue fork or bamboo skewer which he uses to spear pieces of meat and then dip the meat into the hot oil to cook. It takes just a minute. Don't overcook. Then the guest can dip each piece into one of several kinds of sauces. Red Fondue Sauce is a good sauce to start with.

Other Fondue Sauces:
Soft Homemade Butter with garlic juice mixed in.
Mayonnaise flavored with Worcestershire sauce.
Horseradish, sour cream and mayonnaise.
Paprika sauce: Sour cream, paprika, chopped white onion, and a little salt.
Mayhaw jelly with Tabasco sauce.

Venison Fritters con Dos Salsas

3 cups all-purpose flour
1 tsp. baking powder
2 tsp. salt
4 eggs
1 cup stale beer
½ cup whole milk
1 Tbsp. chili powder

1 Tbsp. paprika
1½ lbs. venison backstrap cut in ¼"
   thin slices
oil for deep frying
Smoked Tomato Salsa
Yellow Tomato Salsa

For fritter batter, mix flour, baking powder, and salt in medium bowl. Add eggs and mix well. Add beer and milk and stir until thick. Stir in chili powder and paprika. Heat oil in deep fryer or heavy, deep skillet to 350 degrees. Salt venison and dust with flour. Dip each piece of venison into fritter batter, then slowly lower into hot oil. Fry for about 2 minutes, or until golden brown. Place on paper towels to drain. Serve with Smoked Tomato Salsa and Yellow Tomato Salsa. Serves 8.

Venison in a Blanket

2 (8-oz.) tubes refrigerated crescent rolls

16 small Fat Free Venison and
   Mushroom Breakfast Sausage

Separate the dough into 16 triangles. Place a sausage on wide end of each triangle and roll up. Place, tip side down, on ungreased baking sheets. Bake at 400 degrees 10 to 15 minutes or until golden brown. Recipe can be increased proportionately. Serves 16.

Venison Smoked with Fragrant Spices

2 venison tenderloins
3 Tbsp. soy sauce
3 Tbsp. rice wine or sherry
1 tsp. sugar

½ cup dark brown sugar
2 tsp. cinnamon
2 tsp. powdered aniseed
2 tsp. cloves powder

Cut the venison into small, very thin slices. Place the meat in a shallow pan and add the soy sauce, wine, and sugar. Allow to marinate for one hour. Place the pan over medium heat, turning the meat until it is tender. Place a sheet of heavy aluminum foil in the bottom of a large cast-iron pot. Combine the brown sugar, cinnamon, aniseed, and cloves and spread over the foil. Support a wire inside the pot, about 2" above the spice mixture. Arrange the slices of venison on the rack and cover the pot tightly. Place the pot over a low fire and allow to smoke about 10 minutes. Serve the venison hot or cold. Be sure to turn on the fan or open the windows for this preparation; the smoking pot can be placed on hot coals in the outdoor barbecue. Serves 2.

Venison Nuggets

I always use it at a deer camp as hors d'oeuvres, to precede a meal—I find it to also be a good "conversation builder" as well as tasty eating. This recipe is real fun and enjoyment at a deer camp when feeding a lot of hungry deer hunters.

¾ to 1 lb. venison loin or hind quarter
cold water
baking soda

Konriko "Hot 'n Spicy" Creole Seasoning
flour
vegetable oil

Separate each muscle group; trim away all fat and white tissues. Cut meat across the grain in ¼" to ⅜" thick by 2" to 3½" long pieces. Rinse meat well in cold water and place meat in a large stainless steel or plastic (not aluminum) bowl. Add 1 tsp. of baking soda per quart of cold water and cover meat to at least 3" to 4" above meat level. (1⅛ tsp. salt, per quart of water, can be substituted for baking soda). Refrigerate for at least 4 hours. If an unusual amount of blood is drawn out, remove meat and rinse with water; return meat to bowl and cover with fresh baking soda and water solution. Remove from refrigerator; drain well; dry with paper towels. Sprinkle meat with Konriko "Hot 'n Spicy" Creole Seasoning. Shake meat well in a paper sack containing all-purpose flour. Set sack aside and let meat rest for at least 10 minutes. While meat is resting in flour, heat vegetable oil to deep-frying temperature. Cook only a few pieces of meat at a time. This recipe can be prepared beforehand and frozen for a short period. *Do not overcook.* Serves 2 to 4.

Mr. Van Richardson

Venison Sausage Balls

1 lb. Country Venison Sausage or other
  bulk sausage

2 cups Cheddar cheese, shredded
3½ cups self-rising flour

Crumble venison sausage into a bowl. Microwave on High just until sausage is soft. Add cheese. Microwave until cheese is melted; mix well. Mix in flour. Shape into small balls. Place on a baking sheet. Bake for 15 to 30 minutes or until brown; drain well. Serves 2 to 4.

Venison Fingers

5 lbs. ground venison
4 tsp. Tender Quick salt
2½ tsp. white pepper
2½ tsp. mustard seed
2½ tsp. Seasoning Salt

1½ tsp. Hickory Smoke salt
2 tsp. peppercorns
½ tsp. garlic powder
½ tsp. ground savory
⅛ tsp. curry powder

Combine and mix all spices together. Add to venison and mix thoroughly. Let stand in refrigerator 2 days; turn every day. Divide the venison and make into 5 long fingers. Place on oven rack with pan underneath and bake at 150 degrees for 8 hours. The venison will continue to have a red color when done. Serves 12 to 16.

19

Miscellaneous Venison Recipes

Miscellaneous Venison Recipes contains a collection of different styles of recipes that add a whole new dimension to venison cooking. Some exciting recipes contain shrimp, red beans or cabbage.

Other exciting and change of pace recipes are for Christmas mincemeat pies, scallopini, hash, shish-kabobs, scrapple, ragout, étouffée and chop suey.

If you wish to surprise a venison lover who thinks he has eaten venison every way that it can be cooked, this is the chapter for you.

Braised Venison in Dry Red Wine

1 (3½ to 3¾-lb.) venison round
   roast, trimmed
salt
pepper
½ cup canola oil
1 med. white onion, finely chopped
1 slice smoked bacon, chopped
3 Tbsp. tomato paste
6 bay leaves
4 whole cloves

1 tsp. fresh rosemary, chopped
1 bottle dry red wine
6 cups canned beef broth
4 Italian tomatoes, drained and chopped
olive oil
Swiss chard
16 polenta pieces cut into 1"x1"x½"
   thick triangles

Season venison with salt and pepper. Heat oil in heavy Dutch oven over high heat. Add venison and brown on all sides, about 15 minutes. Transfer venison to platter; reduce heat to medium. Add onion and bacon to Dutch oven. Sauté until onion is golden, about 8 minutes. Mix in tomato paste, bay leaves, cloves and rosemary. Add wine. Return meat and any juices to Dutch oven. Cover and simmer 30 minutes, turning meat once. Mix stock and tomatoes into sauce. Cover and simmer gently until meat is tender, turning occasionally, about 2¾ hours. Transfer venison to warm platter. Cover with foil to keep warm. Strain sauce through fine sieve. Degrease sauce. Return sauce to Dutch oven. Boil until reduced to 32 cups, skimming foam from surface as necessary, about 1 hour. Add any venison juices from platter to sauce. Sauté Swiss chard in olive oil. Place sautéed Swiss chard on serving platter spread out to edge. Sauté polenta in olive oil until slightly browned around edges. Cut venison across the grain into ⅓"-thick slices. Arrange venison slices on top of Swiss chard leaving 1½" border around edge. Arrange 16 triangles of polenta around edge of venison. Spoon sauce over venison and serve. Serve on a bed of sautéed Swiss chard with small triangles of toasted polenta. Serves 8.

Braised Venison Lombard-Style

Venison is larded with carrots and pancetta.

6 medium carrots, peeled and soaked in cold
water for 30 minutes
8 oz. pancetta (Italian-style unsmoked bacon
preserved in salt) or fatty prosciutto,
coarsely chopped.
½ cup canola oil
black pepper
1 (3-lb.) venison roast
2 med. red onions, coarsely chopped
3 med. celery stalks, chopped
4 oz. prosciutto, chopped
1 cup dry red wine

6 juniper berries
2 bay leaves
2 whole cloves
1 tsp. dried thyme
1 tsp. dried marjoram
1 cup fresh Italian plum tomatoes,
quartered or 1 cup canned, drained
1 cup (about) canned beef broth,
warmed
Boiled Holman-Style Beans
bay leaves

Drain 2 carrots and chop finely. Marinate with half of pancetta, ¼ cup oil and pepper in small bowl 30 minutes. Puncture venison 2" deep in 10 places, using a larding needle or a small sharp knife. Enlarge holes with fingers. Drain carrot mixture, reserving oil. Stuff mixture into holes. Tie meat securely with twine to hold shape. Drain remaining 4 carrots and chop coarsely. Heat reserved oil and remaining ¼ cup of oil over medium heat in heavy casserole just large enough to hold venison. Stir in carrots and remaining 4 oz. pancetta, onions, celery and prosciutto and sauté 5 minutes. Pat venison dry and add to pan. Cover and brown on all sides, about 20 minutes. Pour in wine. Wrap juniper berries, 2 bay leaves, cloves, thyme and marjoram in cheesecloth. Add to meat. Cover and simmer 20 minutes. Puree tomatoes through food mill into pan. Pour in enough broth to cover ⅔ of meat with liquid. Cover and simmer gently until meat is tender when pierced with knife, turning occasionally, about 1½ hours, adding more broth if necessary to keep ⅔ of meat covered with liquid. Remove meat from casserole. Degrease cooking juices. Set pan over high heat and boil until liquid is reduced to 4 cups, about 10 minutes. Discard twine and cut meat into ¾" slices. Overlap slices down center of platter. Spoon sauce around venison. Arrange beans around sauce. Garnish with bay leaves. Serves 6 to 8.

Braised Venison with Fall Vegetables

3 lbs. venison, cut 2" cubes
all-purpose flour
Crisco or other shortening
water
1 Tbsp. vinegar

½ cup celery, chopped
½ cup apple
½ cup carrot
½ cup onion

Dredge venison with flour and sear on all sides in Crisco. Add enough water to cover the bottom of the pan; add vinegar. Cover tightly and cook very slowly for about 2 hours, adding a little more liquid as necessary. About 30 minutes before meat is tender, add celery, apple, carrot and onion. This mixture will flavor the gravy and add flavor to the meat. It may be strained from the gravy before serving, if desired. Serves 4 to 6.

Breaded Thin-Cut Venison Skillet Steaks

2 lbs. of venison cut into slices ¼" thick
1 cup fresh lime or lemon juice
salt
black pepper
2 eggs

¼ cup all-purpose flour
2 Tbsp. water
1 cup dry fine bread crumbs
1½ cups Crisco
2 lemons or limes, cut into wedges

Marinate the thin-cut venison in lemon juice for 1 hour. Pat them dry and dust with salt and pepper. Mix and lightly mix the eggs and water. Dip the venison in the egg mix. Then dip in flour and shake off the excess flour. Dip them in the dry bread crumbs. Gently shake off any excess bread crumbs. Refrigerate the breaded venison for 2 hours. Heat Crisco in a large and heavy pan. Add the venison, very quickly cooking on one side and turning over once. *Do not overcook.* Thin venison should be cooked to more than medium-rare. Garnish with lemon wedges and serve immediately. Serves 4.

Caribbean Sweet and Sour Venison

3 Tbsp. safflower or canola oil
2 Tbsp. fresh ginger, peeled and chopped
  fine
1 Tbsp. garlic, chopped fine
1 cup carrots, chopped coarse
1 cup onions, chopped coarse
1 cup green bell pepper, chopped coarse
1 cup crushed pineapple in its own Juice

¼ cup white wine vinegar
1 Tbsp. sugar
½ Tbsp. freshly ground white pepper
1½ cups tomato catsup
½ cup pineapple juice
2¼ lbs. venison filets cut in bite-size
  pieces
boiled rice

In a large saucepan, heat the oil. Add ginger and garlic and sauté over a low flame for 5 minutes, until fragrant. Do not overbrown the garlic or it will taste bitter. Add carrots, and sauté another 5 minutes. Add onion and green peppers and sauté about 3 minutes, until green peppers lose their rawness, but aren't cooked thoroughly. Add cup of pineapple and its juice and vinegar. Bring to a boil over high heat. Reduce heat to medium and cook for 5 minutes. Add the sugar, white pepper, tomato catsup and pineapple juice. Stir well and continue to cook an additional 5 minutes. Cook venison in boiling water for 5 minutes. Drain venison and add to sauce. Cook together for 2 minutes. Adjust seasonings, tasting for salt, pepper and vinegar. Serve over boiled rice. Serves 6.

White tails are, for the most part, a herd animal, and with the exception of some mature bucks or other smaller groups, can be difficult to separate.

Chevreuil Miroton

2 Tbsp. butter
1 onion, sliced coarsely
1 Tbsp. flour
1 cup canned beef broth

salt
black pepper
1 ½ tsp. white vinegar
thin slices of roasted venison

Sauté onions in melted butter. Sprinkle flour over all and mix rapidly with a wooden spoon. Add broth, salt and pepper; stir until boiling. Reduce heat and add vinegar. Simmer about 15 minutes. Arrange slices of roasted venison on a hot platter and cover with the sauce and serve. Serves 4.

Chipped Venison in Sour Cream

½ lb. cooked venison roast or steak
water to cover
2 Tbsp. butter
2 cups sour cream
1 (6-oz.) Jar marinated artichoke hearts, drained and thinly sliced

½ cup dry white wine
1 ½ Tbsp. freshly grated Parmesan cheese
ground cayenne pepper
6 slices buttered toast

Shred chipped Venison Jerky. Transfer to small saucepan and cover with water. Bring to a boil over high heat. Drain, Melt butter in a large skillet over medium-high heat. Stir in sour cream and cook, stirring constantly, until smooth, 3 to 5 minutes; do not boil. Reduce heat to medium-low and add venison, artichoke hearts, wine, cheese and ground red pepper. Stir until heated through. Spoon over buttered toast and serve. Serves 6.

Christmas Venison Mincemeat Pie with Candied Fruits, Sour Cherries and Walnuts

Circa 1890. My grandmother, Mrs. Clyde Lacy Lynch, would make these pies for Christmas presents. For this recipe, Nanny would use beef. Venison works just as well.

Canned Venison Christmas Mincemeat
    with Candied Fruits, Sour Cherries
    and Walnuts

Standard Pastry
brandy

The mincemeat filling needs to be prepared at least 2 weeks in advance. For a smaller number of pies, the recipe can be halved or quartered. Make Standard Pastry and prepare pie plates. With a small Christmas theme cookie cutter, cut out the center of the pastry that will be used for the top. Place the cut on top of the pastry covering and gently press down. Fill pie shells with mincemeat filling and cover with pastry top and crimp around the edges. Bake in a 350-degree oven until the crust is golden brown. Season mincemeat with brandy before serving. This recipe makes about 20 pies.

Creamed Dried Venison

Venison Jerky
Milk & Coffee Gravy

toast
baked potatoes

Cut Venison Jerky across the grain in thin strips. Chop thin strips into small pieces. Combine with a liberal amount of well-seasoned Milk & Coffee Gravy. Heat thoroughly. Serve on toast or baked potatoes. If desired, cooked spaghetti, macaroni, mashed potatoes, or steamed rice may be substituted for toast or baked potatoes.

Curried Venison Pie

2 Tbsp. butter
½ cup hot whole milk
salt
black pepper
3 cups potatoes, cooked and mashed

1 egg, beaten well
3 cups cooked venison, cut into cubes
1 med. white onion, chopped
2 cups Indian Curry Sauce

Melt butter in the hot milk; add salt and pepper to taste. Beat into the mashed potatoes. Add the well-beaten egg and beat until light. Fill a greased 1½-quart casserole with part of the potato mixture. Combine meat, onion and Indian Curry Sauce; turn into the casserole and top with the remaining potato mixture. Bake in a 425-degree oven about 30 minutes or until heated through and lightly browned. Serves 6.

Fried Breakfast Venison with White Sauce

1 cup venison, chopped fine
boiling water
2 Tbsp, butter
2 Tbsp. all-purpose flour

1½ cups whole milk
salt
black pepper

Remove any fiber from the venison; chop fine and scald with boiling water. Drain thoroughly. Melt the butter in a heavy frying pan; add the chopped venison and cook until crisp. Stir in the flour; gradually pour in the milk and stir until boiling. Season with salt and pepper and serve on toast. Serves 3 to 5.

The average reproductive life of a doe is approximately 10 years.

Fried Noodles with Venison Slices, Shrimp and Vegetables

1 egg
½ tsp. peanut oil
1 lb. ramen (or mee) noodles.
4 Tbsp. peanut oil
2 med. onions, chopped
4 med. garlic cloves, pressed
1 Tbsp. fresh ginger, peeled and chopped
1 med. head cauliflower, divided into small florets
1 small head cabbage, thinly sliced
4 leeks, thinly sliced
4 celery stalks, sliced
½ lb. bean sprouts
2 Tbsp. peanut butter

1 Tbsp. Sambal Ulek paste (available at Oriental markets)
2 Tbsp. ground coriander
½ lb. venison round steak, sliced across the grain in thin ½"x 2" strips
½ lb. uncooked medium shrimp, peeled
1 large tomato, chopped
½ cucumber, sliced
1 lemon, thinly sliced
fresh cilantro leaves

Beat egg in small bowl. Heat ½ tsp. oil in 8" omelet pan over medium-high heat. Add egg, tilting pan to coat. Let egg cook until set. Remove; cut into ¼" wide strips. Cook noodles according to package directions. Drain and transfer to platter. Toss noodles with 1 Tbsp. oil. Tent with foil to keep warm. Heat 2 Tbsp. oil in wok over medium-high heat. Add onions, garlic and ginger and stir-fry until aromatic, about 1 minute. Increase heat to high and add cauliflower, cabbage, leeks and celery. Cook until vegetables are crisp-tender, stirring frequently, about 3 minutes. Add bean sprouts, peanut butter, Sambal Ulek and ground coriander and stir until heated through, about 1 minute. Transfer to plate. Heat remaining 1 Tbsp. peanut oil in same wok. Add venison and stir-fry until just brown. *Do not overcook.* Add to vegetables. Add shrimp to wok and stir-fry until just opaque, about 3 minutes. Return venison and vegetable mixture to wok; toss until well combined and heated through. Add noodles and toss to combine. Season with salt and pepper. Divide among plates. Top each portion with omelet strips, tomato, cucumber, lemon and cilantro. Serves 4 to 6.

Venison Pie with Tomatoes and Peas

1½ to 2-lb. venison roast
1 Tbsp. real butter
3 onions, diced
1 clove garlic, minced
1 can tomatoes
1 Tbsp. paprika

pinch of red pepper
1 bay leaf
dash of thyme
1 cup stale beer
3 carrots, sliced
1 cup frozen peas

Cut the venison into 1" pieces. Heat butter in a skillet and quickly brown. Add onions, garlic, tomatoes, seasonings and Budweiser. Cover and cook slowly until the venison is tender, about 1 to 2 hours. Add carrots and peas when venison is almost tender. Remove from heat and pour into a baking dish. Drop on Venison Pie Topping from spoon and bake in 425-degree oven 15 minutes, or until topping is browned.

Venison Pie Popping

1 cup all-purpose flour
¾ cup yellow cornmeal
1 Tbsp. sugar
1 Tbsp. baking powder
½ tsp. salt

¾ cup whole milk
3 Tbsp. melted Crisco or other
    shortening
1 egg, slightly beaten

Combine flour, cornmeal, sugar, baking powder, and salt in mixing bowl. Add milk, Crisco, and egg. Stir until smooth. Serves 4.

Italian Venison Stir Fry

1 lb. venison round steak
2 med. garlic cloves, crushed
1 Tbsp. olive oil
2 med. zucchini

12 cherry tomatoes, halved
¼ cup Italian salad dressing
2 cups spaghetti, cooked
4 Tbsp. Parmesan cheese, grated

Cut venison crosswise and if possible crossgrain into 1" strips. Cut each strip crosswise in half. Thinly slice zucchini. Cook garlic in a large skillet for 1 minute over medium-high heat. Add ½ of the venison strips and stir fry only 1 to 1 ½ minutes. *Do not overcook.* Season with salt and pepper. Remove venison and keep warm. Add zucchini and stir fry 2 to 3 minutes or until tender-crisp. Return venison to skillet. Add tomato halves and dressing; heat through. Serve over hot pasta. Sprinkle with Parmesan cheese. Serves 4.

Pastry Venison Loaf

1½ recipes Standard Pastry
6 cups cooked venison steak, chopped
3 Tbsp. pimiento, chopped
1½ tsp. salt
⅛ tsp. pepper

1 tsp. Worcestershire sauce
6 Tbsp. butter
6 Tbsp. all-purpose flour
1 cup canned beef broth
Mushroom White Sauce

Prepare Standard Pastry and chill. Combine meat, pimiento, salt, pepper and Worcestershire sauce. Melt butter; add flour and mix until smooth; gradually add the broth and continue to cook, stirring constantly, until very thick. Add just enough of the stock mixture to hold the meat together. Shape into a loaf on a shallow pan; chill at least 3 hours. Roll chilled pastry into a large oblong. Place the loaf on the center and fold the pastry up and around the sides and ends of the loaf; square sides and edges; seal the corners. Roll a small piece of pastry to fit the top of the loaf; place it on top; seal and pinch the edges; decorate with pastry cutouts and designs as desired. Chill thoroughly; brush with egg diluted with a little water. Bake in a 425-degree oven 1 hour or until browned. Serve with Mushroom White Sauce. Serves 8.

Quick Venison Red Beans and Rice

1 (8-oz.) pkg. Mahatma Red Beans & Long
   Grain Rice With Seasonings
3¼ cups water
1 Tbsp. butter

1 cup venison, cut ½ inch pieces
Tabasco sauce
salt
pepper

Follow directions on package. Add venison at the same time you add beans, rice and seasonings to water. Add Tabasco, salt and pepper to taste. Serves 4.

Congealed Venison Pie in a Pastry Shell

½ lb. veal stew meat, cut ½" cubes
½ lb. ham, cut ½" cubes
1 small yellow onion, minced
ground nutmeg
salt
pepper

Hot Water Pastry
½ lb. cooked venison, cut ½" cubes
3 hard-boiled eggs, halved across egg
1 egg beaten with 1 tsp. water
1 Tbsp. unflavored gelatin
2 cups canned beef broth

Preheat oven to 400 degrees. Grease a 7" or 8" cake pan with a removable bottom. Combine and mix veal, ham, onion, nutmeg, salt and pepper. Roll ⅔ of warm Hot Water Pastry out to a thickness of ⅛". Wrap remaining pastry in aluminum foil and keep warm. Line the greased cake pan with the pastry. Place ½ of the meat mixture on top of the pastry in the cake pan. Cover with half of the cooked venison. Press a deep trench down the center of the meat filling. Lay the egg halves into the trench. Cover with the remaining venison, then with the remaining meat mixture. Smooth out the top. Roll out the remaining pastry. Lay the pastry over the dish. Trim off excess edge and reserve the dough. Wet the edge with water and crimp to seal. Cut a small hole in center of the pastry. Reroll the reserved dough and cut out appropriate seasonal designs. Wet the underside of the designs with water and arrange on top of the pie. Brush the surface with egg and water glaze. Insert a meat thermometer into the center hole. Bake for 40 minutes.

Reduce the oven temperature to 325 degrees. Brush pie with egg and water glaze again. Continue baking, about 1 hour, until the meat thermometer registers 160 degrees. While the pie is baking, soften the gelatin in ¼ cup beef broth. In a saucepan, heat the remaining 1¾ cups of broth to a simmer. Add the gelatin to the broth and stir until it is dissolved. Remove the broth from the heat. Remove the pie from the oven. Place funnel in vent hole. Slowly pour in broth mixture into the pie until it is full. Turn the pie from side to side to settle the broth. Repeat every 20 minutes with remaining broth. If the broth congeals, melt by reheating. Remove the pie and allow to come to room temperature. Refrigerate the pie overnight. When ready to serve, remove the pie from the refrigerator and allow to come to room temperature. Unmold, place on round serving plate, slice and serve. Serves 8 to 10.

Saffroned Venison and Beans

1 cup dry navy beans
2 tsp. salt
2 Tbsp. canola oil
1 lb. venison, cut in cubes
3 ripe tomatoes, quartered
1 med. onion, thinly sliced

⅛ tsp. pepper
⅛ tsp. chopped saffron
1 tsp. brown sugar
½ cup dry white wine
1 (No. 2) can whole kernel corn
1 med. green bell pepper, thinly sliced

Rinse the beans thoroughly and place in a large saucepan with enough water to cover. Bring to a boil and reduce heat. Simmer for 2 hours. Add 1 tsp. salt and simmer for 1 hour longer or until beans are tender, adding water as needed to keep covered. Heat the oil in a large, heavy skillet. Add venison and brown over high heat. Add the tomatoes, onion, remaining salt, pepper, saffron, brown sugar and wine and simmer until beef is tender. Drain the beans, then add the corn, green pepper and beans to the venison mixture. Cook until green pepper is tender. Serves 4.

Sauerbraten with Venison

3-lb. piece venison round steak
4 oz. ground pork
1 pt. vinegar
3 bay leaves
12 peppercorns
6 whole cloves
1 sprig parsley, chopped

2 Tbsp. flour seasoned with salt and
  pepper
¼ cup butter
1 cup onion, sliced
1½ cups carrots, julienne
1 dozen Gingersnap Cookies
1 Tbsp. sugar
Potato Dumplings

Wipe meat with cloth. Place in a small earthenware crock; add vinegar and enough water to cover; add bay leaves, peppercorns, whole cloves and parsley. Cover and place in refrigerator. Leave 3 or 4 days, turning the meat daily. Drain off liquid, reserving it for the sauce. Rub meat on all sides with seasoned flour. Brown it thoroughly in butter or drippings; add onions, carrots and 2 cups of the spiced liquid. Cover and simmer gently about 2 hours or until meat is tender. Remove meat to a hot platter. Add gingersnaps, rolled into fine crumbs, and sugar to the gravy; cook for about 10 minutes. Add more salt if desired. Pour sauce over meat; surround with Potato Dumplings. Serves 6 to 8.

Scallopini of Venison

2½-lb. venison backstrap, sliced very thin
all-purpose flour
salt
black pepper
paprika

2 med. white onions, sliced
1 tsp. sugar
1 (4-oz.) can mushrooms
1¼ cups tomato juice
1¼ cups hot water canola oil

Cut meat into very thin serving slices. Combine flour, salt, pepper, and paprika. Roll venison slices lightly in seasoned flour. Flatten slightly with edge of plate or meat pounder. Fry until just golden brown on both sides in hot canola oil (it is very easy to overcook these thin slices). Remove meat from pan. Add onions. Place meat and onions in greased casserole dish. Add remaining ingredients. Bake at 350 degrees for 2 hours or until tender. Serves 8 to 10.

Southern-Style Venison and Ham Rolls

6 slices venison round, pounded ¼" thin
3 slices boiled ham, halved
salt pepper to taste
3 Tbsp. butter
1 med. onion, chopped
2 clove garlic, pressed
1 small can tomato juice

½ tsp. salt
½ tsp. chill powder
¼ tsp. basil
⅓ cup creamy peanut butter
½ green bell pepper, sliced
⅓ cup stuffed olives, sliced
Boiled Rice

Place ½ ham slice on each venison slice and sprinkle with salt and pepper. Roll up and secure with cotton string. Brown in butter in a large skillet and pour off excess drippings. Stir in onion, garlic, tomato juice, salt, chili powder and basil and cover skillet. Simmer for 1 hour. Spread peanut butter over venison rolls and add green pepper and olives. Cook for 30 minutes longer or until venison is tender, stirring occasionally. Place Boiled Rice on serving plate. Center venison rolls on the bed of rice, pour sauce over rolls. Serves 4 to 6.

Spicy Venison Shish Kabobs

2 lbs. venison, cubed
juice of 2 limes
4 Tbsp. olive oil
2 Tbsp. onion, grated
2 Tbsp. ground chili pepper
1 tsp. coriander

1 tsp. powdered ginger
3 garlic cloves, pressed
2 tsp. curry powder
3 tsp. salt
mushrooms, tomatoes, onion and bell
  peppers cubed

Cut venison into 1½-inch cubes. Mix lime juice, olive oil, grated onion, chili pepper, coriander, ginger, garlic, curry powder, and salt. Marinate meat in mixture for 2 hours. Alternate venison, tomatoes, peppers, onions, and mushrooms on skewers. Grill to medium done over a charcoal grill for 20 to 35 minutes basting with the marinade juice. Serves 2 to 4.

Spinach and Venison Pastrami Frittata

3 Tbsp. olive oil
2 clove garlic, pressed
1 (10-oz.) pkg. frozen leaf spinach, thawed,
  thoroughly drained and chopped
4 oz. Venison Pastrami or other pastrami,
  cut ¼" thin and diced

7 eggs
2 tsp. Dijon mustard
4 oz. (about 1 cup) Gruyere or cheddar
  cheese, grated
black pepper

Heat oil in a medium skillet over low heat. Add garlic and sauté until fragrant, about 1 minute. Mix in spinach and diced Venison Pastrami. Whisk eggs and mustard together in medium bowl. Pour eggs over spinach mixture in skillet. Stir gently to blend ingredients. Cover skillet and cook until eggs are almost set, about 8 minutes. Meanwhile, preheat broiler. Sprinkle cheese over frittata. Broil until cheese melts and bubbles, about 1 minute. Sprinkle with pepper. Serve frittata warm or at room temperature.

Stir-Fried Ginger Venison with Mushrooms

1 lb. venison steak thinly sliced across
  the grain
3 Tbsp. soy sauce
1 Tbsp. cornstarch
1 Tbsp. Chinese rice wine or dry sherry
1 tsp. sugar
1 Tbsp. Oriental sesame oil
2 Tbsp. canola oil
2 tsp. fresh ginger, peeled and minced

2 garlic cloves, pressed
1 cup green onions, chopped
½ lb. mushrooms, sliced
½ lb. spinach, stemmed
salt
pepper
boiled rice
additional soy sauce

Place venison in bowl. Combine 3 Tbsp. soy sauce and next 3 ingredients in small bowl. Pour over venison and toss. Heat both oils in wok or large skillet over high heat. Add ginger and garlic and stir-fry until aromatic, about 45 seconds. Add venison and marinade and stir-fry until venison begins to brown, about 2 minutes. Add green onions and mushrooms and stir-fry until onions begin to soften, about 2 minutes. Add spinach and stir-fry 45 seconds. Season with salt and pepper. Serve immediately with rice, passing soy sauce separately. Serves 4.

Using claims data, State Farm estimates 2.3 million crashes between deer and vehicles occurred between July 1, 2008 and June 30, 2010— up 21.1 percent from five years ago. West Virginia tops the list of those states where a driver is most likely to hit a deer (1 in 42 chance). Iowa is second (1 in 67), followed by Michigan (1 in 70), South Dakota (1 in 76) and Montana (1 in 82). Drivers in Hawaii are least likely to hit a deer (1 in 13,011).

Tagliarini-Style Venison

1 lb. venison round steak
1 lb. country-style pork sausage
1 green bell pepper, chopped
1 (No. 2) can tomatoes
2 (12-oz.) cans niblet corn
1 jar pimientos, chopped
1 (13½-oz.) jar mushroom pieces
1 jar stuffed olives, sliced
1 cup tomato catsup

1 tsp. chili powder
1 tsp. oregano
salt
black pepper
paprika
½ cup sherry
1½ pkgs. wide noodles
slices of sharp cheese
Mozzarella cheese

Cook venison and sausage in a large cast Iron skillet until done. Add bell peppers and cook until pepper is partially done. Add other ingredients (except noodles and cheese) and bring to a boil. Cook noodles according to package directions. Drain and add meat mixture. Stir well and put into fairly shallow baking dishes or the broiler pan. Cover with slices of sharp cheese and sprinkle with shredded Mozzarella, if desired. Bake at 325 degrees about 20 minutes or until cheese is melted. May be placed in smaller baking dishes and frozen. Omit cheese until time to heat and serve. Serves 15 to 20.

New Mexico-Style Shredded Venison

¼ cup Mazola corn oil
1 large onion, chopped
1 large jalapeño chili, minced with seeds
2 lbs. venison, cut 2" cubes
1 Tbsp, chili powder
2 tsp. ground cumin
½ tsp. ground coriander
½ tsp. dried thyme, crumbled
½ tsp. dried oregano, crumbled

¼ tsp. ground cloves
pinch of ground allspice
4 large garlic cloves, pressed
2 Tbsp. tomato paste
2 (14-oz.) cans stewed tomatoes
2 cups canned beef broth
2 cups canned chicken broth
2 bay leaves
¼ cup fresh cilantro, chopped

Heat oil in Dutch oven over medium heat. Add onion and jalapeño and cook until soft, stirring occasionally, about 5 minutes. Add venison and stir until brown on all sides, about 7 minutes. Mix in chili powder and next 6 ingredients and cook 2 minutes. Add garlic and tomato paste and cook 3 minutes. Stir in all remaining ingredients except cilantro. Reduce heat to low; cover and simmer 1 hour. Uncover and simmer until venison is tender and shreds easily, about 1 hour. Remove venison from liquid using a slotted spoon. Set aside. Increase heat to medium and boil cooking liquid until reduced to 1½ cups, about 35 minutes. Shred venison using fingers. Mix into sauce. Spoon into bowl. Sprinkle with cilantro. Makes about 6 cups.

Mexican-Style Venison Pizza

1 lb. venison, chopped
¼ lb. pork fat, chopped
1 Tbsp. dried onion, minced
1 tsp. dried oregano, crushed
1 tsp. freshly grated nutmeg
1 tsp. dried mint, crumbled

½ tsp. black pepper
6 (8") flour tortillas
6 Tbsp. crumbled feta cheese
¼ cup Parmesan cheese, grated
1 yellow bell pepper, cut julienne

Mix chopped venison and pork fat and grind together. Preheat broiler. Cook venison in a medium skillet over medium heat until brown and crumbly. Drain well. Stir in next 5 ingredients. Arrange tortillas on 2 large baking sheets. Divide meat among tortillas, spreading to within ½" of edges. Sprinkle 1 Tbsp. feta and 2 tsp. Parmesan cheese over each; top each with bell pepper. Broil until cheese melts and browns, about 4 minutes. Serve immediately. Makes 6.

Vegetable-Stuffed Venison Roll with Tomato Sauce

1 (3-lb.) round venison roast
black pepper
1 (⅓-lb.) piece of slab smoked bacon
4 Chinese sausages, halved lengthwise
3 large carrots, peeled and cut into thirds
  lengthwise
2 hard-boiled eggs, quartered lengthwise
1 large green bell pepper, cut into ⅓" strips
1 large red bell pepper, cut into ⅓" strips
16 stuffed green olives

Sauce:
2 cups water
2 cups tomato sauce
2 med. onions, finely chopped
½ cup white vinegar
2 bay leaves
¼ tsp. salt
¼ tsp. black pepper
canola oil (for frying)

To cut venison into 1 long flat piece, insert sharp knife ¾" above work surface. Cut along bottom of meat down full length parallel to work surface, leaving ¾" "hinge" at far long side. Pull back on top of roast and repeat. Continue cutting until roast is opened into one long strip. Pound meat strip to ½" thickness. Sprinkle meat with pepper. Slice slab bacon lengthwise into 4 strips, then halve lengthwise. Arrange bacon, sausages, carrots, eggs, bell peppers and olives crosswise atop meat in alternating rows. Roll meat up tightly, starting at short end. Tie roulade securely at 2" intervals, using kitchen twine.

For sauce: Combine all remaining ingredients except vegetable oil in heavy medium saucepan and bring to boil, reduce heat and simmer 3 minutes. Preheat oven to 350 degrees. Heat ½" oil in deep large skillet over medium-high heat. Pat roulade dry and brown on all sides. Transfer to deep roasting pan. Pour tomato sauce over meat. Cover tightly with foil. Bake until meat is tender, about 2 hours, basting with sauce every 20 minutes. Set roulade on platter; reserve sauce. Let meat cool. Cover and refrigerate until well chilled. Can be prepared 1 day ahead. Preheat oven to 350 degrees. Cut roulade into ¾" slices across grain. Arrange cut side down in single layer in large roasting pan. Bake just until warm, about 15 minutes. Reheat sauce. Spoon onto warm serving platter. Top with meat and serve immediately. Serves 12.

Venison Steak with Sweet Garlic and Caramelized Onions

Venison Steak:
14 large garlic cloves
1 Tbsp. dry mustard
1 Tbsp. paprika
1½ tsp. salt
1 tsp. black pepper
6¾-lb. venison brisket or flank steak
2 med. white onions, peeled, sliced thin
2 cups canned beef stock

Caramelized Onions:
4 med. white onions, sliced thin
3 Tbsp. unsalted butter

1 tsp. sugar
salt
pepper

Sauce:
1½ Tbsp. all-purpose flour
3 Tbsp. tomato paste
2 Tbsp. dry vermouth
½ tsp. dry mustard
3 Tbsp. unsalted butter,
    cut into pieces

Position rack in the center of oven and preheat to 350 degrees. Line heavy large shallow roasting pan with enough heavy-duty aluminum foil to enclose venison steak completely. Finely chopped 2 garlic cloves. Mix garlic, mustard, paprika, salt and pepper in a small dish. Rub mixture over both sides of steak. Spread sliced onions and 6 whole garlic cloves over foil and prepared pan. Top with steak. Cover with remaining onions and garlic. Pour stock into bottom of pan (not over venison). Wrap steak with foil; fold edges to seal. Bake until meat is tender, about 4 hours. Cover and refrigerate steak at least 6 hours and preferably overnight.

To make caramelized onions, melt butter in a large skillet over medium heat. Add onions and sugar and cook until onions caramelize, stirring occasionally, about 20 minutes. Season to taste with salt and pepper.

For sauce, discard solid fat from steak. Remove steak from pan. Transfer onions and garlic from steak and place in a food processor. Add flour and puree until smooth. Add 1 cup pan juices, tomato paste, vermouth and mustard and blend. Transfer sauce to small skillet. Stir in remaining pan juices. Cook over medium-high heat until slightly thickened, stirring frequently, about 5 minutes. Whisk in butter 1 piece at a time.

Thinly slice venison across the grain. Arrange sliced meat in large shallow baking dish. Pour sauce over. (Can be prepared 1 day ahead. Cover steak and onions separately and refrigerate. Bring to room temperature before reheating.)

Position rack in center of oven and preheat to 350 degrees. Tent steak loosely with foil. Bake until hot 30 to 40 minutes. Remove foil. Top with caramelized onions and bake 10 minutes.

As you travel south, the white-tailed deer become smaller in stature.

Venison Cabbage Rolls

Cabbage Rolls:
8 cabbage leaves
1 lb. venison
½ lb. pork
6 saltines
1 white onion
1 tsp. salt
½ tsp. black pepper
1 egg

Tomato Sauce:
1 (16-oz.) can tomatoes
½ cup water
½ bay leaf
½ tsp. salt
dash powdered sage
½ tsp. sugar

Cook cabbage leaves in boiling, salted water for 2 minutes. Drain. Grind venison, pork, saltines and onion in food grinder using fine disc. Stir in egg and seasoning. Place 3 Tbsp. of meat mixture on each leaf of roll. Fasten with a toothpick. Put in large skillet and cover with tomato sauce. Cover skillet and simmer for about 1 hour. Serves 4 to 6.

Venison Cacciatore

1 pt. inexpensive cheap white wine
½ pt. inexpensive Chianti wine
6 med. white onions, quartered
2 cloves garlic, minced
6 med. tomatoes, quartered
1 tsp. salt
2 bay leaves, broken
2 sprigs parsley

1 sprig oregano
1 sprig marjoram
3 lbs. venison, cut 2" squares
black pepper
salt
all-purpose flour
½ cup canola oil
2 cups brown rice

Add wine, onions, garlic, tomatoes, and salt to a covered clay cooking pot. Tie spices in a small spice cooking bag and add bag to cooking pot. Cover and simmer over low heat. Rub venison with salt and pepper and dredge in flour. Sauté meat in oil until venison is brown. Add venison and drippings to clay pot. Cover and bake in a 300-degree oven for 3 to 3½ hours. Remove spice bag. Serve over brown rice. Serves 4 to 6.

Venison Casserole with Mushrooms and Tomatoes

2 lbs. venison, cubed
1 can mushroom soup
pkg. dry onion soup mix
large tomatoes, quartered

salt
black pepper
2 cups Cheddar cheese, shredded

Place venison in the bottom of a casserole dish. Add mushroom soup, dry onion soup mix and tomatoes on top. Cover and bake at 325 degrees for 2 hours. Add Cheddar cheese at end of cooking cycle so that it will have time to melt. Serves 2 to 4.

Venison Chop Suey

1 lb. venison, cut into ½" cubes
¼ cup real butter or margarine
1 cup onions, chopped
1 cup celery, chopped

2 Tbsp. molasses
2 Tbsp. soy or teriyaki sauce
1 can bean sprouts
3 Tbsp. cornstarch

Cook venison in butter; do not brown. Add onions, celery, molasses and soy sauce. Cook for 5 minutes. Drain bean sprouts; reserve liquid. Mix cornstarch and reserve liquid; add slowly to meat mixture. Cook until thickened. Add bean sprouts; heat thoroughly. Serve over rice or chow mein noodles. Serves 6.

Molded Venison Hindquarter with Creamed Horseradish Sauce

1 small venison hindquarter
1½ cups vinegar from pepper sauce
¼ cup safflower oil
6 med. onions, quartered
6 carrots, halved
2 stalks celery with tops
4 bay leaves
⅛ tsp. ground thyme
12 to 14 whole cloves
⅛ tsp. black pepper

⅛ tsp. red pepper
½ cup tawny port or sherry
3 packs unflavored gelatin
water
4 hard-boiled eggs, sliced
3 limes, sliced
½ pt. cream with Homemade Horse-
    radish to taste
salt and pepper to taste

Place hindquarter in a large glass dish and pour pepper sauce vinegar over it. Place in the refrigerator overnight. Turn several times. Remove the venison, drain and save the marinade. Heat the safflower oil in a very large cast iron skillet and brown the venison. Cover the venison with water. Add the onions, carrots, celery, bay leaves, thyme, cloves, black and red pepper and saved marinade. Add sherry and if needed, water to cover. Soften the gelatin in a small amount of water. Bring to a boil and add softened gelatin. Separate the venison into chunks and remove all connective tissues and bone. Select a very large mold and lay the hard-boiled eggs and lime slices on the bottom. Lay the venison pieces on top of the lime slices. Carefully pour the liquid over the venison. Refrigerate for 8 hours. Remove the mold and remove any fat that has congealed on the top. Select a serving platter that is the shape of the mold. Lay the platter, face down on top of the mold. Turn over, as a unit. Gently lift the mold off. Garnish with parsley and other seasonal greens and sprigs of fresh spices. Serve with cream and horseradish sauce. Serves 12 to 16.

 *A old Native American saying: A deer has enough brains to tan its own hide.*

Venison Étouffée—Cajun Style

5 lbs. venison, cut ½" cubes
safflower oil
5 cups white onions, chopped
1 cup green bell pepper, chopped
½ lemon, chopped fine
2 tsp. garlic, chopped fine

1 cup parsley, chopped
salt, to taste
2 Tbsp. Worcestershire sauce
Tabasco sauce to taste
boiled rice

Salt and pepper meat and quickly brown in safflower oil. Put venison in a Dutch oven. Add the remainder of the ingredients. Do not add any more liquid. Stir often to prevent sticking. Cook over very low heat for 6 to 8 hours until venison is very tender. Serve over boiled rice. Serves 4 to 6.

Venison Hash

boiled venison, chopped small
4 Tbsp. canola oil
2 Tbsp. all purpose flour
1 large onion, chopped
¼ cup apple cider vinegar
1 cup tomato catsup
3 Tbsp. Worcestershire sauce

2 Tbsp. yellow mustard
2 cup water
1 tsp. celery seed
½ tsp. sage
salt
black pepper
canned beef broth

Boil pieces of venison backstrap or tenderloin until tender. Cut meat into small pieces. Drain well. Make a sauce by combining and mixing the remaining ingredients. Place the venison in a shallow glass baking dish and pour the sauce mixture over chopped venison. Bake for 2 hours at 135 degrees. Add a little beef broth if needed. Serves 4 to 6.

Venison in Cumin-Scented Spinach Sauce

2 lbs. fresh spinach leaves or mixed greens
(such as mustard greens, kale, collard)
greens and beet greens
5 Tbsp. canola oil
2 med. white onions, finely chopped
2 tsp. ground cumin
6 jalapeño chilies, minced with seeds
1 Tbsp. ground fenugreek (a spice)

¼ to ½ cup heavy cream
1 tsp. garam masala. A spice mixture
available at Indian markets and some
specialty foods stores, or Mogul
Beef Curry, do not include garnish.
½ cup fresh cilantro, minced

Blanch spinach 2 seconds in large pot of boiling water. Drain. Refresh under cold water. Drain spinach; squeeze dry and chop coarsely. Set aside. Heat oil in large skillet over medium-high heat. Add onions and stir until golden brown, about 8 minutes. Add spinach and 2 tsp. cumin and stir 2 minutes. Add chilies and fenugreek. Reduce heat to low and cook until mixture is semidry, stirring occasionally, about 10 minutes. Can be prepared 1 day ahead. Cool, cover and refrigerate. Rewarm before continuing, stirring constantly. Blend in ¼ cup cream if thinner sauce is desired. Stir until heated through. Season with salt. Transfer to large dish. Sprinkle with minced cilantro and serve. Serves 8.

Slow-Cooked Venison
with Cheese and Tortilla Chips

2 lbs. Velveeta cheese, cubed
1 (16-oz.) can enchilada sauce
1 (8-oz.) can chili without beans
2 lbs. venison, chopped

1 large white onion, chopped fine
1 (6-oz.) jar jalapeño peppers, drained &
   chopped
tortilla chips

Combine cheese, enchilada sauce and chili in a slow cooker. Cover over low heat and stir often until cheese melts. Brown venison with onion. Add venison and onion mixture to the melted cheese mixture and stir well. Add jalapeño peppers and stir. Cover and simmer for 1 hour. Serve with tortilla chips. Serves 4 to 6.

Venison Pastry
with Potatoes and Rutabagas

Filling:
1½ lbs. venison, cubed
3 cups potatoes, sliced thin
½ cup rutabaga, finely grated
½ cup white onion, chopped
½ tsp. salt
¼ tsp. black pepper
1 Tbsp. butter
instant unseasoned meat tenderizer

Crust:
3 cups all-purpose flour
⅓ cup Crisco
pinch of salt
⅓ cup water
whole milk

Gravy:
Brown Vegetable Gravy

Mix all filling ingredients together. Do not allow to stand too long or potatoes will turn dark; set aside. Make crust using flour, Crisco and salt. Mix well. Gradually mix in water, using a fork. Pat together into a ball. Divide dough into 4 smaller balls and roll dough out to the size of an 8" pie plate. Place ¼ filling mixture on half of the rolled crust; fold over and seal the edges. Brush with milk and bake at 425 degrees for 20 minutes. Reduce heat to 375 degrees and bake 30 minutes more. Serve with Brown Vegetable Gravy. Serves 4.

Venison and Vegetable Pie

2 lbs. venison shoulder, cut into 2" cubes
¼ cup flour, seasoned with salt and pepper
2 Tbsp. safflower oil
2 med. onions, sliced
3 cups boiling water

⅛ tsp. marjoram
1½ cup string beans
8 carrots, cut into 2" lengths
1 recipe Standard Pastry

Remove all fat from venison and cut venison in 2" cubes. Heat oil in a heavy skillet. Roll each piece of venison in seasoned flour; place in hot fat; add onions. Brown venison on all sides. Pour off oil; add boiling water and marjoram; cover and simmer slowly 1½ hours. Push venison and place string beans on one side and carrots on the other; cover and continue cooking over low heat until vegetables and meat are tender, about 30 minutes. When meat and vegetables are cooked, remove to casserole or baking dish. Pour thickened gravy over meat and vegetables. Cover with pastry dough patted out to ¼" thickness and bake at 425 degrees for 15 to 20 minutes. Serves 4 to 6.

Venison and Beer Ragout

3 lbs. venison
3 Tbsp. canola oil
3 large onions, chopped
5 garlic cloves, chopped
½ lb. smoked bacon
1 tsp. curry powder
1 can tomato soup, undiluted

1½ qts. water
2 tsp. sour mash bourbon
¼ cup Budweiser beer
1 Tbsp. salt
½ lb. fresh mushrooms, sliced
Boiled Rice

Cut venison into cubes about 1½" square. Heat canola oil in electric skillet and add meat, onions, garlic and bacon. Cook until all is richly browned, stirring frequently. Add all other ingredients except mushrooms; cover and simmer for 50 minutes. Add mushrooms and simmer 10 minutes more. Serve over Boiled Rice. Serves 4 to 6.

Venison Scrapple

1 med. white onion, cut fine
¼ lb. beef fat, sliced
2 lbs. sliced venison round steak with bones
2 qts. cold lightly salted water

unsalted water
1 cup yellow cornmeal
1 tsp. salt
⅛ tsp. black or white pepper

Brown onion in beef fat until light brown. Add the browned onions, fat and venison with bones to the salted water and cook until venison is tender. Allow to cool. Skim off fat and remove bones. Chop venison fine. Add enough water to the remaining liquid to make 1 quart. Add cornmeal, salt, pepper and venison. Cook 1 hour stirring frequently. Pour into a mold. Place venison mold in the refrigerator and chill for 6 hours. Remove from the mold and slice into ½" pieces. Fry the slices until brown. Serves 4 to 6.

Venison Shank Crosscuts

2 lbs. venison shanks, cut 1" long
¼ cup all-purpose flour
½ tsp. salt
½ tsp. black pepper
2 Tbsp. bacon grease

1½ cups fresh apple elder
4 carrots, cut into 2" chunks
6 to 10 small potatoes
2 Tbsp. brown sugar

Mix flour, salt and pepper in a shallow pan. Dredge meat in flour mixture. Preheat large heavy skillet and add bacon grease. Brown both sides of crosscuts. Add one cup apple cider. Cover skillet tightly and simmer for 2 hours or until tender. Add carrots, celery, potatoes and remaining 1½ cups apple cider. Sprinkle with brown sugar and cook until vegetables are tender. Serves 4 to 6.

Mrs. Kathryn Breland

Venison Shish-Kabobs

3 lbs. venison backstrap, cubed
½ cup lime juice
1 Tbsp. Worcestershire sauce
1 clove garlic, pressed
12 slices bacon, cut in thirds
1 lb. small onions, boiled

3 green bell peppers, cut in large pieces
16 large mushrooms
1 pt. cherry tomatoes
salt
pepper
Wishbone Italian salad dressing

Marinate the venison in lemon juice, Worcestershire and garlic for 2 hours. On skewers alternate pieces of venison, bacon and vegetables. Season with salt and pepper. Cook on a gas grill. Baste with salad dressing. *Do not overcook.* Serves 6 to 8.

Venison Stewed in Fruit Sauce

1 large orange
1 tangerine
1 large pear
2 lbs. stewing venison, cut in 1" cubes
juice of 1 lemon
4 cloves garlic, minced
1 Tbsp. sugar
⅓ cup ruby port

1 Tbsp. A-1 Steak Sauce
¼ tsp. cinnamon
¼ tsp. aniseed
¼ tsp. ground cloves
¼ tsp. black pepper
½ tsp. salt
1 tsp. fresh gingerroot, minced

Peel the orange and tangerine. Separate the fruit sections and remove the seeds. Peel the pear, seed and cut it into thin slices. Brown the venison quickly in a Dutch oven with the garlic. Add the sugar, port, minced ginger, A-1 Sauce, cinnamon, aniseed, cloves, pepper, and salt. Add the orange, tangerine, pear, and the lemon juice. Stir in 1½ cups boiling water, cover, and simmer gently for 2 to 3 hours, until the venison is extremely tender. Serves 2 to 4.

Venison Strips
in Mustard and Spaghetti Sauce

1¼ lbs. venison round steak, cut in
   thin strips
3 Tbsp. spicy brown mustard
3 Tbsp. butter
1 med. white onion, thinly sliced
1 (15-oz.) can spaghetti sauce with
   mushrooms

¼ tsp. oregano
1 tsp. salt
¼ tsp. black pepper
3 Tbsp. sour cream
cooked egg noodles

Spread meat with mustard mixed with butter; brown meat on all sides. Add onion and cook until tender. Add spaghetti sauce and seasonings. Cover and simmer about 25 minutes or until meat is tender. Stir in sour cream and just heat through. Serve with hot cooked egg noodles. Serves 4 to 6.

Venison with Curry & Applesauce

3 lbs. boneless venison, cut 1½" cubes
½ cup all-purpose flour
salt
¼ cup canola oil
1 med. onion, chopped

1½ Tbsp. curry powder
1 cup canned applesauce
1 (10½-oz.) can condensed chicken
   broth
½ cup half and half

Toss venison cubes in the flour mixed with 2½ tsp. salt until well coated. Heat oil in skillet or Dutch oven. Add venison and sauté until golden brown. Add any remaining flour and mix well. Add next 4 ingredients and put in cooker. Cover and cook 8 to 10 hours longer. Add cream, season with additional salt to taste. Makes 6 to 8 servings.

Venison with Horseradish

4 venison round steaks, cubed
1 large onion, sliced
2 Tbsp. butter
salt and pepper to taste
2 Tbsp. teriyaki sauce

½ cup sherry
1 cup sour cream
2 tsp. horseradish
2 tsp. fresh dill, chopped
boiled rice

Brown the cubed venison round steaks and onions lightly in butter in a skillet. Add the salt, pepper, teriyaki sauce and sherry and cover. Simmer for 20 minutes. Combine the sour cream, horseradish and dill and stir into the steak mixture. Heat through and serve on boiled rice. Serves 4 to 6.

Venison with Egg Noodles and Sour Cream Sauce

2 lbs. venison, cut 2" cubes
1 clove garlic, minced
¼ cup Crisco, melted
1 cup celery, diced
½ cup white onion, chopped
1 cup carrots, diced
2 cups water
1 tsp. salt

dash black pepper
1 bay leaf
4 Tbsp. butter, melted
4 Tbsp. all-purpose flour
1 cup sour cream
parsley
hot cooked egg noodles

Melt the Crisco in a skillet and brown the garlic. Quickly brown the venison on all sides. Remove the venison to a shallow baking dish. Add the celery, onion and carrots to the drippings in the skillet and sauté. Stir in water, salt, pepper and bay leaf and pour over the venison. Bake at 350 degrees. Remove the venison from oven. Drain, reserving broth. Mix the butter and flour in a skillet and cook over low heat. Stir until the sauce is smooth and creamy. Add reserved broth and cook until the sauce is thickened. Stir in the sour cream. Pour the sauce over the venison and vegetables. Garnish with parsley. Serve over egg noodles. Serves 6 to 8.

Many pioneer women had to hunt to replenish meat stores when husbands were away to war or men-folk were unavailable. Today, women hunt for sport, alone, in groups, or with family. Women make up about 9 to 10 percetn of all hunters.

20

Venison Sausages and
Sausage Dishes

Normally we think of sausage as being made by a professional meat processing plant. One of the pleasures of working with your own venison is that you will have at your disposal the major ingredient to make your sausage at home. After you finish butchering your venison you will have all those bits and pieces left over. You will be surprised how many pounds of meat you can accumulate by working over the bones and ribs with a narrow-bladed boning knife.

Since venison is virtually fat free, the meat has very little moisture content. The addition of fat is needed to provide the moisture for quality meat loaves. The general rule of thumb is to mix 60% venison with 40% moist meats (15# venison to 10# fat) to 50% venison with 50% moist meats (10# venison to 10# fat). Bacon and pork/beef fat are normally the meats added. My favorite additive is ground smoked bacon.

If you like your sausage for breakfast, but are concerned about the fat content, you must try Mrs. Gene Holger Hohl's Fat Free Venison and Mushroom Breakfast Sausage. Feel free to experiment with substituting mushrooms for the fat in any of these sausage recipes. Mushrooms provide water, which substitutes for fat, in preventing the sausage from tasting dry. Since venison is virtually fat free, with the substitution of mushrooms you can convert most any of these recipes to fat free. This procedure has not been tested on all of the sausage recipes. You will need to experiment. Make your sausage by beginning with 25% (by weight) of mushrooms to 75% (by weight) of venison; break off a small piece and fry it. If the sausage is dry, add more mushrooms to the mixture and test it again. Other sausage recipes can be found in many of the books which specifically address home sausage-making.

If you will be preparing large amounts of sausage, there are butcher supply companies that furnish bulk, commercially prepared seasoning mixes.

If you do not have the time to make your sausage at butchering time, freeze the meat until you are ready to make your sausage. For planning purposes you may wish to weigh the meat and package it in one or two-pound packages. Mark the weight on the packages. This will make your calculations easier when sausage-making time comes around.

Bulk sausage is very perishable and should be either cooked, frozen or preserved the same day it is made. Some sausages can be made into patties; wrapped and frozen with double pieces of wax paper between each patty. Other sausage needs to be stuffed into casings. You can either use a stuffing attachment to your grinder or mixer, or you may be able to talk your butcher into stuffing it for you.

Sausage can be stuffed at home by using plastic wrap or a piece of cheesecloth. Stretch the plastic wrap or cheesecloth on the counter and put the sausage on top. Roll sausage into a log about ½" in diameter and crimp the links by tying the links and the ends with string.

For years I used my grandmother's old hand-cranked meat grinder to grind venison for sausage. This small unit worked fine for small batches. It had no casing stuffing attachment, so I was limited to making my sausage into patties. For making large batches of sausage, I highly recommend that you consider purchasing an electric meat grinder. My Oster® Heavy-Duty Meat Grinder and Sausage Stuffer (see appendix) has served me well for years.

To form professional and consistent sausage patties, use the Tin Can Method of making patties: With an electric can opener, cut both ends out of a tin can. Cut out circles of wax paper 1" larger than the can. Lay one end of the can on the work surface and cover with a piece of wax paper. Set the can shell over the wax paper and the cut out lid. Measure ¼ to ⅓ cup of sausage and place in the can, place another piece of wax paper on the top of the can and lay the other cut out lid on top. Press the wax paper and top down into the can shell, and gently press to spread out sausage into a patty. Gently press down on the cut-out top on the patty, then carefully lift the can shell up and off of the patty. The patty now is consistent in size, about ½" thick, and has a piece of waxed paper on each side. Stack the patties, and freeze in a plastic bag.

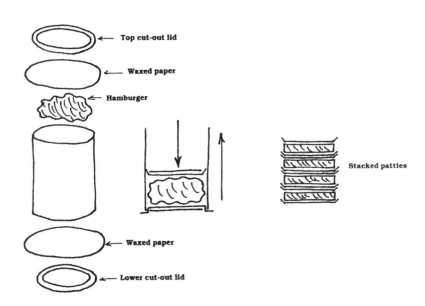

Tin Can Method of Making Sausage and/or Hamburger Patties

A word of caution about making sausage. Take your time and plan well. You may need to purchase/order casing and pork fat or beef suet several weeks in advance. These can be frozen until needed. Making sausage is a labor and equipment-intensive job. You may be using equipment that you will not be familiar with. You may wish to plan on spreading your sausage-making over two days. Day one: Assemble and check out all equipment, inventory required ingredients, and purchase ingredients that you do not have, begin thawing the meat, and set up work area. Day two: Allow twice the amount of time you estimate you will need. Clear the work area, organize your equipment, assemble all ingredients, and enjoy making your sausage.

Natural Casings and Stuffing Procedures

Preparing Natural Casing for Stuffing

Natural casings can be purchased from your local butcher. (See other sources in Appendix). In many areas they must be ordered in advance, so plan ahead. The casings are packed in salt and must be soaked about 1 hour before stuffing. Cut casings in 4-foot lengths for easy handling and stuffing. Before stuffing, flush casings through with cold tap water. Any casings left after making sausage can be re-salted and frozen.

Stuffing Tubes

- *SMALL Stuffing Tube*—Used to make pork or beef breakfast sausage, and Southern-Style sausage. Use with natural sheep casings (about .5 to 1 inch or 21 - 23 mm in size).

- *MEDIUM Stuffing Tube*—Used to make Country-Style sausage, such as Polish, Italian, Bratwurst, Venison, Chorizo, etc., as well as skinless sausages. Use with natural hog casings (about 1 to 1.25 inches or 28 - 30 mm in size).

- *LARGE Stuffing Tube*—Used to make larger skinless sausages or to stuff larger casings.

Stuffed Sausage Yield

- Sheep casings—4-foot length casings make approximately 1½ pounds of stuffed sausage.

- Hog casings—4-foot length casings make approximately 2½ pounds of stuffed sausage.

- Link Sausages Without Casings (Skinless Sausages)

Sausage may be prepared without casings. Put meat through food hopper. Pinch sausage off into desired lengths. Brown on all sides and serve. Uncooked links may be frozen on a cookie sheet until firm, then wrapped in plastic swap or freezer bags. When ready to use, brown frozen and serve.

Casing Volumes

1 hank hog casings will make 120 lbs. to 130 lbs. of sausage
1 hank sheep casings will make 50 lbs. to 60 lbs. of sausage
1 box of bulk beef suet weighs 55 lbs. to 60 lbs. per box
1 box of bulk pork fat weighs 55 lbs. to 60 lbs. per box

How to Prepare Casings Before Stuffing

Before casings are stuffed, they should always be soaked in warm water. This soaking makes them pliable, and they will stretch to their utmost limit when being stuffed. If they are properly soaked, they will stretch considerably and will not burst as easily as they will if they are not properly soaked. The casing should be soaked in warm water about 90 degrees temperature Fahrenheit, from one to two hours, depending upon how old and dry they are. If the casings are very old and dry, they will have to be soaked until they are perfectly soft and pliable. When casings are soaked in water that is too hot, the casings are scalded and become tender and will burst when being stuffed, and the heavy sausage will tear loose in the smokehouse.

HOMEMADE VENISON SAUSAGE RECIPES

Country Venison Sausage

2 parts venison, ground
1 part lard, diced
thyme
coriander
summer savory

sweet marjoram
bay leaf, pulverized
black pepper
sausage casings (optional)

Chill venison and lard, then grind together. Season with spices. Fry a small piece of sausage, then taste. Check by placing a piece of the cooked sausage in your mouth, then inhale to get a good whiff of each ingredient. If it has enough of a particular spice, your nose will tell you; it will smell almost medicinal. If it can use a pinch more, the aroma of the spice will enhance the flavor of the sausage. Add additional seasonings a pinch at a time and smell again. Remember, the goal is balance, and moderation is the key. Add seasonings as your taste dictates. Make into patties and either cook, wrap separately or use casings and freeze.

Country Venison Sausage with Sage and Cayenne Pepper

½ to 1 tsp. cayenne pepper
3 Tbsp. salt
2 tsp. black pepper
2 tsp, dried sage

6 lbs. boneless venison
4 lbs. boneless pork butt or shoulder
1 lb. bacon slices or smoked bacon slab

Sprinkle combined seasonings over meat cubes in a large bowl. Toss until well coated. Grind with fine grinding disc and stuff casings or bulk pack for making patties. Freeze in meal-size portions.

Herbed and Spiced Venison Sausage

1½ lbs. ground venison
¾ lb. ground fat pork
2 tsp. salt
½ Tbsp. dried sage, powdered
½ Tbsp. dried oregano, powdered
1 tsp. black pepper

¼ tsp. red pepper
2 tsp. dark brown sugar
2 Tbsp. parsley, chopped
sausage casings (optional)
Pan-Browned Potatoes
Fried Apples

Mix all the ingredients together well and pack into a container with a cover. Place in the refrigerator overnight so that the mixture can absorb the flavor of the herbs. The next day, shape into patties and brown well on both sides in a skillet. Serve the sausage for breakfast or for supper with Pan-Browned Potatoes and Fried Apples. Can be frozen in patties or links. Serves 4 to 6.

Fat Free Venison and Mushroom Breakfast Sausage

This recipe is virtually fat free and still has the taste and texture of old-style breakfast sausage.

4 lbs. venison, red meat only
2 lbs. mushrooms, chopped
2 cloves garlic, minced
2 tsp. black pepper
2 tsp. chili powder
2 tsp. cayenne pepper
2 tsp. marjoram

2 tsp. basil
4 tsp. salt
2 Tbsp. sage
2 Tbsp. parsley
2 onions
6 Tbsp. ice water
hog casings 2 tsp. thyme

Cut meat and mushrooms into chunks, add seasonings, and grind with medium cutting plate. Grind onions. Knead ground meat and onion in bowl and add ice water to give a soft dough consistency. Stuff into hog casings. Store in refrigerator or wrap casings in plastic wrap and freeze. Serves 4 to 6.

Mrs. Gene Horger Hohl

Garlic Venison Sausage

1 small white onion, quartered
2 lbs. boneless venison
¾ lb. pork fat
4 cloves garlic, minced
2 tsp. salt
1 tsp. black pepper

1 tsp. sage
½ tsp. thyme
¼ tsp. ground nutmeg
¼ tsp. ground ginger
⅛ tsp. ground allspice

Grind onion with coarse disc into large bowl. Add meat, fat, and seasonings. Toss until well coated. Grind with coarse disc and stuff into casings or shape into patties. Cook or freeze. Makes 2½ lbs.

Italian Parmesan Sausage

4 lbs. venison
2 lbs. pork fat or beef suet
1½ cups grated Parmesan cheese
¼ cup parsley, finely chopped

2 tsp. cayenne pepper
1½ tsp. salt
1 tsp. black pepper
1 Tbsp. water

Combine all ingredients, except water in large bowl. Toss with water to coat meat. Grind with coarse disc and stuff into casings or shape into patties. Cook or freeze. Yields 4 lbs.

Hard Venison Sausage

2½ lbs. potatoes, peeled and cooked
2½ lbs. lean venison
2½ lbs. lean pork
2½ lbs. pork fat

2 Tbsp. salt
1 tsp. saltpeter
2 tsp. coarse-ground black pepper
sausage casings

Cook potatoes and allow to cool overnight. Chop and mix together venison, pork, and pork fat. Add potatoes, salt, saltpeter and pepper. Fine grind 3 times. Fill sausage casings and smoke over hickory chips at 140 degrees for 24 hours. Hang in a cool dry place for 1 to 2 months, to cure. Makes 10 lbs.

Smoke-Flavored Venison Summer Sausage

3 lbs. venison, ground
2 lbs. pork sausage
1 cup water
¾ tsp. black pepper
½ tsp. garlic salt

1½ tsp. onion salt
1 Tbsp. peppercorns
4 Tbsp. Tender Quick salt
2½ Tbsp. mustard seed
3 Tbsp. McCormicks hickory smoke salt

Mix all ingredients and grind with a fine blade together. Form into 5 rolls. Wrap in aluminum foil and refrigerate for 3 or 4 days. Place in a shallow baking dish and bake in a 140-degree oven for 8 hours. Remove from the oven and allow to come to room temperature. Leave in the aluminum foil and freeze until ready to serve.

Homemade Red Wine Sausage

9 ft. sausage casings
1 (2¾-lb.) venison roast, cut 1½" cubes
1½ lbs. bacon, cut 1½" pieces
¾ cup Italian dry red wine

3 Tbsp. fresh Italian parsley, minced
4 tsp. garlic, pressed
3½ tsp. salt
1⅛ tsp. black pepper

Rinse casings under cold water. Soak in warm water 1 hour, changing water occasionally. Mix all remaining ingredients. Rinse casings. Slip one end of casing over faucet and run cold water through. Clip out or tie any sections with holes. Blot dry. Fit meat grinder with coarse blade. Attach stuffing horn to grinder. Place one end of casing over horn. Gradually push casing onto horn, leaving 1" overhand. Tie knot in end, with fine string. With right hand feed sausage mixture through meat grinder while anchoring casing to horn with left thumb, allowing casing to unroll as mixture is extruded. Twist and tie with string at 4" intervals. Remove from horn and tie knot in end of casing. Cut sausage into links. (Can be prepared ahead and refrigerated 2 days or frozen 1 month. Thaw sausage before cooking.) Prepare hot fire in barbecue or preheat grill to high. Pierce sausage with fork. Grill until cooked through, turning occasionally, about 10 minutes. Serve sausages hot. Makes about 18 sausages.

Hot Italian Sausage

2 tsp. salt
1 tsp. black pepper
4 tsp. fennel seeds
4 tsp. oregano
1 tsp. garlic powder

1 tsp. cayenne pepper to taste
1 tsp. red pepper flakes, finely chopped
6 lbs. boneless venison
2 lbs. boneless pork butt or shoulder
1½ lbs. bacon or pork fat

Sprinkle combined seasonings over meat cubes in a large bowl. Toss until well coated. Grind with desired grinding disc. Shape in casings or patties. Freeze in meal-size portions.

Old Time Hunter's Venison Sausage Patties

2 Tbsp. salt
2 tsp. black pepper
¾ tsp. mace
¼ tsp. ground nutmeg
¼ tsp. ground cloves

½ tsp. ground allspice
½ tsp. garlic powder
4 lbs. venison, cut in 1½" cubes
4 lbs. boneless pork butt or shoulder,
    cut 1½" cubes

Sprinkle combined seasonings over meat cubes in a large bowl. Toss until well coated. Grind with a fine disc and shape into patties or stuff into sheep casings. Freeze in meal-size portions.

Indiana Farm Venison Sausage

This herb-flavored sausage is delicious fried for breakfast, especially with eggs, pancakes and syrup.

4 lbs. venison
2 lbs. pork fat, or smoked bacon slices
2 cloves garlic, minced
2 tsp. black pepper
2 tsp. chili powder
2 tsp. cayenne pepper
2 tsp. marjoram
2 tsp. thyme

2 tsp. basil
4 tsp. salt
2 Tbsp. sage
2 Tbsp. parsley
2 onions
6 Tbsp. ice water
hog casings

Cut meat and fat into chunks, add seasonings, and grind with medium cutting plate. Grind onions. Knead ground meat and onion in bowl and add ice water to give a soft dough consistency. Stuff into hog casings. Store in refrigerator or wrap casings in plastic wrap and freeze. Serves 4 to 6.

Mexican Breakfast Venison Sausage

1½ lbs. venison
¾ lb. pork fat or bacon
1½ tsp. kosher salt
⅛ tsp. ground white pepper
¼ tsp. cayenne pepper
½ tsp. red pepper flakes
½ tsp. ground coriander
¾ tsp. ground cumin

3 Tbsp. paprika
½ tsp. brown sugar
3 Tbsp. balsamic vinegar
2 garlic cloves, minced
1 tsp. chili powder
⅛ tsp. ground cloves
casings or plastic wrap (optional)

Have your butcher grind venison and pork fat. Place meat in a large bowl and add spices. Mix all ingredients together by hand until the ingredients are evenly distributed. When you have thoroughly mixed the sausage, pinch off a small piece and fry it. Taste it for flavor balance. Is there enough undertone of garlic? Can you taste the chili powder? Check by placing a piece of the cooked sausage in your mouth, then inhale to get a good whiff of each ingredient. If it has enough of a particular spice, your nose will tell you; it will smell almost medicinal. If it can use a pinch more, the aroma of the spice will enhance the flavor of the sausage. Add additional seasonings a pinch at time and smell again. Remember, the goal is balance, and moderation is the key. Sausage can be stuffed in casings using a stuffing attachment to your grinder or mixer. You may even be able to talk your butcher into stuffing it for you. You can stuff your sausage the easy way, using plastic wrap or cheesecloth. Stretch the plastic wrap or cheesecloth on the counter and put the sausage on top. Roll it into a log about ½" in diameter and crimp the links by tying the links and ends with string. The sausage can now be frozen and individual links can be unrolled as needed. If you wrap your sausage in cheesecloth you can smoke it before freezing. Roll cheesecloth wrapped sausage in plastic wrap before freezing. Serves 6 to 8.

Mississippi Country Venison Sausage

2 small yellow onions
1 Tbsp. butter
3 lbs. venison
1 lb. pork fat
2 Tbsp. sage
1 Tbsp. salt

1½ tsp. chill powder
1½ tsp. marjoram
1½ tsp. thyme
½ tsp. garlic powder
¼ tsp. cayenne pepper
sheep casings

Grind onions with coarse disc and sauté in pan with butter. Combine onions, meat, fat and seasonings in a large bowl. Toss until well coated. Grind with coarse disc and stuff casings or shape into patties. Cook or freeze. Yields 4 lbs.

Turkish Venison Sausage

2 lbs. venison
2 lbs. boneless lamb
1 lb. beef fat
1 med. yellow onion

3 tsp. crushed mint leaves
2 tsp. salt
1 tsp. garlic powder
½ tsp. black pepper

Sprinkle combined seasonings over meat and fat cubes in a large bowl. Toss until well coated. Grind with coarse disc and stuff into casings. Cook or freeze. Yields 5 lbs.

Old World Italian Sausage

2 tsp. salt
1 tsp. black pepper
4 tsp. fennel seeds
4 tsp, oregano
1 tsp. garlic powder

1 tsp. cayenne pepper
6 lbs. venison
2 lbs. boneless pork butt or shoulder
1½ lbs. bacon or pork fat

Sprinkle combined seasonings over meat cubes in a large bowl. Toss until well coated. Grind with desired grinding disc. Shape in casings or patties. Freeze in meal size portions.

Venison Bratwurst

8½ tsp. salt
5 tsp. black pepper
2½ tsp. grated nutmeg
2½ tsp. mace
1 tsp. garlic salt

1 tsp. mustard seed
6 lbs. venison
2½ lbs. veal
½ lb. beef fat
hog casings

Sprinkle combined seasonings over meat cubes in a large bowl. Toss until well coated. Grind with desired grinding disc and stuff into casings.

Southwestern Venison Sausage

2½ lbs. venison
1 lb. beef or pork fat
5 cloves garlic, minced
5 chili peppers, chopped
½ cup yellow onion, finely chopped
¼ cup brandy
⅓ cup chili powder

1 tsp. black pepper
1 tsp. ground coriander
1½ tsp. cumin
salt to taste
½ tsp. Tabasco sauce
½ cup apple cider vinegar

Grind venison and fat together with a coarse cutting plate. Combine garlic, peppers, onion, brandy, and seasonings. Mix into meat along with the Tabasco sauce and cider vinegar. Stuff into casings, tying off each link at 4" intervals. Hang in a warm, breezy, insect-free place and dry for 24 hours. Store in refrigerator or freeze. Serves 4 to 6.

Old-Fashioned Venison and Pork Sausage

4 lbs. venison
2 lbs. pork fat
½ tsp. salt
6 tsp. sage
3 tsp. black pepper

1½ tsp. sugar
¾ tsp. ground cloves
⅔ cup cold water
hog or sheep casings

Thoroughly chill venison and fat and put them separately through grinder with ½" cutting plate. Chill meat again. Combine all seasonings and mix into meat, then put through grinder with ⅛" cutting blade. Mix seasoned venison and fat in a bowl and add just enough water to make a soft dough. Stuff into casings, taking care to avoid air bubbles. Hang sausages in a cool dry place (or in the refrigerator) for one to two days. These sausages gain from being smoked at about 80 degrees for 10 to 14 hours until they turn a deep, dark brown. Store under refrigeration or in freezer. Cook before serving. Serves 4 to 6.

Venison and Potato Sausage

4 lbs. venison, chopped
2 lbs. beef, chopped
1 lb, pork, chopped
1 large yellow onion, chopped
1 gal. potatoes, chopped

2 Tbsp. salt
1 tsp. black or white pepper
1 tsp. ground allspice
hog casings

Mix all ingredients and grind with a coarse blade in your sausage grinder. Change grinder to a fine blade, attach sausage stuffer and fill sausage casings. After stuffing, tie the ends of the sausages with cotton string. Submerge the sausage in large pot of cold water and bring to a boil. Boil for an hour. Prick each sausage with a fork after the first 10 minutes of boiling. Sausages can be frozen. Serves 6 to 8.

Venison and Smoked Bacon Sausage

4 lbs. venison
2 lbs. smoked bacon
2 cloves garlic, minced
2 tsp, black pepper
2 tsp. chili powder
2 tsp. cayenne pepper
2 tsp. marjoram
2 tsp. thyme

2 tsp. basil
4 tsp. salt
2 Tbsp. sage
2 Tbsp. parsley
2 yellow onions
6 Tbsp. ice water
hog casings

Cut venison meat and smoked bacon into chunks, add seasonings, and grind with medium cutting plate. Grind onions. Knead ground meat and onion in bowl and add iced water to give a soft dough consistency. Stuff into hog casings. Store in refrigerator or wrap casings in plastic wrap and freeze. Serves 4 to 6.

Venison Frankfurters

1½ lbs. venison
Brine Cure for Pork
1 lb. pork fat
2 Tbsp. salt
1 tsp. white pepper

½ tsp. coriander
½ tsp. nutmeg
½ tsp. cinnamon
sheep or hog casings

Cure meat for 3 days in the Brine Cure for Pork; then grind it 2 times, along with the fat, through a coarse cutting plate. Mix in salt and seasonings, and grind again through a medium-fine cutting plate. Slowly add 1 cup of ice water and mix thoroughly. Stuff into hog casings about 18" long. Secure at both ends and twist in the middle to make 2 long, thin sausages from each length of casing. Hang to dry for 24 hours; then cold smoke for 8 hours or until sausages turn deep brown. To cook, simmer in boiling water for 10 minutes. Serves 4.

Venison Summer Sausage with Spices

6 lbs. venison
2 lbs. lean pork
10% brine
2 lbs. beef suet
3 Tbsp. cloves

3 Tbsp. ground ginger
3 Tbsp. ground nutmeg
3 Tbsp. ground coriander
2 tsp. white pepper
2 cups Burgundy

Place the lean venison and pork in an enamel or clay crock and cover completely with the 10% brine solution. Place a plate on top and weigh it down. Store at 35 degrees for 10 days. Stir every 2 days. After 10 days, remove meat, rinse briefly in cold water, dry and store on a stainless steel rack in the refrigerator 6 hours until the meat is well chilled. Cut into small chunks. Cut beef suet into small chunks. Mix well meat, fat and spices. Grind twice and place in casings. Cool smoke for 13 to 15 hours. The sausage will lose considerable weight. After smoking, hang in a refrigerator at 35 degrees for 2 weeks before eating. The sausage can be kept for many months in a cool dry and dark place. If a mold develops on the sausage wipe it off with a cloth dampened with vinegar. You may wish to discard the casings before cooking.

Venison Summer Sausage with Red Wine

6 lbs. venison
Sweet Pickle Brine
4 Tbsp. salt
4 tsp. garlic powder
3 Tbsp. white pepper
2 lbs. lean pork

2 lbs. pork fat
8 whole black peppercorns
2 Tbsp. coriander seed
pinch mustard seed
2½ cups dry red wine

Cut the venison into 2" chunks and place in a crock. Cover with brine; use weight to keep meat submerged. Remove the meat and stir the brine every 4 days. After 8 to 12 days remove venison, rinse it, and place it in the refrigerator to drain for 24 hours; then cut it into smaller chunks, and mix with the salt, garlic powder, and white pepper. Grind the venison, pork, and pork fat twice through a ³⁄₁₆" plate, and mix. Mix in other seasonings and wine; let stand for 48 hours in refrigerator. Stuff into muslin or natural casings. Cold smoke at 80 degrees for 12 to 14 hours until the skin turns dark brown (sausage will dry and shrink by as much as ⅓). Hang sausage in a refrigerator or other cool place for at least 2 weeks. Store in refrigerator or freeze. Serves 8 to 10.

Deer have their eyes on the sides of their head, giving them a 310 degree view. This wide view makes it hard for deer to focus on a single point. Deer have good night vision, which is useful in the early morning and near dusk.

Venison Sausage with Lemon and Spices

½ lb. venison
½ lb. pork fat
½ lb. lean veal
1 cup bread crumbs
grated rind of 1 lemon
¼ tsp. sage
¼ tsp. sweet marjoram

¼ tsp. thyme
⅛ tsp. summer savory
½ tsp. black pepper
4 tsp. salt
⅛ tsp. fresh grated nutmeg
sausage casing (optional)

Grind meat twice with the finest blade. Mix other ingredients in a separate bowl. Add ground meat to this mixture and form into a loaf. Store covered in the refrigerator overnight. Either make patties or stuff casings. Cook or freeze. Recipe can be doubled. Serves 6 to 8.

Designing Your Own Sausage

Sausage has and can be made from about any meat. Spices are added to provide flavor and to a larger or lesser degree to assist with curing. The curing process is what determines if the sausage can be preserved with or without freezing. Today, most cooks have home freezing appliances and there is little need to worry about curing if the rules of cleanliness are followed and if your sausage is frozen as soon as it is made. Many butcher supply houses have prepackaged sausage spices, or you may wish to develop your own sausage recipes. Listed below are a selection of possible ingredients that you can select from. Fry a small piece of your sausage and adjust the spices to your own taste. If it tastes good, then it is good.

Most sausage makers use the ratio (by weight) of 35% - 50% of moist meat to 65% - 50% venison. I prefer 40% moist meat to 60% venison.

Spices:

1. allspice
2. basil
3. bay leaf
4. chili powder
5 cloves
6. coriander
7. cumin
8 dark brown sugar
9. fennel
10. garlic powder
11. garlic salt
12. ginger
13. hickory smoked salt
14. mace
15. marjoram
16. mint leaves
17. mustard seed
18. nutmeg
19. onion powder
20. onion salt
21. oregano
22. paprika
23. parsley
24. parsley, Italian
25. pepper, black
26. pepper, cayenne
27. pepper, red flakes
28. pepper, white
29. peppercorns
30. sage
31, salt
32. salt, kosher
33. summer savory
34. sweet marjoram
35. thyme
36. Tabasco sauce

Vegetables:

1. garlic
2. lemon
3. mushrooms
4. onions
5. potatoes

Liquids:

1. wine, Italian Chianti
2. brandy
3. wine, dry red
4. water
5. venison blood

Venison/Fill Meats:

1. lamb, boneless
2. pork, boneless butt
3. pork, lean
4. pork sausage
5. pork, shoulder
6. veal
7. venison blood
8. venison, lean

Fat & Fillers:

1. bacon slices
2. bacon, smoked slab
3. beef suet
4. lard
5. mushrooms
6. pork fat

RECIPES WITH VENISON SAUSAGE

Apple and Venison Sausage Omelet

½ lb. Country Venison Sausage
½ cup applesauce
1 French Omelet

1 Tbsp. sausage drippings
1 tsp. pimento, chopped
½ tsp. parsley, chopped

Cook venison sausage in 10" omelet pan or skillet until browned. Drain, reserving 1 tbsp. drippings. Crumble sausage with applesauce; set aside. Prepare French Omelet using reserved sausage drippings in place of butter. While top is still moist and creamy-looking, spread sausage-applesauce mixture over half of the omelet. With pancake turner fold omelet in half or roll turning out onto a platter with a quick flip of the wrist. Sprinkle remaining sausage over the top. Garnish with chopped pimento and parsley. Serves 2.

Baked Apples Filled with Venison Sausage

3 large tart apples
1 cup Hunter's Venison Sausage Patties

1 tsp. salt
2 Tbsp. brown sugar

Preheat oven to 375 degrees. Cut a slice from the tops of the apples. Scoop out the cores and pulp, leaving shells ¾". Cut the pulp from the cores and chop it. Combine chopped apple with sausage. Sprinkle apples with salt and brown sugar. Fill the apples heaping full with the sausage/apple mixture. Bake until tender. Serves 6.

Cabbage with Venison Sausage Sauce

1 lb. Old World Italian Sausage
1 green bell pepper, chopped
1 cup onion, chopped
1 cup tomato juice
1 (14½-oz.) can diced tomatoes
   with liquid

2 Tbsp, fresh minced oregano or 2 tsp.
   dried
¼ tsp. salt
dash black pepper
¼ cup butter
1 medium head cabbage, sliced

In a skillet, cook sausage, green pepper and onion until the sausage is browned; drain. Stir in tomato juice, tomatoes, oregano salt and pepper; simmer for 1 hour. Melt butter in a Dutch oven; sauté cabbage over medium heat until tender, about 15 minutes. Transfer to a serving platter; top with meat sauce. Serves 4 to 6.

Baked Fennel with Goat Cheese and Italian Venison Sausage

½ lb. Old World Italian Sausage
1½ lbs. fennel bulbs, trimmed and cut lengthwise into ¼" wide slices
1 tsp. fresh lemon or lime juice
2 Tbsp. unsalted butter
1 Tbsp. olive oil
¼ tsp. fennel seeds, crushed
½ cup water
2 Tbsp. all-purpose flour

1½ cups whole milk
freshly grated nutmeg
salt
pepper
¼ tsp. fresh tarragon minced or a pinch of dried, crumbled
4 oz. fresh goat cheese (such as Montrachet)
3 Tbsp. grated Parmesan cheese

Cook sausages in large skillet over medium heat until cooked through and golden brown. Transfer to paper-towel-lined plate using slotted spoon and drain thoroughly. Toss fennel with lemon juice in large bowl. Melt 1 Tbsp. butter with oil in same skillet over medium heat. Add fennel seeds and sauté until fennel is translucent, about 3 minutes. Add ½ cup water. Cover and simmer until fennel is just tender, about 15 minutes. Transfer fennel to bowl using slotted spoon; reserve cooking liquid. Melt remaining 1 Tbsp. butter in medium saucepan over medium heat. Add flour and stir 3 minutes. Remove pan from heat. Gradually whisk in milk and reserved fennel cooking liquid. Whisk over medium heat until sauce boils and thickens, about 5 minutes. Season with nutmeg, salt and pepper. Mix in fennel and tarragon. Transfer mixture to 6-cup shallow baking dish. Top with sausage and dollops of goat cheese. Sprinkle Parmesan cheese over. Preheat oven to 375 degrees. Bake until knife pierces fennel easily and top is light brown, about 20 minutes. Serves 6.

Baked Venison Sausage Ring

3 Tbsp. cornflakes
1 lb. Herbed & Spiced Sausage
1 Tbsp. white onion, minced
¾ cup fine bread crumbs
2 Tbsp. parsley, chopped

1 egg beaten
8 eggs, scrambled
parsley, chopped
paprika

Preheat oven to 350 degrees. Lightly grease a 7" ring mold. Cover bottom with cornflakes. Combine sausage, onion, bread crumbs, parsley, and beaten egg. Place these ingredients in the mold. Bake the ring 15 minutes. Drain the fat and bake 15 minutes longer until well done. Invert the ring onto a hot platter and fill the center with scrambled eggs and garnish top with chopped parsley and paprika. Serves 2 to 4.

Due to habitat destruction—not hunting—the panpas deer of the Netherlands are very rare and are threatened.

Creamy Baby Lima Beans with Venison Sausage and Gruyere Cheese

7 cups frozen baby lima beans (about 3 ½ 10-oz. packages)
½ lb. Old World Italian Sausage, casings removed
¼ cup green onions, finely chopped

2 cups half and half
1 cup grated Gruyere cheese (4 oz.)
salt
black pepper
fresh parsley, minced

Cook baby lima beans in large saucepan according to package directions. Drain. Cook sausages and shallots in 3 qt. saucepan over medium heat until sausages are cooked through, crumbling with fork, about 10 minutes. Pour off drippings from saucepan. Add half and half and cheese to sausage. Simmer 2 minutes, stirring constantly. Add beans. Season with salt and pepper. Cook over low heat until sauce thickens slightly and beans are heated through, stirring mixture gently, about 8 minutes. Transfer to bowl, Sprinkle with minced parsley and serve. Serves 8.

Four Cheese and Venison Sausage Baked Pasta

12 bacon slices, chopped
2½ lbs. Old World Italian Sausage
1 large yellow onion, chopped
1 tsp. dried thyme, crumbled
1 tsp. dried rosemary, crumbled
½ tsp. fennel seeds, chopped
1½ lbs. dried tricolored fusilli or rotini pasta
2 large carrots, peeled, sliced on diagonal into ¼" thick pieces
1 bunch broccoli, cut into florets
1 (6½-oz.) pkg. creamy garlic and herb cheese, room temperature

½ cup heavy cream
1 cup chicken stock or canned broth
2 cups grated Fontina or Monterey Jack cheese
1½ cups crumbled blue or Gorgonzola cheese
1 (28-oz.) can Italian plum tomatoes, drained and chopped
1 cup grated Parmesan cheese
salt
black pepper

Cook bacon in large skillet over medium heat until crisp, stirring over medium heat about 10 minutes. Transfer to paper towel using slotted spoon. Add sausages to drippings in skillet and cook until brown on all sides, about 20 minutes. Transfer to paper towel. Pour off all but 3 Tbsp. drippings from skillet. Add onion, thyme, rosemary and fennel seeds to skillet. Cook until onion is tender, stirring occasionally, about 6 minutes. Set aside. Bring large pot of salted water to boil. Add pasta and cook 4 minutes. Add carrots and cook 2 minutes. Add broccoli and continue cooking 2 minutes. Drain and refresh pasta and vegetables under cold water. Drain well. Preheat oven to 400 degrees. Butter 6 qt. casserole or baking dish. Place herb cheese in large bowl. Gradually whisk in cream. Stir in stock. Add pasta mixture, bacon, onion and herb mixture, Fontina, blue cheese, tomatoes and ⅔ cup Parmesan. Cut sausages on diagonal into 1" pieces. Add sausage to pasta mixture. Season with salt and pepper. Toss to combine. Transfer pasta mixture to prepared dish. Sprinkle top with remaining ⅓ cup Parmesan. Cover and bake until cheese bubbles, about 50 minutes. Serves 10.

Homemade Red Wine Sausage
with Broccoli Di Rape

2 lbs. fresh cranberry beans, shelled or 1 cup
  dried cannellini or Great Northern beans
2¾ lbs. broccoli di rape or escarole
  Discard tough large leaves and bottom of
  stalks
16 uncooked Homemade Red Wine
  Sausage

½ cup olive oil
4 tsp. garlic, minced
⅛ tsp. red pepper flakes
salt
black pepper

Place dried beans in large bowl. Cover with water and soak overnight. Rinse beans. Place in medium saucepan. Add enough cold water to cover by 2". Bring to boil. Reduce heat, cover and simmer until just tender, about 25 minutes for fresh or up to 1½ hours for dried. Cool. (Can be prepared 1 day ahead and refrigerated.) Cut leaves and tender stalks of broccoli di rape into 1½" pieces. Leave flowers whole. Blanch leaves, stalks and flowers in large saucepan of boiling salted water until wilted, about 1½ minutes. Drain, reserving ½ cup cooking liquid. Rinse with cold water and drain. (Can be prepared 4 hours ahead.) Heat vegetable oil in large heavy skillet or Dutch oven over low heat. Add garlic and cook 2 minutes, stirring occasionally. Mix in pepper flakes, then beans, broccoli di rape and ¼ cup reserved broccoli di rape cooking liquid. Season with salt and pepper. Top with Homemade Red Wine Sausages. Cover and simmer gently until sausages are just springy to touch, stirring occasionally, 15 to 20 minutes, adding remaining ¼ cup of broccoli di rape cooking liquid if dry. Adjust seasoning. Drain off any excess liquid. Serve immediately. Serves 8.

Jambalaya with Venison Sausage

1 Tbsp. canola oil
1 lb. Herbed and Spiced Venison
  Sausage, sliced
1 lb. med. shrimp, peeled
1 med. onion, chopped
1 small green bell pepper, cut into thin strips
½ cup celery, thinly sliced
2 cloves garlic, minced
1 (10-oz.) package frozen cut okra, thawed

1 (14½-oz.) can Del Monte Cajun-
  Style Stewed tomatoes, undrained
1 (8-oz.) can tomato sauce
1 tsp. Tabasco sauce
1 tsp. Creole seasoning
1 bay leaf
1½ cups quick-cooking rice,
  uncooked
2 Tbsp. parsley, chopped
salt and pepper to taste

Heat oil in a large skillet over medium-high heat. Add sausage and cook to ½ done. Add shrimp and cook 2 to 3 minutes or until done; remove sausage and shrimp from skillet. Add onion, green pepper, celery, and garlic to skillet. Cook until onion is tender, stirring occasionally. Add okra, tomatoes, tomato sauce, Tabasco sauce, Creole seasoning, bay leaf; bring to a boil. Reduce heat to low; cover and simmer 5 to 10 minutes. Stir in rice, sausage and shrimp. Cover, remove from heat; let stand for 5 minutes. Fluff with fork. Sprinkle with parsley. Serves 6.

Mexican Breakfast Venison Tacitos

The first time I was served these tacitos was after Hurricane Allen hit Robstown, Texas in 1980. Hector Rayes, the Nueces County Civil Defense Director, cooked these for me as a going-away present. As simple as these are to make, they are a real surprise the first time you try them.

1 lb. Mexican Breakfast Sausage
8 eggs
12 steamed tortillas

jalapeño peppers
Tabasco or Mexican hot sauce
1 cup Cheddar cheese, shredded

Steam the tortillas by wrapping them in a cloth dish towel and placing the bundle on a covered steaming rack for 10 to 15 minutes. Break up sausage and fry in a heavy skillet until done and remove. Beat eggs together in a bowl. Begin scrambling eggs in skillet until about ½ done; add cooked sausage and continue cooking eggs until done. Place 2 Tbsp. of the egg and sausage mixture in a steamed tortilla and roll into a ½" tacito roll. Serve hot with a few drops of Tabasco sauce of top of each tacito, cheddar cheese and jalapeño peppers on the side. Makes 12 tacitos. Plan on 3 to 5 tacitos per serving.

Pasta with Italian Venison Sausage

8 ozs. ziti or mostaccioli pasta
1 lb. Old World Italian Sausage
1 large white onion, coarsely chopped
2 cloves garlic, minced
1 large red bell pepper, cut into 1" squares
1 large green bell pepper, cut into 1" squares
1 (14½-oz.) can Italian-style tomatoes,
   diced and undrained

1 (6-oz.) can tomato paste
¼ cup chopped fresh or 2 tsp. dried
   basil
2 cups (8 oz.) mixture of various Italian
   cheeses or Sargento 6 Cheese Italian
   Recipe Blend

Cook pasta according to directions; drain. Meanwhile, cut sausage into ½" pieces; discard casings. Cook sausage in 12" skillet over medium heat until browned on all sides, turning occasionally. Pour off drippings. Add onion, garlic, and bell peppers; continue to cook 5 minutes or until sausage is cooked through and vegetables are crisp-tender, stirring occasionally. Add tomatoes and tomato paste; mix well. Stir in pasta and basil; transfer to 13"x9" baking dish. Cover with foil; bake at 375 degrees for 20 minutes. Uncover and sprinkle cheeses evenly over casserole. Continue to bake 5 minutes or until cheese is melted. Serves 6.

In the Adirondacks, most of the fawns die every winter. Deer persist in the region because adults live 12-15 years and only need one or two mild winters in their lifetime to replace themselves.

Quick Spinach-Venison Sausage Quiche

1 Tbsp. butter
1¾ cups mushrooms, sliced
1 (12-oz.) pkg. frozen spinach soufflé, thawed
½ lb. Old World Italian Sausage, casings
  removed, cooked and crumbled

¾ cup Swiss cheese, shredded
2 eggs, beaten to blend
3 Tbsp. whole milk
1 baked 9" deep-dish pie crust

Preheat oven to 400 degrees. Melt butter in large skillet over medium-high heat. Add mushrooms and cook until softened, stirring occasionally, about 7 minutes. Remove from heat. Mix in spinach soufflé, sausage, cheese, eggs and milk. Spoon into crust. Bake until tester inserted in center comes out clean, about 30 to 35 minutes. (Wrap edges of crust in foil if browning too quickly.) Let quiche stand at room temperature 5 to 10 minutes to firm before serving. Serves 6.

Sausage and Sour Cream Omelets

8 oz. Mississippi Country Venison
  Sausage, casings removed, cut
  into bite-size pieces
2 Tbsp. green onions, chopped
½ cup sour cream

4 eggs, beaten
2 Tbsp. water
½ tsp. celery salt
1 Tbsp. canola oil

Cook sausage and onions in medium skillet over medium-high heat until meat is browned, stirring frequently, 8 to 10 minutes. Remove sausage mixture and drain on paper towels. Transfer to medium bowl. Mix in sour cream. Do not wash skillet. Whisk eggs with water and celery salt until well blended. Heat sausage drippings over medium-high heat. Pour half of egg mixture into skillet, using spatula, lift eggs as they cook, letting uncooked part run underneath until omelet is cooked but still creams. Spoon half of sausage mixture over half of omelet. Slide out onto plate, folding omelet over filling. Keep warm. Heat oil in same skillet over medium-high heat. Repeat process for second omelet. Serve immediately.

Venison Sausage and Wild Rice Casserole

1 lb. Venison Sausage With Lemon
  And Spices
½ cup celery, chopped
½ cup white onion, chopped
½ cup mushrooms, sliced
2 cups water

1 (10¾ oz.) can cream of mushroom
  soup
1 cup wild rice
1 cup cheddar cheese, grated
salt
black pepper

Preheat oven to 325 degrees. Cook sausage in heavy large skillet over medium-high heat until browned, breaking up with spoon. Add celery, onion and mushrooms and cook until tender, stirring occasionally. Pour off drippings from skillet. Mix in water, soup, rice and cheese. Season with salt and pepper. Transfer to 9"x13" glass baking dish. Bake until rice is tender and top of casserole is browned, about 1½ hours. Serves 6 to 8.

Seafood and Sausage Paella

Shrimp:
1 cup dry white wine
2 plum tomatoes, seeded and chopped
2 Tbsp. olive oil
2 garlic cloves, minced fine
½ Tbsp. saffron threads, crushed
black pepper
1½ lbs. large shrimp, raw and peeled

Rice:
4 Tbsp. olive oil
1½ cups white onion, chopped
4 garlic cloves, minced
6 cups canned chicken broth

½ Tbsp. saffron threads, crushed
1 bay leaf, broken
3 cups long-grain rice
mesquite or hickory chips, soaked 1
    hour in water and drained
2 large green, red and/or yellow bell
    peppers, quartered lengthwise and
    seeded
1 lb. smoked Old World Italian Sausage
1 (8-oz.) pkg. frozen peas, cooked 15
    seconds in boiling water and drained
1 lb. Steamed Mussels
fresh parsley, minced

To Make Shrimp: Bring first 7 ingredients to simmer in a small saucepan. Pour into glass dish. Add shrimp and let marinate 2 hours at room temperature or overnight in refrigerator, turning shrimp over occasionally.

To Make Venison-Rice: Heat 3 Tbsp. oil in a large pot. Add onion and 4 minced garlic cloves and sauté 2 minutes. Add stock, ½ tsp. saffron and bay leaf and bring to a boil. Mix in rice. Reduce heat to low, cover and cook until all liquid is just absorbed, about 15 minutes. Transfer rice to large bowl. Cool completely, fluffing rice with fork occasionally. Heat barbeque grill to high heat. Add wood chips. Brush peppers with remaining 1 Tbsp. oil. Place peppers skin-side-down on grill and cook just until skin begins to darken in spots, about 7 minutes. Cut peppers julienne. Skewer shrimp; reserve marinade. Place shrimp and venison sausage on grill and cook until sausage is cooked through and shrimp are just pink. Shrimp will cook quicker than the sausage. Cool shrimp and sausage slightly.

Peel and devein shrimp. Return shrimp to marinade. Cut sausage into 1" thick rounds. Add sausage and peas to rice and toss gently. Can be prepared 1 day in advance. Cover peppers, shrimp and rice mixture separately and refrigerate. (Bring to room temperature before continuing with recipe.) Set aside 6 shrimp. Toss remaining shrimp and marinade with rice mixture. Transfer to large platter. Arrange mussels on half shells around border. Arrange roasted peppers in center. Top with reserved shrimp. Sprinkle with minced parsley and serve. Serves 6.

Venison Sausage,
Sweet Potato and Fruit Casserole

4 large boiled sweet potatoes
1 lb. Venison Sausage with Lemon
  and Spices
1 Tbsp. bacon, minced
2 large apples, pared and cut in thick slices

6 slices canned pineapple rings
salt
dark brown sugar, divided
whole milk

Preheat oven to 350 degrees. Peel and slice boiled sweet potatoes into thin slices. Grease baking dish. Cover the bottom with half the sweet potatoes. Shape venison sausage into 4 flat cakes and brown lightly in a skillet. Add meat cakes on top of sweet potatoes and cover with fruits and bacon bits. Sprinkle lightly with salt and brown sugar. Add remaining sweet potatoes on top of fruit. Brush with milk. Sprinkle with brown sugar. Bake about 45 minutes. Makes 4 servings. Recipe can be doubled. Serves 4.

Boudin Noir Chevreuil

A fine French black pudding or blood sausage. Either eat or freeze at once.

¾ cup yellow onions, finely chopped
2 Tbsp. lard
⅓ cup cream
¼ cup bread crumbs
2 eggs, beaten
black pepper

½ tsp. fresh thyme, minced
½ bay leaf, pulverized
1 tsp. salt
½ lb. lard, cut into ½" cubes
2 cups fresh venison blood
sausage casings

Cook onions in 2 Tbsp. lard gently without browning. Cool slightly and mix in whipping cream, bread crumbs, eggs, pepper, thyme, bay leaf and salt. Add cubed lard and venison blood. Fill casings only ¾ full; the mixture will swell during the poaching period. Without over-crowding, put the sealed casings into a wire basket. Bring to a boil a large pan half full of water or half milk and half water. Remove pan from heat and plunge the basket into the water. Now return pan to very low heat for 15 minutes. Test for doneness by piercing sausage with a fork; if blood comes out, continue to cook about 5 minutes more or until barely firm. Should any of the sausages rise to the surface of the simmering liquid, prick them to release the air that might burst the skins. Split and grill them very gently. Serves 4 to 6.

European nobles depended on deer herds as a source of nourishment for their troops.

21

Corned Venison

Corned venison is delicious. Corning venison is not easy. It is messy, and labor and equipment intensive. If you make a mistake, you can create meat that is spoiled and will be unedible. It is highly recommended that before you embark on this adventure, you obtain one of the excellent books on the market that specifically address all the aspects of this interesting way of preserving meat. Properly done, corned venison will provide you with a meat that will rival the best corned beef.

Corned Venison I

My father, Harold W. Webster, Sr., told me that this is a very old family recipe and that this recipe had been used by his great-great-great-grandmother and grandfather. He did not know their names or where they had lived. After my father's death, I began my search into my genealogy and I found out that my great-great-great-great grandfather was Jacob D. Curry; he and his wife, Nancy Ragland Curry, lived on the west bank of the west fork of the Amite River in Spanish West Florida in the 1790s.

50 lbs. venison
4 qts. coarse salt
⅛ lb. saltpetre

⅛ lb. saleratus
½ qt. sorghum molasses or 1 lb. brown sugar

Choose a time of the year when the temperatures range between 34 and 40 degrees. Cut venison hindquarters across the grain in 2" to 3"-thick pieces. Remove all fat. Rub all sides of the venison with salt. Scatter some salt in the bottom of a 5-gallon crock. Add a layer of venison. Alternate salt and venison until all is used. Let remain overnight. Dissolve saltpetre and saleratus in a little warm water with the molasses or brown sugar and pour over meat to cover. Place a large plate with a clean brick or other heavy weight on top of the plate so that the venison will stay under the brine mixture. The corned venison will be ready in 12 days. In warm weather use a little more salt. Remove venison and pat dry. Package in zip-lock bags and freeze.

Corned Venison II

2½ lbs. salt
10 lbs. venison
1 gal. water

1 lb. brown sugar
4 cloves garlic, sliced
4 Tbsp. pickling spices

Rub 2 lbs. of the salt into the venison brisket, then place meat in a clean plastic or ceramic container for 24 hours. Boil water, and mix in sugar and remaining salt. Let cool, then pour brine over meat. Add garlic and spices, weigh meat down, and cure for 30 days in refrigerator at 38 to 40 degrees, turning meat every 5 days. Remove meat as needed; rinse in fresh water for a few hours before cooking. Keep remaining meat submerged in brine at 38 to 40 degrees.

Corned Venison and Cabbage Pot Pies
with Puff Pastry

14 oz. cabbage, cored and cut ½"x4" strips
3 Tbsp. unsalted butter
3 Tbsp. all-purpose flour
1 cup whole milk
1 cup Gruyere cheese (4 oz.)
1 Tbsp, plus 1½ tsp. coarse-grated mustard
¼ tsp. freshly grated nutmeg

¼ tsp. dried dillweed
cayenne pepper
8 oz. very thinly sliced cooked Corned Venison II, cut into ½"x4" strips
Quick Puff Pastry or 2 lbs. purchased pastry
1 egg beaten with 1 tsp. cold water (glaze)

Cook cabbage in large pot of lightly salted boiling water until tender, 5 to 8 minutes. Drain. Squeeze dry in towel. Melt butter in heavy large saucepan over medium heat. Add flour and stir 3 minutes. Whisk in milk. Cook until mixture is smooth and very thick, whisking constantly, 4 to 5 minutes. Gradually mix in Gruyere. Add mustard, nutmeg, dill and cayenne pepper. Stir in Corned Venison and cabbage. Cool.

Divide filling among six 1-cup ramekins. Cut Quick Puff Pastry in half. Roll 1 piece out on lightly floured surface to thickness of ⅜" (refrigerate second piece). Cut out 3 rounds 1¼" larger in diameter than ramekins, using bowl as a guide. Reserve scraps. Brush 1 side of round with glaze. Arrange glazed side down atop ramekin, pressing firmly against sides of ramekin and pushing up slightly at rim; do not press down on the rim. Press pastry to sides of ramekin with tines of fork to seal. Trim pastry overhang to ¾". Repeat with remaining 2 pastry rounds. Roll out second piece of pastry. Cut and assemble as above. Reserve scraps. Brush tops and sides of pastries with glaze. Score tops in grid pattern; do not cut through pastry. Gather scraps. Roll out ⅜" thick on lightly floured surface. Cut out twelve 2" shamrocks. Brush with glaze. Arrange on baking sheet glaze side up. Place pies on baking sheet. Refrigerate shamrocks and ramekins at least 30 minutes. (Can be prepared up to 6 hours ahead.) Position rack in center of oven and preheat to 400 degrees. Place baking sheet with pies and shamrocks in oven and bake until pastry is golden brown and filling is hot, 20 to 25 minutes. Transfer pies to plates. Arrange 1 shamrock atop each pie and 1 on each plate. Serves 6.

Corned Venison and Mixed Vegetables

1 (3- to 4-lb.) Corned Venison II, trimmed
8 peppercorns
½ tsp. oregano
¼ tsp. pepper
¼ tsp. freshly grated nutmeg
¼ tsp. dried dillweed
8 small red potatoes
3 med. carrots, cut 2" pieces

3 celery ribs, cut 2" pieces
2 Tbsp. celery leaves, chopped
2 turnips, peeled and cut into wedges
1 med. head of cabbage, cut into 8
   wedges
½ lb. fresh green beans
4 ears fresh corn, halved

Place corned venison in a Dutch oven and add peppercorns, oregano, pepper, nutmeg and dill weed. Cover with water and bring to boil. Reduce heat; cover and simmer for 2 hours or until meat is tender. Add potatoes, carrots, celery, celery leaves and turnips; return to a boil. Reduce heat; cover and simmer for 20 minutes. Add cabbage, beans and corn; return to a' boil. Reduce heat; cover and simmer 20 minutes or until vegetables are tender. Serves 8.

Reuben Omelet
with Corned Venison

1½ oz. Corned Venison II,
   sliced thin and torn into bite-sized pieces
⅓ cup sauerkraut, drained
¼ tsp. caraway seeds

2 slices Swiss cheese, cut into strips
1 French Omelet
2 cherry tomatoes, halved
2 slices Kosher Dill Pickles

Prepare Corned Venison II, sauerkraut, caraway seeds and Swiss cheese before making omelet; set aside. Prepare French Omelet. While top is still moist and creamy-looking, top with corned venison, sauerkraut, caraway seeds and Swiss cheese. With pancake turner, fold in half or roll, turning onto a platter with a quick flip of the wrist. Garnish with cherry tomatoes and Kosher Dill Pickles. Serves 2.

Deer hunting in the U.S. generates revenue for states and the federal government from the sales of licenses, permits and tags. The 2006 survey by the U.S. Fish and Wildlife Service estimates that license sales generate approximately $700 million annually. This revenue generally goes to support conservation efforts in the states where the licenses are purchased. Overall, the U.S. Fish and Wildlife Service estimates that big game hunting for deer and elk generates approximately $11.8 billion annually in hunting-related travel, equipment and related expenditures.

Corned Venison Hindquarter

2½ lbs. salt
1 (10-lb.) venison hindquarter
1 gal. water

1 lb. light brown sugar
5 med. cloves garlic, sliced
4 Tbsp. pickling spices

Debone and butterfly hindquarter. Rub 2 lbs. of the salt into the venison brisket, then place meat in a clean plastic or ceramic container for 24 hours. Boil water, and mix in sugar and remaining salt. Let cool, then pour brine over meat. Add garlic and spices, weigh meat down, and cure for 30 days in refrigerator at 38 to 40 degrees, turning meat every 5 days. Remove meat as needed; rinse in fresh water for a few hours before cooking. Keep remaining meat submerged in brine at 38 to 40 degrees.

Corned Venison with Beans on Cornbread

1 egg
½ cup whole milk
1 (10-oz.) package easy cornbread mix
¾ lb. Corned Venison II, chopped
1 (1-lb.) can kidney beans
1 (1-lb.) can stewed tomatoes

1 tsp. salt
½ tsp. oregano
¼ tsp. black pepper
1 tsp. cornstarch
fresh Parmesan cheese, shredded
parlsey sprigs

Preheat oven to 425 degrees. Place the egg and milk in bag of cornbread mix. Squeeze upper part of bag to force air out and close top of bag by holding tightly between thumb and index finger. Place bag on a table and mix, working bag vigorously with fingers, for about 40 seconds or until egg is completely blended. Squeeze bag to empty batter into ungreased aluminum pan contained in package. Bake for about 20 minutes. Brown the Corned Venison in a skillet in a small amount of fat, then drain off excess drippings. Drain the kidney beans and add to corned venison. Add the tomatoes, ¼ cup water, salt, oregano and pepper and cook over medium heat for 20 minutes. Mix the cornstarch with small amount of water and stir into corned venison mixture. Cook for about 5 minutes longer or until slightly thickened. Cut the cornbread into 6 pieces. Slit each piece horizontally and toast. Place 2 pieces of cornbread on each serving plate and spoon corned venison mixture over cornbread. Sprinkle with shredded Parmesan cheese and garnish with parsley. Serves 6.

Corned Venison Casserole

1 (8-oz.) pkg. noodles
12 oz. Corned Venison II, flaked
½ lb. American cheese, diced
1 (10½-oz.) can cream of mushroom soup

1 cup whole milk
½ cup chopped onion
1 cup buttered bread crumbs

Cook noodles according to directions on package. Drain well. Add corned venison, cheese, soup, milk and onion. Pour into buttered 2 qt. casserole dish. Top with buttered crumbs. Bake at 350 degrees for 45 minutes. Serves 6 to 8.

22

Venison Jerky

Jerky is the end product of drying the meat, not cooking, until most of the moisture is removed. Once the moisture is removed, jerky will keep for years if stored in a cool and dry place. The author recommends a refrigerator or freezer for periods over 30 days. For additional preservation and flavors, you can salt-cure or marinate the jerky in a variety of mixtures.

Many people become perplexed when they discover that the hindquarter of venison that they began with produced only a fraction of that weight in jerky. The author's rule of thumb is: a 10 lbs. hindquarter of venison, with bones, gives 5 lbs. of lean meat with all fat, white, and connective tissue removed. This 5 lbs. of prepared red meat produces 2 lbs. of dry venison jerky. Plan on your clean red meat losing about 60% of its weight in the drying process.

One time I used my Grand Dad's Hot and Spicy Venison Jerky Marinade recipe and my Oven Drying Method to make venison jerky for a friend. My friend supplied the meat. I supplied the labor, the know how, $25.00 worth of marinade makings, and 12 hours of gas to operate my oven. We agreed that I would get ½ of the finished product.

To this day, my friend thinks that I stole most of his meat. I could never make him understand, that from the 20 lbs. hindquarter that he brought me, that his finished share was only 2 lbs. of jerky.

That was the day I have stopped making jerky for my friends and began giving them my recipe so that they could make their own. Now they give me samples of their jerky to see if I like it as much as I like my own.

I haven't lost any more friends. And, I haven't had to make any jerky for a long time.

Jerky Drying Methods

The Home Dehydrator and Attic Drying Methods are the author's preferred methods of making jerky. With these methods, temperatures hardly ever go over 130 degrees. You do not have to worry about overdrying. If you have to leave for the day, your jerky will be okay until you return. Vermin and insects are not a problem.

Home Electric Dehydrator Jerky Drying Method

Ben Johnson, of Johnson Gun and Pawn Shop in Neely, Mississippi, taught me about using a dehydrator to make venison jerky. I gave Ben my recipe for Hot and Spicy Venison Jerky Marinade. Ben and his wife Dorothy made their first batch of jerky using their dehydrator. Ben changed the recipe, because it was too spicy for his taste, and the jerky was still outstanding. As Ben tells it, he and Dorothy finished off the whole batch in two days.

The author has found that the home dehydrator is the easiest, cleanest, safest, and most economical of all drying methods. If you are drying 10 lbs. to 20 lbs. of jerky or are planning to make jerky over a long period of time, this may be the method you may wish to use. The price for home dehydrators, without additional trays, ranges from $30.00 to $114.00. I have used a Gardenmaster® Dehydrator (see appendix) for some years. And, considering the cost of gas or electricity for the oven, or the cost for building materials for other drying methods, the one time investment is minimal.

Home electric dehydrators are available through many discount department stores. If you plan on making jerky for several years, or if you and your family also have plans for dehydrating vegetables and fruits, you will be well served by purchasing one of these units. Most home dehydrators come with 2 to 4 drying trays and are expandable to 12 to 30 trays. Marinated jerky has the tendency to drip surplus marinade during the early drying process, so check to see if the dehydrator has a drip tray. Some dehydrators have a temperature control. This control is a very handy item and allows you to adjust drying temperatures for different drying applications.

Attic Venison Jerky Drying Method

An easy way to dry jerky is in the attic. Late spring to early fall are the best times of the year. During this period, your attic temperature will reach 100 to 160 degrees. This is a perfect temperature, you don't use any utilities, and you will not accidentally overdry or cook your jerky.

Marinate the meat using any marinade.

Run strings or wire back and forth across your attic at 2" to 3" intervals. Lay a piece of heavy plastic sheeting on the attic floor to catch the marinade drippings. Hang each piece of meat from its own opened up 'S'-shaped paper clip. For 10 lbs. of meat, you may need 200+ clips. Try not to let pieces of meat touch each other.

In the summer, if you hang your venison early in the morning, the meat will usually be dry by 9:00 p.m. If all your meat is not dry in the evening, don't worry about it. Just let all the meat continue to hang during the night and throughout the next day until dry. Be patient. It will be worth it.

Old Refrigerator Venison Jerky Drying Method

This drying method uses an old refrigerator to provide an insulated drying chamber, and an electric hot plate placed underneath to supply the warmth for drying.

Remove the motor, compressor and mechanical cooling equipment from refrigerator. Remove all interior equipment. Drill twenty ½-inch holes all the way through the top of the refrigerator. Make wooden pegs to fit in the holes. Measure the area on the bottom of the refrigerator floor that will be directly over the hot plate and drill closely spaced 1-inch holes directly over the hot plate area. Make a drip pan that will set 6 inches above the inside floor of the refrigerator and leave a 2" space around the edge of the drip pan for the warm air to rise around. Install as many wire drying racks as you wish. Drill a hole through the top that will allow a meat thermometer to stick all the way through. Turn on the hot plate using the lowest temperature setting on your hot plate. Adjust inside temperature by opening and plugging the vent holes drilled through the top of the refrigerator. Maintain drying temperature between 120 and 140 degrees on the meat thermometer. With a little practice you will discover what setting to place your hot plate on, and how many holes you will need to leave open to maintain the proper drying temperature. Load the racks with the marinated venison. You should be able to process at least 50 lbs. of meat at a time. You can also use your dryer to dry fruits and vegetables.

Oak Ridge, Mississippi, Venison Jerky Drying Method

(This method was used in rural Mississippi in the 1860s and may well have been used by Webster ancestors as early as the 1790s. My father told me that when he was growing up in Oak Ridge, Mississippi, his grandfather, Napoleon "Pomp" Bonapart Webster, would cut venison into long, thin strips and soak them overnight in a marinade made from water, salt and a "whole lot" of black pepper. The meat was then hung from a fence, tree branches, in the attic, or from the rafters of the barn until dry. I understand that "Pomp" learned this method of preserving venison while he was serving with the Confederacy during the War of Northern Intervention. He was captured, placed in a Federal prison, paroled, exchanged, then re-joined his Confederate unit so he could fight again. Websters have always been a little hard to convince. My father told me that he would eat this jerky as is or his mother would use it in stews or as a seasoning for cooking Poke Greens).

A large 8" long x 4" wide x 4" high boneless venison roast is cut down through the top to make long 4" wide strips of jerky. The object is to end up with a 4" wide by ¼" thick by several yards long strip of meat. The method is to cut down across the center width to within ¼" of the bottom. Turn the knife, side down. Then cut outward along the bottom, in one direction, unwrapping meat until a long ¼" thick x 4" wide strip is made from ½ of the chunk. Knife is then reversed and the other half is cut the same way.

Open-Air Venison Drying Method

¼ to ½ venison carcass   4 Tbsp. allspice
3 lbs. salt   5 Tbsp. black pepper

Separate the meat by using the French method of following muscle groups. Remove all fat and connecting tissues. Cut the groups into long thin pieces. The pieces should be no more than ½" to ¾" thick. Mix the spices and roll the pieces of venison in the spice mixture. Rub this mixture into the meat, then shake off any excess. You can either drape the strips over a wire or you can hang the venison from wire or strings. About one month is needed for the meat to dehydrate and to absorb the seasoning. In dry areas the time may be less; in damp areas of the country the time may be more. Slice thin for chewing, and soak overnight for stews and soups. When stored in an airtight and dry environment, venison which has been air-cured can be stored for many years.

Oven Venison Jerky Drying Method

A gas oven works better than an electric oven. With a gas oven you use the heat from the lower broiler section to supply the drying heat. The meat is placed on wire racks in the upper baking section. The heat travels up through the racks and provides relatively even drying for all levels.

In an electric oven you have to dry with the upper element, because when you place an aluminum foil tray on the lower element to catch the drippings, you cannot use the lower electrical element to supply the heat. An electric oven will increase your drying time. The upper levels of the meat will dry first. You will need to check often and remove the dry meat from the top level and move the less dry meat up.

For 10 lbs. of meat you will need 3 racks in your oven. You may need to buy some ½"x½" wire hardware cloth to go on top of your oven racks so that the smaller pieces of meat will not fall through.

Make a tray from heavy duty aluminum foil, and place this tray on the bottom of the gas oven to catch the moist drippings as they are released from the meat.

To load the trays with the marinated jerky, lay plastic sheeting or several layers of newspaper on the floor. Remove trays from the oven and lay them on the plastic or newspapers. Lay meat on the trays, trying not to let pieces of meat touch each other. Let the meat rest for 30 minutes to allow as much of the surplus marinade to drip off. Place the loaded trays in the oven.

Turn the oven on at the lowest possible temperature, usually 140 to 150 degrees. Remember you are not cooking the meat. You are drying or evaporating the moisture out of the meat. Open the top oven door slightly to let the moisture out. You may need to prop the door open. Most oven doors are designed to close tightly. Place a meat thermometer inside and adjust the door opening to maintain the proper temperature.

Drying will take from 8 to 14 hours. 1 usually marinate my meat on a Friday night and dedicate my Saturday to drying. You are looking for meat to turn dark chocolate brown with the consistency of very tough but pliable leather. Do not dry to the brittle stage. Since pieces of venison will dry at different times, you will need to begin checking the jerky at about the 4th hour so that you can remove the pieces that dry first. Check every hour thereafter. Store jerky in a sealed container in a dry and cool place. It will keep for many months. You shouldn't have to worry much about keeping it for very long. Your jerky will be gone in several weeks.

Sun-Drying Venison Jerky Method

Make a wooden drying frame. String thin wires or string placed at 2" to 3" intervals. Hang the frame over a large piece of heavy plastic sheeting. Hang jerky on opened "S"-shaped paper clips from the wires. Try not to let the pieces of meat touch each other.

Cover loosely and completely with cheesecloth netting. The netting keeps insects and other small critters and birds away.

This method works best during the hot days of the summer. It may take several weeks, depending on the humidity, for all the moisture to leave.

At night cover the frame with a piece of plastic sheeting to prevent dew from forming on jerky.

Sticky Fly Paper

From a turn-of-the-century sausage and meat-curing supply catalog.

If you are drying jerky or hanging venison where there is a chance that insects may come in contact with the meat, you may wish to use the following recipe for making fly paper.

Every butcher can make his own Sticky Fly Paper with very little trouble. It is made as follows:

1 lb. rosin   3½ oz. boiled linseed oil
3½ oz. molasses

Boil the three together until they get thick enough, and then spread on heavy manila paper. The proper and quickest way is to take a sheet of heavy manila paper and spread the mixture on half of the surface of it, then double the paper over; the mixture put on the half will be quite sufficient to coat the other half that is doubled over on it. The cost of making the sticky fly paper is very small, and in an hour, any butcher can make enough Sticky Fly Paper to last the entire summer.

VENISON JERKY MARINADES

Hot and Spicy Venison Jerky Marinade

The basic proportions for this recipe were given to the author by Mr. Don Blake of Las Vegas, Nevada while the author was deer hunting and living in that area.

INGREDIENTS:	PROPORTIONS:					
Venison (red meat)	2½ lbs.	5 lbs.	10 lbs.	15 lbs.	20 lbs.	25 lbs.
Teriyaki sauce	½ cup	1 cup	2 cups	3 cups	4 cups	5 cups
Water	½ cup	1 cup	2 cups	3 cups	4 cups	5 cups
Tabasco sauce	¼ tsp.	½ tsp.	1 tsp.	1½ tsp.	2 tsp.	2½ tsp.
Liquid Smoke	1 dash	¼ tsp.	½ tsp.	¾ tsp.	1 tsp.	1¼ tsp.
Lemon pepper	4 Tbsp.	8 Tbsp.	16 Tbsp.	24 Tbsp.	32 Tbsp.	40 Tbsp.
Cayenne pepper	1 tsp.	2 tsp.	4 tsp.	6 tsp.	8 tsp.	10 tsp.
Crushed red pepper	½ Tbsp.	1 Tbsp.	2 Tbsp.	3 Tbsp.	4 Tbsp.	5 Tbsp.
Garlic powder	¼ tsp.	½ tsp.	1 tsp.	1½ tsp.	2 tsp.	2½ tsp.
Coarse black pepper	1 Tbsp.	2 Tbsp.	4 Tbsp.	6 Tbsp.	8 Tbsp.	10 Tbsp.
Dark brown sugar	½ cup	1 cup	2 cups	3 cups	4 cups	5 cups

Remove *all* fat and white tissues from meat. Cut meat across the grain in ¼" thick pieces. Mix all ingredients very well in a plastic or glass container or bucket. Put venison into the marinade. Stir well. Refrigerate for 24 hours. Stir and rotate the venison 4 or more times during the 24-hour period.

Mild and Sweet Venison Jerky Marinade

Developed especially for Mr. Curtis V. Breland and Miss Anne S. Lipscomb,

INGREDIENTS: PROPORTIONS:

Venison (red meat)	2½ lbs.	5 lbs.	10 lbs.	15 lbs.	20 lbs.	25 lbs.
Teriyaki sauce	½ cup	1 cup	2 cups	3 cups	4 cups	5 cups
Water	½ cup	1 cup	2 cups	3 cups	4 cups	5 cups
Liquid Smoke	1 dash	¼ tsp.	½ tsp.	¾ tsp.	1 tsp.	1¼ tsp.
Lemon pepper	4 Tbsp.	8 Tbsp.	16 Tbsp.	24 Tbsp.	32 Tbsp.	40 Tbsp.
Garlic powder	¼ tsp.	½ tsp.	1 tsp.	1½ tsp.	2 tsp.	2½ tsp.
Coarse black pepper	1 Tbsp.	2 Tbsp.	4 Tbsp.	6 Tbsp.	8 Tbsp.	10 Tbsp.
Dark brown sugar	½ cup	1 cup	2 cups	3 cups	4 cups	5 cups

This recipe can be ½, ¼, ⅛, doubled, or tripled. Remove *all* fat and white tissues from meat. Cut meat across the grain in ¼-inch thick pieces. Mix all ingredients in a plastic container and mix very well. Put venison in marinade. Stir well. Refrigerate for 24 hours. Stir and rotate meat 4 or more times during the 24-hour period.

Tabasco & Worcestershire Sauce Marinade

CAUTION: This is a very potent, intense and powerful marinade. It is very strong on pepper, soy sauce, and hickory smoke. This recipe IS NOT for the novice/average jerky lover. If you really like soy sauce and fire breathing pepper, this recipe is for you.

INGREDIENTS: PROPORTIONS:

venison (raw red meat)	10 lbs.	20 lbs,	30 lbs.	40 lbs.
Tabasco sauce, (2-oz. bottle)	½ btl.	1 btl.	1½ btl.	2 btl.
Worcestershire Sauce, (5-oz. bottle)	2 btl.	4 btl.	6 btl.	8 btl.
soy or teriyaki sauce (10-oz. bottle)	2 btl.	4 btl.	6 btl.	8 btl.
liquid hickory smoke, (4-oz. bottle)	¼ btl.	½ btl.	¾ btl.	1 btl.
cayenne pepper, (1.75-oz. bottle)	½ btl.	1 btl.	1½ btl.	2 btl.
onion salt, (5.12-oz. bottle)	½ btl.	1 btl.	1½ btl,	2 btl.
water	to cover	to cover	to cover	to cover

Mix all ingredients and pour over venison. Mix together well. Refrigerate and allow to stand overnight. Dry until venison has dehydrated.

CONCENTRATED JERKY

Venison Mincemeat

3 lbs. venison, cooked and ground fine twice
1 lemon, ground
3 lbs. seedless raisins
½ lb. red currants
1 lb. ground beef suet
6 lbs. apples, pared and chopped
1 pt. grape juice

1 qt. apple juice
2 tsp. ground cinnamon
1 tsp. ground cloves
1 tsp. ground allspice
1 tsp. salt
3 cups white sugar

Combine and mix all ingredients. Cook in large pot pan on low heat for 3 hours, or until the apples are tender. Remove from the stove and allow to cool. Pack into jars or airtight freezer bags. Store mincemeat in refrigerator or freezer. Makes about 8 quarts.

Venison Pemmican

equal parts pounded venison Jerky and
    rendered beef fat, by weight.

dried berries
sausage casings

Pemmican is one of the classic and old time ways of preserving venison in a way that it provides almost a complete concentrated food. Pound venison jerky into a mass of pulp. Make rendered fat by cutting beef suet into 1 "-sized chunks and heating it in the oven. Be careful not to let the melted fat boll up. Pour an equal amount, by weight, of rendered beef fat over the pounded jerky until you have the consistency of ordinary sausage. Do not add salt. Dried berries have traditionally been added for flavor. Pack the pemmican in commercial hog casings or sealable plastic freezer bags. Pemmican will provide practically every food element, with the exception of Vitamin C. The average healthy person can do without Vitamin C for at least two months. When supplemented with foods containing Vitamin C, scurvy can be prevented for long periods of time.

The most famous fictional deer is Bambi. *In the Disney film, he is a white-tailed deer, while in Felix Salten's original book,* Bambi, A Life in the Woods, *he is a roe deer. No matter what kind of deer he is, he is positively an endearing little fawn.*

23

Freezing, Canning, Smoking & Curing Venison

Other than making jerky, freezing, canning, smoking and curing are the other options available to you for putting your venison by until you are ready to prepare it.

Freezing bulk food in the home became feasible in the early 1950s when affordable volume home freezers became available on the consumer markets. Without a large freezer, you can still store a large number of small packages in the freezing unit of your home freezer.

Canned meat was used in 1850s during the American Civil War as a means of providing meat for the troops. The results were less than acceptable. The reason for the marginal success was not a lack of knowledge of the mechanical process of placing and sealing meat in airtight metal cans. The problem was an incomplete understanding of how to stop the bacteria from acting on the meat after it was processed and canned. Upon arrival at the scene of battle, when some of the canned meat was opened, the product was found to be very tasty and nourishing. In other lots, the cans were swollen and ruptured.

Today we understand the cause of this problem. Not only do the work area, canning equipment, and containers have to be sterile, but the meat must be brought to the proper temperature and held at that temperature for the appropriate length of time.

Home canning venison is not difficult, but there are certain canning rules that cannot be violated. There are many outstanding home canning books available to the home canner through bookstores and the manufacturers of home canning equipment. These books address all of the safety factors and techniques involved in the home canning process.

The author recommends that the home canner read and understand these resources before embarking on this project. Home canning is equipment intensive. Neither the reasonable cost of the equipment nor the investment in time is out of proportion to the fine results that can be obtained.

Next year, when the venison in the freezer is long gone, you will still be enjoying the fruits of your labor.

FREEZING

Basic Freezing Procedure

Freezing venison is the least labor intensive way to put your venison by . Freezing is quick and inexpensive and your venison can be kept for long periods of time if it has been properly wrapped and frozen. You can freeze any size piece of venison that you can get into your freezer.

Freezing meat that will be used within a month is easy. Freezing venison for 6 months or more and having it thaw in a usable condition calls for care and proper packaging methods.

The objectives of freezing are to (1) quickly stop the growth of bacteria, (2) protect the meat while it is in the freezer, (3) prevent "Freezer Burn," (4) provide for easy selection and identification, and (5) allow your valuable venison to thaw in a usable condition.

After cleaning and aging your venison in a 34 to 36-degree cold room for 4 to 6 days, butcher your meat in single recipe-size cuts. After butchering, freeze your venison as soon as possible. If you have to travel, wrap your meat in two heavy plastic bags and pack the bags in an ice chest with plenty of ice. Add more ice during the trip. When you get home, take the time to properly wrap and freeze your venison BEFORE you unpack your hunting equipment from the car. The cold room has begun a tenderizing process that you now need to stop as soon as you can.

Proper wrapping will protect your meat and in 6 months or more, you will have little or no freezer burn. Freezer burn is the process by which cells that have been broken during freezing process give up their fluids to evaporation. Meat that has freezer burn feels soft and light. Meat with freezer burn appears white and feels somewhat like a sponge, and may have a unique smell. If you have ever filled an ice tray in the freezer and returned several months later, you found that the ice tray was empty. While frozen, the water evaporated from the tray and the water is now the frost on the freezer walls. This is what can happen to your venison if you do not package it properly. Sometimes a portion of the meat is still usable. The burned meat can sometimes be cut off and the remainder may be salvageable.

Your goal in preventing freezer burn is to put a solid vapor barrier between your venison and the cold air in the freezer. Butcher paper has a plastic vapor barrier on the side closest to the meat. With butcher paper, there is some air exchange through the folds and wraps of the paper. Ziplock freezer bags work well if you add a little water and exhaust all the air before sealing. It is difficult to exhaust all air from the ziplock bags, and sometimes the seals leak air back inside. Butcher paper and ziplock bags are not recommended for freezing meat for longer than 3 to 6 months.

For longer freezing periods, you will need to guarantee a 100% vapor and liquid-proof barrier. I have used this method of wrapping venison, and after 2 years I have had little or no freezer burn. Use heavy plastic wrap. Lay the meat on the plastic wrap and roll the meat over, wrapping it completely in the wrap. Fold one end of the wrap up over the package and press with your hands to seal. Stand the package on the folded end and pour in just enough water to cover meat. Work meat to release all air bubbles. Add a little more water if needed. Fold over and seal the open end of wrapping. Lay the meat on another piece of plastic wrap and roll the opposite way. Repeat the wrapping/water procedure. Place the twice-wrapped venison in a ziplock freezer bag; add a little water; exhaust all air and seal. Label the bag as to date, cut of meat, number of pieces, and weight.

Vacuum food sealers have been on the consumer market for some years. Only recently have I been experimenting with one. Without a doubt this is the best piece of packaging equipment you can invest in. My vacuum sealer virtually eliminates the worry about freezer burn forever. I add a little water to the bag to assist with eliminating any possible contact of the meat with air and freeze the bag before sealing. Precut bags and rolls for making your own custom bags are available. I use my vacuum sealer not only for freezing venison, but for packaging and freezing everything from vegetables to soups, fruits, and anything else that I want to freeze for a long period.

Package smaller cuts of meat in the quantities that you would expect to use in one recipe. If in doubt, make package smaller—you can always thaw two packages. Mark each package with a waterproof marker indicating date frozen, type of cut, and number of pieces. You will thank yourself later.

When placing the packaged venison in the freezer, place it in single layers rather than in one large pile. A one-square-foot of meat may take several days to freeze. After the venison packages have frozen, you can then restack them to conserve freezer space.

When you are ready to cook, do not rush the thawing process. Plan ahead. Place the sealed meat package in the refrigerator section to thaw. A 2-pound package will need 24 hours to thaw. Larger pieces will take proportionately longer amounts of time to thaw. Faster thawing, especially in hot water, affects the tissue quality and allows bacteria to grow.

CANNING

Basic Canning Procedure

The newer methods of canning may be extended to include the canning of meats, poultry and fish. It is convenient to have the meat in a ready-to-eat form. Canned meat is cooked during the canning process and retains most of its original flavor and texture, and after opening, can be prepared in many different ways.

Meat may be packed raw or first browned, then packed. If the meat is to be used for stews and soups, the method of packing raw is satisfactory. If the cut is tender and a browned appearance and flavor are desired, the meat should be quickly seared in deep fat, in the broiler, or in a hot oven. The object of this searing is to obtain a browned surface; no attempt is made to pre-cook the meat.

1. Allow meat to cool to air temperature. Kill 6 hours before canning.
2. Wipe meat with damp cloth; do not wash.
3. Cut in sizes suitable for serving.
4. Pack raw, or sear and pack loosely to within ½" of jar top.
5. Add 2 tsp. salt to each quart of raw meat; 1 tsp. to each quart of seared meat.
6. No water is added to meat.
7. Partially seal jars and process 3 hours in hot water bath, or for 60 minutes in pressure cooker at 15 lbs. pressure.
8. Remove from canner, seal, and cool as quickly as possible without danger of breaking jars.

Canned Chopped Venison

Put meat through food chopper. Turn into hot skillet with small amount of fat. Stir until seared. Add from 1 to 1½ cups boiling water, or meat stock, or tomato puree and 1 tsp. salt to each quart of ground meat. Pack into hot jars. Process 60 lbs. pressure or 3½ hours in a hot-water bath; then complete seal.

Canned Country Venison Sausage

Make Country Venison Sausage with Sage and Cayenne Pepper, but leave out the sage. Form into patties using Tin Can Method. Brown in a 350-degree oven or in a heavy skillet over moderate heat, pouring off fat as it collects. Hot-pack canning jars. Cover with boiling pan gravy and water. Leave 1" head space. Process pints for 75 minutes, or quarts for 90 minutes in a pressure canner at 10 lbs. of pressure.

Canned Venison Meatballs

6 lbs. chopped venison
½ lb. chopped fat
1 onion

1 Tbsp. salt
½ tsp. black pepper
1 cup cracker meal

Mix ingredients and form into balls of uniform size. Drop balls, few at time, into boiling water. Cook 5 minutes. Pack into hot jars. Cover with water in which cooked. Process 60 minutes at 15 lbs. or 3½ hours in hot-water bath; then complete seal. Note: Meatballs may also be precooked by baking or by browning in fat. Cover with gravy or tomato sauce.

Canned Venison Mincemeat
with Spices and Brandy

5 qts. venison, fine ground
2 qts. apple cider
1 pt. molasses
1 pt. Cider Vinegar
3 lbs. raisins
5 qts. apples, chopped
2½ cups sugar
1 Tbsp. salt

1 tsp. black pepper
1 Tbsp. ground nutmeg
1 Tbsp. allspice
4 Tbsp. ground cinnamon
1 Tbsp. ground cloves
1 pt. red wine
1 pt. brandy
12 quart canning jars and lids

Cook venison in a skillet until done and store with juices in the refrigerator overnight. Mix remaining ingredients and place in a roasting pan and cook for 2 hours or until reduced down. Add red wine and brandy. Scald jars and lids. Pack jars with cooked venison and fill to within ½" of top with liquid. Cold pack jars for 15 minutes. Makes 10 quarts.

Canned Venison Stew

Cut meat into cubes of uniform size. Brown quickly in small amount of fat. Cover with boiling water. Boil 5 minutes. Add seasonings. Pack into hot jars. Process 60 minutes at 15 lbs. pressure or 3½ hours in hot-water bath; then complete seal.

Or: Cubes of raw meat may be covered with boiling water; boil 8 to 10 minutes before packing.

Or: Vegetables which have been boiled 3 to 5 minutes may be added to stew as it is packed into the jar. A better stew is made by combining meat and vegetables when needed for serving.

Canned Venison Christmas Mincemeat with Candied Fruits, Sour Cherries and Walnuts

This 1890s recipe was used at Christmastime at my grandmother's house. Christmas was always a very special time of the year. Nanny did not have much money. She took great pleasure in cooking and giving her efforts to her friends as Christmas presents. For this recipe, Nanny would use beef. Venison works just as well.

9 qts. apples, peeled and sliced
4 lbs. venison, chopped
2 lbs. beef suet chopped
3 lbs. sugar
2 qts. apple cider
4 lbs. seeded raisins
3 lbs. currants
1½ lbs. candied citron, chopped
½ lb. dried, chopped candied orange peel
½ lb. dried, chopped candied lemon peel

juice and rind of 1 lemon
1 Tbsp. cinnamon
1 Tbsp. mace
1 Tbsp. ground cloves
1 tsp, salt
1 tsp. black pepper
2 whole nutmegs, grated
1 gal. sour cherries with Juice
2 lbs. broken walnut bits
1 tsp. powdered coriander seeds

Except for the brandy, mix and simmer all ingredients for about 2 hours. Stir frequently. Do not allow to scorch. Ladle into hot canning jars. Allow ½" headroom. Process in a pressure canner for 20 minutes at 10 lbs. If you are using the hot water boiling method, process for 90 minutes. This recipe can be halved or quartered. (See Christmas Venison Mincemeat Pies.) Makes enough filling for about 20 pies.

Canned Venison Sausage

Form sausage into cakes or stuff casings. Cook until lightly browned. If in casings, prick before re-cooking. Pack into hot jars. Process 60 minutes at 15 lbs. pressure or 3½ hours in hot-water bath; the complete seal.

Note: do not add large amounts of sage and spices to sausage which is to be canned.

Canned Venison Soup Stock

8 lbs. venison
8 lbs. bones
6 qts. cold water
1 Tbsp. whole black pepper

¼ pod hot pepper
1 tsp. mixed whole spices
1 Tbsp. salt

Use equal portions of bone and lean meat. Crack bones. Cut meat in small pieces. If brown stock is wanted, brown meat in enough fat to prevent sticking. Cover the meat (either browned or raw) with the water. Add salt and let stand 30 minutes. Add seasonings and simmer until liquid is reduced to about 4 quarts. Strain through cheese cloth. Chill. Remove fat. Boil 5 minutes and pour in hot jars. Process 50 minutes at 15 lbs. pressure or 3 hours in hot-water bath; then complete seal.

SMOKING

Smoking can be used to either add flavor to venison, or it can be a cooking process. Depending on how high the temperature is and how long you keep your venison in the smoker, you can either smoke for flavor or end with a finished product. The flavoring agents are usually based around wood chips such as mesquite and hickory. Some recipes call for the addition of spices and wines. The smoking process consists of placing the venison on a rack and closing the smoker; then placing wood chips that have been soaked in water either on the smoldering fire or in a pan above an electrical heating element. I inherited my smoker from my mother, but Brinkman® makes fine charcoal or electric smokers.

Virtually any cut of venison, including sausages, can be smoked. Each manufacturer of smoking equipment encloses an instruction and recipe book with their smoker. I am especially fond of smoking my deboned quarters, backstraps, ribs and sausages. Smoking does not necessarily mean that the meat has been cooked and is ready to eat. Most meats that have been smoked will need to be cooked after they are smoked. The exception is for those meats that have gone through a curing process that allows you to store them without refrigeration. Even with these meats, most cooks prefer to use some type of cooking during the preparation process. If you have never smoked your own meat, you are in for a real surprise.

Deboned and tied roasts that have been smoked/cooked are a real treat. Smoke/cooking not only imparts flavor but also cooks the meat. The temperatures that you use may be higher and the smoking time longer than you would use if you were just smoking your venison. You may wish to insert a meat thermometer into the thickest part of the meat to obtain the desired degree of doneness. When smoke/cooking meat of various sizes, insert the thermometer into the smallest cut of meat first. When it is done, remove the meat and insert the thermometer into the next smallest. By doing this, you are able to correctly cook each piece of meat without having some pieces overcooked and others still raw. Since venison does have a tendency to dry out during cooking, you may wish to lay a few pieces of bacon over large cuts while they are smoke/cooking. After you have finished, not only will you have smoke/cooked venison, but you will have smoked bacon as well.

Years ago when I was living in Nelliesburg, Mississippi, I built an old-fashioned smokehouse. I built a little 4'x4'x6' high smokehouse on top of a little rise behind my grandmother's house. The smokehouse was built out of old plywood, with holes cut around the top edge of the sides to let the smoke circulate out; it had a small door, and the whole arrangement was covered with screen to keep the bugs out. An old 55-gallon drum would have served my purpose just as well. A 10"x10" trench was dug out from the bottom of the smokehouse and down the slope for about 20 feet and was lined with tin and covered with dirt. At the end of the trench I dug a 2'x2'x2' fire pit which I also lined with tin. The drop from the smokehouse to the fire pit was about 3'. This smokehouse arrangement acted like a chimney, and created a draft at the top of the smokehouse which pulled the smoke up from the fire pit over the meat and out the top of the smokehouse.

I cured just about any cut of venison and pork in this old smokehouse that you can imagine. The trick was to keep the hickory chips smoldering without them going out or flaring up into a fire. Needless to say I had to spend a lot of time monitoring the fire. The smoking process could take as long as 5 to 6 days. The results were outstanding. With today's modern charcoal and electric smokers, the burden of continually monitoring the fire is greatly reduced. A modern metal smoker costs considerably less and is more efficient than my home-built smokehouse. My reward was serving my friends meats that I had smoked in a smokehouse that I had built myself. Today these friends probably do not remember that I built a smokehouse, but I am sure they remember the meals that I served to them.

An interesting variation is to smoke your bacon, beef or pork fat. These smoked meats are especially good when making recipes which call for additive meats for burgers, meatloaves, meatballs and sausages. Smoked bacon sides are available, but they are expensive. By smoking your own additive meats, you save money and you can control the amount of smoked flavor in the meat.

Smoked and Stuffed Venison Ribs

venison ribs	½ lb. butter
mesquite chips	1 cup soft bread crumbs
1½ cups celery, diced	1½ tsp. poultry seasonings
½ cup yellow onion, minced	1 cup carrots, sliced
1 tsp. salt	2 cups hot water
1 small can mushroom stems	2 beef bouillon cubes

Soak mesquite chips in water for 2 days. Heat coals in the barbeque pit until you can hold your hand over the fire for 10 to 15 seconds. Sprinkle soaked hickory chips over coals and close cover and allow smoke to fill pit. Place ribs on grill; close cover and smoke/cook very slowly until ribs are tender, 1 to 2 hours. Remove ribs from pit and allow to rest until cold. Cut ribs in serving portions; arrange close together in a large roaster. Preheat oven to 450 degrees. Make dressing from celery, onion, salt, mushrooms and butter. Sauté for 15 minutes; remove from heat and stir in bread crumbs and poultry seasonings. Brown ribs in the oven for 10 minutes. Then remove the ribs long enough to spread carrots and celery over the bottom of roaster. Arrange the ribs tightly together on top, their more raw sides uppermost. Cover with the dressing, smoothing it down evenly, and brown for another 10 minutes. Dissolve bouillon cubes in hot water then pour over ribs. Cover the roaster and return to the oven. Turn the heat down to 300 degrees and bake for 2 hours, adding more stock if necessary.

Smoked Hot Italian Sausage

Hot Italian Sausage   mesquite chips

Soak mesquite chips for 2 days in water. Follow smoker directions regarding pre-heating and loading of soaked wood chips in an electric smoker. Light charcoal in smoker and allow smoker to heat for about an hour. Fill water tray in smoker. Sprinkle a handful of soaked hickory chips on charcoal. Place Hot Italian Sausage Links on the top grid and do not open the smoker for about 3 hours. Do not let fire go out and make sure the water tray is always full. Remove sausage and let rest for 10 minutes or let cool to air temperature and wrap and freeze.

Smoked Indiana Farm Venison Sausage

Indiana Farm Venison Sausage   hickory chips

Soak hickory chips for 2 days in water. Follow smoker directions regarding preheating and loading of soaked wood chips in an electric smoker. Light charcoal in smoker and allow smoker to heat for about an hour. Fill water tray in smoker. Sprinkle a handful of soaked hickory chips on charcoal. Place Indiana Farm Venison Sausage on the top grid and do not open the smoker for about 3 hours. Do not let fire go out and make sure the water tray is always full. Remove sausage and let rest for 10 minutes or let cool to air temperature and wrap and freeze.

Smoked Venison

venison (any cut)   1 tsp. black pepper
dry red wine   sour cream
½ cup canola oil   Blackberry Hot Pepper Jelly
¼ cup lime juice

Marinate venison in wine for at least 24 hours. Prepare a light fire in covered grill. Place meat on spit and cook, basting with sauce made with oil, lime juice and black pepper. When the meat gets warm, add wet hickory chips to the fire (and more briquettes as necessary to keep an even heat). Smoke venison for 3 hours with continued basting. Remove meat from spit and baste with wine. Wrap in foil and allow meat to cool to room temperature. Reheat, when ready to serve, in foil for 20 minutes at 250 degrees. To serve, place a dab of sour cream and a tsp. of Blackberry Hot Pepper Jelly on each piece of meat.

White-tail deer have good eyesight and acute hearing, but depend mainly on their sense of smell to detect danger. They have numerous scent glands on their legs for intraspecies communication, and secretions become especially strong during the rutting season.

Smoked Venison Backstrap

2½ to 3 lbs. venison backstrap
3 cloves garlic, pressed
4 cups Burgundy wine
½ cup teriyaki sauce
½ cup Worcestershire sauce
4 oz. Allegro marinade
hickory chips

Marinate venison in garlic, Burgundy, teriyaki sauce, Worcestershire sauce and Allegro marinade in the refrigerator 24 hours, turning every 6 to 8 hours. Less tender cuts of meat may need to be marinated for 2 days. Soak a double handful of hickory chips in water for two days. Light charcoal in smoker and allow smoker to heat for about an hour. Fill water tray in smoker. Sprinkle a handful of soaked hickory chips on charcoal. Place venison on the top grid and do not open the smoker for about 3 hours. Do not let fire go out and make sure the water tray is always full. Serves 6 to 8.

Smoked Venison Backstrap
with Blackberry Catsup on Biscuits
Made with Buttermilk

hickory chips
1 tsp. ground thyme
½ tsp. ground nutmeg
1 tsp. black pepper
½ (2 lbs.) venison backstrap
Biscuits Made With Buttermilk
butter
Blackberry Catsup
red pickled apple slices, halved
parsley sprigs

Soak hickory chips in water for 2 hours. Mix thyme, nutmeg and pepper. Rub backstrap with mixed seasonings. Heat coals in the barbeque pit until you can hold your hand over the fire for only 5 seconds. Sprinkle soaked hickory chips over coals and close cover and allow smoke to fill pit. Insert a meat thermometer into the thickest part of the backstrap. Place backstrap on grill; close cover and cook for about 30 minutes or until meat thermometer registers 155 degrees. Remove meat from pit and allow to rest for 5 minutes. Slice 6 pieces ½" or less pieces on a diagonal. Slice open Biscuits With Buttermilk; spread with butter and toast. Spoon a little Blackberry Catsup on ½ of individual each serving plate. Gently lay a slice of smoked backstrap on the Blackberry Catsup; drip a little stream of Blackberry Catsup on the top of the smoked backstrap. Overlap two halves of biscuit on the other side of the plate. Garnish with ½ slice of pickled apple and parsley. Serves 6.

Biologists estimate there are 26 million white-tailed deer living in North America—more than are believed to have existed when Christopher Columbus arrived in the New World in 1492.

Stuffed and Smoked Venison Roast

1 (4 to 6-lb.) venison roast
1 cup Burgundy
1 med. yellow onion, chopped
1 bell pepper, chopped
2 large garlic cloves,
    quartered
2 Tbsp. dried parsley
1tsp. mint, crushed
6 drops Peychaud's bitters

2 Tbsp. Worcestershire
    sauce
1 Tbsp. liquid smoke
2 large clove garlic,
    sliced
fresh red peppers
green onions
salt
cayenne pepper

Remove all the fat and connecting tissues from the venison. Make a marinade by mixing Burgundy, onion, bell pepper, parsley, mint, bitters, Worcestershire sauce and liquid smoke. Place roast in a large glass container and cover with the marinade. Refrigerate overnight. Remove the roast and pat dry.

Make small slits over the roast and insert a slice of garlic, red peppers and green onions into the slits. Rub salt and cayenne pepper over the whole roast. Follow your smoker's directions for smoking large roasts. Fruit woods such as apple, wild cherry, and mesquite make excellent smoking woods. Cover the roast with bacon strips to retain moisture. Serves 6 to 10 depending on the size of the venison roast.

Smoked Venison Spareribs with Pineapple

2 lbs. venison spareribs
soy sauce
1 Tbsp. all-purpose flour
½ cup pineapple juice
¼ cup sugar

¼ cup vinegar, distilled
½ cup water
1 cup pineapple chunks
cornstarch binder

Soak mesquite chips in water for 2 days. Follow directions for electric or charcoal smoker or heat coals in the barbeque pit until you can hold your hand over the fire for 10 to 15 seconds. Sprinkle soaked hickory chips over coals and close cover and allow smoke to fill pit. Place ribs on grill; close cover and smoke/cook very slowly until ribs are tender, 1 to 2 hours. Remove ribs from pit and allow to rest until cold. Cut ribs in sparerib serving portions. Dip the spareribs in soy sauce, drain, then sauté for 5 minutes. Stir in the flour, then add the pineapple juice, sugar, vinegar, and water. Stir, cover, and simmer for about one hour, or until ribs are tender. Season with salt. Add the pineapple chunks, heat, then thicken the sauce with cornstarch binder. Serves 2.

Smoked Venison Stew

3 to 4 lbs. venison roast
hickory chips
all-purpose flour
3 Tbsp. bacon fat
1½ cups hot water
1 cup red wine
1 tsp. mixed dry thyme, marjoram and basil

1 tsp. dried parsley
1 large white onion, sliced
1½ tsp. salt
½ tsp. black pepper
3 carrots, scraped and quartered
3 potatoes, peeled and quartered

Soak hickory chips in water for 2 days. Heat coals in the barbeque pit until you can hold your hand over the fire for 10 to 15 seconds. Sprinkle soaked hickory chips over coals and close cover and allow smoke to fill pit. Insert a meat thermometer into the thickest part of the roast. Place roast on grill; close cover and smoke/cook until meat thermometer registers 100 degrees. Remove meat from pit and allow to rest until cold.

Remove sinews and bones from venison, cut meat into 2"-size pieces, and roll in flour. Brown in hot bacon fat in deep kettle. Add hot water, wine, herbs, onions, salt and pepper. Cover pot and bring to a boil. Lower heat and simmer 2 hours. Add carrots and potatoes. Cover and simmer 1 hour, adding more hot water if needed. When meat is tender and vegetables done, serve hot. Serves 6.

Meat from very young deer does not need to be hung very long, if at all. But meat quality in older deer will be improved considerably if allowed to hang for several days.

CURING

Curing whole hind and forequarters with bones inside can be a trying experience. The problem with curing these two cuts of meat is that it is very difficult to get enough of the curing ingredients deep enough to cure the meat which is next to the bone. Professionals and experienced home processors use an injecting needle to distribute the correct amount of the curing mixture deep inside. If you wish to cure whole quarters, I recommend that you obtain one of the fine publications that are available that address this particular aspect of curing.

On the other hand, do not be afraid to experiment with curing roasts, steaks, and de-boned quarters. Before you use your venison, you may wish to use very lean beef for your first efforts at curing.

Dry Cured Venison

From Harold W. Webster, Sr., an old 1800s Webster recipe from Oak Ridge and Amite County, Mississippi.

For every 10 lbs, of meat allow:
salt, as needed
2 bay leaves
2 coriander seeds
4 whole cloves

6 peppercorns
1 cup salt
¼ cup sugar
2 tsp. saltpetre

Dry curing is more tolerant to warmer temperatures than brining. In Oak Ridge, dry curing was done in late fall or early spring. Ideally dry curing should only be done when temperatures can be depended on to be between 36 and 40 degrees. To be on the safe side, limit dry curing temperature to 36 to 40 degrees. During the warmer months, you can remove the racks from your refrigerator and place the crock inside. Use a refrigerator thermometer for several days prior to test for temperature range. Make setting adjustment as needed.

Place the meat on racks and sprinkle them very lightly with salt. Cool completely. Pulverize bay leaves, coriander seeds, cloves and peppercorns. Mix ground spices, salt, sugar and saltpeter. Cover meat completely with the curing mixture; rub the meat repeatedly with the mixture. Gently place the meat in a sterilized crock, being careful not to disturb the salt and spice coating. Cover crock with a loose fitting cloth cover. Recoat the heavier cuts of meat with the curing mixture in 6 to 8 days. Cure for 3 days for each pound of meat. If the temperature should go below freezing, add that amount of time to the curing time. Leave the meat in the crock even after all of the curing mixture has been absorbed.

After venison has cured, it can be left in the crock until used. It may be scrubbed and hung in a cool, well-ventilated place to dry out before storing or smoking. Large cuts of venison such as hindquarters should be hung at least 25 days before smoking. If the venison will not be smoked, then wrap each piece in muslin and then in several layers of heavy paper. Hang in a dark, cool well-ventilated room. Hindquarters should be left to hang for 2 years. Smaller cuts of venison can be used after 6 months.

Home Cured Venison Roast

1 (4 to 6-lb.) venison shoulder or
  hindquarter roast
1cup Morton's sugar cure mix
  (do not substitute)
3 cups water

1 tsp. salt
Kitchen Bouquet
Wesson oil
glass, enamel or glazed vitrified clay pot

Trim all fat from the roast. Wash and place in large container. Make enough brine to cover the venison by making a brine using the curing mix and water. Cover the venison and place the bowl in the refrigerator from 9 to 12 days, turning the meat 2 or 3 times. After curing time is completed, drain the meat and place in a large cooking pot; cover with water, add salt and boil until the venison is tender. Serve with Homemade Horseradish or other sauce. The roast may be cooked in an un-covered roasting pan in a 300-degree oven until tender. Brush with equal parts Kitchen Bouquet and salad oil several times during the roasting process. Serves 6 to 8. (Morton's sugar cure mix cannot be substituted.)

Salt Cured Venison

Remove all fat and connecting tissues from the venison. Cut the lean red venison into long ½" thick strips. Make a brine by dissolving all the salt possible in boiling water. Immerse the strips, a few at a time, for 3 minutes in the boiling water. Hang the meat to drain. Make a mixture of pepper, oregano, basil and thyme and rub onto the venison. Hang the venison to dry in the sun for several weeks until it is hard and almost black on the outside. It will keep almost indefinitely away from damp and flies. The venison can also be hung in the attic to dry. If hung outside in the sun, cover with plastic at night to keep the moisture off. The dried venison can be bitten off and eaten as is or it can be also be cooked in stews. This venison is very concentrated and a little goes a long way as an emergency food. It is not a good food for long consumption, as it lacks the necessary fat and other essential vitamins and minerals.

Venison Pastrami

1½ gal. water
3 lbs. salt
3 cups light brown sugar
4 Tbsp. pickling spices
8 cinnamon cloves, crushed
6 garlic cloves, crushed

2 tsp- black pepper
1 tsp. onion powder
½ tsp. red pepper
12 lbs. venison round steak, cut 2"–4"
  thick

Mix all ingredients except venison. Submerge venison in brine and cure for 42 days (3 to 4 days for each pound of venison). Rinse and dry. Cold smoke for 4 hours, then finish by cooking in slow oven until center of meat reaches 140 degrees. Store in refrigerator.

24

Venison Marinades

There are good reasons for people to marinate venison. Three of the reasons have validity, one does not. Marinades can be used to impart a particular flavor, tenderize older game and sometimes minimize a mild wild taste. Ignorance of proper meat processing is not a valid reason.

There are going to be times when the only venison you have available to you is a tough old buck who was run all day and harvested at full stride with a pack of dogs hot on his heels. We usually give this meat to people whom we don't see very often. If you have been blessed with such a gift, have heart. Through no fault of your own, you have to find a way to rectify the errors of others. You have a 90% chance of making something good out of it. But you also have a 10% chance of having a piece of meat that nothing will help.

The best way I have found to determine the quality of the venison is to smell the raw meat. If the raw meat smells exceedingly strong, you have a challenge on your hands. For meat with a strong smell, you may wish to use one of the stronger wine or vinegar marinades.

All-Purpose Venison Marinade

1 cup water
2 Tbsp. vinegar
2 small limes, sliced
½ tsp. peppercorn, crushed
3 carrots, sliced
1 stalk green celery, chopped
1 bay leaf, crumbled

3 sprigs parsley
3 whole cloves crushed
1 Tbsp. Tony's Creole Seasoning
3 large cloves garlic
1 yellow onion, chopped fine
2 Tbsp. olive oil

Marinate venison in the refrigerator overnight. Remove, drain and cook.

Apricot Venison Marinade

½ lb. dried apricots
3 large onions, sliced
1 clove garlic, minced
2 Tbsp. butter
1 Tbsp. curry powder

2 Tbsp. dark brown sugar
½ tsp. salt
3 Tbsp. vinegar
pinch red pepper
2 Tbsp. lime juice

Cook and puree apricots in a food processor. Sauté the onions and garlic in butter until golden. Add the curry powder and cook for 1 more minute. Add apricot puree, sugar, salt, vinegar, red pepper, and lime juice. Bring to a boil, then remove from heat and cool completely before pouring over raw venison.

Basic Venison Marinade

1 cup salad oil
1 cup apple cider vinegar
2 med. onions, sliced
1 cup celery, chopped
1 clove garlic, chopped

1 tsp. salt
1 tsp. black pepper
1½ tsp. Worcestershire sauce
2 bay leaves

Combine all ingredients and marinate venison overnight. Before cooking, drain, and wipe dry. DO NOT WASH.

Beer and Bourbon Venison Marinade

1 cup beer
1 cup sour mash bourbon
1 cup cooking oil
1 tsp. salt
½ tsp. garlic powder

½ tsp. onion salt .
1 med. yellow onion, sliced
½ tsp. black pepper
venison
2 Tbsp. cornstarch

Make the marinade by mixing all ingredients (except venison and cornstarch). Pour marinade over venison. Cover and refrigerate for 2 weeks. Turn meat daily. After refrigerating, cook the venison and marinade in a covered pan at 300 degrees for about 5 hours. If needed, thicken the pan juices with cornstarch.

Bourbon & Balsamic Vinegar Venison Marinade

3 Tbsp. dark brown sugar
1 tsp. salt
1 tsp. black pepper
1 bay leaf

¼ cup Jack Daniel's sour mash
  bourbon
1 tsp. garlic, chopped fine
1 Tbsp. Worcestershire sauce
⅛ cup balsamic vinegar

Mix all ingredients to make the marinade. Refrigerate and marinate venison for 4 hours.

Bourbon & Lime Juice Venison Marinade

½ cup teriyaki sauce
¼ cup Ezra Brooks, black, bourbon
1 Tbsp. lime juice

¼ cup dark brown sugar
salt
black pepper

Mix all ingredients to make the marinade. Heat marinade over very low heat until the brown sugar is dissolved. Cool to air temperature. Marinate venison in the refrigerator for 2 days, turning often. Marinade can be used for basting while cooking.

New Orleans Venison Marinade

1 Tbsp. peppercorns, crushed
3 bay leaves
½ tsp. allspice
6 whole cloves

1 cup brandy
1 cup dry red wine
1 cup corn oil

Mix together all ingredients to make the marinade. Marinate the venison for 24 hours. Venison will keep in this solution from 1 to 2 weeks if kept refrigerated at 36 degrees.

Brown Sugar and Port Venison Marinade

venison round steaks
1 lb. dark brown sugar

ruby or tawny port wine

Place venison steaks in a 2-gal. container and spread brown sugar between pieces of venison round steaks. Fill container with port wine. Refrigerate and let stand 24 hours. Remove the venison and cook.

Buttermilk Venison Marinade

Cultured buttermilk has been used for hundreds of years to tenderize and remove much of the wild flavor that has been associated with venison. In a glass container, cover the venison completely with cultured buttermilk. Steaks and chops should marinate 4 to 5 hours. Four-pound and heavier roasts should marinate 12 hours. After the meat has marinated, wipe off excess buttermilk. Cook the meat according to your favorite recipe.

Deep South Plantation Venison Marinade

1 haunch of venison, 6 to 7 lbs.
5 Tbsp. salt butter
1 large onion, chopped
2 Tbsp. green onions, chopped
1 carrot, chopped
4 whole cloves
½ tsp. dried thyme

¾ tsp. dried marjoram
¼ tsp. dried tarragon
½ tsp. dried basil
½ tsp. dried rosemary
⅛ tsp. sugar
1 cup dry red wine

Wash and wipe the venison dry. Make the marinade by melting the butter and sautéing the onion, green onion, and carrot in a saucepan over low heat until soft. Remove the marinade from the heat and add the cloves, thyme, marjoram, tarragon, basil, and rosemary. Stir well; add the dry red wine and mix again. Brush the venison with olive oil and sprinkle generously with salt, black pepper, and cayenne pepper. Put the venison into a large glass bowl and pour the marinade over. Cover the bowl and refrigerate for 8 hours. Remove the venison from the marinade and drain before cooking.

Cooked Marinade for Venison

1 cup celery, chopped
1 cup carrots, chopped
1cup onions, chopped
1½ cups olive oil
3 cups cider vinegar
2 cups water
½ cup parsley, coarsely chopped
4 bay leaves

1 Tbsp. Thyme
1 Tbsp, basil
1 Tbsp. cloves
1 Tbsp. allspice berries
pinch mace
1 Tbsp. peppercorns, crushed
6 cloves garlic, crushed

To make the marinade, sauté the celery, carrots and onions in olive oil until golden brown. Add remainder of the ingredients and simmer for 1 hour. Strain and cool to air temperature before pouring over the venison.

Old World Venison Marinade

3 cups claret wine
1½ cups water
1 tsp. black pepper
2 bay leaves

¼ tsp. rosemary
¼ tsp. tarragon
¼ tsp. thyme
¼ tsp. mustard seeds

Mix all ingredients and marinate meat in a covered glass dish overnight.

 Reindeer are believed by many to be one of the first domesticated deer. A 9th-century letter from Norway's King Ottar to Alfred the Great mentioned his fine herd of over 600 reindeer.

Gourmet Venison Spice and Red Wine Marinade

5 Tbsp. butter
1 (6 to 7 lb.) venison roast
1 large onion, chopped
2 Tbsp. green onion, chopped
1 carrot, chopped
4 whole cloves
½ tsp. dried thyme

¾ tsp. dried marjoram
¼ tsp. dried tarragon
½ tsp. dried basil
½ tsp. dried rosemary
⅛ tsp. sugar
1 cup Burgundy wine

Make marinade by melting the butter and sautéing the onion, green onions, and carrot over low heat until soft. Remove vegetables from the heat and add the cloves, thyme, marjoram, tarragon, basil, and rosemary. Mix well, then add the Burgundy and mix well. Allow to cool to air temperature.

olive oil
salt

black pepper
red pepper

Brush the venison with olive oil and sprinkle generously with salt, black pepper, and red pepper. Place the venison into a large glass bowl and pour the marinade over. Cover the bowl; refrigerate for 8 to 12 hours. Remove the venison from the marinade and allow to drain before cooking. Strain marinade and use in making Red Wine, Currant Jelly, & Brandy Sauce.

Juniper Berry and Burgundy Venison Marinade

2 cups Burgundy
1 cup canned beef broth
1 med. yellow onion, chopped
2 large garlic cloves, chopped fine

2 bay leaves, broken
8 juniper berries, crushed
1 tsp. salt

Make marinade by mixing all ingredients. Place venison in large bowl. Cover with marinade. Place venison in the refrigerator for 24 hours. Remove venison and strain marinade and reserve for basting.

Marinade for Game

From an 1850 hand-written recipe from Providence, Rhode Island.

1 onion, sliced
2 carrots, sliced
4 green onions, chopped
¼ cup parsley, chopped
1 tsp. salt

10 or 12 peppercorns
4 juniper berries, crushed
¼ tsp. dried thyme
1 cup red wine
1 cup olive oil

Mix all ingredients to make the marinade. Marinate venison in the refrigerator for at least 12 hours, turn several times. Wipe venison dry before cooking. Venison backstrap or a small forequarter roast is especially good when marinated in this mixture for 24 hours. Cook over a charcoal grill until just pink in the center. Makes about 4 cups of marinade.

Olive Oil and Wine Vinegar Venison Marinade

7 or 8 lbs. of venison round steak cut no
    less than 1½" thick
2 Tbsp. olive oil
½ cup wine vinegar
1 rounded tsp. oregano

1 medium onion, sliced thin
⅛ tsp. salt
⅛ tsp. black pepper
⅛ tsp. cayenne pepper

Mix all ingredients to make the marinade. Place the venison in the marinade, lay onions on top and marinate in the refrigerator overnight.

Venison Sauerbraten Marinade

4 lbs. venison pot roast, cut 3" to 4" thick
2 cups red wine vinegar
2 cups water
2 cups yellow onions, sliced
4 bay leaves

16 whole cloves
1 Tbsp. salt
¼ tsp. black pepper
2 Tbsp. dark brown sugar

Cover venison with vinegar and water, onions, bay leaves, cloves, salt, pepper, and sugar. Let stand in refrigerator for 24 hours.

New England Style Venison Marinade

1 qt. red wine vinegar
1 qt. water
1 Tbsp. cayenne pepper
1 Tbsp. black pepper
1 Tbsp. salt
3 cloves garlic, chopped
3 bay leaves

1 tsp. cloves
1 tsp. allspice
1 tsp. mustard seed
1 tsp. thyme
½ cup sour cream
½ cup Currant Jelly
1 Tbsp. brandy

Make marinade by mixing all ingredients. Pour marinade over venison, cover and refrigerate for 12 hours. Turn several times. Remove, drain and dry before cooking.

In Germany, women have a long association with the hunt; Diana is the goddess of the hunt, and for a male hunter to refer to a woman as a "Diana" is without a doubt the ultimate compliment a man can bestow on a woman who hunts.

25

Venison Sauces & Gravy

These sauces complement venison. The sauce can add that special touch to a fine venison meal. Many dishes experience a name change just by changing the sauce. For many recipes, the sauce is what defines the dish. We do need to remember that the major ingredient in the recipe is the focal point, not the sauce. Use your sauce to complement the dish, not the dish to complement the sauce. Many delicate recipes can be ruined if we make the sauce the focal point.

Most milk and flour-based sauces tend to skim over if they are not served soon after making. If you determine that need to prepare your sauce ahead of time, exclude the air from the top of the sauce by laying a thin piece of kitchen plastic wrap on the surface of the sauce. Before reheating the sauce, remove the plastic wrap and stir frequently during the reheating.

Some sauces can take rough handling and approximate measuring. Other sauces are very intolerant of even the slightest deviation from the recipe. There are times when the air temperature and humidity can affect a delicate sauce.

There are two schools of thought on preparing sauces. One school teaches you to treat each sauce as a delicate work or art. The other school advises you to rough your way through the process, and serve it as it comes out. I suspect that the truth is somewhere in-between the two for most sauces. My recommendation is to do your best on timing and preparation, and you will be rewarded with fine sauces.

Apple-Orange Cranberry Liqueur Sauce

juice from ½ orange, shell reserved
2 cups water
1 Granny Smith apple, peeled, cored and
  quartered
3 cups fresh cranberries

1¼ cups sugar
½ tsp. sugar
½ tsp. cinnamon
¼ tsp. ground cloves
2 oz. cranberry or orange liqueur

Remove the membrane from the inside of the orange shell and discard. Cut the shell into small diced pieces. Put into a saucepan with water, bring to a boil and cook for 10 minutes. Drain and set aside. Chop the apple into small pieces and place in saucepan. Sort the cranberries, discarding any soft ones, and add to the chopped apple together with the diced orange peel, orange juice, sugar, cinnamon, cloves and cranberry or orange liqueur. Place over medium heat and bring to a boil. Then reduce heat and simmer gently, partially covered, until thickened, the apple is tender, and the cranberries have burst, 10 to 15 minutes. Transfer to a bowl and let cool before serving. (Can be covered and refrigerated but should be brought back to room temperature before serving.) Serves 6.

Barbeque Sauce

An American Colonial 1794 recipe.

½ lb. butter
juice of 3 lemons
¼ cup Homemade Horseradish
¼ cup tomato catsup

¼ cup white vinegar
1 Tbsp. Worcestershire sauce
4 tsp. salt
Tabasco sauce to taste

Combine all ingredients. Keep sauce warm and stir frequently as it tends to separate. Simmer for 1½ to 2 hours. Makes about 3 cups.

Bar-B-Q Sauce with Apple Sauce

This recipe was given to the author by Joe Spivey while we were working as Red Cross volunteers in the aftermath of the 1989 floods in Elba, Alabama.

¼ cup tomato catsup
¼ cup Worcestershire sauce
¼ cup mustard

¼ cup apple sauce
Tabasco sauce to taste

Mix all ingredients and bring to a gentle boil. Remove from stove and cool. The sauce may be frozen.

Barbeque Sauce with Fresh Pineapple

¾ cup fresh pineapple
3 Tbsp. butter
3 Tbsp. fresh ginger, minced

1 bottle teriyaki sauce
¼ cup pine nuts, coarsely chopped
4 cloves garlic, pressed

Mix all ingredients and bring sauce to a boil over low heat. Cool to air temperature. Marinate venison for 1 hour. Grill venison to no more than medium. The remaining sauce can be used for basting while grilling.

Béarnaise Sauce

4 egg yolks
juice of 1 lemon
2 cups butter, melted
salt

white pepper
2 Tbsp. capers
¼ cup parsley, chopped
1 Tbsp. tarragon vinegar

In top half of a double boiler, beat egg yolks and lemon juice. Cook slowly in the double boiler over very low heat, never allowing water in bottom pan to come to a boil. Slowly add the melted butter to above mixture, stirring constantly. Add salt, white pepper (to taste), capers, parsley and vinegar. Stir to blend. Makes 2 cups.

Black Bean & Tequila Salsa

1 cup dry black beans
1 bay leaf
1 large clove of garlic
2 tsp. cumin, ground
¼ tsp. red pepper flakes
2 tsp. salt
⅓ cup white onion, minced

½ tsp. garlic, pressed
½ medium tomato, seeded and diced
⅓ cup radishes, chopped
2 Tbsp. cilantro, chopped
1 Tbsp lime juice
1 tsp. jalapeño pepper, chopped
1½ oz. dark tequila

Cover beans with 2" of water and soak overnight. Drain and cover with fresh water and bring to a boil. Add bay leaf, garlic, cumin and pepper flakes. Reduce heat and simmer until the beans are tender, 1 to 1¼ hours. Remove from heat and stir in 2 tsp. salt. When cool, drain beans discarding liquid, bay leaf and garlic. Add to beans minced onion, minced garlic, tomato, radishes, cilantro, lime juice, jalapeño and tequila. Simmer to boiling and remove from heat and serve. Makes 4 cups.

Blackberry Sauce with Nutmeg and Cloves

½ cup fresh or frozen blackberries
¼ cup rice wine vinegar
2 Tbsp. dark brown sugar
¼ tsp. cinnamon, ground

⅛ tsp. nutmeg, ground
⅛ tsp. cloves, ground
⅛ tsp. cayenne pepper
¼ tsp. salt

Rub blackberries through a fine sieve or use a food mill to separate the juice from the pulp and seeds. In a small saucepan, combine all ingredients and cook until slightly thickened. Serve hot or at room temperature.

Blackberry Sauce with Bourbon

4 (14½-oz.) cans chicken broth
1 (10-oz.) jar Blackberry Jelly
½ cup sour mash bourbon
¼ cup Blackberry Wine

2 Tbsp. black peppercorns, cracked
¼ tsp. dried thyme
2 Tbsp. reserved pan drippings

Combine first 6 ingredients in a saucepan; bring to a boil over high heat. Reduce heat, and simmer about 1 hour or until liquid is reduced to 4 cups. Pour mixture through a large, fine-wire mesh strainer into a 4-cup liquid measuring cup. Discard seeds. Stir in 2 Tbsp. reserved pan drippings. Makes 4 cups.

Brown Vegetable Gravy

fat
flour
V-8 vegetable juice

salt
pepper
grated onion

Make brown gravy by using 2 Tbsp. of fat for each cup of gravy required. Add 2 Tbsp. of flour for each 2 Tbsp. of fat. Blend fat and flour over low heat until it is rich brown. Stir frequently and take care not to scorch it. Complete the browning before adding liquid. Remove from heat. Gradually stir in liquid, preferably cold, allowing 1 cup liquid for each 2 Tbsp, fat and flour. In addition to any juice left in the pot after the meat is cooked, add V-8 vegetable juice. Season to taste with salt and pepper; add a little grated onion; return to heat and cook, stirring constantly, until thick and smooth.

Beurre Meunière Sauce

A 1783 American Colonial recipe.

⅓ cup Clarified Butter

1 Tbsp. lemon juice

Brown the butter in a heavy saucepan until it becomes a rich brown. Add lemon juice and pour over vegetables.

Beurre Noir Sauce

¼ cup Clarified Butter
1tsp. lemon or lime juice

1 Tbsp. capers, chopped

Cook Clarified Butter very slowly, until dark brown. Stir in lemon juice and capers. Serve on meat immediately.

Burgundy and Bouillon Sauce

2¼ Tbsp. cornstarch
1 cup water
2 beef bouillon cubes
⅛ tsp. dark brown sugar

¾ cup Burgundy
½ tsp. salt
⅛ tsp, black pepper

Combine ingredients and cook, stirring constantly, over medium heat until mixture is thick.

Cranberry Meatball Sauce

1 (16-oz.) can jellied cranberry sauce
1 Tbsp. lime juice

3 Tbsp. light brown sugar
1 cup tomato catsup

Heat ingredients for the sauce until smooth. Pour over meatballs. Bake at 350 degrees for 1 hour.

Cranberry Sauce

4 cups cranberries   2 cups sugar
2 cups boiling water

Wash and pick over the cranberries. Place the cranberries in a saucepan and cover with water. As soon as the water begins to boil again, cover the saucepan with a lid. Boil the berries 3 or 4 minutes or until the skins burst. Put them through a strainer or ricer. Stir the sugar into the pureed cranberries. Place the mixture over heat and bring it to a rolling boil. For cranberry sauce, remove the pan from the heat at once. If you want to mold cranberry jelly, boil the mixture for about 5 minutes. Skim and pour into a wet mold. The cooking periods are correct for ripe berries. Very ripe berries may require cooking for a few minutes longer.

Mrs. Clyde Lacy Lynch

Currant Mint Sauce

1 Tbsp. mint leaves, chopped   1 (6-oz.) glass of Currant Jelly
grated rind of ½ orange

Stir 1 tbsp. chopped mint leaves with the grated rind of half an orange into a 6-ounce glass of Currant Jelly.

Fresh Lemon and Orange Sauce

½ cup butter   ½ cup fresh orange juice
2 egg yolks   ¼ tsp. salt
1 Tbsp. boiling water   ¼ tsp. paprika
2 Tbsp. fresh lemon juice   2 Tbsp. grated orange rind

Place butter in a saucepan and warm and mix until it is soft and fluffy. Beat in the egg yolks, one at a time. Stir in boiling water; then add the lemon juice. Stir and cook 1 minute over low heat. Add orange juice, salt, and paprika. Mix well. Cook over low heat until the sauce is the consistency of heavy cream. Serve with venison or asparagus. Yields 1¼ cups.

Among the native Tlingit of southeast Alaska, the deer is a symbol of peace, because a deer does not bite or get angry, and is gentle.

Grand Marnier Cream Sauce
for Venison Roasts

2 Tbsp. butter
¼ cup fine chopped green onion
½ cup white wine
1 cup heavy cream

3 Tbsp. Grand Marnier
1 tsp. salt
½ tsp. black pepper
pinch red pepper

Sauté onions in melted butter until very soft. Add white wine and simmer for about 15 minutes. Gradually stir in cream; add the Grand Marnier, salt, black and red pepper; reduce to ⅓ volume over medium-high heat. Serve hot over sliced venison roast.

Green Yogurt Salad Dressing

1 cup unflavored yogurt
½ cup extra virgin olive or canola oil
3 Tbsp, red wine vinegar
1 bunch parsley

1 tsp. cumin
1 tsp. cinnamon
salt to taste
white pepper to taste

Place yogurt in a food processor, and process for 10 seconds until completely smooth. Add oil, vinegar and parsley, and blend or process until pureed. Add cumin and cinnamon. Mix well, and season to taste with salt and white pepper. Makes about 2 cups.

Harold's Favorite Spaghetti Sauce

2 onions, chopped
2 cloves garlic, minced
2 Tbsp. canola
1 (28-oz.) can tomatoes
1 cup water
½ tsp. dried basil
¼ cup parsley, chopped

½ tsp. thyme, crumbled
2 tsp. salt
¼ tsp. black pepper
¼ tsp. red pepper flakes
1 (6-oz.) can tomato paste
venison meatballs
12 oz. spaghetti, cooked and hot

Sauté onion and garlic until golden in hot oil in large saucepan. Add tomatoes and bring to boil. Simmer, uncovered, 20 minutes, stirring occasionally. Put in crock pot cooker, add remaining sauce ingredients and browned Harold's Favorite Venison Meatballs, cover and cook on low 6 to 8 hours. Add more seasoning, if desired. Serve on hot cooked spaghetti. Makes 6 servings.

Hawaiian Pineapple Sauce

1½ tsp. cornstarch
½ cup pineapple juice
¼ cup vinegar

½ cup sugar
2½ tsp. soy sauce

Combine all Ingredients and reduce over low heat until sauce thickens.

Jezebel Sauce

1 (10-oz.) jar pineapple preserves
1 (10-oz.) jar apple jelly
6 oz. Homemade Horseradish

½ can dry mustard
1 tsp. black pepper

Mix all ingredients together; let set in refrigerator 1 hour. Serve cold on hot meat.

Hollandaise Sauce

4 egg yolks
2 Tbsp. lemon or lime juice
½ lb. butter, melted

¼ teaspoon salt
salt and pepper
pinch of cayenne pepper

In top half of double boiler, beat egg yolks and stir in lemon juice. Cook very slowly in double boiler over low heat, never allowing water in bottom pan to come to a boil. Add butter a little at a time, stirring constantly with a wooden spoon. Add salt and pepper (to taste). Continue cooking slowly until thickened. Makes 1 cup.

Mrs. Anne Lynch Webster

Hot Cole Slaw Dressing

⅓ cup finely chopped onion
⅓ cup French salad dressing

¼ cup sugar

Combine all Ingredients and let sit in refrigerator. It will be better if allowed to sit for 3 days before using. To make a creamier dressing, 3 Tbsp. of mayonnaise may be added. Heat before serving over venison. Yields 1 cup.

Mrs. Clyde Lacy Lynch

Hot Cumberland Sauce

1 tsp. dry mustard
1 Tbsp. light brown sugar
¼ tsp. powdered ginger
pinch red pepper
¼ tsp. salt
¼ tsp. ground cloves
1½ cups tawny port
½ cup seedless raisins

½ cup blanched almonds, slivered
2 tsp. cornstarch
2 Tbsp. water
¼ cup Currant Jelly
1 Tbsp. grated orange and lemon rind
¼ cup orange juice
2 Tbsp. lemon juice
2 Tbsp. Grand Marnier

Combine mustard, brown sugar, ginger, cayenne, salt, cloves, port, raisins, and almonds; simmer covered 8 minutes. Dissolve cornstarch in water and stir into sauce. Let sauce simmer for about 2 minutes and stir in Currant Jelly, orange and lemon rind, orange juice and Grand Marnier. Serve hot. Pour on top of servings of venison.

Hot Red Wine and Currant Jelly Sauce

2 Tbsp. butter
½ cup Currant Jelly
juice of ½ lemon
½ cup water

1 tsp. salt
red pepper
½ cup Burgundy

Simmer butter, Currant Jelly, lemon juice, water, salt, and red pepper together with drippings in a pan. Blend into a smooth gravy. Remove from fire, add wine and serve over venison.

Indian Curry Sauce

¼ cup butter
¼ cup onion, chopped fine
½ cup apple, chopped fine
¼ cup celery, chopped fine
1½ to 2 tsp. curry powder
⅛ tsp. ground ginger

2½ cups canned chicken broth
3 Tbsp. all-purpose flour
2 egg yolks, slightly beaten
½ cup cream
salt
black pepper

Melt butter over low heat; add onion, apple and celery and cook 5 minutes. Blend in curry powder and ginger. Add 2 cups of chicken bouillon and simmer 15 minutes. Blend flour with remaining chicken bouillon; stir into the sauce. Cook, stirring constantly, until thick and smooth. Stir a little of the hot sauce into the slightly beaten egg yolks; add to remaining sauce. Cook, stirring constantly, over very low heat for 2 minutes. Add cream and season with salt and pepper to taste. Serve at once. Makes about 3 cups.

Marchand De Vin Sauce for Venison

1 mushroom gravy mix
½ cup dry red wine

½ cup water
2 Tbsp. butter

Mix all Ingredients in a saucepan and bring to a boil over low heat; reduce heat and simmer until thickened.

Madeira Wine and Green Onion Sauce

2 Tbsp. butter
2 Tbsp. green onions, chopped fine
1½ cups canned beef gravy

2 Tbsp. lime or lemon juice
¼ cup Madeira wine

Melt the butter in a saucepan, add green onions and cook until the onions are just tender. Add the gravy and lime or lemon juice and bring to a boil. Add Madeira and heat. Makes approx, 1½ cups sauce.

Milk & Coffee Gravy

3 Tbsp. Crisco
3 Tbsp. all-purpose flour
1½ cups whole milk

½ cup very thick & strong coffee
salt
black pepper

Warm Crisco in a heavy skillet. Add flour; heat, stirring until bubbly. Add milk and coffee; cook, stirring, until thickened. If it is too thin add a little flour. If it is too thick add more milk. Season to taste with salt and pepper.

Molasses & Bourbon Sauce for Smoked Vegetables

1 cup hickory chips, soaked in water
1 large white onion
5 large mushrooms
2 tomatoes
1 tsp. garlic, pressed
2 Tbsp. butter
2 Tbsp. sorghum molasses
2 Tbsp. red wine vinegar

1 tsp. teriyaki sauce
2 Tbsp. tomato catsup
2 Tbsp. bourbon
¼ cup canned beef broth
½ tsp. chili powder
salt
pepper
cayenne pepper

Smoke onion, mushrooms and tomatoes by placing soaked wood chips on coals and arranging onion, mushrooms and tomatoes on cooking grate. Cover grill and smoke for about 15 minutes. Chop finely the onion, mushrooms and skinned and cored tomatoes. In a small saucepan, sauté the smoked onion, garlic and smoked mushrooms in butter for 2 to 3 minutes. Add all other ingredients; simmer over low heat for 15 minutes. Season to taste. Adjust thickness with water.

Mrs. Ann Lynch Webster

Molasses Sauce for Venison

Mix 1 quart of water, 3 Tbsp. sorghum molasses, 1 Tbsp. Apple Cider Vinegar, 2 tsp. salt and ¾ tsp. powdered dry mustard. Heat to the boiling point.

Mrs. Ann Lynch Webster

Mushroom-Red Wine Venison Sauce

½ lb. mushrooms, sliced
2 Tbsp. green onions, finely chopped
¼ cup plus 1 tsp, butter,
   divided
3 Tbsp. all-purpose flour
1½ cups whole milk

¼ cup dry red wine
1 Tbsp. fresh parsley, minced
½ tsp. salt
pinch of dry whole tarragon
¼ tsp. white pepper

Sauté mushrooms and onions in 2 Tbsp. butter in a heavy skillet until tender. Remove from skillet; set aside. Melt 3 Tbsp. butter in a saucepan over low heat. Add flour, stirring until smooth. Cook 1 minute, stirring constantly. Gradually add milk and red wine; cook over medium heat, stirring constantly, until thickened and bubbly. Stir in sautéed vegetables and remaining ingredients. Makes 2 cups.

Mushroom White Sauce

2 cups mushroom caps, sliced
2 tsp. onion, grated
4 Tbsp. butter
4 Tbsp. all-purpose flour

1 tsp. salt
¼ tsp. white pepper
2 cups whole milk

Cook mushrooms and onion in butter for 5 minutes; add flour, salt and pepper; stir until well blended. Remove from heat. Gradually stir in milk and return to heat. Cook stirring constantly, until thick and smooth. Makes 2 cups.

Mustard and Lemon Hollandaise Sauce for Venison

1½ tsp. powdered mustard
1 Tbsp. water
¾ cup butter
1½ Tbsp. lemon or lime juice

3 large egg yolks, well beaten
1/16 tsp. salt
1/16 tsp. black pepper

Mix mustard and water and let stand for 10 minutes. Divide butter into three pieces. Place one piece in the top of a double boiler and melt. Add lemon juice and egg yolks. Cook slowly over hot water, beating constantly with a rotary beater until the butter has melted. Add the second piece of butter and continue beating. As the mixture thickens, add the third piece of butter. Remove from water at once. Stir in salt, black pepper, and mustard. Serve over cooked vegetables, or venison. Yields 1⅔ cups.

Poivrade Sauce

⅓ cup carrots, chopped
⅓ cup white onion, chopped
4 Tbsp. parsley, chopped
3 Tbsp. olive oil

1 cup dry red wine
2½ cups canned beef gravy
1½ Tbsp. black pepper
Cognac and juices from venison roast

Sauté vegetables in oil 5 minutes. Add wine and simmer until reduced by ½, Add gravy and cook over low heat for 30 minutes. Strain. Add pan juices, dash of cognac and pepper and serve with venison roast.

Poppy Seed Salad Dressing

2 cups sugar
2 Tbsp. dry mustard
3½ tsp. salt
¼ cup white onion, finely chopped

1¼ cups red wine vinegar
3 ⅓ cups canola oil
8 tsp. poppy seeds

Mix all ingredients in a blender. Makes about 3 pints of dressing.

Red Eye Gravy

This recipe was given to me by my father. He stated that it was given to him by his grand-mother in Oak Ridge, Mississippi, who told my father that it was given to her by her grand-mother. This recipe has been in the Webster-Thompson-Andrews-Curry family in Mississippi for at least 6 generations, or since about 1790 or before.

3 Tbsp. leftover salted ham or bacon fat
  (include bottom of the skillet scrapings)
1½ cups strong black coffee

salt
pepper

After frying salt cured bacon; heat fat and bottom scrapings in a cast iron skillet. Stir in coffee. Salt and pepper to taste. Serve over grits, mashed potatoes and venison.

Red Fondue Sauce

¾ cup tomato catsup
2 Tbsp. Cider Vinegar

½ tsp. Homemade Horseradish
½ cup light brown sugar

Mix together. Simmer over low heat until mixture bubbles. Remove from heat and serve.

Red Raspberry Sauce

4 (14½-oz.) cans chicken broth
1 (10-oz.) Jar Red Raspberry Jelly
½ cup Ezra Brooks sour mash bourbon
¼ cup Raspberry Wine

2 Tbsp. red peppercorns
¼ tsp. dried thyme
2 Tbsp. reserved pan drippings

Select ripe raspberries. Combine the first 6 ingredients in a saucepan; bring to a boil over high heat. Reduce heat, and simmer for about 1 hour or until the liquid is reduced to 4 cups. Pour the mixture through a fine-wire mesh strainer. Discard seeds. Stir in 2 Tbsp. reserved pan drippings. Makes 4 cups.

Currant Jelly & Brandy Sauce for Venison Roast

any red wine and spice
   marinade
Pan drippings
¾ cup Burgundy
¼ tsp. ground ginger

¼ tsp. ground cloves
1½ tsp. lemon or lime Juice
½ cup Currant Jelly
3 Tbsp. all-purpose flour
1½ Tbsp. brandy

Make the sauce by pouring the liquid left from the strained red wine and spice marinade from the roasting pan into a large saucepan. Add the sauce ingredients and cook over low heat until the Currant Jelly has melted. Raise the heat slightly until the sauce begins to simmer, then lower it Just enough to keep a simmer going. Cook until the sauce is reduced by about ⅓. Pour about 2 or 3 tbsp. of the sauce over each slice of venison.

Remoulade Venison Fondue Sauce

1 cup Mayonnaise
1 hard-boiled egg, chopped fine
1 tsp. dry mustard
1 tsp. anchovy paste

2 tsp. capers
1 tsp. tarragon leaves, chopped
1 tsp. garlic, minced

Place Mayonnaise in a mixing bowl and stir in hard-boiled, chopped eggs. Then stir in dry mustard, anchovy paste, capers, tarragon leaves, and garlic. Stir until anchovy paste disappears. Makes 1 cup.

Sauce Espagnole for Roast Venison

A 1746 American Colonial recipe.

4 Tbsp. butter
1 onion, chopped fine
1 carrot, chopped fine
2 Tbsp. all-purpose flour
½ cup dry white wine

Bouquet Garni
2 Tbsp. tomato paste
4 cups canned beef broth
salt
black pepper

Melt butter in a saucepan and cook onion and carrot until they are browned. Stir in flour; then add wine and 3 cups beef broth. Add bouquet garni and simmer for 1 hour. Remove from heat and strain through cheesecloth. Return the sauce to the pan and add tomato paste, the remaining cup of beef broth, salt, and pepper. Simmer for 30 minutes. Serve hot with roast venison.

Brown Sugar and Lemon Sauce for Venison

½ tsp. teriyaki sauce
1 cup canola oil
½ cup Apple Cider Vinegar
½ cup Homemade Catsup
½ cup Worcestershire sauce
1 tsp. chili powder
1 cup light brown sugar

juice of 2 lemons
1 tsp. tarragon leaves, chopped
1 tsp. garlic, minced
1 tsp. salt
1 tsp. black pepper
1 tsp. red pepper

Mix all ingredients and bring to boil and simmer for 5 minutes. Serve warm on sliced venison. Makes 3½ cups.

Smoked Tomato Salsa

1 (12-oz.) can whole peeled tomatoes, juice reserved
1 large red onion, halved
2 fresh jalapeño peppers
1 bunch fresh cilantro
1 Tbsp. garlic, minced

juice of 2 limes
1 bunch green onions
2 dps. liquid smoke
hot red pepper sauce to taste
salt
black pepper

Smoke whole peeled tomatoes (reserve juice from can) and red onion on a grill or smoker for about 20 minutes. Let cool. Dice tomatoes and onions, and place in blender with reserved juice from can. Seed jalapeños and add to blender with cilantro, garlic, lime juice, and green onion. Puree about 1 minute. Season to taste with hot red pepper sauce and salt and pepper.

Spicy Tomato Catsup Sauce for Venison

1 cup tomato catsup
3 cups water from soaking vegetables
3 Tbsp. sugar
2 tsp. salt

1 Tbsp. onion, chopped
mix pinches of ground cloves, allspice, mace and cayenne pepper to make ¼ tsp.

Mix all ingredients and bring to the boiling point.

Mrs. Ann Lynch Webster

Orange and Italian Tomato Sauce

1 cup fresh tomatoes, peeled, seeded
  and chopped
1 cup canned Italian tomatoes seeded,
  drained and chopped
1 large seedless orange
1½ tsp. olive oil
3 large garlic cloves, minced
½ tsp. ground cumin

¼ tsp. ground coriander
⅛ tsp. pepper flakes
1 tsp. tomato paste
½ tsp. salt
¼ tsp. sugar
black pepper
½ cup green onion, sliced

Chop tomatoes and allow to drain. Peel orange and make seven 2" wide strips. Finely chop 3 strips (set ½ tsp. aside) and set the other 4 aside. Remove each orange section and cut in thirds and set aside to drain (save orange Juice). Heat oil in a sauté pan and add garlic, cumin, coriander, pepper flakes, and 4 strips of orange peel; sauté for less than one minute. Add orange sections, tomatoes, tomato paste, salt and sugar and sauté for 2 to 3 minutes. Remove and discard the orange strips. Add black pepper, onion and saved chopped orange peel. Add salt and pepper to taste. Makes about 2 cups.

Tomato Sauce

¼ cup canola oil
½ cup onion, chopped
½ cup green pepper, chopped
¾ cup carrots, diced
¾ cup celery, diced
1 clove garlic, chopped fine
2½ cups (No, 2 can) whole canned
  tomatoes

1 can tomato paste
1 tsp. salt
¼ tsp. black pepper
⅛ tsp. ground cloves
dash red pepper
1 bay leaf

Heat oil in a heavy skillet and add onion, green pepper, carrots, celery, and garlic; cook until lightly browned. Add the remainder of the ingredients and simmer over low heat, uncovered, about 1 hour or until thickened. Serve with venison spaghetti or with other venison sandwiches.

White Cream Gravy

2 tsp. bacon fat or pan drippings
½ tsp. all-purpose flour
1 cup half & half

salt
black pepper

Melt fat and remove from heat. Whisk the flour into the milk and slowly add to the fat, stirring constantly, until thick. Cook over direct heat 5 minutes, stirring occasionally. Add salt and pepper to taste.

Wild Mint Sauce

1 cup wild mint leaves, chopped
2 Tbsp. sugar
¼ tsp. salt

¾ cup white vinegar
¼ cup lemon or lime juice

Process mint leaves in a food processor until chopped fine, then mash mint into sugar and salt. Add the white vinegar and lemon juice. Set aside for 4 to 6 hours before using.

Wild Onion Sauce

¼ cup real butter
1½ cups wild onions, sliced thin

¼ cup port or sherry

Melt the butter in a small sauté pan. As soon as the butter begins to change color, add the wild onions. Lower the heat, and sauté until they are just slightly crisp, pour in wine. Bring to a simmer and serve over broiled venison.

Yellow Tomato Salsa

3 large yellow tomatoes, diced
1 med. white onion, diced
2 fresh jalapeño peppers, diced
1 bunch cilantro
1 Tbsp. garlic chopped fine

juice of 2 limes
salt
pepper
Tabasco sauce

Place vegetables in a blender and puree 1 minute. Season with salt, pepper and Tabasco sauce to taste.

Whitetail deer antlers are one of the fastest growing tissues known, having been recorded to grow as fast as ½ inch per day. While a whitetail's antlers are growing, they are soft and covered with velvet, a living tissue that supplies blood to the antlers. Bucks shed their antlers annually, usually in January or February, after the breeding season. A new pair of antlers will start growing in the spring. By August or early September, antlers are fully-grown and become hard once the velvet falls off.

Wine, Mushroom & Pecan
Venison Roast Sauce

1 cup seedless white grapes
1 cup water
4 Tbsp. real butter
½ cup ruby or tawny port

⅛ tsp. ground cloves
2 Tbsp, mushrooms, chopped fine
½ cup pecans, chopped fine

Place grapes and water in a saucepan and bring to a boil. Reduce heat and simmer for 5 minutes. Drain off water and add the butter, wine and cloves. Cover and simmer for 5 minutes. Stir in mushrooms and simmer for 5 minutes. Stir In pecans and simmer for 5 minutes. Serve immediately over sliced venison roast. Makes 2½ cups.

Venison Soufflé Cream Sauce

3 Tbsp. butter
3 Tbsp. all-purpose flour
1 cup whole milk
1 small yellow onion

3 whole cloves
1 small bay leaf
salt
white pepper

Melt butter over low heat. Blend in flour and heat for 4 minutes; allow to cool. Scald milk. Stir milk into butter and flour mixture very slowly. Stud onion with whole cloves. Add onion and bay leaf to mixture. Cook and stir the sauce with a whisk until thickened and smooth. Place in a 350-degree oven and cook slowly for 20 minutes. Strain the sauce. Season to taste with salt and white pepper. Makes 1 cup.

Venison Soufflé Tomato Sauce

3 Tbsp. olive oil
1 large Vidalia or yellow onion, chopped
2 celery ribs with leaves, chopped
1 carrot, cut into small pieces
½ green bell pepper, chopped
1 garlic clove, chopped

6 large tomatoes, peeled, seeded and
   drained
1 sprig thyme
1 tsp. salt
⅛ tsp. pepper
1 tsp. sugar

Heat olive oil over low heat. Add onion, celery, carrots, green bell pepper and garlic; heat and stir for 3 minutes. Add tomatoes, thyme, salt, pepper and sugar; cook gently, uncovered until thick. Stir frequently to keep bottom from burning. Put sauce through a strainer. Add additional seasonings if needed.

26

Side Dishes

These side dishes are some of the author's favorites. Venison can be prepared and served at any time of day and for any occasion. These side dishes were developed and selected to complement venison.

There is a side dish which will complement every venison occasion. Some of these early American recipes were served with venison by the English, French, and Spanish colonists prior to the 1700s. Explore Abigail Adams' 1774, Winter Squash Soup and the 1750 Hot Potato Salad. If you have been unsure about whether or not you like sweet potatoes, Trudy Webster Lipscomb's Sweet Potato Soufflé will make you a lifetime devotee of this sweet potato recipe.

Enjoy these recipes and experiment. Preparing venison may be a new experience for you. So why not go all out and explore new side dishes also. You will not be disappointed.

Baked Cheese Grits

This simple, cheesy side dish is wonderful with breakfast—and the garlic gives it added zip.

3 cups water
¾ cup Quaker Quick Grits, uncooked
¼ tsp. salt
1 egg, beaten
1 cup (4 oz.) shredded cheddar cheese

2 Tbsp. margarine
⅛ tsp. garlic powder
dash red pepper sauce or ground red
 pepper

Heat oven to 350 degrees. Grease 1½-quart casserole or baking dish. Prepare grits according to package directions. Add small amount of grits to beaten egg. Return grits mixture to pan. Add remaining ingredients. Cook over low heat an additional minute or until cheese is melted. Pour into prepared casserole; bake 30 to 40 minutes, or until top is set and lightly puffed. Let stand 5 minutes before serving. Serves 4 to 6.

 *The Key Deer (Odocoileus virginianusls) of Florida lives in isolation on Big Pine Key. The harsh sub-tropical island environment has produced a smaller-than-average deer, seldom exceeding 30 inches in height.*

Italian Style Boiled Beans

2 cups dried cannellini beans or lentils
water
6 cups cold water

1 Tbsp. olive oil
1 medium garlic clove, minced
coarse salt

Cover beans with cold water and soak overnight. Pour beans into a colander and allow to drain. In a large saucepan, add 6 cups of water and soaked beans, oil, garlic and salt and bring to boil. Reduce heat, cover and simmer until beans are tender, about 2 hours. Serve hot. Makes about 6 cups.

Boiled Rice

To make rice in any volume; use 2 parts water to 1 part rice.

2½ cups water
½ tsp. salt

2 tsp. olive oil
1¼ cups long grain rice

Bring water, salt and olive oil to a rolling boil. Add rice. Stir briefly. Reduce heat to a low simmer. Cover and cook for 18 minutes. Do not uncover during cooking. Before serving, fluff cooked rice with a fork. Serves 3 to 4.

Boston Baked Beans

This is a 1764 Colonial American recipe.

4 cups pea beans
1 large onion, studded with 8 cloves
½ lb salt pork
1 cup brown sugar

3 tsp. dry mustard
2 tsp. salt
1 tsp. pepper
½ cup dark molasses

Soak beans in water overnight. Drain in a colander. Place beans in a large saucepan; cover beans with water and cook until the skins burst when blown on. Drain the beans and place in a ceramic bean pot. Press the onion into the center of the beans until it is just covered. Make long cuts into the salt pork every ½" and spread out. Push salt pork slightly below the surface of the beans. Pour ¾ cup brown sugar, mustard, salt, pepper, and molasses mixture over the beans. Pour 1 cup of boiling water over the beans; stir slowly. Add enough boiling water to cover the beans. Cover the bean pot and bake in the oven at 250 degrees for 4 to 5 hours. Uncover for the last half hour. Sprinkle with the remaining brown sugar to brown and crisp the pork. Add water as needed during baking. Serves 10 to 12.

Brown Rice Pilau

1½ cups brown rice
3 cups canned chicken broth
1 tsp. turmeric, ground
⅓ cup currants, dried
¼ cup Madeira wine

½ cup green onions, chopped
⅓ cup pinion pine nuts
1½ Tbsp. dried gingerroot, minced
2 Tbsp. real butter

Cook rice in chicken broth and ground turmeric until done, about 45 minutes. Remove from heat and add the rest of ingredients. Let rice stand for 15 minutes before serving. Serves 4 to 6.

Carrot Soup with Sherry and Sour Cream

13 carrots, sliced in ½" pieces
8 potatoes, diced into cubes
3 ozs. unsalted butter
½ cup white onion, diced
1 Tbsp. garlic, chopped
1 tsp. ground coriander
4 cups canned chicken broth

½ tsp. sugar
¼ tsp. salt
2 cups whole milk
black pepper
3 Tbsp. sherry
½ cup sour cream
¼ cup fresh cilantro, chopped

Melt butter in a large saucepan over medium-low heat; add the onion and sauté until just tender. Add the garlic and sauté until just tender. Add the carrots, potatoes and coriander and sauté for about 2 to 3 minutes. Add the chicken broth, sugar and salt; partially cover and cook over medium heat until the vegetables are soft. When cooked, remove vegetables and broth, and process in a food processor in small batches to a smooth puree. Return the vegetables to the saucepan and add the milk and pepper to taste. Place over medium heat and heat almost to a boil. Taste for seasoning and adjust if necessary. If too thick, add more milk. Just before serving, stir in the sherry. Ladle soup into warm soup bowls with 3 Tbsp. sour cream and a generous sprinkling of chopped cilantro on top. Serves 6 to 8.

Cauliflower du Barry

1 head of cauliflower
1 cup Mashed Potatoes
¼ cup cream
2 Tbsp. real butter

salt
black pepper
Beurre Meuniere Sauce
1 Tbsp. parsley, chopped

Break the cauliflower into sections and cook in salted water until just tender. Drain and puree in a food processor. Mix cauliflower, potatoes, cream, and butter. Season with salt and pepper. Serve from a large serving platter and cover with Beurre Meuniere Sauce. Sprinkle with chopped parsley. Serves 6 to 8.

Southern Corn Pudding

4 cups fresh sweet cut corn	¼ lb. real butter
4 eggs	salt and pepper
1 Tbsp. pimento, diced	paprika
1 cup whole milk	2 Tbsp. green bell pepper, diced

Cut corn from fresh sweet cob and then scrape and save the juice until you have 4 cups of corn and liquid. Canned cream-style corn or whole kernel corn, or a combination of the two may be substituted. Beat eggs and add to corn with pimento and bell pepper. Pour milk, add salt and pepper and mix thoroughly. Spread ⅓ of this mixture in the bottom of a casserole. Dot with pads of butter. Repeat with two more layers. After the butter has been added to the top layer, sprinkle generously with paprika. Bake in a 350-degree oven until firm.

Cranberry-Rice Stuffing

A 1760 American Colonial recipe from the New England colonies.

1 (6-oz.) pkg. long-grain and wild-rice mix	¼ cup sugar
1 cup fresh cranberries	1 tsp. orange rind, grated
1 cup celery, sliced thin	⅓ cup green onions, chopped

Cook rice with its enclosed seasonings according to package directions. Add fresh cranberries and heat till they begin to split. Stir in the rest of the ingredients. Mix well and spoon into a greased or oiled 4-cup casserole dish. Cover and bake in 350-degree oven for 30 to 40 minutes. Excellent accompaniment to venison roasts. Serves 6 to 8.

Senegalese-Style Creme Soup

A spicy cold-weather soup that will warm the whole body.

½ cup real butter	2 Tbsp. Worcestershire sauce
½ cup all-purpose flour	1 tsp. salt
½ cup curry powder	½ tsp. cayenne pepper
8 cups whole milk	parsley, chopped

Melt butter in a 4-quart saucepan and stir in flour. Cook over low heat for 10 to 12 minutes stirring constantly, but do not brown. Blend in curry powder and cook for 1 to 2 minutes more, stirring constantly. Slowly add milk, stirring constantly to keep smooth. Add Worcestershire sauce, salt and pepper; simmer for 10 minutes. Remove from heat; strain through 3 layers of cheesecloth. Serve hot and garnish with chopped parsley. Makes about 2 quarts.

Creme Vichyssoise Glace

4 leeks
1 white onion, sliced
2 Tbsp. butter
6 medium potatoes, sliced
1 qt. canned chicken broth

1 Tbsp. salt
2 cups whole milk
1 cup half & half
1 cup heavy cream
chives, chopped fine

Wash leeks very carefully and discard green stalks. Slice the white part, combine with onion, and cook in melted butter until limp but not brown. Add potato slices, chicken broth, and salt. Bring to a boil and boil 35 minutes. Rub through a fine strainer or puree in an electric blender, return to heat, and add milk and half & half cream. Season to taste and bring to a boil; do not cook further. Finally, add the whipping cream and chill thoroughly in the refrigerator. Serve in cups with a sprinkling of finely chopped chives on top. Serves 8.

Mrs. Ann Lynch Webster

Old Style Yams

4 boiled sweet potatoes
¼ cup real butter
2 slices of lemon or lime

½ cup sugar
½ cup water
red food coloring

Peel and slice the yams in about ¼" thick slices. Make a syrup by cooking butter, water, lemons and sugar for about 3 minutes, and add one drop of red food coloring. Put sliced yams in a shallow baking dish and pour the syrup over them. Bake in a 350-degree oven for about 30 minutes. Spoon the syrup over the yams two or three times during the baking. The food coloring gives the yams a bright and fresh look.

Potatoes—Rue Royal

½ cup boiling water
⅓ cup real butter, melted
pinch salt
½ cup all-purpose flour

1 egg
¾ tsp. salt
¼ tsp. fresh ground nutmeg
1¾ cups cooked, mashed potatoes

Boil water over high heat in a medium-sized saucepan, then reduce heat to low and add the butter, salt and flour, stirring constantly until the mixture forms a compact ball. Remove the saucepan from heat and allow to cool to air temperature. Add egg, salt, nutmeg and beat until it is smooth. Add the mashed potatoes and mix thoroughly. Chill in the refrigerator. Roll mixture into 1½" balls and drop into hot fat and fry until golden brown. Serves 4 to 6.

Deviled Eggs

6 hard-boiled eggs, cut into halves
½ tsp. salt
½ tsp. black pepper
½ tsp. dry mustard

2 tsp. parsley, minced
2 Tbsp. chopped sweet pickles
about 3 Tbsp. Mayonnaise

Mash egg yolks and mix with all other Ingredients. Refill egg whites with mixture. Garnish with a sprinkling of paprika. Refrigerate. Serve cold. Deviled eggs can turn bad very quickly in warm weather. Makes 12 Deviled Egg halves.

An 1890s recipe of Mrs. Anna Lilly Sinclair Lynch

Eggplant Pie

2 eggs
2 cups boiled eggplant, peeled and mashed
½ cup bread crumbs
2 Tbsp. real butter
1 tsp. fresh thyme, chopped
1 Tbsp. parsley, chopped

1 Tbsp. onion, sautéed
salt and pepper to taste
½ cup cracker crumbs
2 Tbsp. sharp cheese, grated
1 Tbsp. real butter

Beat the eggs and add them to the eggplant. Add the bread crumbs, butter, thyme, parsley, onion, salt, and pepper. Pour the eggplant mixture into a greased glass ovenproof dish, sprinkle with cracker crumbs, and grated sharp cheese, and dot with butter. Bake in a 350-degree oven until golden brown. Serves 6 to 8.

Eggs with Roquefort Cheese and Green Onion Stuffing

4 hard boiled eggs
2 Tbsp. crumbled Roquefort cheese
1 tsp. prepared mustard
1 tsp. green onion, chopped fine
½ tsp. rosemary leaves

2 Tbsp. Mayonnaise
salt
pepper
paprika

Hard boil eggs and allow to cool. Remove the shell from the eggs. Split the eggs lengthwise and remove the yolks. Combine the yolks with the cheese, mustard, chives, rosemary and mayonnaise. Mix very well. Season to taste with salt and pepper. Fill egg whites with the cheese and onion mixture. Sprinkle a little paprika on top of each egg filling. Makes 8 stuffed egg halves.

Onion Pie - Idaho Style

4 eggs, slightly beaten
1⅔ cups sour cream
1 (2-oz.) jar pimento, drained and finely
    chopped
1 tsp. caraway seed
1 envelope onion soup mix
1 cup Cheddar cheese, shredded
1½ cups all-purpose flour

½ cup Pillsbury Hungry Jack Mashed
    Potato Flakes
½ tsp. baking soda
½ tsp. salt
½ tsp. garlic salt
½ cup butter
⅓ cup sour cream
6 strips crisp bacon, crumbled

Make filling by mixing together eggs, sour cream pimiento, caraway seed, onion soup mix and Cheddar cheese. Set aside and make pie crust. In a large mixing bowl; mix dry ingredients. Cut in butter until mixture resembles coarse crumbs. Add sour cream, stirring until dough forms into a ball. Press into 12-inch pizza pan. Bake at 375 degrees for 12 to 15 minutes. (Can be baked in 10-inch pie pan at 375 degrees for 30 to 35 minutes or until center is firm.) Remove from oven. Stir filling and pour over crust. Sprinkle bacon evenly over filling. Return to oven. Bake 25 to 30 minutes longer. Serve warm.

French Omelet

4 eggs
¼ cup whole milk
½ tsp. salt

dash black pepper
1 Tbsp. butter

Mix eggs, milk, salt and pepper with a fork. Heat butter in 10" omelet pan or skillet until just hot enough to sizzle a drop of water. Pour in egg mixture. Mixture should set at edges at once. With pancake turner, carefully draw cooked portions at edges toward center, so uncooked portions flow to bottom. Tilt skillet as it is necessary to hasten flow of uncooked eggs. Slide pan rapidly back and forth over heat to keep mixture in motion and sliding freely. While top is still moist and creamy-looking, with pancake turner fold in half or roll, turning out onto platter with a quick flip of the wrist. Serves 2.

Harold W. Webster, Sr.

Fried Grits

A traditional Southern use for leftover grits.

Prepare 6 servings of grits as package directs. Pour into 8"x4" or 9"x5" loaf pan. Cover; refrigerate several hours or overnight. Unmold; cut into ½" thick slices. In small amount of margarine or drippings, fry grits over medium-high heat about 10 minutes per side, or until golden brown. Serve with syrup. Serves 6.

Fried Red or Green Tomatoes

A 1781 American Colonial recipe.

½ cup yellow cornmeal
½ cup all-purpose flour
2 Tbsp. sugar
1 tsp. salt

¼ tsp. black pepper
very firm red or green tomato slices
Crisco

Mix all ingredients except tomatoes. Coat both sides of tomato slices with cornmeal mixture. Fry in melted Crisco until brown on both sides. Serve hot.

Garlic Potatoes

1 cup cream
1 whole head of garlic, cloves separated and
   peeled
1½ to 2 lbs. new potatoes

6 Tbsp. butter
salt
black pepper to taste

Bring cream and garlic to a simmer in a large saucepan and cook until reduced by half. Peel and cook potatoes in boiling salted water until very tender. Remove and drain. Puree milk and garlic mixture in a blender. Pass potatoes through a potato press. Add pressed potatoes to the milk mixture, and whip in butter. Season with salt and pepper. Serves 4 to 6.

Pearl Onions, Green Beans,
& Roasted Chestnuts

1 lb. pearl onions, trimmed and peeled
salt
1 lb. green beans, cut into 2" lengths
2 Tbsp. unsalted butter

1 jar (1½ cups) Williams-Sonoma
   whole roasted chestnuts*
1½ tsp. fresh ginger, grated
2 Tbsp. fresh mint leaves, chopped

Fill a saucepan ¾ full of water and bring to a boil. Add the onions and 2 tsp. salt, lower heat and simmer until onions are almost tender, 8 to 12 minutes. Drain and set aside. Fill a large saucepan ¾ full with water and bring to a boil. Add the green beans and 2 tsp. salt and cook until the beans are bright green and just tender, about 5 to 7 minutes. Drain the beans and plunge into cold water to stop the cooking. Drain and set aside. Just before serving: In a large sauté pan, or deep frying pan, over medium-high heat, melt butter. When hot, add the onions and chestnuts and sauté, stirring occasionally, until lightly golden, about 12 to 15 minutes. Add the beans, ginger and mint and continue to cook while tossing until very hot. Season to taste with salt and pepper. Transfer to a warm serving dish and serve immediately. Serves 6 to 8.

*(see appendix for source)

Pan Fried Potatoes

From Harold W. Webster, Sr., an old Oak Ridge, Mississippi Webster family recipe, circa 1850.

3 large potatoes, sliced ¼" thick   salt
canola oil (lard was originally used)   pepper

Fry potato slices in canola oil in a heavy skillet until golden brown. Remove cooked potatoes and drain on paper towels. Serves 4.

Hot Potato Salad

A 1750 American Colonial recipe.

8 potatoes
1 stalk of celery, diced
2 hard-boiled eggs, sliced
1 white onion, minced
2 Tbsp. Dijon mustard
1 Tbsp. fresh parsley, minced
4 slices bacon, diced

2 eggs, well beaten
1 cup sugar
½ tsp. salt
¼ tsp. black pepper
½ cup vinegar, diluted with ½ cup
    water

Boil, peel and dice the potatoes. Add the celery, hard-boiled eggs, onion, mustard, and parsley. Fry the bacon until it is crisp; remove bacon and crumble. Beat the eggs; then add the sugar, salt, pepper, and vinegar and water. Mix well. Pour the egg mixture into the hot bacon fat and stir until the mixture thickens. Pour over the potato mixture and mix lightly. Add crisp bacon. Serves 10 to 12.

Mashed Potatoes

My grandmother told me that this was one of my great grandfather's favorite dishes. From the late 1890s to the 1930s, Tom was the engineer on the Southern Railroad passenger train run from Meridian, Mississippi to New Orleans, Louisiana. The story, as it was told to me, was that one evening in 1910, Tom came home for dinner after a run and was served mashed potatoes. He stated that was not the way that they were served at the Roosevelt Hotel in New Orleans. He went out in the yard and cut the tops off the wild onions growing in the front yard, went back into the kitchen and chopped them up and added them to the mashed potatoes.

6 medium-sized potatoes, pared
water
½ tsp. salt
2½ Tbsp. butter, melted

3½ Tbsp, chives or wild onions,
    chopped
¼ cup heavy cream

Wash potatoes, remove sprouts and blemishes, then peel. Cook potatoes covered 30 to 40 minutes in salted water until tender. Put potatoes, butter and chives through a food processor, blender, electric mixer or potato ricer. Add cream and beat with fork or heavy whisk until the potatoes are creamy. To help fluff potatoes, place in pan, cover, and place over very low heat about 5 minutes. Serves 6.

Mashed Potatoes & Turnips

As the first grandchild, I had the honor of naming Nanny. Born on January 1, 1900, Nanny was one of those rare individuals who worked all her life, never had very much, never complained, and always had all the riches that this life could give. This 1918 recipe was served on special occasions by Mrs. Clyde Lacy Lynch.

2 potatoes, peeled and sliced	2 Tbsp. oil
2 turnips, peeled and sliced	salt
2 cups turnip greens, washed and chopped	black pepper
1 Tbsp. garlic, minced	Tabasco sauce to taste

Boil potatoes and turnips in lightly salted water. Drain and mash. Place in a saucepan; keep warm. Sauté the greens and garlic in olive oil for about 10 minutes, until wilted. Puree in a food processor; stir into potato-turnip mixture. Season to taste with salt, pepper and Tabasco sauce. Makes 4 servings.

Mashed Potatoes and Parsnips Royal

3 lbs. potatoes, peeled and cut into large chunks	salt
	⅓ to ¾ cup whole milk, warmed
2 parsnips peeled and cut into ½" thick pieces	black pepper
	fresh parsley sprigs, chopped

In a large heavy saucepan put the cut potatoes and parsnips and cover by 1" with water. Add 2 tsp. salt and bring to a boil over medium-high heat. Reduce heat to medium and boil until they are tender. Remove potatoes and parsnips and drain well. Using a potato press, press the potatoes through. Return the mashed potatoes to the saucepan and return to low heat. Gradually add the milk, a little at a time, and beat until the potatoes are smooth and fluffy. They should not be soupy. Season with salt and pepper to taste. Set aside and keep warm. Spoon the potatoes into a serving dish and sprinkle parsley on the top. Serves 6 to 8.

Potato Croquettes

2 cups Irish potatoes, cooked and mashed
1 egg yolk
1 tsp. parsley, minced
1 egg
2 Tbsp. real butter
salt

paprika
½ tsp. onion juice (scrape onion with
   a spoon)
bread crumbs
green onions, minced

Combine mashed potatoes with butter, egg yolk, seasonings, and flavorings. Make into either round or cone-shaped croquettes. Dip croquettes into egg, then into bread crumbs and fry golden brown in deep hot fat. Drain and garnish with chopped green onions. Serves 4.

Mrs. Ann Lynch Webster

Potato Dumplings

2 cups potatoes cooked and riced
2 Tbsp. all-purpose flour
1 Tbsp, melted Crisco
1 egg, slightly beaten

½ tsp. salt
dash black pepper
⅛ tsp, ground nutmeg

Combine and mix all ingredients thoroughly. Divide the mixture into 12 equal portions and shape into balls and chill in the refrigerator. Drop into gently boiling stew or sauerbraten, Cover and steam for about 12 minutes. Makes 12 medium-sized dumplings.

Primos' Creamy Grits

Primos Restaurant at North State and Fortification Streets, Jackson, Mississippi no longer exists. In 1994 it burned and was not rebuilt. For over fifty years, Primos was famous for its creamy grits. The secret to their grits was their use of Half & Half milk instead of water.

	1 Serving	4 Servings	6 Servings
Half & Half Milk	1 cup	3 cups	4 cups
Quaker Quick Grits	3 Tbsp.	¾ cup	1 cup
Salt	dash	¼ tsp.	½ tsp.

Slowly stir grits and salt into barely boiling milk. Reduce heat to medium-low; cover. Cook 5 to 7 minutes or until thickened, stirring occasionally. Serve with: margarine, butter, cheese, red-eye gravy or as a hot cereal with milk and sugar. Note: Pour leftover grits in a mold and chill overnight; then slice, fry or cook in a toaster oven until golden brown. Serve with syrup for a traditional breakfast.

Red Cherry Omelet Flambé

¾ cup red cherry pie filling
1 French Omelet
1½ tsp, confectioners' sugar

2 Tbsp. brandy
½ tsp. cherry liqueur

Warm pie filling while preparing omelet. Prepare French Omelet. While top is still moist and creamy-looking, spread ¼ cup cherry pie filling on half of omelet. With pancake turner fold omelet in half. Spread omelet with remaining pie filling and sprinkle with confectioners' sugar. Pour brandy over the top of the omelet. With a long match, carefully light brandy by tilting pan so brandy will light. Allow brandy to burn out. Add cherry liqueur. Serve immediately from the pan. Serves 2.

Almond Rice
with Apple-Orange Cranberry Sauce

2½ cups water
½ tsp. salt
2 tsp. olive oil
1¼ cups long-grain rice

1 Tbsp. almond slivers
1 Tbsp. green onions, chopped fine
Apple-Orange Cranberry Sauce

Bring water, salt and olive oil to a rolling boil. Add rice, almond slivers and chives. Stir briefly. Reduce heat to a low simmer. Cover and cook for 20 minutes. Do not uncover during cooking. Before serving, fluff cooked rice with a fork. Serve with Apple-Orange Cranberry Sauce. Serves 3 to 4.

Sautéed Bok-choy

1 small head Chinese cabbage
½ tsp. sugar
2 Tbsp. rice wine

1 tsp. salt
1 tsp. teriyaki sauce
⅓ cup hot water

Wash the cabbage, then slice the stems at an angle into 1" lengths. Reserve the leaves. Sauté the white stems 2 minutes, then add the leaves. Sauté for another minute. Sprinkle with salt and sugar, then add the teriyaki sauce, rice wine, and hot water. Stir, cover and cook for 2 minutes longer. *Do not overcook*, or the cabbage will lose its crunchiness.

Pressed and Baked Shiitake Mushroom and Potato Roundel

2 Tbsp. unsalted butter
¾ lb. fresh shiitake mushrooms, stemmed
    and sliced
⅓ cup Parmesan cheese, freshly grated

1 Tbsp. fresh basil chopped
2 large potatoes, peeled, sliced thin
    crosswise
salt and black pepper

Preheat the oven to 350 degrees. Line cookie sheet with aluminum foil and butter. Melt 2 Tbsp. butter in heavy large skillet over medium heat, add the shiitake mushrooms and sauté until they are just tender. Add the Parmesan cheese and basil.

Arrange half of potato slices in 9" round pile on the buttered foil, overlapping the potato slices. Cover with mushroom mixture, pressing as flat as possible. Season with salt and pepper. Lay on another layer of potato slices. Cover with another piece of buttered foil and another cookie sheet. Place a brick or a heavy pot filled with water on top of the cookie sheet. Bake until the potatoes are tender (a little more than 1 hour). Remove from the oven and allow to cool, leave the brick and the top cookie sheet in place. Preheat the oven broiler. Remove the brick, top cookie sheet and top piece of aluminum foil. Broil roundel until crisp and brown, about 2 minutes per side. Cut into 6 to 8 wedges. Serves 6 to 8.

Spanish Rice

½ cup green pepper, chopped
¾ cup white onion, chopped
⅓ cup ham, chopped
½ tsp. Spanish saffron
⅓ cup real butter

3 cups Boiled Rice
½ tsp. white pepper
⅓ cup pimiento, chopped
1 Tbsp. liquid from pimiento

In a 9" skillet over medium heat, sauté green pepper, onion, ham and saffron in butter until just tender. Stir in Boiled Rice, white pepper, pimiento and pimiento liquid, continue cooking until heated through. Serves 4 to 6.

Squash and Peanut Pie

A 1798 American Colonial recipe.

3 lbs. tender young squash
1 medium white onion, chopped fine
¼ cup butter
½ cup cream
1 tsp. salt

½ tsp. grated nutmeg
⅛ tsp. cayenne pepper
½ cup salted peanuts, chopped fine
½ cup dry bread crumbs
2 Tbsp. real butter, melted

Slice the unpeeled squash. Cover the sliced squash with water and boil until just tender. Remove squash and drain. Mash or mix in a blender the squash; add onion, butter, cream, salt, nutmeg, cayenne pepper, and ¼ cup of the peanuts. Pour into a buttered pie plate or a shallow baking dish. Combine remaining ¼ cup of peanuts, bread crumbs, and melted butter. Sprinkle over the squash mixture. Bake in a 375-degree oven for 30 minutes or until the top is lightly browned. Serves 6 to 8.

Stuffed Baked Potatoes

2 large potatoes
4 strips bacon, quartered
¼ cup green onion, chopped
2 Tbsp. Parmesan cheese, grated
½ cup sour cream

½ tsp. salt
½ tsp. white pepper
real butter, melted
paprika

Bake potatoes in a 400-degree oven for 1 hour. While the potatoes are cooling slightly, fry the bacon pieces until crisp. Drain off the excess bacon drippings; leaving 3 Tbsp. in the skillet. Add the onion and sauté slowly. Remove the skillet from heat. Cut a lengthwise slice in each potato and carefully spoon out the insides. Mix potato pulp cheese, sour cream, salt and pepper. Press potato and cheese mixture through a potato ricer. Return mixture to skillet and heat through. Stuff the mixture into the potato shells and drizzle with butter and dash of paprika. Bake at 350 degrees for 15 to 20 minutes. Serves 2.

Sweet Potato Croquettes with Walnut Topping

2 cups sweet potatoes, mashed
1 egg yolk
1 tsp. parsley, minced
1 egg
2 Tbsp. real butter
salt

paprika
½ tsp. onion juice
1 egg, lightly beaten
bread crumbs
shortening for frying
walnut meat, sliced fine

Mix potatoes with butter, egg yolk, seasonings, and flavorings. Form into croquettes into small loaf shapes. Dip croquettes into the egg, then into the bread crumbs and fry golden brown in deep hot fat. Drain and garnish with walnut slices.

Sweet Potato Soufflé

Mrs. Trudy Webster Lipscomb. This is the sweet potato recipe that I really love.

2 cups cooked sweet potatoes, mashed
1½ cups sugar
2 eggs, beaten
½ cup milk
6 Tbsp. butter, softened
½ tsp. cinnamon

½ tsp. nutmeg
½ cup Rice Krispies
½ cup pecans, chopped
6 Tbsp. butter
½ cup packed brown sugar

Combine sweet potatoes, sugar, eggs, milk, softened butter and seasonings in a bowl; mix well. Spoon into 10" buttered casserole. Combine Rice Krispies, pecans, remaining 6 Tbsp. butter and brown sugar in small bowl; mix until crumbly. Sprinkle over sweet potato mixture. Pre-heat oven to 350 degrees and bake for 20 minutes. Serves 6. When recipe is doubled, use a 9"x13" buttered casserole.

Imgedara

This is the dish for which Essau sold his birthright.

1 cup lentils
1 onion
1 Tbsp. butter

¾ cup rice
saltwater

Wash lentils and let them soak in cold water several hours. Then boil until tender. Brown the sliced onion in butter, add to the lentils with rice, and salt to taste; cook until rice is done, adding enough water to make the thickness of succotash.

Traditional Dumplings

2 cups sifted all-purpose flour
1 Tbsp. baking powder
1 tsp. salt

1 Tbsp. real butter
¾ cup whole milk

Mix and sift together flour, baking powder and salt. Cut in butter. Make a cavity in the center of the flour and pour in milk. Using fingertips mix everything together using a folding motion. Have stew gently simmering. Drop tbsp. full of the batter into the stew. Cover at once and allow the dumplings to steam for 15 to 20 minutes. Dumplings can be served on the side with gravy.

Turnips Au Gratin

1½ lbs. (4 cups) turnips, pared and sliced
3 Tbsp. real butter
¼ cup onion, chopped
¼ cup green bell pepper, chopped
¼ cup celery, chopped
3 Tbsp. all-purpose flour
1 cup cream

½ cup sharp Cheddar cheese, grated
salt
pepper
seasoned bread crumbs
paprika
snipped parsley

Cook turnips in boiling/salted water until tender. Remove to a colander and drain. Melt butter and sauté vegetables until golden. Blend flour in slowly. Add cream to make the desired consistency. Add cheese and salt and pepper, cook over low heat until the cheese is melted into sauce. Place turnips in a serving bowl and pour cheese mixture over. Top with seasoned bread crumbs. Dust top with paprika and sprinkle with parsley bits.

Mule deer of both sexes normally do most of their feeding in early morning before sunrise, or in late afternoon and evening after sundown. They spend the middle of the day bedded down in cool, secluded places.

Tuscany Bean Hors D'Oeuvres

1 clove garlic	pepper
¼ cup onion	Tabasco sauce
¼ cup parsley	4 oz. pimentos, drained, coarsely 1 can
white kidney beans, drained	chopped
2 Tbsp. lemon juice	4 bagels, halved
salt	stuffed green olives, sliced

Finely chop garlic, onion and parsley in a food processor. Add kidney beans and lemon juice; salt, pepper and Tabasco sauce to taste. Process until beans are just smooth. Fold in pimento pieces. Lightly butter and toast bagels and cut each into 8 pieces. Fill a large tipped pastry bag with bean mixture and make a rosette on each bagel piece. Place a stuffed green olive slice on the side of each rosette. Serve cool.

Mr. Hank Holmes

Wild Onion Soup

½ stick butter	1 qt. canned beef broth
1 cup wild onions, sliced thin	sourdough bread
1 Tbsp. all-purpose flour	Parmesan cheese, grated

Melt butter in a saucepan and brown onions until just tender. Sprinkle onions with the flour and cook over low heat until done. Add the beef broth and cook over low heat until the onion is tender. Cut 4 slices of sourdough bread as thin as possible. Cover the bread with a generous amount of freshly grated Parmesan cheese and melt this quickly under the broiler. Place the soup in a warm soup tureen and float toasted bread slices on top.

Winter Squash Soup

A 1764 Colonial American recipe by Abigail Adams, Quincy, Massachusetts.

3 large onions, chopped	1 tsp. fresh rosemary
1 cup celery, chopped	1 tsp. fresh savory
1 clove garlic	2 Tbsp. fresh parsley, chopped
4 Tbsp. butter	2 cups cream
3 cups canned chicken broth	salt and pepper to taste
2 cups cooked squash, mashed	fresh grated nutmeg

Sauté onions, celery, and garlic until done in 2 Tbsp. of the butter. Add to chicken broth with cooked squash, rosemary, savory, and parsley. Bring to a boil; simmer for 10 minutes. Add 2 Tbsp. butter. Remove from the heat and add cream. Season with salt and pepper. Sprinkle with nutmeg and serve in a warmed soup tureen. Serves 6 to 8.

27

Salads

Anne's Favorite Salad

6 leaves of iceberg lettuce
1 cup no fat cottage cheese
1 banana sliced into 4 pieces
6 strawberries, cleaned and quartered
2 fresh, 1" slices pineapple, cubed

Poppy Seed Dressing
salt
pepper
2 maraschino cherries

Break lettuce into bite-sized pieces. Place ½ of the lettuce in each bowl. Arrange ½ cup of the cottage cheese across the center of the lettuce. Group ½ of the bananas, strawberries, and pineapple around the edge of the cottage cheese. Pour Poppy Seed Dressing across the top of each salad; sprinkle lightly with salt and pepper. Center a cherry on the top of the cottage cheese. Serve cold from the refrigerator. Serves 2.

Cole Slaw

4 cups cabbage, shredded
½ cup mayonnaise
2 Tbsp. lemon juice
1 Tbsp. onion, grated
½ tsp. celery seed

1 tsp. sugar
½ tsp. salt
⅛ tsp. pepper
paprika
green onion rings

Shred cabbage and crisp in ice water. Combine mayonnaise, lemon juice, grated onion, celery seed, sugar, salt and pepper. Drain cabbage thoroughly and mix with the dressing. Serve in lettuce cups. Garnish with a dash of paprika and green onion rings. Makes 6 to 8 servings.

Mrs. Clyde Lacy Lynch

The only female deer that regularly grow antlers are reindeer. Farm-raised reindeer are curious and friendly animals. They are easy to fence, feed, and train to pull, so are often used for exhibitions at Christmastime.

Greek Potato Salad

3 med. potatoes, sliced ¼" thick
1 cup dried tomato halves, cut
Lemon Dressing
1 cup cucumber, sliced

½ cup red onion, sliced
1 cup (4 oz.) feta cheese, crumbled
½ cup Greek olives

In a 2-qt. saucepan, cook potatoes, covered in 2" boiling water over medium heat until tender. Drain and set aside. Cover tomatoes with boiling water and soak at least 10 minutes. Make Lemon Dressing. Drain tomatoes and pat dry. Add potatoes, tomatoes and cucumber to dressing and toss. Mound potato mixture on a plate. Arrange onion, cheese and olives on top. Serves 4.

Mrs. Ann Lynch Webster

Red and Green Cabbage Cole Slaw

½ head red cabbage
½ head green cabbage
vinegar
sugar
mayonnaise
whole milk

Dijon mustard
salt
pepper
poppyseed
1 green bell pepper, chopped fine

Slice and chop cabbage as finely as possible. Mix equal amounts of vinegar, sugar, mayonnaise, and milk, seasoned with a little Dijon mustard, salt, pepper, and poppyseed. Mix peppers with cabbage and pour in enough dressing to saturate cabbage well. Let stand overnight in the refrigerator. Serves 4.

Mrs. Ann Lynch Webster

Broiled Lemon Salad

4 lemons
¼ cup sugar
1 bunch parsley, washed and dried

¼ cup extra virgin olive oil
salt
pepper

Slice the ends off of the lemons. Slice the lemons into the thinnest possible rounds; remove the seeds. Combine lemon and sugar in a small bowl and mix well. Let stand for 2 hours. Pick leaves off the stems of the parsley. Grill the lemon slices over a medium to low fire or place lemon rounds in a single layer on a cookie sheet and broil until slightly browned. Remove lemon rounds and combine with parsley, olive oil; salt and pepper to taste. Toss gently. Serves 4.

Mrs. Ann Lynch Webster

Potato Fresh Spice Salad

1½ lbs. potatoes, well scrubbed
½ to ¾ cup olive oil
2 Tbsp. fresh rosemary, finely chopped
2 Tbsp. fresh basil, chopped fine

2 Tbsp. fresh chives, chopped fine
1 Tbsp. garlic, minced
salt and pepper to taste
Balsamic vinegar to taste

Cook potatoes in boiling water until tender. Slice potatoes while still warm. Place potatoes in a large bowl and add the next 5 ingredients, seasoning with salt and pepper and adding vinegar to taste. Serves 4 to 6.

Red and White Onion Rings

2 cups Cider Vinegar
¾ cup raw sugar
4 tsp. salt
½ tsp. garlic salt

¼ tsp. white pepper
2 cups red onion, sliced
2 cups Vidalia onions, sliced

Mix all ingredients except onions and bring to a boil. Drop in onions and turn off heat. Cool and keep in the refrigerator until ready to serve. Serves 4.

Potato Salad

3 cups boiled potato chunks
3 Tbsp. onion, grated
1 Tbsp. lemon or lime juice
1 Tbsp. Dijon or yellow mustard
½ cup sweet pickles, chopped
4 hard-boiled eggs, chopped

⅓ cup French salad dressing
mayonnaise
salt
black pepper
lettuce
paprika

Mix potatoes, onion, lemon juice, mustard, pickles and eggs; add French salad dressing. Chill for several hours. Add enough mayonnaise to moisten. Season with salt and pepper and serve in lettuce cups. Garnish with paprika. Serves 6 to 7.

Mrs. Clyde Lynch Lacy

It is estimated that there are 1,750,000 deer in Mississippi and over 175,000 licensed deer hunters. In 2002 over 320,000 deer were harvested in the state.

Tomato Aspic Salad

2 (3-oz.) bars Philadelphia cream cheese
1 tsp. grated onion
1 tsp. pickle relish
2 Tbsp. mayonnaise
Tabasco sauce to taste
5 Tbsp. gelatin
1 cup water
6 cup canned tomato juice
3 med. white onions, chopped
3 ribs celery, chopped

3 Tbsp. vinegar
1 Tbsp. Worcestershire sauce
juice of 2 lemons
3 bay leaves
1 tsp. sugar
salt to taste
cayenne pepper to taste
Tabasco sauce to taste
parsley
carrot curls

For cheese balls, mix together cream cheese, grated onion, pickle relish, mayonnaise, and Tabasco sauce. Place the gelatin in the water and allow to swell. In a large saucepan, mix together tomato juice, onions, celery, vinegar, Worcestershire sauce, lemon juice, bay leaves, sugar, salt, and Tabasco sauce. Heat over low heat until it comes to a boil. Remove from the heat and strain. Add gelatin and pour into molds. After the molds have cooled to lukewarm, drop in cheese balls. Let aspic salads set in the ice box for at least 6 hours. Unmold and serve on lettuce leaf with a dab of Mayonnaise. Decorate with a sprig of parsley and carrot curls. Serves 4 to 6.

 *The states with the greatest number of hunters also have the largest deer herds. Pennsylvania, for example, which has more than a million deer hunters, also has more than a million deer.*

28

Breads

There is no mystery to making excellent bread. Home cooks have been making bread for thousands of years. The only time you will have a problem is if you substitute ingredients or measure your ingredients incorrectly. When a recipe calls for milk, use whole milk. Do not substitute skimmed milk. Whether your recipe calls for either lard, butter, margarine, shortening, olive oil or bacon drippings, use what your recipe recommends.

Don't let baking terminology disturb you. Kneading, punching, beating down or slashing are just what they sound like. If you have a cookbook that specifically addresses baking skills, you may want to read through it. Please do not be unduly concerned about doing it exactly right. If you diligently follow your recipe, your bread will not be bad. There will be occasions when you will make outstanding bread. At other times your bread will be less than outstanding—but never bad.

When I began exploring baking recipes, I was frustrated that proven recipes did not always act the same. There were times when the recipe would not use all the measured flour. At other times I needed more flour than the recipe called for. The controlling factors were temperature, humidity, time of year and types of flour. For these reasons, bread making may be an exact science, but these inconsistencies are common around the world.

Armenia Bread

1 pkg. active dry yeast	1 Tbsp. sugar
1 cup warm water	1 Tbsp. shortening
3 cups all-purpose flour, sifted, divided	whole milk
1 tsp. salt	sesame seeds

Combine yeast and water and let stand 5 minutes. Add 1½ cups sifted flour, salt, sugar and shortening and beat until smooth. Add another 1½ cups sifted flour. If the dough is too stiff to beat, knead in the flour by hand until it is smooth and elastic, about 5 minutes. Place dough in a greased bowl, cover and let rise until double in bulk, about 45 minutes. Punch dough down and divide into 2 balls. Flatten the dough evenly in 2 greased 8" layer cake pans. Slash in a decorative pattern on the top of dough and brush with milk. Sprinkle with sesame seeds. Let dough rise again until almost doubled in bulk. Bake in a preheated 425-degree oven about 20 minutes. Flatbread is best eaten warm. Reheat before serving.

Basic Crepes

1½ cups all-purpose flour
¼ tsp. salt
2 cups whole milk

3 eggs
2 Tbsp. real butter, melted
canola oil

Mix well flour, salt, and milk. Add eggs and butter. Beat or whisk until smooth. Refrigerate the crepe batter for at least 2 hours. Pour the batter into a wide and shallow dish. Brush the outside bottom of a rounded bottom skillet with oil. Gently dip the bottom of the pan in the batter and lift up and out of the batter. Turn the pan upside down and place the inside of the pan over a gas burner. The test for doneness is when the edges of the crepe are brown and the surface is no longer tacky. Remove the pan from the heat and lift off crepe and place on waxed paper to cool. Repeat until all the batter is used. Makes 24 (6") crepes or 18 (8") crepes.

White Bread

½ cup whole milk
1½ Tbsp. sugar
1¼ tsp. salt
3 Tbsp. Crisco

½ cup warm water
1 pkg. active dry yeast
3 cups all-purpose flour

Warm milk; stir in sugar, salt and Crisco until melted. Cool to lukewarm. Pour warm water into large bowl; add yeast, and stir until dissolved. Stir in lukewarm milk mixture. Add 1½ cups flour and beat vigorously until smooth. Stir in most of remaining flour. Turn out on lightly floured board. Knead until dough is non-sticky, smooth and elastic, about 8 to 10 minutes. If necessary, add more flour while kneading. Put dough in greased bowl and lightly grease top. Cover bowl and set in warm place to rise until dough doubles in bulk (about 30 minutes). Punch dough down and squeeze out air bubbles. Roll into an oblong loaf and place loaf into a greased bread pan. Cover and let rise in a warm, draft-free place until almost doubled in bulk (about 45 minutes). Bake at 375 degrees for 50 minutes or until golden brown.

Mrs. Ann Lynch Webster

Santa Claus's reindeer are a team of flying reindeer traditionally held to pull the sleigh of Santa Claus and help him deliver Christmas gifts. Named Dasher and Dancer, Prancer and Vixen, Comet and Cupid, and Donder and Blitzen, they are based on those used in the 1823 poem A Visit from St. Nicholas, *arguably the basis of reindeer's popularity as Christmas symbols. The subsequent popularity of the Christmas song* Rudolph the Red-Nosed Reindeer *has led to Rudolph often joining the list.*

Biscotti

Biscotti is a fine early-morning, coffee-dunking, sweet bread.

1 cup butter, softened	¼ tsp, salt
1½ cups dark brown sugar	3 tsp. baking powder
1 Tbsp. anise seed	⅛ tsp. ground cinnamon
6 eggs, beaten	⅛ tsp. ground nutmeg
grated peel of 1½ limes	whole milk
6 cups all-purpose flour	almond slivers (optional)

Cream butter and sugar. Add anise seed. Beat in eggs and lime peel. Combine flour, salt, baking powder, cinnamon and nutmeg. Add to egg mixture, alternating with milk. Beat until smooth. Dough should be fairly soft. Roll dough on a floured surface into oblong loaf (4"x9" approximately). Place on greased cookie sheet. Bake at 350 degrees for 20 minutes until golden. Remove from oven. Cool slightly and cut loaf into 1" slices. Place slices on a cookie sheet and toast slices at 450 degrees for 3 to 4 minutes, or until lightly brown. Watch carefully so that they do not burn. Makes 30 to 35 biscotti.

Mrs. Ann Lynch Webster

Stew Biscuit Topping

A substitute for dumplings in stew.

1 cup all-purpose flour	½ tsp. salt
¾ cup yellow cornmeal	¾ cup whole milk
1 Tbsp. sugar	3 Tbsp. melted butter
1 Tbsp. baking powder	1 egg, slightly beaten

Combine flour, cornmeal, sugar, baking powder, and salt in mixing bowl. Add milk, butter, and egg, and stir until smooth. Drop Biscuit Topping batter from spoon into stew and bake in preheated 425-degree oven for 15 minutes or until topping is nicely browned.

Biscuits Made with Buttermilk

2½ cups all-purpose flour	3 Tbsp. Crisco
1 tsp. salt	⅞ cup Buttermilk
4 tsp. baking powder	

Preheat oven to 500 degrees. Combine flour, salt and baking powder in a large bowl with a fork. With two knives, cut cold Crisco into dry ingredients. Mixture should have large flakes and be slightly uneven. Add Buttermilk and stir to combine until you have sticky dough. Turn dough out onto a well-floured board and knead for about 30 seconds. Roll out to ½" thickness and cut into small biscuits with a juice-glass-sized biscuit cutter. Place biscuits on a well-greased baking sheet and bake for 10 minutes or until golden.

Mrs. Clyde Lacy Lynch

Buttermilk Biscuits

These large, soft biscuits are a natural with butter and honey. Serve straight from the oven with fried venison and gravy, barbecued venison ribs, or on their own,

2 cups sifted unbleached all-purpose flour
2 tsp. baking powder
¼ tsp. baking soda

¼ tsp. salt
6 Tbsp. Crisco
1 cup Buttermilk

Position rack in center of oven and preheat to 450 degrees. Sift flour, baking powder, baking soda and salt into a medium bowl. Cut in Crisco until mixture resembles coarse meal. Make a well in the center. Pour Buttermilk into well. Stir just until mixture is moistened. Flour hands. Divide dough into 6 pieces. Lightly toss each piece back and forth between hands to form a ball. Arrange balls on an ungreased baking sheet. Flatten to 1" rounds; sides should touch. Bake until light brown, 18 to 20 minutes. Cool biscuits for 5 minutes on rack before serving. Makes 6.

Cheese and Herb Bread

1 (13¾-oz.) pkg. hot roll mix
1 egg, beaten
2 Tbsp. all-purpose flour
½ cup Parmesan cheese

½ tsp. dry rosemary leaves, crushed
½ Tbsp. caraway
½ Tbsp. sesame seeds

Pour water as directed on package into large bowl and stir in yeast from packet until dissolved. Blend in egg. Add flour from package, then 2 tbsp. flour, cheese, and rosemary. Stir until well blended. The dough will be stiff. Cover bowl with waxed paper, and let dough rise in a warm place until doubled (about 45 minutes). Turn out on lightly floured board; knead until smooth and elastic, 8 to 10 times. Shape into a 3"x6" loaf. Place dough in a greased bread pan which has been sprinkled with sesame seeds. Brush the top of the loaf with butter and sprinkle with caraway and sesame seeds. Cover and let dough rise in a warm, draft-free place until almost doubled in bulk (about 45 minutes). Bake at 375 degrees for 35 to 40 minutes.

Chili Biscuits

1 Tbsp. unsalted butter
1 med. white onion, minced
3 med. garlic cloves, pressed
2 cups sifted all-purpose flour
1 Tbsp. baking powder
  2 tsp. chili powder

1 tsp. salt
¼ cup Parmesan cheese
2 Tbsp. fresh cilantro or parsley, minced
⅓ cup cold Crisco or cold lard
¾ cup whole milk

Melt butter in heavy small skillet over medium-low heat. Add onion and garlic and cook until soft, stirring occasionally, about 10 minutes. Cool mixture 10 minutes. Sift flour, baking powder and salt into large bowl. Stir in cheese and cilantro. Cut in Crisco or lard with pastry blender until mixture resembles coarse meal. Blend in onion mixture. Make well in center of flour mixture. Add milk to well and mix with fork just until dough comes together. Turn dough out onto lightly floured surface and knead 3 to 5 times. Roll dough out to ½" thickness. Cut out biscuits using 3" floured cutter. If using this recipe in another recipe, stop here. If cooking biscuits alone, heat oven to 450 degrees. Bake until biscuits are puffed and lightly browned, about 15 minutes. Makes 6 to 8.

Crackling Bread

This 1850 recipe came to me from my grandmother, Mrs. Clyde Lacy Lynch. "Nanny" told me that this recipe was as old as her antique furniture that she said was buried during the Civil War to keep the Yankees from stealing it! The house was burned, but some of the furniture and some of the silver were saved.

¾ cup all-purpose flour, sifted
2½ tsp. baking powder
2 Tbsp. raw sugar
¾ tsp. salt
1¼ cups yellow cornmeal
1 extra large egg

3 Tbsp. melted Crisco (lard was
  originally used)
1 cup whole milk
½ cup cracklings, smoked ham, or
  bacon bits
butter or Red Eye Gravy

Preheat oven to 425 degrees. Grease a 9" covered cast iron skillet with lard. Place skillet in the oven until sizzling hot. Sift together flour, baking powder, raw sugar, and salt; add cornmeal and sift again. Beat egg in a separate bowl. Fold into beaten egg, melted lard, milk, and meat. Pour batter into the hot skillet, cover and bake for about 30 to 40 minutes. Cut and serve immediately with butter and/or Red Eye Gravy.

Deer farms have existed in China since about 2,000 BC.

Cuban Bread

5 to 6 cups all-purpose flour
2 pkgs. dry yeast
1Tbsp. salt

2 Tbsp. dark brown sugar
2 cups hot water
sesame or caraway seeds

Place 4 cups of flour in a large mixing bowl and add yeast, salt and sugar. Stir until they are well blended. Pour in the hot water and beat for 3 minutes with a mixer. Gradually add the remaining flour (using fingers if necessary), ½ cup at a time, until the dough takes shape and is no longer sticky. Sprinkle the work surface with flour. Work in the flour as you knead, keeping a dusting of flour between the dough and the work surface. Knead for 8 minutes by hand until the dough is smooth and elastic. Place the dough in a greased bowl, cover with plastic wrap, and put in a warm place (80 to 100 degrees) until it doubles in bulk, about 15 minutes.

Punch down the dough, turn it out on the work surface, and cut into 2 pieces. Shape each into a round. Place dough on a baking sheet. With a sharp knife or razor, slash an X on each of the loaves and brush with water and sprinkle with sesame seeds. Place the baking sheet on the middle shelf of a cold oven. Place a large pan of hot water on the shelf below, and heat the oven to 400 degrees. The bread will continue to rise while the oven is heating. Bake for about 50 minutes or until the loaves are a deep golden brown. Thump the bottoms of the crusts to test for doneness. If they sound hollow, they are baked. Turn the loaves out onto metal racks and cool before slicing. Since the bread has no shortening, it will not keep beyond a day or so. Even though it may begin to stale, it will make excellent toast for several days. It will freeze well.

Mrs. Gene Horger Hohl

Daddy's Own Pancakes

2 cups all-purpose flour
2 tsp. baking powder
¼ tsp. salt
⅛ tsp. soda

2 eggs, separated
2 cups whole milk
2 Tbsp. cooking oil
1 tsp. sugar

Separate eggs. Mix all dry ingredients. Add beaten egg yolks, milk and cooking oil. Whip egg whites until they form stiff peaks. Fold into mixture. Cook on a griddle at about 375 degrees. Makes about 14 medium pancakes.

Mr. Bill P. Williams

The white-tailed deer population will normally continue to expand until the increasing lack of nutrition begins to initiate controlling influences.

D'Daddy's Corn and Dill Muffins

Circa 1940. D'Daddy, Roselyn Sinclair Lynch, my grandfather, was born in Weiner, Arkansas, from a family that arrived in Exeter, New Hampshire in 1654. John and Mary Sinclair came from Edinburgh, Scotland. Sinclair Castle is located outside of Edinburgh and on the grounds is Roselyn Chapel. I have a postcard from Edinburgh dated in the late 1890s to my grandfather's mother, Rosa Lilly Sinclair Lynch, which suggests to her that if the child is a boy, he should be named Roselyn after the chapel, and Sinclair after the castle. The families' ties with Scotland continued for over 250 years. For some reason, the communications ceased around 1900.

1 cup all-purpose flour	1 cup heavy cream
1 cup yellow or white cornmeal	1 egg
3 Tbsp. sugar	¾ cup fresh or frozen corn kernels
1 Tbsp. baking powder	¼ cup butter, melted
1 tsp. salt	1 tsp. fresh dill, chopped

In a bowl, mix together flour, cornmeal, sugar, baking powder and salt. Set aside. In a small bowl whisk together milk, egg, corn kernels and vegetable oil until blended. Add to dry ingredients along with dill and stir until blended. Spoon into buttered muffin plaque, filling each cup ⅔ full. Bake in preheated 400-degree oven until toothpick inserted into muffin comes out clean, about 15 minutes. Cool for 3 minutes, then remove. Makes 15 muffins.

Drop Biscuits

1 cup all-purpose flour	½ tsp. salt
¾ cup yellow cornmeal	¾ cup whole milk
1 Tbsp. sugar	3 Tbsp. melted Crisco
1 Tbsp. baking powder	1 egg, beaten

Combine flour, cornmeal, sugar, baking powder, and salt in mixing bowl. Add milk, Crisco, and egg, and stir until smooth. Drop biscuit batter from a large serving spoon onto a baking pan and bake in 425-degree oven 15 minutes, or until topping is nicely browned. Serves 4.

French Bread Pizza Style

1 pkg, active dry yeast
1½ cups warm water
1 cup Harold's Favorite Spaghetti
  Sauce
1 Tbsp. sugar
1 Tbsp. Parmesan cheese, grated

½ tsp. garlic powder
½ tsp. sweet basil
½ tsp. leaf oregano
3 Tbsp. safflower oil
6¾ to 7 cups all-purpose flour

In large mixing bowl, dissolve yeast in warm water. Stir in all ingredients, adding flour gradually to form a stiff dough. Knead on floured surface 3 to 5 minutes until smooth. Place in greased bowl. Cover; let rise in warm place until light and doubled in size, about 1 hour. Divide dough into three parts. Shape each part into a long, thin loaf, about 12 inches long. Place on greased cookie sheets, Cover; let rise in warm place until light and doubled in size, about 45 minutes. Bake at 375 degrees for 30 to 35 minutes until deep golden brown. Remove from cookie sheets; cool. Brush with melted butter. Dough may also be shaped into 3 round loaves and baked on cookie sheets.

Broiled or Grilled Chapati Bread

1⅓ cups whole wheat flour
⅔ cup all-purpose flour

⅔+ cup water

Mix and sift both flours, Make a crater in the center of the flour and gradually add water and mix with fingertips to make a crumbly mixture; 1 Tbsp. more water may be needed. Knead until smooth. Divide dough into an 8" long loaf. Wrap the loaf in plastic wrap and refrigerate for 1 hour. Slice Chapati dough into 16 pieces. Roll each piece into a 5" round and stack each piece between plastic or waxed paper. Heat barbecue grill to medium-high heat or oven broiler to 300 degrees. Remove dough rounds from plastic and grill until each is puffed and dry, about 1 minute per side. Serve warm. Makes 16.

Grilled French Bread Rolls

¾ cup olive oil
6 large garlic cloves, crushed

18 large Italian-Style Wheat Rolls
black or white pepper

Heat olive oil in a medium-sized skillet over medium-low heat. Add garlic cloves to oil and cook until they are just brown. Remove and discard the garlic. Heat the barbecue grill to high heat. Split Italian-Style Wheat Rolls in half horizontally and brush surfaces with garlic-flavored oil. Sprinkle each roll generously with pepper. Grill rolls, oiled-side-down, until golden brown. Serve hot, Makes 18 rolls.

Hoe Cake

An old-time country recipe and Civil War staple.

2 cups yellow or stone ground cornmeal   hot water
1 tsp. salt

Put cornmeal and salt in bowl and mix well. Moisten with hot water until the dough can be handled. Let dough stand for an hour. Shape dough, by spoonfuls, into flat cakes about ½" thick. Fry the cakes on a hot greased skillet until golden brown on both sides. Serve hot. Serves 4 to 6.

Hush Puppies with Whole Kernel Corn

Circa 1900 to 1915. The author's father related that eating Hush Puppies, made by his grand-mother in Oak Ridge, Mississippi, was one of his fondest childhood memories. Harold Sr. was a self-taught fly fisherman and his favorite form of recreation was on a summer's evening to load up a wooden flat-bottom boat in the back of his station wagon and head off, with 6-yr.-old Harold Jr. in tow, to fish for large hand-sized bream in the old cut-off lakes in the Mississippi Delta. Dad would have the cook at Nick the Greek's Restaurant in Belzoni clean and fry the bream and make Hush Puppies to this recipe. Fishing with dad and eating these Hush Puppies at Nick's is one of the author's fondest childhood memories.

½ cup all-purpose flour   1 egg
2 tsp. baking powder   ½ cup whole milk
1 tsp. salt   3 Tbsp. cooking oil
1½ cups plain cornmeal   red pepper flakes (to taste)
½ cup drained whole kernel corn   dash of garlic powder
¾ cup white onion, diced

Combine all ingredients. Cover and let set for 30 minutes. After frying fish, form into 1" to 1½" balls and drop into hot grease. When golden brown, remove and allow to drain on paper towels. Serve hot. Makes about 10 servings.

Hush Puppies with Cornmeal and Onions

2 cups yellow corn meal   1 medium onion, chopped fine
2 tsp. baking powder   ¼ cup bacon drippings
½ tsp. sugar   3 eggs
1 tsp. black pepper   1 cup boiling water
1 tsp. salt   shortening

Mix and sift all dry ingredients together. Add onion, bacon drippings, eggs and water. Shape into 1½" balls. Deep fry in shortening until the hushpuppies float to the top.

Irish Soda Bread

2 cups all-purpose flour
2 Tbsp. light brown sugar
1 tsp. baking powder
½ tsp. baking soda
¼ tsp. salt

3 Tbsp. butter
2 eggs
¾ cup buttermilk
⅓ cup seedless raisins

In a bowl, combine flour, brown sugar, baking powder, baking soda and salt. Cut In butter until crumbly. Combine 1 egg and buttermilk; stir into flour mixture just until moistened. Fold in raisins. Knead on a floured surface for 1 minute. Shape into a round loaf; place on a greased baking sheet. Cut a ¼" deep cross on top of loaf. Bake at 375 degrees for 30 to 35 minutes or until golden brown. Serves 6 to 8.

Italian-Style Bread

This recipe can be divided into 2 parts and made into 2 round loaves.

½ cup warm water
1 pkg. active dry yeast
1½ tsp. sugar
3 Tbsp. butter, cut in
　　small pieces

1 tsp. salt
3 cups all-purpose flour
½ Tbsp. butter
1 Tbsp. yellow cornmeal

Pour warm water into a large bowl; stir in yeast and sugar. Melt butter; cool to luke-warm. Stir butter and salt into yeast mixture. Stirring vigorously, add flour, one cup at a time, until dough almost comes away from sides of the bowl. Turn out onto lightly floured board. Using a spatula, scrape under flour and dough, fold over and press with free hand. Continue turning and pressing until dough has absorbed enough flour so it is easy to handle. Knead dough about 4 minutes. When dough is soft and smooth, let rest 4 to 6 minutes. Roll or pat dough into 8"x12" rectangle. Starting with narrow end, roll dough tightly, jelly-roll fashion. Pinch-seal dough about every half turn. Pinch-seal ends very well. Grease a cookie sheet and dust with cornmeal. Place dough loaf on cookie sheet. Brush top of loaf with water and dust with cornmeal. Cover and let dough rise in a warm place until almost doubled in bulk (50 to 60 minutes). Bake at 425 degrees for 45 to 50 minutes.

Italian-Style Wheat Rolls

1 oz. dry yeast
½ cup lukewarm whole milk
1½ tsp. light brown sugar
3½ cups all-purpose flour
½ Tbsp. salt
4 Tbsp. of safflower oil

1 egg, beaten
1 tsp. anise
1 tsp. cumin
1 tsp. fennel
½ cup lukewarm water
1 Tbsp. yellow cornmeal

Crumble the yeast and dissolve in milk; add sugar and mix well. Put the flour in a bowl and make a hollow in the center. Pour milk mixture into center of the flour. Scatter salt around hollow. Add safflower oil, egg, anise, cumin, fennel and water. Mix to make a dough of average consistency. Dust with flour; cover and let rise in a warm place for 20 minutes. Work the dough again on a floured baking board; divide it into as many rolls as you want. Dust them lightly with flour, arrange them on a baking sheet sprinkled with cornmeal. With a very sharp knife, score a cross on the top of each roll. Cover and leave them to rise in a warm place for 15 minutes. Preheat the oven to 400 degrees and bake until brown.

Joe's Famous Bread

1½ tsp. active dry yeast
1 cup plus 2 Tbsp. water, 105 to 115 degrees
3½ cups Gold Medal Bread flour, sifted,
    divided
1½ tsp. salt

3 Tbsp. honey
1 tsp. lemon juice
3 Tbsp. oil
milk

Combine yeast and water and let stand 5 minutes. Add 1½ cups of the sifted flour, salt, honey, lemon juice and shortening and beat until smooth. Add another 1½ cups sifted flour. If the dough is too stiff to beat, knead in the flour by hand until it is smooth and elastic, about 5 minutes. Place dough in a greased bowl, cover and let rise until double in bulk, about 45 minutes. Punch dough down and divide into 2 balls. Flatten the dough evenly in 2 greased 8" layer cake pans. Slash in a decorative pattern on the top of dough and brush with milk. Let dough rise again until almost doubled in bulk. Bake in a preheated 425-degree oven about 20 minutes. Flatbread is best eaten warm. Reheat before serving.

Mr. Joseph J. Packa

White-tailed deer remain the most popular large game animal throughout most of the US. These deer may bound at speeds of up to 40 miles per hour, and are good swimmers, often entering streams and lakes to escape predators.

Johnny Cake

The bread that won and lost the Civil War.

1 cup yellow or stone ground cornmeal
1 cup all-purpose flour
½ tsp. salt

2 cups sour whole milk
2 Tbsp. sorghum molasses
2 eggs
½ tsp. baking soda

Mix and sift the cornmeal, flour, and salt together. Add the baking soda to sour milk and stir until it foams. Then add milk to the meal and flour. Add the sorghum molasses and unbeaten eggs and mix well. Pour the batter into a 13"x 9"x12" inch oiled baking pan. Bake in a 400-degree oven for 20 minutes or until golden brown. Serves 8 to 10.

Kate's Rolls

¼ cup sugar
3 Tbsp. oleo
1 cup hot water
1½ cups regular flour, divided

1 tsp, salt
⅓ cup dry milk
1 pkg. dry active yeast

Put sugar and oleo in a mixing bowl. Add hot water and stir until oleo melts. When water is lukewarm, add ¾ cup flour, salt, dry milk and yeast. Stir well, and then beat. Add enough of the remaining flour to make a thick, cake-like batter. Cover and let rise in a warm place until double in bulk. Then add enough flour to make a stiff dough. Cover and put in refrigerator for 2 hours. Spread flour on a floured cloth and roll out. Cut out rolls. Place on a greased pan and let rise. Cook about 20 minutes in a 350-degree oven.

Mrs. Milma Wiselogel

Kentucky Biscuits

2 cups all-purpose flour
2½ tsp. baking powder
½ tsp. baking soda
dash salt

1 Tbsp. granulated sugar
½ cup butter or shortening
¾ cup buttermilk
1 Tbsp. butter, melted

Mix flour, baking powder, baking soda, salt and sugar in a mixing bowl. Cut in butter or shortening with a pastry blender. Add buttermilk. Mix quickly to make a soft dough. Turn out onto a lightly floured surface. Knead a few times to make soft dough (don't overknead or biscuits will turn hard and dry). Roll out to a 6"x 6" square. Place on an ungreased baking sheet. With a knife, cut dough into 12 even portions. Do not separate. Bake at 400 degrees until golden brown, about 15 minutes. Dust with flour when biscuits come out of oven. Serve piping hot with butter, jam and/or honey.

Mrs. Milma Wiselogel

Mrs. Lipscomb's Tea Rolls

An 1899 recipe of Mrs. Annabelle Sturdivant Lipscomb of Columbus, Mississippi.

1 cup boiling water
1 cup tepid water
½ cup sugar
1 cup shortening
6 cups all-purpose flour

2 pkgs. yeast
2 whole eggs
2 tsp. salt
butter, melted

Cream shortening and sugar and add boiling water. Let cool. Dissolve yeast in tepid water, mix well and add to cool shortening and sugar mixture. Add beaten eggs, flour, and salt and knead well. Place dough in a greased bowl and put in the refrigerator until ready to use. Roll dough out to ¼" to ⅜". Cut out with circular cutter. Fold cut-out over itself to make a "half moon." Gently press down. Place cut-outs on a baking sheet. Let rise at room temperature, to about double in size, about 1½ hours. Preheat oven to 325 degrees. Brush with melted butter; bake until lightly browned, about 20 minutes. Depending on the size of the cutter, makes 12 to 20.

One Hour Rolls

2 cups all-purpose flour
2 Tbsp. sugar
1 tsp. baking powder
1 tsp. salt

¼ cup Crisco
1 pkg. yeast
¼ cup warm water
¾ cup buttermilk

Mix and sift all dry ingredients together. Cut in Crisco until the particles are fine. Dissolve the yeast in warm water and add to the buttermilk and mix well. Stir yeast mixture into the dry ingredients. Turn dough out on a floured board, and knead dough until it is smooth and blistered. Roll dough to ¼" thick and cut with biscuit cutter. Spread dough with melted butter and fold double. Place dough on an ungreased baking sheet, and let rise 1 hour. Bake in 400-degree oven for 12 to 15 minutes until golden brown. Makes 24 rolls.

Poochie's Spoon Bread

1 cup yellow cornmeal
2½ cups scalded whole milk
2 eggs, separated
1 Tbsp. butter

1 Tbsp. baking powder
½ tsp. salt
1 tsp. sugar

Pour scalded milk over meal. Add egg yolks, butter, baking powder, salt and sugar to meal and milk mixture. Fold in egg whites and bake in a casserole dish at 350 degrees for 45 minutes to 1 hour.

Peppy Lemon Batter Bread

½ cup Pillsbury Hungry Jack Mashed Potato
    Flakes
1 Tbsp. sugar
1½ tsp. salt
1 tsp. grated lemon peel
½ tsp. coarsely ground black pepper
2 Tbsp. Crisco
1 pkg. cream cheese

1 cup boiling water
½ cup whole milk
2 eggs
1 pkg. active dry yeast
¼ cup warm water
3½ cups all-purpose flour
real butter, softened
coarse salt

In large mixer bowl, combine potato flakes, sugar, salt, lemon peel, black pepper, shortening, cream cheese and boiling water; blend well. Add milk and eggs. Dissolve yeast in warm water; add to potato mixture. Blend in 2 cups flour; beat White-tailed bucks need a 13 percent to 16 percent crude protein diet to develop their full genetic potential.2 minutes at medium speed. By hand, stir in remaining flour to form a stiff batter. Cover; let rise in warm place until light and doubled in size, about 45 minutes. Stir batter vigorously, about 35 strokes. Spoon batter into a well-greased 2-quart casserole. Cover; let rise in warm place until dough rises almost to top of casserole about 30 minutes. Bake at 350 degrees for 40 to 45 minutes until deep golden brown and loaf sounds hollow when tapped lightly on top. Remove from casserole. Brush with butter and sprinkle with coarse salt.

 *White-tailed bucks need a 13 percent to 16 percent crude protein diet to develop their full genetic potential.*

Petits Brioches

Small French dinner rolls.

½ cup whole milk
½ cup real butter
⅓ cup sugar
1 tsp. salt
¼ cup warm water
1 pkg. active dry yeast

3 whole eggs
1 egg yolk
3½ cups unsifted all-purpose flour
1 egg white
1 Tbsp. sugar

Scald milk and cool to lukewarm. Cream butter in large mixing bowl. Gradually add sugar and salt until dissolved. Measure water into a small warm bowl. Sprinkle or crumble yeast and stir until dissolved. Add lukewarm milk, dissolved yeast, eggs, egg yolk and flour to creamed butter mixture. With a wooden spoon beat vigorously for 2 minutes. Cover bowl and let rise in a warm place, free from draft, until more than doubled in bulk (about 2 hours). Stir down and beat vigorously for 2 minutes. Cover tightly with aluminum foil and refrigerate overnight.

In the morning beat down the dough. Turn soft dough out on a lightly floured board. Divide into 2 pieces, one about ¾ of the dough and one about ¼ of the dough. Cut large piece into 24 equal small pieces. Form into smooth balls. Place balls in well-greased medium-sized muffin pans. Cut smaller piece into 24 equal pieces. Form into smooth small balls. Make a deep indentation in center of each large ball. Dampen slightly with cold water. Press a small ball into each indentation. Let rise in a warm place, free from draft, until doubled in bulk, about 50 minutes. Heat oven to 375 degrees. Beat together 1 egg white and 1 tbsp. sugar. Brush top of each brioche lightly with beaten egg. Bake 15 to 20 minutes, or until lightly browned and baked. Turn out of pans immediately to cool. Makes 2 dozen brioches.

Quick Batter Rolls

2 pkg. fresh yeast
1¼ cups warm water
¼ cup sugar
1¼ tsp. salt

1 egg, unbeaten
3 cups all-purpose flour
2 Tbsp. melted Crisco (cool to
    lukewarm)

Dissolve yeast in warm water in a large mixing bowl. Add sugar, salt, and unbeaten egg. Add flour gradually; mix well. Add Crisco and continue to beat until thoroughly mixed. Spoon batter into greased muffin pans, filling about ⅓ full. Let rise in a warm place until batter is level with tops of muffin pans. Bake in a 375 to 400-degree oven for 20 minutes.

Quick Dumplings

1½ cups Bisquick Original Baking Mix
½ cup yellow cornmeal

⅔ cup whole milk
½ tsp. sugar

Mix all ingredients until soft dough forms. Roll out and cut into 1"x 2" rectangles. Use as you would any dumplings.

Rapid Mix French Bread

3 to 3½ cups unsifted all-purpose flour
4 tsp. sugar
1½ tsp. salt
1 pkg. active dry yeast
2 Tbsp. real butter

1¼ cups very hot tap water
yellow cornmeal
1 egg white, slightly beaten
1 Tbsp. water

Mix 1 cup sifted all-purpose flour, sugar, salt and active dry yeast. Add butter. Gradually add very hot tap water to the dry ingredients and beat, in an electric mixer at medium speed for 2 minutes. Add 1 cup sifted all-purpose flour, or enough to make a thick batter. Beat at high speed for 2 minutes. Stir in 1 cup sifted all-purpose flour to make a soft dough. Cover bowl tightly with plastic wrap and let stand 45 minutes.

Stir down dough and turn out onto a heavily floured board. Make Into an oblong, 15 inches long. Taper ends. Sprinkle a baking sheet with cornmeal. Place dough on the baking sheet. Cover and let rise in a warm draft-free place until doubled in bulk, about 40 minutes. Heat oven to 400 degrees. With a sharp knife, make diagonal cuts on top of the loaf. Bake for 25 minutes. Combine beaten egg white and cold water and brush top of loaf. Return loaf to the oven and bake for 15 minutes longer, or until done. Remove loaf from the baking sheet and cool on wire rack. Makes 1 large or 2 small loaves.

Rye Flour Bread

½ cup warm water, 105 to 115 degrees
2 pkgs, active dry yeast
2 cups whole milk
2 Tbsp. butter
1 Tbsp. alfalfa or wild-flower honey

2 tsp. salt
6 cups rye flour, divided
1 egg, beaten
2 Tbsp. caraway seeds
2 Tbsp. sesame seeds

Combine water and yeast. Scald milk; as it cools, add butter, honey and salt. Add the yeast mixture and stir in 2 cups rye flour. Cover; set in a warm draft-free place for 1 hour. While stirring, add slowly 3 cups rye flour, caraway seeds and sesame seeds. Cover; set in a warm draft-free place for 2 hours. Divide into 2 parts. Form into loaves and place on a well-greased baking sheet. Crease the tops of the loaves, cover and allow to rise about 2 hours more. Bake in a preheated 350-degree oven about 1 hour. Test for doneness by tapping the bottom of the pan to release the loaf and then tapping the bottom of the loaf; if a hollow sound is heard, the bread is done. Cool loaves on cake racks.

Spaetzle

2 eggs
1½ cups flour
½ cup water
½ tsp. salt

¼ tsp. baking powder
dash ground nutmeg
dash ground ginger
butter

Beat the eggs and combine with flour, water, salt, baking soda, nutmeg and ginger; beat well. Drop small amounts of batter from a spoon into boiling salted water. Batter can also be pressed through a spaetzle press, through a colander with large holes, or lightly streamed from a small pitcher spout. Spaetzel should be very light. Cook several pieces and if it is too heavy, add water to the batter. Boil in water. Do not overcrowd. Spaetzles are done when they float to the top. Remove and place in a bowl of warm water. Drain and cover with a light coating of melted butter when ready to serve. Serves 4.

Skillet Buttermilk Cornbread

1 cup sifted all-purpose flour
½ tsp. baking soda
1½ tsp. baking powder
1 Tbsp. sugar
1 tsp. salt

¾ cup yellow cornmeal
1½ cups Buttermilk
2 eggs
4 Tbsp. butter, melted or
    bacon drippings

Preheat oven to 425 degrees. Grease a 9" covered skillet with butter, oil or fat drippings. Place skillet in the oven until sizzling hot. Sift together flour, soda, baking powder, sugar, and salt; add cornmeal. Combine and beat in a separate bowl buttermilk, eggs and butter or drippings. Combine all ingredients with a few rapid strokes. Pour batter into hot skillet, cover and bake for about 20 to 35 minutes. Serve immediately with butter.

Sourdough Flapjacks

1 pkg. active dry yeast
1 cup very warm water
all-purpose flour
1½ eggs, unbeaten

¼ tsp. soda
¾ tsp. salt
6 Tbsp. sugar

Dissolve yeast in very warm water and stir well. Add enough flour to make the batter as stiff as waffle batter. Cover and let stand overnight at room temperature. The next morning add eggs, soda, salt, and sugar. Mix well and cook in the same way as other pancakes. Serves 8.

Small Loaf French Bread

2 pks. dry yeast
2¾ cups warm water

7 cups unbleached white flour
4¼ tsp, salt

Soften yeast in ¼ cup warm water. Mix flour and salt in a large bowl. Add warm water and mix well. Add yeast mixture. Blend into dough. Turn onto floured board and knead until dough is smooth and elastic. Put kneaded dough in a covered bowl and let rise until doubled in size. Punch dough down and let rise a second time until doubled. Punch down. Turn onto a floured board and shape as desired. You can make one large loaf, two small loaves or you can cut the dough into three pieces and braid and sprinkle with poppy seeds on top of buttered bread. Bake at 400 degrees for 25 minutes, or until golden brown. Mist loaves with water 3 or 4 times during baking for a fine crust.

Spider Cornbread

A recipe from 1763 Colonial America.

1½ cups white stone ground cornmeal
1 Tbsp. sugar
1 tsp. salt
1 tsp. baking soda

2 eggs, well beaten
2 cups Buttermilk, non-cultured
1½ Tbsp. real butter, melted

Preheat the oven to 450 degrees. Put an iron skillet in the oven to warm. Mix and sift together cornmeal, sugar, salt, and baking soda. Add buttermilk to the beaten eggs, then stir into the cornmeal mixture until the mixture is smooth. Add melted butter. Grease the skillet and pour mixture into the warm skillet. Bake for 30 minutes at 450 degrees. Serves 6 to 8.

Sweet Cornbread

An old 1850 Webster family recipe from the Oak Ridge area of Mississippi.

¾ cup all-purpose flour, sifted
3½ tsp. double-acting baking
   powder
4 Tbsp. raw sugar
¾ tsp. salt

1¼ cups yellow, stone-ground
   cornmeal
1 egg
¼ cup Crisco or lard, melted
1 cup whole milk

Preheat oven to 425 degrees. Grease an 8x8" heavy pan with shortening. Place pan in the oven until sizzling hot. Sift together flour, baking powder, sugar, and salt; add cornmeal. Combine egg, melted shortening and milk; pour into flour mixture and stir just enough to moisten the dry ingredients. Do not beat. Pour batter into hot pan and bake for about 30 to 40 minutes. Cut into squares and serve immediately.

Sweet Dough Rolls

5 to 6 cups all-purpose flour
2 pkgs. active dry yeast
½ cup sugar
1½ tsp. salt

½ cup real butter, softened
1½ cups very hot tap water
2 eggs (at room temperature)

Combine 2 cups flour, active dry yeast, sugar and salt in large bowl. Blend well. Add soft butter. Add hot tap water to ingredients in bowl all at once. Beat with electric mixer at medium speed for about 2 minutes. Add eggs and 1 more cup of flour. Beat with electric mixer. Stir in remaining flour gradually. Use just enough flour to make a soft dough which leaves sides of bowl. Turn out onto floured board. Knead dough 5 to 10 minutes or until dough is smooth and elastic. Cover bowl and let rise for 15 to 20 minutes. Punch down. Shape into rolls. Place close together on 2 greased 8" square pans. Refrigerate 2 hours to overnight. When ready to bake, remove from refrigerator. Uncover and let stand for 10 minutes. Preheat the oven to 375 degrees and bake for 30 to 35 minutes or until done. Bake on a lower oven rack for best results. Remove from pans and cool on wire racks. Makes 32± rolls.

Yvonne's Special Waffles

Circa 1945. When Erin Ladner was a child, she lived in Hattiesburg, Mississippi and she would babysit Mrs. Yvonne Owens' children. Frequently, Erin would be asked if she would like to help Mrs. Owens bake. When Erin married in 1983, Mrs. Owens gave her a waffle iron and this fine recipe for a wedding present. Erin tells the story that after her son had read Green Eggs and Ham, he adds a different cake coloring each time Erin cooks these waffles.

2 cups flour
1 tsp. salt
1 tsp. baking soda
1 tsp. baking powder
4 eggs

1 cup milk
1 cup sour cream (instead of milk and
   sour cream you can substitute 2
   cups of buttermilk)
½ lb. butter

Sift together flour, salt, baking soda, and baking powder. Add eggs, milk, and sour cream or Buttermilk and butter. Heat waffle grill and spoon waffle mix on grill and cook until golden brown. Serves 8.

29

Desserts

We do not serve as many desserts with our meals as we have been served in the past. Today desserts are usually reserved for special occasions. These desserts will provide a proper finale for any occasion.

If you like your desserts with less calories and good taste, Anne's Chocolate, Mint & Banana Pie and Raspberry Swirl Peach Soup are the perfect accompaniments for light summer dinner or brunch.

From the flamboyant Bananas Foster and Peaches Flambe to the understated elegance of Abigail Adams' 1768 Ginger-Apple Custard, Miss Dabney Anne Lipscomb's Triple Chocolate Delight Pie to Senator John C. Stennis' traditional Southern Pecan Pie—you will enjoy all of these desserts.

Baked Cherry Alaska

Pound Cake
6 " square Vanilla Custard Ice Cream,
    frozen very hard
prepared cherry cake icing

Meringue
2 maraschino cherries, halved
1 thin slice lime, quartered

Lay a piece of heavy paper on a small flat ovenproof dish. Place a layer of pound cake, cut at least 1" thick, on the plate. Spread a ¼" layer of the cherry icing on top of the block of ice cream. Turn the block over and set it icing-side-down on the layer of pound cake. Cut excess cake off from around edges of ice cream. Cut ½" to ¾" thick pieces of pound cake and fit to cover sides and top of ice cream and remove. Spread a ¼" layer of cherry icing on the pieces of pound cake and affix them to ice cream block with the icing next to ice cream. Return to freezer for 1 hour. Preheat oven to 500 degrees. Remove from freezer and cover completely with a thick coating of meringue. Place baking sheet in preheated oven for 3 to 5 minutes or until meringue is touched with gold. Garnish with cherry halves and quartered lime slices. Serves 6 to 8.

Banana Ice Cream

Make a custard with 2 pints milk and 4 eggs and thicken well over a very slow fire. Mash 6 ripe firm bananas to a smooth pulp with 1 teaspoon lime juice and add to the custard when cool. Sweeten to taste and freeze.

Bananas Foster

This recipe was given to Harold W. Webster. Sr. by Mr. Robaire; Mr. Webster's favorite waiter at Brennan's Restaurant, New Orleans, Louisiana. As late as 1972, a photograph of Mr. Webster and Mr. Robaire was displayed in Brennan's Restaurant Kitchen. Mr. Robaire has since retired and has returned to his native France.

2 Tbsp. brown sugar
1 Tbsp. butter
1 ripe banana, peeled and sliced lengthwise
dash cinnamon

½ oz. banana liqueur
1 oz. white rum
1 large scoop Vanilla Custard Ice Cream

Melt brown sugar and butter in flat chafing dish. Add banana and sauté until tender. Sprinkle with cinnamon. Pour in banana liqueur and rum over all and flame. Baste with warm liquid until flame burns out. Spoon bananas and liquid over a generous portion Vanilla Custard Ice Cream. Serve immediately. Serves 1.

Blackberry Pie

2 Tbsp. cornstarch
1 cup sugar
⅛ tsp. salt
½ cup cold water

3 cups blackberries
2 pie shells, uncooked
real butter

Mix cornstarch, sugar, and salt. Blend in the cold water. Bring this slowly to a simmer and, stirring, cook a minute. Combine with blackberries; pour into an uncooked pie shell, cover with slices of butter. Top with a second layer of pastry. Pierce top of pastry shell several times with a fork. Preheat the oven to 450 degrees and bake for 10 minutes. Then reduce the heat to 350 degrees and bake for 30 minutes more or until done.

Mississippi-Style Blueberry Turnovers

2 pie crusts
1 cup fresh, frozen or canned blueberries
    drained
⅓ cup sugar

2 Tbsp. all-purpose flour
1 tsp. lemon or lime Juice
⅛ tsp. salt
Vanilla Custard Ice Cream

Roll pastry to ⅛" thickness, cut in eight 5" squares. Combine blueberries, sugar, flour, lemon juice and salt; place a heaping tbsp. on each square. Fold pastry in half diagonally, seal edges with fork. Cut slits for steam to escape. Place turnovers on baking sheet. Bake for 20 to 30 minutes at 400 degrees. Serve hot with Vanilla Custard Ice Cream. Makes 8.

Chocolate, Mint & Banana Pie

A special pie for that special occasion: when you want to serve something spectacular and you don't have a lot of time. This pie has just that hint of mint in the chocolate and banana; it is a pleasant surprise.

4 cups skim milk, divided
½ tsp. peppermint extract
1 (1.3 oz.) package of sugar-free chocolate pudding & pie filling
1 (9 oz.) graham cracker crust
¾ cup graham cracker crumbs
½ tsp. banana extract

1 (1.3 oz.) package of sugar free vanilla pudding & pie filling
1 (8 oz.) Extra Creamy Cool Whip
1 Tbsp. shaved sweet chocolate
1 cherry
8 mint leaves

Pour 2 cups skim milk and peppermint extract into mixing bowl. Add chocolate pudding mix. With a whip or rotary beater, beat at slow speed until well blended, 1 or 2 minutes. Pour chocolate mixture into graham cracker pie shell at once. Wait 5 minutes. Smooth on graham cracker crumbs on top of chocolate filling. Pour 2 cups skim milk and banana extract into mixing bowl. Add vanilla pudding. With a whip or rotary beater, beat at slow speed until well blended, 1 or 2 minutes. Pour vanilla mixture on top of graham cracker crumbs at once. Refrigerate for 2 hours. Before serving spread on Cool Whip, center cherry on top of Cool Whip. Sprinkle on shaved chocolate. Garnish with mint leaves. Serve cold. Serves 8.

Mrs. Anne Lipscomb Webster

Chocolate Mousse

A real chocolate lover's dream. This smooth dessert gets topped off with a generous portion of light whipped topping, chocolate curls and cherries.

1¼ ounce envelope unflavored gelatin
¼ cup water
1 cup skim milk
½ cup unsweetened cocoa
⅓ cup NutraSweet Spoonful

2 cups light whipped topping
6 cherries
Light whipped topping
sweet chocolate curls

Sprinkle gelatin over water in a small saucepan; let stand 2 or 3 minutes. Cook over low heat, stirring constantly, until gelatin is dissolved; cool. Stir ¼ cup of milk into cocoa to make a paste; gradually stir in remaining milk. Stir in gelatin mixture and NutraSweet Spoonful. Refrigerate until mixture begins to thicken, 20 to 30 minutes. Fold in 2 cups whipped topping. Spoon mixture into stemmed glasses or serving bowl. Refrigerate 2 to 4 hours. Garnish with whipped topping, chocolate curls and cherry. Serves 6.

Mrs. Ann Lynch Webster

Coffee Ice Cream

2½ cups whole milk
1½ cups sugar
2 eggs, beaten
½ cups strong cold coffee
½ tsp. salt

1 cup Whipped Cream
1 tsp. vanilla
3 Tbsp. Mount Gay, Barbados rum
shaved sweet chocolate

Scald milk over low heat, but do not allow to boil. Stir in sugar until dissolved. Pour the milk mixture over beaten eggs. Beat until well blended. Stir and cook in a double boiler over (not in) boiling water until thick enough to coat the back of a spoon. Chill and add cold coffee, salt and Whipped Cream. Partly freeze in an ice cream machine and when almost frozen add vanilla and rum. Finish freezing and garnish with curls of shaved sweet chocolate.

Cold Blackberry Soup

2 cups fresh or frozen blackberries
½ cup sour cream
1 cup sherry

1 cup cold water
sugar or NutraSweet

Press berries through a fine sieve. Discard seeds and pulp. Then stir in sour cream. Pour in sherry and water and sweeten to taste with sugar or NutraSweet. Place in refrigerator for at least 2 hours. Serve in cold bowls.

Almond and Cream Soufflé

3 cups cream
6 Tbsp. white sugar
6 egg yolks
½ tsp. almond extract

pinch of salt
4½ oz. blanched whole almonds,
    toasted
½ cup light brown sugar

Heat cream in a heavy saucepan. Add white sugar and stir until dissolved. Beat egg yolks until light and creamy. Add the hot cream to the egg yolks gradually; whipping constantly with a wire whisk. Stir in the remaining ingredients, except the brown sugar. Pour into a 6 cup soufflé dishes and sprinkle brown sugar on the top. Bake at 325 degrees for 45 minutes, or until done. Makes 6 servings.

Maine's big bucks continually draw over 200,000 hunters annually to the rugged back country, areas which other visitors seldom visit.

Custard Sauce

3 egg yolks
2 cups whole milk
⅛ tsp. salt

½ cup sugar
1 tsp. vanilla extract

Beat the egg yolks. Add milk, salt, and sugar and cook slowly over low heat until thick. Stir constantly. Mix in the vanilla extract. Cool and store in the refrigerator until ready to serve.

Eggnog Ice Cream

Borden's canned eggnog
sour mash bourbon (optional) to taste

fresh ground nutmeg
cinnamon sticks

Fill ice cream maker to proper level with Borden's eggnog. When ice cream is made, stir in 1 tsp. bourbon per serving. Pack with towels and let set for 1 hour. Serve with a sprinkle of fresh ground nutmeg on top. Garnish with a cinnamon stick in each serving.

Chocolate Soufflé

¼ cup blanched almonds
3 Tbsp. all-purpose flour
3 ozs. semi-sweet chocolate, chopped fine
½ cup unsweetened Dutch-process cocoa
1 cup sugar
½ cup boiling water

2 large egg yolks, room temperature
1 Tbsp. Napoleon brandy
4 large egg whites, at room temperature
¼ tsp. cream of tartar
6 maraschino cherries, chopped
powdered sugar

Position rack in lower third of the oven. Preheat oven to 375 degrees. Place a round of parchment paper in the bottom of an 8" spring form pan. Spray the sides with vegetable oil spray. In a food processor or blender, grind the almonds with the flour until very fine; set aside. Combine the chopped chocolate, cocoa and ¾ cup of the sugar in a large mixing bowl. Pour in the boiling water; whisk until mixture is smooth and chocolate is completely melted. Whisk in egg yolks and brandy. Set aside. Combine egg whites and cream of tartar in remaining sugar; beat on high speed until stiff but not dry. Whisk the flour and almonds into the chocolate. Fold about a quarter of the egg whites into the chocolate mixture to lighten it. Fold in remaining egg whites. Scrape the batter into the pan; level top if necessary. Bake in a 375-degree oven for 30 to 35 minutes, or until a toothpick inserted into the center comes out with a few moist crumbs clinging to it. Cool in the pan on a wire rack. Torte will sink like a soufflé. Taking care not to break the edges of the torte, slide a knife between the torte and the pan; run it around the pan to release the cake completely. Invert the cake onto a plate; remove the pan and paper liner. Turn right-side-up on a platter. Torte may be stored, covered, at room temperature, for 1 day or frozen up to 2 months. To serve, sift 2 or 3 tbsp. of powdered sugar on top. Sprinkle with chopped maraschino cherries. Serves 10.

French-Style Strawberry Ice Cream

6 egg yolks
2 cups whole milk
1 cup sugar
pinch of salt

4 cups cream
2 cups crushed fresh strawberries
1 Tbsp. lemon or lime juice

Mix the egg yolks, milk, sugar, and salt in a double boiler and heat to make a thick custard. Cook until the mixture coats the back of a spoon evenly. Allow to cool. Add cream. Pour into an ice cream maker and make until it is half frozen. Add crushed strawberries and lemon juice and continue to stir-freeze. Allow to set a few hours before serving. Makes 2½ qts.

Fresh Blackberry Sherbet

1½ cups fresh blackberries
⅓ cup powdered sugar
⅔ cup sweetened condensed milk

2 Tbsp. fresh lime juice
2 egg whites, beaten stiff

Mix blackberries with powdered sugar. Allow to stand for 15 minutes. Crush and press the blackberries through sieve or food mill. Combine sweetened condensed milk and lime juice with the blackberry juice. Chill until the mixture begins to thicken. Fold the beaten egg whites into the chilled mixture; place in refrigerator tray and chill until partially frozen. Remove and beat until it is smooth. Keep in the freezer until frozen. Serves 3 to 4.

Ginger-Apple Custard

5 cups country bread, chunked
2 cups Buttermilk
2 cups whole milk
3 lbs. apples, peeled, cored and sliced
¼ cup water
½ cup sorghum molasses
⅓ cup sugar

4 eggs, lightly beaten
¾ tsp. ginger
1 tsp. cinnamon
¾ tsp. nutmeg
⅛ tsp. ground cloves
⅛ tsp. black pepper
¼ tsp. salt

Place broken bread in a bowl and pour the buttermilk and milk over it. Set aside. Place apples and water in a skillet. Cover and cook over low heat until the apples start to soften but still retain their shape. Remove from the stove and allow to cool slightly. Beat the remaining ingredients into the bread mixture. Fold in the apples. Pour into a greased 3-quart baking dish. Bake at 350 degrees for 50 to 60 minutes, or until set. Serve warm and topped with Custard Sauce for dessert. Serves 12.

Abigail Adams, Quincy, Massachusetts, 1764

Gingersnap Cookies

¾ cup shortening
¾ cup brown sugar
¾ cup molasses
1 egg
3 cups all-purpose flour, sifted

¼ tsp. salt
1½ tsp. baking soda
⅓ tsp. ground cloves
1 tsp. ground ginger

Cream shortening and gradually add sugar. Add molasses and egg and mix well. Add sifted dry ingredients and blend thoroughly. Form cookies on ungreased cookie sheets (if available, use a fillable cookie press). Sprinkle with sugar. Bake at 370 degrees for 12 to 14 minutes.

Mrs. Anna Lillie Sinclair Lynch

Harold's Key Lime Pie

4 egg yolks
1 (14-oz.) can sweetened condensed milk
3 oz. Key lime juice
3 drops green food coloring
1 pre-made graham cracker crust

1 pint Whipped Cream or
 whipped topping
1 fresh lime
1 cherry

Separate eggs; combine yolks with condensed milk. Add food coloring to lime juice; add lime juice mixture to condensed milk a little at a time, and stir until filling is smooth and creamy. Pour filling into graham cracker crust. Bake in preheated 350-degree oven for 15 minutes. Chill in refrigerator for 2 hours. Cover pie with a generous covering of Whipped Cream or whipped topping and garnish with a cherry in the center surrounded by thin slices of lime. Serves 6 to 8.

Italian-Style Ice Cream
with Raspberry Sauce

1 (8-oz.) pkg. cream cheese, room
 temperature
1 cup real butter, room temperature
1 cup powdered sugar
½ cup golden raisins

½ cup raisins
2 tsp. fresh lime juice
1½ tsp. vanilla extract
1 (8-oz.) pkg. frozen raspberries, thawed
 (undrained)

Beat cream cheese and butter with an electric mixer until well combined. Beat in sugar, raisins, lime juice and vanilla extract. Refrigerate until well chilled. Scoop onto serving plates. Surround with raspberries and berry juice. Serves 4 to 6.

Hot Cross Buns

1 pkg. dry yeast
¼ cup very warm water
¾ cup whole milk
1 stick real butter
⅓ cup sugar
½ tsp. salt

4 cups sifted all-purpose flour
1 tsp. ground cinnamon
¼ tsp. ground allspice
¼ tsp. cardamom
1 egg
½ cup red currants

Dissolve yeast in water. Heat milk in a 3-quart saucepan until it is bubbling around the edges. Add butter, sugar, and salt. Remove from the stove and cool to lukewarm. Stir in yeast mixture. Mix and sift together the flour, cinnamon, allspice, and cardamom. Add half the flour mixture to butter mixture. Beat well. Blend in egg and red currants. Add the remaining flour and stir in to make a soft dough. Turn dough onto a lightly floured board and knead until it is smooth and elastic. Place dough in a bowl which has been greased with butter. Twirl dough to grease its surface. Cover and let rise until it doubles in bulk. Punch dough down, turn and let rise again. Divide dough into 24 pieces. Form each piece of dough into a round bun. Place the buns on a baking sheet which has been greased with butter. Brush the surfaces of buns with slightly beaten egg white. Cut crosses on top of the buns. Let buns rise until they are double in bulk. Bake in 350° oven until golden brown. Add enough sifted powdered sugar (about 1½ cups) to remaining egg white to make a thick frosting. With a cake decorating bag, pipe crosses onto the top of the warm buns. Serves 24.

Key Lime Sherbet

juice of 4 limes
grated rind of 1 lime
1½ cups sugar

2 cups whole milk
2 cups cream

Mix lime juice, grated rind and sugar with a rotary beater. Add milk and cream slowly. Beat well and place in a freezing tray; when partly frozen, put back in electric mixer and beat again. Re-freeze; when partly frozen again, put back in electric mixer and beat a third time. Re-freeze.

Lemon Cream

2 cups cream
2 egg yolks, well beaten
½ cup sugar

rind of 1 lemon, grated
juice of 1 lemon
2 egg whites, stiffly beaten

Mix and beat together cream, egg yolks, sugar, and grated lemon rind. Bring this mixture to a boil, remove from the stove, and stir until cool. Put the lemon juice into a bowl and slowly pour the cream mixture over it, stirring until mixed. Gently fold in the egg whites. Sprinkle with additional grated lemon rind. Refrigerate for 1 hour. Serve chilled. Pound Cake is an excellent accompaniment to this simple dessert. Serves 6.

Lemon Flummery

1 cup boiling water
1 (3-oz.) pkg. lemon flavored gelatin
¾ cup dry white wine or tawny port

¼ cup cream
½ cup sweetened whipped cream for
  topping

Add boiling water to the lemon flavored gelatin and stir to dissolve gelatin completely. Add wine and cream. Mix thoroughly and pour into five 4-ounce serving molds. Refrigerate for 1 hour to set. Serve, topped with sweetened whipped cream. Serves 5.

Miss Dabney's Triple Chocolate Delight Pie

Keebler Chocolate Pie Crust
chocolate pie filling
Chocolate Miracle Whip

sweet chocolate shavings
1 cherry

Fill chocolate pie crust with chocolate pudding mix. Place in the refrigerator. Just before ready to serve, spread a very generous layer of cold Chocolate Miracle Whip (available at supermarkets). Garnish with sweet chocolate shavings and a cherry. Serves 6 to 8.

Miss Dabney Anne Lipscomb

Mocha Chocolate Chip Cheesecake

1½ cups finely crushed creme-filled
  chocolate sandwich cookies (about 18)
3 Tbsp. butter, melted
3 (8-oz.) pkgs. cream cheese, softened
1 (14-oz.) can sweetened Eagle Brand
  condensed milk
3 eggs

3 (1-oz.) squares semi-sweet chocolate,
  melted
2 Tbsp. instant coffee dissolved in 1
  Tbsp. warm water
2 Tbsp. vanilla extract
1 cup mini chocolate chips
  Whipped Cream

Preheat oven to 300 degrees. Combine cookie crumbs and margarine and press onto the bottom of a 9" spring form pan. In a large mixing bowl, beat cream cheese until it is fluffy. Gradually beat in the sweetened condensed milk until it is smooth. Add the remaining ingredients except chips and whipped topping and mix well. Stir in ¾ cup chocolate chips. Pour mixture into pan. Bake 1 hour or until center is set. Cool and chill in the refrigerator. Garnish with whipped topping and remaining ¼ cup of chocolate chips. Serves 6 to 8.

Mrs. Ann Lynch Webster

Southern Pralines

1 lb. light brown sugar
1 (6-oz.) can evaporated milk
2 Tbsp. light corn oil

¼ cup real butter
1 tsp. vanilla extract
1½ cups pecan halves

Mix sugar, evaporated milk and corn syrup in a two-quart saucepan. Cook over medium heat, stirring constantly, until the mixture comes to a boil. Continue cooking, stirring occasionally, until the temperature reaches 238 degrees on a candy thermometer. Remove from heat. Add butter, but do not stir. Cool to 110 degrees. Add vanilla extract and beat until creamy. Stir in pecan halves. Spoon onto waxed paper. Allow to cool completely before serving. Makes about 1½ lbs. of candy.

British Colonial-Style Shortcake Biscuits

2½ cups sifted all-purpose flour
½ cup unsalted butter,
   chilled
⅓ cup sugar
2 Tbsp. Citrus Sugar

1 Tbsp. plus 1 tsp. baking powder
½ tsp. cream of tartar
¼ tsp. salt
¾ cup chilled whipping cream

Preheat oven to 375 degrees. Line a large cookie sheet with aluminum foil. Generously butter foil. Mix the first 7 ingredients until the mixture resembles coarse meal. Place the mixture in a food processor. Pour cream evenly over mixture. Process until dough forms moist clumps. Transfer dough to lightly floured work surface. Knead gently until dough holds surface together. Pat out to 1" thickness. Cut into 3" rounds using floured biscuit cutter. Gather scraps and pat out and re-cut. Transfer biscuits to a cookie sheet, spacing 3" apart. Bake until light brown, about 18 minutes.

Old-Fashioned Strawberry Short Cake

strawberries
sugar
British Colonial-Style Shortcake Biscuits

Whipped Cream

Clean, trim and slice strawberries in half. Place strawberries in bowl and sprinkle with sugar. With a fork, mash about 25% of the sugared strawberry halves. Let the strawberries set in the refrigerator to cool for at least 20 minutes. Slice Old-Fashioned Shortcake Biscuits into halves. Place sugared strawberries on the bottom ½ of the biscuit and cold Whipped Cream on the top ½ of the biscuit. Lay the top ½ with the Whipped Cream over onto the bottom ½ with the sugared strawberries. Spoon 1 Tbsp. cold Whipped Cream on the outside center of top of the sandwich. Add ½ strawberry to Whipped Cream on top.

Peaches Flambé

2 large canned peach halves
2 Tbsp. all-purpose flour
½ cup real butter

2 thin slivers orange peel
2 thin slivers lemon peel
2 ozs. Brandy

Dredge peach halves in flour. Sauté in butter in small skillet or omit butter and deep-fry in hot oil (375 degrees) until golden brown. Place peach halves, cut-side-down, on warm platter. Garnish with orange and lemon peel. Pour brandy over peaches and ignite, basting until flame burns off. Serve with remaining warm brandy. Serves 1.

Pound Cake

A 1770 American Colonial recipe from Charleston, South Carolina

1 cup real butter
½ cup Crisco
3 cups sugar
5 large, or 6 medium eggs
2 tsp. lemon extract

¼ tsp. salt
3 cups, plus 5 Tbsp. sifted flour
1 cup whole milk
½ tsp. baking soda
1 tsp. cream of tartar

Cream butter, Crisco, and sugar together well. Add eggs, one at a time, blending just enough to mix. Add lemon extract and salt. Add flour and milk alternately, ending with flour. Sprinkle baking soda and cream of tartar sifted together on top of the butter and fold in gently. Pour into a large, greased and floured tube pan and bake at 315 degrees for 1 hour and 15 minutes. Do not open the oven until the cake is done. Cut out a paper stencil, place on top of cake and sprinkle powdered sugar through the design.

Raspberry-Blackberry Chilled Creme Dessert

2 cups whipping cream
1 cup plus 2 Tbsp. sugar, divided
1 envelope unflavored gelatin
1 tsp. vanilla extract
1 tsp. almond extract

2 Tbsp. brandy
2 cups sour cream
½ cup fresh or frozen raspberries
½ cup fresh or frozen blackberries
8 fresh mint sprigs

In a saucepan, combine cream and 1 cup sugar. Cook and stir constantly over low heat until candy thermometer reads 160 degrees or steam rises from pan. Do not boil. Stir in gelatin until dissolved; add vanilla and almond extracts. Cool 10 minutes. Stir brandy into sour cream. Whisk sour cream mixture into cream and vanilla/almond mixture. Pour into eight dessert glasses. Chill for at least 2 hours. Before serving, combine berries and remaining sugar; spoon over each serving. Garnish each glass with a sprig of fresh mint. Serves 6 to 8.

Mrs. Ann Lynch Webster

Raspberry Swirl Peach Soup

This recipe was given to the author by Mrs. Trudy Webster Lipscomb. A first course that's different and delicious—chilled peach soup with swirls of raspberry purée. So easy and so stunning.

2 cups fresh or frozen peaches, peeled,
    seeded and diced
1 (12-oz.) can peach or apricot nectar
⅓ cup NutraSweet Spoonful
1 cup fresh or frozen raspberries

2 Tbsp. water
2 Tbsp. NutraSweet Spoonful
powdered or fresh ground nutmeg
mint sprigs

Process peaches, nectar and ⅓ cup of NutraSweet Spoonful in a blender or food processor until smooth: lay a piece of plastic wrap across the surface to retain the color and refrigerate until very chilled. Process raspberries, 2 Tbsp. NutraSweet, 2 Tbsp. water in a blender or food processor until smooth; strain and discard seeds; lay a piece of plastic wrap across top of purée to preserve color: refrigerate until very chilled. Spoon peach mixture into bowls; place 6 to 8 random-size drops of raspberry purée on top of peach soup; with the point of a knife, hook a little tail on each drop (like a comma). Sprinkle lightly with nutmeg; garnish with mint. Serve in cold bowls as a first course or as a treat on a hot summer day. Serves 3.

Sherry Cake

1 box yellow cake mix (Duncan Hines)
1 (1.3-oz.) pkg. instant vanilla pudding mix
¾ cup Mazola oil

4 eggs
1 cup sherry, divided
1 cup powdered sugar

Preheat oven to 350 degrees. Mix cake and pudding mix. Mix oil, eggs, and ¾ cup sherry. Stir oil, egg, and sherry mixture into cake and pudding mixture. Pour cake mixture into a Bundt cake pan. Place cake on the middle oven shelf. Bake for 55 minutes. Allow cake to cool until the sides of the cake pull away from the sides of the pan. Mix together ¼ cup sherry and powdered sugar. Remove cake from the pan and with a toothpick, punch holes at 1" intervals on top of cake. Pour sherry and powdered sugar mixture over cake.

Mrs. Anne Lipscomb Webster

Sicilian Ice Cream

½ cup whipping cream
¼ cup powdered sugar
½ cup mixed candied fruits, diced small
½ tsp. raspberry liqueur

1 egg white
1 pt. Vanilla Custard Ice Cream
¾ pt. chocolate ice cream

Whip heavy cream and stir in powdered sugar, candied fruit and liqueur. Beat egg white stiff and fold it thoroughly into the whipped cream mixture. Line the bottom and sides of a 1½-quart mold with ½" Vanilla Custard Ice Cream. Cover with a ½" layer of chocolate ice cream. Fill the hollow with the cream and egg-white mixture. Smooth the top, and cover it with wax paper. Seal with the mold lid. Freeze until the ice cream is firm throughout. Unmold and slice into wedges.

Soft Molasses Cakes

A 1773 American Colonial recipe.

2½ cups sifted flour
2 tsp. baking soda
1 tsp. ginger
1 tsp. cinnamon
¼ tsp. salt
½ cup butter, softened

½ cup sugar
½ cup sorghum molasses
1 egg
¼ cup cold water
1 cup golden raisins

Mix and sift together flour, baking soda, ginger, cinnamon, and salt. Beat butter, sugar, sorghum molasses, and egg together until light and fluffy. Add the sifted ingredients alternately with cold water and beat until blended. Stir in the raisins. Drop by rounded Tbsp. 3" apart onto a greased cookie sheet. Bake for 10 to 12 minutes at 350 degrees.

Southern Pecan Pie

A 1976 recipe by John C. Stennis, Mississippi United States Senator 1946 to 1988.

3 eggs, beaten
1 cup sugar
1 cup light or dark corn syrup
½ tsp. salt

1 tsp. vanilla
1 cup pecan halves
1 unbaked 9-inch pie shell

Beat eggs and sugar until thick. Add corn syrup, salt, vanilla and pecan halves. Pour into pie shell and bake in preheated 300 degree oven 50 to 60 minutes or until filling is set.

Spanish Caramel Custard

This flan recipe was given to the author by the chef in a little restaurant in Tampico, Mexico, in the summer of 1968. The author was traveling with and studying little-visited archeological sites in Central and Eastern Mexico with the artist, writer, educator and one-of-a-kind friend, Professor Homer Castille, Jr. of Canton and Meridian, Mississippi

3 cups sugar
½ cup boiling water
6 eggs
1 Tbsp. anisette
1 tsp. vanilla extract

pinch nutmeg
pinch salt
2 cups scalded whole milk (raw milk
    today) was originally used, not
    recommended

Melt 1 cup of sugar in a heavy skillet over low heat, stirring constantly. When mixture is light brown, remove from heat and slowly add boiling water; stir and boil until caramel is dissolved in the water. Pour caramel into 8 custard cups. Cool the cups for 30 minutes in refrigerator. Beat eggs until frothy. Add remaining sugar, anisette, vanilla extract, nutmeg, and salt; beat well. Scald milk and add gradually to egg mixture. Remove caramel cups from the refrigerator and pour custard into caramel cups. Place cups in a pan of water and bake at 350 degrees for 30 to 40 minutes or until the custard is set. Air cool. Then chill custard cups for at least 1 hour in the refrigerator.

When ready to serve, remove cups from the refrigerator and loosen around the edges with a spatula and turn mold upside down on individual serving saucers. The caramel will be on top of the custard. An alternate preparation method is to coat the sides and bottom of a baking dish with some of the warm caramel. Cool caramel coated dish by placing it in the refrigerator for 30 minutes. Add the custard mixture; place the baking dish in a tray of water and bake at 350 degrees for 30 to 40 minutes or until the custard is set; air cool. Chill the baking dish for at least 1 hour in the refrigerator; when ready to serve, remove the baking dish from the refrigerator and cut individual square servings. Place each serving on a serving plate and pour remaining caramel over each individual serving. Serves 8.

Strawberry Custard Pie

1 baked 10-inch pie shell, cooled
1 pkg. vanilla pudding and pie filling mix
8 ladyfingers, split in half
1 pt. strawberries
½ tsp. strawberry liqueur
10 oz. Currant Jelly

2 tsp. water
whipped cream
1 strawberry
sprig fresh mint

Prepare and bake pie shell in a 10-inch glass pie plate; allow to cool. Prepare vanilla pudding and pie filling mix and pour into cool baked pie shell. Slit and place ladyfinger halves, cut side down on top of pie filling. Wash, hull, and cut strawberries in ½, add liqueur. Arrange strawberry halves close together, cut side down, in circles over top of ladyfingers. Heat Currant Jelly with water until softened. Blend until smooth. Cool, then spoon over berries. Chill. Just before serving, place whipped cream in a pastry bag and border the pie. Garnish center of pie with a strawberry and a sprig of fresh mint.

Strawberry Flambé

slice of Pound Cake
strawberries
sugar

meringue
absinthe
brandy

Cover a slice of pound cake with strawberries that have been marinated in sugar and water. Build up over strawberries a peak of meringue, sweetened to taste and flavored with absinthe. Put under broiler to brown. In peak of meringue, set a half egg shell filled with brandy. Light brandy as dessert is brought to table. Serves 1.

Strawberry Shortcake

2 cups all-purpose flour
3 tsp. baking powder
¾ tsp. salt
3 Tbsp. sugar
1 (3-oz.) pkg. cream cheese, softened
3 Tbsp. real butter, softened

1 egg, beaten
about ½ cup whole milk
real butter, melted
strawberries sweetened with sugar
whipped cream

Mix and sift together flour, baking powder, salt, and sugar. Cut in cream cheese and butter. Pour beaten egg into a measuring cup and add enough milk to measure ¾ cup. Gradually stir egg and milk mixture into the flour mixture. Knead the dough for about 20 seconds. Divide the dough into two parts; roll each part to ½" thick. Cut 6 circles from each half of dough. Spread one circle with melted butter and place another circle on top. Bake at 425 degrees for about 15 minutes. When done, separate the layers. Spread each layer with butter. Put sweetened strawberries on one circle and top with other circle. Add strawberries and top with whipping cream. Serves 6.

Vanilla Custard and Fruit Trifle

A 1796 recipe.

2½ cups vanilla custard
1 sponge cake sliced or 24 ladyfingers
¾ to 1 cup medium sherry
8 ozs. raspberry jam
¾ cup candied cherries, sliced

¾ cup sliced almonds, toasted
1 cup cream
3 Tbsp. sugar
½ tsp. vanilla extract

Make a thin vanilla custard. If needed add extra milk. In a 2-quart, straight-sided glass or crystal bowl, arrange a layer of sponge cake or ladyfingers on the bottom, and line the sides. Sprinkle with ½ cup sherry. Pour half of the custard over cake. Dot with raspberry jam, half of candied cherries, and ⅓ of almonds. Arrange another layer, and repeat, saving 12 cherry halves for top decoration. Whip the cream, sweetened with sugar and flavored with vanilla extract. Spread enough to cover the top of the trifle, and decorate with cherry halves. Must be made and refrigerated at least 6 hours before serving. Serves 6 to 8.

Vanilla Custard Ice Cream

In Clarksdale, Mississippi, before the days of electric ice cream makers, the author's grandfather, Roselyn Sinclair Lynch, converted a hand-cranked ice cream maker to electric by mounting their wooden ice cream maker and an electric motor on a board, and installed a large diameter belt wheel on the ice cream maker and a small diameter belt wheel on the motor, with an automotive fan belt attaching the two. This wooden ice cream machine was still in fine working order as late as 1975.

2 cups sugar
4 Tbsp. all-purpose flour
¼ tsp. salt
3 cups sweet milk

4 eggs, well beaten
3 pts, light cream (half and half)
7 tsp. vanilla extract

Mix sugar and flour. Add salt, then milk. Cook about 10 minutes in top of a double boiler, stirring constantly. Add some of the cooked mixture to the beaten eggs, return to double boiler, and cook an additional 2 or 3 minutes. Cool. Add cream and vanilla. Pour mixture into 1-gallon crank freezer and crank until ice cream is made. When ice cream is made, remove the dashers, pack and Insulate over the top of the ice cream container with towels, and let set 1 hour before serving. Makes 1 gallon.

Germany imports about 16,000 tons of venison annually. This represents about half of the world total and half of Germany's annual consumption.

30

Drinks and Punches

Whether it be an elegant Christmas dinner, a fall brunch or a summer cookout with friends, the drinks we choose make a statement about us, our friends, and the food we serve.

For a real taste of history, you may wish to try the non-alcoholic 1690s recipe for Syllabub and my family's 1700s Sassafras Tea, or try the 1700s mildly alcoholic Colonial Caribbean Ginger Beer, an 1860s Confederate Veterans Blackberry Wine, or the Powerful New England Puritans' 1600s Hot Buttered Rum.

New Orleans has a long history of blending the good of many of the cultures. The drinks of New Orleans are as diverse as its cultures. Try these three New Orleans favorites: Cafe Brulot, Milk Punch, and Ramos Gin Fizz. Make your own Homemade Hot Chocolate.

DRINKS WITHOUT ALCOHOL

Blackberry Fizzle

An 1800s Mississippi recipe.

5 oz. tartaric acid (obtained at drugstore)	12 lbs. blackberries, mashed
2 qts. water	sugar

Dissolve tartaric acid in water. Pour into the blackberries and let stand for 2 days. Strain mixture through 3 layers of wet cheesecloth. To each pint of clear juice, add 1 cup sugar. Bring juice to a rolling boil for one minute. Pour the juice into clean glass soft drink bottles and seal tightly. Refrigerate. Makes a nice summer drink, served either cold, over crushed ice, or as a party punch.

Fruit Punch

8 cups water	1 shredded pineapple
4 cups sugar	1 box strawberries
8 oranges	2 grapefruit, chopped
3 lemons	2 qts. Apollinaris water

Boil the water and sugar and allow to cool. Add the remaining ingredients. If too strong, this punch may be diluted.

Cold Coffee Punch

3 oz. Nescafe Classic Instant Coffee
1 (16-oz.) can chocolate syrup
1 cup sugar
4 cups boiling water

2 cups cold whole milk
2 qts. cold whole milk
1 qt. Vanilla Ice Custard Cream

Combine instant coffee, chocolate syrup and sugar with boiling water in a saucepan. Cook until instant coffee and sugar are dissolved, stirring constantly. Cool. Combine with 2 cups milk and refrigerate 6 hours or until cold. Pour into punch bowl. Stir in remaining 2 quarts of cold milk. Top with small scoops of vanilla ice cream. Ladle into punch cups. Serves 30 to 35.

Ginger Ale Julep

cracked ice or small ice cubes
Mintade

ginger ale
fresh mint sprigs

Fill tall glasses half full of cracked ice. Add 1 Tbsp. of Mintade to each glass. Fill the glasses with chilled ginger ale. Garnish each glass with a sprig of mint.

Gingerroot Beer

4 oz. dried gingerroot
1 gal. water
juice of 1 lemon or 2 limes

1 pkg. active dry yeast
½ lb. sugar

Pound the gingerroot to make it soft and then boil the roots in ½ gal. water for about 20 minutes. Remove from stove and set aside to cool. Mix the lemon juice and dry yeast in a cup of warm water in which gingerroot was boiled. Pour in remaining root water and let mixture sit for 2 days. Strain out the root and stir in the sugar. Seal in clean glass soft drink bottles and place in refrigerator to chill. Keep stored in the refrigerator. Makes approx. ten 12-oz. bottles.

Harvest-Time Switchel

Switchel is a old-time thirst quencher. Circa 1700s.

2 cups white sugar
1 cup sorghum molasses
¼ cup apple cider vinegar

1 tsp. fresh ground ginger root
1 gal, water

Mix all ingredients in a large pot with 1 qt. of water, and heat until dissolved. Add the remaining water. Chill in the refrigerator for 3 hours. Serve as is or over ice. Makes 1 gallon.

Homemade Hot Chocolate

A circa 1800 Shaker recipe.

2 ozs. unsweetened baking chocolate
2 Tbsp. hot water
⅔ cup white sugar
2 tsp. ground cinnamon
½ tsp. salt

2 cups coffee
3 cups hot whole milk
1 tsp. vanilla extract
whipped cream
cinnamon sticks

Melt chocolate with hot water in a double boiler. Stir in mixture of sugar, cinnamon and salt. Add coffee; mix well. Cook for 5 minutes over simmering water. Stir in hot milk and vanilla. Cook over simmering water for 30 minutes. Beat until frothy. Pour into cups. Garnish with whipped cream and cinnamon sticks. Serves 6.

Homemade Soda Pop

Circa 1800s. Before the day when Coca-Cola first was bottled in Vicksburg, Mississippi, a mixture of bicarbonate of soda and tartaric acid was added to a drink to make it fizz.

1 qt. water
4 tsp. cream of tartar
4 cup sugar
1 Tbsp. vanilla extract

whites of 3 eggs, beaten until stiff
fresh lemon or lime juice
bicarbonate of soda

Dissolve cream of tartar and sugar in boiling water. Remove from the stove and add the vanilla extract. When this mixture has cooled, add the egg whites and stir thoroughly. Bottle in clean glass soda pop bottles with screw-type tops and refrigerate. To make the actual soda pop, dissolve 2 Tbsp. of syrup plus ½ tsp. lemon or lime juice per 8-oz. glass of ice cold water. Then add ½ tsp. of bicarbonate of soda.

Hot Spiced Cranberry and Apple Punch

2 qts. cranberry juice cocktail
2 qts. apple juice
¼ cup light brown sugar, packed

2 cinnamon sticks, broken
6 whole cloves
cinnamon sticks

Mix all ingredients in a large saucepan or stock pot and simmer for 1 hour. Strain and serve hot. Use long cinnamon sticks for stirrers. Serves 16 to 18.

Iced Russian Chocolate

1 pt. strong coffee
1 pt. whole milk
2 squares (ounces) chocolate, grated
½ cup sugar

½ tsp. vanilla extract
pinch of salt
sweetened whipped cream

Combine the coffee and milk; add the chocolate. Cook in a double boiler until the chocolate has melted, beating occasionally with an egg beater. Add the sugar and salt; cook 2 or 3 minutes longer; stir in the vanilla extract; cover and chill. Serve very cold with a topping of whipped cream.

Mint Punch with Lime Juice

1½ cups sugar
2 cups boiling water
1 cup dried mint leaves
1 tsp. orange rind, grated

2 cups orange juice
1¼ cups lime juice
1½ bottles (67 oz.) of ginger ale
fresh mint sprigs

Add the sugar to the water and boil until the sugar is dissolved. Add mint leaves and orange rind. Stir in orange juice and lime juice. Steep, covered, for 20 minutes. Chill in the refrigerator overnight. Strain and pour into a punch bowl. Add ice. Add ginger ale; mix gently. Ladle into punch cups garnished with fresh mint sprigs. Punch can be frozen in a decorative ring or in ice trays and added to punch. Serves 16 to 20.

Mint and Fruit Punch

This is a 1700 American Colonial recipe of President James Monroe.

½ cup water
⅓ cup sugar
½ cup fresh mint leaves

1 cup grape juice
1 cup orange or sweet grapefruit juice
½ cup lime or lemon juice

Boil water and remove from the stove. Add the sugar and most of the mint leaves (reserve a few leaves for a garnish). Stir the mixture until the sugar is dissolved. When the liquid cools, strain out the mint; add the grape, orange or sweet grapefruit, and lime or lemon juice. Chill overnight in the refrigerator. Serve the punch over ice with a mint leaf on top. Serves 4 to 6.

Mintade

½ cup water
⅔ cup lemon juice
½ cup sugar

6 Tbsp. fresh mint, chopped
green food coloring

Boil sugar and water for 5 minutes. Add chopped mint leaves and lemon juice and allow to stand overnight. Strain and color with a few drops of green food coloring. Pour into a jar and store in refrigerator. Add to iced tea, lemonade, punch or any combination of fruit juices.

Orange Julius

⅓ cup frozen orange juice concentrate
½ cup whole milk
½ cup water

6 ice cubes
¼ cup sugar
½ tsp. vanilla extract

Chill serving glasses in the freezer for 1 hour. Combine all ingredients and process in a blender till smooth. Pour into frozen glasses and serve immediately. Makes 3 cups.

Rainbow Ice Cubes

strawberry soda
raspberry soda
cherry soda

orange soda
grape soda

Pour the sodas into separate bowls; let stand about an hour to allow the carbonation to pass off. Then pour each flavor into separate ice cube trays and freeze until hard. Can be used to cool flavored drinks and punches.

Russian Tea

½ gal. hot water
⅛ lb. Lipton's tea

2 lbs. sugar
6 lemons, grated and Juiced

Steep tea in boiling hot water. Mix together the lemon juice, sugar and grated peel of 3 lemons, 3 cups of water, and boil for 10 minutes. Strain tea leaf from the tea and add the sugar mixture. When cold, strain. Serve either hot or cold. Makes 2 gal. of tea. Serves 15 to 30.

Sassafras Tea

This is an old Webster/Lynch/Sinclair (St. Clair) recipe that was given to me by my grandfather, Roselyn Sinclair Lynch. Mr. Lynch stated that this recipe had been in his family for many, many generations. This recipe may date back to the 1650s when John Sinclair and his wife Mary landed in Exeter, New Hampshire from Edinburgh, Scotland. It is interesting to note that my father, Harold Webster, Sr. also spoke of drinking Sassafras Tea in Oak Ridge, Mississippi, and, that it was an old family recipe. I have been given this recipe from both sides of my family. This drink was very popular in Colonial America. Today we can taste sassafras without going to the trouble of digging and drying the roots. It is the flavoring used in root-beer soft drinks.

6 dry sassafras roots
1 qt. water

sugar or sorghum molasses, to taste

Wash roots well and let dry for several months. Put dry roots in a coffeepot with water. Soak overnight. Then place on fire and boil slowly till fairly strong. Dilute and sweeten to taste. Serves 7 or 8.

Sparkling Fruit Juice Cocktail

¾ cups sugar
1 cup water
1 cup grapefruit juice

1 cup pineapple juice
1 qt. ginger ale
chunks of cherries, strawberries or
    pineapples

Mix sugar and water in saucepan; bring to a boil. Cook for 5 minutes. Remove from the stove and cool. Add fruit juices to syrup and chill in the refrigerator for 3 hours. Add ginger ale just before serving. Garnish with chunks of cherries, strawberries or pineapple.

Syllabub

This recipe, with very few variations, can be easily traced to before 1690.

3 cups apple cider
¼ cup lemon or lime juice
3 Tbsp. grated lemon or lime rind
1 cup sugar
1 tsp. corn syrup

2 egg whites
¼ cup sugar
2 cups whole milk
1 cup heavy cream
fresh ground nutmeg

To make the cider mixture, mix together the apple, lemon or lime juice, lemon or lime rind, sugar and corn syrup. Stir or gently beat until the sugar is dissolved. Chill for 2 hours in the refrigerator. To make the meringue, beat egg whites with a mixer until foamy. Add ¼ cup sugar, 1 tbsp. at a time, beating until eggs will make stiff peaks. Add milk and cream to the cider mixture and beat until it is frothy. Pour cider mixture into a cold punch bowl. Spoon meringue over the top. Sprinkle with nutmeg. Serves 16 to 20.

Turkish Punch

1 qt. canned apricots
1 cup sugar
1 cup water
2 cups canned apple juice or cider

juice of 1 orange
juice of 1 lemon
carbonated water

Rub the apricots through a coarse sieve or food mill. Boil the sugar and water together for 10 minutes; add to the apricots. When cool, add the other fruit juices. Let stand 2 hours and then dilute with ice water or charged water. Makes 20 small punch cupfuls.

Christmas Punch

1 qt. water
1 qt. cranberries
juice of 3 oranges

1 Tbsp. liquid from maraschino cherries
sugar, to taste

Cook the cranberries in water until tender. Press through a sieve or food mill. Add to this pulp the juice of 3 oranges, cherry liquid and sugar to taste. Cook just long enough to dissolve the sugar. Cool, freeze, and serve in sherbet glasses decorated with sprays of holly or with the handles tied with green ribbon and a few holly berries. Or insert a tiny Yuletide candle in the center of the punch.

Whitetail deer breeding begins in mid October and peaks in mid-to-late November. A buck may mate with several does. Fawns are born after a gestation period of about 201 days, from early May through late September, with about 60 percent of the total born in June. By early November a male fawn weighs about 85 pounds and a female about 80 pounds. The average reproduction rate of well-nourished prime-age does is 1.73 per year.

DRINKS WITH ALCOHOL

Homemade Applejack

This is an old-time recipe that has been made since the first time a man left his hard cider outside and let it freeze. Applejack is hard cider whose alcoholic content has been increased beyond what fermentation alone will produce.

Place an open bucket of Hard Cider in the freezer until a slushy ice forms on the top. Remove the ice and you have Applejack. Some people have been known to repeat this process several times in an attempt to raise the alcohol content even higher.

Blackberry Wine

From a Confederate Veteran's widow. Circa 1800.

To each water bucket of washed and mashed berries, pour a quart of boiling water; put in a stone crock or glass container, tie a piece of cloth over the top and let it stand for 3 days. Then strain through a jelly bag, but do not squeeze. To each gallon of juice, add 3 lbs. of sugar. Put back in crock and let stand for 15 days. When it may be bottled, put into jugs laid on the side and put away in a dark, cool place.

Coffee Brulot

1 cinnamon stick, mashed
12 whole cloves
peel of 2 oranges, cut in thin slivers
peel of 2 lemons, cut in thin slivers
6 sugar lumps
8 oz. brandy
2 oz. curacao
1 qt. strong, black coffee

In a chafing dish add cinnamon, cloves, orange and lemon peel and sugar lumps and mash together. Add brandy and curacao and mix well. Carefully ignite brandy and stir until the sugar is dissolved. Gradually add the black coffee and continue stirring until the flame goes out. Serve hot in demitasse cups. Makes 10 to 12 servings.

Chatham Artillery Punch

A circa 1778 recipe. The Chatham Artillery was organized in 1776 and is one of the oldest military organizations in the United States. George Washington visited with this unit when he toured Georgia in 1791. The author's great-great-great-great-great grandfather, Jacob Curry served with this unit before he located in Spanish Mississippi around 1795.

1 lb. green tea	1 gal. gin
2 gal. water	5 lbs. dark sugar
3 gal. Catawba wine (other fruit wine)	2 qts. maraschino cherries
1 gal. dark rum	3 dozen oranges, sliced and seeded
1 gal. brandy	3 dozen lemons, sliced and seeded
1 gal. rye whisky	10 qts. champagne

Steep the green tea in 2 gal. of cold water overnight. The next day strain tea through 3 layers of wet cheesecloth into 4 (5-gal.) buckets. Mix strained tea and all the other ingredients except the champagne. Allow this mixture to mellow for at least 2 weeks in a cool dark place. To serve, pour the punch over ice and add 1 qt. of champagne for every gallon of punch. Makes 12 gallons. Serves 250 to 350 strong drink lovers.

Ginger Beer

A 1700 English Colonial Caribbean recipe.

¼ lb. ginger	4½ pts. boiling water
few grains rice	sugar to taste

Use ginger that has been dried for a day in the sun after digging. Peel and pound until soft. Pour on boiling water. Leave overnight and half of next day. Strain, and add sugar to taste. Put into bottles, and to each bottle add two or three grains of rice to produce fermentation. Cork bottles and stand in the sun for a day before putting in the fridge to chill for use.

Hard Cider

Fill a 5-gallon water bottle with fresh unpasteurized cider, leaving about 10% of the container empty to allow room for expansion. Cover and tie the opening loosely with a piece of cloth, and store in a cool dark room where the temperature stays between 40 and 50 degrees. Check the temperature frequently. High temperatures will produce rapid fermentation and a bitter flavor. Temperatures that are too cool may prevent fermentation and the cider will not harden. The cider should start to ferment in a day or less. You can hear hissing and tiny bubbles will appear in the liquid. If the cider seems to be fermenting too quickly, the hissing will be loud and the bubbles large. Move the cider to a cooler place. If little or no fermentation appears to be taking place, dissolve a cup or two of sugar in some fresh cider and add it to the bottle. The hard cider is ready when the hissing and bubbling have completely stopped. Winemakers use a winemaker's saccharometer to determine when the hard cider is made. It is made when the instrument indicates a sugar content of about 17 percent. Siphon the hard cider off carefully. Leave the residue in the bottom of the container bottle in clean glass soft drink bottles that have screw-on-type caps. The hard cider can be drunk as is, but if you will allow the hard cider to age for several months, it will be much better.

Hot Buttered Rum

Circa 1600s. This powerful drink is an old-time New England idea of one portion, for one man. It has been said that this old Puritan's drink will make a man see double and feel single,

1 tsp. powdered sugar
boiling water
¼ cup Puerto Rican or Mt. Gay dark rum

1 Tbsp. butter
nutmeg, freshly grated

Place the powdered sugar in a very large hot mug. And ¼ cup boiling water, rum and butter. Fill the remaining mug with boiling water. Stir well. Garnish the top with freshly grated nutmeg.

Irish Coffee

1 oz. Irish whisky
1½ tsp. Demeara or pure cane sugar

fresh strong coffee
chilled Whipped Cream

Mix the whisky and sugar and heat, but do not boil. Mix well and serve in a pre-warmed coffee cup. Fill the cup with coffee to within ½" of top. Stir until sugar is dissolved. Spoon chilled whipped cream on top.

Mr. Harold W. Webster, Sr.

Homemade Elderberry Wine

18 oz. dried elderberries
15 oz. raisins
5 lbs. sugar
2 Tbsp. citric acid

2 Campden tablets
2 tsp. yeast nutrient
2 gallons water
1 pkg. wine yeast

Mix together the first 6 ingredients and place the mixture in a large clean plastic container that has a loosefitting lid. Boil the water and pour over the mixture. Mix well and make sure that all of the sugar is dissolved, cover with the lid and stand overnight in a room where the temperature will stay between 65 and 70 degrees. Next morning sprinkle the yeast on the surface of the mixture and let stand, covered, for 24 hours. Let the mixture ferment for 6 or 7 days; stir the ferment twice a day. On the fifth day make a sugar solution by mixing 2 parts sugar to 1 part water. Add 1 cup of the sugar solution and let stand for 2 days and then add another cup of the sugar solution. Let stand for 2 more days and strain the ferment through a fine sieve lined with 2 layers of cheesecloth. Let stand overnight. The next day siphon the wine into 1-gallon glass jars and place fermentation locks on the jars. Let set for 3 weeks in a dark cool place. Then siphon wine into clean gallon jugs and replace fermentation locks. Let the wine stand for 3 months, siphon the wine into clean gallon jugs and replace fermentation locks. Let the wine stand until the wine is clear and stable. Add 3 Wine-Art stabilizer tablets per gallon and siphon off into glass bottles and seal.

Milk Punch

1¼ oz. bourbon
3 ozs. half and half or cream
1 tsp. superfine powdered sugar

1 dash vanilla
fresh grated nutmeg

Mix all ingredients and shake thoroughly. Strain into 8-ounce highball glass, and top with nutmeg.

Mr. Harold W. Webster, Sr.

Mint Julep

2 oz. sour mash bourbon
4 sprigs fresh mint
½ oz. Simple Syrup

sprig of fresh mint
slice of orange
cherry

Place the bourbon, sprigs of mint and simple syrup into a tall 14-ounce glass or silver mug. Fill the glass with shaved ice and stir with a mixing spoon until the outside of the glass or mug is coated with frost. Garnish with a generous sprig of mint, a slice of orange, and a cherry.

Mr. Harold W. Webster, Sr.

Muscadine Wine

1 gal. muscadine berries
1 qt, boiling water

sugar

Add the muscadine berries and boiling water and let stand 24 hours. Crush berries and strain through 3 layers of cheesecloth. To each gallon of juice, add 3 lbs. of sugar. Cover loosely and let stand until it quits fermenting. Siphon off wine and store in clean glass soft drink bottles with screw-on lids.

Prof. Homar Castille

Gin Fizz

1 oz. lemon Juice
2 tsp, superfine granulated sugar
1 egg white
1 dash vanilla extract

2 dashes orange flower water
2 oz. cream or half and half
1 oz. Beefeaters gin

Mix and shake together thoroughly and strain into an 8-ounce highball glass.

Mr. Harold W. Webster, Sr.

Cafe Parfait

fresh dark roast drip coffee grounds
¼ cup Simple Syrup
rum
Vanilla Custard Ice Cream

Coffee Ice Cream
whipped cream or whipped topping
maraschino cherries

Make the coffee syrup by making a pot of dripped coffee. Make another pot of coffee by pouring the first pot of coffee over fresh grounds; repeat the process until the coffee is thick. Add simple syrup to the thick coffee to make the coffee syrup. Mix equal parts of rum and coffee syrup. In a parfait glass, pour 2 tsp. of the rum-coffee syrup mixture into the bottom of a glass. Fill the glass ½ full of Vanilla Custard Ice Cream. Pour ½ Tbsp. of the rum-syrup mixture on top of the ice cream. Fill glass to top with Coffee Ice Cream. Top with Whipped Cream or whipped topping and a maraschino cherry. Serve with a long spoon. Serves 1.

Mr. Harold W. Webster, Sr.

The white-tailed deer is thought to have arisen in Eurasia and migrated across the Alaskan land bridge. The modern white tail is considered to be a New World descendant of those early travelers.

Roman Fruit Punch

1 cup sugar
1¾ cups water
grated rind of 1 orange
grated rind of 1 lemon
juice of 2 oranges

juice of 2 lemons
½ cup sugar
¼ cup water
1 egg white
½ cup light rum

Boil sugar, water and rind of orange and lemon for 5 to 6 minutes. Allow the syrup to cool. Add orange and lemon juice. Freeze the mixture in an ice cream freezer. Combine ½ cup sugar with ¼ cup water. Boil the syrup until it registers 240 degrees on a candy thermometer. Beat the egg white until it is stiff. Gradually pour the hot syrup into the egg white, beating constantly until the mixture is cool and thick. Add this meringue to the frozen sherbet and mix together well. Return it to the freezer again before serving. Stir in rum and serve in punch cups.

Homemade Raspberry Wine

2 water buckets raspberries
boiling water

sugar
clean glass bottles with screw-on tops

Wash raspberries and remove any foreign particles. For each bucket of raspberries, boil 1 quart of water. Mash berries and place in a large ceramic crock. Add boiling water. Tie a piece of clean cloth over the crock and let stand for 3 or 4 days. Strain the juice through 4 layers of moistened cheesecloth and let drip overnight. DO NOT squeeze. To each gallon of juice, add 3 lbs. of sugar; mix well. Place the sugared juice back into the cleaned crock and let stand for 15 days or until fermentation stops. Siphon off the wine into sterilized glass bottles with screw-on caps. Seal bottles and lay them on their sides in a cool dark place. The wine needs to age for at least 3 months. Master homemade winemaker, Mr. Tom Percy of Phippsburg, Maine, lets his wine age for 1 year—if his friends don't drink it all up. Serve chilled.

Sazerac Cocktail

2 dashes Simple Syrup
1 dash Angostura Bitters
2 dashes Peychaud Bitters

1¼ oz, rye whisky
3 dashes absinthe

Mix and stir together the Simple Syrup, Angostura Bitters, Peychaud Bitters and rye whiskey in a mixing glass. Put 3 dashes of absinthe into a chilled Old Fashioned glass. Roll around to coat inside of glass and discard. Then strain drink from mixing glass into Old Fashioned glass and add a twist of lemon peel. Serve as is. Do not add ice.

Mr. Harold W. Webster, Sr.

31

Lagniappe
(A Little Something Extra)

Lagniappe contains some new recipes and a few very old recipes that have been modified for today's cooks. Also included are recipes for ingredients or unique recipes that can be made from scratch or used in other recipes. Some recipes are just fun to make.

Blackberry Catsup

2 cups fresh or frozen blackberries
½ cup cider vinegar
¼ tsp, ground red (cayenne) pepper
⅛ tsp. ground ginger

2 Tbsp. dark brown sugar
½ tsp. salt
½ tsp. ground cinnamon

Process blackberries through a food mill. Discard the seeds and skins. Mix all ingredients and place them in a saucepan. Simmer for about 15 minutes or until the catsup is thickened to the consistency of tomato catsup. Freeze in half pint jars.

Mrs. Clyde Lacy Lynch

Blackberry Jelly

Put 1 quart of fresh, and slightly underripe whole blackberries in a pan with no sugar or water and cook over low heat until soft. Press through jelly bag and strain. Measure juice and bring to a boil. Add 1½ cups sugar for each cup of juice. When juice and sugar mixture begins to boil, remove from heat immediately and stir until all sugar is dissolved. Pour into sterilized ½ pint jelly jars. Fill to within ½" of top. Seal with paraffin. Put on cap, screw band down firmly. Process in a boiling water bath for 5 minutes. Makes 3 to 4 (8-oz.) jelly glasses.

Mrs. Clyde Lacy Lynch

Blackberry Hot Pepper Jelly

Use above recipe, add 1½ tsp. crushed red pepper flakes and seeds when adding sugar.

Mrs. Clyde Lacy Lynch

Bouquet Garni

1 bay leaf, broken
½ tsp. fresh thyme leaves, chopped
½ tsp. fresh rosemary leaves, chopped
½ tsp. fresh ginger root, sliced

½ tsp. fresh lemon basil leaves, chopped
3 sprigs parsley, chopped
cheesecloth or infuser

Tie spices in cheesecloth. Place in stew, soup or sauce; simmer and remove the bouquet before serving.

Brine Cure for Venison or Pork

2 gals, water
3 lbs. salt
1 lb. dark brown sugar

2 Tbsp. black pepper
5 crushed cloves
1 Tbsp. white pepper

Mix and dissolve all ingredients in water.

Butter Pastry

3¾ cups all-purpose flour, sifted
1 tsp. salt
1 cup cold butter

2 Tbsp. Crisco
¾ cup (about) ice water

Combine and sift the flour and salt in a bowl and cut in the butter and Crisco until particles are fine. Add water, 1 tbsp. at a time, to make a stiff dough. Cover and chill in the refrigerator.

Mrs. Ann Lynch Webster

Dill Pickles

20 lbs. cucumbers (3" to 6")
¾ cup whole mixed pickling spice
3 bunches fresh dill weed
8 large garlic cloves, peeled and quartered

2½ cups Apple Cider Vinegar
1¾ cups canning salt
2½ gal. sterilized water

Remove any blossoms or stems from cucumbers. Cover with cold water and gently wash with a soft brush. Drain until dry. In a 5-gallon crock or jar, place ½ the pickle spices and a layer of dill. Fill the crock with cucumbers to within 3" or 4" of top. Place remaining dill, spices and garlic on top of cucumbers. Mix vinegar, salt and water and pour over cucumbers. Cover cucumbers with a close-fitting heavy plate and use a weight to hold the cucumbers under the liquid. Cover loosely with a piece of cloth. Store pickles at room temperature, Scum may start to form in 3 to 5 days. When it forms, gently skim it off each day. Do not stir the pickles. Make sure that they stay completely covered with the brine and weighted down. If brine evaporates, make additional brine. In about 3 or 4 weeks the pickles will become a dark green and ready to can. If brine has become cloudy, you may wish to strain it through cheesecloth before using it to fill the canning jars. Sterilize the jars, bands and lids. Pack the pickles along with some to the dill weed and garlic into quart jars. Do Not pack the pickles too tightly. Cover to within ½" of jar rim with boiling brine. Adjust jar lids and bands. Bring water in bath to a boil. Place jars in the boiling bath and process for 15 minutes. Remove hot jars from bath and place on wire racks to cool. Makes 9 to 10 quarts.

Mrs. Clyde Lacy Lynch

Buttermilk, Cultured

Today buttermilk is made from pasteurized skim milk and contains about 8.5% milk solids. A culture is added to the milk to develop flavor and to produce a heavier consistency than the skim milk from which it is made. Buttermilk differs from skim milk mainly in its greater amount of lactic acid. Its protein is in the form of a fine curd. It is also more quickly digested than skim milk. Commercial buttermilk frequently has cream or butter particles added,

1 qt. skim milk, 70 to 80 degrees
½ cup cultured buttermilk, 70 degrees

⅛ tsp. salt

Combine ingredients and stir well and cover. Let stand at 70 degrees until clabbered. Stir until smooth. Refrigerate before serving. Store as for fresh milk. In recipes calling for sour milk, you may substitute buttermilk.

The Yearling, *written by Marjorie Kinnan Rawlings, was about a boy's relationship with a baby deer. The Pulitzer Prize-winning 1938 novel was later adapted to a children's film that was nominated for an Academy Award for Best Picture.*

Non-Cultured Buttermilk

My father, Harold W. Webster, Sr., would fill a glass ¾ full with Skillet Buttermilk Cornbread, then fill the remainder of the glass with buttermilk, season with salt and pepper and eat it with a spoon.

Non-Cultured Buttermilk is the liquid left after making butter. After making your butter, save and treat this buttermilk as you would any other milk. Use the buttermilk in recipes. Cold, it is a delicious warm-weather drink.

Canned Baked Beans

You can use any of the dry (navy, kidney or yellow-eye) beans. Wash beans and cover with boiling water and boil for 2 minutes. Remove beans from heat and let soak for 1 hour. Heat to boiling point again and drain. Lay small pieces of salt pork, smoked ham or bacon in an earthenware crock or a pan; add beans; add enough sorghum or dark molasses to cover beans. Cover crock and bake for 4 to 5 hours in a 350-degree oven. Add water as may be needed about every hour. Sterilize jars, bands and lids. Pack hot beans to within 1" of jar rim. Adjust jar lids and bands. Process in a pressure canner at 10 lbs. of pressure (240 degrees); quart jars for 100 minutes; pint jars for 80 minutes.

Mrs. Ann Lynch Webster

Canned Dry Beans with Spicy Tomato or Molasses Sauce

You can use any of the dry (navy, kidney or yellow eye) beans. Wash beans and cover with boiling water and boil for 2 minutes. Remove beans from heat and let soak for 1 hour. Heat to boiling point again, drain and save liquid for making sauce. Sterilize glass canning jars, bands and lids. Fill jars ¾ full with hot beans and add a small piece of salt pork, ham or bacon. Fill to within 1" of top with either Tomato Sauce or Molasses Sauce. Adjust lids and bands. Process in a pressure canner at 10 lbs. of pressure (240 degrees); quart jars for 75 minutes; pint jars for 65 minutes.

Mrs. Ann Lynch Webster

Canned Hominy

Sterilize canning jars, bands and lids. Pack hot hominy to ½" on top of canning jars. Add ½ tsp. of salt to pint jars, and 1 tsp. salt to quart jars. Cover with boiling water to within ½" of top of canning jars. Adjust lids and bands. Process in a pressure canner at 10 lbs. of pressure (240 degrees); quart jars for 70 minutes; pint jars for 60 minutes.

Mrs. Ann Lynch Webster

Canned Mushrooms

Trim the stem ends and discolored parts from mushrooms. Wash and soak the trimmed mushrooms in cold water for 10 minutes. Wash again in clean water. Cut large mushrooms in halves or quarters; leave small mushrooms whole. Steam for 4 minutes in a covered steamer. Save steaming liquid. Sterilize jars, bands and lids. Pack hot mushrooms to within ½" of jar rim. Add ¼ tsp. salt to half pints and ½ tsp. salt to pints. Add crystalline ascorbic acid to preserve color; ¹⁄₁₆ tsp. to half pints and ⅛ tsp. to pints. Add boiling hot steaming liquid or boiling water to cover mushrooms to within ½" of jar rim. Adjust jar lids. Process in a pressure canner at 10 lbs. of pressure (240 degrees); half pint jars for 30 minutes; pint jars for 30 minutes.

Mrs. Ann Lynch Webster

Canned Tomatoes

Select only firm, ripe and red tomatoes. Do not use overripe or tomatoes with soft spots or decayed areas. Loosen skins by dipping into boiling water for about ½ minute. Then quickly dip in very cold water. Cut out stem ends and peel tomatoes. Either leave tomatoes whole or cut in halves or quarters. Sterilize jars, bands and lids. Pack tomatoes to within ½" of jar rim, pressing down gently to fill spaces and release trapped air. Do not add water. Add ½" tsp, salt to pints and 1 tsp. salt to quarts. Adjust jar lids. Process in a boiling water bath (212 degrees); pint jars for 35 minutes; quart jars for 45 minutes.

Mrs. Ann Lynch Webster

Canned Tomato Juice

Select only firm, ripe and red tomatoes. Do not use overripe or tomatoes with soft spots or decayed areas. Wash tomatoes; remove stem ends and cut into pieces. Simmer tomatoes until soft; stir often. Put tomatoes through a vegetable masher/strainer. Add 1 tsp. salt to each quart of juice. Reheat to boiling point. Sterilize jars, bands and lids. Fill jars with boiling juice to within ½" of jar rim. Adjust jar lids. Process in a boiling water bath (212 degrees); pint jars for 10 minutes; quart jars for 10 minutes.

Mrs. Ann Lynch Webster

Canned Whole Potatoes

Select potatoes that are 1 to 2½" in diameter. Wash, peel, and cook potatoes in boiling water for 10 minutes. Sterilize jars, rims and lids. Pack hot potatoes to ½" of jar rim. Add ½ tsp. salt to pints and 1 tsp. salt to quarts. Adjust lids and bands. Process in a pressure canner at 10 lbs. of pressure (240 degrees); pint jars for 30 minutes; quart jars for 40 minutes.

Mrs. Ann Lynch Webster

Apple Cider Vinegar

Open a bottle of sweet apple cider and let it stand at about 70 degrees. After about 5 weeks it will turn to hard cider, then to vinegar. You can speed the process by adding a little of the cloudy clump of the bacteria that forms on the surface of natural vinegar from a previous batch or from a friend's cider vinegar.

Citrus Sugar

2 oranges   1 cup sugar
3 limes or 2 lemons

Peel oranges and limes or lemons in long strips. Place peels and the sugar in a food processor and process until the peels are chopped as fine as the sugar. Seal in plastic ziplock bags and refrigerate. Makes about 1 cup.

Clarified Butter

butter or other commercial real butter

Melt butter completely over very low heat. Remove from heat and let stand a few minutes, allowing the milk solids to settle to the bottom. Skim the butter fat from the top; strain and save the clear yellow liquid into a container.

Mrs. Ann Lynch Webster

Cranberry and Almond Conserve

1 pkg. frozen cranberries   1 cup water
1 large and sweet orange, coarsely chopped   ¼ cup almonds, toasted and slivered
¼ cup sugar

Mix cranberries, orange, sugar and water in a non-aluminum saucepan. Heat to a boil and stir to dissolve the sugar. Reduce the heat to a simmer and cook and stir until the cranberries split. Remove from heat. Stir in toasted almond slivers. Serve warm or at room temperature as a tasty fruit relish. Makes 3½ cups.

Currant Jelly

4 cups red currant juice   3½ cups sugar
  (about 2½ qts. currants)

Wash currants and discard any overripe berries. Drain. Measure 2½ qts. currants and place them in a large stock pot with no more than ¼ as much water as currants. Cook the currants over moderate heat until they are soft and translucent, stirring occasionally, about 10 minutes. Place the currants and their juice in a damp jelly bag and allow to drip overnight; do not squeeze. Measure 4 cups of juice into a large stock pot and boil rapidly until the jelly sheets from a cold spoon. Remove from the heat and skim off the foam. Pour immediately into hot sterilized canning glasses leaving ⅛" of head room, and cap with 2-piece screwband lids; invert and let cool upright to form the seal. Makes 5 to 6 medium glasses.

Dark Roux

1 cup flour   ½ cup olive oil

Mix flour and oil in a heavy cast iron skillet. Cook over low heat, stirring constantly with a flat-edged wooden spatula. Cook slowly as the roux changes from a cream color all the way to the color of dark chocolate. The trick to making roux is to brown the flour slowly without burning it. For a thick roux use 3 parts flour to 1 part oil. For a thin roux, use 2 parts flour to 1 part oil. For oil you can use bacon drippings, olive oil, lard, safflower oil or any type of oil that is your favorite.

Duxelles

1 lb. mushrooms, chopped fine   2 tsp. all-purpose flour
¼ cup green onion, chopped   dash black pepper
¼ cup butter   ¼ cup canned beef broth
½ tsp. salt   2 Tbsp. parsley, chopped
¼ tsp. marjoram   ½ cup cooked ham, finely chopped

Sauté the mushrooms and onions in butter in a saucepan until the liquid evaporates. Stir in the salt, marjoram, flour, pepper and broth. Cook, stirring constantly, until the mixture comes to a boil and thickens. Remove from heat and stir in parsley and ham. Set aside and allow to come to room temperature.

Filé Powder

Filé powder is a thickening and flavoring agent which is sprinkled on gumbo by the individual diner.

fresh sassafras leaves

Gather new and tender sassafras leaves in the late spring of the year. Sassafras leaves are easily identified because the leaves are large and consist of three rounded lobes. Hang the leaves in the attic to dry. Crumble the leaves, discarding the stems and veins. Powder the leaves with a mortar and pestle. Sift the powder; return the portion that does not pass through the sieve to the mortar and grind again.

French Venison Wellington Pastry

4 cups all-purpose flour
1 tsp. salt
½ cup butter

½ cup Crisco
1 egg, lightly beaten
ice water

Mix flour, salt, butter, and Crisco with a pastry blender or with your fingers until the mixture resembles large bread crumbs. Add beaten egg and just enough ice water to form a ball. Wrap in plastic wrap and refrigerate. Can be made one day in advance.

Homemade Horseradish

You have to try this to believe how good it is.

fresh horseradish roots
Apple Cider or white vinegar

salt

This recipe is best prepared out of doors with a fan to blow the horseradish fumes away. Stand between the fan and the work area. Peel and chop fresh horseradish roots. Grate the chopped roots in a food processor. Add enough vinegar to make a moist consistency. Add salt to taste. Seal in sterilized canning jars. Store in refrigerator.

In Tibet, the deer is a very important symbol in the Buddhist Faith. Chenrezi is the white Buddha form which represents the enlightened mind's loving kindness and compassion. He sits on a lotus. He wears the silks and ornaments of a Bodhisattva, representing all his special qualities, and a deer skin over his shoulder. His eyes see all beings.

Homemade Butter

As a child, I would watch Mrs. Ramey, in Nelliesburg, Mississippi, make homemade butter in her wooden churn. Occasionally she would give me a piece of her Sweet Cornbread with her Salted Butter spread inside. I can't remember anything tasting or smelling as good. I make pretty good Sweet Cornbread and Salted Butter myself. But there was just something about sitting on the wooden bench at Mrs. Ramey's kitchen table and eating her cornbread and butter. Whether you make Salted or Sweet Butter, you will enjoy the smell and taste your ancestors enjoyed. Homemade Butter is easy and quick to make, and a real joy to eat.

3 pts. whipping cream
2 Tbsp. buttermilk
2 to 3 trays ice cubes

cold water
¼ to ½ tsp. salt

Pour whipping cream in a large glass mixing bowl; add buttermilk and stir. Cover with a clean cloth and let stand in a warm place 48 hours. Keep covered and cool in the refrigerator for 12 hours. With an electric mixer set on full speed, mix until cream begins to thicken. When mixer begins to slow, watch very closely. The butter will begin to make all at once (should take from 15 to 20 minutes). As the butter begins to make, the mixer will begin to splatter the liquid out of the bowl. Reduce the mixer speed to slow, and with a cold spatula direct the thickened cream through mixer blades until all the butter is made. Place ice in a large mixing bowl and fill ¾ with cold water. Place a colander in another large mixing bowl and pour the butter and buttermilk into colander and allow to drain. Lift colander with butter and place in the bowl containing the ice water. The liquid remaining after draining is Non-Cultured Buttermilk; save the buttermilk to either drink or to use in other recipes. With a cold fork gently break up cold butter into smaller pieces. Wash butter very well in the ice water. Transfer the butter from the colander to another bowl and place the bowl back in the ice water. Squeeze the butter through your fingers and pour off the water that collects in the bottom of the bowl. Continue squeezing until you think you have removed all the water. You now have Sweet Butter,

For Salted Butter sprinkle ½ tsp. salt over the butter and work it in with your hands. The salt adds flavor and also acts as a preservative. You may wish to make one large piece of butter or several smaller serving pieces. Select a mold or possibly measuring cups and line the mold(s) with a piece of plastic wrap, leaving enough overhang to wrap the bottom after molding. Press the butter into the mold removing as much air as you can. Fold the edges of the plastic wrap over the exposed bottom. Turn mold upside down and bump until the wrapped butter drops out. Place the butter in your freezer until ready to use. Frozen butter is very hard, you may wish to let your butter soften several hours before serving. Sweet or Salted Butter will keep frozen for about 6 months. Traditionally homemade butter was eaten the day that it was made. If the butter was to be kept for longer periods, no salt was added and it was stored in a brine solution made by dissolving 1½ cups salt in 1 gal. of water or 6 Tbsp. salt in a quart of water. Store Sweet Butter, weighted down in the brine solution, in a cool place. Makes 1½ cups of butter.

Hominy

2qts. dry field corn   2 oz. Red Devil lye (other lye is okay)
8 qts. water

Place the dry field corn in a glass or glazed vitrified clay crock. Add the water and lye. Boil vigorously for ½ hour, then allow to stand for 20 minutes. Rinse off lye 3 times with hot water. Rinse with cold water until the corn is cool enough to be handled. Work the hominy with your hands until the dark tips of the kernels are removed. Float the dark tips off the corn in water by placing the corn in a coarse sieve and washing thoroughly. Add enough water to cover the hominy by 1". Boil for 5 minutes; change the water and repeat 4 times. Then boil for ½ to ¾ hour until the kernels are soft and drain. Makes about 6 quarts of hominy.

Mrs. Clyde Lynch Lacy

Hot Water Pastry

3½ cups all-purpose flour   1 cup water
1½ tsp. salt   4 oz. Crisco or lard, coarsely chopped

Combine flour and salt in large bowl and make well in center. Simmer water and lard until lard melts, and then bring to a boil. Pour liquid into the well. Gradually draw flour from inner edge into the center with your fingertips until all flour is mixed. Knead the dough until it is smooth, about 3 minutes. Roll out and use while dough is still warm.

Mayhaw Jelly

I had always heard my father talk about his mother making mayhaw jelly at their Oak Ridge, Mississippi plantation. But I had never seen any—much less eaten any—until Curtis Breland, the best solicitor and barrister in Greene County, and Malcomb Murphy, the best solicitor and barrister in George County, carried me to a mayhaw gathering one fine Saturday in April of 1990. Greene County Gold, that's what they call it down there. It can't be bought, it can only be bartered, traded or given as a gift. I have been told that mayhaw jelly will make you do things that you never thought you would do. I have no personal knowledge of this; but, I do know that mayhaw jelly is the king amongst kings when it comes to jelly. Your life will never be complete until you make and enjoy this divine jelly; and afterwards it will never be the same.

3 lbs. mayhaw berries　　　　　　　　　5½ cups (2 lb. 6 oz.) sugar
4 cups water　　　　　　　　　　　　　1 box Sure-Jell fruit pectin

Follow the recipe exactly. Do not double. Measure exactly. Wash and sterilize 4 more jars, bands and lids than the recipe calls for in boiling water for 10 minutes. Crush berries one layer at a time; add water. Cover and simmer 10 minutes, stirring occasionally. Place fruit in a dampened jelly bag or several thicknesses of cheesecloth. Let drip overnight. Measure 4 cups of juice. If juice measure is short, add water to pulp in bag and squeeze again. Pour measured juice into a 6 or 8-quart saucepan or pot. Measure sugar and set aside. Stir Sure-Jell fruit pectin into juice. Saucepot must be no more than ⅓ full to allow for full rolling boil. Bring to a full boil over high heat, stirring constantly. At once stir in sugar. Stir and bring to a full rolling boil (a boil that cannot be stirred down) and boil hard for 1 minute, stirring constantly. Remove from heat. Skim off foam with a large metal spoon. Immediately ladle juice into hot glass jars, leaving ½" space at top of glasses and ⅛" space at top of jars. Wipe with a damp cloth, wipe away any spills on rim or threads of jars. Quickly seal jars by spooning ⅛" hot paraffin onto hot jelly surface; make sure paraffin touches all sides and prick any air bubbles. Quickly seal jars by covering with hot lids; screw bands on firmly. Let jelly stand to cool. Check seals. Jar lids should be slightly concave or remain so when pressed; paraffin should cling to glasses and contain no air bubbles. Remove bands from jars. Cover paraffin sealed glasses with caps. Store jelly in a cool dry place. Makes approximately 6 cups.

Mr. Curtis V. Breland, Esq.

The North American Deer Farmers Association has members in 42 states, five Canadian provinces and three countries outside North America.

Lemon Salad Dressing

¼ cup olive or canola oil
¼ cup water
2½ Tbsp. lemon or lime juice
2 med. garlic clove, pressed

1 Tbsp. fresh oregano, chopped
1 tsp. salt
½ tsp. black pepper
Greek Potato Salad

Whisk or beat together all ingredients, Serve on Greek Potato Salad or as a dressing for mixed green salads.

Mrs. Ann Lynch Webster

Mayonnaise

From 1900 until the 1960s, the author's grandmother would make mayonnaise on the first Saturday of every other month. Mrs. Lynch would use her Wesson Oil crock, with the lettering in blue on the side. No one, except grandmother, was allowed to touch her mayonnaise crock. Mrs. Lynch believed, and so do I, that mayonnaise made in anything else just didn't taste the same. When she finally stopped making mayonnaise, I asked her why she was buying mayonnaise. She told me that the store mayonnaise was cheaper. It was cheaper. But it was not as good.

2 egg yolks
1 pint Wesson oil
juice of 1 lemon
1 tsp. Cider Vinegar

¼ tsp. paprika
dash of cayenne pepper
1 tsp. salt
1 tsp. boiling water

Scald and cool the bowl you will be using. Chill eggs and Wesson oil. Chill beater. Beat eggs until they are thick. Slowly add a small amount of oil until mixture becomes thick. Add lemon juice a few drops at a time, then add more oil. Repeat this process until ½ of the oil and all of the lemon juice and vinegar are used. Add the paprika, cayenne pepper and salt. Mix well. Add remaining oil slowly. After all oil has been added, add 1 tsp. boiling water. The water will keep the mayonnaise from separating. Refrigerate. Makes 1 pint.

Poppy Seed Salad Dressing

1 cup olive or canola oil
juice of 2 lemons or limes
¼ cup vinegar
1½ tsp. onion juice (scrape onion with the
   side of a spoon)

½ tsp. salt
½ tsp. grated lemon or lime rind
¾ cup sugar
1 tsp. dry mustard
1¼ Tbsp. poppy seeds

Add all ingredients to a quart jar and seal. Shake vigorously until all ingredients are mixed. Serve on fruits and salads. Store in refrigerator.

Meringue

4 egg whites
dash of salt

1 cup sugar

Beat egg whites with salt until they hold a soft shape. Add sugar, a little at a time, and continue beating until meringue stands in peaks.

Mrs. Ann Lunch Webster

Pickled Eggs

Circa prior to 1850. Mrs. Gabra Ella Martha Andrews Webster would place her pickled eggs in the spring house to cool. Up until the early 1900s the residents of Oak Ridge, Mississippi relied on subsistence farming and home preservation of foods to feed their families. See other preservation recipes for venison, butter, etc., which were used in early Mississippi

2 cups apple cider vinegar
4 Tbsp. brown sugar
1½ tsp. salt
1 tsp. pickling spices
1 tsp. red pepper flakes

1 clove garlic, peeled
8 whole cloves, peeled and quartered
1 dozen hard boiled eggs, peeled
beet juice, and/or green food coloring
    for Christmas

Place all ingredients in a saucepan and simmer for 5 minutes. Place eggs in a large jar and pour mixture over eggs. Place eggs in the refrigerator for 4 weeks. Remove and strain off spices. Return eggs to strained vinegar mixture and place back in refrigerator. Beet juice may be added for color. Makes 12 pickled eggs.

Puréed Chestnuts

1 lb. fresh chestnut meats
1 tsp. safflower or canola oil
1 Tbsp. apple cider vinegar
3 stalks celery, coarsely chopped
1 small yellow onion, coarsely chopped

2 Tbsp. butter
¼ tsp. black pepper
3 Tbsp. cream
salt

Make a cut on the flat side of each chestnut, place them in a pan with the oil, and shake until well coated. Heat in a preheated 350-degree oven until the shells and inner skins can be removed easily. Shell the chestnuts, cover with water, and add the vinegar, celery, and onion. Boil until tender. Drain, discard celery and onion, and purée or mash chestnuts until free of lumps. Beat in butter, pepper and cream. Add salt to taste. A fine addition to roast venison.

Mrs. Ann Lynch Webster

Quick Puff Pastry

Use for making Venison Chops in Puff Pastry.

2 cups plus 2 Tbsp. unsalted Homemade
   Butter
2 cups all-purpose flour

⅔ cup cake flour
1 tsp. salt
¼ cup± ice water

Slice butter into very thin slices. Freeze butter for 15 minutes. Use a mixer to mix both of the flours and the salt. Add butter and mix until the butter is covered with the flour and stays in lumps. Slowly mix in just enough water to make the dough into a lumpy mass. Roll the dough out on lightly floured surface into a 8"x18" rectangle; lumps of butter will show through. Fold the dough into thirds, alternating sides as you fold. Repeat rolling and folding 3 more times. Wrap dough in plastic wrap and refrigerate for at least 40 minutes. Makes about 2 lbs.

Mrs. Ann Lynch Webster

Red Raspberry Jelly

2½ qts. red raspberries, yielding 4 cups
   juice

5½ cups sugar
1 box Sure-Jell fruit pectin

Follow the recipe exactly. Do not double. Measure exactly. Wash and sterilize 4 more jars, bands and lids than the recipes calls for in boiling water for 10 minutes. Crush berries one layer at a time. Add water. To extract juice, place crushed fruit in a dampened jelly bag or several thicknesses of cheesecloth. Let drip overnight. Measure 4 cups of juice. If juice measure is short, add water to pulp in bag and squeeze again. Pour measured juice into a 6 or 8-quart saucepan or pot. Measure sugar and set aside. Stir Sure-Jell fruit pectin into juice. Saucepot must be no more than ⅓ full to allow for full rolling boil. Bring to a full boil over high heat, stirring constantly. At once stir in sugar. Stir and bring to a full rolling boil (a boil that cannot be stirred down) and boil hard for 1 minute, stirring constantly. Remove from heat. Skim off foam with a large metal spoon. Immediately ladle juice into hot glass jars, leaving ½" space at top of glasses and ⅛" space at top of jars. Wipe with a damp cloth, wipe away any spills on rim or threads of jars. Quickly seal jars by spooning ⅛" hot paraffin onto hot jelly surface; make sure paraffin touches all sides and prick any air bubbles. Quickly seal jars by covering with hot lids; screw bands on firmly. Let jelly stand to cool. Check seals. Jar lids should be slightly concave or remain so when pressed; paraffin should cling to glasses and contain no air bubbles. Remove bands from jars. Cover paraffin-sealed glasses with caps. Store jelly in a cool dry place. Makes approximately 6 cups.

Mrs. Ann Lynch Webster

Puffed Roquefort Cheese Gougeres

1½ cups water
7 Tbsp. unsalted butter,
   cut into pieces
½ tsp. salt
pinch white pepper

1½ cups all-purpose flour
4 large eggs
6 oz. Roquefort cheese, crumbled
1 egg beaten with ½ tsp. water

Place the oven rack in the center of the oven and preheat the oven to 400 degrees. Spray a large baking sheet with Pam or another non-sticking vegetable spray. Place the water, butter, salt and white pepper in a saucepan and bring to a boil. Remove the pan from the stove and mix in the flour. Return the saucepan to the stove and cook over medium heat until the mixture pulls away from the sides of the pan. This should take about 1 minute. Remove from the heat and transfer the dough to a large bowl. Add eggs 1 at a time, blending well after each addition. Beat in all but 2 Tbsp. Roquefort cheese. Place dough into pastry bag fitted with ¾" plain tip. Pipe dough onto the prepared sheet into 2½" rounds, pipe it 1½" high in center. Space the rounds 2" apart. Brush the gougeres with the beaten egg and water mixture; press the tops gently to slightly flatten. Sprinkle with the remaining 2 Tbsp. Roquefort cheese. Gently press the cheese so that it will adhere to the top. Bake for 20 minutes in the preheated oven. After 20 minutes, reduce the heat to 375 degrees. Continue baking until the gougeres puff and the tops are browned. Turn the oven off. Cut a 1" deep slit into one side of each gougere. Return the gougeres to the turned-off oven; leave the door ajar and let stand for 10 minutes. Use a bread knife and cut the tops off. If the centers are very moist, scrape out center and discard. Serve hot. Makes about 12.

Seasoning Salt

This is an outstanding seasoning for most wild game recipes.

1 tsp. nutmeg
2 tsp. black pepper
2 tsp. red pepper
2 tsp. oregano
2 tsp. garlic powder
2 tsp. onion powder

2 tsp. celery salt
2 tsp. dry mustard
2 tsp. ground thyme
2 tsp. ground savory
2 tsp. curry powder
½ to 1 cup salt

Mix all ingredients and process in a blender until the consistency is the same as salt. Adjust the amount of salt to taste.

Mrs. Ann Lynch Webster

Simple Syrup

1 part water   2 to 4 parts sugar

Boil water and sugar for 5 minutes. Keep the syrup in a bottle in the refrigerator and use as needed.

Homemade Sauerkraut

about 50 lb. cabbage   1½ cups Morton's Kosher salt

Remove outer and damaged leaves from cabbage heads; wash and drain. Slice cabbage heads into halves or quarters and remove the core. Shred cabbage into thin shreds. Place 5 lb. of shredded cabbage in a large container and mix in 3 Tbsp. of salt and let stand for several minutes to wilt slightly. The wilting allows cabbage to be packed in the quart jars without breaking or bruising. In a 5 gal. crock, pack the salted cabbage in firmly and evenly. Using a wooden spoon or your hands, press down firmly until the juice comes to the top. Repeat the shredding, salting, and packing until the crock is filled to no closer than 3" to 4" from the top. Cover the cabbage with a cloth and tuck the edges down inside the container. Cover a cloth with a plate that just fits inside the container and weighted down with enough weight so the brine comes to the edge of the plate. Gas bubbles indicate that fermentation is taking place. Store the cabbage at room temperature (68 deg. to 72 deg.) for 5 to 6 weeks or until fermentation is complete. Heat sauerkraut to simmering; do not boil. Sterilize jars, bands and lids. Pack hot sauerkraut into jars to within ½" of jar rim. Adjust jar bands and lids. Bring water in bath to a boil. Place jars in the boiling bath and process (15 minutes for pints and 20 minutes for quarts). Remove hot jars from bath and place on wire racks to cool. Makes 16 to 18 quarts.

Mrs. Clyde Lacy Lynch

Standard Pastry

2 cups all-purpose flour   ⅔ cup Crisco or lard, chilled
1 tsp. salt   6 Tbsp. cold water

Sift flour; measure; add salt and sift again. Using a pastry blender cut in half of the Crisco thoroughly or until mixture resembles coarse corn meal. Cut in the remaining Crisco until the particles are about the size of peas. Sprinkle water, 1 Tbsp. at a time, over small portions of the mixture; with a fork press the flour particles together as they absorb the water; do not stir. Lay aside pieces of dough as they are formed and sprinkle the remaining water over the dry portions. Use only enough water to hold the pastry together. It should not be wet or slippery. Press all the pieces of dough lightly together. The less the dough is handled, the more tender and flaky the pastry will be. Chill dough before using.

Mrs. Clyde Lacy Lynch

Steamed Mussels

⅔ cup dry white wine
⅓ cup green onions, minced
2 Tbsp. olive oil

3 garlic cloves, minced
½ tsp. salt
1 lb. live mussels, scrubbed and
    debearded

Mix the wine, onions, olive oil and garlic and heat in a large saucepan over medium heat. Add the cleaned mussels. Cover and cook for about 6 minutes until some of the mussel shells open. Shake the pan occasionally. Remove the mussels that have opened. Cook the remaining mussels for about 5 minutes more. Remove and discard mussels that have not opened. Remove from heat and allow to cool completely. Remove and discard the upper shells. Makes 1 lb.

Stewed Plum Tomatoes

2 Tbsp. butter
3 cloves garlic, pressed
1 small white onion, sliced thinly
2 (2-lb. 3-oz.) cans plum tomatoes, drained
    and juice reserved

1 Tbsp. sugar
1 tsp. salt
black or white pepper, to taste

Melt butter in a saucepan. Add garlic and onion; cook until just tender. Add reserved tomato juice and boil until reduced to 1⅔ cups. Add tomatoes, sugar, salt and pepper. Heat to serving temperature. Serves 6 to 8.

Mrs. Ann Lynch Webster

Sweet Pickle Brine

4 oz. pickling spices
2½ gals. water
2½ lbs. salt

. 3 cloves garlic, crushed
1 lb. sugar

Mix the pickling spices and 1 gal. of water in a large stock pot and simmer for 10 minutes. Mix in the remaining water, salt, garlic and sugar. Remove from the heat and chill the brine to 35 degrees. Add the venison. Maintain temperature throughout curing.

A survey of urban and rural Missouri citizens revealed that of all animals outside a zoo, people most prefer to see the white-tailed deer. The whitetail was selected as the state mammal by vote of school-age children. Each year hunters in Missouri take nearly four million trips to the field pursuing the whitetail, and while helping to control the growing population, they contribute hundreds of millions of dollars to the economy.

Brining Solution for Venison

Circa 1850s. An old Webster/Andrews, Oak Ridge, Mississippi recipe.

The purpose of soaking meat in a brine solution is to draw the moisture and sugar out from the venison. The process forms lactic acid. The lactic acid will protect the venison from spoiling. A 10% brine solution is made by dissolving 1½ cups salt in 1 gallon of water. Test the solution to see if it will float a 2 oz. egg so that the shell barely breaks the surface. When soaking venison in a brine, use a ceramic crock. The salt reacts with aluminum. If an enamel pot is used, make sure that there are no cracks; the salt will react with the steel.

Tomato Catsup

1 gal. fresh tomatoes
1 qt. white vinegar (use less if too strong)
1 qt. granulated cane sugar
½ tsp. cayenne or red pepper

1 tsp. allspice
½ tsp. black pepper
1 Tbsp. salt

Crush tomatoes through colander or sieve. Discard seeds, skins and pulp. Combine all ingredients in a large pan and cook slowly until thick. Bottle in plastic containers and freeze or process in a pressure canner using canning jars.

Mr. Harold W. Webster, Sr.

Tomatoes Stuffed with Horseradish Cream

8 small tomatoes
½ cup cream
1 Tbsp. Homemade Horseradish

½ tsp. prepared French-style mustard
dash of salt

Cut tops from the tomatoes and scoop out the pulp and seeds. Turn upside down and allow to drain. Whip the cream until stiff and fold in the horseradish, mustard and salt. Fill the tomatoes with the horseradish cream mixture just before serving.

In Michigan $2 from each deer hunting license goes into the Deer Range Improvement Program (DRIP). Established in 1972, that program has been the prime factor in boosting Michigan's deer population from an estimate of less than 400,000 to about 1.5 million today.

Venison Forcemeat Filling

¼ cup butter
¼ cup yellow onion, chopped
½ cup mushrooms, chopped
¼ cup cognac
½ lb. venison, ground fine
½ lb. pork, ground fine
1 egg lightly beaten
¼ cup cream

¼ cup parsley, chopped
1 tsp. salt
¼ tsp. basil
¼ tsp. thyme
¼ tsp. rosemary
⅛ tsp. allspice, ground
⅛ tsp. black pepper

Melt butter in a saucepan. Add onion and cook until just tender. Add mushrooms and cognac and cook over medium heat 5 to 10 minutes. Place mixture in a bowl and add the remainder of the ingredients and lightly but thoroughly mix. Cover with plastic wrap and refrigerate until ready to use.

Venison and Vegetable Soup Stock

6 lbs. venison shin and marrow bones
1 cup venison, cut in 2" cubes
8 qts. cold water
10 black peppercorns
6 whole cloves
3 bay leaves

1½ tsp. thyme
3 sprigs parsley
2 med. carrots, diced
1 cup canned or fresh tomatoes, drained
1 med. yellow onion, diced
1 white turnip, diced

Cut the bones in pieces and brown in a 350-degree oven. Place the bones, meat and water into a large stock pot and bring to a rolling boil. Reduce the heat and simmer, uncovered, for about 30 minutes. Remove the scum by pushing it to the side of the pot and removing it with a large spoon. The last bit of foam can be removed by slipping a piece of paper towel under the foam and gently lifting it up. Add the remaining ingredients and bring to a boil. Reduce heat to simmer and cook partly covered for 6 to 8 hours. Strain the stock. Freeze stock in 1-quart portions for future use. Makes about 2 quarts.

Venison, Wine and Juniper Berry Soup Stock

2 lbs. venison bones, cracked
2 lbs. venison, cubed
3 stalks celery, split
1 large yellow onion, quartered
2 large carrots, quartered and split
10 sprigs parsley
3 bay leaves, broken

½ tsp. dried thyme
½ tsp. whole peppercorns
1 cup Burgundy wine
1 gal. of water .
1 Tbsp. lemon or lime juice
10 juniper berries, cracked

Brown the cracked venison bones under the broiler. Brown, but do not burn. Place the bones in a large stock pot, and add the remainder of the ingredients. Simmer covered for 6 to 8 hours. Add additional water as may be needed. Strain through 3 layers of wet cheesecloth or through a wet jelly bag. Stock may be frozen or canned for future use.

Watermelon Rind Pickles

rinds from ½ large watermelon
¾ cup salt
3 qts. water
2 trays ice cubes
9 cups sugar
3 cups white vinegar

3 cups water
1 Tbsp. whole cloves
6 (1") pieces stick cinnamon
1 lemon or 2 limes, thinly sliced with
    seeds removed

Cut the red edges from the watermelon rinds and cut the rinds into 1" squares. Place the rind pieces in a 5-gallon glass or glazed vitrified clay crock. Make the pickling brine with salt and 3 qts. water. Cover rind pieces completely. Add the ice cubes and let stand for 6 hours. Drain the rind pieces and rinse them in cold water. Place the rind pieces in a large pot and cover with water. Cook for about 10 minutes or until the rind can be pierced easily with a fork. *Do not overcook.* Remove the rind pieces and drain. Place the cloves and cinnamon in a loose cheesecloth bag. Mix sugar, vinegar, and water; add the spice bag and boil for 10 minutes and pour liquid and spices over rind pieces; add lemon slices and let stand at room temperature overnight. Bring watermelon rind and liquid to a boil and cook until the watermelon is clear. Sterilize canning jars, bands and lids. Pack melon loosely into pint jars. Open the spice bag; remove cinnamon sticks and add one piece of cinnamon stick to each jar. Cover pickles with boiling syrup to within ½" of jar rim. Adjust lids and bands. Bring water bath to a boil; add jars and cook for 5 minutes. Process for 5 minutes. Remove hot jars from bath and set on wire racks to cool. Makes 4 to 6 pints.

Mrs. Clyde Lacy Lynch

Basic Homemade Pasta Dough

Use for making ravioli, cannelloni, and lasagna.

4 cups all-purpose flour
3 eggs, lightly beaten

2 tsp. salt
¼ to ½ cup water

Sift flour into a wide bowl and make a well in the center. Pour eggs into the center; add salt. Combine eggs and flour by sprinkling a little flour at a time over the eggs and mixing with the fingers. Add water a few drops at a time until dough is just soft enough to knead. Place the dough on a floured board and knead with the heel of the hand for at least 10 to 12 minutes or until the dough is smooth and elastic. Divide the dough into 4 parts and roll out as directed for each pasta recipe. Should make enough pasta for 4 to 6 servings.

Whipped Cream

1 cup cream
½ tsp. Mexican vanilla

2 Tbsp. sifted confectioner's sugar

Prepare at the last minute JUST BEFORE serving. Chill the cream, bowl and beaters in the refrigerator for at least 2 hours. In warm weather place the mixing bowl in a large bowl filled with ice cubes. If the cream is warmer than 45 degrees, it may turn to butter. Mix the cream, vanilla and sugar. Beat the cream mixture in an electric mixer on medium-high speed until the chilled cream begins to thicken. Do not over whip. Whip just to the point where the whipped cream falls in large globs and makes soft peaks.

Mrs. Ann Lynch Webster

Raisin, Apricot & Onion Stuffing
for Venison Crown Roast

Depending on the size of the crown roast, this recipe may have to be adjusted in volume.

1 cup raisins
¼ cup dried apricots, chopped
7 cups soft bread crumbs
¾ cup butter
1 cup onion, chopped
1 garlic clove, chopped
1 cup celery, chopped

3 cups tart apples, diced
¼ cup parsley, chopped
1½ tsp. salt
¼ tsp. paprika
⅛ tsp. nutmeg
⅛ tsp. ginger

Boil raisins and apricots in water for 5 minutes; drain and add to bread crumbs. Melt butter and sauté onion, garlic and celery. Add sautéed vegetables and remaining ingredients to bread crumbs.

Kosher Dill Pickles

3 lbs. pickling cucumbers
¾ cup Morton Coarse Kosher Salt
2 qts. water
3 cups distilled white vinegar
5 cups water

12 cloves garlic
2 Tbsp. whole mixed pickling spices
6 sprigs fresh dill
6 small hot peppers

Wash the cucumbers. Slice the cucumbers ¾" thick and discard the blossom ends. Place cucumbers in a large bowl. Dissolve the Morton Coarse Kosher Salt in 2 qts. of water; pour water over the cucumbers. Cover and let stand for 24 hours. Remove the cucumbers and drain. In a large stock pot, combine the vinegar with 5 cups of water. Add the garlic and pickling spice tied in a cheesecloth bag. Bring to a boil. Meanwhile, place 1 sprig of dill and 1 pepper in each hot sterilized jar. Pack cucumbers in jars. Discard spice bag; pour hot liquid over jars. Close jars as manufacturer directs. Process 10 minutes in a boiling water bath. Makes 6 pints.

APPENDIX

WEIGHTS OF PARTICULAR CUTS OF VENISON

Weights are for an "average" Mississippi White Tail buck. White Tail deer in other parts of the state and country can weigh as much as 300 pounds. Mule deer in the western states will weigh considerably more. Weight below is measured in pounds.

Cut of Meat	Weight	Cut of Meat	Weight
Rough carcass	120.00	1½" Top Round Steak	2.07
Dressed carcass	72.00	1" Top Round Steak	1.38
After 4 days cold storage	64.00	¾" Top Round Steak	1.05
Final cut & packaged	52.75	½" Top Round Steak	.69
Whole side	32.00	1½" Chop	.63
Hindquarter with bones	10.75	1" Chop	.50
Hindquarter w/o bones	8.50	¾" Chop	.38
Forequarter with bones	5.00	½" Chop	.25
Forequarter w/o bones	3.00	Crown roast	4.00
Loin (backstrap) (25"x3½"x1¾")	3.75	Neck Roast (8½"x5"x5")	3.00
Tenderloin (13"x3"x1")	.75	Whole strip of back chops	6.00
2" Top Round steak	2.75	Side of ribs (16"x 12")	3.00
Brisket	1.00	Flank	1.38

RATIOS FOR GROUND VENISON TO ADDED MOIST MEATS

Venison to Moist Meat	Pound Conversions	Uses
50% to 50%	10# to 10#	Sausage
60% to 40%	15# to 10#	Sausage
66% to 33%	10# to 5#	Burgers, Meatballs
70% to 30%	14# to 6#	Meatballs and Meat Loaves
75% to 25%	15# to 5#	Meatballs and Meat Loaves

OVEN TEMPERATURE CONVERSION CHART

DESCRIPTION	DEGREES FAHRENHEIT (°F)	DEGREES CENTIGRADE (°C)
Keep warm (Lo-Temp) oven	140-170	60.0-76.7
Warm oven	200-225	93.3-107.2
Very slow oven	250-275	121.1-135.0
Slow oven	300-325	148.9-162.8
Moderate oven	350-375	176.7-190.6
Hot oven	400-425	204.4-218.3
Very hot oven	450-475	232.2-246.1
Extremely hot over	500-525	260.6-273.9
Maximum temperature	550-575	287.8-301.7

OVEN ROASTING TIMES

(Cooking times may vary due to size and weight of meat)

Very rare	5 minutes per pound
Rare	20 minutes per pound
Medium rare	22 minutes per pound
Medium	25 minutes per pound
Medium well	27 minutes per pound
Well done	30 minutes per pound

Index